MODERN ITALY

MODERN ITALY

A Political History

DENIS MACK SMITH

YALE UNIVERSITY PRESS
NEW HAVEN AND LONDON

Set in Linotronic Bembo by Fakenham Photosetting, Norfolk, England.
Printed in Great Britain by St. Edmundsbury Press Ltd.

British Library Cataloguing in Publication Data

Mack Smith, Denis, 1920–
    Modern Italy: a political history. – New ed.
    1. Italy – Politics and government – 1870–
    I. Title   II. Italy
    945'.08

    ISBN 0–300–07377–1 (hbk.)
    ISBN 0–300–04342–2 (pbk.)

ACKNOWLEDGMENT is made to the following for permission to quote from the works
listed: Pietro Nenni, for quotations from the books by him in the bibliography; Nazareno
Padellaro, for *Libro della 111 classe elementare*; The Bodley Head, for *Mazzini's Letters to an
English Family*; Hodder & Stoughton Ltd., for *The Memoirs of Francesco Crispi*; Weidenfeld &
Nicolson Ltd., for *Mussolini's Memoirs, 1942–43*, ed. R. Klibansky; G. Bell & Sons Ltd., for
The Roman Journals of Ferdinand Gregorovius 1852–74, ed. F. Althaus, tr. by Mrs. Gustavus
Hamilton; Hutchinson, for *Benito Mussolini, My Autobiography*, tr. R. Washburn Child; G.
Allen & Unwin Ltd., and also Little Brown & Co., and Franz J. Horch, for Emil Ludwig's
Talks with Mussolini, tr. by Eden & Cedar Paul; Edward Arnold Ltd., for Salandra's *Italy and
the Great War*; Deputazione subalpina di storia patria, for *Le carte di Giovanni Lanza*; Tom
Antongini, for his biography of G. D'Annunzio; Arnoldo Mondadori, for quotations from
D'Annunzio, Albertini, and C. Sforza; La Nuova Italia, for works of G. Fortunato; Rizzoli,
for L. Albertini's *In difesa della libertà*; Edizioni scientifiche Italiane, for F. S. Nitti's
Rivelazioni, and *Meditazioni dell'Esilio*; Licinio Cappelli, for G. Massari's *Diario 1858–60
sull'azione politica di Cavour*; G. C. Sansoni, for works of G. Gentile; Aldo Garzanti, for works
of F. Crispi and G. Giolitti; E. Mariano, director of *Il Vittoriale*, for works of G. D'Annunzio;
Istituto per gli studi di politica internazionale, Milan, for D. Farini's *Diario 1891–95*; La
Fenice, for *Opera omnia di Benito Mussolini*; Giuseppe Laterza & Figli, for works of Benedetto
Croce and Luigi Blanch; Doubleday & Co., Inc., for *Ciano's Diaries* ed. by Hugh Gibson,
copyright 1945, 1946, by Doubleday & Co., Inc.; and also William Heinemann Ltd., and
Methuen and Co., Ltd., for *Ciano's Diaries*.

Contents

Preface

The best starting point for a political history of modern Italy is March 1861 when, at long last, Count Cavour was able to proclaim that a united Italian kingdom was in existence. In every previous century each individual region of this Mediterranean peninsula had had its own separate history and relations between them were often characterized by bitter rivalries and civil war. Only after 1861 was it possible for a unified national state to take its place in the European community. During the first sixty years this new kingdom was governed by a liberal parliamentary oligarchy. Then for two decades after 1922 it was a fascist dictatorship until Mussolini's regime suffered catastrophic military defeat in World War II, after which a national referendum changed the kingdom into a democratic republic. Not only was this referendum an explicit repudiation of fascism, but Italian voters in 1946 also turned against the liberal-conservatives whose forbears had united Italy during the *risorgimento*. This was the very first election ever held by universal suffrage, and the victor was a relatively new party of Christian democrats that hitherto had played only a minor role on the margin of politics. So began the last of three successive regimes that each put a distinctive mark on modern Italian history—one of them being liberal, elitist, and moderately anticlerical; the second being illiberal and totalitarian; and the third being predominantly Christian-democrat until the 1990s.

Count Cavour's ambitious aim in 1861 had been to create a liberal and prosperous country that would become one of the great powers of Europe. This objective was achieved but only long after his death and not without setbacks and disappointments along the way. National unification had at first been greatly admired by many foreigners, but enthusiasm waned when social tensions and unresolved constitutional weaknesses prepared the way for Mussolini's nationalist revolution with its acceptance of war as desirable and beneficial. The fascist aim to make Italy feared as well as admired then led to the pursuit of goals in foreign and domestic policy that left the country isolated, enfeebled, and internally divided. This in turn brought about a reaction against militarism, colonialism, and authoritarianism. In the fifty years since 1945, Italy has done a great deal to encourage international co-operation and European integration. Not only do the amenities of civilized living in Europe owe much to what Italians have contributed in these years since World War II, but their country was entirely changed by an economic revolution that created a more satisfactory balance between social classes and removed some of the alienation and internal divisions that had been such a burden in the past.

If Italy today is an immeasurably healthier society than in 1861, this is because her people have shown the same qualities of resilience and enterprise that were so much admired in earlier centuries. Many problems still remain, in part because of a failure to establish the checks and balances needed for a workable system of representative government. The ineffectiveness of the parliamentary opposition and the permanence of a single party in office between 1946 and 1992 allowed corrupt practices to develop in many areas of society and encouraged extravagant expenditure that created a huge national debt. Also a lack of political will permitted a formidable growth in organized crime by the mafia and *camorra*. As parliament lost some of its moral authority, many different suggestions were made for modifications in the constitution that would assist the proper functioning of a democracy, but these were not taken with sufficient seriousness until a revolt by the electorate in 1992 led to a collapse of the existing parties and made radical changes inevitable. Some politicians began to talk of reversing the achievement of 1861 and creating either a federal state or possibly a complete separation between North and South. A very small minority even looked back with nostalgia to the more authoritarian practice of Mussolini. But the great majority preferred to hope that minor constitutional changes would make possible an improved Second Republic by learning from past mistakes and renewing the idealism that in 1861 had led to the unification of Italy.

An earlier version of this book was published in 1959 but its continued existence in print has prompted a request that it be revised and brought up to date. Encouragement also came from Italy where over a dozen editions in translation have been a recommended text in schools and universities. A few cuts and alterations have therefore been made so as to find room for new chapters on the fifty years after 1945. Proximity to such recent events makes it difficult to put the half-century since Mussolini's death into perspective. Yet there are advantages in treating the whole period since 1861 as a continuum in which certain themes recur even when the nation itself and ideas about national identity have continued to change. What has no pretence to be more than an outline of recent history, oversimplified and filtered through personal inter-pretation, may help to explain how present-day Italy has emerged from its past.

Denis Mack Smith

SECTION ONE: ITALY BEFORE 1861

I The "Geographical Expression"

Until 1860 the word Italy was used not so much for a nation as for a peninsula, and Metternich wrote disparagingly of this "geographical expression." It is with geography that any history of this country must begin. Too often have poverty and political backwardness been blamed on misrule and foreign exploitation instead of on climate and the lack of natural resources. We need not go so far as to believe that the destinies of a nation are altogether shaped by its wealth and position: a peninsular situation in the Mediterranean may suggest but does not compel a particular choice of allies, the lack of raw materials can make a country either weak or aggressive (or both), an unkind climate may as easily stimulate as depress. But geography is one factor in defining the scope of a nation. It has always been historically important that the Apennines divide Italy and the Alps cut her off from the rest of Europe.

Italy was a territorial unit many centuries before she became a national state—unlike the Netherlands which was politically a state before it was either a nation or a geographical entity. The natural frontiers of Italy are more or less clearly defined, three sides bounded by the sea, and the fourth following the long chain of the Alps. There have been certain ambiguities within these limits. Corsica and Nice have sometimes been claimed from France, Canton Ticino from Switzerland, Malta from Great Britain; and southern Tyrol, Trieste, and Fiume have been disputed with Austria-Hungary and Yugoslavia. Italian claims to these disputed provinces were sometimes grounded on geography, sometimes on history or ethnology. Even a physical barrier so formidable as the Alps by no means coincides with the linguistic frontier. Large cisalpine areas have been French, German, and Slav by speech, while smaller communities still speak Albanian, Ladino, and even Catalan.

Neither the existence of these contested frontier provinces nor that of tiny enclaves in San Marino and the Vatican City weakens the compactness of Italy so much as do the differences and sometimes the animosities between its component regions. This parochialism is the product of both geography and history. The various regions still preserve something of their individual customs and literature, their peculiar type of economy and methods of land tenure. Even under the highly centralized government of Mussolini, a fascist party secretary could arouse keen dislike for being too typically a southerner, and when Marshal Badoglio announced over the radio in 1943 that the fascist regime had collapsed, there were people whose first reaction was to resent his Piedmontese accent. The natural speech of most Italians has been dialect until quite recently, and most of the dozen or so dialects are largely unintelligible outside their particular district. Up to 1859–61 the regions were still politically divided, with different historical traditions of government and law. Weights, measures, and coinage varied everywhere, the ducato of Naples differing from the oncia of Sicily, the papal scudo from the Piedmontese lira. Dozens of different customs barriers existed along the course of the River Po—a striking example of that municipalism or *campanilismo* which impeded national unification and the modernization of agriculture and industry.

★

Of all these regions, the matrix of the new Italy was Piedmont in the northwest, with Turin its capital. Piedmont, since 1720, had been joined politically with Sardinia and, since 1815, possessed the important shipping center of Genoa which was the great rival of the Austrian-held port of Trieste. Farther east, in the great plain of Lombardy, was the town of Milan, eventually to become the financial, commercial, and artistic pivot of the new kingdom. Well placed at the intersection of trade routes, Milan was in close touch with the transalpine world. Its people were active and practical, and the Lombard plain was watered by the largest Italian river and contained the best and most populous agricultural land in the kingdom. Although Lombardy was wrested from Austria by Piedmont in 1859, it was not until 1866 that Austria surrendered the adjoining region of Venice which she had held for seventy years. Immediately to the south lay the region of Emilia and Romagna with its major towns of Bologna and Ravenna. Below this were Umbria and the Marches, conquered from the Pope by Piedmontese troops in 1860. To the west was Tuscany, which also in 1860 joined this growing nucleus of a united kingdom. Tuscany, a grand duchy with its capital at Florence, had been for centuries the chief cultural focus of the peninsula, and Livorno, known to the English-speaking world as Leghorn, was an important commercial and shipbuilding town. South of Tuscany was the sacrosanct region of Rome where the Pope ruled over a truncated state until 1870.

The islands of Sardinia and Sicily were distinct regions by reason of climate and history and by the character of their people. This difference between North and South was fundamental. For many years after 1860 a peasant from Calabria had little in common with one from Piedmont, and Turin was infinitely more like Paris and London than Naples and Palermo, for these two halves of the country were on different levels of civilization. Poets might write of the South as the garden of the world, the land of Sybaris and Capri, but in fact most southerners lived in squalor, afflicted by drought, malaria, and earthquakes. The Bourbon rulers of Naples and Sicily before 1860 had been staunch supporters of a feudal system, thinly glamorized by the trappings of a courtly and corrupt society. They feared the traffic of ideas and tried to keep their subjects insulated from the agricultural and industrial revolutions of northern Europe. Roads were scanty or nonexistent, and passports necessary even for internal travel. In the *annus mirabilis* of 1860 these backward regions were conquered by Garibaldi and annexed by plebiscite to the North.

In the Mediterranean there has probably not been any drastic change of climate over recent centuries, but agricultural conditions have altered for the worse, largely owing to political catastrophes, bad methods of tillage, and neglect of soil conservation or a proper rotation of crops. Heavy deforestation has occurred in southern and central Italy owing to the requirements of shipbuilding, and because of the *carbonari* with their charcoal pits, and the wild goats which cropped the young trees. This created erosion and dustbowl conditions. Agriculture in the South has to reckon not only with less rain than the North, but with more unpredictable rainfall and a worse seasonal distribution. The southern Apennines contain no natural or artificial lakes, and the winter rain pours off them in torrents which dry up in the hot summer and are useless for irrigation. Where no trees remain to hold the moisture, the soil is washed down the mountain slopes and avalanches devastate the valleys. Few Italian rivers are useful for navigation. Along the Adriatic, ports have silted up, and Ravenna, once a headquarters of the Roman fleet, has become an inland city. Many large areas have been subject to floods. The still water of marshland bred several deadly species of anopheles mosquito, so that people were driven up into the hill towns leaving the lowlands untended and desolate. In these conditions nothing like the intensive agricultural system of France or Lombardy was possible, and there was a basic poverty which not even liberal government after 1860 could easily change.

Comparing favorably with these depressed areas, the northern plain of Lombardy had seen a successful fight against nature. Generations of industrious peasants turned the northern marshes into paddy fields and built an extensive and constantly maintained network of waterways. Realizing that prosperity was precarious and a few years of neglect would be ruinous, they had developed an advanced community sense: for example, a right of aqueduct, by which water might be carried across other people's property, had long been established by law. Luckily, the River Po relied less on winter rain than on glaciers producing a summer flow. In Lombardy, too, there were flourishing cities and trade centers from which investment capital was always returning to the countryside. This compared well with the predominantly agricultural South, where income was derived almost exclusively from agriculture and barely sufficed for replacement and running expenses.

These facts help to explain the poverty of so much of Italy, and show why so many millions of her people have chosen to emigrate. Italy was a poor and relatively overpopulated country in 1860, a fact which political unification was slow to change despite many rhetorical promises and extravagant hopes. The country possessed only a fraction of the resources of France and far less cultivable land, yet the population of France, which in 1850 was still one and a half times that of Italy, was to be outpaced by the latter after 1900. In other countries there was much more of an expanding industry which could absorb surplus labor from agriculture, but in Italy the raw materials of industry were lacking. From the time that wood and charcoal gave way to iron and coal, craftsmanship to mass production, Italy fell behind economically and, as most of her population therefore remained in agriculture, the high proportion of mountainous and barren land was the more disastrous in its effect.

★

Geography was also important in helping to define Italy's relation with other countries. The foreign policy of the united state was bound to be concerned chiefly with countries along her land frontier, especially France, Austria, and Serbia. Each of these was potentially dangerous, but each could be played off against the others. The length of her sea coast, about 4,100 miles as against 1,290 miles of northern frontier, not only left her very sensitive toward other Mediterranean powers such as France and Britain, but also made her a maritime, and sometimes a would-be imperial, power. Nearly all her imports came by sea until roads and railways could be built through the Alps. To the east there was the historical memory of Venetian domination over Dalmatia and the Levant. The Balkan mainland is only fifty miles distant from Italy at the narrowest point in the "canal" of Otranto, while North Africa is only three hours distant from Sicily by sea. Not surprisingly, therefore, Cavour and his disciples had occasional "geopolitical" visions. Italy was altogether enclosed in the Mediterranean, and was sometimes called a promontory "which links Europe with Africa." Ever since the influence of Turkey and the Barbary corsairs began to decline, and especially when the Suez Canal became a fact, some people could wonder if the old Roman Empire might not be recreated in North Africa.

There were indeed some advantages in being a "geographical expression." Metternich's own Central European empire was not even that, and Austria-Hungary was to be broken in pieces by the new nation states, of which Italy and Germany were the largest and most spirited.

2 The Idea of National Unity

Italy had always been a unit geographically. In religion, too, she had been practically homogeneous since Pope Gregory the Great in the sixth century A.D., and something of a common culture and literary language had existed from Dante onward. Until 1861, however, she had never been a political entity, and hardly was one even then. As the Neapolitan historian Luigi Blanch wrote ten years before, "the patriotism of the Italians is like that of the ancient Greeks, and is love of a single town, not of a country; it is the feeling of a tribe, not of a nation. Only by foreign conquest have they ever been united. Leave them to themselves and they split into fragments." Some national consciousness had certainly existed on and off for centuries, but had been vague and tenuous, something manifested in the wilder speculations of a Dante or Machiavelli, and many Italians had argued on the contrary that national unity would be ruinous rather than profitable. Not much national feeling had existed before the nineteenth century, and even an Italian customs union such as the German *Zollverein* was impracticable until Piedmont imposed its own system in 1861. Government had for centuries been parceled out between autonomous cities and foreign dynasties, all of whom had an interest in resisting every patriotic movement not led by themselves and fighting against any neighbor who became too threatening.

Yet successive foreign invaders gradually took on the color of their surroundings and became absorbed by the *genius loci*, until by 1861 these many cities and provinces, only excepting Venice, Trieste, and Rome, stood united in a single state. True enough, there were still important internal divisions and more than one civil war lay ahead. It is true also that unification was achieved by a forcible imposition which some Italians disliked. Nevertheless, many people would have agreed that the five great powers of Europe had by 1861 become six, and in every free country people looked with sympathy and admiration at the rebirth of Italy. The how and why of such an achievement provide one of the fascinating themes of modern history.

★

Italy of the nineteenth-century *risorgimento* was a far cry from the divided Italy of the Renaissance. In the later Middle Ages, Italians made their country the main center of European religion, art, and literature, and also of the new capitalist, urban civilization developing around the Italian inventions of banking and credit. Yet, while inhabitants of the medieval Italian communes consciously belonged to a wider community, their loyalty was by no means to a nation, but first to the city and then to Christendom. No threat of invasion by Saracens, Normans, or Germans succeeded in forcing them into a common resistance and a common front for mutual aid, and some local rulers always sided with every invader for the sake of their own private advantage. Italy had thus become the most invaded country in the world, and Lombardy one of the world's great battlefields. Even where temporary leagues of cities could be formed in self-defense, they were never lasting, but melted away with the danger that engendered them or with a new danger which required a new political alignment. By 1500, however, the eighty city-states scattered through Italy had been more or less united into a dozen regional states by the more successful and unscrupulous of the local tyrants and civic oligarchies.

Italy in the sixteenth century drifted into a period of relative somnolence during which she lost her commercial and cultural primacy. This was due at least in part to her failure to constitute a national state like contemporary France and Spain. Machiavelli might dream of a more united country, but in practice his ideal prince did not succeed in rallying enough of Italy to combine and play the new game of power politics in Europe. Instead, the French invasion of 1494 from the north, countered at once by that of Spain from the south, opened a new era of civil war and foreign subjection, in which Italy became the cat's-paw, the battlefield, even the private perquisite, of one European nation after another. Once again, one party in every local quarrel was always ready to side with an invader in order to curb a rival faction or a neighboring province. Milan tried and failed to become master of northern Italy. Successive papal families attempted by force of arms to win a temporal hegemony, but Cesare Borgia made too many enemies and failed. Then it was the turn of Venice, only to be crushed by France and a confederacy of other jealous provinces. So strong were these internal jealousies that Florence was left alone to resist a Spanish invasion, while her leading family, the Medici, chose to support the Spanish emperor against their own native city. Florence and Rome were both put to the sack by foreign soldiers and the civilization of the Renaissance was shocked to a standstill.

At the same time the Ottoman Turks and the corsairs of Greece and North Africa were obstructing the trade routes that Venice and Genoa had used for their prosperous commerce with the Levant. The commercial center of Europe was shifting away from the Mediterranean to the Atlantic seaboard where ports looked out to a new world largely discovered by Italians. But Italy herself failed to meet this challenge. Although still the richest country in Europe, although Venice had for centuries sent ships into the Atlantic, and though Genoa was not much further from the Spice Islands than was Amsterdam or London, nevertheless internal political rivalries did not allow the necessary adjustments to be made. The interests of Italy were subordinated to those of her new Spanish overlords, and the inherited splendor of centuries was largely dissipated in profitless civil war.

In the two centuries before the *risorgimento*, only the different regions had their individual history, and this was often a pale reflection of trans-alpine Europe. After the death of Michelangelo in 1564, and from the time when Giordano Bruno was burned at the stake in 1600 and Galileo silenced by the Inquisition in 1632, Italy lived in a backwater. Certain regions managed to retain some political independence, for example Venice sheltered behind her lagoons and Genoa screened by the Maritime Alps, but only as shadows of what they had once been. Venice decreased in population between 1500 and 1860. The Venetians failed to retreat in time from the commitments of their Levantine empire; instead of fastening onto the mainland of Italy, they wore themselves out trying to maintain their overseas dominions. Most of northern Italy fell to the Austrian Habsburgs, and southern Italy to a Bourbon dynasty from Spain. In between, right across from sea to sea, stretched the states of the Church where the Pope ruled as a supranational sovereign and as a solid barrier against national unification. Spain, France, Austria, and the Pope would scarcely look sympathetically on any movement toward union or independence. Nor was it likely that they would fail to prevent such a movement in any foreseeable circumstances.

It was with the Napoleonic intrusion into Italy, between 1796 and 1814, that the various regions of the peninsula were forced back into the mainstream of European history. Napoleon even created a prototype "kingdom of Italy" based on Milan. This was an artificial, puppet state, with a population of only six million. But the Napoleonic armies brought with them the germs of liberalism fostered by the French Revolution of 1789, and introduced a minor industrial revolution sufficient at least to provide some of the war equipment required by this foreign emperor. Experience of Napoleonic rule convinced some people how much Italy stood to gain from strong centralized government, for the French brought more efficient methods of administration and a far more enlightened code of law. Customs barriers were broken down and the decimal and metric systems of measurement were introduced. The mercantile classes appreciated this, as they appreciated the better roads, the enlarged market, and the destruction of entails which at last made possible the free transfer of land. Fortunes were made on a scale hitherto impossible while liquid capital reappeared and sought an outlet in profitable enterprise.

But neither the novelty nor the permanence of Napoleon's contribution should be exaggerated. Some of these reforms had been anticipated in Italy during the eighteenth-century Enlightenment, and the rest, once Napoleon had gone, mostly lapsed. The Kingdom of Italy split up again into its constituent elements and the emperor's laws were usually repealed. Most Italians were glad to be rid of him, less because he was a "foreigner" than because heavy taxes and conscription were obnoxious, and because they hoped that the milder government of pope or duke would be less interfering and easier to disobey. In one real sense, moreover, his legacy was one of division, in that he brought north Italy still further within the economic ambit of France and his road over the Simplon pass drew Milan nearer to Paris. This notwithstanding, shortly after Napoleon's final defeat the German scholar Niebuhr could write from Rome that Italy was bound to be united in the course of a generation or two, and Stendhal, for many years a French consul in Italy, noted the same trend. That such a revolution was at last conceivable is to be ascribed in part to Napoleon's influence, and some of the future leaders of Italian patriotism came from families who became rich under his regime.

★

One cannot give wholly satisfactory reasons for the rise and fall of nations. No simple answer will explain why Spain, whose share in defeating Napoleon was infinitely greater than that of Italy, derived thereby no stimulus to a national rebirth like the *risorgimento* and received no similar inspiration from the new ideas of patriotism, liberalism, and romanticism. In Italy these ideas caused a ferment compounded of bitter criticism and boundless enthusiasm. Politically, the 1814–15 Restoration might be called a disaster: the Viennese emperor returned to Lombardy, the Bourbons to Naples, the Austrian grand duke to Tuscany; Venice was no longer a free republic but a province of Austria, and Genoa became a dependency of Piedmont; nor was Piedmont, which still possessed Savoy north of the Alps, a wholly cisalpine and Italian power. Everywhere the aristocracy recovered their privileges and power. But on the nonpolitical plane new forces were at work. There was a feeling of *italianità* which thinkers were beginning to rationalize and statesmen to exploit. There was the liberating wind from the French Revolution blowing freely through the world with its message of political deliverance. There was also an expanding commercial and agricultural middle class with new needs generated by increased prosperity and the revival of trade routes in the Mediterranean.

Without this small middle-class minority it is difficult to see how enough backing could have been found for national unification. They found it irksome to have eight separate states in Italy, each with tariff barriers, individual coinage and systems of measurement. Not only the merchants and textile manufacturers of northern Italy, but also some landowners realized that economic progress presupposed a larger internal market. They quickly recognized the advantages of a centralized government which could build roads and railways and defend their interests abroad. The commercial classes of Lombardy had done well out of "foreign" rulers but nevertheless felt that the Austrian government, for all its relative honesty and enlightenment, exploited their province, and some of them expected more consideration if only they could be governed by Italians.

Economists such as the Piedmontese aristocrat Cavour were at the same time looking forward to the excavation of a Suez Canal, calculating that the shortest route from England to India might include the railroad they wanted to build from Turin to Brindisi. The canal was not finished until 1869, but long before then another obstacle disappeared with the destruction of the Barbary pirates. At last it seemed as if the Mediterranean might recover its importance as the main highway of world trade. At a time when Turkish power was declining, it was the more important that a united Italy should be ready to capitalize these potential advantages, for by the 1830s both Greece and Serbia had won their autonomy from Turkey, and Mehemet Ali in Egypt and France in Algeria were threatening to alter the Mediterranean balance of power. As things turned out, the canal was in fact to bring few immediate advantages to Italy; there was no great influx of trade from the East, and ships did not stop to bunker in a country which lacked the necessary coal. It was none the less important that these changes were, in advance, thought likely to make Italy's fortune if only she were sufficiently united to exploit them.

Quite as impressive as these economic factors, and by and large affecting different people, was the common Italian culture now more in evidence, and there was discussion in literary and intellectual circles about possibly creating a United Italy. In 1825–27 Alessandro Manzoni published *I promessi sposi*, the most influential novel ever written in Italian. Manzoni was from Lombardy, but soon after publication he visited Florence and in the next edition fifteen years later he had corrected the style to conform more with the language as spoken in Tuscany. This in the end proved decisive in confirming Tuscan as the classic prose style for Italian literature. Some of the purists objected, but like all masterpieces this book carried its own compulsion and another essential step had been taken toward national consciousness. Meanwhile Grossi and Guerrazzi found the educated public avid for tales of medieval Italian heroes who once beat the French and the Saracens, and Leopardi's patriotic odes had to be confiscated by the Austrian and Piedmontese censorship lest they should incite people to revolt. Literature thus helped to reassure Italians that they were not so unfit for war and politics as some of them had imagined.

Nor were these littérateurs content with Italy as the legendary land of romance. The Abbé Gioberti in 1843 wrote a celebrated work, *The Moral and Civil Primacy of the Italians*, to claim that Italy alone was morally worthy to head a federal Europe. As he said, "a nation cannot hold its due position in the world unless it could become more self-confident." His grandiose vision was a compensation for the reality of weakness, a protest against foreigners such as Lamartine who called Italy a land of the dead, but it was fanciful and far from real life. The literature of the romantic movement preferred historical legends of past greatness, and gave little thought to the revolution of 1848 or the colorful deeds of Garibaldi. To many of the romantics, contemporary events seemed cheap and shoddy when compared with their ideal of what Italy ought to be, and perhaps their attitude also betrays a secret shame at their own lack of practical support for Garibaldi and the revolutionaries. Their moral contribution was, however, beyond controversy. National consciousness would never have become practically effective without visionaries and evangelists to implant it by degrees in the minds of those few people who had the strength, the skill, and the courage to act.

3   Mazzini, Garibaldi, and the Revolutionaries

Before this economic and cultural revival could develop into a political *risorgimento*, someone had to transmute ideals into action. Centuries of foreign rule had left Italy not only without a territorial nucleus around which a national movement could gather but without experience of free government. Forty years of trial and error were necessary after the Napoleonic period in order to test the various methods and parties which gradually became engaged in the crusade for independence. At one extreme there was the orthodox means of open war and diplomacy; at the other, plotting, piracy, and assassination. As well as conservative monarchists, there were anarchists, republican agitators, starving peasants, discontented soldiers and students, all with different aims and methods, but all helping, often unintentionally, to create a united Italy. Of these it was Mazzini and the revolutionary republicans who first persuaded people that unification might be feasible, and who then, by many isolated and courageous acts of revolt, forced the conservatives and the lukewarm to join with them in half-unwilling alliance.

Very soon after the Restoration of 1814–15, a handful of secret societies became active in undermining the European settlement agreed at Vienna in 1815. In Genoa and Sicily, which had lost their previous autonomy, to Piedmont and Naples respectively, even some conservative aristocrats had an interest in revolt. So had discharged officers of Napoleon's Italian army and the civil servants who staffed his government. In 1820–21 therefore, and again in 1831, uprisings took place in several of the larger Italian cities to remedy various local and individual grievances. But they lacked cohesion and co-ordination. Certain towns in Sicily preferred to side with the Bourbons at Naples against the island capital, Palermo, of whose predominant position they were jealous, and in Bologna the "foreign" refugees from Modena were disarmed even though both cities were fighting against Austria.

By 1848, the next year of widespread revolutions, some of the malcontents had realized the need for sacrificing local animosities in a common cause. Soldiers from insurgent Naples joined with Tuscans, Romans, and the Piedmontese army in trying to save the gallant insurrection of Milan, and an elected Sicilian parliament invited a Piedmontese duke to be their king. Once more, however, all ended in mutual recrimination, Milan accusing Piedmont of treachery and selfish aggrandizement, Piedmont replying that the Milanese were clouding the straight issue of independence with a controversy over republicanism upon which patriots were divided. Province was divided against province, class against class. The poor were not interested in political independence but much more in the price of salt and flour; landowners fell back on the old dynasties rather than countenance the occupation of their land by the peasants in arms; and as for the merchants, they might have wanted greater freedom, but not at the price of forced loans and inflation. In 1849, therefore, the old regimes were again restored, and although some people had tasted liberty and learned to fight on the barricades, the bitterness of civil war and defeat soured the cause of patriotism.

It is not possible to identify many of those who took part in these insurrections of 1848. No doubt it was a small minority, for the wars and risings of the *risorgimento* had little obvious appeal to ordinary people. If not the intellectuals, it was at least the intelligent, in particular the professional classes, the lawyers, doctors, and shopkeepers who manned the Palermo barricades in 1848—so observed William Nassau Senior, the economist, who spent much time in the country. Italian lawyers were not as conservative as English lawyers: they were poor in money and esteem, usually excluded from the judicial bench and high society, full of abstract ideas, and hence ready to accept change and revolution. Furthermore, they were a numerous body, for most respectable families were ensnared in hereditary lawsuits, and universities were equipped to teach only medicine and the law. Lawyers were therefore an often subversive element in society.

University students, too, were rebellious by nature. They were the first to join Garibaldi's volunteers, and no university would be bold enough to refuse them a degree if some successful patriotic escapade made them miss their examinations. Patriotism offered a glorious relief from the crabbed, patriarchal system which kept them, even after marriage, cooped up in ancestral *palazzi* with generations of relatives. When ruled by austere, authoritarian parents, such as those of the poet Leopardi, the young were bound to be in revolt. Little travel was possible for them before the age of railroads, and there was no sport except the very necessary art of fencing. In their drab lives a town riot was a tonic and an intoxicant, and in between riots they could show their national enthusiasm by refusing to buy taxed tobacco, by cheering arias of Verdi which hinted at patriotic rebellion, or by wearing the conical Calabrian hat after its prohibition by the Austrians as a patriotic symbol. The student population of Italy, as of many other countries, was an ideal revolutionary force. While students had less to lose than citizens with responsibilities, their education fitted them to understand the need for protest, or at least enough to make it seem glamorous. Besides being persecuted by governments as a source of seditious infection, many of them had small hope of profitable employment in existing society and understandably wished to build a brave new world where brains were as important as birth, and where the white-collared man was king.

★

The great teacher and inspiration of rebellious youth was Giuseppe Mazzini, a republican, a patriot, and by far the greatest prophet of the *risorgimento*, who also believed that a united Italy would pave the way for a federal union between all the countries of Europe. Mazzini was born at Genoa in 1805, and lived as a revolutionary agitator, sacrificing personal comfort, the company of his family, and the lives of his friends. Exiled from Genoa and Piedmont in 1831, he was then expelled from Switzerland and France, and spent most of his remaining years planning the resurrection of Italy amid the fogs of London. He launched numerous societies and newspapers to convince people that Italy could and must be unified through the exertions of ordinary people. No trust, he maintained, should be placed in princes or in political alliances nor in any appeal to mere self-interest, for the problem was moral more than political, and ordinary citizens must learn that they alone by their own sacrifices could redeem themselves. A nation should be something spiritual; not like America which "is the embodiment, if compared to our own ideal, of the philosophy of mere *rights*: the collective thought is forgotten: the *educational* mission of the state overlooked. It is the negative, individualistic, materialistic school." Mazzini, on the contrary, made national unification a religious duty, and convinced his disciples that it was part of God's providence, in which belief they discovered an invaluable sense of inevitability and self-confidence.

Mazzini's practical application of patriotism was by means of continual insurrections, thereby making people conscious of their power and of how to use it in executing God's purpose. He sometimes managed to visit Piedmont surreptitiously, defying a sentence of death, and frequent uprisings testified to the valor of his lieutenants and to his own idealism and personal fascination. There exists today an edition of his writings in over a hundred volumes, ranging from a manual on guerrilla warfare to thousands of incendiary letters which kept conspiracy alive. The mildest of men, sad, lonely, and affectionate, he was amongst the most feared and hated personalities in Europe, although to many young Italians, one of the more admirable.

It is easy to say with his detractors that Mazzini was a failure. Not only were many of his disciples killed in insurrections which seemed hopeless from the start, but his enemy Cavour was to oust him from the revolutionary leadership, and in 1872 Mazzini died an unhappy and disillusioned fugitive. During the last twenty years of his life he possessed little apparent influence and was known better in England than Italy. He had proved impossibly utopian in believing that the populace would rise against tyranny on their own initiative and resolve all the problems of national and class selfishness. When they did rise, it was usually for selfish and non-national reasons of their own, and he found them to be far from the progressive force he had hoped. His disillusionment was profound. "I had thought to evoke the soul of Italy," he said, "but all I find before me is its corpse." The country had turned out to be "rotten with materialism and egoism." Worse still, Mazzini knew that his failure was partly due to his own intractable nature, to his distrust of compromise, and to the temperamental obstinacy which ultimately alienated even his former friend Garibaldi.

Recognition came posthumously, when conservatives and monarchists needed no longer to fear him and when the king could personally approve the erection of a statue in Rome to this republican Apostle of Unity. Mazzini's influence could then be truly appreciated. His theory of popular initiative had been vindicated in central and southern Italy during 1859–60. Cavour, the prime minister of Piedmont, would not have conceived it possible that a thousand men, armed only with a few rusty flintlocks, could land in Sicily and conquer a large, disciplined army. But Mazzini had believed in the impossible, and Garibaldi's success in 1860 frightened Cavour into seeing that his only hope of forestalling a democratic and republican revolution was to invade the Papal states and the South, and to proclaim that Rome should one day become the capital of United Italy. Here was Mazzini's revolutionary program almost to the letter, enacted by an orthodox diplomat who, as lately as 1856, had called the idea of national unity "complete nonsense." Mazzini's success lay in defining the goal and arousing enthusiasm among more practiced soldiers and statesmen. Cavour as well as Garibaldi was his unacknowledged and ungrateful pupil.

★

Italians found their greatest general of modern times in Giuseppe Garibaldi, the inspired leader of guerrillas. Garibaldi was rough and untutored, with little grasp of politics, but with remarkable flair for the tactics of irregular warfare. His success with his men, who loved him and believed him invincible, was above all one of character, for he lacked calculation and guile, was unambitious for himself and devoid of cheap ostentation. He was an honest man with the reputation of being one, whereas Cavour never freed himself from the suspicion of double-dealing and unscrupulousness. No one could meet Garibaldi without recognizing his single-minded and disinterested love of Italy, and few people failed to be charmed by his courtesy and simplicity of manner. He was temperate even to parsimony, and when his headquarters in 1860 was at the magnificent Palace of Caserta he would still wash his own shirt and sleep on hay with his saddle for a pillow. There was seldom any need in his army for routine discipline, and as he himself was fearless and tireless, so he seemed to turn ordinary men into supermen.

Southern Italians venerated their deliverer as a saint, and in distant countries workmen who had never seen Garibaldi gave up their half-holidays to make arms for him. No one else in the world was so admired or so widely known by name. English dukes begged for his portrait; one of them, himself a cabinet minister, had a son who ran off to join Garibaldi's volunteers; and their wives even raided Caserta to comb out the hairs from his brush for keepsakes. The romancer Dumas followed him around to get copy for novels and, in return for this privilege, equipped a yacht on which to make red shirts for the revolutionary troops. It was Garibaldi's generous good nature that won public opinion in Europe to favor the deeds of a buccaneer. Frenchmen, Poles, Hungarians, South Americans, and a battalion of British volunteers joined the bravest of Italian youth in the fantastic army which he could conjure up from nowhere and then as magically disperse again. Chivalrous enthusiasts linked up with professional adventurers, for it was not least among Garibaldi's services that, alongside the patriots, he could enroll those social outcasts who are in the van of any revolution or counterrevolution, most of them idealists, others thriving on disorder, and who from the *carbonari* to the fascist *squadristi* have been among the most combustible and explosive elements in Italian society.

Garibaldi called himself a republican and a socialist. In practice, however, he loyally served the monarchy, and to Mazzini's disgust meekly surrendered to the king the dictatorial powers over the half of Italy which he conquered in

1860. Whether this was naïveté or common sense it greatly helped the process by which most of the republicans and revolutionaries rallied to the throne—a dozen of his famous volunteer Thousand were later to become generals in the regular Italian army, although he himself crumpled up the notice of his own appointment and threw it out of the window. Away from the battlefield, his own political beliefs, for all their honesty, were trite and shallow. He distrusted Mazzini and hated Cavour. As he was quite unable to understand the difficulties of Cavour's position, he blasted him as a coward, a traitor, and a fomenter of civil war. Where Cavour believed in parliaments, Garibaldi was all for a dictatorship and looked on the Italian parliament as thoroughly unrepresentative and unserious. He genuinely believed in what he called liberty, and yet thought that freedom could and should be forced on people for their own good. Unskilled in public speaking—except from balconies—he had no patience with the talk and the delays of parliamentary government, and so dictatorship was the natural form of government he chose for southern Italy in the wartime emergency of 1860. This would-be republican, anticlerical democrat that he was, had presided from the royal throne during pontifical high mass in the Cathedral of Palermo, claiming the royal rights of apostolic legateship (although a notorious heretic), clad in red shirt and with sword unsheathed as the Gospel was read.

Under all his panache, Garibaldi had neither the ruthlessness nor the ambition and intelligence of Cromwell or Napoleon. In later years he turned up rarely in parliament, sometimes wearing his poncho and red shirt to the dismay of the frock-coated deputies, but he was far happier back on his farm, away from the smart men of politics, awaiting some new call to arms. His real work was finished when Cavour took over the Italian revolution; and like Mazzini he became disillusioned with the Italy which Cavour and the moderates had made. The liberals who eventually ruled Italy regarded him as crude and vulgar, a model *condottiere* and truly great of soul, but a child in politics and slightly ridiculous, a relic from a former age of violence, and now only an embarrassment or an exhibit. Such was his popularity that every town had a street or square called after him; even the bed on which he died in 1882 was later surrounded by iron railings and preserved as a national monument. Nevertheless his share in the *risorgimento*, though no less important than that of Cavour or Mazzini, was depreciated by officialdom as something of which to be a trifle ashamed.

4 Cavour and the Expansion of Piedmont

Germany and Italy became unified states at much the same time. The methods employed by Italian patriotism are generally said to be more liberal than those used in Germany and more diversified, which may suggest one reason why the Italian nation was less firmly established, for liberalism does not always exactly coincide with patriotism. The constituent elements of the new state were notably variegated. But out of this jumble of regions and parties, Piedmont was eventually to emerge as a nucleus around which the rest of Italy could gather. Until such a center of attraction existed, Mazzini's sermons and Garibaldi's swordplay were insufficient. Piedmont and her ambitious, warlike dynasty were needed to put some blood and iron into the movement for independence.

Surprisingly enough, this chosen region was one with no great tradition of *italianità*, but was a largely French-speaking area which straddled the Alps and had existed only on the borderline of Italian history. Rome would have been a more obvious center if only the Romans had showed a glimmer of interest in the prospect. But Rome proved in practice to have either been inured by centuries of clerical despotism, or else to be already satisfied with a position as the capital of a religious empire far larger and grander than Italy. A cynic might say that many Roman citizens were content with their virtual monopoly of jobs at the headquarters of the Church, while the poorer classes exploited the pilgrims and the Grand Tour trade, making a passable living out of alms, lodging houses, and religious trinkets. After Rome, Naples might have been conceivable as a center of United Italy. Naples was the largest city in the peninsula, capital of the biggest and most populous Italian state, but was also provincial and retrograde, and ruled hitherto by a Spanish dynasty which until the previous century had considered this region as almost an appurtenance of Spain.

If prosperity was the criterion, Milan would have been a much more likely capital than Piedmontese Turin. The Austrians who ruled Lombardy until 1859 had long since abolished the more abused aristocratic and clerical privileges. Tax farming had been reformed, a census instituted, and the area was being welded into something like an economic unit by the suppression of internal trade barriers. This was way ahead of the rest of Italy. Tuscany, too, had an administration under her Austrian grand duke which until the middle of the century was more enlightened and liberal than that of Piedmont. The legal and penal system of Tuscany was a model to Europe; its universities gave the best education in Italy; there was less police intrusion than elsewhere, more tolerance of Jews and Protestants, and in general a higher standard of welfare and culture. Many foreigners wintered in Florence and brought with them liberal ideas, so that even its theologians tended toward unorthodoxy. Tuscany, however, was linked to Austria by dynastic ties, and was slow to sense that urge toward political independence which was at the heart of Italian patriotism.

It was political independence which distinguished Piedmont from other regions and eventually enabled the House of Savoy to lead the Italian revolution. This dynasty was the oldest ruling house in Europe. Until the eighteenth century its center of gravity had been on the French side of the mountains. The Savoy duchy, a buffer state controlling the Great and Little St. Bernard passes, had kept its independence because of the rivalries of France, Spain, and Austria. Through marriage and alliance with these powers in turn, additional territory had spasmodically been incorporated, and, since France formed a strong barrier to the north, expansion was now easier toward Italy. The acquisition of Sardinia early in the eighteenth century brought to the duke of Savoy the title of king; and when by 1748 his land frontier had reached the River Ticino and Lake Maggiore, the new Kingdom of Sardinia had its center of gravity in Italian Piedmont rather than in French Savoy. There was, however, no exclusive feeling for Italy in its almost French rulers, only the dynastic ambition to expand anywhere. They styled themselves "Kings of Sardinia, Cyprus, Jerusalem, etc." But Napoleon's victories temporarily frustrated their ambitions and made Savoy-Piedmont a colony of France for twenty years. Cavour, Mazzini, and Garibaldi were, for this reason, born subjects of France, and Napoleon's sister stood godmother at Cavour's christening.

Piedmont played no very active part in Napoleon's defeat, but the settlement of 1815 left her well placed for intervention in Italian affairs. Not only was she the Italian region with greatest freedom from Austrian patronage, but in 1815 she was gratuitously presented with Genoa and so obtained one of the four largest ports in the Mediterranean. She thereby also became more markedly an Italian power. The Concert of Europe, moreover, having deliberately recreated this subalpine kingdom as a necessary buffer between France and Austria, would not easily permit its destruction. Piedmont could therefore follow an audacious foreign policy, knowing that this tacit guarantee gave her everything to gain from war and little to lose. The full implications of this fortunate position were not grasped at once, for Piedmont in 1815 appeared to be merely an appendage of the Holy Alliance between Austria, Russia, and Prussia, in other words a satisfied and conservative power which, having profited by the Treaty of Vienna in 1815, stood to gain by defending rather than attacking it. Not until public opinion had been converted to look upon Austria as the arch-enemy was conservative Piedmont given any inducement to become revolutionary, but Austrian hegemony in the peninsula made this change inevitable sooner or later. After 1815 the balance of power was upset by the eclipse of France, and this was bound to bring Austria more effectively into Italy and hence ultimately into conflict with the Piedmontese, though not until France was strong enough to return into Italian politics could the buffer state again play her accustomed role of *tertius gaudens*. Italian unification in fact required the reappearance of

France as a major power, and that meant waiting until Louis Napoleon became emperor in 1852.

A premature attempt was made in 1848, when Milan revolted against Austria and gave King Carlo Alberto of Sardinia his chance to march into Lombardy in support of the rebellion. The result was a disastrous defeat at Custoza in July. Bad tactical direction and inefficient staff work would have been quite enough to ruin the campaign even without tragic political differences with the radical Milanese, for the wars of the *risorgimento* were, one after the other, to show that the Savoy dynasty lacked all the military virtues except courage. Mazzini and the radical republicans also questioned the motive which led Carlo Alberto into the war: they held that it was not fellow feeling for Italians, but mainly the old selfish dynastic aggressiveness which saw good reasons for annexing the fertile grainlands of Lombardy. The radicals ascribed the king's defeat to his greater dislike of Milanese republicanism than of Austrian imperialism, and they fairly concluded that he was putting the interests of monarchy and of himself before national sentiment.

It was, however, significant that other European states would not let Piedmont lose any territory in the peace settlement of 1849, and soon afterward Louis Napoleon restored to Europe a more nicely equivalent balance of power. This momentary equipoise gave just the opportunity needed by a man of Cavour's stamp to establish the fortunes of his country. Fifteen thousand men were therefore sent in 1855 to fight the Russians in the Crimea. No great Italian interest was at stake there; rather the reverse, since Russia was a useful check upon Austria, and the very next year Cavour was entreating the Czar to an alliance. But the expedition served to win a seat at the Paris peace congress in 1856, and there Cavour took his opportunity to assert in public that Piedmont had as much right as Austria to intervene in the other regions of Italy. Following up this success, in 1859 he carefully and imperturbably provoked a second war against Austria with France as his ally, and so won the long-coveted region of Lombardy. Louis Napoleon, for his part, welcomed this creation of a compact north Italian state in which French influence would replace Austrian. It was thus by exploiting the rivalries of other European countries that Piedmont compensated for her own weakness and began to annex one province after another, and this set a tradition of foreign policy which Cavour's successors had good reason to follow.

★

Count Camillo di Cavour is the most interesting and effective politician in modern Italian history. By birth the younger son of an aristocrat, he became an engineer officer in the army, but retired early and took up agriculture. Quite unexpectedly, the events of 1848 drew him by way of newspaper editorship to the forefront of Piedmontese politics. He was a cabinet minister in 1850, prime minister by 1852, and thereafter remained almost continuously at the head of affairs until his death in 1861. Far more amiable and sympathetic than Bismarck, his counterpart in Germany, Cavour was no less sure of touch, no less self-confident, and almost as unscrupulous when occasion demanded.

Like Garibaldi, Cavour had an imperfect knowledge of the Italian language and he preferred to write in French. Other people had to revise his newspaper articles, and his secretary found it painful to hear him speak Italian in public. Until quite lately, the Italian language had been unacceptable in Turin society, and Cavour was not untypical in being more at home in French literature and English history than in Italian. He was, for that reason, admirably equipped to interpret to Italy the liberal and industrial revolutions which he had studied in England and France. He was equally fitted, by close study of the national interests of the various powers, to insert the Italian question into the crisscross of European diplomacy. Cavour exploited the rivalries between England and France, France and Austria, Austria and Prussia, and sometimes he thereby managed to give his country a deceptive and counterfeit strength as a make-weight in the balance of European power.

Piedmont acquired in Cavour a novel and invaluable spirit of enterprise. A man as great in energy as in vision, he was a gambler who had once lost a substantial fortune by speculating in French securities on a chimerical rumor of war, though he was on other occasions a clever and fortunate speculator. He was particularly interested in financing banks and railroad development. At times he was audacious in politics to the point of folly, yet this was usually counteracted by common sense, realism, and political tact. He had a remarkable sense of what was possible, and would always compromise with his ideals if that seemed advisable; nor was he ever frightened out of changing his mind by the accusation of opportunism.

One is not surprised to find that Bentham was the favorite philosopher of Cavour's youth and that he once defined Christianity as orthodox utilitarianism. From such a standpoint he was bound to oppose a doctrinaire such as Mazzini, for not only was Mazzini adamant upon the utopian dogma of national unity, but Cavour by comparison could seem a trimmer, materialistic and even irreligious. The conflict of ideas between these two men was as great as the clash of their personalities, and yet it was Cavour's trimming, his materialism, and in part even his irreligion which eventually translated Mazzini's dogma into practical politics.

Between 1850 and 1855 Cavour rendered an indispensable service to Piedmont through his internal reforms. Hitherto the country had been in many respects backward. If the other Italian states did not rush to join Piedmont in the years before 1850 as they were to do in 1859–60, the reason was the unenlightenment of her administration quite as much as her deficiency in national consciousness. It is surprising to find that the first Italian steamboat, the first big iron bridge, and the first railroad had appeared not in Piedmont but in Naples under the patronage of the "reactionary" Bourbons, and the first electric telegraph joined Leghorn to Pisa in 1847. There was clearly the need in Piedmont for a strong injection of Adam Smith as well as Bentham, and also of what Cavour himself (aristocrat though he was) called the immortal principles proclaimed by the French Revolution in 1789.

On his farm at Leri, Cavour had already shown himself a bold and successful innovator and had introduced modern accounting methods, crop rotation, experiments in subsoil drainage and livestock breeding, and machinery for making beet sugar and polishing rice. He showed the same spirit when he was a cabinet minister after 1850 and demonstrated that the *risorgimento* was not simply a revolt against foreign oppression, but first of all an internal revolution designed to introduce economic, political, and civil liberty. So doing, he brought Italy into line with the most advanced countries in Europe and established Piedmont unquestionably, for the first time, as chief among the states of the peninsula.

Cavour's confessed aim was to convince Europe that Italians knew how to govern themselves without Austrian tutelage. He thus consciously compared the role of Piedmont in Italy with that of Prussia in Germany. To assert Piedmontese superiority, the legal codes were reformed and ecclesiastical immunities drastically curtailed. Exiles from other Italian states were welcomed so long as they rejected Mazzini, and it was important that the careers most easily open to these exiles were in the ill-paid though powerful fields of journalism and education where they could instruct public opinion in *italianità*. Some of the more distinguished obtained posts at Turin university; others became editors of important newspapers; while Farini and Minghetti eventually reached cabinet rank. Turin temporarily assumed the leadership in intellectual life hitherto maintained by Florence, and the books published in this city soon began to reflect her patriotic ambitions.

No great industrial enterprise had hitherto appeared in Piedmont but Cavour inaugurated a new bank to provide credit for industry. He reduced tariffs considerably, so that exports and imports tripled in value over the period 1850–59. The railroad network by 1857 stretched from the French to the Swiss and Austrian frontiers, thus facilitating the mobilization and military campaign of 1859. Piedmont, indeed, by 1859 included half the railroad mileage of Italy, and the Mont Cenis tunnel was shortly to bring Paris within one day's journey. Cavour also laid the foundations of an armament industry, sending engineers to learn in England how to make naval engines, armor plate, and rifled cannon. In 1857 a start was made on the famous Cavour canal which was to irrigate a large area around Vercelli and Novara and make it some of the most fertile land in the country. An important effect of such enterprise was that Rothschild of Paris and Baring and Hambro of London put their money into these developments and so obtained an interest in underwriting Piedmontese advancement.

In carrying through such reforms Cavour was hardly typical of his colleagues and fellow citizens, but his own expansive character created the impression that Piedmont was more enlightened and liberal than was in fact true. Although its center of gravity had shifted from Chambéry in Savoy to the less illiberal milieu of Turin, the royal Court was still full of reactionary Savoyard generals from across the Alps. With clericals and reactionaries under Solaro della Margherita on one political wing and, on the other, radicals such as Depretis who were tinged with Jacobinism, Cavour had no easy passage for his favorite doctrine of the golden mean in everything.

In the end his good sense was invincible. "You will see, gentlemen," he had told parliament in March 1850, "how reforms carried out in time, instead of weakening authority, reinforce it; instead of precipitating revolution, they prevent it." He contended that the only real progress was slow and wisely ordered, and that by social reforms alone could socialism be resisted. He was no democrat, but he realized that, for better or worse, democracy was in the long run irresistible; while he would concede no natural right of participation in government, he was ready to extend the suffrage to all who accepted existing institutions. This was his customary pragmatic approach. All governments, he saw, would in future rely either tacitly or explicitly on public support. At a time when his protector Louis Napoleon was establishing plebiscitary dictatorship in France, Cavour was prudent enough to foster constitutional monarchy as "the only type of government which can reconcile liberty with order." Public opinion as revealed in parliament showed him the direction of popular sympathies, and out of the free conflict of ideas he would choose the policy which had most support. "I have no faith in dictatorships, especially civilian dictatorships," he wrote. "I think one can do many things with a parliament that would be impossible with absolute power ... and I never feel so weak as when parliament is shut."

Although Cavour expressed the hope that Italy could be created without a Cromwell, his actions were sometimes a good deal less liberal than his theories. This was important, because Cavour was to earn the reputation of being the one really successful Italian politician, and it was his practice which set the tone for political life after 1861. A shrewd fellow deputy called him a cross between Robert Peel and Machiavelli, and some later Italians were even to praise him as the great authoritarian. If he avoided repressive measures where possible, this seems to have been not so much because they were inherently bad, as because he knew that repression often defeated its own purposes. While he was sincere in his liberal beliefs, he was too practical a person to be doctrinaire and unyielding about them. The liberal method was good because "free institutions tend to make people richer," and it was this practical test of success which would justify any means so long as the end were desirable. Thus corruption in politics might well be legitimate, and in any case public and private life each had their separate code of morals: "If you must resort to extraordinary means, then adopt them as energetically as possible, so that the grandeur of your aim may make up for the hateful methods you employ, and so that your government will not appear ridiculous as well as odious." Machiavelli would have applauded.

Cavour appreciated the value of the free conflict of ideas; yet though he wrote that he felt weaker when parliament was shut, in practice he was glad to rule without it when he most needed to feel strong. In theory he claimed to admit that the Mazzinians would be less dangerous inside than outside parliament, yet in practice he drove the extremists into clandestine conspiracy by preventing the free expression of their opinions. When the last surviving republican paper was studiously careful not to give him legal grounds for suppression, he first tried to bribe the printer to cease publication and then ordered the Genoese authorities to compel the editor into bankruptcy by "frequent and almost daily sequestrations, legal or illegal." The Mazzinians said that they wanted national unity far more than they wanted a republic, but Cavour on the contrary said that he would refuse an alliance with them even at the price of leaving Italy divided and launching a civil war. Sometimes he connived at their insurrections, sometimes he went to the other extreme and warned Austria or her satellites of Mazzini's plans. At all costs, however, the revolutionaries had to be kept powerless and discredited, and used merely to frighten Europe into tolerating his own "conservative revolution" in preference.

★

Cavour's theoretical liberalism and practical Machiavellism both helped in realizing national unification. For many years he had believed that Italy might in the distant future become an independent nation, but until 1859–60 his own plans were for an enlarged kingdom of northern Italy linked by alliance with other Italian states. The fact was that he disliked revolutionary republicanism more than he loved national unity. He feared that Mazzini's insurrections would embroil him with France and undermine the predominance of Piedmont which depended on French support. Luckily he was met halfway by some of the more practical revolutionaries who abandoned Mazzini's utopianism. Unsuccessful republican uprisings, for instance those of the Bandiera brothers in 1844 and Pisacane in 1857, convinced radicals such as Manin that a national revolution could succeed only if supported by the Piedmontese army, and accordingly they placed their hopes on convincing Cavour that public opinion was now ready for a unified Italian kingdom. It was Garibaldi's conquest of Sicily in 1860 which finally persuaded him that Manin was right.

Cavour at first did all he dared to stop Garibaldi from sailing on this madcap venture, and even after the landing in Sicily he remained for a while unhelpful and skeptical. But, as always, he was clever enough to let events take their course without implicating himself too far, and, while fully prepared to disown the revolutionaries if necessary, was equally ready to lend a hand and reassert his influence should they prove victorious. His diplomatic tact had already been shown earlier in 1860, for against much opposition he had sacrificed the two northeastern provinces of Savoy and Nice to France, and so won the French emperor Napoleon III for an accomplice in the acquisition of central Italy as a *quid pro quo*. Plebiscites had then been held in Tuscany and Emilia to confirm their annexation. And not content with this, Cavour then suggested to Britain that, while France wanted no more than a state of northern Italy as a check upon Austria, it might be a British interest that an even larger Italy should emerge as a counterpoise to France in the Mediterranean.

The sudden news of Garibaldi's overwhelming success made Cavour decide that the best chance of controlling the revolutionaries was to outdo them at their own game. While still pretending to treat with the Bourbon regime in Naples, he sent secret agents to try to forestall Garibaldi with a more conservative insurrection, offering promotion to officers in the Neapolitan army and seducing local politicians from their loyalty by offers of money. When Garibaldi arrived at Naples first, Cavour was not to be outdone. He quickly engineered popular uprisings in the Papal states as a pretext to invade Umbria and the Marches, and annexed most papal territory except the area around Rome; because this enabled him to advance southward and force Garibaldi by the threat of civil war to yield Naples and Sicily as well. If the latter resisted, the order was that his volunteer soldiers should be "exterminated."

Legitimists and Catholics everywhere were profoundly disturbed by this invasion of the Papal states, but Cavour gave the ingenious excuse that only thus could the anticlerical Garibaldi be prevented from overthrowing the government of the pope in Rome. "The aim," he said, "has been holy, and perhaps this will justify any irregularities in the means which we have had to use." Almost before people could see what he was about, Cavour had unified most of Italy and held rigged plebiscites to regularize the fact. When parliament met early in 1861, a new kingdom of twenty-two million people could be officially declared in existence. Only Rome with its French garrison, and Venice together with the Trentino and Trieste under Austrian rule, remained outside.

SECTION TWO: THE POLITICAL AND ECONOMIC SCENE

5 The Constitution, the King, and Parliament

A written constitution had been granted by Carlo Alberto to his Kingdom of Sardinia in 1848. There was some agitation in 1860–61 for a constituent assembly to draw up a new scheme of government for the united kingdom, but Cavour was determined not to have a complete breach with tradition and feared what would happen if basic institutions were called in question.

The *statuto* of 1848 therefore constituted the fundamental law of the realm for the next hundred years. Despite the claim in its preamble to irrevocability, the details and the spirit were in fact altered, first in a liberal, later in an authoritarian sense. Specific articles guaranteed a right of public assembly and a right to freedom of expression in the press, though in practice even under Cavour himself such liberties were not inviolate. Ministers were technically responsible to the king and not to parliament, but in practice this "constitutional government" based on royal power soon gave way to "parliamentary government." Such flexibility could work either way, and all depended on the character of successive sovereigns and their ministers.

Vittorio Emanuele II, while less powerful than the rulers of Prussia, had more authority than most constitutional monarchs. Article 65 of the *statuto* laid down that "the king nominates and dismisses his ministers"; he was under no obligation to follow their advice, and the constitution contained only the vaguest generalities about ministerial power. By not being too definite about who had the chief initiative in legislation, the path was left open for an empirical development of constitutional conventions. The king possessed the power of issuing decrees having the force of law. He personally chose all members of the Senate. The king summoned and dissolved parliament, and could even preside at cabinet meetings. Article 5 provided that:

> The king alone has the executive power. He is the supreme head of the state, commands all the armed forces by sea and land, declares war, makes treaties of peace, of alliance, of commerce, but giving notice of them to the two Houses as far as security and national interest permit. Treaties which demand any financial burden, or which would alter the territorial boundaries of the state, shall not have any effect until after the two Houses have consented to them.

Although some treaties were put before parliament, the king retained a dominating influence in foreign affairs: the foreign minister was usually his personal nominee, and sometimes the sovereign conducted a private policy which was independent of or even contrary to that of his prime minister.

A further channel of royal influence was the army and what was loosely called the Court party, with whose help the king could resume a personal direction of government in moments of crisis. After the Treaty of Villafranca in 1859, after the Turin riots of September 1864, and again in 1867, 1898, and 1943, the king at critical moments handed over government to one of the army commanders. Until the twentieth century, moreover, the ministers of war and of the navy were invariably generals and admirals, people who had sworn a military oath to obey the king and so were in a special way his servants. These military officers commonly remained in office from one ministry to the next, as placemen of the crown.

The monarch was usually surrounded by army officers and in public rarely wore civilian clothes. The Court was not unlike a military encampment, and the heir to the throne was educated under martial discipline. Instructed in spartan habits, successive kings were men of simple and modest tastes, but this military atmosphere bred the morals and politics of an army clique and often a barrackroom language and behavior. It also perpetuated the absurd and dangerous notion that war was a gentlemanly and desirable occupation. The national economy was to be crushed by ruinous expenditure on army and navy, often without parliamentary sanction, and wars could be lightheartedly provoked even when Italy was in no position to fight.

Vittorio Emanuele became King of Sardinia in 1849, and King of Italy in 1861. He died in 1878. Because of the challenge of republicanism and the need to overshadow Garibaldi in popular esteem, an official apologetic and panegyric was developed to inflate his reputation. The true picture hidden behind clouds of incense is of a puny and usually insignificant man, good-natured and shrewd, but superstitious and ill-educated, possessing a rough-hewn and by no means despicable character but little of the luster and aureole of majesty. He said in private that Italians were quite unsuited to parliamentary government and could be governed "only by bayonets or bribery." His own enthusiasm was chiefly reserved for women, horses, and hunting. When his ancestral province of Savoy had to be ceded to France, his first anxiety was the loss of his hunting grounds. Like his forebears and his son he publicly maintained a mistress and illegitimate children, and seemed to think that this conduct was expected of a real king. He used to tell his friends the unlikely story of how Queen Victoria's daughter fell in love with him but knew too much Greek and Latin for his tastes. His own preferences were more rude and proletarian—"too much the father of his people," said the wags.

There were obvious weaknesses in his position after 1861. He was resented by adherents of other Italian dynasties which he had displaced. A long tradition of republicanism existed in some areas, and only Piedmont and Naples were strongly monarchist. Divine right was no longer what it had been in his father's time, and after the plebiscites the king technically held office by will of the people as well as by the grace of God. He did not possess those natural allies of monarchs, a strong aristocracy and a royalist priesthood, especially once the Church had excommunicated him for his armed invasion of the Papal states.

Vittorio Emanuele's strength lay in the guarantee of political stability which he afforded. Opposition from the radical Left was reduced by Garibaldi's belief that the king was a God-given instrument to end the temporal power of the Papacy. Opposition from the clericals of the Right was partly neutralized by the monarch's possibly sincere but not very energetic attempt to behave as a good Catholic. Cavour skillfully used this counteraction between the two extremes to make the king rely more on the liberals of the Center. The king was never very friendly with Cavour: they came to an open breach over foreign policy, and again when the royal mistress and Cavour tried unsuccessfully to exclude each other from their respective offices. But although the king's temperament repeatedly led him to intervene in government, for much of the time he kept fairly narrowly within constitutional bounds, and in his attitude toward Mazzini and Garibaldi he showed more tolerance and sometimes more common sense than Cavour himself.

★

A special instrument for the exercise of royal influence was the Senate. Entirely chosen by the king, it was a conservative body made up of ex-deputies, army officers, and other prominent male citizens, and, as only the elderly and moderate were chosen, it lacked liveliness and sharp conflict. Financial measures had to be first introduced in the Lower House, and though otherwise both Houses were equal in status, this financial initiative soon gave the Chamber a distinct primacy. A Senate vote of no confidence did not compel resignation. Cavour, who would have preferred an elected Senate, several times led the Chamber in collision with the Upper House, and when he died in 1861 the latter body evidently possessed little more than a delaying power. Out of thirty subsequent prime ministers, only Menabrea in 1867–69, Pelloux and Saracco in 1899–1901, and Badoglio in 1943–44 were senators.

Ministers of the crown could speak in either House but vote only in that to which they properly belonged. Ministers were selected by the king and in theory were responsible to him alone, but parliament developed a degree of control by interrogating them in "interpellations" as well as by votes of no confidence and general debates on finance. The prime ministership was an office not mentioned in the constitution, but Cavour made it all-important. The prime minister usually came to hold executive responsibility by also taking a powerful departmental post, either finance or the interior. Collective cabinet responsibility was not thought essential; an individual minister might resign if his department was censured and the prime minister could then reform his cabinet in a *rimpasto*. The American James Lowell wrote that each single minister was less a member of a group than a free lance fighting on his own behalf at the head of his retainers. This made governments highly unstable, and altogether there were thirty-three different cabinets in the thirty-five years between 1861 and 1896.

Parliament itself had respectable medieval progenitors, but its roots in history had withered, and the strongest national traditions were those of paternal monarchy. Cavour had a great gift for parliamentary government and had closely studied constitutional practice abroad. He worked to increase the power and responsibility of the Chamber, for he recognized it to be his main check on the king and on his chief enemies, Mazzini, Garibaldi, and the clericals. By 1861, therefore, convention had settled that the ministers should normally be the expression of a majority in the Lower House.

Parliamentary life in 1861 and after was strongly influenced by the alliance of Right Center with Left Center upon which Cavour had first embarked nine years earlier. His opponents in 1852 had called this move an unscrupulous intrigue for power, and there is no doubt that he had acted behind the back of his cabinet colleagues and in order to supplant D'Azeglio in the premiership. But Cavour himself claimed this *connubio* as his political masterpiece since it consolidated the constitution by allying the Center groups against both extremes. It made for moderation and political consensus. It also set the fashion for basing power on mutable alliances within an amorphous government majority, rather than on a single party with a tight and consistent program. Instead of resigning if their policy failed to gain support, prime ministers tended to change that policy and try to build another compromise coalition. Cavour's shifting majority thus comprised many shades of opinion: it contained central-izers such as Ricasoli and Spaventa, together with decentralizers such as Farini and Minghetti; it contained Jacini of the Catholic Right, and Rattazzi of the anticlerical Left; Sella who wanted state control over the Church, and Lanza who wanted a free church in a free state. One result of this was to inhibit the growth of a clear-cut party system and an organized parliamentary opposition.

Cavour was not a party man, but rather an opportunist who took care never to be very far behind or ahead of public opinion. If no well-articulated parties were to appear before socialism and fascism, this was largely because differences of principle were thus discounted and fluctuations were deliberately encour-aged on the pretense of putting national before sectional interests. Any group not adopting these coalition tactics was out of the game, and any challenge on points of major principle might be rendered impotent. Some of the clericals, for instance, when, in 1857, they tried to take part in parliamentary politics, were not encouraged to do so but were treated as traitors who had to repudiate opposition or else stand aside. Similarly the republicans and believers in regional autonomy were muzzled, and their views kept as far as possible from public scrutiny. Coalition government was in practice aided by the fact that, out of a population of twenty-two million, there was an electorate of only half a million, of whom only 300,000 voted, and these constituted a narrow class which did not often contain strong divergencies of view. Instead of a two-party system, therefore, moderates of both the so-called Right and Left used to combine in every cabinet, and the government majority was perpetually being modified as the many small groups rallied for tactical reasons around one strong personality after another.

The philosopher Benedetto Croce and others were to justify this practice as an admirable and peculiarly Italian type of parliamentary government. Nevertheless, quite apart from producing highly unstable cabinets, it left governments sometimes dangerously free from opposition and criticism. There seldom existed any alternative government ready to take office with a completely different composition and policy. Parties were mostly clusters of clients around their patrons, and both policy and tactics were altered *en passant*. Political life therefore revolved less around principles than around persons, and parliamentary history was a tale of shifting loyalties, not of party conflict. Major oppositions of principle were often buried altogether, with surprising results, and though some individual politicians of both Right and Left regarded this as unsatisfactory, they could do nothing to alter what became a regular political practice.

★

Right and Left are generalized categories which mark the rough division of deputies into conservative-liberal and radical-democrat. The patriots who carried out the *risorgimento* were polarized into two wings, liberal and radical, which represent a fairly clear division in Italian history. The liberals, some of them on the Center Right and others on the Center Left, had sometimes before 1848 made a temporary and uneasy alliance with the radical revolutionaries against the unenlightened despotism of the *ancien régime*; but then, after the autocrats disappeared in 1859–60, the liberals were revealed as the chief beneficiaries from the revolution and became increasingly conservative of results achieved. The radicals, on the other hand, were more democratic and believed in equal rights for all, especially when they themselves failed to win any substantial positions of power. They also thought that, if economic matters were left unregulated as the liberals taught, progress would be too slow to be sure. They looked to reforms in the future, while the others were more conscious of history and tradition.

Conservative-liberals such as Cavour and Minghetti had been slow to accept Mazzini's ideas of national unity, and D'Azeglio continued to believe that the North should stop short of annexing Rome and the South. While they had taken a necessary share in the Italian revolution, these liberals had been less single-minded in their revolutionism, and had sometimes repudiated the liberal cause when straight political issues were confused by social revolution. Nevertheless, it was upon the conservative-liberals that success eventually depended, for they represented the cautious trimmers who made up "public opinion" in Italy. Cavour and Ricasoli were seen as safer and more realistic than Mazzini and Cattaneo: they knew how to husband resources, and how to wait for the moment when Italy could profitably intervene in the crosscurrents of European diplomacy. Although not the people to initiate a revolt, they might join if it looked like succeeding.

★

Cavour's majority after the elections of January 1861 was very substantial, and its focus was somewhere a little to the right of center. The "opposition" was small and various. On the extreme right-wing benches were about twenty illiberal reactionaries or "ultras," representing those few adherents of the pre-1860 dynasties who had not gone off into quietist abstention. Among them were some Piedmontese disciples of Solaro della Margherita who were almost more monarchical than the king himself. They deplored that their divinely appointed ruler should have stooped to accept a revolutionary and popular resettlement of Italy; they resented popular sovereignty manifested in the plebiscites, and could hardly bear to see the Turin parliament invaded by "Italians." It was perhaps unfortunate that the extreme Right was so doctrinaire and ineffective. Still worse, the Catholics were boycotting politics because the pope refused to recognize a state which had filched two-thirds of his domain; and Cavour himself, in a misguided fear of opposition, had once persuaded parliament to annul the election of extreme Catholic deputies. Italy therefore lacked a strictly conservative party. Equally important, this meant that a quite inadequate representation was accorded to those Italians whose political heirs under universal suffrage in 1948 were eventually to give an overwhelming majority to a Catholic party. Politics in Italy remained to this extent unrepresentative and "undemocratic." In France, by contrast, the liberals were forced closer together by the presence of a "reactionary" opposition in the legislature, whereas in Italy the weakness of such opposition allowed many fractional center groups to retain their individual loyalties, thereby making the government coalition often characterless and always liable to disintegration.

Rattazzi and Depretis were the principal leaders of the Left Center. They were liberal before they were radical, and always within or near the borders of Cavour's coalition. Beyond them were groups on the extreme Left, comprising fifty ill-assorted federalists, Garibaldians, and semirepublicans, the radical democrats of Tuscany under Guerrazzi, those of Piedmont under Brofferio, and a handful of Sicilians around Crispi. The loyalties of these groups were sometimes as much regional as political. Mazzini himself was still in exile, an outlaw under sentence of death.

Garibaldi in April 1861, when he turned up in parliament flaunting his red shirt and poncho, caused an uproar by accusing Cavour of dividing the country and threatening it with civil war. This outburst was in character, and it reflected the frustration of some who remained outside the government coalition. Garibaldi's lack of political tact threatened to carry Italy into dangerous revolutionary waters, for he still meant to start another private war for the conquest of Venice and Rome. Cavour and subsequent prime ministers, in their dealings with Garibaldi, showed equal tactlessness and incomprehension. The ex-Dictator of the Two Sicilies therefore resigned from parliament where, as he said, intrigue and talk were substitutes for action. He retired to write an autobiographical poem and to campaign for universal peace and a world state, his followers distributing themselves over the political spectrum.

This miscellaneous left-wing opposition was hamstrung by Cavour's able parliamentary maneuvers. Its leaders had served well enough on the battlefield, but their political energies had been perverted by years of conspiracy, exile, and imprisonment. Their good qualities were moral rather than political, and although full of fine intentions and popular appeal, they lacked the moderation and skill for parliamentary business. Italian politics thus lacked a strong Left as well as a strong Right, and opposition from either quarter tended to be irresponsible and utopian. The radical democrats were generals without an army and, because of the restricted suffrage, had no possibility of organizing a strong national party. Their program consisted of various paper schemes for universal suffrage, compulsory education, a progressive income tax, and economic assistance to Italy's backward regions.

Not only was this extreme Left inherently weak in both numbers and leadership, but Cavour and his successors freely used local-government machinery to rig elections and defeat them. The Left complained that a quarter of the minuscule electorate were in one sense or another government pensioners or amenable to official direction. When, despite this, Mazzini was repeatedly elected *in absentia* at Messina, the safe majority of official placemen could be relied on to veto his election. Bribery and intimidation of the press was another weapon. Cavour did his best to do without martial law, but could not avoid it at Naples after 1861, and police regulations were enforced harshly when less subtle politicians succeeded him as minister of the interior. Arbitrary government was made necessary by the unfriendliness of the rural population, and was defended by politicians who knew that, had the will of ordinary people prevailed, there might have been no *risorgimento* at all.

★

It was this general hostility or indifference of the masses which precluded any extension of the suffrage. Even among the enfranchised 2 per cent, public spirit was weak. There had been no political education under the Habsburgs in Lombardy or the Bourbons of Naples, and even in Piedmont there existed no solid basis of local self-government to educate people in applied liberalism. Without a widespread class of independent smallholders, another prerequisite of liberal parliamentary government was lacking. In the North, public-spirited landowners such as Cavour and Minghetti lamented that the regular practice of dividing real property among male children prevented the formation of a stable class of rich landlords trained to carry out the tasks of public life. In the South, there was rich landlordism in plenty but little social or political conscience. Local government in the South after 1861 was exploited by cliques who created jobs for their relatives, managed the communal lands and local charities in their own interests, and built roads at public cost for their private benefit. Those who ran municipal administration regularly arranged that taxes were levied chiefly on basic foodstuffs and so fell principally on the poor.

In all classes the absence of a community sense resulted from a habit of insubordination learned in centuries of despotism. Even the nobles and the rich had become accustomed to the politics of obstruction and hence thought that governments could be fairly cheated without moral obliquity so long as the cheating were successful. In December 1861 a special warning had to be issued against the private agencies which claimed to help people evade government regulations. Instead of recognizing that taxes had to be paid, the attitude was rather that if one group of people had discovered a profitable evasion, then other groups had better look to their own interests. Each province, each class, each industry thus endeavored to gain at the expense of the community. Before such traditional habits of mind could be changed, a slow and costly course of political education was necessary for both rulers and ruled.

6   The Social Hierarchy

The cause of national independence in Italy was associated with the liberalizing of government; it was also connected with urbanization and a social transformation in which new classes broke through a hitherto stifling political and social hierarchy. Before the *risorgimento*, the ruling classes had mostly consisted of a landowning aristocracy in alliance with the Church, whereas by 1861 a professional and mercantile element, allied to a new middle class of landed gentry, was much more prominent.

The bourgeoisie had hardly appeared as a force in politics before the Napoleonic period, but they were bound to discern in patriotism and liberalism an attractive ideology which would justify their advance toward prosperity and power. Lombard merchants had been cut off by Austria from the "foreign" port of Genoa, and toward the north, they met a discrimination in favor of textiles and other industrial exports from Bohemia. Patriotism therefore had a special advantage for them in combating restrictive monopolies and unenlightened protection. For the newly rich it meant expropriating the huge domains of the Church and purchasing them cheaply in a buyers' market: this was particularly true in Sicily, where neither Napoleon nor the principles of 1789 had ever reached, and where ecclesiastical land held in mortmain amounted to a tenth of all cultivable ground. Similarly with the common lands in each village, the more enterprising landowners wanted an "enlightened" government which would let them enclose and appropriate the commons. Whereas the Bourbons had favored the poor against the middle classes—for example by forbidding export of grain to keep bread cheap—after 1861 a free market was created which allowed agricultural prices to rise. Economic progress demanded that free trade should thus succeed paternalism, but the change-over was effected in a way which was as harsh on the underprivileged as it was agreeable to many of their betters.

The *risorgimento* was, as one would expect, a movement not of the populace but of an elite. In Garibaldi's Thousand there were no peasants, but rather students, former soldiers, independent craftsmen, and *litterati*. The backbone of the national revolution was made up of ex-officers such as Cavour and Pisacane, sailors such as Bixio and Garibaldi, medical doctors such as Bertani and Farini, lawyers like Crispi and Rattazzi, writers and scholars like Amari and De Sanctis. On the other hand few men of great possessions were listed in the secret societies, because the *risorgimento*, while anything but popular, was largely a revolution of the disinherited, of the starry-eyed, of the educated unemployed and underemployed.

★

The nobles in Italy had little political importance as a general category, not possessing the same feudal or military privileges as their equivalents in Germany, nor the habit of government as in England. Nobility did not imply wealth or power, and certainly there was nothing of a standardized aristocratic caste. Count Cavour, as a younger son, had to carve out his own fortune in finance and agriculture. The Marquis d'Azeglio, his predecessor as prime minister, was a successful painter and novelist. At Rome, the first of the princely Torlonia family had begun by selling castoff clothes in the city before he advanced to management of the lucrative salt and tobacco monopolies and ultimately became a millionaire. In Sicily, with a population of less than four million, there were sixty dukes, a hundred princes, and innumerable barons and marquises, many of them as illiterate as their grooms. In each province the nobility had a different character, and so never formed a caste barrier against the advance of democracy. In Piedmont or Tuscany it was sometimes liberal, just as it was usually clerical in Rome and feudal in Naples.

Far from having common interests with their counterparts in Piedmont, the titled families of Milan and Naples resented the surrender to Turin of the offices and patronage which before 1860 they had enjoyed in their provincial capitals. The multiplication of minor titles after 1861 also helped to break any remaining caste feeling. As the king once said, he could never refuse a cigar or a title to a gentleman—and the cynics added that he was not too punctilious about their being gentlemen. Cavour recognized that the ineffectiveness of the Italian aristocracy ruled out anything like a House of Lords, and there was never any suggestion that hereditary peers should sit in the Senate by right.

Economically as well as politically the old families were in decline. They did not readily enter commerce or industry, and there was little incentive to improve farming techniques when labor was plentiful and cheap. They were therefore increasingly left behind by new men, such as Pirelli, Orlando, and Breda, who rose through industrial enterprise to the dignity of the Senate. After 1815, Piedmont and Naples had tried to rehabilitate the landed aristocracy by restoring entails and primogeniture, but wars and the subsequent depression left most of the big estates heavily mortgaged. After 1815 they partly won back their social position, but any former economic power was waning. Few Roman aristocratic families retained much of their former affluence. Many had wasted their fortunes at faro or *trente et quarante*, trusting that the papal government would save them from bankruptcy. The princely families who owned the rural estates around Rome lived in the city and farmed out their estates to the wealthy *mercanti di campagna*, who in their turn, if they ended by owning property, made it a point of honor and social prestige to hire out the management to others.

An American diplomat in 1860 specially noted the contempt with which practical agricultural pursuits were regarded by the Neapolitan nobility. The Sicilian aristocracy, like the Spanish dons from whom many of them descended, would not stoop to the professions, let alone to trade. They had led the feudal revolution of 1812, but the succeeding revolutions of 1848 and 1860 found the professional middle classes more in command. Between the years 1820 and 1860, according to the British consul Goodwin, the number of landowning families in Sicily had risen from two thousand to twenty thousand, and the size of estates was smaller in proportion. What was happening here was happening elsewhere, and whether in the army, or in administration and diplomacy, the middle classes were assuming the position to which their numbers, enterprise, and ability entitled them.

A decayed social status alone was left to the nobility. If too poor to own a carriage or a gondola, they would hire one for the afternoon *passeggiata* and affix their own special door or emblem bearing the family coat of arms. In the North they were merging rapidly into the rest of society. In the South they were often lazy, corrupt, and ignorant good-for-nothings who on rare visits to their estates played the *gran signore* in a fortress surrounded by armed retainers. Thus Consul Goodwin described them in 1860:

The Sicilian nobleman, brought up at home by a priest and allowed to herd with menials, has no companion among his equals. Thrown into the hands of a pedagogue, he merely learns to read and write, then passes into the care of a friar who teaches him his catechism and the rudiments of Latin, and he finally goes to a school of nobles where he obtains a mere smattering of *Belles Lettres*. Then his education finishes. Coming home at 16 or 17, he throws aside his classics, betakes himself to novel reading, and sets up as a man about town. Prevented by class prejudice from entering the army or navy, he learns neither to command or obey; and excluded as he is from the magistracy by his legal ignorance, he neither administers justice nor enforces the laws. None of the nobility live on their estates. Most of the Sicilian towns serve for the residence of the neighbouring landlords on whose scanty outlay they depend for their subsistence. The family mansion standing on the deserted market place shows traces of former splendour in painted ceilings, gilt doors and embossed furniture. Here, lost in space, dwell the present possessors, ignorant of what is going on in the political world, falling gradually to the lowest level. They are destined to be supplanted by men of business and industry on a not distant day.

These men still considered local government their perquisite, but they were not of the caliber to influence national politics.

★

Because the *risorgimento* was a civil war between the old and new ruling classes, the peasants were neutral except in so far as their own perennial social war became accidentally involved. They had no love for United Italy and probably no idea what the term signified until it came home to them in higher prices, taxes, and conscription. Their instinctive tendency was to oppose any patriotic army which requisitioned their scanty food supplies and hence were usually a counterrevolutionary force in politics. In 1848 the Lombard peasants opened the irrigation dikes against the invading Piedmontese. In 1849, as in 1799, they had fought for the old dynasties in both North and South, because their dislike of royal tyranny was less than their hatred of the local lawyer, the usurer, and the factor who managed the landowner's estate, all of whom represented a more immediate and more effective oppression. Pisacane, the patriot, had been killed in 1857 by the very Neapolitan peasants he had hoped to liberate, the same rustic churls who sometimes hindered Garibaldi and who stripped and robbed the fallen soldiers of both sides on every battlefield.

Since Italy was a land of agriculture, peasants made up the great bulk of the population—national figures like Verdi, Pope Pius X, and Mussolini never quite threw off their humble origins. Garibaldi and even the king had more in common with rustic plebeians than with intellectual landowners such as Cavour. During long periods of the year, most agricultural workers were unemployed, and overpopulation kept their wages at a mere subsistence level. Though legally emancipated from feudalism, they had lost rights as well as duties thereby, because feudal landlords had formerly assumed obligations and responsibilities which now lapsed. The poor had the worst of both worlds: whatever the law might say, the peasant still labored at the *corvée*; his family could still be the virtual property of the landlord, kept in a state of personal dependence by armed *campieri* and *mazzieri* who wore their lord's livery. The laborer who lacked animals and tools was also at the mercy of the richer peasant, and in a year of bad harvest only the moneylender stood between him and starvation.

Sonnino in 1877 described how peasants in the lower Po Valley ate corn almost exclusively. In Apulia the day laborers consumed little but black barley bread baked two or three times a year. Since they could not buy, industry was deprived of a potential market and industrial development was consequently retarded. Thus there was no outlet for the surplus labor which impoverished the countryside. Only the Church and a few philanthropists bothered about the submerged nine-tenths of Italian society. It took time before the doctors linked pellagra with consumption of corn, nor did they understand what caused the malaria which infected several million Italians with chronic tertian and quartan fevers and kept perhaps four million acres uncultivable. Hundreds of thousands of people lived in caves, or in windowless wattle-and-daub huts, or in the damp cellars of the Neapolitan *fondaci*, and figures given to parliament in 1879 imply that some working-class areas in Rome had a population density of ten people per room.

In the southern agricultural regions nearly everyone was illiterate. The saying went there that a donkey cost more to maintain than a man, and Garibaldi's town-bred Thousand were astonished to find shepherds clad only in goat skins. Roads were nonexistent even between some of the chief cities; there was little commerce, only sparse cultivation, the surrounding sea was a highway for pirates, and the land resembled North Africa more than north Italy. W. S. Gilbert, librettist of the Gilbert and Sullivan partnership, was in youth captured by Calabrian brigands. The combination of malaria, brigands, and lack of water forced people to cluster in large villages perhaps as much as a dozen miles' walk from where they worked. Parts of the South in 1861 still possessed an economy where money was unessential. Rent, the services of the priest, the "protection" given by the lords' *campieri*, and the interest due to usurers, could all be paid in kind. Feudal conditions easily survived in such an environment; there was great inequality of wealth and little pretense of equality before the law. It was a Counter-Reformation world where the clergy had great influence over a hand-kissing population of serfs, where people learned their scanty morals and politics in church, and children had no chance of attending school. Conditions of life and work reduced the peasants permanently to the verge of revolt, and no political upheaval occurred but they rose to exploit it in a parallel insurrection that could be far more cruel and destructive.

However unsympathetic these peasants were toward the political aspirations of liberalism, without their unintended help the political revolution itself might have failed. In their eyes, insurrection meant a chance for sack and arson, an opportunity to attack their lord's bailiff and the police, to burn the town hall with its tax rolls and title deeds, to occupy their lord's land and divert water from his mill. Sometimes, driven by hunger, they ignited the first spark of what later became political rebellion, for they alone had everything to gain and little to lose by open class war. The driving force of the *risorgimento* was therefore by no means merely the heroism of Garibaldi and the brains of Cavour; to a lesser extent it was also personal or social vendettas and competition between families for control of local government.

Both peasants and city intellectuals had an interest in starting a revolution, the one with a social, the other with a political objective. Once insurrection had begun, however, the success of one class spelled ruin for the other. The rebellions of 1820–21 and 1848–49 had failed principally because the middle classes had not completed their political revolution before the peasants, profiting from the ensuing anarchy, started a separate grudge war of their own. Liberal landowners had therefore been forced to change sides and hope that the Austrians or the Bourbons would succeed in repressing social disorder. It was fortunate for Italy that circumstances were different in 1859–60.

The 1860 revolt in southern Italy is of great interest for its illustration of the attitude and the importance of the peasants. A combination of urban unemployment riots with anarchical *jacqueries* disintegrated local government and forced the terrified Bourbon police to run for their lives. This was an unintended but indispensable condition for the success of Garibaldi's invasion. A few days of rick burning, cattle stealing, land occupation, and assassination followed, but this outraged owners of property, even those who were liberals and patriots. As was said of Catania, the wealthier citizens "wanted liberty, but only if it could be won without sacrifice or inconvenience to themselves and without any social insurrection that might expose their houses to robbery." Garibaldi at first played for peasant support, and his early decrees in Sicily and Naples cleverly promised land distribution and cheaper food. But he soon found that his sole chance of permanent political victory lay in the support of the landlords who were chiefly interested in enforcing law and order, and many of whom by this time were interested in little else. So he altered course and executed the "communists" on the estates belonging to Admiral Nelson's family at Bronte. This was the price the landowners demanded in exchange for backing a patriotic revolution that otherwise meant little to them.

A peasants' revolt was in this way not only instrumental in undermining the Bourbons at a decisive moment, but also in compelling some of the old ruling classes to turn toward victorious Piedmont as the defender of social order against their serfs. These peasants soon realized that Garibaldi was not so much a rebel on their side, but rather appeared to represent a new and perhaps equally oppressive government. By that time, however, the forces of order were back in control. The middle classes, whether conservative or radical in politics, were at one on the social question. Cavour had correctly analyzed this:

> In Italy a democratic revolution has little chance of success. To appreciate this it is enough to examine the elements making up the party which wants political change. This party meets with little sympathy among the masses

which, except for one or two sections in the towns, are generally attached to the old institutions of the country. Its main strength resides almost exclusively in the middle and a part of the upper classes. And both of these have many interests to defend. Property, thank heaven, is not in Italy the exclusive privilege of any one class. If social order were really threatened, if the great principles on which society reposes were challenged, I am sure that we should find even the most extreme republicans in the forefront of the conservative party.

By its own logic, therefore, a movement which had partly grown out of peasants rebelling against landowners ended up on the side of the landowners against their peasants—indeed this was one important reason for its success. The common people were otherwise irrelevant to patriotism, and this helps to explain why few patriotic leaders except Garibaldi did very much to win their support. Cavour, in his early days at least, had spoken of competing with the socialists in offering social reform, but he confined himself to vague admonitions. Mazzini, too, since only for a few months of 1849 in Rome did he ever wield executive authority, had to rest content with sincere but theoretical statements, as that liberty implied equality, and that political revolution would be ineffective without major social changes. Except for Pisacane, Garibaldi, and Mazzini, the early radicals paid too little attention to social reform and the condition of the poor.

For some time after 1860 social problems remained in the background. The middle classes had, as it were, gained a premature victory over the feudal landlords. Feudalism had been destroyed before its successor, capitalism, was ready to take over the management of society, and before labor was sufficiently articulate to state its needs. According to Sonnino, the only social legislation in the first decades of United Italy was a measure on postal savings banks in 1870, and an ineffective act of 1873 about child employment in industry. So far as one can see, the general standard of living showed little or no improvement for some time. Insufficient money was spent on public works, and political instability discouraged any impartial study of social and economic problems. Deeper still lay a dangerous cast of mind which associated liberalism with the interests of the rich. History was to show, for instance, that night work in the textile industry was prohibited only when overproduction gave factory owners a real interest in reducing output.

To become an inherent part of Italian life and consciousness, the political *risorgimento* required a supplementary social revolution, one which could attract popular sympathy to the government and convince the ruling classes that social remedies might be a prerequisite of political stability. To complete the process of unification, the common people had to be brought into the mainstream of national life, and reluctance to learn this lesson was to bring severe trials upon Italy in the next ninety years.

7 Agriculture and Industry

The great majority of Italians lived by agriculture, yet Italy was not self-sufficient in food; the basic cause of this was the scarcity and misuse of capital. Rather than improve existing landholdings, wealthy proprietors preferred to extend them or buy titles, for those were the best ways to purchase social esteem. Savings disappeared in interest on mortgages, which in 1860 was thought to consume as much as one-third of the revenue from the soil, and this ineffective use of credit was a crippling burden on the major national industry. The most popular types of cultivation were not always the most profitable, for the most lucrative crops needed a greater outlay than the average farmer could afford—vines, olives, and almonds, for instance, took ten years or more to mature. In some areas there was no money to build roads to the local market and transportation difficulties added to the cost of marketing. Although labor was cheap, borrowing was expensive and people often lacked the resources or the will to cultivate their land with more than moderate efficiency. Rivers were left without embankments because it paid no one to build and maintain them, and large areas which might have absorbed the surplus agricultural population were abandoned to malarial marsh and swamp. After two of three crops had been extravagantly raised on recently cleared land, it might be deserted, its owner preferring to exploit other virgin soil rather than stay and pay his quota of land tax.

A prerequisite of improvement was a new attitude as much as new capital. Certainly state help was required wherever land reclamation was beyond the capacity of individual proprietors. Great areas would have to be drained or irrigated, water supplies regulated, and mountains saved from erosion by tree planting. Quite as important was a change of outlook among the cultivators themselves. The Italian laborer was one of the hardest working in the world, and when employment was insufficient at home he made seasonal expeditions abroad to build the Suez Canal, the Forth Bridge, the railroads of America, the Alpine tunnels, and the harbors of Calais and Marseille. But no permanent improvement was likely at home until domestic agriculture could be made more efficient and enterprising or became more able to provide for an industrial population.

Peasant families still spun and wove their clothes from home-grown hemp and flax. Subsistence agriculture had to cover almost all their needs, and this restricted the possibilities of improvement. Even after 1860 and on the big farms of Lombardy the wooden plough and the hand flail were in general use. A Sicilian nobleman who imported subsoil ploughs found that his workers broke them to avoid a reduction in jobs, and well into the next century sowing and reaping were done by hand. The southern peasant distrusted innovations, often believing, for instance, that machine-made cloth could not be durable. He still prayed to one saint against hail, to another against drought, to St. Cataldo before threshing, to St. Erasmo if his ass were ailing. Even in the twentieth century, villages have been known to change their patron saint if they received less rain than other nearby districts. This psychological conservatism accompanied technical ignorance as further factors which limited any advance in agricultural efficiency and standards of life.

Among methods of land tenure, the extensive farm or *latifondo* of the South had survived two thousand years of war and revolution, despite frequent changes of ownership and some hostile legislation. The legal abolition of feudalism by Napoleon had temporarily broken up some of these *latifondi*, but intensive agriculture was limited by natural conditions. Hence, as before and since, large estates continued or reappeared around the only people with access to capital. Where three harvests regularly failed out of ten, the peasant had insufficient reserves to work on his own; a balanced farm unit would have been too large for his resources, and it was difficult on small holdings to rotate crops efficiently or to grow enough fodder for the necessary oxen. Napoleon's government had therefore been unable to prevent people selling back their parcels of land once the estates had been divided. Common land belonging to each village, wherever it was distributed in lots to the peasants, frequently passed to land speculators who had ready cash, or else landowners used their control of local government to enclose the commons without any pretense of equity. The large estates increased in size, while the peasants lost rights of grazing and wood collecting on the common land which had been important in their economy.

Only a small proportion of farm workers owned property more extensive than a hovel and a back yard, and many more were casual day laborers whose lot was miserable. In Tuscany and elsewhere a beneficial system of *métayage* or *mezzadria* had been developed, by which the owner gave the seed, vines, and olive trees, perhaps the cattle, and would pay all rates and taxes, while the tenant supplied tools and labor. No cash rent was involved, but produce was divided half and half, or more favorably to the landlord. This sharecropping hardly encouraged investment in land, since either party knew that the other would gain half of the return on any improvement. In compensation it certainly helped social stability, and it was often therefore called an ideal type of collaboration. But as markets became wider and tools more expensive, the security of tenure given by the *mezzadria* did not compensate for the low output per unit of land. It usually meant that crops were grown for subsistence alone, vegetables indiscriminately among the vines, without incentive to specialization.

The principal crops in Italy were cereals, silk, and grapes. Cereals, needing little capital outlay, were grown even in areas which were thoroughly unsuitable and took up nearly half the country's productive acreage. Nassau Senior in 1851 found that in Sicily sixteen bushels of wheat to the acre were produced every other year, the land laying fallow the next, and he commented that this was no more than in the time of Cicero. Except on the great northern plain, vines, olives, and fruit would have better suited the prevalent conditions of scanty and uncertain rainfall. In some years more wine was exported from Italy than from France, although Italy suffered from the insufficient skill of growers and manufacturers. There was little selection of vines, and because of the fear of theft and hail the grapes were often harvested too early. Types of wine varied too much from year to year, and there was little attempt to study foreign taste. Silk had the great advantage that it was even more an export crop which helped the accumulation of capital and the balance of payments. The other chief export products of Italian agriculture were oil, fruit, and cheese. Hemp and flax were grown in considerable quantities, and there was a momentary boom in cotton when the American Civil War created the illusion that Sicily and Sardinia could supply the north Italian textile industries.

★

Before 1860, Italy had hardly begun to share in the industrial revolution. The country was deficient in raw materials, and though labor was abundant, skilled technicians were rare, for the worst-paid lawyer or white-collar worker thought himself far superior to the most skilled artisan. The progressive industrialist who brought over machines from England might find no one to assemble or maintain them, and a surplus of ordinary manpower lessened the incentive to make improvements. In any case power would be lacking for a new age of steam and electricity and machinery from abroad was expensive.

The mental attitude of both rich and poor was unfavorable to great industrial development. As Cavour complained, too much investment had been diverted from industry to real estate. People who were brought up under the *ancien régime* had been taught to think speculation improper and credit something uncanny or unholy—King Ferdinando of Naples had been irritated by the very mention of bills of exchange. Paper money continued to be distrusted and coins hoarded long after 1860; cattle and farm produce went on being exchanged by barter; over fifty different coins continued in occasional use—ducat, piastre, oncia, scudo, lira, marengo, and florin. Alongside the new decimal and metric systems, the old illegal weights and measures survived in country districts until the end of the century.

Such industry as existed was never far removed from agriculture. Town dwellers continued to own small holdings outside the city walls, and agricultural laborers during winter would often seek part-time employment in the towns. Quarrying and mining were generally undertaken by part-time farmers, and the Lombard silk industry was largely operated by women who worked for much of the year in the fields. Even when cottage industries gave way to a factory system using power looms, silk throwing remained a seasonal occupation for agricultural workers. The 1861 census recorded nearly eight million agriculturists but only three million workers engaged in craftsmanship and manufacture, and of these three million most were women working part-time. Ellena calculated in 1880 that only 20 per cent of industrial workers were adult males. For some years after 1861, the number of textile workers doing piecework in their homes must actually have grown. The workers were the first to protest against factory employment, because auxiliary domestic jobs were precious to a farming family which had to reckon with seasonal unemployment, and many people were afraid of losing independence and security in factory life. They could not appreciate that factories held out the potential benefit of combination in trade unions, whereas in cottage industry their wages would be tied to the rates prevailing in agriculture.

The money which might have promoted an industrial revolution had for centuries been hidden in the countryside, often unproductively. Potential investors had been deterred by the unsympathetic attitude of the pre-1860 regimes and by the wars and unrest of the *risorgimento*. In Lombardy, which was unusual in having a regular surplus of exports over imports, Cattaneo estimated that in 1850 there was five times as much investment in agriculture as in industry. Three out of the four big Italian railroad companies were to be completely financed from abroad, and the fourth largely so; the first installations of gas in Italy were the product of foreign enterprise, and foreign houses owned much of the textile and shipping industries. English capital was sunk in the sulphur, wine, and essential-oil trades of Sicily, as well as in Venetian hotels and glass. French investment was directed mainly to Piedmont and Naples, German and Swiss to Lombardy, in a process which incidentally had the not unimportant effect of binding to the fortunes of Italy some of the chief banking houses and capitalists of Europe.

Cavour constantly complained that there was so little enterprise by Italians. He pointed out that the national debt and property mortgages absorbed savings that should have gone into agriculture and industry. Government stock and the purchase of land were thought safer, and ironically the desire for safety also caused Italian money to flow abroad into French bonds. Cavour himself was partly responsible, for in a sense this fact was part of the cost of the *risorgimento*. Cavour had created the national debt; he also set the fashion of immobilizing so much of the national wealth in relatively unproductive military expenditure. As there was never enough capital invested in production, there was never enough employment, salaries were too low and the rate of interest too high.

In an age of iron and steel, Italy suffered, and her few natural resources could not be properly exploited until hydroelectric power became cheap. The situation was not improved by the governmental protection given before 1860 to inefficient methods and industries. Cavour in Piedmont had set a different example by freeing trade and giving encouragement to a few selected industries. When this policy was applied to the rest of Italy after 1860, inefficient concerns were ruined and the industrial life of the country remained concentrated in the triangle between Milan, Turin, and Genoa. Water power was more accessible in this northern area, transport easier, and markets nearer. The North had more industrial traditions than elsewhere, more financial experience, and more readiness to speculate and improve.

A good example is provided by the history of the Orlando family, who began making agricultural machinery in Sicily, but soon moved to Genoa where the government was less restrictive and the market more attractive. There the Orlandos deliberately set themselves to prove that Italians, as well as forming a nation, possessed industrial skill and enterprise, and could produce textile machinery, marine engines, and armaments equal to the best anywhere. The cause of patriotism naturally found this family enthusiastic. Cavour at once saw their value, and though they were tainted politically with Mazzinianism, he set them to dredge ports and reorganize the Ansaldo engineering works. Luigi Orlando, who in 1848 had aided insurrection by constructing prefabricated movable barricades and iron-ringed wooden cannon, in 1855 was experimenting with ironclads, and the next year made Garibaldi captain of the first Italian screw-propelled ship. By 1860 he was employing a thousand workers and was able to equip Garibaldi's volunteer army with arms made secretly and largely at his own expense. His brother, Giuseppe, was chief engineer on one of the two paddle steamers which carried Garibaldi's troops to Sicily. Constantly fed by government orders, the Orlando workshops became the most important factory for armaments and locomotives in Italy.

Textiles were, however, of more importance in the Italian economy. From 1816 onward, jennies driven by water power were being used, and the industry spread in small rural townships where fast-flowing rivers and part-time female labor were available. The creation of a larger domestic market and the appearance later of steam-driven looms then made big urban factories more economic. The woolen industry was most prosperous in Piedmont, and here an important stimulus was the need for uniforms during the Crimean war of 1855 and the Austrian war of 1859. More important was silk manufacture, which was found all over Italy but particularly in Lombardy and Piedmont. In the days of government protection the export of raw silk had been prohibited, as a result of which Lyons had become the European center of silk manufacture, but in an age of freer trade, raw and manufactured silk again became the chief Italian export.

Italy's second export industry was the sulphur mining of Sicily, in which ten thousand workers were engaged about 1861, half of them young boys. This sulphur industry lacked an adequate incentive to greater efficiency until it met competition from the United States later in the century. The ore was extracted by methods which wasted one-third, and there was little attempt to regulate supply with demand. No advantage, moreover, had been taken of Sicily's monopoly position to set up refineries or capacity for sulphuric acid manufacture. Another mining industry which enjoyed a quasi-monopoly was that of marble. Deposits of coal were negligible, and though a little iron was found in

Sardinia, Elba, and the Val d'Aosta, before long the mines were going to need protective duties which raised the price of the raw material at the expense of the Italian consumer.

★

The impact of unification on the Italian economy disappointed some people who had been led by the romantic and heroic aspects of the *risorgimento* to hope for too much. There had been a popular illusion that independence would automatically bring more pay and a lower cost of living, perhaps even less work and lighter taxes. The abolition of internal customs barriers and the reduction of tariffs were undoubtedly advantageous, as were decimal measurements and a uniform currency. Yet long-term benefits had to be purchased by short-term losses.

Naples felt the pinch at once, and with the disappearance of its royal court lost many of the public services, building contracts, and bureaucratic appointments which had formerly provided an artificial prosperity. Naples was the largest town in Europe after London, Paris, and St. Petersburg, and before 1861 had been the capital city of a kingdom of eight million people. This Neapolitan kingdom had possessed four times the merchant shipping of Piedmont and a considerably larger navy. But owing to the unenlightened protection enjoyed by Neapolitan industry before 1861, severe losses were sustained when the new Italy eliminated marginally productive industries by allowing free competition from the North. Some of the southern textile producers had been accustomed to 100 per cent protection, whereas Piedmont by 1860 had reduced her duties to about 10 per cent by value.

The prevailing school of economists in the North believed wholeheartedly in free trade. Under their influence the liberal fiscal system of Piedmont, designed to suit a relatively prosperous community, was extended after 1861 to more backward areas. The other regional banks successfully fought against the Bank of Turin being given a monopoly of note issue, but southern industrialists were not united enough to press their common interests in parliament. Northern industries, already accustomed to freer trade, were in a fine competitive position when other provinces had to reduce their tariff on iron from twenty or thirty lire a kilogram to three. It was even said that the general application of the low Piedmontese tariff was intentionally designed to sweeten the pill of unity for the North, which now obtained a new and defenseless market.

Competition thus drove out of circulation many local products in the South, and even in some of the lately annexed northern towns, Modena and Parma for example, native industry proved too fragile. It is true that for short while the cheapness of northern goods was partly offset by high freight charges, and as late as 1872 cotton manufacturers in the North could still tell a commission of inquiry that unification had not yet improved their sales. But gradually the "conquest" of the South by northern industry and finance was creating the unified market upon which general prosperity depended. Milan and Turin were bound to prevail in the end. Protection was introduced again during the eighties, but, like free trade in the sixties, this was again designed to aid the richest and most powerful regions of the country at the expense of the poorest.

In agriculture, though output increased and prices rose after 1861, improvement was not unqualified. When many ecclesiastical estates were nationalized and thrown cheaply upon the market, this encouraged farmers to go for quick returns irrespective of damage done to the land. Contact with a wider world progressively exposed southern agriculturists to world economic crises. Cotton was ill-advisedly planted for a short-lived American market, and a vast acreage in the South was given over to vineyards after phylloxera ravaged those of France. In each case the gain was temporary, and valuable long-term investments in olives and fruit trees were sacrificed to meet momentary changes in world demand. This was part of the price paid for greater economic unification of the peninsula.

It was a price which in the long run was well worth paying when the benefits of improved communications were felt. Italy had missed the canal age because of its mountains and because irrigation had a prior claim on water supplies. This made it the more deplorable that land communications were so poor. In the Kingdom of Naples about 1860, according to Nisco, 1,621 out of 1,848 villages had no roads at all, and there were only a hundred miles of railroad, with no services operating on saints' days or in Holy Week, and no tunnels lest public morality should suffer. The railroad track from Milan to central Italy stopped at Bologna. Venice was still cut off from Emilia. The Tuscan network was isolated both to north and south, and a journey southward to Rome still involved travel by ship or post chaise. In Sicily and Sardinia there were no railroads at all. Not until railroad construction proved a less risky investment did Italian capitalists budge from what Cavour called "culpable apathy" in this matter.

Not only prosperity, but also the free commerce of ideas and the moral gain of feeling truly united were dependent on these developments, and after 1861 a general railroad boom gradually overcame many forces making for inertia. Brigands saw their livelihood threatened and sometimes tore up the track. Contractors exploited bureaucratic ignorance and built badly. Parliamentarians courted powerful electors by arranging uneconomic branch lines in their constituencies. Local authorities undermined each others' projects in the competition to secure a place on the main railway lines. But the tracks were laid. Most of the necessary investment came from abroad, most of the companies engaged went bankrupt, and the return per mile progressively declined. But in the last resort the state paid rather than let a line stop short. The building of the Mont Cenis tunnel at government expense between 1857 and 1871 linked the Italian with the French system; the St. Gotthard between 1872 and 1882 joined Italy to Central Europe; and when the Simplon tunnel was built in the years 1898–1906, the network was substantially complete.

8   Immediate Political Problems

On February 18, 1861, a parliament representing all the recently united provinces met at Turin. A month later, with no dissentient voice, it officially conferred on Vittorio Emanuele the new title of King of Italy by grace of God and will of the people. It was also declared that Rome should one day be taken from the pope and become the national capital.

Cavour's first difficulty was the dearth of good subordinates. Lieutenants had to be promoted into colonels almost overnight, junior teachers into headmasters, small-time lawyers and professors into cabinet ministers. For the *risorgimento* had not thrown up enough leaders of first-class caliber, and some of the best had either been killed in war or else had been soured in frustrating conspiracy and exile. It was sometimes admitted that too little of their success had been due to the Italians themselves, and too much to a fortunate international situation, so that they lacked enough practical experience of administration and statesmanship. Cavour himself did not have the time or the skill to educate a new class of governors, preferring to concentrate power and take three or more portfolios in his own direct control. He had alienated other prominent more radical future leaders such as D'Azeglio, Rattazzi, and Ricasoli, and could not abide the men of the future such as Depretis and Crispi. When considering possible names for his new cabinet he lamented to the British ambassador that there was not a single Lombard or southerner who was both reputable and pliant enough for his needs.

Cavour himself in 1861 was worn out with playing Atlas and less fertile in the expedients for which he had been renowned. The other leaders of the *risorgimento*, men such as D'Azeglio and Garibaldi, were becoming old and embittered, and there were few new figures to catch the enthusiasm of a younger generation and solve the many problems attending the birth of a new state. Cavour's sudden death in June 1861 was for this reason a shattering blow—Bismarck, who was only five years younger, still had thirty years of power ahead of him. The making of Italy was due in great measure to Cavour's personal skill, and he alone among Italian statesmen comprehended the difficulties of resettlement. He may have died opportunely for his own reputation, but for Italy his loss was irreparable.

*

Cavour left his successors no stable majority, for much of his following had been personal. Until 1876 governments went on chiefly being formed from his own group of liberal conservatives on the moderate political Right. These men, though they had used revolutionary and conspiratorial means to overthrow the old regime, were determined to allow no further revolution against themselves, and despite appeals from Verdi among others, Mazzini remained an outlaw and threatened with execution if he should be caught. The governmental *consorteria* (as it was called) was a loose union of interests. In its fifteen years of rule, cabinets were to be constantly overthrown by internal quarrels, and repeated attempts were made by one subgroup or another to break loose and form an alternative political alliance. No single leader possessed Cavour's charm and fascination, his sense of the practicable, and his ingenuity in compromise and timing. They were honest, hard-working men and most set an invaluable example of loyal service and probity, but on the whole they were narrow and unimaginative, and their personal rivalries caused a confusion of political issues which did not help the emergence of healthy parliamentary debate. The extreme Right and the extreme Left occasionally united in common opposition, and whenever these were joined by a secession from the government majority, any cabinet was likely to fall.

Cavour had not belittled such problems as reconciliation with the Church, the annexation of Venice and Rome, and the fusion of North and South, but he had no time to prepare a comprehensive and effective policy. Personally, he knew far more about agricultural conditions in Ireland than about those in Sicily or Sardinia, and far more about politics in Paris than in Rome. Had he lived he would perhaps have learned to improvise as successfully in domestic as in foreign policy. But his successors neither improvised well nor gave much evidence of a sense of considered purpose. The very existence of a "southern problem" was denied. It was recognized that Rome must be won but there was no agreement about how, and relations with the Church were allowed to drift from bad to worse. Though professedly Catholic, the leaders of the new state were excommunicated, and the friar who attended Cavour's deathbed was punished for this action by his superiors.

Faced by parliamentary indiscipline, with vested interests ready to resent any preferential treatment of others, commitment to a definite policy was difficult. Seven different financial systems had to be unified; some of them were quite chaotic and they possessed different tax structures and methods of accounting. Care had to be taken to divide the jobs, decorations, and contracts not too unfairly between the different provinces. The petitions placed before parliament show the strength and variety of these sectional interests. Many towns and regions were squabbling about who should have preference in railroad construction. Not untypical was that Syracuse claimed recognition against Noto as the administrative capital of its province. At Naples, Nigra thus described what he found on his arrival as governor in 1861:

There is a continual clamor: "Simplify, improve, moralize the administration, dismiss Bourbon employees, replace them with the victims of Bourbon tyranny, give the people work and bread, give us roads, schools, industry, and commerce, repress the hostility of the clergy, organize the municipalities, give arms to the National Guard, send us troops and gendarmes." One side

49

cries, "Hurry up with unification, destroy every vestige of local autonomy, give the central government entire responsibility for local affairs." The other side replies, "Respect the traditions and institutions already in existence, keep all that is good in local administration, and do not turn away destitute all the old servants of the Bourbons."

Nigra's comment was that

> ... one cannot improvize in a few months a whole system of railroads; one cannot create schools without schoolmasters; one cannot base industry and commerce on anything but general confidence and the slow but sure action of free institutions; one cannot change in one moment a people who have been for ages subjected to slavery and ignorance, nor suddenly make them civilized and cultured; public opinion can only be built up gradually by the exercise of freedom.

In all the newly annexed provinces many interests had been damaged by the revolution. Local oligarchs had been displaced by rival families who had been quicker to turn their coat, and great numbers of public servants had been abruptly discharged. When former political prisoners were clamoring for jobs, it was a delicate question whether to appoint new and inexperienced officials or the trained employees of the former despotic dynasties. Time was needed before former judges and ministers could sit in the same courtroom or cabinet with people they had once condemned to torture and the galleys. The lawyers were disgruntled at having to use an unfamiliar code of law; local officials were discomfited by dependence on far-off Turin; while at Turin itself the central departments were quite bewildered by so many diverse problems and local circumstances. Landowners sometimes found their estates forcibly occupied by their own hired men, and they resented being ruled by lawyers instead of representatives of their own privileged class.

No government could have appeased so many various interests, nor was there time to be entirely consistent. Promises were made of decentralization, and at the same time many steps had to be taken toward greater centralization. At Naples the civil servants of both Francesco di Borbone and Garibaldi often had to be retained simultaneously in lieu of granting unemployment relief, despite the cost and the dangerous multiplication of officialdom. Senatorial and ministerial posts were distributed geographically, and higher administrative officials too were chosen less for their competence than so as not to offend regional susceptibilities. The poor *lazzaroni* were set to work building railroads, and the rich *latifondisti* kept quiet by the cheap sale of ecclesiastical estates. But placating all parties was a complicated business and sometimes proved self-defeating.

One especially embarrassing problem was amalgamation of the old provincial armies into a new Italian army along with Garibaldi's volunteers. When Cavour halted Garibaldi at Naples in 1860, one avowed reason had been his fear that the prestige of the monarchy and the regular troops might suffer if these irregulars and near-republicans were too successful. The government, therefore, not only tried to deflate Garibaldi's prestige, but disowned him in front of Europe and even confessed that a civil war against him was not out of the question. Although the volunteers had conquered half the peninsula for the king, the defeated Neapolitan army was treated better, because the Piedmontese generals were jealous of the astonishing success of these irregular troops, preferring to amalgamate with regular soldiers who were officers and gentlemen and had been through the orthodox military academies. The Neapolitan Nunziante became a general in the Italian army, despite the fact that much of his life had been spent repressing liberalism, and despite the last-minute betrayal of his king and his military oath when he deserted the Bourbons and joined the victors. Garibaldi's guerrillas, on the other hand, had to submit to rigorous screening which, while no doubt useful for excluding undesirables, drove many excellent men to despair.

★

The nation was to thrive on the store of energy and healthy rivalry produced by regional divisions; nevertheless, especially in these early years, the old traditions of municipalism weakened the sense of national unity. It is noteworthy and paradoxical that so many among the motives which brought about national unity were non-national in origin. The overmastering urge of Sicily to break free of Naples had enormously helped Garibaldi in 1860, and Garibaldi's own animosity—as a Niçois and a convicted felon—against the Piedmontese government lay behind his breach with Cavour and his conquest of Sicily and Naples. This pervasive regionalism and individualism became exasperated when the result of the national revolution led to an increase in centralized government. Some of the regions were made to feel conquered and exploited and were not happy in subordination to Turin. It was easy for them to doubt the adequacy of a single administrative system in a country containing such diverse traditions and levels of social development.

The backwardness of the South illustrated this difficulty of applying uniform laws. Virtually the whole southern agricultural population was illiterate. Yet it was impossible to apply the Piedmontese law of 1859 which had specified two years' compulsory education, because parents would not have co-operated even if the teachers and schools could have been found. Indeed, in defiance of subsequent regulations, forty-five years later almost one-quarter of the children of Italy were still not attending school, because education was made a charge upon the villages, and village taxpayers often neither wanted it, nor could afford to pay for it.

Political education, too, was rudimentary in direct proportion to low standards of living. Maxime du Camp at Naples in 1860 heard people in the streets shout "long live Italy" and then ask their neighbor what the word "Italy" meant. Another observer heard people asking if "Italia" might be the name of the king's wife. The introduction of the jury system was especially difficult in backward areas. Very often no witnesses could be found, let alone jurymen to convict, because private vengeance against witnesses was more fearful and more certain than the legal penalties for crime or perjury.

It was understandable that the government should wish to centralize and standardize administration more quickly than was expedient, for these internal divisions were potentially dangerous and national consciousness was still weak. Even many educated Italians knew little of their country except from books. There was still no standard language that was intelligible to the majority or that was normally spoken by more than one Italian in twenty. Manzoni had spent a month as far south as Florence, and Cavour several days there, but neither of them ever went to Rome or Naples, let alone Sicily, Calabria, or Apulia, and both would have felt infinitely more at home in Paris than anywhere beyond the Apennines.

The Lombard radical, Cattaneo, would therefore have preferred a federal constitution with regional autonomy. He prophesied—and Gladstone and Lord John Russell were privately saying much the same—that a centralized Italian state would tend to put national power before personal freedom, and that foreign wars might even lead to a dangerous militarization of society. Cattaneo's analysis was often profound and farsighted, and it is a reminder that other solutions were proposed to the Italian question than those of the republican unitarists or the royalist Piedmontese. But in practice federalism remained an intellectual concept only, and after the conversion of former enthusiasts such as Balbo and Gioberti, had little influence on politics. Cavour himself was ready to accept federalism as late as 1859, but the events of 1859–61 settled that Italy was to be a centralized monarchical state instead of a federal republic.

★

The new government of Italy countered these deep-rooted regional sentiments by an administrative centralization which perhaps exceeded in the urgency of the moment what was justified or wise. Already in November 1859, without waiting for any parliamentary debate to justify such an arbitrary act, Piedmontese laws had been hastily applied to Lombardy in the teeth of local opposition, and other regions were similarly treated after 1860. The Piedmontese administrative and judicial systems, copied from France, had proved adequate enough, and it was thought undesirable to waste time in comparative study of other systems in the peninsula. Local separatism and municipalism had to be soundly beaten, and a centralized or even autocratic control was needed in combating the brigandage and disaffection rife in the South. The Franco-Piedmontese system of departments could also be superimposed across former regional boundaries and had the advantage of creating novel territorial units devoid of traditional loyalties and sentiment.

Even where the arguments for regional devolution were intellectually accepted, the argument from convenience and speed still told decisively against them. In the case of education, for example, administrative convenience made it desirable for the universities to adopt uniform courses, to restrict optional subjects and lectures, and to make professors into state officials who were centrally appointed and who took a formal oath of obedience to the king. In those few educational matters where initiative was left to the localities, responsibility for primary education was given to villages whose first anxiety was to limit expenditure and minimize the rates.

This failure to develop a vital local self-government stifled local initiative and was to hinder the growth of parliamentary democracy, while the appointment of a government-controlled prefect in each province was said by many Italian liberals to be incompatible with true liberalism. Centralization also meant that much parliamentary time was wasted on parochial matters. But the chief objection raised by opponents of centralization was that theory and logic were allowed to prevail over local custom and a more empirical attitude, a fact which contributed to making the national movement dangerously rootless and revolutionary.

Cavour's views here are uncertain, for like a true empiricist he was hesitant to commit himself irrevocably. Having cleverly hinted to waverers in the South that he would allow considerable local autonomy if only they joined United Italy, he then was caught off balance by the suddenness of success and changed his mind. He knew that some Piedmontese would hardly support the *risorgimento* unless the primacy of their own laws and traditions was clearly recognized. Farini and Minghetti, two leading members of his cabinet, neither of them Piedmontese by origin, had prepared in 1860 a project for administrative devolution. This was based on six regions "which represented the old autonomous states of Italy." But the scheme was dropped the following year. One reason was that some people associated regional autonomy with national disintegration. Another was the fear that local self-government would play into the hands of corrupt local cliques who coveted the patronage involved in the multiplication of minor offices. Individual communes, too, saw that they would retain more independence of Florence, Naples, and the other regional capitals if power lay not in the regions but in a central government. A royal decree of 1861 therefore changed the old intendants into prefects, and—apparently against cabinet advice—abolished the last relics of autonomy in Naples and Tuscany.

This imposition of the Piedmontese administrative system reinforced the impression that one region had virtually conquered the rest. The Milanese federalist, Ferrari, acidly called this the last of the barbarian invasions. Jurists confirmed that the Kingdom of Italy in 1861 was legally not a new state, but merely an extension of the Kingdom of Piedmont-Sardinia. In deference to dynastic vanity the Italian constitution remained exactly that granted to the

Piedmontese in 1848, and the parliament of 1861 was the eighth not the first by official reckoning. The king also continued to style himself Vittorio Emanuele *the Second* and kept his jubilee in 1874, though critics pointed out that James VI of Scotland had been gracious enough to call himself James the First of England, and Henry III of Navarre became Henry IV of France.

Outside Piedmont this was not popular. Cavour's successor, Baron Ricasoli, regretted that his fellow Tuscans were heavily outnumbered on the commissions set up to study the new administrative and legal changes, and complained that the Piedmontese only understood French institutions and talked a different language. At Milan, the historian Cantù noted that the Piedmontese and Lombards did not mix in society. At Bologna, thirty-five professors refused to take an oath of loyalty to the new government and were dismissed from their posts. As for Neapolitans, many would allow no other city to take precedence over Naples except Rome, and many books and pamphlets were written to show that Turin was of all cities the least Italian in history and character. Crispi, a future prime minister, claimed that the southern provinces were ahead of the North as regards their legal codes and administration. Everywhere there were grumbles that Piedmont received too many government contracts, that the South paid more than its fair share of taxation, and that all local institutions and customs were being brushed aside in the interests of uniformity. The very process of "piedmontization" thus provoked a revival of local sentiment, and Cavour's attempt to replace the Bank of Naples failed completely, for southerners were reluctant to use northern banknotes, and southern branches of the Turin Bank soon began to run at a loss.

Some of the critics later admitted that Piedmont had behaved much better than report said, and they could not deny that the North had a great deal to offer the South. Though the Piedmontese administration was uninspiring and unimaginative, it was comparatively honest, reasonably efficient, and in most cases stood for a moderate and tolerant ideal of civil and economic liberty. Though her legal codes may have been less finished and somewhat less humane than the Tuscan, a free press and a jury system was a novelty for some other regions, even if an illiterate population made juries unworkable in any liberal sense. The king, too, made a slight effort to italianize his family. At least he arranged for his grandson to be born at Naples and to be given among many other names that of the local saint, Gennaro; and instructors were later brought from Tuscany to correct the worst asperities of the prince's thick northern accent. Although Savoyards and Piedmontese predominated in Court circles, the king used to go on circuit through other regions and stay part of each year hunting in the several provinces.

As may well be imagined, this could not prevent a burden of misunderstanding and recrimination between North and South accumulating for the future, and there continued to exist a tense rivalry between the center and the localities which was a mixed blessing and curse. The Neapolitan historian, De Ruggiero, was still able to conclude in the next century that, after more than sixty years of existence as a single state, the Italian people were not yet an organic unity. After so many centuries of division, this was hardly surprising, nor was it essentially unhealthy, but it is a fact which is easily forgotten, and without which an understanding of modern Italy is impossible.

SECTION THREE: THE FIRST DECADE,
1861–1871

9 Ricasoli, Rattazzi, and Minghetti, 1861–1865

Bettino Ricasoli, who became prime minister in June 1861, was like Cavour a notable agriculturist—his castle of Brolio gave its name to one of the most famous wines of Chianti. Unlike Cavour, he was a deeply religious man who would even preach to his tenant farmers, and he was a radical tory with less of his predecessor's whig intolerance of Mazzini. Ricasoli, indeed, might have been the person to attract both radicals and clericals into parliamentary politics. His concern for the welfare of the poor, as well as his sincere intention to bring Mazzini back from exile, earned him some support on the Left, and as a Tuscan he voiced the feelings of those who were irked by Piedmontese domination.

Ricasoli copied Cavour in seeking support from both Right and Left, and this deprived him of a secure basis in policy and principle. The "Iron Baron" lacked Cavour's parliamentary experience and *tact des choses possibles*; integrity by itself was insufficient, and more finesse and subtlety were required in order to make this type of coalition work. Cavour had sharply criticized his conduct as governor of Tuscany in 1860, and now in 1861 Ricasoli was to prove too rigid a statesman to maintain such a broad government majority.

In 1861 this Tuscan aristocrat formed the first of a series of short and unstable cabinets, and it soon appeared likely that he would fall between two stools, king and parliament, being too proud for the one, too inflexible for the other. He treated the libertine king with an air of superiority and moral condescension, and publicly boasted that his ancestry was longer and—by implication—better than the House of Savoy. He neglected to comply when the king asked him to wear the customary ministerial uniform, saying that his forebears had never worn anyone's livery. Out of the same pride he refused to take his salary or even to use the free railroad tickets which members of parliament were allowed.

Vittorio Emanuele was soon plotting to overthrow a prime minister who tried to confine him within constitutional bounds. Court circles preferred Rattazzi, who though much more of a radical was at least a courtier and a Piedmontese. Before long the king was actively intervening to break up Ricasoli's coalition, and reports of cabinet meetings were even communicated surreptitiously to the palace by one of the junior ministers. This alliance of the Court with Rattazzi was welcomed by those Piedmontese deputies who did not like government by a Tuscan. The clericals also began to think that Ricasoli's religious enthusiasm verged on the Jansenist heresy, while other conservatives feared his coquetting with the Left and his refusal to break up democratic meetings. It was not in Ricasoli's nature to chase popularity, and despite a large majority vote in the Chamber, he chose to resign in February

1862. Ferrari in parliament called this a royal *coup d'état*, and such in effect it was.

★

Urbano Rattazzi, who followed, was a man much distrusted. The British ambassador thought him a "cunning, scheming, low political attorney." Cavour had for five years made Rattazzi his chief lieutenant, but believed him devoid of principles and firmness of direction, arguing that "Rattazzi exaggerated the parliamentary system, so that deputies won too much influence in administrative matters. . . . Though he has singular qualities of mind and heart, he entirely lacks initiative. He would be an admirable legal or political adviser, indeed the best I know, but he cannot run an important department of state."

The new premier inherited Cavour's ingenuity in forming coalitions, and his cabinet included Sella from the Right and Depretis from the Left, but once again, not for the last time, this confusion led to disaster. Rattazzi's aims are still unclear, but his administration was a byword for what Sir James Lacaita termed "corruption, jobbery, and intrigue unprecedented in the parliamentary history of Piedmont." Lacaita continued:

> In every principal Italian city he sought supporters amongst the worst and most disreputable set of politicians and demagogues. Public money has been squandered in the most scandalous manner. Had I not been here and ascertained many facts, I would never have believed them. The moral sense of the Nation was roused against him, and he has fallen under the pressure of public morality.

Rattazzi's fall resulted from his mismanagement of another Garibaldian insurrection for the capture of Rome. Undoubtedly Rattazzi and the king connived at it, and exposure of this fact was a blow to the regime. Garibaldi had always claimed—and Cavour tacitly allowed—that when the government could not take the next step toward national unification, the volunteers had a right to act on their own. In 1862 he was encouraged to go on thinking that the same implicit arrangement still held good by which the government would deny him openly, yet secretly would hope for and perhaps even help his success.

Rattazzi, like Cavour, found it useful to keep Garibaldi on the point of insurrection. The prime minister hoped thereby to convince Napoleon III that France should let the Italians occupy Rome lest the radicals capture it by force of arms and push Italy leftward in the process. Garibaldi was therefore given secret hints of support, and probably more tangible help, which he misinterpreted. The tragedy which ensued came about through deliberate governmental equivocation. King and minister both incited Garibaldi to action (the king confessed as much to foreign diplomats), and were determined either to appropriate his success or to disclaim and punish his failure.

When Garibaldi sailed for Sicily in June 1862, some politicians realized what might happen if he were not distinctly told where he must stop. Instead, the military and naval authorities were given the impression that he was under secret orders from the king. Many responsible officials were on vacation, and there was a noticeable lack of co-ordination between Palermo and Turin. Partly by error, partly on purpose, the government postponed action until all control over events had been lost.

When, in July, Garibaldi reviewed the National Guard at Palermo, he still had no overt revolutionary program. Only when a voice from the crowd cried "Rome or death" was he intoxicated by the exciting atmosphere, and he adopted this exclamation as a war cry and a policy. There were sixty battalions of infantry in the South. Yet, although Garibaldi's intentions were now public, no action was taken to prevent him from drilling volunteers, and several merchant ships were requisitioned under the very eyes of the navy. Parliamentary deputies were informed by the naval command that no orders had been sent to stop him, and he was therefore able to embark three thousand men in front of cheering crowds at Catania, while two warships stood off the port in idle and purposeless expectation. Rattazzi later explained how he himself had assumed that the fleet had instructions to arrest Garibaldi, but the orders given by Vice-Admiral Persano were deliberately ambiguous: "Take any steps which may be necessary, but always remember to put king and country first." Persano was a minister in the cabinet; he later put the blame on the two unfortunate captains and dismissed them for their inaction.

When Garibaldi landed his force in Calabria, Rattazzi was reluctantly forced either to brand him as a rebel or to brave the French and take responsibility for a march on Rome. However unpleasant the alternative, only once choice could be made, and Cialdini's troops advanced to disperse the volunteers. The two forces met at Aspromonte. Heavily outnumbered, and astonished by what he took to be a breach of faith, Garibaldi told his men not to return Cialdini's fire, and although badly wounded himself he took off his hat to cry *"viva l'Italia"* before lighting a cigar and yielding himself a prisoner. The regular troops shamelessly pretended that there had been a real battle though only a dozen men had been killed in this one-sided affray. One officer was promoted to general on the spot in reward for his magnificent services, and seventy-six medals for valor were bestowed on the victors. Garibaldi was imprisoned, and some of those who had deserted the army to join him were summarily executed—although two years earlier in similar circumstances the government had rewarded deserters very differently. The world-wide sympathy for Garibaldi was a condemnation of Italian action in this sorry affair, and the king took the first occasion to grant a partial amnesty to the volunteers when his daughter married the King of Portugal.

Vittorio Emanuele now sacrificed Rattazzi as he had done Ricasoli. Prime ministers had to learn that the dynasty must be served in its own despite, and the king's responsible ministers must take the blame for the king's own irresponsible actions. The next premier, for want of anyone else, was Farini, a safe man and one of Cavour's liberal-conservative disciples. This was the first of a number of occasions when the absence of party organization enabled the sovereign to choose a weak stopgap minister and avoid dependence on the more powerful parliamentary leaders. Farini had contributed signally to the *risorgimento* both as writer and politician, and now became prime minister for three months. At once it became clear, however, that he was already in an advanced state of mental derangement and cabinet meetings became a tragic farce, though the pretense had to continue for a while so as not to alarm the financiers who were being asked for a loan. But when Farini threatened the king with a knife to force a declaration of war on Russia, he was hastily persuaded to resign.

★

Marco Minghetti, his successor, was another of those moderates who had been unenthusiastic for national unity until Cavour made patriotism socially conservative. He was a cultured, traveled man who was said to know his Dante by heart. Compared with Rattazzi he was politically well to the Right, and, though usually tolerant and easygoing, after sharp words in parliament in June 1863 he wounded Rattazzi in a duel. A native of Bologna, Minghetti sympathized with the idea of regional devolution, and this challenge to Piedmontese supremacy was not easily forgiven. The Piedmontese profited from Turin being the seat of government; they also possessed the unconcealed favor of the king and had more experience than others of parliamentary procedure. On the other hand, Tuscan deputies were again urging that the capital be moved to somewhere more central and more Italian. Minghetti agreed with them.

The growth of this feeling led in September 1864 to a convention with France by which Napoleon III promised to withdraw his troops from Rome if Italy would transfer her capital to Florence. The French had been garrisoning Rome to protect the Holy Father from invasion, but England was suspicious of this occupation, especially when a military expedition to Mexico revealed the wide-ranging ambitious nature of Napoleon. For this reason, and in order to obtain French Catholic support and the friendship of Italy as a client state, the emperor proposed to withdraw his troops. He insisted, however, on the humiliating condition that Italy should promise never to attack papal territory, and even that she should bind herself to defend it against Garibaldi or any other aggressor. He also insisted on the change of capital as a pledge that Italy had given up her ambitions on Rome. Napoleon could not know that Minghetti, in bad faith, merely wanted the French out of the way so that the rest of the Papal states could be annexed at leisure.

Cavour had half admitted that Turin was geographically and temperamentally too close to France and that, also, it possessed insufficient historic associations to remain for long as the national capital, but he himself had no wish to move from his home town and he confessed to private doubts about transferring to the corrupt atmosphere of Rome. Minghetti and other non-Piedmontese ministers would have been content with the capital at Naples, but Sicilians were opposed to any renewal of Neapolitan domination. Florence was therefore the obvious choice.

Minghetti's embarrassment was indicated by the fact that, until negotiations were complete, he told neither the king nor apparently the full cabinet what was being arranged. In the end Rattazzi voted for this convention, but it was bitterly resented by other deputies on the Left as an apparent surrender of national claims to Rome. The Piedmontese were even more disgusted, for different reasons; now that they were called upon to sacrifice their own pre-eminent position, Left and Right in Piedmont were at one. Turin was faced with a catastrophic drop in property values as well as a blow to her regional superiority complex, and in two days of quite unexpected civil rioting, twenty-three people were killed and hundreds wounded. Piedmontese deputies broke from the *consorteria* to form a federation of groups known as the *permanente*, a secession which weakened the government and again exemplified regional loyalties cutting across differences of political principle. The king abruptly dismissed Minghetti by telegram, just as if parliament were irrelevant. He was particularly angry that his Court ball was hissed by the irate townspeople of Turin and his guests manhandled as they arrived.

The next prime minister was an army officer of the Court party. General Lamarmora, as a Piedmontese, disliked the change of capital—he was another of those Italian statesmen who had to learn Italian almost as a new language. But he was a loyal servant of the crown and dutifully accepted the move, because it was imperative that France should not be offended and that Rome should be liberated of her French garrison. Lamarmora managed to find new accommodation at Florence for the various ministerial departments, and effected the removal of all government staff and papers in six months. Administratively as well as politically it was a formidable undertaking.

★

The abandonment of Turin severed one more link with the past and weakened the stabilizing force of tradition. The new kingdom was not making a very strong start. It was surviving, which was more than some observers expected, but in four years there had been no striking success except the grim farce of a civil war against Garibaldi. The disaffection in some southern provinces still necessitated the presence there of an army of occupation—90,000 troops was the figure given by the minister in November 1862. Unity and independence sometimes appeared to be only what Gladstone called the "upthrow of a political movement which some following convulsion may displace," rather than, as he later believed, "the long prepared and definitive results of causes permanent in their nature." Disaster occasionally seemed so imminent that the king's abdication was sometimes expected.

As the monarch held his new office "by will of the people," through plebiscites, popular disaffection might almost throw doubt on Italy's right to exist. The provincial plebiscites of 1859–60 had always given a 99 per cent majority for "Italy one and indivisible," but it was suspicious that many constituencies had recorded no negative votes at all. Often there had been no properly drawn up electoral registers, so that people of any age or any nationality could and did vote. Opposition newspapers had been muzzled, and as the ballot was public and many voters could not so much as read their voting papers, influence was easily exercised by presiding authorities who had already taken an oath of loyalty to Vittorio Emanuele and made not the slightest pretense of impartiality. The landowners and the National Guard officers often marched their men to vote en bloc, as Ricasoli himself had done. Some foreign observers thought that most southerners who could understand the issues had wanted much more local autonomy, but that the wording and manner of the vote left people quite unable to express their true wishes. Sicilian peasants had sometimes simply fled into the hills on polling day, as this strange new device looked to them like a novel preparation for collecting more tax.

Not only was the act constituting the new kingdom called in question, but the Italy resulting from these plebiscites seemed artificial and deficient in national character. Italian culture still lacked a distinct identity of its own: the intellectual classes looked to France for their lead, and other liberal politicians to England. Regional self-sufficiency could not be broken down quickly, and there had been no social revolution to convince the peasants that they were participants in, not victims of, the new order. The great southern liberal, Giustino Fortunato, lamented that Italy was several centuries behind other civilized nations, and the speed of her national revolution had allowed it to penetrate only skin-deep: unification had been "improvised," it had been a "miracle" going against both history and geography, and for the next fifty years he went on expecting that the new nation might break up again. As D'Azeglio indicated, though Italy was made, it nevertheless remained to make Italians. To such men the new state was scarcely stable or permanent, and they were almost frightened of what they had done and of what Europe might think. D'Azeglio on the Right and Ferrari on the Left hoped fervently that Rome might remain independent, and others wanted the whole South to be abandoned for being insufficiently "Italian." Quite apart from the clericals who opposed on principle, many moderate conservatives were ashamed of Cavour's deceitful methods; and from the other extreme, Mazzini and Garibaldi, though now representing only an unimportant fringe, were in open opposition to the movement which they themselves had initiated.

As the *risorgimento* had aroused too many hopes, this disillusionment was inescapable. After the civil wars of 1860, the defeated parties, whether autonomists, federalists, republicans, Garibaldians, Catholics, or Bourbonists, all nursed varying degrees of indignation. National unity had cost the savings of more than one generation. The naïve expectation had been that political change would suddenly release a great store of hidden wealth, but in fact it had only accustomed Italians to spending more than they could afford. Meanwhile, the nation appeared to outside observers as little more than a French satellite, and it suffered mortification in having to countenance the presence of a French garrison in Rome and Austrian rule at Venice. As achievement fell short of hopes, the essential weakness of the country disillusioned many of those who had grown up on the heroic national myths.

Typical of this protest against the prosaic outcome of the glorious revolution was the early poetry of Giosuè Carducci. This man had been inspired by Mazzini's republican fervor but now feared that heroism had been almost in vain, bringing forth only a ridiculous mouse. It was unfortunate that the first great national poet should have given expression to such a disillusioned mood. Apparently, the birth of a nation was not portentous enough to evoke great art or literature, or at any rate the Italian creative genius was not rising to the occasion. Manzoni wrote surprisingly little between 1827 and his death in 1873; just as Rossini likewise produced almost nothing after *William Tell* in 1829, and until he died in 1868 spent empty years in Paris, often disparaging the *risorgimento* as an unfortunate mistake. Even Verdi, though he was idolized as a national hero, stood outside politics; he was elected a deputy, but resigned after several weeks, and never carried out his duties as a senator. Through literature and the arts, some of the infelicities, egoisms, and disappointments which were bound to accompany such a revolution might have been purged or idealized. Unhappily, the person of Vittorio Emanuele hardly caught the imagination except on the crudest level. It was possible to think that his principal motive had been not patriotism but dynastic ambition, and certainly he had been placed on his new throne less through his own merits than by Napoleon III and Garibaldi, to whom he was thus beholden. Carducci's acid reference to such awkward points was to earn him temporary suspension from his professorial chair in 1867.

To many people it was a bitter thought that the *risorgimento* had "cost more in money than in blood," and they compensated for this with a hagiology which described the national heroes as prodigies of valor and wisdom. History was falsified to prove that the revolution had been a purely liberal and liberating movement and that Italy was by natural endowment a great power. This myth overemphasized the heroism, just as the pessimists exaggerated the humdrum qualities of the new state. Sonnino could write in 1880, as D'Azeglio in the 1860s, that if only the liberals had known the country better they might not have found the courage to unite Italy, but this was an unverifiable guess at the other extreme. The simple truth was that political unification did not complete, nor could it have completed, the *risorgimento*. A stupendous and slow task of reconstruction still lay ahead, the forging of a national consciousness, the discovery and fostering of national interests abroad and raising standards of living at home. Such activity did not always lend itself to poetry or heroics.

And yet, after discounting exaggerated hopes and fears, the nation already justified itself. Italy was widely regarded elsewhere as a textbook liberal creation. Gladstone, for one, recognized the initial difficulties and achievements. "May God prosper and bless the work," was his comment in 1862; "seldom, I believe, has there been one in the sphere of politics charged with deeper interest to his creatures."

10 Counterrevolution and Brigandage, 1860–1865

The first important threat to the stability of the new regime came from the South. In 1860, Francesco the ex-king of Naples had fled with his numerous brothers and uncles to seek sanctuary in Rome, where an observer inside St. Peter's basilica likened them to a little heap of withered leaves. From there they made one last effort at counterrevolution, relying on open or covert support among both the aristocracy and the peasants in their former kingdom.

Cavour had chosen rashly when in October 1860 he sent the ailing and unstable Farini to Naples to crush the Garibaldians and Bourbonists. Garibaldi had hoped to continue as royal vicegerent in southern Italy until the time came to march on Rome, but Cavour had many personal and political reasons for preventing this. His first concern was to subdue Garibaldi and to merge the administration of South and North, if necessary overriding any opposition from the radical democrats or from local sentiment. He and Farini were well aware that the governments of Europe, as well as potential investors and railroad contractors, were waiting to see how Italy dealt with her first really vital problem.

Cavour therefore told Farini to use the army at the least sign of unrest and if necessary to "exterminate" the Garibaldians. He also decided to close down the advisory comittee of Neapolitans which Garibaldi had established to facilitate the process of union. Military government alone was thought to be adequate for what Cavour called "the weakest and most corrupt part of Italy," and instructions came from Turin that the local press should be curbed and "some rough military treatment would be a salutary medicine." In the long run Naples was to benefit from the efficiency of her new administrators, but police repression after 1861 was often more rigorous and sometimes almost as illiberal as that of the Bourbons.

Local opposition was bound to ensue. Although Naples had taken little share in its own military liberation, there was shocked alarm when the province found itself simply "annexed" as a conquest of Piedmont. A broadly representative committee of Neapolitans recommended that the South should be given some local autonomy, but Farini introduced northern laws as fast as possible so that parliament could be presented with a *fait accompli*. The northern carpetbaggers had themselves to thank when they became highly unpopular. They themselves had to recognize that most Neapolitans (and Farini said almost all) lacked enthusiasm for the new Italy. Newspaper correspondents wrote as if another movement for independence might break out at any moment. Lacaita—who despite his British title was a landowner from Apulia—wrote Cavour in December 1860 that

> the friends of annexation are in a very small minority; you must not be deceived by the results of the recent plebiscite, which were due to the general abomination of the perjured dynasty, the aversion to Mazzinianism ... and in some part also to intimidation. ... Farini's misgovernment, which has split the Liberal party, has accentuated the anarchy of the provinces, and brought the annexation into ridicule and contempt.

Another liberal Neapolitan, Fortunato, concluded that not even the middle classes of the South positively desired national unity, and that the *risorgimento* had been due less to popular feeling than to a few intellectuals and a fortunate alignment in European diplomatic relations.

The South had originally turned against the Bourbons on the grounds of misgovernment. When the same symptoms of apparent misgovernment persisted after 1861, many people began to wonder if this might derive from something intractable about the South and its inhabitants. Too late did many Neapolitans discover that they had misconceived their own wishes and wanted not better government but less government and still lower taxes. Hence the derisory comment that this incursion of northerners was another barbarian invasion; hence the dislike of Piedmont, much as some southern Germans disliked Prussia. When a big scandal was unearthed in 1864 over railroad contracts in the South, it was noteworthy that none of the five deputies who had to resign was a southerner whereas Count Bastogi, the person chiefly involved, had been in Cavour's cabinet, and the opinion gained ground that the North was battening corruptly on this defenseless area. The accusation was exaggerated. A more just criticism was that the ministers and advisers whom Cavour chose from the South, De Sanctis, Amari, Massari, Spaventa, and Scialoia, had been cut off from their home provinces in long years of exile, and had even learned to despise their fellow Neapolitans. Another factor in the breach was a tactless letter written in August 1861 by the former prime minister, D'Azeglio:

At Naples we overthrew a sovereign in order to set up a government based on universal suffrage. And yet we still today need sixty battalions of soldiers to hold the people down, or even more, since these are not enough; whereas in other provinces of Italy nothing of the sort is necessary. One must therefore conclude that there was some mistake about the plebiscite. We must ask the Neapolitans once against whether they want the Piedmontese or no.

The South was in fact rapidly becoming the scene of insubordination and quareling.

★

Political issues fomented but did not create the social phenomenon of brigandage. During the Napoleonic wars the British, with political intent, encouraged the Neapolitan brigands against the French, and the Bourbons later had to treat with Fra Diavolo as with a sovereign power. Now the exiled King Francesco exploited banditry as a weapon of political counterrevolution and relentlessly stirred up a class war against the rich. The brigands in their turn exploited Francesco, taking his money and enjoying the political sanctuary offered inside the papal frontier. The pope understandably regarded the Piedmontese as the real brigands since they had stolen most of his dominions. False money was coined at Rome in the name of Francesco, and Neapolitans were enrolled in his legitimist army from the migrant workmen who crossed the frontier for seasonal employment in the Agro Romano.

The most notable leader, Borjès the Spaniard, who had fought on the Carlist side in the Spanish civil war, was enlisted abroad by royalist agents, made a general, and authorized by the ex-king to appropriate public funds in any Neapolitan town. For three months he marched the length and breadth of the South, meeting other brigand bands but discovering few people motivated by genuine loyalty to their ex-king, and receiving the ridicule of straightforward professional brigands such as Crocco. Nevertheless, any rebel could rely on the anarchic sentiments which set village against village, countryside against town, Church against state, taxpayer against tax collector. Some popular support was forthcoming in this last flickering of feudal and separatist reaction against the nation state, and the memory of Neapolitan counterrevolutions in 1799 and 1849 made some people afraid to adopt the patriotic cause too quickly. The result may properly be called a minor civil war, and it helped to perpetuate the unfortunate impression that Italy might collapse at any moment.

Much more than a political rising, it was a product of unemployment and of a tradition of highway robbery activated by a revolt of the plebs. Many brigands had first adopted their métier in order to settle accounts with some local enemy, and had then fled from justice to the mountains. There were men such as Carmine Donatello, galley slave and murderer, who for a time in 1860 had helped Garibaldi, hoping for pardon and reward; there were renegade priests who celebrated clandestine mass in the woods; there were revengeful peasants who found banditry more rewarding than toiling for a pittance on other people's land. Most of those involved were merely seasonal brigands who took to the *maquis* in the months when agriculture offered scanty employment. There were also the unemployed ex-Bourbon soldiers, together with deserters and fugitives from conscription, jail breakers, and those enticed by the lure of booty.

Many ordinary citizens, while not active themselves, regarded the brigands as legitimate combatants in the ceaseless war against landlords and against an impossibly remote, almost foreign government. Amid all the excesses and hatreds of this futile fight, some believed that the rebels were fighting for the Church and the legitimate dynasty. The Piedmontese were excommunicate; they had arbitrarily introduced their own secularist legislation into the South; and they persecuted the clergy, the chief friends of the poor. The patriots affected a pious abhorrence at the Church encouraging brigandage, but it was naïve to imagine that they could despoil the clergy without the latter resisting.

Massari described the peasants "to whose admiring eyes the brigand becomes something different, a fantastic being, a symbol of their frustrated aspirations, the vindicator of their wrongs. He is no longer the assassin, the thief, the man of sack and rapine, but the person whose own powers suffice to get for himself and for others the justice which the law fails to give. And the man who protects him becomes a hero." To further his revenge on society, the peasant would readily give food, information, and shelter to such men. When soldiers came in sight, malefactors would put their rifles behind a hedge and take up hoes with other workers in the fields. Not until a sense of security and a fear of justice could be instilled would country folk co-operate effectively with the government: until that moment, fear, honor, and human sympathy restrained them.

The ferocity of this kind of war knows no bounds. When the Piedmontese entered Neapolitan territory in October 1860, one of the first actions of General Cialdini was to shoot every peasant found carrying arms. This was a declaration of war on people who needed arms to defend their property, and it reaped the whirlwind. Captured soldiers were sometimes tied to trees and burned alive; others were crucified and mutilated. Times had not changed much since the days of the brigand Mammone, who had been wont to drink out of a human skull, and never to dine without a freshly severed human head decorating his table. The law of the jungle prevailed, and the soldiers were stirred to excesses in retaliation. No quarter was given, but terror was used against terror. Men were shot on suspicion, whole families were punished for the actions of one of their number, and villages were sacked and burned for sheltering bandits.

Successive viceroys from Farini onward, before dealing with this social war in the provinces, first had to control the city of Naples itself. There they tried every policy, siding first with the old aristocracy, and then with the radicals; they attempted to suppress the secret fraternity known as the *camorra*, and then tried handing over to this nefarious body the duties of the police. Before long, numerous petitions described the chief result of annexation as being the disintegration of society. This was not an easy challenge to meet, but in the middle of 1861 the secret political funds which Garibaldi had abolished were restored to the prefects, and a more conciliatory attitude was adopted toward the clergy. The government even had to open a public subscription list to help pay for a more rigorous policy, and the dangerous expedient was adopted of encouraging landowners to form private armies in self-defense. At the beginning of 1862, according to papers captured on an English adventurer, there was an organization of over 80,000 rebels in the Neapolitan provinces. Against these men total war was declared and fought with great loss of life and reputation.

★

In January 1863, a parliamentary commission of inquiry under Massari left Genoa for Naples. Its report, read in secret session to parliament, is an invaluable document about conditions in the South. Among many interesting conclusions, the commission established that brigandage was weakest where relations between worker and employer were satisfactory, for instance near the relatively wealthy port of Reggio Calabria, or wherever the *mezzadria* system of land tenure was established and the laborers were not nomadic but bound to the soil by ties of interest:

> But wherever large estates are the rule, the proletariat is very numerous ... and many people are at their wits' end to make a bare living. ... The existence of a bandit has many attractions there for the poor laborer ... and brigandage becomes a savage protest against centuries of injustice by men reduced to the utmost poverty. With such people there is an absolute lack of confidence in the law and the exercise of justice. ... Corruption in communal and provincial administration, justice not always honestly administered, and the hopeless inadequacy of the local police, are new and powerful contributions to the spread of brigandage. ... The barons and their retainers have set the example of lawlessness, and now people have learnt to reserve their greatest respect for men who have committed the worst crimes and atrocities.

The report was quite clear that the papal government had helped the brigands with money and recruitment from Rome, and had used the Neapolitan episcopate for transmitting instructions.

Massari's report suggested that long-term remedies be at once applied, for people must be shown the unmistakable advantages of liberty and be convinced that greater freedom would bring eventual prosperity and employment:

> You must extend education and see to a fairer distribution of the land. Roads must be built, marshes reclaimed, public works begun, the forests looked

after. ... It is absolutely necessary that the old customary laws should be repealed, and large areas of common domain such as the Tavoliere di Puglia be broken up into small holdings. ... Freeing the land from such primitive communal restrictions would help to eradicate the savage proletariat who are driven by hunger to know no law but that of rapine. It is also indispensable to settle the disputes about communal land which for so long have divided every village against itself.

Ecclesiastical property held in mortmain had to be broken up so that landless highwaymen could become peasant cultivators. The police profession had to be raised in public esteem in the same manner as could be observed in England. Communications would have to be vastly improved, "for you know, gentlemen, how Scotland after its union with England was similarly given over to brigandage until roads were built."

Above all, the government had to provide security and prove that there was neither fear nor hope of a Bourbon restoration, for without this conviction people were too fearful of reprisals to organize communal action against banditry. Prison reform was indispensable "from the moral and hygienic point of view, but also from that of security, since the ease of escaping is a great source of recruitment to brigandage." Jailers were miserably paid and often no less criminal than their prisoners. Massari's commissioners reported that they had found people kept in prison at Naples for three years without trial, even when this period was longer than the maximum sentence for the crime of which they had been accused. Not only had government to be efficient, but justice had to be done and be seen to be done or else people would continue to look on their new rulers as enemies instead of friends.

These were long-term measures and, until they could take effect, martial law was indispensable; money should be made available for espionage and bribery, and the normal rules of war disregarded. Short-term severity was something more obviously urgent and more easily understood in distant Turin. As a result, the Pica law was passed, which made harsh repression not something exceptional but a measure on the statute book:

The government shall be empowered to confine under house arrest for anything up to a year any vagabond or unemployed person, or anyone suspected of belonging to the *camorra* or harboring brigands. ... In those provinces declared by royal decree to be infested with brigands, any armed band of over three persons organized for criminal purposes and their accomplices shall be punishable by a military court.

This suspension of constitutional liberties was passed into law after very little debate, because the deputies were impatient for their summer vacation. There were soon 120,000 soldiers concentrated in Sicily and the South, almost half the national army.

By 1865 the war was virtually over. Crocco fled to the Papal states leaving his bands leaderless, and the foreign adventurers who had fought in misguided enthusiasm for Francesco melted away. Highway robbery remained a feature of the South, and Turiello in 1882 wrote that not only were escorts necessary for travel, but roads were more dangerous than before 1860. Yet landowners could usually collect their rents once more; farm laborers could report evil deeds and bear witness without a certainty of reprisal; it was no longer necessary to take hostages, to evacuate whole villages, or to expose the heads of executed criminals at the crossroads.

The North had outwardly pacified the South, and yet the underlying regional animosity was intensified. A civil war is one of the cruelest events that can take place in any country, and the *risorgimento*, during which many Italians continued to fight as part of the Austrian army, had been a succession of civil wars of which this was the most cruel, the most protracted and costly. Among the casualties of this simple fight against brigandage, there were more regular soldiers who died from malaria than were killed in all the campaigns of 1860, and more people perished in it than were killed in all the other wars of the national *risorgimento*.

11   The War for Venice, 1866

From 1861 onward, Italian foreign policy never left Venice and Rome far out of sight, and the only doubt was how long a wait would be necessary before a third war of liberation was fought against Austria. There was no easy passage to great-power status. Cavour had longed for another European war which would give scope for his own diplomatic skill and allow Italy to count for something in the balance of power. During the last few months of his life he had been intriguing with Kossuth and Klapka to stir Hungary into insurrection against Austria, and had employed the Italian diplomatic service to smuggle cargoes of arms into the Balkans. When found out, he denied all knowledge of this illicit traffic and tried to blame Garibaldi, but unfortunately the captured crates of munitions were all clearly labeled as special consignments from the royal arsenal at Genoa. Cavour had usually known how to couple audacity with caution. He did not flinch at the thought of taking on Austria single-handed, since he calculated that Italy had more to gain than Europe could afford to let her lose. "We have conquered the world before now," he once said in an unguarded moment, "and shall do so again." On one desperate occasion he even spoke of allying with the United States and proceeding to defeat Britain as well as Austria.

After Cavour's death Italian foreign policy became far more timid. French backing was less substantial, for Napoleon was becoming respectable and Italy was already large enough for France to feel slightly apprehensive. The king, with Rattazzi's encouragement, continued to push his dynastic claims in the Iberian Peninsula, and even tried to replace King Otto in Greece by the Prince of Carignano or the Duke of Aosta. He also thought of persuading England to cede Malta, as she was giving the Ionian Islands to Greece. But for Italians generally, the conquest of Venetia was the one acquisition necessary for self-respect.

Mazzini and Garibaldi urged the king to march directly against Venice, threatening to resume their republican propaganda if he delayed. Mazzini argued that Austria was in grave financial difficulties, and that Slav and Hungarian disaffection was such that Austria would be outnumbered by Italian troops on her southern frontier. Half-persuaded, the king in 1863–64 entered into secret communication with Mazzini himself. His ministers were kept in the dark about this, but were unscrupulously trying to goad the Western powers into a war against Russia from which Italy could perhaps snatch some advantage during the general confusion. Opinion hardened still further against Austria when the Italian elections of 1865, reflecting a disillusionment with the *consorteria*, reinforced the radical Left.

★

The king, who like his father had married an Austrian archduchess, first demanded that Austria be sounded by negotiation. He knew that the British believed in a strong Austria for maintaining the stability of Europe, and hence a war might not be easy. Some farsighted Austrian statesmen and financiers also realized that the Prussian threat and a financial crisis made it advisable to placate Italy. As the two countries were not yet on diplomatic terms, negotiations were opened through private individuals, but the talks broke down because Italian politicians preferred war to anything less than complete Austrian surrender. Lamarmora was in any case engaged in simultaneous military discussions with Prussia, a fact which Austria knew from intercepted messages. The government even sent officers in disguise over the Austrian frontier in order to prepare for hostilities.

From Bismarck's point of view, an Italian alliance would help to establish Prussian hegemony in Germany. The two countries had a common enemy, and as yet no conflicting interests. Cavour and Mazzini had both appreciated the value of a Prussian alliance. Bismarck kept in touch both with the government of Italy and with the Mazzinians, and while secretly paying Italian agitators to stir up trouble, made doubly sure by negotiating with the king behind the prime minister's back.

Italy's mistake in treating simultaneously with Austria and Prussia was underlined when Austria at the last moment offered to cede Venice peacefully in exchange for continued Italian neutrality. The prime minister, General

Lamarmora, had to refuse this generous offer because he held that Italian honor was by then pledged to aid Prussia in war. As a soldier, the idea of simple barter was unwelcome to him, and he also miscalculated that, with Prussian aid, a war would win the Trentino as well as Venice. He was well aware of the sentiment which Gregorovius had lately expressed at Rome in his diary, that not until the Italian revolution had achieved a great victory would the not always reputable means used to attain nationality be forgotten. Military victory would be a tonic to Italy and a demonstration of strength to the outside world at large.

A secret alliance was therefore signed with Prussia in April 1866, by which Italy obtained a good hope of annexing Venice, though unfortunately Bismarck excluded the Trentino on the grounds that it was a partly German-speaking territory. Lamarmora therefore meant to fight his own war and rejected the suggestion that he should collaborate in the Prussian strategic plan. Bismarck was known to agree with Garibaldi in wanting Italian forces to cross the Adriatic and promote rebellion by Hungary and the Slavs. Lamarmora, however, was a product of the Turin military academy; not only did he intend to organize his own campaign, but the fomentation of rebellion was objectionable on "every principle of humanity, morality, and sound policy." He vetoed outright General Türr's mission in Serbia and Croatia which Bismarck and Vittorio Emanuele had actively promoted, and this helps to explain why Italy failed to derive full military benefit from her Prussian alliance.

Lamarmora deceived himself into greatly overestimating Italian military capacity. In five years the army had more than doubled and was now nearly 400,000 strong, considerably larger than the forces of the whole British Empire, and certainly larger than the industrial potential of Italy warranted. It considerably outnumbered the forces which Austria could oppose to it, and the Italian fleet was twice as large as the Austrian. Yet there were serious weaknesses in organization and morale. The component regional elements had been intermingled in the army but the new units were not yet properly fused; they lacked *esprit de corps* as well as adequate equipment and experienced generals. The Piedmontese and Neapolitan armies had too recently been fighting each other for a proper harmony of sentiment, and both disliked the Garibaldians for their unorthodoxy, their political unreliability, their popularity and success. Italian regular soldiers were looked upon as a caste apart in society and had not yet become the civilian army that popular imagination seized on after De Amicis wrote his *Vita militare* in 1868. To many civilians they could seem a hated army of occupation and the executors of martial law. Almost half of the Sicilians drafted for military service regularly escaped to the hills, while in the Basilicata the proportion was nearer three-quarters (even fifty years later it was still one-fifth in these unreconciled southern provinces).

★

General Lamarmora was a fine man but an indifferent commander and he plunged headlong into war without any of the requisite preliminaries. Supply was mismanaged and preparatory planning was wholly insufficient. Disregarding the lessons of 1848 and 1859, the Italians again chose direct attack against the quadrilateral of fortress cities upon which the Austrian defense system in north Italy was based. With false confidence the annual draft had also been delayed in order to improve the budget figures. Such was the mutual jealousy of the generals that the prime minister had to become chief of staff himself. Moreover General Cialdini agreed with Bismarck in opposing the plan for a direct attack and was therefore given a practically independent command on the Po, while the king and Lamarmora led the main forces on the River Mincio. The king was commander in chief under the terms of the constitution and was thus able to intervene in strategic decisions without having immediate responsibility for their execution. The generals were alarmed by this for they knew that the king had no military talent or experience; yet dynastic reasons demanded that he should figure prominently in the campaign.

At the last minute Italy's eager plan to start a war was nearly wrecked when Napoleon III proposed to settle the dispute by discussion, but a stupid reply by Austria lost any hope of a peaceful settlement. Hostilities began in June. Lamarmora began his frontal advance without waiting either for Cialdini to act or for information about the Austrian dispositions. A few hours after the declaration of war a battle was fought near the village of Custoza, in which the Archduke Albert with half the number of troops repulsed Lamarmora's advance guard. The latter was unrealistic enough to think that this small encounter, in which fewer than 750 Italians were killed, was a major defeat. He fell back behind the Mincio, and Cialdini, against Lamarmora's express injunctions, began a retreat without even going into action.

There was no further big engagement for it took a month to reorganize the army, and only the former Bourbonist general Pianell succeeded in not losing his reputation. Cialdini showed himself proud, arrogant, intractable, and quite ready to disobey orders alike from king and government. Had he crossed the Po at the right moment, as the king desired, he might yet have threatened the Austrians and allowed Italian numerical superiority to prevail, but he chose to give the war up for lost and petulantly criticized royal intervention as the cause of defeat. The Austrians at once took this unexpected opportunity and entrained many of their men back over the Alps to where Prussia, though a smaller country than Italy, won a crushing victory at Sadowa on July 3. Bismarck had some excuse for deriding the retreat of his Italian allies and their exaggeratedly fearful communiqués.

Many people had clamored from the first for Garibaldi to take a prominent part in the war, but the army and the king begrudged him his share of the limelight and only a few of his volunteers were allowed to take the field. For as long as possible they were kept well away from the scene of action. They were then belatedly concentrated on a subordinate front where they continued a slow but steady advance through the mountains, and once more showed that, while they lacked the discipline of a regular corps, they compensated for this by dash and enterprise. These Garibaldians in the Trentino included some of the most enthusiastic among the younger generation of patriots including people such as Boito the composer, later the librettist of Verdi's *Otello* and *Falstaff*; also Pirelli, soon to become world-famous in the Italian industrial revolution. Once again Garibaldi's men came off more honorably than the regular army, and when finally given the order to fall back were at the gates of Trent itself.

After the defeat of Custoza the navy was ordered to provoke an action with its superior forces, for it was important for Italy to claim some kind of success before Austria surrendered. Unfortunately Admiral Persano was distrusted by other officers, and with reason. He owed his position to favoritism more than merit and had once run a warship aground with the royal family on board. As minister of marine he paid small regard to parliament, and as admiral in chief he had prepared no plan for offensive action against Austria. The Austrian vice-admiral Tegetthoff was more than ready, and his ships, though lighter, less numerous, and slower, appeared before Ancona where Persano's fleet was lying. But the Austrian fire was not even returned, Persano pleading trouble among his engineers and insufficient coal. The crews rapidly lost their enthusiasm through this inaction and the admiral was accused of cowardice. Driven on by government reproaches, Persano finally left port, still manifestly trying to avoid contact with the enemy. After returning to Ancona he received peremptory instructions and a threat of dismissal, and so set out once more, without plan or even accurate maps, to meet defeat off the island of Lissa on July 20.

This was the first large engagement ever fought between ironclad steam fleets. The Austrians had seven ironclads against twice as many but their gunnery and tactics were greatly superior. Persano placed his ships in a single line and allowed the Austrians to choose several concentrated points of attack. The Italian admiral, who had contrived not to be on his flagship when it was rammed and sunk, dared not then risk the further action which some of his captains urged. Public opinion was dumbfounded, and matters were not improved when Persano began blaming his subordinates in public. When the Senate, acting as a court of justice, dismissed him from the service with loss of pension and decorations, Italy's discomfiture was complete.

★

Bismarck's policy for the future demanded Austrian friendship and he therefore did not press his victory. After Sadowa, unknown to his ally, he made approaches for peace, realizing that Italy must accept whatever terms he concluded. It was agreed that Austria should surrender Venice, but to France, not directly to her defeated enemy. This horrified Lamarmora. It would be dishonorable, he said, to receive Venice as a gift from France, for the country would become ungovernable and the army would lose all its prestige. But the Austrians were now able to send more troops to their southern sector and compel Italy to accept an armistice at the end of July. Venetia was to be Italian, but Austria retained the Trentino and Garibaldi therefore had to withdraw from territory he had already conquered. The northeastern frontier of Italy was still exposed and vulnerable. What was worse, too many people had been led to look on war as a test of progress and civilization, and there was a grave loss of morale when it appeared that other countries made better weapons and knew better how to use them.

Italy was fortunate to gain as much from the treaty as she did. Austria at last recognized the new kingdom, Venice was won and the "quadrilateral" was no longer in foreign hands. Yet military defeat had shaken confidence in the armed forces and in the king himself, especially as it was followed by an undignified and public wrangle among various generals and admirals, each trying to blame the others. Italy secured no glory out of Prussia's success, and could not even point to that "heroism in defeat" which had illumined earlier pages of the *risorgimento*.

Some patriots would later lament that the war had not lasted longer and so toughened and inured the national character. Garibaldi was outraged that the Venetians had not risen of their own accord, not even in the countryside where it would have been easy, but had waited passively for deliverance, and he noted how some "Italians" from the Trentino had actually fought against Italy as they had done in 1848 and 1859. Garibaldi looked back over his experience since 1848 and reflected that only in Sicily and Calabria had the peasants backed Italian patriotism, and even there they had been moved by social and regional more than by national feeling. Elsewhere they had usually been the enemies and not the friends of national unification. He had seen with his own eyes how many of them rejoiced at the return of the Austrians after a short interval of national "liberation," and how they often deserted as soon as a war began to go badly. Italy in their eyes too often meant just the landlords and a hostile government. They possessed little in common with the upper classes who had reasons for grievance against Austria, and even less in common with the intellectuals who forged patriotic myths as retrospective justification of national liberation. Unfortunately these peasants represented a majority of the Italian nation.

Italy was now one step further toward winning her "natural frontiers," but the war had not penetrated deeply enough to create a firmer national consciousness. Verga has a story about a Sicilian fisherman who lost his son at the battle of Lissa without being able to understand where or why this had happened. Ordinary citizens were not greatly enthusiastic when Austria presented Venice to a French commissioner, and the only satisfaction was that the inevitable plebiscite showed only sixty-nine votes against union with Italy.

12   Financial and Other Problems, 1866–1867

At the end of the war, patriotic expectations were further damaged by a revolt at Palermo which bore some resemblance to earlier Sicilian outbreaks in 1820, 1848, and 1860. The same bands of irregulars, which formerly had helped Garibaldi, re-emerged as if to undo his work, for in their eyes all governments were tarred with the same brush. Already in 1861 the first parliamentary elections provided ominous examples of bloodshed in Sicily. Administrators from the North reported that three-quarters of the population was semi-barbarous and nearly everyone was estranged from the government of Turin. Lack of roads put large areas of the island beyond easy reach of the law, and people still customarily traveled in caravans for safety. Tens of thousands of deserters were at large, and the mafia continued to organize resistance and a system of private justice. The legend grew that Sicily was ungovernable, and successive administrations had to collude with the *mala vita* as their sole means of exercising sufficient authority.

In 1863 the army was forced to take the field against this disorder as well as against brigandage in Naples. General Govone was a Piedmontese who had learned on the mainland that severity and even cruelty might be required, and Sicily therefore had to endure six months of large-scale military operations. Families and villages were held hostage and subjected to dragonnades. Govone cut off water from villages in the middle of the Sicilian heat and used torture to exact information, even burning people alive in their houses. Matters became worse when he explained publicly in his defense that Sicilians were barbarous and had to be treated roughly.

The result of these operations was the capture of four thousand out of the twenty-five thousand refugees dodging military service. Thousands of people were found wrongly inscribed on the electoral lists and a substantial sum was collected in tax arrears. This achievement, and even more the methods used, added fuel to a mounting feud against the mainland. Martial law and the enforced exile of hundreds of Sicilians seemed to belie clauses in the constitution. Northerners had little idea of the social and economic derangement which unification had brought to the South, and when feelings of revolt became more intense, this was treated as simple lawlessness calling for police repression.

The end of the Austrian war in 1866 came only just in time for more troops to be transferred south. In September there was a "march on Palermo," when numerous armed bands from the hills erupted into the city and overcame the garrison just as Garibaldi had done in May 1860. This time, however, they acknowledged no single leader and had but the vaguest intentions; there was only a sullen hatred against the government, against its taxes, its attempt to dissolve the monasteries, its remoteness and severity. Escaped prisoners, deserters, dismissed Bourbon employees, autonomists, even the Mazzinians and the dispossessed clergy raised their several cries of *"viva Francesco secondo," "viva la repubblica."* Manifestos reviling "the gang of thieves which has been ruling Italy for six years" incited the populace to assault police stations, arms magazines, and customs houses.

The government was caught by surprise, and the National Guard, immobilized by fear, in many places surrendered their weapons. Some of the wealthier citizens seem to have been sympathetic but to have reversed their views when the elements of class war became more pronounced, especially when forced to pay heavy protection money to the various gangs. The rebels set up a provisional government in which six princes, two barons, and one *monsignore* were induced to sit. Only the port, the palace, and the prison were still held by the twenty-seven-year-old Marquis di Rudinì who was then mayor of Palermo.

Finally, an expeditionary force from Genoa and Leghorn put down the revolt, a surrender being negotiated through the French consul. The government found it prudent not to probe too deeply into the causes of the revolution, which were therefore neither remedied nor even properly understood. Di Rudinì, a Sicilian himself, confessed that he had to deal with the most corrupt people in all Italy and so was none too scrupulous in his repressive measures. Many thousands were kept in prison under suspicion. The Archbishop of Monreale and many other churchmen were arrested, and several hundred friars were exiled to Genoa. Worse still, cholera killed 7,800 people in Palermo alone—the superstitious citizenry said that this infection was introduced of malice and on purpose.

★

The prime minister in office was Ricasoli who had returned to succeed Lamarmora in June 1866. The events in Sicily lost Ricasoli much good will, and when the elections of March 1867 depleted his coalition, he resigned. This brought back Rattazzi and the constitutional Left to office for a few months, because personal squabbles divided Minghetti, Lanza, Sella, and the other leaders of the *consorteria*.

Although Rattazzi's former governments were blamed for the two national calamities of Novara in 1849 and Aspromonte in 1862, he had done the state some service by educating the Left in the practice of constitutional government. While keeping clear of the extreme radicals, he had usually entered into the group system that constituted the government majority. The extreme Left disapproved of such a transparent political maneuver, but these irreconcilables had lost their *raison d'être* along with their monopoly of the national unification program. They were bound to become less important when new weapons and military techniques ended the age of barricades and guerrilla leaders. Garibaldi

79

himself resigned from parliament in disgust at the harsh treatment given to Sicily.

Mazzini, repeatedly elected, had his election more than once overruled by parliament, and he therefore returned to the political sterility of uncompromising republicanism. As well as republicanism, he had consistently advocated social reform, liberty of conscience, equality between the sexes, and European federation, but he was a visionary and too far ahead of the times. At Italian request he had been extradited from one country after another and found refuge only in England. In 1870 he was at long last caught and imprisoned after a final attempt at insurrection in Sicily. Two years later he died, a lonely, disappointed man.

★

Neither Right nor Left could differ much over the really urgent questions of national finance. The Austrian war of 1848–49 had cost some 200 million lire, the Crimean war 50 million, the war of 1859 250 million, and that of 1866 nearly 800 million. Against this, the annual revenue of the state had remained stationary for three years at about 480 million, but rose to 600 million by 1866. Cavour had once confessed that finance was more important even than foreign policy. He knew how to be enterprisingly spendthrift on occasion, in building the Fréjus tunnel, the Cavour canal, or the new naval port at La Spezia, but Piedmont had almost bankrupted itself in achieving unification, and now Cavour's successors, with less financial acumen, had to meet expenses many times the sum of those paid by all the individual states together before 1860.

Italy was determined to justify her claim to be a great power, and therefore the public debt, which in 1861 stood at 2,450 million lire, had more than doubled four years later. But while human decision could make expenses grow out of all measure, revenue was more intractable. Almost a third of this revenue went in servicing the national debt, and more than a quarter on the armed forces. The deficit between 1861 and 1864 was as much as 47 per cent of the total state expenditure, and in 1866 was well over 60 per cent. Since the national credit was not buoyant, government bonds paid up to 8 per cent interest and had to be offered at 70 per cent or less of their par value.

Quintino Sella, who was finance minister in 1862 and 1864, was the most able of Cavour's disciples. He was a mining engineer and mineralogist rather than a financier, but was the first to realize what sacrifices and economies would be necessary to pay for the making of Italy. Sella was an excellent example of the honest, hard-working middle classes, with a high sense of public service and a carelessness about unpopularity in their insistence upon efficient administration. But Rattazzi's ministry of 1862 had fallen before Sella could try out his economies or his scheme to stop tax avoidance. This was one of the tragedies of the Italian political system in which unstable coalitions quickly succeeded each other and in which a minister was seldom in office long enough to plan and carry out any reform. The next finance minister, Minghetti, though apt enough in circumventing individual problems, was not forceful enough in character to propose a comprehensive remedy and brave the consequences.

This was another of the vices of Italy, that the greatest beneficiaries of the *risorgimento* were unwilling to pay for it. The rich who monopolized politics found it easy to put the greater burden of taxation on the poor who had gained least from the national revolution. Italy could boast almost the lowest wages in Europe, along with about the highest indirect dues payable on food, and the reformers all agreed that taxes fell disproportionately on consumption rather than on income or property. Even some conservatives confessed that the less a man owned the more he seemed to pay, and Sonnino admitted in the Chamber that the tax collector and the policeman were the only contact the brutish peasantry had with the state, whereas the rich could bribe impoverished revenue officers and rely on an inefficient system of checking tax returns.

Instead of devising a more rational plan of assessment and collection, the state simply recouped some of its losses with yet more numerous taxes and so made legislation more complex. New taxes often overlapped the old, and were based on so many varying systems that they were wasteful as well as exorbitant. The uneven efficiency of local tax offices meant variation in yield, and as so much depended on the arbitrary assessment of some ignorant official, uncertainty was added to unfairness. Later in the century, Fortunato computed that on average over 30 per cent of individual incomes went in taxation, and this was said to be probably more than anywhere else in the world.

An economic crisis was not long in coming after 1861. Railroad building, the brigandage campaign, transferring the capital to Florence, the war of 1866, all these caused exorbitant expenditure. The Anglo-Italian Bank, of which Ricasoli himself was president, collapsed. Reconstruction loans became increasingly expensive as European banking houses shied away from them, and government stock after Lissa fell to 37 from its nominal price of 100. Confidence could only be restored by bringing a better balance into the government accounts, but it was not easy to see how. An increased land tax would meet fierce resistance from landowning deputies, and in any case would require a lengthy new cadastral survey. Free-trade principles ruled out any rise in customs revenue. There had already been a great leveling upward of taxation to Piedmontese standards, and this had aroused fury in other provinces. An attempt to raise the tax on salt and tobacco led only to a decrease in sales.

Sella ultimately decided, against Lanza's advice and tremendous left-wing opposition, to restore the hated tax on the grinding of wheat and corn. This had been the cause of many rebellions before 1860 and had been abolished by the national state as an earnest of future prosperity. But it had the great advantage of being easy to impose and difficult to evade. Sella expected to obtain from it a hundred million lire a year. Where he went wrong was in his confident prophecy that the tax would not cause hunger. The middle classes, having won their own freedom from feudalism, were hardly aware that a social question existed, and were ignorant about the common people who lived on bread, pasta, and polenta.

The grist tax was approved by 182 votes against 164 and came into force in January 1869. At once rioting began, and after two weeks there had been 250 deaths, 1,000 people wounded, and 4,000 rioters were in prison. Cries were heard of "long live the pope and the Austrians." Country vicars and newspaper editors were among those arrested for showing sympathy with the rebellion, and an army corps under General Cadorna had to be mobilized in Emilia. But the tax went on being collected. It was coupled with the farming out of the tobacco monopoly at very unrewarding terms to the state, and the private company which exploited this monopoly was notoriously corrupt, its share price quadrupling almost at once.

The chief financial result of the 1866 war was a large-scale resort to credit. Scialoia had to issue 650 million lire worth of paper money and compel acceptance of nonconvertible notes of the Banca Nazionale. Four-fifths of the money hitherto in circulation had been coin, and this new temporary measure did at least result in making paper money more acceptable. It also made obtaining foreign loans still harder, and this emphasized the need to balance income with expenditure and borrow more at home. As an immediate result, money lost much of its value, and the "forced currency" further lowered national credit. The bank gained handsomely, but coin left for France at an alarming rate, and the inflationary effect of a fall in money values reduced the real wages of the people. Although the salaries of king and ministers were cut to show their good intentions, this was small consolation to the genuinely poor.

★

Another governmental money-making device was the sale of ecclesiastical property. A vast extent of agricultural land had accumulated in mortmain through possession by ecclesiastical bodies and charitable trusts. The breaking up of such estates, it was now argued, would benefit agriculture, and lawyers decided that the state might properly requisition such a national asset to meet the capital expense of a national war. An act was passed in 1867 and the land sold, but in such quantity that land values fell so that the proceeds were less than expected. By 1880 over a million acres had been alienated in this way, and the state had irretrievably spent its most lucrative capital gain.

These ecclesiastical estates had by law to be sold in small lots, if necessary with deferred payments so that poorer farmers could buy. But in practice the ruling consideration was fiscal and the land went chiefly to speculators and existing landowners. Smallholders found it difficult to borrow money for their purchases, since moneylenders discovered a far better investment in direct acquisition of real estate at this price. Often the auctions were openly rigged. Even when the small farmer was successful in purchasing a plot of land, he possessed little capital for running expenses and so might have to sell out after the first poor harvest. His discomfiture was the greater in that the common lands belonging to individual villages, which had furnished him hitherto with pasture and firewood, were often enclosed as private property, and in addition, instead of paying rent to the Church, he now had to reckon with more businesslike and exorbitant owners.

It was not the old families any more than the peasant who gained from this land distribution, nor even the parish priest whose meager stipend was meant to be augmented out of the proceeds, but rather the financiers and middle-class businessmen who regarded cheap land as a hedge against inflation and a means of social climbing. Since prestige was conferred more by broader acres than by improvement of existing estates, the result was to increase the extent of the *latifondi* and to divert money away from more useful work. In a country where there was little saving and where savers were timid, this was serious. Purchase money had to be borrowed at 6 per cent or more, and this payable interest was often higher than the gross income from the land; at least it never left much margin for settling any debts incurred.

13   The Capture of Rome

By express provision of the constitution "the Catholic, Apostolic, and Roman religion is the sole religion of the state," and yet the *risorgimento* passed for an anticlerical movement. Even the devout Catholics of Ricasoli's circle wanted a reform in the Church, and most other national leaders were heretics, deists, or skeptics. Patriotism stood for secularization of the state as well as for destruction of the pope's temporal power. By 1860, therefore, patriotic Italians found themselves under collective excommunication, theoretically barred from the sacraments and religious burial, and until 1929 the Vatican refused to recognize the existence of Italy.

Cavour shrewdly and correctly foresaw that lay Catholics and even the lower clergy would pay little mind if the Holy See condemned the national movement. He himself was not a good practicing Catholic. Believing that the contemplative religious orders were now "useless and even harmful," he had already gone far toward secularizing Piedmont before 1860, dissolving most of the monasteries and abolishing clerical privileges at law. He sharply cautioned the clergy that civil war might follow if they intruded into secular politics. Personally, he was ready to give up the old jurisdictional claim to intervene in episcopal appointments, but he stipulated in return that the laity should be sovereign in Italy. Mistakenly thinking that he held all the cards, he confiscated papal territory and killed the pope's subjects when they tried to defend themselves, yet still apparently thought that Catholics would meekly surrender to the triumph of liberalism and to his formula of "a free Church in a free state."

Garibaldi and Mazzini had realized the inherent incompatibility from the first. Mazzini was far more naturally religious and Garibaldi more anticlerical than was Cavour. Garibaldi used to call the priests wolves and assassins and the pope not a true Christian. He blamed the national backwardness on clerical ascendancy in the schools and the consequent predominance of classical and rhetorical studies over technical and physical education. At Naples in 1860 Garibaldi had shocked the faithful by allowing the importation of bibles and the construction of a Protestant church, and in the North he had even baptized children with his own hands. Crispi and Bixio kept up his cry in parliament that Rome be invaded and the cardinals thrown into the Tiber, while the young poet, Carducci, wrote a *Hymn to Satan* in which the Church was the great enemy and patriots were pictured as fighting not only against the papal states but against religion itself.

Unification brought the extension of Piedmontese secularist laws to the newly annexed provinces. Without waiting even so much as to consult parliament, the new northern proconsuls unilaterally denounced the Neapolitan concordat, and within a few months sixty-six bishops had been arrested in these southern provinces alone. Many more ecclesiastics had to wait years without receiving the royal exequatur permitting them to enter upon their office, and the revenue of their sees was thus forfeit. Don Bosco, soon to be beatified, was held by the police for questioning, and five cardinals were prosecuted in as many years. Ricasoli ordered the cardinal of Pisa to celebrate independence day with a solemn *Te Deum*, and when the cardinal barred his cathedral in protest, the chancel was forced and the service sung without him. Then he himself was taken under arrest to Turin.

Such actions did not assist the successive attempts to negotiate with the pope. Nor was the wholesale confiscation of Church property a good advertisement for liberalism. Many Catholics realized that reforms in the relation between Church and state were overdue, but injustice was bound to be caused by so sudden and severe a secularization in a land containing so many clergy when changes were effected by unilateral action.

Cavour secretly sent considerable sums to Rome for bribing the ecclesiastical authorities, and at one point opened negotiations with the papal secretary of state himself, the affluent and more than disreputable Cardinal Antonelli. Some prelates were favorable to a negotiated solution of the "Roman question," among them the theologian Cardinal Santucci. The pope, however, remained adamant on retaining his temporal power, even though this was not declared an article of faith. The Church after 1848 had entered a conservative phase in both politics and religion, and ideas of liberal Catholicism had been suppressed after the early writings of Rosmini and Gioberti.

In December 1864 the papal encyclical *Quanta cura* appeared together with a syllabus of errors including all the major principles of liberalism. Among the eighty propositions advanced, number 79 suggested that freedom of discussion would corrupt the soul; and number 32 hinted that the clergy had a natural right to avoid military service. Religious toleration, freedom of conscience and the press, the validity of secularist legislation, were all condemned, along with socialism, rationalism, and bible societies, and it was denied that the pope either could or should come to terms with "progress, liberalism, and modern civilization."

This syllabus aroused great indignation. Although the less illiberal church-men threw doubt on both its significance and its authority, most of the hierarchy took it as an infallible pronouncement. Subsequent apologists tried to explain that it did not prevent a Catholic styling himself a liberal in politics. Indeed, since the condemned propositions were spreading fast, the Church was likely to have to change tack and come to terms with liberalism and modern civilization before very long. Its original publication, however, seemed a blow to compromise and provoked an outburst of anticlericalism. Crispi pedantically told parliament that Christianity must be purged of the vices of the Roman Church or else it would perish. Successive govern-ments proposed that seminaries should submit to government inspection, that prefects might interfere even in ritual if necessary, and that priests could be indicted for refusing absolution to those excommunicated for political offences.

A law of 1866 then declared that most religious orders should have their houses dissolved and their goods confiscated. Some thirteen thousand ecclesias-tical bodies had already been suppressed, and under this ruling another twenty-five thousand followed. It was explained in justification that some Church endowments ought to pass to the state now that the latter intended to assume responsibility for education and charity. Parish revenues were left intact, but cathedral chapters and bishops were compelled to follow the monasteries in surrendering their capital to the state, receiving 5 per cent in return (after three-tenths of the capital had first been deducted for educational and charitable purposes). Seminarists were also made liable to military service, and the new civil code denied legal sanction to such marriages as were not performed in a civil ceremony.

★

This still did not solve the Roman question. Cavour wanted to make Rome the future capital of Italy, but the convention of 1864 with France seemed to carry a moral obligation to renounce this aim. The more religious-minded among the liberals, Jacini for instance, agreed with the more anticlerical such as D'Azeglio in disliking the whole idea of making Rome into Italy's capital city. The project seemed to give undue weight to sentimental and historical as against cultural and economic arguments. "Thank God, this will rid us of Rome," had been the reaction of the Catholic Count Pasolini to the convention of 1864. On the other hand the doctrinaire patriots insisted that Italy without Rome was no true nation, and Bismarck abetted them so as to create a diversion and prevent anticlerical Italy from joining with Catholic Austria and France against him. A man such as Cavour might have used this split between Bismarck and Napoleon III to denounce the convention and annex Rome, and Rattazzi the new prime minister knew as much, but did not dare or understand how to do it.

Apart from Rattazzi's hesitancy, the main reason for Garibaldi's defeat in his third attempt to march on Rome was the indifference of the Roman citizens and the fact that their faith and their interest kept them loyal to Pius IX. Even some of the lukewarm patriots in Rome were so fearful of social revolution that they split away from the adherents of Mazzini and Garibaldi, and on occasion delated them to the police. Rome was still the "parasite city" of clerics, hotelkeepers, and beggars. Half of its population existed on official hand-outs, and the governing classes of clergy exempted themselves from taxes and had a highly privileged position to defend. Had there been a stronger lay middle class, or even had the moderates and radicals been more in agreement, Garibaldi might not have failed so dismally.

It is almost incredible that a catastrophe similar to that of Aspromonte should have been allowed to happen again in 1867. Rattazzi was in office on both occasions. Once again he hoped that Rome would rise of its own accord and declare itself annexed with a mock plebiscite, and at least he hoped to let things go so far as to persuade Napoleon that Garibaldi would become ungovernable if the popular demand for Rome went unsatisfied. But his chief desire was that of not compromising himself irretrievably either way, and so once again he failed, neither convincing Europe that Italian eagerness for Rome was irresistible, nor demonstrating that Italy could control her own revolutionaries without foreign interference. He again permitted the "spontaneous" enrollment of volunteers, with arms sometimes officially provided. Garibaldi testified that the government even incited him to invade the Papal states as a pretext for the national troops to move in and "restore order." Rattazzi denied this story, but the king's statements to the French and British ministers confirm it in detail and add the refinement that the king intended to use this excuse to "massacre" the Garibaldians as well as defeat the papal mercenaries. The memoirs of Finali confirm authoritatively that the secret service funds were used to stir up a local rising which was to give the excuse for this operation.

Humiliated by the vicarious acquisition of Venice, the ingenuous but noblehearted Garibaldi had been anxious to show that the voluntary initiative of the Italian people could complete the work of national unification. Urged on by the government, bands of volunteers collected on the papal frontier in the late summer of 1867. Mazzini did not usually err on the side of caution, but for once counseled Garibaldi to stay quiet, because he was sure that Rattazzi, like Cavour, would disown the rebels if they failed and would merely exploit and then crush them if they won. In September the government arrested Garibaldi and sent him back home to Caprera, but as he was not put in strict custody, and as the volunteers remained on the frontier, this was again considered a ruse to deceive foreign diplomats.

Rattazzi may have hoped in this way to make time for the Romans to rise and give him an excuse for intervention. The liberals in Rome, however, did not stir, and Napoleon reluctantly deferred to French public opinion and sent back to the Holy City the armies he had withdrawn after the convention of 1864. If the Italians were not going to keep their word and defend the papal states, then he must do it himself. The possibility of French intervention had been discounted by the king and his government. Rattazzi thought that he was still in charge of the situation and realized too late that he had gone either too far or not far enough. When confronted with the choice of arresting the volunteers or invading the papal states before the French could arrive, he panicked, and resigned office in October.

At this point Garibaldi suddenly reappeared on the mainland and ordered his bands to advance. So free were his movements that they seemed to have official blessing, and the king in fact was still guardedly weighing his chances. But the people under papal rule evidently did not want "deliverance". In particular the peasants remained sullen and reluctant to give help or information to Garibaldi. Gregorovius, the German historian then living at Rome, wrote in his diary:

> It is a fact that no rising has anywhere occurred in the provinces. No one will compromise himself. Rome remains entirely quiet. ... The tumult that was expected to break out yesterday evening, and which had been announced the day before, was, it is said, put off on account of the rain. Two young men asserted that the rising would break out in an hour, since something must necessarily take place to redeem the Romans from the charge of cowardice ... but the night passed quietly; the great deed of heroism remained unperformed.

In contrast to this apathy, the invaders performed many deeds of courage, and two of the Cairoli brothers became a national legend when one was killed and the other badly wounded trying to run guns into the city; but the volunteers fought poorly and many deserted.

When Napoleon finally embarked French troops for Rome, Vittorio Emanuele inexpertly tried to save appearances by ordering his troops to march against Garibaldi and calling the French his good allies. General Cialdini crossed the frontier in pursuit of the "rebels," only to be ordered back by the French, and on November 3 the volunteers were defeated at Mentana. The French were back in Rome and the chances of Italian occupation seemed infinitely reduced. Political cleavages in Italy had been sharpened. Furthermore, the *papalini* could now argue plausibly that the Romans evidently had little wish for union with Italy and hence that the vaunted liberal justification for a national movement was merely a blind for something much less creditable.

★

This catastrophe forced Rattazzi out of politics, though his three-day speech in self-defense was long remembered for its eloquence. In the emergency the king turned to another general, the Savoyard senator Menabrea. The shock of Mentana, coming after the military defeats at Custoza and Lissa, had compromised the dynasty, and the king looked to the Court party to tide him over some awkward parliamentary debates. Menabrea himself and several of his cabinet were former officials of the royal household, and yet, although some people demanded suspension of the constitution, the king himself had little hope of restoring absolutism. In 1869, Lanza and Sella were allowed to overthrow the government of this royal aide-de-camp. Here was an auspicious symptom of growth in parliamentary experience.

The king was opposed to a further move toward winning Rome, especially as Garibaldi's failure had damaged his alliance with France. He also had an affectionate regard *"pour ce pauvre diable de Saint Père,"* and when gravely ill in 1869 he very properly married his mistress and plied Rome with telegrams for papal benediction. As a Catholic and a loyal vassal of Napoleon, he had eventually turned against Garibaldi's invasion in 1867, and in 1869 was still trying to negotiate a formal alliance with France which would have excluded him from acquisition of the Holy City. Even after the outbreak of the Franco-Prussian war in 1870, the king continued to hope he could join a war against Prussia. In the Senate, Cialdini spoke for the Court party in terms which seemed to challenge parliamentary government itself. Lanza privately confessed that the king's ideas about foreign policy were threatening disaster: "The king is in practice his own minister of foreign affairs and keeps up a secret correspondence with our ambassadors and with Napoleon. This may not be constitutional, but it is unfortunately a fact." Vittorio Emanuele in fact not only secretly promised the French that he would join them in fighting against Prussia, but had recently asked the Prussians if he could join them in fighting against France, and also told the Austrians he was ready to fight against both France and Prussia.

Throughout August 1870 the French troops were leaving Rome again, this time because they were needed on the Rhine front, but still the king taunted his ministers with cowardice because they tried to prevent him fighting against his late ally, Prussia. He was now banking on a French victory, and hoped once again to be on the winning side in a European war. Indeed, only the news of Napoleon's crushing defeat at Sedan suddenly forced upon him a more realistic view. Sella threatened to resign if this heaven-sent chance to defy the French and occupy Rome were not seized. Ominous threats also came from the prefects about possible revolution, and the Left hinted that they might abandon parliament altogether. Manifestly, the French alliance was now a double handicap, so the king nimbly changed sides, taking care to explain to the pope how he was being forced into annexing Rome against his own better judgment. Lanza's letters show that once again the secret service funds were used to precipitate a local uprising which would give a pretext for having "to restore law and order," but nothing happened and the army had to attack Rome uninvited, the papalists losing nineteen men and the Italians forty-nine.

Italy thus casually gained Rome, like Venice, as just another by-product of Prussian victory. The patriots could not understand why Aspromonte, Mentana, and the bombardment of the Porta Pia had successively passed without much spontaneous support from the Roman people, and it all seemed an unsatisfactory ending to the wars of liberation. Pelloux, a future premier, was awarded a military cross for opening up the walls with his batteries, but there could be no real glory in defeating the merely token resistance of this tiny papal army. Once again, too much had been due to fortune and foreigners, and the national energy expended seemed almost disproportionately small for such a substantial success.

Whatever the expense, Italy was at last substantially united and complete. One English writer calculated the total financial cost of unification as forty million pounds sterling; Fortunato on the basis of official figures estimated the cost at only six thousand dead and twenty thousand wounded between 1848 and 1870—the German army lost more in one day of August 1870. Nevertheless the result was impressive. A new nation of twenty-seven million people had appeared, alongside Britain with thirty-two million, France with thirty-six, and Germany with forty-one million. It remained to be seen what would be the effect on international politics.

★

The destruction of the temporal power of the papacy was the climax of the *risorgimento* and one of its most important achievements. Ever since the time of Petrarch, Italians had looked on Rome not only as the center of the world and of true religion, but as the heart of Italy. Machiavelli had reviled the temporal power of the Church as the greatest obstacle to national unity. But when papal sovereignty collapsed in 1870, patriots such as Jacini and Capponi could still dislike the bullying tone given to this national triumph by the bombardment of Rome. When the pope refused to hand over the keys of the Quirinal and fulminated against the king as a new Attila, the government had to break open the palace and confiscate newspapers which printed the papal decree. In October, however, another plebiscite gave an inevitable endorsement of the invasion. Out of a population of 220,000 there were 167,000 eligible voters, of whom 133,000 approved and only 1,500 disapproved. Those who believed in plebiscites could now feel happier.

It was not wholly by chance that temporal defeat for the pope came simultaneously with the proclamation of papal infallibility as a dogma of the

Church. In the first place, the meeting of the Vatican Council at the end of 1869 frightened even Catholic Europe with the specter of ultramontanism; and this let Italy take Rome without active opposition from the other Catholic powers. In the second place, the loss of territorial power left the Pope with less need to temporize and greater freedom to speak as a religious leader. By 1870 the strongest current of opinion in the Church was that of the Jesuits in favor of increased centralization and clericalism, and a declaration about papal infallibility was the natural upshot. The new dogma did not produce any schism of importance in Italy as it did in Germany, though many liberal conservatives such as Sella, Bonghi, and Minghetti sympathized with those bishops who constituted the dissentient minority.

A special law was passed by the Italian state to regularize the pope's position in a Rome over which he no longer ruled. His person was declared inviolable. He was to have the honors due a king, free communication with Catholics throughout the world, and diplomatic immunities for foreign ministers attached to the Vatican. An income of over three million lire per annum was assigned him in perpetuity. The state also gave up most of its restrictive controls over Church action and renounced the hereditary apostolic legateship which the king had claimed to exercise in Sicily. State and Church were to exist separately. Church property was to be secularized, and ecclesiastical salaries paid (after deduction of fairly heavy expenses) out of a nationalized *fondo per il culto*.

Successive popes, however, utterly repudiated this settlement. They could not take a pension from Italy without appearing to be her lackey, or without seeming to sanction this violation of the sanctuary. Not having been consulted, Pius IX preferred the role of an invaded and aggrieved party as "the prisoner of the Vatican." On the other hand, not only Crispi and the Left, but Sella and many others feared that the pope had been granted too much by this offer of exemption from ordinary Italian law, and thought that the new clerical liberties were an unjustified diminution of national sovereignty. When the pope rejected the Law of Guarantees, they welcomed this fact as a release from further obligation.

A *modus vivendi* was gradually found, papal honor being satisfied by refusal to recognize the new kingdom, while the Church continued to enjoy a usually benevolent interpretation of existing laws. Legal fictions circumvented the prohibition against religious orders holding property, and an increase in the wealth of these orders was one sign of a new flowering of religion. Deprivation of temporal power was proving, as Cavour had foretold in the teeth of clerical opposition, to be a help and not a hindrance to propagation of the faith.

★

The Church meanwhile boycotted domestic Italian politics with resolution and tried hard to prohibit Catholics from sharing the full duties of citizenship. The Abbé Gioberti had vainly hoped that the Church would once more stand actively in politics for popular welfare and against tyranny, and Jacini had sought, also in vain, to find in Catholicism the basis for an active conservative party. Cavour himself had, theoretically, welcomed clerical participation in elections as a sign that the Church was coming inside the orbit of parliamentary government where it would assimilate liberal precept and practice. But when in 1858 he vitiated this theory by annulling the election of certain Catholic deputies, the latter understandably decided that their protest would be more effective outside parliament. The editor of the leading Catholic paper in Turin, Don Margotti, coined the phrase "neither electors nor elected," which later became an official prohibition against Catholics intervening in national politics. If clerical deputies entered parliament, so the argument went, they would have to swear loyalty to the conquerors of papal territory; tenure of any office in the state might likewise involve them in excommunication, and even as mayors of villages they would have to marry people by a civil ceremony which the Church did not recognize. In 1866 the Sacred Penitentiary had conceded that a Catholic might sit in parliament if he added to his oath the words "so far as divine and ecclesiastical law allow," but when the following year Count Crotti tried to use this formula, he spoke too loudly and pandemonium broke out. His oath was disallowed and he was expelled from the Chamber.

It cannot, therefore, be blamed upon the Church that Catholics remained aloof, for the state was the aggressor in this war, and indeed some politicians suggested that practicing believers should be excluded from public office. In the elections of 1874 the Vatican declared it "inexpedient" for Catholics to vote, and this *non expedit* later became a formal prohibition, though many of the faithful continued to disobey. Most of the electorate exercised their vote, and the percentage was not materially increased when the ban was eventually lifted. Much the same proportion also held good for local elections where there was no veto at all.

The veto was sterile in fact but quite valid in theory. The Church had to protest against injustice, especially as she continued to assume that the Italian occupation was temporary and God would yet restore his own. She could not refrain from censure when a Protestant church was built in Rome in 1873 and a Masonic temple two years later. In his pose as a prisoner, the pope did not stir from the Vatican and he admitted no good-will envoys from the king. The last official act of Pius IX was a defiant protest. Leo XIII, who was pope from 1878 to 1903, protested over sixty times, and on at least four occasions allowed a rumor to spread that he might remove from Rome as his predecessors had moved to Avignon five hundred years earlier. Up to 1929 this formal protest was maintained and the very suggestion of compromise repudiated. When the celebrated Jesuit, Padre Curci, changed from attacking Italy to defending it, he was straightway expelled by his order.

Lay statesmen called the pope's attitude merely the melodramatic pose of a would-be martyr, especially since both sides in practice dropped their condemnations and co-operated in many matters. Practicing Catholics were partly cut off from the rest of the nation, with separate schools, a distinct social life, and without full exercise of their rights and duties as citizens. A disaster for the state, this was even more a disaster for the Church. Yet the novels of the Catholic Fogazzaro show how easy it was for clerical influence to remain important in local politics. Complete non-co-operation would have been disastrous: on the one hand it would have given the anticlericals free rein, and on the other the nation would have been divided against itself. Even the majority of anticlericals were proud of having the pope in Rome and abated their reforming zeal when he threatened to leave.

SECTION FOUR: THE NATION ASSERTS
ITSELF, 1870–1882

14   The Last Years of the Right, 1870–1876

The elevation of Rome into a national capital created special problems. The city was divided into "blacks" and "whites" as in the time of Guelphs and Ghibellines, family rivalries here mixing with religious feeling. The "black" aristocracy, which had done little enough to defend the pope, now compensated by holding aloof from the royal Court, and the Quirinal palace and its chapel were placed under interdict. The families of the Orsini and Colonna were internally divided, but the Chigi, Borghese, and Barberini, which had thrived through papal nepotism, put their religious before civil allegiance. The fabulously rich Prince Torlonia changed the livery of his household so as not to resemble the royal colors, and "black" ladies paraded their carriages along Corso only in the summer months when good royalists were away in the country. Of all the Roman nobility, the Duke of Sermoneta alone had been a confessed liberal before 1870. From then onward there was to be a gradual process of assimilation, but for many years there were two distinct social sets as well as two Courts and two *corps diplomatiques*.

Vittorio Emanuele was too simple and unsociable to cut much of a figure among these grandees. He suffered from being morganatically married to a commoner, as well as from his temperamental lack of grace and glitter. Even more he suffered from having declared war on the pope while trying to have it both ways by posing as a humble churchman. He had been brazenly aggressive; he seemed a bully for attacking the weak, a coward for waiting before doing so until France was in desperate difficulties. His conquest was in any case legally and morally hard to defend, especially after 1864 when he had undertaken in a treaty to defend the papal frontier against all comers.

Successive governments nevertheless tried hard to catch the imagination and sympathy of the common people in the capital. Great sums of money were spent on spectacular buildings to give employment and gild the pill of northern occupation. Forty thousand state officials had somehow to be housed, and a consequent attempt to modernize the old city started a wave of speculation in land. Romans soon found that their taxes had doubled and house prices more than trebled. Cardinals and princes competed to buy up the large private gardens on the Quirinal and Esquiline hills, and then sold them profitably for building. The results were effective, if not always in good taste: *palazzi* were converted into government departments, the flora of the Colosseum (on which an Englishman had written a whole book) was stripped off, and excavations began on the site of the forums. Augustus Hare was later to write that a few years of Italian rule had done more to destroy Rome than the Goths and Vandals together.

But attempts to make Rome a capital in the style of Paris were to fail, for the rival allegiance to the Vatican was an almost insuperable difficulty. Strong regional sentiment still left Turin and Milan as more important as centers of national life. Rome lacked the resources to become industrial and remained provincial in culture. Its university had never been of much note, and the city never became the principal center for books and newspapers. Its climate and geographical situation were poor, and though it was the seat of parliament, parliament itself was in a sense cut off from the real life of Italy. Rome remained a city of the past—ancient, medieval, or baroque. It was not a town of theaters and banks, but of churches, palaces, and monuments. Some people called it too southern, others too international, others too corrupt, and it soon became fashionable to lament that the capital was not somewhere else.

★

Fortunately, the surface of politics remained tranquil during these years. Lanza succeeded Menabrea in office for an unusually long period, from 1869 to 1873, and fell only when Depretis of the Left joined Minghetti in voting to multiply fourfold the grant proposed for the new naval dockyard at Taranto. Minghetti, who followed Lanza, also remained in power for the uncommon duration of three years. The Right, however, was not a compact body, and though arbitrary government influence was used even more than usual in the elections of 1874, the potential opposition increased by about 30 seats, thus commanding about 233 votes in the Chamber against 275. Minghetti therefore survived precariously in fear of a defection by some of his supporters.

The Right always had a tendency to dissolve into regional elements. One dissident element was the Piedmontese *permanente* which had broken away after the abandonment of Turin in 1864. Another rebellious group, larger and more discontented, was formed by those southern deputies disillusioned by the steeply increased taxation and the small economic gain which union had meant for the South. A Tuscan group under Peruzzi made a further grievance out of the removal of the capital to Rome and demanded compensation for the many Florentine speculators who had suffered by the transfer. Florentine lawyers thereby lost a valuable legal practice and their city lost many indirect sources of revenue. When Minghetti's minister of public works, Spaventa, proposed to nationalize the railroads, this threatened the investments in railroad construction of the Tuscan banking houses. Influential financiers such as Bastogi feared that Spaventa was attacking their monopoly of railroad development in southern Italy, just as Correnti and the Lombard merchants feared that this nationalization presaged a general departure from well-established free-trade principles.

Despite these grievances, the statesmen of the Right, whose term of office was drawing to its close, had set a great example of patriotism. During these early difficult years they had helped to create traditions of parliamentary government and political rectitude. Seldom in Italian history has the country possessed rulers so upright and incorruptible as the agriculturist Ricasoli, the doctors of medicine Farini and Lanza, Sella the geologist, and Ferrara the professor of economics. Not often did prime ministers hand over to their successors such a large balance in the secret service fund as did Lanza, although he was under no obligation to account for his expenditure. He was as thrifty with the state's finances as with his own, living modestly, and left office a poor man. "This spiritual aristocracy of upright and loyal gentlemen," as Croce called them, never sought cheap popularity, but remained courageously disinterested in their conduct of public affairs, even at the price of losing office.

It would be incorrect to label these men as unqualified conservatives. The national movement had been so revolutionary that to call oneself conservative was to invite political failure, and deputies for this reason used to compete for seats near the center of the Chamber. The old aristocracy had either become liberal or else was unimportant in politics. The new industrialists could not be conservative, at least not yet, for they were still in the process of overthrowing feudal and aristocratic Italy, and were not yet entrenched in established industries under state protection. The Right was in fact composed of people who were liberal before they were conservative. True enough, they had insufficient notion of the needs and interests of ordinary citizens. They were invariably moderate, prudent, and fearful of change, but some were more "progressive" than the so-called Left, as Cavour had been more "revolutionary" than Rattazzi. Spaventa tried to nationalize the railroads despite radical opposition, and Scialoia in 1874 tried to make elementary education compulsory. Minghetti was taxed by the radical anticlericals with "Vaticanism," but was able to reply that, of 94 requests by bishops for the royal exequatur, he had granted only 28, and shortly afterward he expelled 33 prelates from their sees for failing to secure such permission.

This necessity to be at once revolutionary and conservative had its disadvantages. It meant that issues in politics remained blurred and the electorate could rarely choose between alternative policies. It meant also that the Right had no very firm basis in ideology and was thus peculiarly brittle. Some of its constituent groups were permeated with Hegelianism and were insufficiently concerned to defend the individual against the state. Some had already abjured the free-trade tradition stemming from Cavour, as others ignored his injunctions against administrative centralization and rejected his "free Church in a free state." In consequence, when the Right fell from power in 1876, it found itself without a coherent program.

Italian parliamentary life was in fact continuing to develop a special character in which the government majority included many diverse groups held together by loose and evanescent ties. The leading politicians were too independent in their views for a strict party system. Lanza had sat on the Left when first elected to parliament. Sella was close to the Left on Church policy and on franchise reform. Yet, at the same time, Sella was well over to the Right on matters of finance and the grist tax. Minghetti, on the other hand, was ready to abolish the grist tax, and was divided from most of the others by his leaning toward the idea of partially autonomous regions. Sella and Minghetti never sat in the same cabinet because there were also personal differences between them. Such a situation, in which private relations counted for more than policy, was typical; the groups inside the Right were kept from open breach only by their common distrust of Depretis and his still more radical associates.

★

The Right had many achievements to its credit: the annexation of Venice and Rome rounded off the united kingdom; an industrial and agricultural revolution had been initiated; in fifteen years the revenue had been tripled; and at last in 1876 the budget could be given the appearance of balancing.

Against these achievements must be set the fact that the country was more stringently taxed than any in Europe, and taxed with less concern for general economic welfare. By now most of the domanial and ecclesiastical lands were sold, and yet a huge debt had accumulated which drained away more and more money from land improvement and industry. Francesco Ferrara, the greatest economist of the time, lamented that there was no sign in the economic life of the country to suggest that the nation had been finally unified. The more conservative Villari painted a much blacker picture. In science, letters, industry, commerce, and education, Italy was lagging behind the other civilized powers, yet still (so he said) thought that she was better than them all. Armaments, ships, and engineers had to be imported from abroad. Italian books were not read beyond the Alps, so Villari complained. Italy's generals were incompetent, her administrators were often appointed by favor or nepotism. Another pessimistic statement came from Rattazzi in 1873 just before he died, when describing to parliament what remained to be done:

> In ten years we have spent thirteen billions and we have still not built an adequate army or fleet, nor have we obtained public security at home, nor are our frontiers in a proper state of defense, nor above all have we enough schools. ... No one in Europe regards us as a great power. ... Our magistrates are intellectually despicable, and their moral standards deplorable. And Austria has beaten us by sea and land.

Apart from internal divisions, another reason for weakness of the Right was its haughty condescension toward the radicals as uneducated and socially impossible, and its unwillingness to entice more than a selected few of them inside the government majority. The system of government by coalitions depended on a proper "circulation of elites," but Lanza made no overtures to the Left comparable with those once made to him by Cavour. The radical-democrats therefore remained as a factious and irresponsible opposition, while the liberal-conservatives continued self-righteously to profess a monopoly of patriotic fervor. Garibaldi was becoming a frustrated, gouty, and eccentric old man. In 1870 he wrote to offer "what is left of me" to the French Republic in fighting Germany and acquitted himself well, for which service he was elected to the French Assembly. But at home, apart from a mild flirtation with socialism, he passed the time tending his bees and beans on Caprera, or campaigning for some lost cause like diverting the course of the River Tiber.

Most of Mazzini's followers had by now been realistic enough to renounce their republicanism and swear the oath of loyalty as deputies. Crispi and Bertani of the radical *estrema* were fighting inside the Chamber for increased democracy in the state. Another future leader of the extreme democrats, Cavallotti, accepted the oath in 1873, adding the rider that he looked upon it as null and an infringement of popular sovereignty. Such radical thinkers found much sympathy among young men excluded from the closed shop of politics.

Other miscellaneous symptoms of discontent could be found. Many independent liberals, including those inclined toward Freemasonry, envied the process of parliamentary reform in Britain, and some of them believed that the greatness and prosperity of their own nation needed active participation by the working classes in national elections. Meanwhile protest by the *avant garde* helped to diffuse a sense of bitterness and frustration among the intellectuals. Cavour's last minister of education, Professor De Sanctis, had by now deserted the government majority, and proclaiming the necessity of a two-party system he had ranged with the left-wing opposition from about 1865. Another observer on the Right, Sidney Sonnino, echoed Rattazzi's indictment of the government when he wrote in 1872 that political education was actually diminishing rather than increasing; he noted an indifference to everything that related to representative government and the exercise of a citizen's rights; there was a confusion in parties, an instability and weakness in the government, and a general loss of confidence. This was one result of ten years of parliamentary rule. Sonnino also observed that in the lowest and most populous section of society there existed an accumulation of discontents and hatreds which had to be taken into account if it was intended to give a secure basis to parliamentary institutions. Even Sonnino had to admit that Depretis and the politicians of the Left were temperamentally more fitted to understand these popular discontents.

The tactics of coalition government might have suggested a more imaginative program to a prime minister in this situation. But Minghetti remained strict and unyielding, and instead of adapting his tactics to win over the more moderate of his opponents, made only a halfhearted approach toward the Left. On the other hand a notorious incident took place at the Villa Ruffi near Rimini, when a number of people were arrested on the quite unjustified suspicion of plotting a republican revolt. They included Fortis, a future prime minister, and Saffi, one of the triumvirs who had governed the Roman republic in 1849. After a panic decision for their arrest, they were hustled handcuffed into a crowded railroad compartment and spent the night on straw. It was a severe setback for the government when after some months in prison they were acquitted.

In 1875, Depretis, who had succeeded Rattazzi as leader of the constitutional Left, laid down a challenging program in a famous speech at Stradella. Among other things he claimed to stand for free and compulsory education, an extension of the suffrage, decentralization of administration, and more local self-government. This obtained a good press, and as the speech betrayed the slightly vaporous language of Correnti, it suggested that certain group leaders on the Center Right were wavering in their allegiance. A temporary coalition was forming of Left, Right, and Center deputies such as had overturned Menabrea in 1869 and Lanza in 1873. Matters were working toward a climax when, in March 1876, Minghetti was defeated over the *macinato* tax and his project of railroad nationalization. Ironically, this defeat came just after his greatest success in announcing that for the first time expenditure was less than revenue. The Right had completed their task of tightfisted and unspectacular administration. New times called for new men.

15   Depretis and Transformism, 1870–1880

The accession to power of the Left was a healthy sign for constitutional development. Technically, there was no obligation under the 1848 *statuto* for governments to hold themselves responsible to parliament, but the king shrewdly recognized the advantages of broadening the basis of the political class. He privately reassured his entourage that he would still keep a hand on the reins himself, so they need not be frightened of Depretis in power.

The center of gravity of the state therefore shifted a little. Some of the more obstreperous radicals such as Nicotera and Crispi were at last enticed inside the governing classes, and in particular the South gained far greater representation in the government. Certain important sectional groups thus moved over to defend the new order instead of wasting themselves in factious opposition, and an avenue for legitimate ambition was opened for younger men. Most of the new cabinet had never held ministerial rank before, and the practice of the spoils system now advanced many other new people to minor office. With Agostino Depretis as premier there was little danger of another *consorteria* being formed, since, far from being rigid and exclusive, he went to the other extreme of promoting too easy an amalgamation among all manner of groups and interests. The Left soon revealed itself even more than the Right as a political party without fixed composition and policy.

Among the many worthy men who took office with Depretis were Zanardelli at the ministry of public works, the Neapolitan jurist Mancini at the ministry of justice, Professor Coppino at the ministry of education, and the naval engineer Benedetto Brin in the admiralty. Depretis personally was one of the most upright politicians in modern Italian history. Even when prime minister he continued to live in a top-floor apartment 120 steps up. Compared with the doctrinaires and ideologues he was always sensible and matter-of-fact, and his approach to every problem was calm, self-possessed, and usually cautious. Experience of administration as an official in various departments had taught him much. He was not a great man—and Italy needed a great man at this moment—but he was adroit in maneuver, fertile in expedients, and always moderate enough not to do much harm. Depretis gained as well as lost from his habitual attempt to circumnavigate a problem rather than face it squarely. He possessed few strong opinions of his own, and people usually left his presence with the impression that he agreed with them. Pareto wrote of him as someone with a skeptical turn of mind, who never embarrassed himself with principles or convictions. Always ready to follow any route that would assure him of a majority, he enjoyed in the later years of his life what Pareto called the most absolute dictatorship possible under a parliamentary regime. These comments were intended as criticism, but they might almost have been said of Cavour by some of his admirers.

★

While in opposition, the Left had possessed less a program than an accumulation of grudges—at least, ever since their anticlericalism and enthusiasm for national unification had been taken over by Cavour. In foreign affairs the Left had not much room nor much reason to depart very far from traditional policies. At home Depretis had vaguely projected certain democratic reforms, and the more rash and forthright Crispi had argued for universal suffrage as well as for an elected Senate and elected judges. Abolition of the grist tax and increased expenditure on public works had often been demanded from the radical benches, and also a diminution of state controls. The state should be "felt and seen as little as possible," said Crispi, against those of the Right who were advocating the nationalization of some private enterprises.

Once in office, the Left, which had risen to power only with help from dissident groups inside the Right, found reform harder to practice than to preach. The king's opening message to parliament in November 1876 spoke once more of administrative decentralization, but this was only talk. Depretis tried hard to make his ministry look more progressive than its predecessor, yet could do little more than promise to study possible reforms and to use less authoritarian methods of law enforcement. Nor was this last promise kept. Undoubtedly, under his administration Italy became more democratic, but this tendency was, for the most part, independent of official policy, as Cavour and others had foreseen. After the Law of Guarantees, the Left was hardly more anticlerical than the Right; indeed the fact that the Left and the clericals had sometimes combined when in opposition made it plausible to accuse Depretis of making undue concessions to the Vatican. The usual practice of coalition government, the same which had caused Cavour to move leftward and take over the policy of national unity from the democrats, now made Depretis move the other way and borrow from the Right.

When in opposition, Depretis had condemned the use of government "influence" at election time, but in the six months before November 1876 the prefects were strictly enjoined to use their administrative authority to manipulate the elections. Recalcitrant local government officials were transferred to less pleasant regions, or reduced to conformity by the threat of such transfer and its hampering effect on their future careers. In most principal cities, the prefects were changed at once. It was intimated that special favor in the matter of schools, railroad concessions, and other government contracts would be shown to those constituencies which voted the right way. The minister of the interior, Nicotera, left nothing to chance, and so won for his friends an overwhelming majority of about 380 deputies against 130. Many leaders of the Right, including Bonghi, Spaventa, and Massari, failed to be returned, and in southern Italy, where corrupt influence was most easily wielded, only four deputies of the Right were elected. It soon appeared, indeed, that victory had been too complete, for the lack of an effective conservative party impaired the political education of both sides. The absence of opposition and the presence of so many inexperienced deputies left this great majority exposed to the same internal disintegration which has sapped so many other ministries in Italian history.

The complete reconstitution of the Lower House brought with it some decline in quality among the deputies. The conservatives used to say, spitefully but not altogether untruthfully, that this triumph of the Left introduced nothing into politics except intrigue, corruption, and a moral vacuum. During almost sixteen years of opposition, Depretis had become accustomed to seek allies indiscriminately and to promise too much to too many. His chief strength lay in southern Italy where political life had always been unhealthy, where men had learned their politics in the school of conspiracy or else by cringing under a corrupt Bourbon despotism. His electoral success was incontestable, but instead of expressing a general reaction against the *consorteria*, it rather reflected a marriage of expediency between Nicotera and dominant clienteles in local government. Deputies henceforward were too frequently in collusion with local *notabili* and were the mouthpieces of parish-pump politics; they would trade their votes to each ministry in turn so long as private interests were placated. Depretis persuaded parliament to vote for building two thousand kilometers of railroad, which he then parceled out in return for votes. Another of his first measures was to increase the sugar tax, a few days after which some seventy deputies were raised to the dignity of *commendatore* or *cavaliere*: the connection seemed obvious. Depretis perhaps used no more violent pressure than Farini had done in 1861 or Minghetti in 1874. But he created an electoral machine which henceforward rarely failed to register the desired result.

★

This employment of government influence in elections was the first principle of Depretis's administration. A second was the formation of a new parliamentary majority by "transforming" the old groups into a new government coalition. In an election speech of October 1876 he said: "I hope my words will help bring about the fertile transformation of parties, the unification of all shades of liberal in parliament in exchange for those old party labels so often abused and so often decided only by the topography of the Chamber." Here again Depretis was exploiting a trend which already existed, and the word *trasformismo* was coined merely to express or rationalize that absence of party coherence and organization which had itself brought about the fall of the Right. Transformism was more or less a continuation of Cavour's practice. Most of the prime ministers since 1852 had not been strictly party men but had been willing to accept support from anywhere except the two extremes.

Each prime minister had the same problem of creating a government coalition which would be both liberal and conservative, and the differences among them therefore lay mostly in emphasis. One reason put forward to explain these inevitable coalitions is the absence from parliament of the extreme clericals and Mazzinians, the most powerful catalysts available. The need to keep these extremes out of politics drove all varieties of progressive-liberal and conservative-liberal into a common refuge where they laid aside their quarrels and joined in parceling out power and jobbery. The self-confidence of strong men such as Cavour and Depretis aided this process, for their domination of the political scene was connected with the elasticity of these center groups and the refusal by all politicians to stand too much on principle. Even Minghetti, who believed in a two-party system, thought strong government to be of overriding importance, and rallied many conservatives behind Depretis in their common fear of radicals and clericals.

Whatever the reason, political controversies were clearly not taking the form of party conflict. De Sanctis was another of Cavour's ex-colleagues who deplored this fact. In 1877 he wrote: "We have now reached the point where there are no solidly built parties in Italy except those based on either regional differences or the personal relation of client to patron; and these are the twin plagues of Italy." Existing groups were composed of elected representatives who might change their allegiance as occasion demanded, a fact which made election results unreliable. Depretis argued that this was quite proper since the existence of a well-organized opposition would retard governmental activity and divide the best elements of the nation into two ineffective halves.

Transformism is one method of parliamentary government, and this kind of constant Center coalition undoubtedly tended to make politics less con- troversial and more moderate. But occasionally some of the liberals recognized that, as De Sanctis and Croce taught in the different fields of literature and aesthetics, the lack of clear controversy could be deadening and stultifying. Cavour had been blamed for purposely splitting up existing parties as a means of increasing his own power, and Menabrea and Saracco had from two quite different angles criticized his eclectic policy and "game of political seesaw." Now Zanardelli accused Depretis of "confounding political parties which are necessary to national greatness, and of exhausting the political passions which are the lifeblood of free government." Transformism was attacked for degrading the practice of compromise, because what had been a patriotic duty in the common struggle against Austria was now being debased into a mere political habit to cover an absence of conviction. Spaventa and Di Rudinì of the defeated Right made much of this charge and began to pay unaccustomed compliments to a notional two-party method of government.

Giolitti added to this argument that an initially laudable attempt to create a coalition of moderates soon deteriorated into a mere instrument of ambition for Depretis. Crispi, too, began attacking *trasformismo* on the same grounds, only to adopt the technique himself when he succeeded to power on Depretis's death in 1887. Depretis, Crispi, and then Giolitti himself, all in turn had recourse to this method to prevent the growth of an organized opposition, as any prime minister who felt under threat would be tempted to reinforce his supporters by a *combinazione* with other dissident minorities. This absence of any well-articulated opposition had unfortunate effects, and so did the consequent quick succession of cabinets, for an apparently solid but undisciplined majority was sometimes dispersed almost overnight.

The primary intention of Depretis was to create the benevolent "parliamentary dictatorship" which Italy had known under Cavour, and in this he partly succeeded. A decree of July 1876 for the first time accorded legal status to the President of the Council, who became quite as much of a prime minister as his counterpart in England or France, receiving special responsibility for cabinet decisions and the execution of government policy. Depretis then announced his technique of government—perhaps realizing that these were almost the very words of Cavour himself: "Whereas it used to be said that the government represented a party, we intend to rule in the interests of everyone ... and will accept the help of all honest and loyal men of whatsoever group." Accordingly, while Depretis's coalition extended leftward almost as far as Bertani, he also approached Peruzzi and the dissident Tuscans who had helped unseat their former colleagues on the Right. Twenty-five years earlier Depretis had deplored Cavour's *connubio* with Rattazzi; yet to reproach him now with inconsistency would be irrelevant, for at last power was within his grasp and he believed he could use it to Italy's advantage.

Indubitably, this imparted an element of peacefulness to parliamentary life. Depretis's temperament inclined him to soft-pedal personal feuds and shun the clash of rival theories. He was above all an administrator, who preferred always to establish the admitted facts of a case, and then try empirically to secure broad agreement without allowing preconceived ideas to influence his decision. Effective though this was, by avoiding conflict and opposition he deprived government of a desirable check, confusing principles and destroying clarity of ideas. He had much more chance of remaining in power if he could cloud the issues and seem to agree with everyone; but in the effort to soften discord and polemics he sometimes suffocated all idealism. Like Cavour, he shied away from formulating a rigid policy which could be voted down, and preferred expedients which might be abandoned by dropping an unpopular minister and changing his cabinet. Small wonder that Depretis was called the wizard of Stradella and the Robert Walpole of Italy.

★

For a time the leaders of the Right held out against the transformation of political groups which Depretis was effecting. They could not yet believe that the elections of 1876 represented a final loss of power. But under Minghetti and Sella the hundred-odd deputies of this right-wing opposition never became a well-constituted body. In the Senate they still had a majority, yet instead of redoubling their efforts, the senators of the Right tended to absent themselves from parliament, while Depretis gradually used the powers of royal nomination to pack the Upper House with his own supporters. Now that the hope of spoils and perquisites was diminished for right-wing deputies, their abstention indicated that many people considered politics as a profitable perquisite for those in power and hence saw little point in mere opposition. This defeatism was the more easily exploited by Depretis because Sella, Minghetti, Spaventa, Bonghi, Sonnino, and Villari had so little in common. Once he was clearly the master in parliament, some of these conservatives were always ready to support his coalition. Of the rest, a good number retired to continue their criticism on a purely academic level. They would write articles for magazines such as the *Rassegna Settimanale*, or for the *Corriere della Sera*—that great achievement of Italian journalism which was launched by a group of Milanese industrialists in 1876.

The radicals to the left of Depretis were much weaker now that Rome was won and the monarchy settled in the Quirinal Palace. The two southerners Nicotera and Crispi, who had once endured exile for their republican faith, were appointed ministers of the crown in 1876 and 1877 respectively. Former conspirators such as General Medici and Visconti-Venosta had become respectable marquises, and Carducci, another notable ex-republican, began to write odes of humble loyalty to the royal house. Garibaldi himself, since his friends were in office, hastened to accept what he had hitherto refused, a substantial sum of money from the state for his former services.

There were still a few deputies on the extreme Left who stood aloof from the process of transformism. Bertani in eight successive parliaments and also Cavallotti in ten tried to give some coherence to these democrats who made up what was called the *estrema*. Their task was to goad the government into fulfilling its early program of social reform. Though they had little corporate discipline, they included some of the most forthright and attractive Italian politicians, and these radicals, republicans, and (later) socialists constituted a pressure group more powerful than their numbers might suggest.

★

It was in part due to the stimulus of the *estrema* that Depretis at the beginning of 1877 introduced a measure to abolish arrest for debt, and set up at Bertani's request a special committee to inquire into agricultural conditions. Another noteworthy reform was the Coppino law which made education free and compulsory for children between the ages of six and nine. Only twenty deputies voted against this law, but its negligent enforcement enabled the critics to say that Depretis was trying to acquire the fame of a progressive liberal without being one in fact. Many Catholics demurred at the spread of lay education as a possible threat to the faith, especially as this law abolished compulsory religious teaching in elementary schools. But there was also a general inertia among local authorities which made the bill only partly effective.

The liberal spirit behind these measures was contradicted by the harsh methods of Baron Nicotera, the minister of the interior. His overbearing conduct antagonized moderate members of the Left such as Cairoli, and convinced Spaventa that political standards were sinking further below those elsewhere in Europe. Nicotera prohibited public meetings whether socialist or Catholic. When a meeting of protest against the grist tax was announced, he forbade it on the grounds that public order might be endangered, and then asked parliament to absolve him for thus infringing the constitution. In December 1876 he defended in parliament his system of *domicilio coatto*, a form of internal exile that he had taken over from his predecessors. He sent labor agitators to the penal islands. He also banned some newspapers, forbade employees of his ministry to read others, and bought the favor of opposition journals with the secret funds of his department.

This policy was not very far removed from that once followed by Spaventa himself, and it confirmed what many intelligent men had prophesied, namely that the Left in power, despite their paper policy of reform, would prove no more liberal than the Right. From the common people's viewpoint, it strengthened the impression that the government of United Italy was still the same oppressive conspiracy of the powerful against the weak, of the rich against the poor, and that the police, far from being defenders of liberty, were sometimes almost its enemy.

As soon as this authoritarian attitude began to weaken the ministry in the eyes of public opinion, Depretis in December 1877 replaced the unpopular Nicotera by Crispi, taking as his pretext the scandalous revelation that the former had been tapping private telegraph messages. Crispi had until now condemned the "parliamentary incest" by which the radical Nicotera had been transformed into a pillar of conservative government. But Crispi surrendered to transformism quite as easily. Nicotera took his revenge by showing that his successor had once gone through a mock marriage under a forged signature with a lady whom he had then left in order to legitimize his daughter by another woman. Crispi had to resign until people could forget this peccadillo.

Such animosities soon broke up the false majority of the Left. Every suggested reform merely created fresh political divisions. In 1877 Garibaldi was already accusing Depretis of preferring wasteful expenditure on a large army rather than aiding the poor in winning a decent livelihood. In November, Zanardelli resigned from the cabinet as a protest against extravagance in apportioning railroad contracts. A group of about eighty deputies around Benedetto Cairoli moved away from Depretis toward the twenty other deputies composing the *estrema*. In 1879 the finance minister, Grimaldi, resigned when the grist tax was finally abolished, because he maintained that this put politics before finance. There was tension between laissez-faire liberals such as Zanardelli and the authoritarian Nicotera. Personal disagreements separated Crispi from Cairoli, yet both of them favored a much larger extension of the suffrage than Depretis and Nicotera would have tolerated. The two leading writers on the Left, Carducci and the great literary critic De Sanctis, both castigated Depretis for his lack of idealism and his policy of expedients. Owing to these divisions, instead of transformism bringing stability, one cabinet quickly followed another, and each ex-minister became the leader of a group potentially hostile to his successor. Collective cabinet responsibility was even weaker than before.

No obvious political crisis had brought the Left to power, nor was it over any clear issues of policy that five separate ministries fell in less than two years. The second ministry of Depretis, formed in December 1877, resigned after four months when his candidate for the post of Speaker in the Chamber was not approved. Cairoli then took office in March 1878, along with Zanardelli and De Sanctis. On Cairoli's resignation, Depretis took over at the end of the year; then there were two more Cairoli ministries in 1879, one of which included Depretis as minister of the interior. These unstable cabinets caused great scandal among the main body of liberals, especially as there was so little connection between their formation and any vote in parliament. There was little to distinguish one from another, or even from their various predecessors before 1876. Despite election promises, the Left continued the policy of centralization and the practice of decree laws, and interfered quite as much with the press and with personal liberty. Turiello was not alone in concluding that the Left was more conservative and less revolutionary than the old Right.

It would be more accurate to say that the Left in office became more pragmatic and less irresponsible. At the other wing of the Chamber, Spaventa and Bonghi were equally ready to accept some moderate reform proposals.

Right and Left depended in fact on much the same class of people. They had common interests against clericals and reactionaries on the one hand, and against radicals and socialists on the other. Every prime minister in turn depended on this fact until Mussolini altered the rules of the game.

★

One sign of a new age in 1878 was the accession of two new potentates in Italy, King Umberto and Pope Leo XIII. Vittorio Emanuele probably died of malaria, a symptom of the unhealthiness of his new capital amid the Pontine Marshes. Special permission was given by Pius IX for him to receive the last sacraments and for ecclesiastical censures to be momentarily lifted, and the whole Court by custom filed before his bed as he lay dying.

The new king was more dutiful and dignified than his father, less original in his notion of kingship, and far less interesting as a personality. Umberto had made a dynastic and loveless marriage with his cousin Margherita, a proud and beautiful woman who lived long enough to back Mussolini. Margherita had hard words for parliament and was religious to the point of bigotry. She also became a fervent nationalist who looked forward to the day when Italy would be feared in the world. But she also charmed such ex-republicans as Carducci and Crispi, and at the Court ball in 1875 she inaugurated a new epoch by dancing the first quadrille with the one-time republican Nicotera—though it remained her grumble that the leaders of the Left were inexpert dancers. Rosina, the second wife of Vittorio Emanuele, had been a coarse *popolana*, daughter of a sergeant in the army, but the new royal consort was a queen to her fingertips, and a leader of fashion whose toilettes were copied assiduously.

Umberto and Margherita set up an impressive royal household at Rome which tried to rival that of the Vatican. Three deep bows before the king, and walking backward out of his presence, were *de rigueur*. Fox-hunting parties in the English manner became fashionable, with red coats and sandwich lunches, and were regularly attended by foreign ambassadors as a means of diplomatic contact. Together the royal couple tried to win over both the "blacks" on the Right and the "reds" on the Left and to reconcile Roman society to the national revolution.

16   Foreign Policy, 1860–1882

The near identity of views among Italian politicians about foreign affairs is explained by certain compelling facts. That Austria owned Italian territory constituted one such fact. The general benevolence of most other European countries toward Italy was another. Unification had become possible only because France, Britain, and Prussia had competed in favoring Italy because of their own mutual fears and jealousy. When Queen Victoria inveighed against Lord John Russell's sympathy for "this *really bad*, unscrupulous Sardinian government," he retorted that either Italy would have to be united or it would again become Austrian or French. British statesmen were satisfied that "another Prussia has arisen in the South of Europe, which will in all probability be a new guarantee for the Balance of Power."

The sympathy of Europe had given Italy a deceptive advantage and led her statesmen to plan policy on two mistaken assumptions: that their country was inherently strong, and that other nations would continue to find their interests promoted by Italy's continued expansion. At first she was able to run risks in the confidence of being considered a natural ally by both France and Britain, and when this advantage ceased to apply she thought herself harshly used. In such artificially favorable circumstances it was difficult to take proper stock of her interests and it was tempting to devise a foreign policy involving risks too great for her strength. She also had to discover which of the powers was her most likely ally. Possibly she would have to continue the traditionally fickle policy of the House of Savoy if she wished to carry more influence than her capabilities warranted.

Up to 1870 Italy continued to be a protégé of Napoleon III. She shared with France the enmity of Austria and a kinship in Romance culture and language. More tangibly, in her legal code, her metric system of measurements, even in her tricolor flag and her fashions of dress and behavior, Italy imitated her sister country. The royalties of French authors in Italy were large, and as late as 1900 there was a prime minister whose native language was French. The military aid of France had been indispensable for the conquest of Lombardy in 1859, and the king obstinately maintained his entente with France until Napoleon's defeat in 1870.

Almost as necessary was the friendship of England. Not until 1935 did an understanding with England cease to be a more or less fixed point in Italian policy, because Italy was highly sensitive to blockade by sea and most of her imports came through channels dominated by the British navy. The generation of Cavour had a great admiration for England. From the very beginning of his political career, according to his secretary, Cavour tried to model Piedmont upon English institutions. This admiration and good will waned slightly with the years. None the less it was reciprocated in Britain, even though fear of Russia and France forced Britain into an Austrian alliance which made a complete understanding with Italy impossible. Italy was valued by Great Britain as another potential check upon France. English liberals and whigs agreed as early as 1860 that the time was ripe for Italy's annexation of Venice, and in 1861 the Italians had been told that Rome could be occupied at once as far as Great

Britain was concerned. Unofficial opinion in England as in America was wildly enthusiastic over the achievement of Italian independence. Mazzini lived most of his adult life in London. Half a million Londoners lined the streets to cheer Garibaldi when the *invitto Duce* paid a visit in 1864: in no other country had any one person ever received such a welcome.

★

By 1866, when the backing of Prussia was added to that of France and Britain, Italians were no longer content with the prospect of a neutral position in Europe like that of Belgium or Switzerland, and in the hope of being treated as a great power their foreign policy became more pugnacious. Some of their leaders became oversensitive about whether Italy was receiving due admiration and respect, and not only resented criticism but imagined it where it did not exist. They were incensed by the thought that their country might be seen as a museum of ruins, as a tourist paradise, a country of opera singers, organ-grinders, ice-cream vendors, beggars, and touts; and in reaction against this supposed reputation, politicians were sometimes tempted to become adventurous and bellicose. Cavour had preached the dangerous doctrine that seldom was anything gained by neutrality. Vittorio Emanuele issued the ominous pronouncement, heartily echoed by Umberto and Margherita, that "Italy must not only be respected, she must be feared."

This attitude was comprehensible, but it led to a forceful foreign policy that proved expensive. Former allies therefore became more grudging of their assistance. Hitherto Italy had always been able to retreat if conflict threatened, but after pretending to greatness her honor would be at stake and withdrawal would be less easy. Some detached and careful observers perceived this trend. Fortunato was brave enough to say that Italy was at fault in her vanity and desire to cut a figure. In 1900 he pointed out that 21 per cent of government expenditure was for military supply, compared with 17 per cent in Germany; also that 33 per cent of Italy's budget went on debt service compared with 20 per cent of Germany's, and national income was only a third of the French. He therefore advocated spending less on the army and navy, showing how odd it was to claim parity with France and Germany. Mazzini had argued that nationalism was a malignant perversion of patriotism. Garibaldi, too, toyed with pacifism and internationalism in his old age, even arguing that the army took too many peasants away from the fields and so weakened Italy by making her dependent on foreign food. On the other hand, General Cialdini resigned in protest against economies in army expenditure, and called them a monument of political incompetence.

Successive governments tended to support Cialdini. Under an illusion about her own wealth and power, Italy launched into the race for armaments. After 1870, General Ricotti reorganized the army on the Prussian model and extended conscription to all able-bodied men. On German advice he decided that Italy could not be defended easily and hence needed to attack, notwithstanding the expense. Naval construction was based on holding a superiority over Austria-Hungary. It was never debated whether Italy could afford simultaneously a front-rank army and navy. Neither was it foreseen that every technical invention would mean disproportionate expense for a country which lacked iron and fuel, nor that each increase in armaments would involve her prestige more deeply. As the illusion of national strength grew, legitimate patriotism eventually developed into aggressive nationalism, and as much as a third of state expenditure was allocated to provision for war between 1860 and 1940.

The French alliance was wearing thin by the time Italy made her treaty with Prussia in 1866. Ill-feeling grew after the return of French troops to Rome in 1867 and victory of the *chassepot* rifle over Garibaldi at Mentana. A sense of rivalry with France began to show itself in North Africa, and economists also feared that Italy's dependence upon French investment was too exclusive. Prussia, on the other hand, was not a Mediterranean power and had no common frontier with Italy over which friction could arise. She was also a rapidly growing nation and, like Italy, was determined to upset what was left of the Vienna settlement of 1815. When Prussian ministers expressed doubts about Cavour's invasion of the Papal states in 1860, the latter replied that Prussia was similarly situated and might one day thank Piedmont for this example of national unification. Out of this community of sentiment emerged the alliance which defeated Austria in 1866.

Italy thus returned to the practice that Piedmont had always adopted in the distant past, where her own support, if judiciously marketed between the two titans France and Germany, might be priced above its real worth. From the War of the Spanish Succession to the Triple Alliance she proved remarkably adroit in knowing when to change her allegiance and join the winning side. But this was a dangerous game, and when the balance of Europe tipped too heavily, as it did after 1870 against France and after 1918 and 1945 against Germany, Italy's illusion of strength was exposed. Her better foreign ministers were not lured by ambition to attempt more than preserving this balance or righting it when upset. And though nationalists and later the fascists held such unheroic behavior up to shame, in fact it succeeded, whereas Mussolini, like Crispi, led his country into disastrous defeat.

Before the time of Crispi, both Right and Left were generally agreed in playing safe. Visconti-Venosta, the foreign minister of the Right, insisted that Italy should be "unadventurous"; Cairoli of the Left believed in a policy of "freedom from ties and commitments"; Depretis thought foreign affairs a bore, and ranked diplomats with professors as the people he liked least. The older men of the Right tended toward the francophile tradition of Cavour, while the younger radicals welcomed Bismarck as an anticlerical and an exponent of state socialism. But this difference was not pushed very far.

Continuity in foreign policy was assisted by the fact that the king kept a special prerogative of supervision in this field. Not only was the foreign minister generally a royal nominee, but the sovereign might carry out a personal policy by corresponding with ambassadors without his ministers' knowledge. Either way the cabinet as a whole was as a rule unconsulted and uninformed; and Cavour had shown that this could work satisfactorily. Vittorio Emanuele was usually too "correct" and too indolent to object when the diplomats of the Palazzo della Consulta developed ideas of their own. Purely dynastic ambitions did, however, continue to weigh with him. His daughter Clotilde was married to the rakish Prince Napoleon, Maria Pia to the King of Portugal; and in 1870 his second son Amedeo accepted an invitation to become King of Spain until forced to abdicate three years later.

★

Umberto's mother and grandmother were Austrian princesses and this may have helped predispose him to a partial reconciliation with Austria-Hungary, but there were also more solid reasons for not pressing traditional animosity too far. Whereas France after 1870 was a defeated republic and therefore doubly undesirable as an ally, Germany and Austria were both ruled by successful conservative monarchs. In 1873 Vittorio Emanuele made a state appearance in Vienna and Berlin, and, when in 1875 Franz Joseph responded by visiting the former Austrian possession of Venice, his action was hailed as recognition that the hard feelings of the war of 1866 were dead. Even though Austria still ruled the "unredeemed lands" of Trent and Trieste, King Vittorio's speech to parliament in 1876 mentioned "the cordial friendship and sympathy between our two peoples," and privately he told the emperor that Italian irredentist claims would now be dropped.

This *rapprochement* with Austria took place under Minghetti before the Left came into power. Not everyone approved of it, and though it continued as official policy for forty years, there were always independent and opposite forces working in other directions. The European balance of power had swung heavily toward Germany in 1870, and some people thought that Italy should try to redress this swing rather than join with the dominant power. Other politicians would have preferred a war to annex Trieste and the Trentino, and could not willingly ally with the hereditary foe while these *terre irredente* were still in foreign hands. In 1877 Crispi, for instance, went to see Bismarck and tried to embroil Germany against Austria, but without success.

The influence of this Sicilian radical, Francesco Crispi, was to be ruinous for Italy. He was one of a new generation of lawyer-politicians. By temperament he was blustering, assertive, often impetuous, without the educational advantages of Minghetti and his friends on the Right or their wide European outlook. Even before Crispi obtained office he was agitating for an aggressive policy. In 1877 he urged Depretis that

it is of paramount importance that Europe should esteem us as sufficiently powerful to make our strength felt should complications result from war in

the East. .... At no matter what cost Italy must complete her armament. ....
My regret is profound when I reflect that as far back as 1870 the ministry of
the Right turned a deaf ear to my petition to arm the country in anticipation
of mighty events.

After a talk with Vittorio Emanuele, Crispi wrote to tell the prime minister
how "the king feels the need of crowning his lifework with a victory which
shall give our army the power and prestige it now lacks in the eyes of the
world."

Crispi was already ambitious to be a man of destiny and his grand designs
were not unwelcome at Court. Unfortunately for him, Bismarck had chosen to
side with Austria-Hungary. One result of the overwhelming Prussian victories
of 1866 and 1870 was that Italians could no longer play off Germany against
Austria or France against Germany, and Crispi's mission to Friedrichsruh only
resulted in Crispi coming dangerously under Bismarck's fascination. When the
Congress of Berlin met in 1878, Italy was unable to make her influence felt, for
she had neither an ally to support her nor scope for maneuver. In any case the
Italian parliamentary system was such that no cabinet remained in office long
enough to develop a policy to meet the new balance of forces in Europe.

The Congress of Berlin took place when Cairoli was prime minister and his
schoolfriend Count Corti was foreign minister. Corti arrived unbriefed on the
various problems for consideration. So while Austria won a protectorate over
Bosnia and Herzegovina, while Britain acquired Cyprus and France secured
recognition of claims in North Africa, Italy left with clean but empty hands. A
tentative demand was made for the Trentino, but this only provoked Gort-
chakov's jibe that Italy must have lost another battle if she was asking to annex
another province. Bismarck suggested that she might compensate herself in
Albania; Britain cynically proffered an alternative, Tunis. But Cairoli, who had
once fought among Garibaldi's volunteers, made a poor diplomat and was too
straightforward to stoop to the barter of territories and the sharing of
"compensation" in secret treaties. His was a praiseworthy idealism, but this did
not make for worldly success.

This apparent failure to assert national interests left Italians feeling touchily
aggrieved for not many of them approved Cairoli's policy of "clean hands." It
was not sufficiently appreciated that their country was sitting for the first time as
an acknowledged power in the Concert of Europe. Nor did they recognize
that, as Italy was not involved in the Eastern crisis which led to the Congress, it
was hardly a defeat if she did not emerge with large gains. Failure lay not so
much in empty-handedness abroad, but rather in the inability at home to
recognize Italy's true interests and in the belief that more expenditure on
armaments was an easy and sure path to great victories. Crispi's criticism of
Cairoli merely fostered the unwarranted suspicion that his countrymen had
suffered a diplomatic reverse, and when this was confirmed by a second

apparent reverse over the French occupation of Tunis in 1881, Italy abandoned her policy of "no commitments" and unadventurousness. She committed herself to Bismarck and in May 1882 became a very junior partner in the Triple Alliance.

★

By joining Germany and Austria, Italy hoped to secure her back door while she fished for colonies and improved her international position. As the rest of Europe was not yet ready to satisfy Italian hopes for Trent and Trieste, the next best thing was to shelve them in exchange for a guarantee by Catholic Austria against a resumption of papal sovereignty in Rome. Another motive for the alliance was pique and alarm at being forestalled in Tunis. The politicians of the Left were severely shaken by this French colonial victory and needed some counterbalancing success to underwrite their parliamentary position. Italy needed to emerge from diplomatic isolation, and the king had reasons for preferring monarchical and militarist Germany to republican France. Depretis entered into the *Triplice* reluctantly and tried to conceal its existence lest France should take alarm. The treaty was not officially admitted until some years later, and the actual text was not published until after its repudiation in 1915.

By express intention the pact was a guarantee against French aggression. It also expressly guaranteed the existing social order in Europe and the institution of monarchy against republicanism. With the amplifications subsequently added during its thirty-three years of life, military aid was promised if one signatory through no fault of its own were attacked by other powers, and benevolent neutrality if one of them felt obliged to initiate a war. A particular importance was to attach to what later became Article 7:

> Austria-Hungary and Italy undertake to use their influence to prevent all territorial changes which might be disadvantageous to one or the other signatory power. To this end they agree to interchange all information throwing light on their own intentions. If, however, Austria-Hungary or Italy should be compelled to alter the *status quo* in the Balkans, whether by a temporary or by a permanent occupation, such occupation shall not take place without previous agreement between the two powers based on the principle of reciprocal compensation for every advantage, territorial, or otherwise.

By mutual agreement the treaty was stated to be in no way directed against Great Britain.

Quite obviously such an engagement would favor Germany more than Italy, for while France might attack Germany to reconquer Alsace-Lorraine, a French invasion of Italy was hardly credible except to Crispi's torrid imagination. Italy might thus have to fight for Germany, but not Germany for Italy. In return for very doubtful gains, Italians had to renounce their irredentist claims on Austria.

Another disadvantage of the treaty was that, though ostensibly a measure for peace, its effect was to increase tension and enlarge military expenditure throughout Europe. Italy's interest in peace was buried by Crispi's magniloquent insistence on prestige and by the military obsessions of the Court. The king had come back from Berlin an enthusiast for the German war machine, and one of his retinue heard him grumble that the worst soldier in the Prussian Hussars looked more impressive than the best soldier in the whole Italian army. The Italian taxpayer was henceforward expected to make good this deficiency.

Above all, the Triple Alliance curtailed the freedom of action which was one of Italy's chief assets, for in alienating France she endangered her ability to befriend both sides. Instead of striving to keep a general equilibrium, she was helping to overturn it, and while this may have made her more feared, it also earned her a reputation for untrustworthiness. Other nations were not easily persuaded that an alliance formed by Bismarck had no aggressive purpose, and they hardly thought that Italy would have given up her demands upon Austria without hope of fairly sizable compensation to be wrested from France.

Depretis was, of course, in a poor bargaining position. He had to rest content with the feeling of security conveyed by the alliance, and with its comfortable acknowledgment that the temporal power of the papacy had now probably gone for good. Some Italians hoped that, if not offensive in intention as yet, the alliance would soon become so, with Austria advancing into the Balkans in return for adjustment of Italy's northeastern frontier. Others supported the treaty on the quite different grounds that it deterred France and Russia from breaking the peace. Another claim was that it brought economic advantages. But in fact trade with France had been substantial, whereas Italy was to receive little from Austria, and the influx of capital and industrial goods from northern Germany was not without its economic and political dangers.

The Triple Alliance boosted Italian morale but seldom had much influence on the actions of its signatories. The chief satisfaction which it bestowed on Italy was recognition by the great powers that she was of their number. This desire for prestige was a sentimental more than a material consideration. Though understandable enough, it was to bulk far too large in foreign and colonial policy.

17 Colonial Enterprise, 1860–1882

As soon as United Italy became self-conscious, ancestral memories of earlier colonial expansion were revived to support the argument that prestige demanded active emulation of past victories. Rome had conquered Hannibal and Jugurtha; medieval communes had fought against Saracens and Barbary pirates along the North African coast; the empire of Venice had stretched through Greece to Constantinople, while the discoveries of Columbus and Vespucci gave some Italian historians an almost proprietary feeling about the New World.

The nineteenth century found these past memories very much alive. Large Italian settlements still flourished at Cairo, Alexandria, and Tunis. The tradition of maritime enterprise was manifested in Garibaldi, who as a ship's captain had cruised to Newcastle, Constantinople, China, and Peru, and who had lived for many years in North and South America and North Africa. The Mediterranean had seemingly become a backwater at the beginning of modern times but now a new generation intended to restore its importance. Moreover, Spain and Turkey, which had fought successfully against the Italians in the sixteenth century, were now in decline, and this left a gap which a rising nation might fill. On the other hand, the Italian language, once a lingua franca throughout the Mediterranean, was being displaced in the Levant by French, in Malta by English and Maltese; while the political expansion of France into Algeria and beyond was another trend which had to be resisted if resurgent Italy were to receive what was thought to be its due. The nation which, geopolitically speaking, seemed best placed to predominate in the Mediterranean, found the three outlets of this sea, Gibraltar, the Bosporus, and Suez, all controlled by outsiders.

Italians in the eighteenth century had recognized the importance to them of Malta and Tunis, but it remained for Cesare Balbo and Gioberti to argue that geography and history offered Italy a natural leadership in the Mediterranean. In the 1830's Italian missionaries were established at Massawa on the Red Sea. Padre Massaia penetrated into Ethiopia and at Cavour's wish established friendly relations with local chieftains. Cavour was often farsighted in initiating small measures which might one day turn out profitably. In the early 1850s he subsidized the Rubattino shipping company and even lent it naval vessels to inaugurate a shipping service from Genoa to Tunis. Less wisely, he set up a government-subsidized transatlantic shipping service which quickly went bankrupt. He was similarly conscious of Italian interests on the Austro-Hungarian coast of the Adriatic, and his participation in the Crimean War was partly planned as a move in a larger Mediterranean policy toward which he was groping.

After Cavour's death, governments almost lost interest in colonialism, in part perhaps because unification was the work of landbound Piedmont which had no seafaring tradition. Desultory negotiations began with Portugal for concessions in Angola and Mozambique, with Britain for the Falklands and for a station in Nigeria, with Denmark and Russia for a share in the Nicobar Islands, the Antilles, and the Aleutians. Menabrea mildly encouraged the traveler

Cerruti to seek out possible spheres of influence in the Indian and Pacific oceans. Private individuals were active, and explorers and missionaries from Italy did important work between 1860 and 1875 in Burma, Siam, Borneo, and New Guinea. There was talk in 1867 of making Sumatra into a convict settlement. More realistically in the same year an African society was founded at Naples, and a number of explorers were sent to trace the sources of the Nile. Through the activity of private individuals, public opinion began hesitantly to reflect an interest in colonial enterprise.

The beginning of work on the Suez Canal gave another impetus to colonialization, and Cavour intended that the Italian merchant marine should be in the van of opening up this passage to the East. Some Italian historians state that the most important contribution toward the canal was made by Italians. But although Italian labor was largely employed, there was comparatively little Italian capital or initiative in the venture. Negrelli, who did so much to further it, was despite his name a loyal Austrian subject and director of the Austrian railroads, and his object was to create a trade outlet from Central Europe through Trieste. When after fifteen years' work the canal was finally opened, it did not in fact do nearly so much for the advancement of Italy as had been hoped. Perhaps Cavour's policy of giving interest-free loans to shipping companies left them too comfortably subsidized to bother. In 1870 only 1.3 per cent of the tonnage going through the canal was Italian, and in the year 1913 only a hundred Italian ships used this route as compared with nearly three thousand British vessels.

The missionaries, however, supported the chamber of commerce at Genoa in encouraging the government to set up trading and refueling stations in the Red Sea. Sapeto was allowed to make a reconnaissance in a naval ship with Vice-Admiral Acton as his technical adviser, ostensibly on behalf of the patriotic Genoese shipbuilder and shipowner, Rubattino. They sailed in one of the first vessels to pass through the canal and finally chose the Bay of Assab as the most promising station for a service between Genoa and the Indies. Rubattino purchased a concession of land in the bay, because the government expected less diplomatic difficulty if this private company appeared to be working on its own. But almost at once Egypt protested, and the Italian government was forced to show its hand and make Egyptian troops withdraw from the area. Before politicians had decided whether colonization was wise, and if so whether Assab was the best place to begin, the Italian flag was committed and retreat was impossible without loss of face. As soon as a few marines were killed there, the government would be obliged to buy up the rights of Rubattino and proclaim Italian sovereignty. This was to become a familiar story.

★

There was no lack of partisans to justify such casually incurred obligations, for already the imperialists were using the argument of surplus population in Italy, and missionaries and philanthropists spoke of the need to civilize backward races. Scientists were excited by the search for new lands, and some jurists wanted penal settlements for captured Italian brigands, especially when the death penalty was abolished. It was said with meaningless rhetorical exaggeration that Italy had to be "either the prisoner of the Mediterranean or its conqueror."

Other public figures, no less patriotic, argued strongly against any such extension of national commitments. As soon as traders and missionaries began to involve Italian prestige with native tribes and to collide with other foreign expeditions, national feeling was likely to be dangerously aroused. Available military resources might have been better occupied in preparing for a possible rectification of Italy's northern frontier. Financial difficulties in any case made it impossible to invest enough in colonies to ensure a sufficient return, for Italy lacked certain prerequisites of expansion: her industry was not adequate even for the domestic market, and was quite unable to compete with that of Britain or France, while the British also had enough surplus production to make colonies less a luxury than an economic requirement. Italy had no comparable need yet for new markets or fields for foreign investment, and indeed was hardly able to absorb the raw materials which colonies might supply. Whereas elsewhere colonialism was motivated by a surplus of capital, in Italy it grew out of poverty and from the illusion that here was a quick way to get rich.

Ricasoli had warned his countrymen in 1864 that they were spending too much on luxuries, and he mentioned the San Carlo theater at Naples. Rattazzi agreed that prestige ventures abroad were less important than raising the standard of living in the South. Garibaldi also insisted that the latifondi and marshlands of Italy were the first areas in need of colonization, and he reiterated that colonialism not only put prestige before welfare, but would mean increased expenditure on army and navy and a continual risk of war. The settlement of Assab therefore found public opinion at first largely indifferent or hostile. Responsible statesman such as Sella and Minghetti became restive as one commitment led to another, and rightly prophesied that this would mean additional taxes which the country could not afford. A special commission discussed the whole colonial question for sixteen months in 1871–72, but its members could not agree one way or the other and the advocates of expansion again took heart.

★

On strategic grounds, Tunisia was much more important than Assab. Cape Bon jutted out from Africa almost within sight of Sicily. Many Sicilians had settled there. A proposal had been made in 1864 for a partition of Tunis between France and Italy, to which the government at first gave favorable consideration, but after pondering the costly colonial war to which France was committed in Algeria, Visconti-Venosta backed down. Instead he decided on economic penetration and in 1868 a treaty was signed between Italy and the Bey of Tunis, followed by attempts to obtain fishing and tobacco-growing rights. But this was to reckon without France. It was not appreciated that, though Italian settlers were more numerous, France had far more investments to defend in Tunisia and a political interest arising out of the need to control her restless subjects in neighboring Algeria.

In 1876 Austria tried to embroil Italy with the French by suggesting that she might declare a protectorate over Tunis, and the Austrians may have hoped that this would also fend off any Italian request to be compensated in the Trentino for Austrian expansion into Bosnia. In the next year, Russia and Britain made much the same suggestion so as to compensate Italy in advance for their own forward policy in parceling out the disintegrating Ottoman empire. But Italian opinion was still unenthusiastic about colonial enterprise. Depretis and Cairoli refused even to discuss Mediterranean affairs in the preliminary talks before the Congress of Berlin, and then neglected to profit from the hard bargaining which accompanied the Congress. In Cairoli's famous comment to the Austrian ambassador, "Italy will go to Berlin with her hands free, and wishes to leave it with her hands clean."

To Crispi and the imperialists this attitude was a scandal. Some of them would have liked to profit from Napoleon's defeat in 1870 to assert Italian claims in North Africa, but other leaders of the Left feared an economic struggle with France and preferred the alternative policy of winning French support to make Austria yield the *terre irredente*. Not until 1882 did they abandon irredentism in favor of an Austrian alliance, and in the intervening years France was free to establish her protectorate over Tunis.

Cairoli's first mistake in 1878 was to imagine that Italian and French interests could for long coexist there without friction. Then he allowed France to state unilaterally that she would never allow any country but herself to establish a protectorate in Tunisia. If Italy had made a similar declaration the position might yet have been retrieved, but England and Germany, having received no response to their previous suggestions to Italy, reconciled themselves to French occupation. Cairoli said nothing: either he had been inexcusably ignorant of French ambitions, or else was afraid to confess how he had failed to nurse Italian interests in North Africa.

When, too late, he realized the turn events were taking, he sent an armed guard of marines with orders to push Italian interests in Tunis to the limit. The French consul was then given similar instructions and direct conflict was only just avoided. An English company which owned a railroad in Tunis was agreeably surprised to encounter a prestige competition for its purchase: the French bid was first accepted, at a price far above its real worth, but then Cairoli had the contract declared invalid by the English courts. A small mishandled colonial squabble was thus turning into a direct threat to peace.

Understandably enough, France decided to put an end to this dubious and dangerous situation, and the railroad dispute gave her the excuse she needed. Her intention was to declare a protectorate over Tunis, guessing that Depretis and Cairoli dare not push matters anywhere near the verge of war. Profiting therefore by incidents on the doubtful frontier between Tunis and Algeria, French troops were landed and in May 1881 won recognition of their claims from the Bey by the Treaty of Bardo. Cairoli, now back in office, protested, but he was assured that there was no idea of permanent occupation, so he had to pretend to himself and parliament that no alteration had been made in the Mediterranean *status quo*. The *Rassegna Settimanale*, on the contrary, declared that "the subjection of the north coast of Africa to France will bring with it as a necessary consequence the destruction of Italy's future as a great power." This feeling of helplessness, exacerbated by the public affront, helped to clinch negotiations for the Triple Alliance in the following year. Not until 1896 was recognition given to the French protectorate in Tunis, and some Italians continued to claim that the colony was still theirs by right.

★

Egypt was the other country in North Africa in which there were substantial Italian settlements and financial interests. Important public men, the writers Marinetti and Ungaretti among them, were born in Alexandria, and one prominent politician, Scialoia, left Italy to become a servant of the khedive. When after 1876 England gradually intruded into Egyptian affairs, Italy kept in close touch with the local patriots. In 1879, Khedive Ismail fled to Italy, and Arabi Bey then became for the Italian press an Egyptian equivalent of Garibaldi, as was the Mahdi in the Sudan.

This helps to explain why Mancini in July 1882 refused a British proposal for joint military intervention in Egypt. Crispi, Minghetti, Sonnino, and Visconti-Venosta from their various standpoints disapproved of this refusal and called it one of the greatest failures in Italian foreign policy, but Mancini knew that he had neither troops nor money for the scramble after colonies. Only when Britain emerged unexpectedly successful in Egypt did he let it be known that his earlier refusal no longer stood. Britain, however, was in no mood to share her responsibilities after she had borne the risk and expenses of the campaign.

Once again, by refusing another British offer to help offset the power of France in North Africa, Italy saw the balance of the Mediterranean weighted against her. The paramount position in that sea which Cavour and Gioberti had prophesied for their country was far from becoming a reality. Parliament gave Mancini a vote of confidence, but the debate indicated that a younger generation was thinking more aggressively on the subject of colonial aggrandizement.

SECTION FIVE: THE TROUBLED PERIOD
OF CRISPI, 1880–1893

18 Depretis and Crispi, 1880–1890

The Left majority in parliament was weakened by the elections of 1880. Its unreliable radical wing around Nicotera and Crispi won a hundred seats and the Right increased their representation to about 170. Against this, the Center-Left groups around Cairoli and Depretis mustered some 220 deputies. So confused were the issues of politics that, in constituencies where no candidate had an absolute majority, the extreme Left and extreme Right sometimes voted together in the second ballot.

This partial victory of the Left was, however, taken to confirm their mandate for electoral reform. So restricted was the parliamentary suffrage that in some constituencies the poll was a hundred votes or less—Cavour had noted some deputies being returned by only five or six votes in all. On the other hand the plebiscites of 1860, 1866, and 1870 exemplified the successful working of universal manhood suffrage. Cavour had advocated a widening of the parliamentary franchise, provided that voters had enough education to be independent and enough income to be interested in preserving social order. He argued that a wider suffrage would give citizens a moral dignity and sense of responsibility, and some conservatives therefore supported the moderate measure of reform that Depretis now proposed.

The project which became law in 1882 raised the number of voters from half a million to something over two million. The taxpaying qualification was reduced from forty lire a year to nineteen, the age qualification from twenty-five to twenty-one, and the educational qualification to knowing how to read and write; in other words it enfranchised the petty bourgeois and the educated artisan. A halfhearted attempt was simultaneously made to diminish governmental influence in elections through a new procedure for registering voters and securing the secrecy of the ballot. The method of *scrutinio di lista* was introduced to replace that of voting in small constituencies, and it was hoped thereby to reduce the power of questionable local interests. The resultant enlargement of electoral districts was also accompanied by provisions to secure a more just representation for minorities.

Among the disadvantages of this electoral law, an increased representation of minority groups aggravated the worst features of transformism and made parliamentary manipulation easier. No doubt Depretis had intended as much. Over a third of the deputies returned in 1882 had never sat before and party labels lay lightly on them. On general grounds it was welcome that 7 per cent instead of 2 per cent of Italians now had the vote, but the pessimists feared that this would favor demagogues and pressure groups. The history of Italy, like that of Germany, was to prove that a broadening of the electorate could be harnessed to the cause of the strong state and in practice signified no necessary advance in liberalism. Another result of this reform was to enfranchise cities more than the countryside, the North rather than the South, and this dangerously worsened an existing differentiation, for example making it easier to neglect the interests of southern agriculture when the time came for tariff reforms. Some of its provisions proved less satisfactory in practice than in theory, and the system of *scrutinio di lista* had to be repealed in 1891. But as literacy spread, so the suffrage continued automatically to widen until Giolitti's major reform bill of 1912. The advent of mass democracy, however unwelcome to some of the more conservative liberals, was proving irresistible.

★

One symptom of transformism was that other leaders of the old Right, for instance Sonnino and Professor Villari, lined up with the radicals in wanting even more suffrage concessions than Depretis was ready to allow. The influential *Rassegna Nazionale* at Florence, a paper for "conservatives who are yet friends of progress," showed that some prominent Catholics agreed in supporting political reform. Villari's famous *Letters from the South* voiced a new spirit of realistic appraisal and self-criticism:

> When I think what conservatives have done in England on behalf of the poor and of agriculture, I blush with shame. . . . It is high time that Italy began to realize that she has inside herself an enemy which is stronger than Austria. Somehow we must face up to our multitude of illiterates, the ineptitude of our bureaucratic machine, the ignorance of our professors, the existence of people who in politics are mere children, the incapacity of our diplomats and generals, the lack of skill in our workers, our patriarchal system of agriculture, and on top of all, the rhetoric which gnaws our very bones. It is not the quadrilateral of fortresses at Mantua and Verona which has arrested our path, but the quadrilateral of seventeen million illiterates.

Not even Depretis himself showed so much reforming zeal as this. His promises of decentralization, economies in government, and cheaper food sounded impressive but were simply not being kept, and any public references he made to carrying out his 1875 "program of Stradella" could sometimes be greeted with ironic mirth.

The fact that moderate reform found apologists on either side of the House indicates that transformism was no mere machination of Depretis but something rooted in the electoral system or in Italian attitudes to politics. Depretis said, with some justification, that the former differences between Left and Right had by now been mostly removed; what this statement tried to conceal was that his support now came from the Center and the Right. Since the first socialist was already in parliament, the various bourgeois groups had a joint interest in making common cause. Speeches by Depretis at Stradella and by Minghetti at Legnano implied that their respective parliamentary groups were being transformed into a new government majority. From both sides came the suggestion that moderates on either side should merge during a transitional period until new issues had arisen and a "normal opposition" could be restored.

Other people were doubtful, and while agreeing that transformism might help by shuffling the old parties which had lost their reason for existence, yet deplored that no new parties were arising to replace them. But even Fortunato who took this view could not say where these new parties ought to be found, and the parliamentary situation of an amorphous government coalition of *ministeriali* opposed by miscellaneous *anti-ministeriali* was soon so generally accepted that the word transformism lost some of its pejorative significance. In a speech to parliament in 1883, the conservative Serena said that *trasformismo* had destroyed the Left; at which Crispi contradicted him and said that it had rather destroyed the Right; and the parliamentary records mention an anonymous voice saying it had killed them both.

Depretis's tactical alliance with Minghetti alienated many of his left-wing colleagues, and Zanardelli and Baccarini led those who blamed him for abandoning the principles and the supporters who had brought him to power. They contended that he was confusing issues simply in order to retain office and thereby retarding the nation's political education. Depretis replied that he had not altered his views but had to accept the alliance of those members of the Right who shared much of his program. For good measure he added that he would never "make a criterion of government out of the topography of the Chamber" and the word Left was an archaism which had lost its meaning. Zanardelli and Baccarini therefore resigned from the government in May 1883 and joined with the "historic Left" of Crispi, Nicotera, and Cairoli to form what was called in jest the Pentarchy.

It was the failure of this Pentarchy to make good its high-sounding principles which did most to substantiate the attitude of Depretis. The irascible and ambitious Nicotera fell in public esteem when for an imaginary offence he spat on a junior minister and forced him to fight a duel, a barbarous as well as an illegal practice. Nicotera was to show himself quite ready to treat with the conservatives Sella and Di Rudinì if he could thus reach office, and Crispi too, who while in opposition had criticized the practice of transformism, was shortly to make confusion worse confounded. Crispi used these words in parliament when criticizing the transformism of Depretis:

Since 1878 we have had no political parties in Italy ... only political men and groups, and each group, instead of representing an order of ideas, has been just an association of individuals whose opinions have constantly changed. This state of affairs has been actively encouraged by the government. In the meantime I stood apart with a few friends and held firm beliefs which were not just personal to myself. With the elections of 1882, the disorders of the Chamber penetrated into the country at large. The candidates did not form into parties with definite programs, since they had no principles to defend but were possessed only of the intention to re-enter parliament.

Crispi was unconsciously criticizing himself, for in his turn he separated from Nicotera, Cairoli, and Depretis despite the fact that he had lately been their colleague and was to join Depretis again in 1887. The "wizard of Stradella" had so melted all existing groups that Crispi, as soon as he found it a hindrance to advancement, gave up trying to reconstitute the historic Left. Only the twenty deputies of the *estrema sinistra* had no intention of compromising with this parliamentary game of ins and outs.

Of the old Right, the major part under Minghetti had associated with the government coalition in 1882. A somewhat more extreme group under Bonghi and Spaventa was still independent, and so was a faction of the Center Right under Di Rudinì. This latter group opened negotiation with the Pentarchy, making the condition that Cairoli with his foreign policy of "clean hands" should be replaced by the more assertive Crispi in its leadership. Not that there was any point of principle upon which they disagreed with Depretis—unless it were the dubious expedients used by the minister of finance, Magliani, to cover deficits by the exchequer. Since the grist tax had gone and expenditure had by no means been lowered to balance this loss, Magliani tried to conceal some running expenses under the heading of capital investment. *Finanza alla Magliani* became a byword, and critics here had a target which it was hard to miss.

Depretis in the eleven years after 1876 showed himself a master of tactics and expedients, placid, subtle, with an infinite capacity for assimilating other political groups, able to mold parliament almost at will. Nothing had been seen like this since the death of that other great Piedmontese statesman, Cavour. The chief gift of Depretis to Italy was efficient administration, under which some liberal reforms were unobtrusively carried out without the surface of politics being ruffled by too much violent controversy. In foreign as in domestic policy his natural instinct was, as he put it, to open his umbrella when he saw a cloud on the horizon, and wait till the storm had passed. He developed the tactic of forestalling parliamentary defeat by timely resignation, and successively in 1883, 1884, 1885, and 1887 resigned so as to leave himself free to change direction and remold his coalition. When he formed his eighth and final cabinet in April 1887, he dropped Generals di Robilant and Ricotti of the Right and took on Crispi and Zanardelli of the Left. Crispi in opposition had not stinted his criticisms of Magliani but now had no qualms about becoming his colleague, and the other deputies had lost their capacity for surprise at this tergiversation. By collaborating again with the foxy Depretis after ten years out of office, Crispi abandoned the independent Left and entered the system of *trasformismo*, and he thus marked himself out as the obvious successor to Depretis when the latter died later in the year.

★

In August 1887, at the age of sixty-eight, this extraordinary man became prime minister. Crispi belonged to an Albanian family which had long since emigrated to Sicily, and his grandfather was a priest in the Greek Orthodox Church. Admirers claimed he was a sincere, high-minded politician, and certainly he was a hero to men as diverse as Carducci, King Umberto, and Mussolini. He was undeniably a patriot who had served his country in bitter years of conspiracy and exile.

It was nevertheless Crispi's misfortune to be governed too exclusively by motives of personal and national dignity. He lacked balance and serenity. He was moody, taciturn, quick to anger, and showed what was sometimes called a typical Sicilian characteristic of being excessively proud and oversensitive to criticism. He could be grossly discourteous, not only to the press and parliamentary opponents but to foreign statesmen, and his rudeness and indifference to other people helped to make him a thoroughly bad influence in foreign affairs. He was also simple-minded to a degree, and could be provoked to action by the improbable suspicion that the Sicilian socialists were in alliance with Czarist Russia, or that France planned a surprise attack on Genoa. It must be added that well-founded charges of political corruption and personal immorality were made against him. A notorious scandal developed when he abandoned his common-law wife who had sailed with him among Garibaldi's famous Thousand, and on this and other matters he received much abuse and denigration from his many personal enemies. But his force of character was such that he went from strength to strength until a disastrous military defeat in Ethiopia caused his ignominious disappearance from public life in 1896.

Crispi's politics were nothing if not personal to himself. When asked in the 1860s whether he was a Mazzinian or a Garibaldian, he had replied, "Neither, I am Crispi." He it was who had led the retreat from republicanism with the much-quoted slogan that "the monarchy unites us, the republic would divide us." Out of office he at first sat well over to the Left in parliament, and on many points saw eye to eye with the *estrema* since along with Nicotera and Cairoli he had both a Garibaldian and Mazzinian past. Like the much more ingratiating and persuasive Cavallotti, he remained radical and anticlerical, however much he differed from other radicals over foreign policy. Crispi in his time had fought for internal liberties against the omnipotence of the state and had campaigned for an elective Senate and universal suffrage. Indeed this ex-republican was always to remain a volcanic revolutionary by temperament, but he partly matured into a political conservative once he had to defend the position which his great talents and energy had won him.

Although theoretically he believed in freedom and the alternation in power of fairly well-defined parties as in England, Crispi in practice used dictatorial means to reform his country at home and strengthen it abroad. Full of admiration for Bismarck, he became a confirmed believer in paternal government, anxious to increase the power of the throne "lest parliament should become a tyrant and the cabinet its slave." But before long the real tyrant was none other than Crispi himself, who would lightly dispatch troops to quell labor unrest, or rudely suspend Prince Torlonia from the mayoralty of Rome for daring to congratulate the pope on his jubilee. It was typical of him that, like Cavour, he gave little power and responsibility to subordinates: when over seventy he still ran three major departmental ministries as well as the premiership, and colleagues have described how he bullied his cabinets. Though he had condemned transformism as the ruin of parliament, in 1888 he dismissed his minister of education, Coppino, in favor of Boselli from the old Right. He lavishly purchased the support of the press, paying particular attention to the Stefani news agency, and this same habit of mind led him to explain English unfriendliness by the supposition that he must have spent too little on bribing the *Times*.

Nevertheless, during this first spell of three years in office, Crispi went only part of the way toward setting up a Bismarckian chancellorship. Though he became more and more autocratic in practice, at heart he believed in his own form of liberalism. He had probably been sincere in his reply of November 1877 to an accusation of dictatorialism: "Italy is a country with too solid a foundation of liberty to tolerate a dictatorship, and whoever might dare to attack her liberties, whether from the Right or the Left, would meet a resistance from the great majority of Italians such as would foil all his attempts." Gradually, however, he was to come around to Garibaldi's view that only strong action would hustle a corrupt and ineffective parliament along the path of reform.

Crispi's government introduced many liberal measures. There was the Public Health Act of 1888, a long-overdue prison reform, and the further extension into local government of the elective principle. In 1889 Zanardelli's civil code of law supplemented the penal code of 1865, and set up special tribunals for redress against abuses by the administration, and at last allowed a limited right to strike. Crispi also reformed the numerous charitable institutions run by the Church. He himself, like so many liberals, was a freethinker who died unreconciled to the Church, but he firmly believed in the "usefulness" of religion among the people and made greater efforts than some Christians to solve the impasse with the Vatican. Perhaps these various reforms, the parliamentary situation being what it was, might not have been so easily effected without someone of Crispi's mettle to force them through.

If his ideas were liberal but his methods violent, if finally he came to rule by martial law, the explanation is partly that he was corrupted by power, partly that he became more cynical about his fellow citizens. According to Fortunato's melancholy dictum:

We Italians are authoritarian to the very marrow of our bones, and by tradition, habit, and education we have become conditioned either to command too much or to obey too much. We may learn from books and from foreigners that liberty is something to be desired for its own sake, but we never, absolutely never, feel that this is true deep down in our hearts.

The new criminal code was not submitted to parliament in its final text but the government was simply empowered to draft and promulgate it by royal decree. Parliament likewise gave Crispi the authority to determine by decree what were the powers of the prime minister and how many other ministers there should be. He was allowed to raise taxes by decree and have them retrospectively confirmed by statute, and his successor had to ask for a bill of indemnity to cover expenditure incurred by Crispi without warrant.

This was the very pattern of what was called parliamentary dictatorship, and it differed only in degree whether under Cavour, Depretis, Crispi, or Giolitti, or even under Mussolini during his first years of power. The deputies themselves were usually grateful when a man of action cut through their interminable debates, arbitrated their conflicting views, and relieved them of responsibility for unpopular decisions.

19   Irredentism and Nationalist Fervor

Someone of Crispi's vanity and energy could do particular damage in foreign relations and his germanophile sentiments did not pass long without criticism. Those who had fought three wars against the Habsburgs sharply protested when the king exchanged courtesies and decorations with this traditional enemy and was even seen garbed as an Austrian colonel in Vienna. Right-wing newspapers attacked the Triple Alliance as a breach of tradition and a bar to Italy's freedom in foreign policy, while Zanardelli on the Left was not alone in preferring liberal England and republican France to militarist Germany.

Crispi's rejoinder was to call public opinion a poor judge of foreign policy. This was true enough, yet policy inevitably lost something in strength if unsupported by popular opinion. The public was largely uninstructed in foreign affairs: diplomatic documents were occasionally published in Green Books but, as Petruccelli said, one might understand more before reading a Green Book than after, so deeply buried (and sometimes falsified) was the relevant information. Moreover, parliament was asked to comment, if ever, only after treaty commitments had already been irrevocably made by the king and his government.

★

Dissatisfaction with the Austrian alliance received special support from those bent on the acquisition of Trent and Trieste, and in 1882 the martyrdom of Oberdan gave a great fillip to these irredentists. Oberdan was a republican from Trieste who had deserted from the Austrian army and taken refuge in Italy. In September 1882 he went back to try to assassinate the Emperor Franz Joseph, believing that the cause of Trieste needed a martyr and hoping that his attempt might ruin the treaty which King Umberto, "the Austrian colonel," had just signed. Before he could carry out his design he was arrested and executed but, so sensitive was public feeling, this would-be assassin became a legend and a symbol, and his action took its place in Italian history books as an admirable deed of patriotism.

Certainly, the attempt put Trieste on the map for many of Oberdan's countrymen who hitherto had not heard of it. Many people would have assumed that the absorption of Rome in 1870 had completed Italian unification, not foreseeing that this very act might generate an appetite for still further aggrandizement. Sonnino in the *Rassegna Settimanale* of May 1881 had denied that Italy possessed any serious claims on Trent or Trieste. But a new generation was witnessing patriotic sentiment almost imperceptibly developing into nationalism and imperialism. The moderate Minghetti said in 1884 that Italy "was obliged to follow an expansionist policy." And the ex-Garibaldian Imbriani popularized the phrase "*terre irredente.*"

There was no doubt that the war of 1866 had left the northeastern frontier strategically and ethnically defective. The Trentino was a large Austrian wedge driven southward through the Dolomites and this exposed the peninsula to invasion. Many inhabitants of this wedge spoke Italian and recognized their close links with Italy; yet their separation from Venice in 1866 left them too weak numerically to stop Austria progressively Germanizing the province. The Brenner railroad, the Alpine mountaineering clubs, and the *Volksbund*, all helped to foster Austrian influence there. German language and trade were on the increase. To the countrymen of Goethe and Wagner, the *lago di Garda* was the *Gardasee*. None too soon, rival Alpine societies were established in the Italian interest, with rival guides and alternative mountain refuges to keep the Italian element organized and self-conscious. When the German element in 1891 erected a bronze statue of Walther von der Vogelweide in Bozen (Bolzano), the Italians responded with a monument in Trent to Dante. Italian patriots such as Battisti—as later the young De Gasperi—represented the province in the imperial parliament of Vienna, and voiced the desire to separate this area from the rest of the Austrian Tyrol. But this separatist movement was checked by the Triple Alliance and had to wait until Austria again became the national enemy in the different circumstances of 1915.

Agitation was as yet even less strong for Trieste and the Istrian Peninsula, and still less for Fiume or the rest of the Dalmatian coast along which the medieval Venetian settlements had implanted strong traditions of Italian culture. On ethnic and historical grounds Italy had much the same right to Trieste as to Trent, but strategically it was less urgent, and only when Austria had made Trieste into a great emporium of commerce did it become desirable in itself and a threat to the trade of Venice. Mazzini and Cavour had agreed in hoping that one day Trieste would be Italian; but the paramount obstacles were first that Trieste was an Italian town in the middle of a Slav countryside, and second that Greater Germany found it her best outlet to the Mediterranean. Not only was Trieste the only port in the Austrian empire with a big export trade, but it was a center of finance and banking and an excellent base for any advance into the Balkans. Thus there was a determined refusal by Austrians to recognize the predominant Italian element in Trieste, and every attempt was made to increase the German and subsequently the Slav elements in its population.

Since their naval defeat off the island of Lissa in 1866, Italians had been very sensitive in the northern Adriatic, and though Crispi tried to divert attention from this danger area, the wave of nationalism which accompanied his premiership carried a momentum which he could do little to control. The urban pockets of *italianità* in Trieste, Fiume, Gorizia, and Pola were gradually becoming submerged as the advance of democracy and national consciousness told in favor of the Slovenes and Croats. Italians had long dominated the area, but the Slav middle classes were increasing all the time, while even some of the peasants were becoming literate and politically conscious. Slav schoolmasters were an important force and were often allied with the Church. More and more town councils gave up Italian as their official language, and after 1870 no one could any longer be sure that most newspapers in Trieste and Ragusa (Dubrovnik) would long remain Italian. Italians were edged out of the best jobs and were meeting this challenge by learning Croat and becoming slavized themselves. The process was natural enough, but it produced an understandable bellicosity and touchiness on both sides.

The activities of Battisti in the southern Tyrol, and of Oberdan and Barzilai at Trieste, were the most striking signs of a new outward-turning nationalism after 1880. Advocates of the Austrian alliance tried to divert this nationalism into distant colonial wars, or into the more remote claims which could be made upon Corsica, Nice, and Malta. The use of Italian in the law courts of Malta was a privilege jealously watched, though it was manifestly weakening with the passage of time. Also in the Swiss Canton Ticino, Italian culture was carefully tended, and schools and newspapers were supported against the possible day when Switzerland might break up.

Hard though it was to formulate a general doctrine of irredentism, *ad hoc* arguments were devised to serve each immediate purpose. The argument of natural frontiers was advanced for annexation of Southern Tyrol and held to outweigh the fact that so many of the inhabitants were German by speech and historical tradition. In Dalmatia the opposite proposition was used, namely that Italian communities must be absorbed despite all the obvious geographical difficulties. Corsica and Nice were claimed on the historical ground that they had once been under Italian rule, while with Trent and Malta such historical arguments were understandably rejected. None of the irredentists showed any comprehension of the Austrian claim to Trieste or the Slav interest in Fiume and Dalmatia.

★

The realist Depretis, who looked upon irredentist fancies as merely "*des vieux cancans*," formally renewed the Triple Alliance just before his death. Italy was then in a good bargaining position, what with the existing unfriendliness between Russia and Austria and between Germany and France. In fact Bismarck was so concerned over French nationalism that he himself opened discussions for renewing the alliance. Profiting from this, Italy now obtained special assurances that she would receive compensation if Austria advanced in the Balkans. The Catholic emperor in Vienna also undertook not to play off the pope against Italy, and Depretis received the promise of German support if France ever tried to extend her dominion in the Mediterranean through Morocco and Tripoli. But those Italians were in error who subsequently claimed that Germany accepted an obligation to back Italy's policy of conquest in North Africa.

Crispi was far more of a "triplicist" than Depretis and in general had more interest in foreign policy than any politician since Cavour. When he became prime minister in 1887 he took over in person the foreign office as well as the home office. He had the effrontery to assure the German chancellor that an Italian expeditionary force was ready for war with France, and that (so runs his diary) he would quickly be able to put half a million men into the field, not counting reserves and the militia. His conversion from irredentism seemed to be complete, since he added that he considered Austria's existence necessary for the balance of power, and he was sure that Italy would prove a faithful ally to the Habsburg empire.

Within a year Crispi paid another visit to Bismarck. Just like Mussolini later, he built his policy on German ambitions and military strength, hoping that Italy would gain from any revision of the map of Europe which Bismarck might make. In 1888 he presented to parliament a request for emergency expenditure on army and navy, and partly as a result the fiscal year 1888–89 was the worst for Italian finances since 1870. He contemplated a joint penetration of the Balkans against the Slavs, and in 1889, to curry favor with Austria, dissolved the Roman "Committee for Trent and Trieste." The following year, when his colleague, Seismit-Doda, failed to protest against an irredentist speech made during a banquet he was attending, Crispi dismissed him by telegram. Yet Crispi did not stop subsidizing the irredentists on the secret service account.

Privately, he hoped that the Austro-Hungarian empire would one day break up, to Italy's profit, but he did not believe in anticipating that event. Meanwhile, as he added in an angry oration at Florence in October 1890, irredentism might imperil the unity that Italians had so far achieved: nationalism should not be taken too far as a rule of politics, or else Austria, France, Switzerland, all the countries who possessed Italian minorities, might retort in self-defense.

What chiefly mattered to him was prestige. He claimed of himself in 1888 that "a man has appeared who considers Italy the equal of any other nation and intends to see that her voice shall be respected." This pose as the leader of a powerful country was a piece of self-deceit that only damaged his credibility. In 1889 he fabricated a war scare against France and told England that the French navy was moving on La Spezia. A British admiral was at once dispatched with his fleet to Genoa, and on arrival found that Crispi had acted on an unsubstantiated rumor from a secret agent in the Vatican. The Italian premier had simply imagined or invented the French threat, and perhaps was trying to make the world believe that his disastrous denunciation of the French commercial treaty had been justified.

Crispi's irritability and alarmism were to end in personal and national tragedy. One explanation is that he urgently needed to divert attention from unrest in Sicily and some notorious bank scandals at Rome. As these were endangering his majority he tried to consolidate his coalition by pretending that the country was in danger. In meeting these imaginary threats he had few scruples about the use of martial law and maintained that opposition by the very fact of being opposition must be factious and unpatriotic. As he told parliament, "for twenty years we have gone on merely debating, Left against Right, and forgetting the really important questions which if solved would give our nation not only power but the reputation and consequences of power." Loud cries of "*bravo, benissimo*" greeted this statement.

In fulfillment of his warlike intentions, Crispi did not merely pick a quarrel with France. The very first month of his premiership he made overtures in London for a military convention against Russia. He must have known the almost insuperable difficulty of making Britain commit herself on the Continent, but he seemed determined to fight a war somewhere and be on the winning side. He began to talk of frontier rectifications, of "Italian rights in the Mediterranean," of "the necessity to expand," and after much rhetorical repetition he managed to indoctrinate a large sector of the ruling elite with the glamor of imperialism. It was a lesson that Mussolini learned later, and it was Mussolini who dubbed Crispi the forerunner of resurgent fascist Italy.

The imperialists argued that they were compelled into a more active foreign policy by the French advance in Algeria and Tunis, by the British presence in Cyprus and Egypt, and the Austrian in Bosnia, for the distribution of power in the Mediterranean was being altered against Italy. It was unfortunate that Italy and Germany emerged as nation states just when an industrial revolution, accompanied by an enormous development in communications and popular education, put unprecedented power at the service of aggravated feelings of national self-sufficiency and self-worship. Despite the astonishing success of her national unification, the new Italy began to conceive of herself as a have-not power, and a nation of her quality was said to need colonies if she were to keep up appearances. Mazzini's campaign for "the liberation of subject peoples" might justify Italy's claims to Trieste or Trent, but in Ethiopia or Albania it was assumed that something more exalted and virile was required.

The Triple Alliance, the penetration of Eritrea, the tariff war with France after 1887, all reflected the belief that Italy should play the great power. In fairness to Crispi it must be recognized that others were ahead of him. Pasquale Turiello, for instance, was arguing that, since the fact of unification had not sunk deeply into popular consciousness, military enterprise should be encouraged in order to reinvigorate the national character. One of Turiello's books was entitled *National Virility and the Colonies*. In others he described the inevitable fight for existence between nations, and demonstrated to his own satisfaction that peace and international concord were as illusory as democracy and representative government. The weak should go to the wall since the future was to the strong. Nations had to pervade other areas with their language and culture or else would disappear in the struggle for life.

Another writer who carried weight with the new generation was the brilliant but corrupt and unstable Rocco de Zerbi. He, too, was a man of the Right and an advocate of Italian imperialism. He was the deputy most immediately implicated in the bank scandals. De Zerbi had written: "I speak of my own country in bitterness, for I do not see her eager to carry herself forward to power, but only content with her own smallness. She does not know what she wants, or at least has no idea how to subordinate everything to that end." De Zerbi believed that Italy needed purging and rejuvenation in what he termed a "bath of blood."

★

It was to be expected that many people would react strongly against this aggressive rhetorical nationalism and against Crispi its representative. The more respectable conservatives, for example the Marquis di Rudinì, despised their fellow Sicilian as a conspirator and mischief-maker. Others objected to Crispi's anticlericalism, while Prinetti and Colombo, the representatives of Milanese industry, were aghast at his lavish expenditure on the army and colonies. Meanwhile his own former friends on the Left had been shattered by personal and ideological differences into a confusion of splinter groups. Crispi's coalition was therefore vulnerable and this helped to counteract his extremist policy of repression at home and conquest abroad.

The weakness of this coalition was that it was a personal majority, heterogeneous, with no basic agreement on policy. When Left and Right combined against him, Crispi began to talk of trying to build or rebuild a party system that would help parliamentary debate by providing a principled opposition. Yet he believed that he would go on being accepted as the one necessary man, and in practice continued to manipulate groups in a personal coalition revolving around "the minister's friends." This earned him more criticism from Bonghi and others who had supported transformism as a temporary tactic but found it unacceptable as an end in itself.

Despite a considerable victory in the elections of November 1890, Crispi tripped up when in January 1891 he provocatively upbraided the conservatives with having left Italy disarmed before 1876. He even accused them of having compelled the country to follow "a policy of servility to the foreigner." This was one of those unequivocal statements which destroyed any transformist political system that depended on delicate finesse and compromise coalitions. It shows how Crispi's tactlessness made him at best a mediocre politician, for he could not restrain his desire to wound and taunt.

On this occasion, so unworthy was his remark that one of his own ministers walked straight out of the Chamber and Crispi was challenged by a surprise motion of no confidence. He warned the deputies that "your vote will decide whether Italy desires a strong government, or whether instead she intends to return to the kind of cabinet which has brought discredit on our country by its hesitation and inconsistencies." To his astonishment, parliament did not agree with his own opinion of himself, and despite his large majority in the recent election, he had to resign in favor of Di Rudinì. For several years he returned to the back benches of parliament in what he called "my usual seat on the extreme Left."

20   Agriculture and Industry, about 1880

Some of the more disinterested minds in Italy were deeply disturbed by the excessive concentration upon foreign policy and parliamentary tactics. Jacini repeatedly reminded parliament that agriculture posed by far the most urgent questions for Italy, and Sonnino insisted that the moral and physical welfare of the common people should be the first concern of the privileged classes, even if this meant diverting money which could have bought an extra carriage for their wives or a box at the municipal theater. Sonnino made practical suggestions about forming peasant co-operatives, and he hoped that local administration could be reformed to ensure that the interests of the whole community and not of a single class should prevail.

These conservative reformers were in agreement with those radicals who agitated for a parliamentary investigation into agriculture. Bertani's speech on this topic in 1872 had shocked the deputies by describing how, almost within sight of Rome, fifteen thousand people were living in caves like Stone Age lake dwellers. But neither the commission then appointed, nor individual investigators such as Sonnino, Franchetti, and Fortunato, met with much enthusiasm during their inquiries, because the conscience of the nation was as yet barely touched, and farmers were often afraid to give accurate evidence about agricultural conditions lest this should raise their tax liability.

The parliamentary commission began work in 1877. Its report in fifteen volumes was presented in 1885 and painted a depressing picture. Agriculture was at a standstill. Landowners were consuming their entire revenue and had little margin of profit for new capital to put back into the land. The extinction of communal rights of pasture and wood gathering, and of rights of way for the long-distance migration of herds, destroyed the livelihood of many people. The breaking up of communal lands and of estates held by ecclesiastical and charitable trusts had not produced a stabilizing class of peasant proprietors but rather benefited existing landlords. Local authorities, dominated by richer citizens, had habitually defied the law and allowed the commons to be enclosed by landowners who then would pay a merely nominal rent. In fact the number of people owning land declined substantially between the censuses of 1861 and 1901.

Agricultural strikes and the forcible occupation of land by the peasants continued spasmodically and kept alive an ominous sense of alarm. There was doubtless a crying need to improve conditions of work and living, yet the remedy proposed by the radicals of distributing land among the peasants was hardly economic, because modern methods of reaping, threshing, and making oil and wine needed ever greater resources of capital. Those who obtained possession of some small plot had often to surrender it since they could not afford the expenses of farming, and even the system of *mezzadria* or sharecropping began to fail now that an increasing amount of capital and tools was required.

When times were so hard for the more prosperous peasants, not even a well-intentioned parliamentary commission could suggest an alternative remedy for the landless poor. Corbino discovered from the census returns of 1881 that out of every thousand living in the countryside there were only forty-six *mezzadri* and fifty-nine peasant proprietors. The majority were simple laborers, with luck employed for half the year, whose standard of living was minimal, and who gained nothing when higher prices brought prosperity to those who owned land. There was no public maintenance for those unable to labor, no public provision for the able-bodied poor, while the nationalization of ecclesiastical charities resulted in more money being spent on their administration and less on actual relief than the Church had formerly spent.

Bertani said that there were two races in Italy, those who ate white bread and those who ate black. Most peasants rarely if ever had meat; their food often consisted entirely of rice, beans, bread, pasta, or polenta made from corn. Imbriani drew attention to the fact that only 203 out of the 3,672 Sicilian sulphur miners drafted for military service in 1881–84 were fit enough for acceptance, and much the same proportion might have been found among the grotto dwellers of the Agro Romano, almost all of whom suffered from chronic malaria.

This disease spread rapidly after 1860 as deforestation encouraged mosquitos, and regular fevers were still thought inevitable and natural. Only at the end of the century was malaria found to be treatable. Another plague on the increase was pellagra, a deficiency disease caused by a starchy corn diet, of which there were over a hundred thousand reported cases in 1881. Cholera epidemics killed at least 55,000 people between 1884 and 1887, and only later did people discover the cause in slum conditions. A belated start was made with the *sventramento* or gutting of the old city of Naples and giving it adequate drains and water. But Sonnino was able to show that some of the money provided for this purpose was perverted by speculators, so that behind the showy main streets new slums were built and a larger number of people were fitted into the same disease-ridden area.

★

One of the chief obstacles to progress in agriculture was the heavy indebtedness of the state and the consequently high taxation. Minghetti in 1876 had at last given the national accounts an illusion of balancing though only by excluding expenditure on railroad construction; yet it was said at the time that this surplus on revenue was ruining the country by the excessive taxation which it implied. The wars of the *risorgimento* had still not been paid for. The vast deficits of the years 1861–76 encumbered the national revenue, and the confiscated ecclesiastical lands had by now been sold with not much to show for their sale. Railways, roads, ships, armaments, and schools, all had to be provided in excess of current ability to pay, and it was hard to know the exact point where expenditure became too risky to be advisable.

When the Left came to power in 1876, balancing the budget was given a lower priority. New expenditure was taken on lightly under an excessive illusion about national strength, yet Cairoli decided to repeal the grist tax and so diminish revenue. This levy on the grinding of wheat was aimed at the poor who consumed more bread than the rich and spent much more of their income on farinaceous foods. Financially this tax was so necessary that the Senate at first refused to allow its repeal, but the government responded by appointing fifty new senators and it was allowed to pass when the elections of 1880 confirmed the Left in office. Without sixty million lire a year from the grist tax, and with a reduced tax on salt, the state would again be running at a loss, and the minister of finance, Grimaldi, resigned in protest.

Unfortunately, almost without a break between 1878 and 1888, the treasury was controlled by Magliani who allowed Depretis carelessly to take on new expenditure without balancing this by more taxation. Magliani was the author of a book on monetary theory and a professional illusionist with figures. Closely connected with the foreign bankers Hambro and Rothschild, he helped restore Italian credit abroad, but could not entirely conceal the annual deficit which became serious in 1885 and by 1889 was 238 million lire a year. In 1888 Magliani made some effort to raise taxes so as to meet the deficit, but this would have lost the Left too much popularity, and rather than force the issue he resigned. Agriculture suffered indirectly from this deficit, for, as the wealth of the country lay predominantly in land, it was assumed that taxes on agriculture could remain indefinitely at their high level. In 1883 Magliani also allowed the banks to resume payment in specie, and this hit farmers by sending up the value of the lira, cheapening agricultural imports still further and discouraging exports.

*

But the agricultural slump after 1873 was due only in part to government action. Its more fundamental cause was the lack of capital which was needed for effecting the switch from subsistence farming to production for an international market. As railroad routes through the Mont Cenis and Brenner passes opened Italy to foreign competition and wider price fluctuations, the more backward parts of the country lost the artificial protection which had insulated them. Contacts with the wider world brought land into production during the American Civil War, land that was profitable only at scarcity prices, and severe losses were caused when peace caused another contraction of demand. Again, the new Suez Canal brought an influx of rice and silk from the East which undercut two staple domestic products.

When steam navigation made cargo shipping cheaper during the 1880s, freight charges fell by over 60 per cent, and the cheap cereals which flooded into Europe caused the most severe crisis of all. From 30 lire a quintal in January 1880, the price of wheat fell in several years to 22 lire. The acreage under cereals had been too extensive for efficient production and the yield per acre was little more than a third of that in England. America and Russia produced grain far more cheaply, and as with cotton, flax, and vegetable dyes, foreign competition ruined many domestic growers. Imports made food cheaper and in the long run forced Italian farming to become more efficient, but the immediate effect was catastrophic.

It was not an unmixed blessing that the vine disease of phylloxera in France simultaneously put an artificial premium on Italian grapes and made Italy the chief wine-producing country in Europe. Between 1874 and 1883 the area under vines increased from five to over seven million acres, displacing fruit trees, walnuts, chestnuts, and even century-old olive plantations in Apulia and Sicily. Annual production of wine went up from 27 to 36 million hectoliters and there was a great increase in export to France, where the strength and color of Italian wines made them suitable *vins de coupage* for blending.

Then in 1888 a commercial rupture with France suddenly reversed this trend and caused a crisis of overproduction. Southern Italy was especially vulnerable where the strong sun and cheap labor had made new vineyards particularly extensive. As the expansion had been paid for by expensive borrowing, and had often meant the destruction of olive groves and other long-term investments, an explosive situation was generated. The diseased French vineyards were eventually restocked with hardier American root stock, and the Algerian vineyards also came into heavy production just when Italy herself fell a victim to phylloxera. The new plantations had not been accompanied by improvements in wine manufacture and the cultivation of reliable markets. Too late it was found that the manufacture of wine for export was becoming too technical a process for small growers who knew nothing of foreign tastes or of how to maintain a constant standard. As a result, prices fell abruptly and there were numerous bankruptcies all over the South.

Other difficulties affected the growing of olives and citrus fruit. The yield of olive plantations was irregular, partly owing to ignorance about pruning: trees were often pruned only every third year, mainly as a way of gathering firewood. The oil produced was known to be too heavy for most tastes yet nothing was done to change it. The difficulties which then ensued from the increasing competition of seed oils were also felt more particularly in the South. Seventy per cent of Italy's oranges and lemons came from Sicily, and it was therefore again in the South that a threefold increase in output of citrus fruits between 1885 and 1905 left Italy with an unsalable surplus. Growers in California had better fruit, better sales organizations, and cheaper methods of transportation. Italy as a backward country, and in particular its more backward provinces, was bound to suffer when measured against more progressive and more favored nations, and the slump which followed this agricultural crisis was to have political repercussions.

★

The political troubles of the 1890s were partly connected also with the development of Italian industry. Here it is difficult to find convincing statistics, whether for production, consumption of raw materials, the amount of mechanization, or the number of operatives employed. Facts were sometimes falsified to obtain increased state protection, or to avoid a feared increase in ratable value. There was a national census every ten years, but the different criteria employed each time make the figures incomparable. The census sometimes included under "productive population" people over the age of eleven, sometimes those over nine; some regions reported women working part-time in the fields as productive, others not; peasant families engaged in both farming and weaving could be listed as either agricultural or industrial. Even the official estimates of the total area of Italy varied.

Up to and beyond the new tariffs of 1878 and 1887, industry was still largely built on independent craftsmen working in their own homes. Even in the

North there was no single region which could be called predominantly industrial, and many or most industrial workers spent much of their time on the land. In the language of the people, *industria* had rather the meaning of ploughing or cheese making.

The railroad network did not create what could be called a nationwide market until the late 1870s. Only then was there a sufficient demand for industrial goods and a possibility of local specialization, though the anomalous "medieval" immunities had still not all been abolished in the free ports of Leghorn, Ancona, Venice, and Messina. The most consistent grievance presented to the Royal Commission on Industry in 1871–72 was that the municipal octrois or duties on consumption hindered internal trade. These local tariffs were unfortunately the chief item in the revenue of each commune and took the place of the restrictive regional customs barriers which had been abolished in 1859–61. For example, at Iglesias the commune took 15 per cent of the value of all local coal, which made the small-scale smelting industry of Sardinia unduly expensive.

One other complaint made in 1872 was that foreign industry had gained more than Italian from national unification. Of the locomotives used by the north Italian network in 1878, 702 had been made abroad, only 39 in Italy by the Ansaldo company. The railroad track was almost all imported because the native steel industry was frail and diminutive. Raw materials and machinery were dearer in Italy than elsewhere, and labor, though much cheaper, was inexperienced and uneducated. A period of foreign tutelage was inevitable and in the long run was highly beneficial, but it was frustrating to find that managers and foremen were sometimes Germans, Swiss, or Scotsmen.

The common people of Italy were too poor for there to be a very widespread demand for industrial products, and though farmers were beginning to sell increasingly in a cash market, too much of their earnings went to pay taxes and the interest on loans. Many town families lived on food which they themselves produced outside the city walls; bread was baked at home and the multi-plication of specialist retailers was still to come. The artisan was cushioned against industrial crises by his part-time employment in agriculture, and not until he was ready to forgo this advantage were large factories possible. Yet another prerequisite of progress was a change in social habits, for the middle classes thought the learned professions and clerical work to be far more socially acceptable than commerce and industry.

★

A major advance in industry began around 1879. One sign is that in the following six years coal imports nearly doubled until they stood at about three million tons annually. Giovanni Battista Pirelli, the ex-Garibaldian volunteer, was beginning to create the rubber industry that still carries his family name: his first factory was built in 1872 at Milan and in 1886 he pioneered the production of electric cable. In textiles there were Tosi of Legnano and the wool-masters of

Vicenza and Biella, these industries being the first to gain from the tariff of 1878. Silk manufacture in particular, which had had a long history in Italy, already possessed the requisite skills and techniques and its machines were mostly made in Italy.

The heavier industries grew up either near what few iron mines there were in Elba and the Val d'Aosta, or in later years where hydroelectric energy was easily obtained, as at Terni, or else where the proximity of seaports and ancillary mechanical industries offered special attractions as at Savona and Sestri in Liguria. Since the old iron foundries of Lombardy were weakened by foreign competitors, and as the existing ordnance factories at Brescia and Turin were too near the frontier for security, Vincenzo Breda agreed to create a new armament industry at Terni. The chosen site was securely placed in Umbria, much nearer the new capital at Rome and supplied with water power from a tributary of the Tiber. Fitted out with modern equipment, this large complex of factories was more able to compete with foreign production, even though it existed mainly through not always discriminating state patronage, and by heavy tariffs on imported pig iron.

The Terni steelworks were in production by 1886, a year after Depretis had persuaded the British firm of Armstrong to open a naval shipyard and cannon foundry at Pozzuoli. Only the hypothesis of war justified these armament works, and it soon became clear that efficiency and economy of production had been sacrificed to military requirements and a goal of greater self-sufficiency. A parasite industry had been conjured up at the expense of domestic consumers, and so irrational were the tariffs protecting it that (people used to say) metal was deliberately produced as scrap by foreign foundries for sale in Italy. Perhaps this was inevitable, but as the industry in fact depended altogether on the state for its prosperity, it was from the first a corrupting influence, and it financed newspapers, deputies, and high-ranking officials in order to persuade the government that such a costly, artificial industry was necessary for the country's greatness and should be protected to the limit.

Many liberal economists protested. Some politicians felt that what Italy could afford would never be quite sufficient to guarantee her frontiers and that her prestige in the world would not be the less for having fewer military pretensions. But though the industrialist Colombo in 1896 resigned from the cabinet rather than sanction extra military expenditure, it was politicians such as Crispi with exaggerated notions of military greatness who were in charge and were easily prevailed on by other less high-minded industrialists who wanted the state to underwrite their rickety concerns and keep the armament industry employed.

*

Similar reasons induced the government to subsidize shipping again inevitably, but also with mixed results. Steamships had in general begun to oust sail by 1860, in which year Garibaldi used paddle steamers for his Sicilian venture. But although the Orlando brothers were then trying out the first Italian-built marine engine and experimenting with metal hulls, Italy owned the raw materials for wooden ships only and had to depend largely on foreign construction for ironclads. Italian shipyards mostly continued building sailing ships, although iron steamers were bigger, faster, and more reliable. The merchant marine in 1871 had a million tons of sail, but only 32,000 tons of steam, and even the larger shipping companies could not afford the more expensive methods of construction. By the end of the century, 85 per cent of imports and 70 per cent of exports still traveled in foreign vessels, and Italian ships were mostly bought secondhand from foreign companies.

The two biggest Italian shipping companies, Rubattino and Florio, were given subsidized government contracts in 1862, and in 1881 fused to form the *Navigazione Generale Italiana* which was to dominate Italian shipping for many years. In the same year a commission was appointed under Boselli to inquire into the merchant marine, and on its recommendation the government in 1885 gave fifty-three million lire to subsidize shipbuilding, together with many tax exemptions. Steam overtook sail quantitatively in 1905, but bounties and subsidies still helped to keep inefficient techniques and practices alive.

It was different with the navy. For a time the Italian navy ranked third in the world by tonnage and it remained the most efficient of the Italian fighting services. The first two armor-plated ships for the navy were built in France but, with the construction of the *Duilio* and *Dandolo*, Italy by 1878 took the lead in developing naval ironclads—they were over 11,000 tons apiece and sailed at fifteen knots.

This was largely the work of Benedetto Brin, minister of the navy under Depretis, Cairoli, Crispi, and Di Rudinì. Brin's policy of increased expenditure on armaments met with wide approval even though he did not always work through the normal parliamentary channels. There were only a few cynics who doubted the usefulness of this fine navy and questioned its huge cost. Nevertheless, as armor plate continued to become heavier, Italy's limited resources put her at an increasing disadvantage with other nations. The effort to hold her place was likely one day to prove too costly, as it also made war more probable and an expensive foreign policy less easy to avoid.

21 The Tariff War with France, 1887–1892

On top of all the other inherent difficulties of adjustment, the agricultural community was involved by the government in an ill-calculated tariff war with

France, their chief customer. The revised Italian tariff of 1887 and the consequent repudiation of the French commercial treaty precipitated the economic depression of 1887–90, and this was to trigger off another Sicilian revolution and a banking crisis which together shook Italian society to its foundations.

The north of Italy had earlier gained considerably from Cavour's reduction of customs duties. Inefficient industries had been weeded out, prices kept low, and commerce generally had prospered. There had been in 1878 a small increase in duties. Depretis was at that moment trying to reduce the price of bread by abolishing the grist tax and did not wish to nullify this by putting additional import dues on foreign grain. He was not himself a champion of the doctrine that the national wealth could be increased by introducing protection and he claimed that the 1878 tariff was in fact imposed only to augment the revenue. But other ministers hoped that a further increment in duties might provide a bargaining counter against foreign nations. Industrialists were also increasingly sensitive to the pinch of competition, now made more acute by cheaper transportation, and as foreign markets were difficult to find, they wished at least to make a hedge around the domestic market as more of a monopoly for themselves.

A report on the great Milanese industrial fair of 1881 makes it clear that hardly one industry was without some claim for protection. No sooner had Cavour left the political scene than the silk manufacturers of Lombardy began a campaign for government assistance. The growing steel interests pointed to the existing French commercial treaties as the prime obstacle to their prosperity, and they received ample support from people who wished to make the country more independent of foreign supplies. Other industrialists wanted protection simply because their industries were uneconomic and either could not be made more competitive at all or else could be improved only at a cost they would rather not pay. Soon the question was intricately involved with parliamentary politics, and by 1886 Depretis was forced to think that concession of higher duties might be the only way to maintain his majority. Pareto commented that the new scale of duties was designed less to build up strong industries than to reward the power groups which had supported or might support the government. Above all this meant the steel industry and hence placed a heavy burden on the rest of the Italian economy for many decades. Domestic production of steel needed high coal imports which the country had somehow to afford, whereas the low-coal-using mechanical industries not only received less protection but now had to pay an uncompetitively high price for their iron and steel.

Among the groups seeking sectional gains, even if at some cost to the community, were those agriculturists threatened in their domination over the home market. Producers of oil, wine, raw silk, fruit, and vegetables were on the whole anxious to avoid import duties because they did not want to provoke foreigners to discriminate against Italian goods. But the big grain producers were a good deal more easily organized than other farmers and carried greater weight with the government because of their social position. According to the parliamentary discussions of 1885–86, the experts were agreed that agriculture generally would suffer from protection; yet many landowners thought otherwise. They wanted protection for themselves and were ready to support protection for industrialists in a compact for mutual profit. This was an unholy and unwholesome alliance.

Among the plausible arguments advanced was that any increase in duties could be rescinded when wheat prices returned to normal, and meanwhile agricultural protection would compensate the South for the higher prices of manufactured goods consequent upon the industrial protection conceded to the North. In fact, however, of the agricultural products to be given protection, rice, sugar, and hemp came almost entirely from northern Italy, whereas such wheat as was grown in the South was more for subsistence than for sale. Those among the cereal growers who produced for a market came mostly from the North and Center, and these were the people who profited. Those who lost were consumers everywhere; those who gained were the owners of large farms where the soil was good and yield was high. An increase in import duty from three to five lire a quintal meant a small fortune for such people, and although the more enlightened southern landowners—the Calabrian Fortunato, for instance—spoke strongly against it, the pressure groups at Rome were too powerful.

Economists were not lacking to justify the revision of tariffs. Magliani at first opposed it but was won over. Most of the younger economists were no longer trained in the *laissez-faire* English school as Cavour and Minghetti had been, but in Germany whence they came back imbued with protectionist and authoritarian principles. From 1875 onward, Luzzatti and others of this new school put forward their ideas in the *Giornale degli Economisti* at Padua. In opposition to them the classical school of economists, represented by Bastogi and Ferrara, formed the Adam Smith Society and published the *Economista*. But this latter group became increasingly remote and ineffective: their free-trade principles made them even doubtful about post-office savings banks and about appointing a commission of inquiry on the employment of children in factories.

The tide in favor of protection rose so high in the years 1886–88 that government and parliament outdid each other in advocating a general increase in duties. But prohibitive duties on French goods provoked retaliation so that 40 per cent of Italian exports were affected. The figures of annual exports to France dropped suddenly from a valuation of 500 million lire to 167 million, and imports from France dropped from 366 million to 164 million in value. This hit the agricultural South particularly, and hence one direct result of the new duties was to take capital away from southern agriculture and put it into northern industry. Grain prices of course improved, but this harmed those peasants who suffered as consumers and did not gain as producers. Bread prices rose proportionately and the grist tax had simply come back in disguise, except that this time the profit went to landowners rather than to the state. Sugar beet was henceforward so heavily protected that sugar was said to be beyond the pocketbook of half the population, but the sugar interest flourished exceedingly and soon claimed to own newspapers and deputies, so wielding considerable influence in the affairs of state.

★

Abrogation of the French commercial treaty had been almost incidental but was a deliberate objective of the more extreme protectionists. This treaty had been voluntarily renewed in 1881 but was now declared to discriminate unfairly against Italian economic interests. The advent of Crispi to power in 1887 brought anti-French opinion to the fore. Crispi held that Italy had depended too much on France for her trade and capital investment and had been unduly submissive to the political dependence which this implied: "France must now forget the history of the supremacy and influence which she once possessed on this side of the Alps; she should recognize that the Italian nation is as good as herself and must now be allowed to enjoy her independence and profit from it." Gratitude to France for her assistance in creating this Italian nation was no longer an operative force in politics. The French chargé d'affaires in Rome was shocked to find several Italian children who assured him that the battle of Solferino in 1859 had been won by the Italians fighting against the French, and who had been taught at school that Nice, Corsica, and Savoy were Italian. Crispi's persecution mania, furthermore, made him think that France was seeking a pretext to quarrel and that she intended to spite him personally. The unilateral denunciation of the treaty in 1888 had strong support from Crispi. He was convinced that Italy was strong enough to force acceptance of her conditions and that France would not be able to escape from dependence on Italian silk and wine.

But Italy in fact was far more vulnerable than France and already had a large adverse balance of trade. Only the attempt to base policy on considerations of sentiment and prestige can have blinded Crispi to this simple truth. Pantaleoni, the economist, estimated in 1884 that the Italian national income was only a quarter of the French, and France was well able to turn to Algeria for wine and to the Orient for silk. Even though some industries in northern Italy gained from the war of reprisals and urged the government to continue it, great damage was also done to the raw and spun silk of Lombardy, Venetia, and Piedmont, and there was a fall in the export of rice, cattle, and cheese which came mainly from the North. The vineyards of Apulia and Sicily, however, felt the effects of the breach most severely of all, where farmers had lately made heavy investments in wine for export. The economy of these provinces was less diversified than that of the North, and a rupture with France meant ruin.

Another harmful result was that the French began to sell their Italian securities, and a number of bank failures in 1889–90 was partly due to withdrawal of French capital. Though Germany supported her ally by buying on the Paris bourse to restore confidence, it was not enough nor in time to avert catastrophe. Also the agricultural depression led to a drop in consumption of manufactured goods, and many speculative ventures built on an unwise use of credit began to fail. Crispi was forced in 1890 to admit defeat and to surrender some of the heavier duties he had imposed on French produce. A modified trade war continued, though reduced in scale, until alternative outlets were opened through commercial treaties with Austria, Switzerland, and Germany. These helped to repair some of the damage done by this irresponsible and ill-prepared essay in government protection.

But the duties on cereals remained and an agrarian pressure group used its great influence in politics to increase them still higher. For landowners, the tax of 7.5 lire per quintal on imported grain constituted in effect a reimbursement of the land tax about which they grumbled so much, but for the poor who lived mostly off cereals it spelled hunger and disease. Economists pointed out how this duty made agriculture progressively uneconomic by forcing poor land into inefficient use and exonerating producers from seeking out better techniques in the face of growing world competition. One report at the turn of the century even advised against investing further in agricultural improvements because it might be money wasted.

One result was the Sicilian rebellion of 1892–93. Another was a further exodus from the land to the towns, while a great wave of emigration became a flood. A predominantly peasant society was being brutally disrupted, and revolutionary forces were being built up which had to find some outlet at home or abroad.

22   Corruption and the Banks, 1889–1893

Between 1889 and 1893 the failure of certain important banks developed into a full-scale crisis of political morality, which had something like the effect of the Panama scandal in France, and came near to ruining Crispi and blighting Giolitti's political career before it had almost begun.

Political corruption had flourished under the pre-1860 despotisms and the habit could hardly be cured easily. Northerners, not without reason, thought it specially typical of the South. Cavour's friend, the British ambassador Sir James Hudson, had unctuously written in 1860 that "the Neapolitans are too corrupt, and the entire Civil and Military administration is so abominable that their junction with Northern Italy (where honesty is the rule in the Public Offices) would merely produce a social decomposition, and then a political putrefaction." His prophecy was exaggerated but not beside the point. The deputies at Turin affected shocked surprise when Massari told how "at Naples there exists a class of person who comes between the administration and interested parties and knows how to bribe government officials." But Ricasoli's government soon had to deal with the same contact men in the North. Politicians needed money because they lacked the financial resources for campaigning, not having large parties behind them. Banks and industrial firms therefore put money at the disposal of small groups and politicians in return for services rendered.

People at first ascribed this simply to defective political habits which national unification would alter, yet the passing of years brought no great improvement. In 1875 the deputy Tajani revealed to parliament how judges and police in Sicily connived at the crimes of the mafia and protected *mafiosi* from justice. The following year a parliamentary commission reported that this underworld life was not peculiar to the South, and instanced the *squadrace* of Ravenna and Bologna, the *pugnalatori* of Parma, the *cocca* of Turin, and the *sicari* of Rome. Similar disreputable gangs could also be found in most other countries: what typified Italy was not this professional crime but the universal mistrust and unco-operativeness of people in every social class toward the government. In some areas 20 per cent of the annual draft for the army contrived to disappear altogether. The unscrupulous rich found it relatively easy to pay hush money to the tax collectors, and it was estimated that in some areas only one-tenth of the taxes due was reaching the Treasury. Scandals over the construction of railroads, which had once ruined the ministerial career of Count Bastogi, came close to tumbling Vincenzo Breda himself, and with the enormous expansion of state expenditure and patronage after the 1880s, corrupt practices over government contracts became a byword.

★

The bank scandals of 1889–93 were given unusual publicity, but Italy profited from the exposure, painful though it was. The financial crash of 1889 was immediately due to an overexpansion of the building industry for which the banks had allowed far too much credit. This building craze had begun with the new government offices in Florence and Rome, and had continued with the rebuilding of the insanitary back-streets of Naples. Rome itself, with a population of 220,000 in 1870, nearly doubled in size during the next twenty years and became a mecca for every kind of adventurer. The banks of Turin had disregarded all good financial doctrine when they saw the great profits realized from speculation in land and building, and far too much of the capital which might have gone into agriculture or industry was diverted into this deceptively profitable investment. The Banca Nazionale increased its note circulation from 462 million lire in 1883 to 611 million by the end of 1886, and reserves in bullion dropped from a half to one-third of the total. Crispi then helped this process by lifting legal restrictions on credit, for the profiteers evidently wielded considerable influence in government circles.

At the beginning of 1889 one or two banks began to suspend payment. Once again Crispi intervened unobtrusively and persuaded the larger financial houses to cover the failing Banca Tiberina with a loan of 45 million lire so that it might complete its contracts for public works. A small slump in the Roman building trade had already caused minor riots of unemployed men plundering the shops of the capital, and Crispi feared what would happen if the bubble burst. It was also said, maliciously but not implausibly, that he had the interests of certain influential financiers close at heart. But his action led to a further inflation of credit and made the collapse worse when it came, for loans from the Banca Nazionale could not sustain this inflation indefinitely. Meanwhile, other banks followed his lead and supported semibankrupt enterprises which would better have been allowed to collapse.

The various regions of Italy still jealously guarded their right to a bank of issue and these were private companies with shareholders who sought profit. The governor of the Banca Romana, one of the six such banks, was a certain Tanlongo. He had begun his career as a factor on one of the large estates of the Roman Campagna and had gradually built up estates of his own. Cavour had employed him in an attempt to bribe officials in the papal curia. A none too scrupulous career had finally brought this half-illiterate but skillful and auda-cious man to the point of giving financial advice to a succession of premiers, as well as to cardinals, to the Jesuits, and the king himself; and handsome loans sometimes accompanied this "advice." Tanlongo was one of the quickest to profit from the wave of land speculation that was swamping baroque Rome under a new Humbertine city. He had had the paper notes of the Banca Romana printed in England, and without reference to the government he had been able to order any quantity—"just like a barrel of beer," said Giolitti. The circulation of his bank was 60 million lire in excess of the legal limit, and 40 million in false notes had been issued as a duplicate series.

When the bank failures of 1889 allowed these financial irregularities to leak out, it also became known that a good deal of this surplus had been spent on interest-free "loans" to deputies and ministers. The banks of issue had come to wield considerable political pressure, and deputies were shy of any proposal to control them because it might have exposed the existence of these "loans." The Banca di Napoli, while its circulation was more or less correct, turned out to have incurred debts of some twenty million, much of which had been accumulated by this concealed political bribery. Its director, when accused of peculation, implicated Crispi himself, and it was established that Crispi had at least countermanded an inquiry which should have been made into the state of this bank. Nor was he so simple-minded as not to have known what was afoot. His many enemies connected this concealment with his sudden appointment of eighty-four new men to the Senate, among them many titled names and the captains of industry, Breda, Bastogi, and Orlando.

When the purely financial crisis reached a point where no further postponement of the reckoning seemed possible, the minister Miceli, at the end of 1889, appointed a private commission of inquiry to see if the banks were exceeding their reserves. This commission under Senator Alvisi drew attention to many serious irregularities, but its report was not published and Alvisi's attempt to raise the matter in parliament was ruled out of order. Several ministers later pretended that they did not even read the Alvisi report but had been content with assurances that everything could be hushed up and rectified without public scandal. For several years the matter was allowed to lie dormant, and the fact that so many people kept silent was a poor commentary on the health of Italian public institutions.

★

The administration led by Crispi resigned early in 1891 after three and a half years of power. Di Rudinì, the wealthy Sicilian *gran signore* with the monocle and long red beard who then succeeded as prime minister, had been the most prominent leader of the Right since Minghetti's death in 1886; nevertheless he made the radical Nicotera his minister of the interior. Whereas Crispi's two ministries had shown transformism on the Left, Di Rudinì, who when out of office had objected to this process, now himself used it as a conservative strategy. Though basing his government on the Right Center, he gave the most important of all offices to the architect of the sweeping Left victory of 1876. Transformism once again showed itself to be a moderating but also a confusing practice. The new government was less anticlerical than its predecessor, more eager for a balanced budget, especially anxious for reduced military expenditure, and less authoritarian than Crispi in its domestic policy.

Abroad, Di Rudinì wanted economy, peace and quiet, and restoration of good relations with France. He hoped that commerce and industry might prosper unhindered by war scares or by the breach of trade relations with neighboring countries upon whom Italy's prosperity depended. He cut the funds of Italian schools abroad which Crispi's patriotism had heavily endowed, and in general played down jingoism, putting Italian foreign policy back in the middle of the road. As Jacini wrote: "It was the mania of aggrandizement that led us to ally with the Central Powers, and the Triple Alliance now imposes on us an enormous armament quite disproportionate to our economic resources. ... The high taxes which inevitably follow are drying up our capacity for production, especially in agriculture." To let the Triple Alliance lapse entirely, on the other hand, would have meant diplomatic isolation again, and so in 1891, without consulting the cabinet, it was renewed. Yet counterbalancing it was the fact that irredentist claims against Austria were now infecting the Right as well as the extreme Left, and when the irredentist Dante Alighieri Society was founded in 1889, its name was suggested by the radical Carducci but its first president was the conservative Bonghi.

Crispi resented the greater friendliness with France which followed this renunciation of his policy, and protested to the king that Italian strength and reputation were being discarded wantonly by his successor. Better that Italy should not have been made at all, he said, than reconcile herself to being a second-class power. What was wanted, so Crispi privately told the king, was a strong man as premier who would not hesitate if necessary to govern against parliament and who could impose an uncompromisingly nationalist and authoritarian policy.

Di Rudinì did not fit this definition. Nor was he one of those statesmen who by patience and intrigue could build a firm majority. When his coalition dissolved in May 1892, he was succeeded by Giovanni Giolitti, another enemy of Crispi's but a far more capable tactician. Giolitti was a man of the Center with the reputation of being a safe man who would do nothing rash. Indeed, having very few fixed ideas of any kind, he was the obvious man to come to the top under such a system of broad coalitions. In particular he was *bien vu* by the royalist Court party who welcomed a Piedmontese after two Sicilians. The king's adviser on this occasion was the younger Rattazzi who, following his more famous uncle, had been taken into Court administration and became Minister of the Royal House. For a short time Rattazzi seems to have played at being a Grey Eminence. Although the scope of his activities is still obscure, it seems that he used royal patronage and his influence with the banks to keep Giolitti in power.

Giolitti needed a firm basis of support and so dissolved parliament at the end of 1892. For the new elections he made free use of government influence, even more than Minghetti and Depretis before him. He took the precaution of dismissing or transferring forty-nine out of sixty-nine prefects, and also freely dissolved communal administrations. Help was purchased by the offer of senatorial appointments. It was noted that widening of the suffrage and the return to single-member constituencies made electoral corruption easier. Very few constituencies in all Italy, said Luzzatti, were free from such corruption in 1892. Giolitti argued that, if the government did not use these dubious methods, the elections would be managed by local cliques of *camorristi* with methods that were even worse. He thus began to construct the electoral machine which, by the beginning of the new century, was to make him the arbiter of Italian politics. This time it secured the election of what were estimated to be 380 ministerial deputies out of a total of 508.

Giolitti, however, lacked the experience to weld his majority together. Managed elections of this kind were fought on no clear issue of principle, so that the resultant majority had little cohesion; weakened by the absence of party allegiance, his majority could evaporate at a very moderate temperature. Giolitti, moreover, had not yet perfected the technique of running miscellaneous groups in common harness, for his ministry was weighted to the Left and he failed to offer enough inducements to the other wing of the inevitable coalition. Four ministers of justice and three of finance followed each other in the space of eighteen months. The Senate resented the inclusion of only one senator in his cabinet, and was also shocked by his multiple nominations to the Upper House. The influence of Queen Margherita was used to back the reactionaries; while of the king's two known mistresses, the Countess of Santafiora favored Crispi and the Duchess Litta was for Di Rudinì. The re-emergence of the bank question sealed Giolitti's fate, and Rattazzi was overturned by a faction of royalist courtiers led by Domenico Farini.

★

Rumors of continued malversation had not been appeased by an official statement in June 1891 that the national interests forbade the publication of Alvisi's report. Then in November 1892 came the nomination of Tanlongo to the Senate for services rendered, an appointment published, significantly enough, a few days before Giolitti's first experiment in "making" the elections. Several months later, Tanlongo was in prison. For quite unexpectedly, in December 1892, the deputy Colajanni reopened the whole issue by discovering and publishing Alvisi's conclusions. The faithful deputies voted by 316 to 27 to bury the whole matter again, but the newspapers bit deep into the scandal and concealment became impossible. Colajanni was supported by Di Rudinì, Pareto, and Pantaleoni among others.

Giolitti put himself still further in the wrong by refusing a request for a parliamentary inquiry on the banks. It is interesting that Crispi spoke from the opposition benches in Giolitti's support, saying that a parliamentary investigation would be unpatriotic and would damage Italian credit abroad, but later it turned out that Crispi was himself still "borrowing" from the banks far beyond his capacity to repay. Instead of a parliamentary inquiry, a governmental commission was appointed under Finali. The Banca Romana hastily corrected its books which for twenty years had been grossly falsified, but even so the Finali report indicated that its note circulation was twice that allowed by law, and fifty million lire had been lost through speculations, malversation, and bribery.

In the same year one of the largest credit institutions in the country, the Credito Mobiliare, had to suspend payments since speculative investing had heavily depreciated its capital. Building enterprises and industrial shares at once began to reflect a general loss of confidence. Deputies were being publicly implicated by name, and the popular hero De Zerbi, a champion of the bank in parliament and who owed it half a million, died from "shock." A former director of the Bank of Sicily was brutally murdered in a railroad car as he returned to Palermo. A director of the Bank of Naples disappeared and was arrested attempting to take poison when disguised as a priest. Finally, in March 1893, Giolitti had to let parliament appoint a third committee under Mordini to consider the political implications of what had been revealed.

Eight months of tension went by before the report of this committee was presented in November. Although it had without doubt been inspired by the desire to play the whole matter down, the air was effectively cleared. A number of deputies were blamed because they and their friends were on the payroll of the bank, and many more were implicated less directly. As for Giolitti, his own memoirs were to protest his complete innocence, but the committee decided that he knew the true condition of the Banca Romana yet continued to have financial dealings with it, and in return for its help had made its president a senator. Giolitti's direct transactions concerned no more than sixty thousand lire borrowed from the bank, probably for bribing the French press to favor the Columbus festival of 1892, and this sum had been duly repaid. As for the accusation that he had had an additional sum for electoral expenses, this was "not proven," but the records of the bank must have been in a poor state if it could not be decided one way or the other. Although still undefeated in parliament, he chose to resign, and a subsequent disappearance abroad made some people suspect the worst.

Crispi was far more closely implicated, having been prime minister during the original Alvisi inquiry. As he had used his political position to draw on the bank, his refusal to act on Alvisi's report was highly discreditable to say the least. Now that the pact of secrecy about these political loans was broken, Crispi, resenting the accession to power of this young upstart from the North, tried to throw all the blame on Giolitti, but his accusations rebounded, for he and his wife owed the bank twenty times his premier's salary and he had taken a bribe from another international financier of scandalous reputation. Crispi is said to have left public life in 1896 a poor man, whereas (some historians have suggested) he could easily have used the secret service fund to pay his debts. Yet he required heavy subventions for his own paper *La Riforma*, and his attitude to the press as a purchasable commodity had cost money. What political influence these financiers managed to wield through their activities must remain conjectural. But at least he showed poor judgment in not breaking off from the bank at the first hint of embezzlement, and his effort at concealment made the scandal seem worse than it possibly was.

★

Italy emerged from this inquiry with a cleaner bill than some had feared. Reforms were introduced to reduce the number of banks and bring note circulation under stricter state control, and deputies and senators were henceforth forbidden to become directors of the note-issuing banks. Giolitti had to resign as prime minister, but did not first submit to a parliamentary vote, and the king was therefore able to choose whomever he wished as a successor. Zanardelli was asked to form a ministry, because here was a man respected by all for his integrity. But when Zanardelli submitted the name of General Baratieri as foreign minister, the king vetoed the suggestion in compliance with a warning from Austria, since Baratieri came from the Austrian province of Trentino. Zanardelli would not accept this veto, and Crispi of all people was invited to replace him.

Inculpated himself, Crispi was hardly the man to reassure the country, but another dangerous revolt was brewing among the peasants of Sicily, and many propertied men were prepared (as again in 1922) to sacrifice liberal government if it were the price for having a strong man at the helm. They looked on Giolitti and Zanardelli as dangerous radicals, for in October 1893 Giolitti had even advocated a progressive income tax and had refused to dissolve the Sicilian workers' unions. Crispi had urgent reasons for wanting power in order to avoid prosecution over the unsavory bank episode. He was also supported by industrialists who wanted an expensive program of rearmament. He told parliament that no party considerations would influence the forming of his emergency government: "When the fortunes of the country have been restored we can go back to normal again; but to continue with our personal squabbles now would be a crime. When in danger we must all unite in common defense."

The danger which Crispi referred to was socialism, and against this growing menace he intended to play the strong man and the delivering hero. He took office only on condition that he could dissolve the Chamber if necessary, and as the Giolittian majority knew what would happen if he was allowed to manage the next elections, they dutifully allowed him to govern as he chose. Social disorder had momentarily restored a rough political consensus among the ruling elite, and events in Sicily and Ethiopia conveniently changed the subject so preventing an adequate debate on Mordini's report.

SECTION SIX: COLONIAL DEFEAT AND POLITICAL REACTION, 1893–1900

23 Social Unrest and Crispi's Last Ministry

Socialism was now a force to be reckoned with, and the fear that it inspired helped Crispi into power for his last fatal ministry. Many diverse strands came together in Italian socialism: the enthusiasm for social justice of Garibaldi, the republicanism of Mazzini, the anarchism of Bakunin, the Marxism of Antonio Labriola, and the rough force of the disorganized agrarian revolts that erupted spontaneously all over the country long before there was any doctrine to give them reason and pattern. The peasants were the most rebellious element in Italian society; but hardly yet the target for propaganda from socialist intellectuals. In their animosity toward the new middle-class state, these peasants sometimes discovered an ally in the Church, and it was the clericals as well as socialists who now fought back by stirring up class war.

Alongside the peasants, but with quite different interests and outlook, were the industrial artisans. At first only the printing trade seems to have had a workers' organization, and this looked back to the medieval *compagnonnages* rather than forward to trade unionism. Isolated events, however, pointed toward the future. Thus in 1862, at Intra on Lake Maggiore, the hat-makers met to discuss how they could fight the machines threatening to challenge their livelihood. In 1865 the unemployed wool workers at Arpino invaded one of the new factories to break up the textile machinery which was depriving them of work. During these early years the workers in railroad construction were particularly difficult to manage, especially in the South and on the forgotten island of Sardinia. But such local protest movements were less organized strikes than the natural reaction of semi-agricultural workers against the new and insecure conditions of an industrial revolution. The Sardinian peasants even attacked and demolished one of the first railroad stations, symbolic to them of a new bondage.

The habit of organization developed naturally out of innumerable secret societies and mutual-aid fraternities. Employees in the Sicilian flour mills had an embryonic kind of union and paid a subscription to a fund for sickness, old age, and military service. As with the dreaded mafia, it threatened millowners who did not employ its members, and as with the Venetian gondoliers, members were expected not to compete with or undercut each other. In Sicily and Naples, the mafia and *camorra* had considerable influence, and employers might have to purchase their good will. In the North, employers were better placed, and when the first Chambers of Labor were formed, these workers' organizations were sometimes dissolved and their leaders put on trial. The right of free association, though explicit in the constitution, was first curtailed, and then specifically abolished by parliament in April 1886. Socialism was already something to be feared and suppressed.

Garibaldi was by temperament a man of the extreme Left and naturally ranged himself with the socialists. At first he even adhered to Karl Marx's Socialist International. Though he repudiated the socialist doctrine which called property or inheritance theft, he believed in minimizing all social privilege. Like Mazzini he wanted a United States of Europe where wars and armies would be impossible, and he preached the brotherhood of all men whatever their color or nationality. At first he even regretted that he had not fought for the workers of Paris during the commune of 1871. In that year he wrote that a fourth estate was appearing which would one day include all workers in town and country and carry all before it. No wonder that, to the common people, Garibaldi symbolized the underdog. To them he was the man who, though unprivileged and self-educated, had risen to be on speaking terms with princes, and his picture decorated the humblest cottages as frequently as did portraits of pope and king.

Mazzini, too, always fought strenuously against the many inequities in Italian society. Most of the early socialists first became politically conscious as republicans under the inspiration of Mazzini. Many of his followers were able to think that he must have abandoned his own doctrines when he condemned the Paris commune and Marxism. Some socialists, for example Proudhon, opposed the unification of Italy as a dangerous piece of bourgeois deception, but to Mazzini national unification was a religious duty, whereas class struggle was something materialistic and horrifying. Too religious and mystical for the new revolutionaries, Mazzini by 1870 was old, ill, and still condemned to live in England as an exile. Once the nation was in existence his chief contribution to national history lay in the past.

Alone among the early Italian radicals, Pisacane was claimed by the socialists as a serious forerunner, but he was an isolated figure who died young and with few followers. The Russian anarchist Bakunin came into Italian life almost on Mazzini's introduction, and some years passed before he was a distinct political force of his own. Like that of Pisacane, Bakunin's socialism was atheistic and materialistic. Even though expelled by the Marxists from the Socialist International for being too independent and too individualistic, his brand of revolutionary anarchism continued until after 1880 to attract many of the extremists.

In 1874 Bakunin had instigated an abortive rising at Bologna which became the subject of a famous historical novel by Riccardo Bacchelli. Involved in this rising was Andrea Costa, a fiery revolutionary from Romagna who had seen the inside of French and Italian prisons. Costa's artisan friends founded a "Workers Party" distinct from the disciples of Mazzini and Bakunin. It was unrealistic and utopian, advocating a foreign policy of universal freedom and brotherhood, but Costa was persuaded by Depretis's extension of the franchise that parliamentary government might be workable, and in the elections of 1882 at Ravenna he became the first socialist deputy.

★

Republicanism and anarchism were strongest in Emilia, Italian Marxism in urban Milan. But the most revolutionary part of the kingdom was Sicily. Those few Sicilian deputies who moved among the rural poor knew that they were living on top of a volcano. Blind opposition to the tyranny of absentee landlords was superimposed on anarchic resentment against all government and an insular protest against a mainland which seemed to exploit Sicily as a conquered possession. The politicians in distant Rome, by their irresponsible breach with France, had ruined thousands of southern families. Wine, fruit, and sulphur, the chief exports of Sicily, were all gravely damaged. The sulphur industry was being defeated by American competition and by a new synthetic process for the manufacture of sulphuric acid. A hundred thousand people received their living from the mines, and when the price of sulphur fell from 140 to 60 lire a ton, many of these had to compete for agricultural employment in an already overpopulated countryside.

The gradual spread of education simultaneously contributed to making the rural South disaffected. As railways and roads brought more farm laborers more into touch with the towns, they became more conscious of their poverty, and their sons who returned from military service had learned elsewhere about higher standards of living. Then came the agricultural depression of the 1880s which pushed some of them to the point of starvation where they would have little to lose by revolt. Agrarian strikes spread after 1890 and, in some districts, were accompanied by violence and bloodshed.

The socialists were as little prepared for this peasant revolt as anyone. They were mostly middle-class intellectuals and were hardly convinced yet of the need to enlist the agricultural masses. Indeed they had reason to fear the conservatism of the *contadini*. Naturally they associated themselves with the Sicilian revolt once it had broken out and tried to explain it in their own terms, but Crispi was wrong in ascribing this outbreak to socialist initiative. Workers' groups or *fasci* had existed in the island for some years, and they had no need of socialist doctrine or organization to make them rise in hunger rebellion to reoccupy the communal lands which had been arbitrarily taken from them.

Giolitti realized as much. He commented in his memoirs that the movement was less serious than subsequent outbreaks, but the wealthy were not accustomed to this kind of struggle and mistook economic agitation for social revolution. Landowners had the ear of the government and were more easily organized than the peasantry. Their traditional remedy for agrarian unrest was exemplary repression, and a meeting at Caltagirone even decided that popular education should be prohibited because it left the poor dissatisfied with their inferior status. As Crispi himself was to find, the one change that landowners would resist by even illegal means was reform of the *latifondi*. They first tried to combine in refusing to employ members of the *fasci*, and then persuaded the magistrates that a strike was tantamount to a violent breach of the peace. Meanwhile there was news of refusal to pay excise duties, of telegraph wires cut, of attacks on town halls and customs houses: in one tragic episode the troops opened fire and ninety-two peasants and one soldier were killed. Politicians in Rome began to fear that an organized socialist revolution had broken out, and Crispi encouraged this illusion as an excuse to justify his return to power.

The Sicilian writers, Pirandello and Verga, showed more sympathy and understanding for the troubles of this unhappy island than did the Sicilian politicians, Crispi and Di Rudinì. Pirandello wrote of a peasant from his native Girgenti who, perhaps like many others in actual life, was quite unable to grasp the significance of the *fasci*: thinking only that they must be enemies of the community, he took arms against them and was killed by the very soldiers who arrived to suppress the movement. The novelist Verga knew even better at first hand the rustic Sicilians for whom the state meant little but oppression, yet for whom socialism would have been unintelligible and irrelevant.

★

The bloody outcome of this unrest led to questions in parliament and helped to upset Giolitti's ministry in November 1893. He had tried to keep order, but recognized the right to strike and hoped things would settle down of their own accord. But this was not good enough for the Sicilian landowners, and in Crispi they found a man who was on tiptoe for just such an occasion in order to pose as the national deliverer and divert attention from the exposure of fraudulence in high finance and politics. A dangerous run on the savings banks made a strong interventionist minister even more necessary.

Radical reformer though in some ways he remained, Crispi was unable to envisage that the origin of the rising might be found not in some contrived plot but in economic despair. Unlike Giolitti he never came near to understanding socialism, and while he exaggerated its dangers he was equally mistaken in believing that repressive measures would prevail against it. He told parliament that socialism was unpatriotic, indistinguishable from anarchism, and signified the end of all liberty, adding that the common people were "corrupted by ignorance, gnawed by envy and ingratitude, and should not be allowed any say in politics." When in opposition, Crispi had censured Depretis for inhibiting growth of party politics and an organized parliamentary opposition, but now that he was back in power he claimed to speak for the whole nation and the General Will. He condemned socialism for being a sectional party. He was credulous enough to believe that the Sicilian revolutionaries, as well as receiving money from the American consul, had signed a secret treaty with the Russians and were in league with France and the Vatican; hence that the request for more local self-government in the island was an unscrupulous intrigue to be resisted at all costs.

Such was the general panic that Crispi, in spite of his own implication in the bank frauds, despite even the recent elections which had returned a large Giolittian majority, obtained an overwhelming vote of confidence from the

Chamber by 342 votes to 45. These disorders had come opportunely to rescue his reputation and give him supreme power. Domenico Farini, who presided over the Senate, was genuinely convinced that this man was "the one moral force left in Italy," and when Crispi was told as much it went to his head. He replied that he was ready to rule without parliament if necessary; and the deputies, faced with such determination, meekly did as they were bid. A class of reservists was called up and fifty thousand soldiers were sent to Sicily, martial law being proclaimed as though a civil war were raging. Military tribunals were installed and given retrospective cognizance of offences committed over the previous year. When in January 1894 the marble workers of Massa and Carrara in the North attacked the local barracks, martial law was proclaimed there also.

For seven months these emergency regulations continued and eventually a thousand Sicilians were on the penal islands. It did not increase people's respect for Italian justice that the courts in July 1894 absolved those accused in the bank scandals who had made a public confession of theft; whereas Sicilians were imprisoned on mere suspicion and harshly sentenced. De Felice, a personal opponent of Crispi who had been elected in 1892 by a heavy majority, was given a severe sentence despite his parliamentary privilege of immunity. Crispi was also allowed exceptional powers to control the press and confine political suspects in *domicilio coatto*; and believing that socialism was the chief enemy he used these powers to dissolve the socialist party and prosecute its leaders. At his insistence a hundred thousand voters were disenfranchised. This seemed thoroughly illiberal and provocative, and his former friends of the *estrema* were dumbfounded that he had so far forgotten his own persecution before 1860 at the hands of another arbitrary government.

To rally support against this man, a "League for the Defense of Liberty" was formed at Milan, in which socialists, radicals, and left-wing liberals tried to forget their differences and stand, as Crispi himself had once stood, for liberty against oppression. This drove him still further to the Right. He even made some efforts to renounce his Masonic friends and anticlerical past in order to win clerical support, but the Vatican turned down his approach with scorn. Crispi, like Mussolini, was to learn that a strong man was welcome only while there was immediate peril of revolution or while he was surrounded by the prestige of success. His cry of "the country in danger" could not continue forever as a substitute for a constructive policy.

★

In December 1894, several months after Crispi's dissolution of the socialist party, there came a last flicker of the bank scandals, when Giolitti tried to stage a comeback by laying before parliament his famous *plico*, or bundle of incriminating letters, to prove Crispi's involvement. It was an unfortunate practice of Italian ministers to appropriate official documents when they left office, and Giolitti in particular seems to have carried off many personal details about other politicians whom he could then perhaps blackmail by the threat of exposure. This *plico* included letters from ministerial files, but also many of a personal nature which suggested that Crispi's private life had been under secret surveillance. For instance, there were a hundred letters from Signora Crispi as well as correspondence with Tanlongo, and references to large sums which Crispi and his friends had received from Tanlongo's bank. Giolitti's presentation of these documents to parliament reflected almost as much against himself as against Crispi, and they raised the awkward question of why Giolitti had concealed them from Mordini's inquiry. Too many people had an interest in stopping such disclosures, and powerful interests protested against statesmen continuing to blacken each others' reputations at a time when social unrest and a war in Ethiopia were threatening the country.

Crispi sensed and exploited this feeling. He first told the deputies that he would answer such grave charges, but the very same evening they were astonished to hear that the king had closed parliament after the shortest session on record. One pretext Crispi gave was that the House should not continue discussion while tempers were so heated. His real reason was that, since parliament still had a Giolittian majority, he intended to change the prefects and organize a new general election. Di Rudinì gathered some of the conservative deputies together to register a protest against his action. Further over to the Left, Cavallotti for the radicals and Zanardelli for the liberals drew the obvious conclusion that Crispi was artificially prolonging the state of emergency so as to distract attention from his own corrupt behavior. This belief was further borne out by the suspension of parliamentary government for the next six months, during which even some taxation had to be authorized by royal decree. All this time Crispi continued in office though he lay under the gravest suspicion, and the revelations of the *plico* could thus not be discussed until parliament was recalled in June 1895. His prorogation of parliament showed the grossest contempt for representative government, and it also implicated the king himself who had acted in full cognizance of the facts.

"At my age," said Crispi, "after fifty-three years of service to my country, I have the right to believe myself invulnerable and above all these libelous accusations." This was an astonishing claim. But some people took it seriously just because Crispi claimed to stand as a defense against socialism and anarchism. As he privately told Farini in December 1894, he had come to the conclusion that parliamentary government was not possible in Italy. But in the elections of May 1895 he managed to win about 350 *ministeriali*, including people from the Left, the Center, and even the extreme Right. Coercion on an unprecedented scale was required to give such a result, and two years later a parliamentary inquest into the finances of the ministry of the interior suggested that money voted for the relief of a great earthquake disaster in Calabria might have gone to his election fund. And yet one must assume that, had Crispi not suffered a military defeat in Ethiopia, he would have managed to consolidate his virtual dictatorship. The young journalist, Guglielmo Ferrero, commented that Italians admired Crispi's political courage and strength of will just because they lacked these qualities themselves; and Ferrero concluded that, since so many of the ruling elite liked his shameless treatment of parliament, Italians were not ready for liberty.

Crispi's methods now became increasingly imperious, and his private conversation suggests that his character and even his mind were weakening. In October 1895 he celebrated his seventy-seventh birthday. His advancing senility, lack of tact, together with the personal animus which separated him from Giolitti and Di Rudinì, and finally his invasion of Ethiopia, all these combined to cause his collapse. Grave and detailed moral accusations had been leveled at him publicly, to which he made no adequate answer. Many Catholics were frightened when his irascible nature led him into another contest with the Church over the appointment of bishops. The conservative liberals did not forget that he had been the enemy of Cavour. The Left feared his authoritarianism and his aristocratic pretenses—the daughter of this ex-redshirt married a prince in 1895—and he contemptuously criticized those deputies who neglected to wear the traditional top hat and frock coat. The five socialist deputies elected in 1892 were increased to fifteen in 1895. All Crispi's personal enemies were back in parliament—Cavallotti, Colajanni, De Felice, Costa, and Imbriani—and there had been many previous examples of a large government majority dissolving almost overnight.

Above all there was the fact that Italy was once again overspending her income by a large margin, yet Crispi wanted to incur even more expense on a campaign in Africa. He even said in private that a military success was required in order to prevent the united nation from splitting up. A coalition was therefore forming against him of those who wanted less financial extravagance, together with those who thought money should be spent on colonizing Italy rather than Africa, those who wanted to fight for the Trentino rather than for Abyssinia, and those Milanese who resented the "southernization" of public life. Wealthy citizens might appreciate Crispi as a protection against social disorder, but were to turn against him when he asked for sacrifices to make Italy a major colonial power, and they mercilessly overthrew him when he led them to military defeat in Ethiopia.

24 The Ethiopian War and the Eclipse of Crispi

After the failure to occupy Tunisia and Egypt in 1881–82, the prospects for Italian colonization in the Mediterranean were poor. Libya was still "unoccupied," but it looked like an unpromising desert and several opportunities had been missed for securing international recognition of Italian interests there. In 1882 a first colony was established on the coast of the Red Sea where there was less chance of clashing with other European interests. Considerations of prestige were thought to demand expansion somewhere, and, unprofitable though this particular venture might seem, it was possible to find reasons which, if sophistical and contradictory, were felicitous on the tongue. It was said that Italy must escape from her "imprisonment in the Mediterranean," or alternatively that the "key to the Mediterranean was in the Red Sea." The realities of geography were thus obscured by rhetoric.

This Red Sea settlement dated from the time when the Rubattino company set up a small commercial station at Assab. Cairoli had to state that there was no intention of establishing a military post, but his successor, Depretis, hoped to persuade other countries that this port should be held by a friendly power which could control the traffic in slavery and arms smuggling. In June 1882 it was proposed to the Chamber that Italian sovereignty be declared over Assab. Some of the more independent deputies objected that the Red Sea was remote and profitless; but now that national pride was involved, few parliamentary leaders were rash enough to damage their political future by committing themselves to a policy of dignified withdrawal while it was still possible.

The acquisition of this port was soon said to demand the occupation of the interior in order to ensure its safety. The Triple Alliance worked in the same direction by encouraging Italy to look away from the Austrian frontier and seek compensation elsewhere. When the Khedive of Egypt decided in 1885 that he could no longer keep a garrison at Massawa (another port further up the Red Sea), Italy sent an expedition thither, trusting that the British would welcome Italy's presence as a background support of their campaign against the Mahdi in the Sudan. Mancini reassured the Chamber with his phrase about the Red Sea being the key to the Mediterranean, but Mancini was a lawyer not a politician and never explained the meaning of this extravagant hyperbole.

Mancini's geography was otherwise at fault, for he ordered a sortie from Massawa to Khartoum as though it was but a few miles' journey through friendly country. The defeat by the Mahdi of the British general Gordon then left Italians alone in a hostile country. Commercial stations were soon in need of increasing military support, and this involved Italy with the tribes of Ethiopia as well as the dervishes in the Sudan. The colonial venture which had begun with the Mediterranean in mind was thus compelled to change direction.

In 1887 a rash decision was taken to move the troops from the feverish coastal area to more healthy quarters in the interior highlands. At once Negus John of Ethiopia became alarmed. Already in Massawa and Assab he had lost two natural outlets for the northern provinces of his empire, and he was justifiably sensitive lest this new move should conceal a design on his country's independence. Twenty years earlier the British had sent a successful expedition against Negus Theodore, but never intended to stay because they calculated that such an enterprise would involve much expense for little return. Italy, on the other hand, did not count the cost until too late and underestimated the strength and intentions of her opponent, as she also overestimated the possible gains in commerce and prestige.

Inevitably, the usual "incidents" took place in the indeterminate frontier region. Di Robilant, the minister for foreign affairs, spoke in a classic phrase of sending a punitive expedition against "two or three robbers," and made no allowance for the fact that the same kind of nationalistic pride which drove Italy to conquest might also be inspiring other people to defend themselves. The result was that in 1887 a column of five hundred Italian soldiers was surprisingly destroyed by Ras Alula at Dogali.

This dealt a wounding blow to Italian morale, especially as France had to be asked for help in transporting reinforcements. Worse still, Italy was thereby drawn ever further into a war of conquest. Amid unruly scenes, the Chamber approved an aggressive policy by 332 votes against 40. Approval was given to increased military appropriations, and the minister of war provocatively spoke of putting several million men under arms. As Crispi told Bismarck, "duty" would compel him to revenge. "It will be a war of little importance," he wrote in his diary, "and it is a war we cannot avoid." He claimed to have no idea of permanent occupation, "yet we cannot stay inactive when the name of Italy is besmirched." Bismarck's comment was that Italy had a large appetite but poor teeth.

One minister chose to resign rather than accept Crispi's argument, but Crispi, undeterred, threw himself further into Ethiopian domestic politics. He first suborned the most important tribal chieftain, Menelik, King of Shoa. The poet Rimbaud was for a while engaged in gunrunning for Menelik, and saw more clearly than the Italians that this ambitious local chieftain was an excellent businessman who knew exactly how to profit from any conflict between Italy and the Negus. For awhile fortune seemed to be with Italy, since Negus John was killed by the dervishes in 1889, and Menelik, who was John's son-in-law and claimed descent from Solomon and the Queen of Sheba, succeeded to the Ethiopian imperial throne with Italian support.

Six weeks later, Menelik signed the Treaty of Uccialli which was interpreted by Rome as giving Italy a virtual protectorate over his empire. Menelik had merely wished to secure formal Italian support against possible pretenders, but misinterpreted by Crispi this treaty gave Italians a false sense of confidence. Italian arms were sent to the new emperor, and Crispi ordered the further occupation of Asmara in the interior. This allowed him in January 1890 to proclaim the existence of the first Italian colony, which he called Eritrea. At once most of the other tribal leaders joined Menelik against their common enemy at Rome. It was also discovered that the Amharic text of the treaty made no mention of an Italian protectorate, for the copies in each language had not been properly checked against each other. Yet, ironically, this contested claim to protectorship became something from which Italy could not back down without loss of face.

Crispi had gone characteristically from one extreme to yet another. As a righteously indignant member of the Pentarchy he had once objected to the Red Sea venture and spoken against the annexation of Assab and Massawa, yet he now outdid all others in his imperialistic zeal. In a dangerously false analogy he recalled how easily Garibaldi had conquered Naples with very slender means. A colonial war, he believed, would be good for the prestige of Italy and of himself, and by providing a counterattraction to irredentism would also reinforce the Triple Alliance. He therefore informed the *Almanach de Gotha* that the name of Ethiopia would disappear from the map, and a new silver coinage was struck in anticipation with Umberto wearing the imperial crown.

Parliament was still left in the dark. Little account was given to it of money spent on military provision, and when new grants were requested these were said to be only for defense. The deputies continued to think in terms of a peaceful commercial colony, whereas Crispi was secretly committing the country to a prestige venture under a military governor with aggressive intentions.

★

It would be hard to discover any campaign undertaken with obscurer aims and methods than that which led to the defeat at Adowa. Opinion was divided, official policy inconsistent. Crispi wanted a protectorate over all Ethiopia. General Baldissera, the military commander at Massawa, wanted no more than the Tigre. Baldissera distrusted Menelik, and on his own initiative, backed by the minister of war, made contact with neighboring and rival chieftains. Crispi himself, on the other hand, relied on advice from Count Antonelli which directly contradicted information reaching the War Office.

Finali, a former minister and friend of Crispi, says that the cabinet was never once allowed a full discussion on the colonies while he was in office between 1889 and 1891. Apparently, the cabinet did manage to overrule Crispi when he wanted to occupy Asmara, urging the financial, political, and military reasons against it, and adding that the Italian people were absolutely against making sacrifices for what they saw as neither glorious nor useful. But ministers were surprised to find in August 1889 that, despite their decision, the occupation had taken place. Such were the devious workings of the Italian constitution.

Among other politicians, Giolitti and the finance minister Sonnino opposed any increased expenditure on Eritrea, while Blanc the foreign minister wanted a purely defensive war, and another minister, Saracco, advocated abandoning even Massawa. Opposition came from the patriotic irredentists who disliked colonial wars and from industrialists in Milan who (apart from those engaged in armaments) saw no profitable market or investments in Ethiopia. Above all there were imperative financial arguments, for the government was spending each year a hundred million lire more than Italy could afford out of revenue. The veteran statesman Jacini, who had been a minister with Cavour, spoke up for common sense. It was vain, he said, for Italian newspapers to magnify the promising future of East Africa, and the only arguments they could find were mere phrases and generalities. Other people highly placed in politics and the services were even beginning to say that a minor reverse in Africa would not be unwelcome as a salutary check on this overmighty premier.

The Italian political system discouraged the formation of a large opposition party which could focus these dissentient voices. The conservative leader, Di Rudinì, was unenthusiastic about East Africa and wanted the military budget reduced by at least thirty million a year, yet he felt that the nation could not back down altogether without losing face. When he succeeded as prime minister in 1891 he had sent a parliamentary commission to Africa, but unfortunately it merely recommended no surrender of positions already held. On Baldissera's advice, Di Rudinì chose to support the Tigre faction against Negus Menelik, but then his successor Giolitti returned to the old alliance and so gave Menelik every reason to distrust the changeableness of Italian policy. While both prime ministers were agreed on preventing any further penetration inland, neither was bold enough to draw back, even though military experts on the spot advised that the inland plateau should be evacuated if no further advance was in view.

One explanation of Crispi's return to office in 1893 was that some people objected to Di Rudinì's project for economies on the army. The generals, the armament manufacturers, the king, the enthusiasts for the Triple Alliance, all were agreed on this point. Farini, who was one of the most important and influential politicians in the country, believed that the army should be strengthened for it might be needed against lower-class unrest, and "the army is the only cement which holds the country together." A strong military state had to be created as "a *sine qua non* of Italy's continued existence," wrote Farini. General Cosenz went one better and told the king that the army would become demoralized if it was not given a war to fight.

Crispi realized that a warlike policy in Africa offered him a last chance of political success. An expansionist policy was therefore resumed and the Tigre occupied. Subsequent recriminations make it difficult to trace responsibility for this. Co-ordination between Rome and Massawa was so bad that Crispi could accuse Baldissera's successor of first occupying Adowa against orders, and then of retiring once the home government had become convinced of the need to stay. General Baratieri occupied Kassala in the Sudan, though Crispi confessed that the government's financial situation made this inadvisable, and the critics then blamed the occupation on the general's personal pique after some subordinate had won a minor military victory in his absence.

Crispi for his part went on refusing demands from his generals for money and supplies, while still inciting them to strong action. He explained to them that public opinion insisted on colonies paying for themselves, and reminded Baratieri how Napoleon used to pay for his wars with money extracted from the people he had conquered. This was not wise. Unfortunately Crispi did not want to ask parliament for funds until he could pose as a triumphant conqueror. Yet financial anxiety prevented him from properly reinforcing his generals and so made this sought-for triumph impossible. Giolitti was later able to criticize the inadequate provision of food, clothing, medicine, and arms. He pointed out how

> Crispi's second ministry completely changed our colonial policy, occupying both Kassala and Tigre, forcing the local ruler of Tigre into alliance with the Negus, and inviting the joint opposition of a united Abyssinia and the dervishes. This policy was wrong and its execution even worse. One part of the ministry wanted war, the other just allowed the drift into war while refusing the means necessary to win it. On top of all this there was incredible incompetence in the organization and military direction of the enterprise.

The critical moment came at the end of 1895. Menelik with his Italian-made arms won a small victory at Amba Alagi against heavily outnumbered advanced units of the main Italian forces, and Crispi, who had chosen to disregard military advice over the question of reinforcements, now taunted his commanders with incapacity and cowardice. Politicians in Rome still seem to have been more preoccupied with what terms they would impose than with planning for victory. Crispi had accepted a personal responsibility by his constant provocation of the Ethiopians. He rashly continued to call them rebels who somehow owed allegiance to Italy. He went on thinking that it was a simple colonial war in which the Italians could not be beaten and which therefore did not need serious preparation. He also continued to deceive parliament into permitting further military appropriations by saying that these troop movements were purely defensive, and by insisting that the Ethiopian war would turn out to be a profitable investment.

But he should have chosen another man to taunt with cowardly inactivity than General Baratieri, a man who had been in Garibaldi's Thousand, who was rash as well as incompetent and apparently quite capable of carrying out a blind advance without proper calculation. Suspecting that Baldissera was sent to supersede him, Baratieri tried for a quick success and marched in four badly integrated columns to Adowa. Far from his base at Massawa, with no accurate maps, with thoroughly ineffective intelligence, he led six thousand men to their deaths in a heroic but hopeless engagement. In one single day, nearly as many Italians lost their lives as in all the wars of the *risorgimento* put together.

★

This defeat concluded Italy's first attempt to conquer Ethiopia. Troops were withdrawn and an indemnity paid. The silver coins bearing Umberto's head were melted down and the Ethiopian currency was still to be that bearing the face of the eighteenth-century empress Maria Theresa. In 1897 Kassala was ceded by Italy to Britain. The colony of Eritrea was retained, but the Red Sea was evidently not a key to the Mediterranean. As Di Rudinì told his constituents in March 1897, they had spent five hundred million lire in exchange for bitterness and disillusion. Eritrea was unsuitable as a colony of settlement because of its climate, and instead of paying for itself would devour money; instead of increasing Italy's prestige it had already diminished her reputation in Europe. She had wanted an empire, and had acquired at great expense a desert.

The setback in morale was even more important. General Baratieri hinted at cowardice on the part of his men, hoping thereby to excuse his folly in allowing them to be so hopelessly outmaneuvered and outnumbered; and unfortunately his remark was published in Rome. The general also blamed the government for not giving him enough supplies at the same time as they jeered at him for his reluctance to fight. Baratieri was brought to trial, like General Ramorino and Admiral Persano before him, and though acquitted it was in terms that branded him with incapacity and reflected poorly on the government which had chosen him. Crispi did his best to calumniate this general, yet the official Green Book, despite the "loss" of telegrams from the files, showed that the prime minister was equally at fault. Adowa was a political rather than a military defeat, and the responsibility was Crispi's for thinking that such a war could be won, that it was worth winning, and could be won cheaply.

For the Italian people, this public washing of dirty linen was particularly painful. In a more just perspective they might have looked on Adowa as the British looked on defeats at Khartoum or Isandhlwana, but they were in no mood to balance passion with realism. They had been persuaded to accept war as a test of nationhood and therefore suffered a psychological trauma for which the rest of Europe was one day to suffer.

The news of Adowa reached an Italy already tense with panic over social revolution and political jobbery. The country had turned desperately to a strong man but he had produced only disaster. Jacini called Crispi a megalomaniac, and it was inevitable that many others would blame their leader's futile exaggeration of prestige and national dignity, his lack of foresight or restraint, and his dangerous approximation to military dictatorship. But some of the criticisms were directed less against Crispi's authoritarianism than against his failure to succeed. Some people, Carducci among them, still hoped in 1896 that Umberto would confirm Crispi in office again so that Italian honor could be satisfied in a yet more extravagant campaign, and Crispi himself remained insanely confident. Queen Margherita would have stood by him for she believed in both his "Africanism" and his application of martial law at home. It was noted that the queen and Crispi both refused to contribute to the religious mission which collected money for the Italian prisoners held by Menelik, cruelly alleging that a virile race should liberate its own kin by force or not at all.

Mercifully, these fine sentiments were too rarefied for ordinary citizens. Fortunato called Adowa a well-merited and salutary defeat for a second-class power with grandiose ambitions, and Italy's simultaneous pursuit of prosperity and *grandezza* seemed to him ridiculous. Popular feeling had even led to railroad track being torn up to prevent the embarkation of troops. Italians had been heard to cry "long live Menelik," and the mayor of Milan publicly asked the government to retreat from an enterprise which so much damaged Italy's good name and commerce.

Fortunately King Umberto, who in general approved of the authoritarian-ism, the imperialism, and the pro-German bent of Crispi, was not so close a friend as to let the prime minister continue in office and he was dismissed even before parliament had time to give its views. The same deputies who had applauded Crispi's aggressiveness now witnessed his collapse with little pity, and there was even a call for his impeachment. Finally, in 1898, they officially censured him for his involvement in the bank scandals—the first example of such an outright parliamentary condemnation in Italian history.

Boldness, patriotism, and energy could not make up for Crispi's weaknesses of mind and temperament. He had taken so much power and tried to run so many departments that checks and balances were lacking. Social unrest had become exacerbated, parliamentary government less efficient, and socialism stronger, all unintended results of his premiership, and nationalism had been purposely and dangerously activated. At the age of nearly eighty he left politics unwillingly and had to watch the reversal of all he had stood for. Socialism and Catholicism were now to become stronger in public life, government more tolerant, foreign policy less anti-French, and colonial policy less influenced by considerations of dignity.

In his time Crispi had contributed much to the making of Italy and to the rallying of left-wing radicals to the Crown, and some people felt guilty that he was allowed to die in disgrace. To some liberal historians such as Croce his period of office was disastrous, a break in the normal liberal development of the country. But others were to call him a hero and demonstrated that, far from being a hiatus in Italian history, these few years of aggrandizement and megalomania were by no means wholly unconnected with the earlier traditions of the *risorgimento* and the nationalist fervor of a later generation.

25 Parliamentary Government Endangered, 1896-1900

The obvious successor to Crispi would have been Giolitti, an unenthusiastic colonialist, unopinionated, undemonstrative in domestic policy, and anxious to curb the military and germanophile proclivities of the Court. But Giolitti's attitudes toward tax reform and social reform were too liberal for the parliament elected in 1895. It was a time of emergency, and the king ran true to form in turning to another military leader. General Ricotti was asked to form a nonpolitical cabinet, and chose to take junior office himself under the Marquis di Rudinì, who became premier for the second time.

This brought a welcome sense of relief. A decree of amnesty was published for many Sicilian dissidents who had been re-elected to parliament and a special commissioner was appointed to carry out emergency reforms in the island. Ricotti resigned as minister of war because he wanted the army reduced from twelve corps to eight, a proposal that the king vetoed. The left-wing liberal, Zanardelli, joined the cabinet later in 1897 in order to broaden the ministerial majority. In so far as party labels meant anything, the cabinet included five men of the Right and six of the Left, so there was not much chance of its agreeing on any constructive or forceful policy.

The problem of social disorder was the most urgent of all, as it was also the most difficult for a cabinet of such variegated composition. Contemporary newspapers in 1896-97 tell of the cabmen at Rome and Naples going out on strike against the new streetcars, of a monetary crisis that sometimes led to wages being paid in kind, of people in Sardinia eating grass and dying of hunger, and of fifty arrests at Ancona for pillaging the municipal granaries. In the past twenty years the contrast between riches and poverty had become more conspicuous. Protests were made in parliament against Italian children being exported to work in French factories. We hear again of town halls and local customs houses being burned, of peasants moving to occupy the land on the large grazing estates of the Agro Romano, and of anarchists planning to assassinate the king. On one occasion the minister of education, Gianturco, was mobbed by the students at Bologna and could escape only when soldiers arrived to take over the university. In Rome university the army had to garrison the lecture rooms before professors could lecture undisturbed.

In the face of this turbulence, and especially after successes by the extreme Left in the elections of 1897, Di Rudinì had no plausible social policy. Few politicians since 1861 ever had time to wonder how far a regime of liberty was possible while some people were near to starvation, though in fact the future of parliamentary government depended upon this emergent proletariat being somehow made less revolutionary. The best answer to bread riots would have been to suspend the local excise on grain and flour which was so cruel an imposition in a time of rising prices, but any coalition cabinet risked a split if it proposed such a measure. When at last Di Rudinì dared stand up to the vested interests behind this excise, it was too late.

★

Peasant unrest and an increase in the parliamentary *estrema* went along with the development of Marxist socialism among some of the city workers. Socialism found fertile ground in a new urban society which developed alongside industry under the protection of tariffs. After centuries of relative stability, the leading towns in Italy had once more been expanding as surplus rural population was gradually persuaded to work in the new factories. The population of Milan was under 200,000 in 1871; within a few years it overtook that of Turin and Rome, and by 1921 was over 700,000. Turin doubled its size to 500,000 in the same fifty years. Urban expansion was hectic, and any economic recession would provide material for socialist propaganda among this developing proletariat.

But the tardiness of Italy's industrial revolution meant that socialism was at first more an intellectual than a proletarian movement. At Milan in 1891, Turati, Bissolati, and other socialists who frequented the salon of Anna Kulishov, founded the review *Critica Sociale*, which was to have considerable importance in educating the next generation. Antonio Labriola's lectures at Rome university dramatically and cogently introduced Marxist materialism to the educated world. And on a less intellectual level the humanitarianism associated with Garibaldi and Mazzini influenced some of Italy's foremost writers. The poet Pascoli had gone to prison in 1879 for his propagation of socialist doctrines. De Amicis who was the most widely read Italian novelist, the writer Ada Negri, and the composer Leoncavallo were all sympathizers. The brilliant lawyer, Professor Ferri, was converted in the early nineties. Lombroso the criminologist, Ferrero the historian and sociologist, and for a while Pantaleoni the economist and Benedetto Croce the philosopher, were all influenced by socialist ideas.

For many people socialism came to replace a sense of disillusion and emptiness, to inject greater realism and fruitful controversy into political life. The conservative Villari wrote in the *Nuova Antologia*:

> socialism has faith in itself; it has order and discipline; and what is more, it fights with a program of its own, while other parties lack such a program and are mainly varied groups characterized by the personality of their leaders rather than by an agreed program. . . . Socialism is not only held as a belief by the most cultured and civilized part of the country, but everything is contributing to favor its progress.

Likewise Croce later wrote about this same period that "socialism conquered all, or almost all, the best minds in the younger generation. . . . Indeed to remain uninfluenced by it, or to assume, as some did, an attitude of unreasoning hostility toward it, was a sure sign of inferiority." Marxism acted as a tonic on the decadent liberalism of the 1890s, and as a purgative which eventually overwhelmed the outmoded radicalism and republicanism of the Left.

Some of the old-guard radicals remained in the front line. Cavallotti, for instance, the most combative leader of the *estrema*, wrote pungent articles which helped to make *Il Secolo* for a time the most powerful journal in the country. Cavallotti was widely admired, a man who had fought under Garibaldi in Sicily, honest and polemical, poet and playwright as well as politician. He was essentially a radical yet far from socialism. In 1898, fighting his thirty-second duel, he was killed by the editor of a rival conservative newspaper who was fighting his fifteenth—the continuation of this primitive and grotesque method of controversy was a sure indication of retarded political education among the deputies. The disappearance of this romantic and generous figure symbolized the passing of leadership on the Left from the radicals to the socialists.

In 1892 the new Italian Socialist Party, or PSI, met for its first conference at Genoa. Its deliberations were a little unreal and pedantic, and already there existed a tendency toward debilitating divisions over hairsplitting points of dogma. The chief decision of the conference was to make a clean breach with the anarchists, and a composite program was then formulated, Marxist by inspiration but moderate in tone, to which both extremists and moderates might adhere.

A second congress at Reggio Emilia in 1893 tried with less success to define a socialist attitude toward the radicals. Ferri led one wing of the party which was ready to work with the radicals for social reform. Enrico Ferri was a political mountebank: handsome, eloquent, and vain, he was to change his mind many times before he ultimately flirted with fascism. Fillipo Turati was more of a realist, as he was also a patriot, a believer in gradualism, and above everything he put socialist party unity. After much debate the congress agreed to compromise over whether to collaborate with other parties in making parliamentary government work. It was decided that socialist deputies might sit in parliament but not vote for any bourgeois government.

Social reform found another champion from an unexpected quarter in Pope Leo XIII, during whose pontificate a group of Catholics appeared with the name of *La Democrazia Cristiana*. Leo in 1878 had condemned socialism as a deadly peril for the Church, as his predecessor had condemned liberalism; but in 1891 the encyclical *Rerum novarum* laid down that property should be more equitably divided and that workers' unions were not necessarily bad. The Church thus recognized more quickly than many liberals how important it was not to leave all the good tunes to the devil. Catholic laymen were still not permitted by the pope to vote, but were encouraged to intervene in more public affairs and began to organize very effectively at local level.

★

Although social reform eventually became almost respectable, the generation of Di Rudinì lacked the imagination or the will to put it into practice. The price of bread continued to rise, especially during the Spanish-American War, and a general economic crisis resulted from Crispi's expensive enterprise in Africa. Violence smoldered throughout 1897. Riots in January 1898 led to Rome being put for several days under martial law with troops posted at every street corner. In Parma the mob ran loose cutting telegraph wires and smashing the new electric lights. At Florence they broke into the Palazzo Strozzi where the Queen of the Netherlands was staying, and for one day virtually took over the whole town. A government circular of May 1898 complained that everywhere local authorities were invoking the aid of the army, and sooner or later this was bound to result in casualties. An extra class of conscripts was drafted. Colajanni spoke of tens of thousands in prison, and socialist deputies were camping inside the parliament buildings so as to avoid arrest. Worst of all, in May 1898 a violent clash took place at Milan. After two policemen had been killed in this city, General Bava-Beccaris turned cannon and grapeshot against the unarmed mob, mistaking a concourse of beggars around a convent for a revolutionary army. Eighty people were killed, and minor street fighting lasted for four days.

This tragic episode was, on very slender evidence, attributed to socialist machination, and hence a repressive policy was adopted. The unfortunate general, who had probably just lost his head, was misguidedly rewarded by the king with the Grand Cross of the Military Order of Savoy to signalize his courage and foresight. The *estrema* leaders at Milan, including the radical Romussi and the republican De Andreis, were arrested, together with Costa, Bissolati, and Anna Kulishov. Turati was sentenced to twelve years in prison although convicted of no more than spreading socialist propaganda. Railroadmen and civil servants were put on a military footing so that they could be punished under military law. The universities of Rome, Naples, Padua, and Bologna were closed; chambers of labor, village banks, and philanthropic associations were dissolved, together with some three thousand Catholic groups and organizations. The Milanese *Osservatore Cattolico* was suppressed, its editor being brought before a military tribunal, and among a hundred other newspapers suspended was the radical *Secolo*, though it had not supported the riots. Such procedure was legally irregular, politically inept, and suggested that the government had little understanding of this turmoil. It compared most unfavorably with the failure of the courts and the government to act against blatant examples of political and financial corruption among the rich.

Responsibility lay with Di Rudinì for this abrogation of constitutional rights. Not only was he prepared to use the army to enforce his domestic policy, but he again threatened to make financial appropriations by royal decree. But the king proved too timid and perhaps too sensible to give his ministers as much authority as the queen and others wished. When parliament met in June 1898, he refused to permit a dissolution. Di Rudinì therefore resigned without waiting for a parliamentary vote. He had played the *gran signore* too much to be popular at Court. He was also distrusted for his incongruous *connubio* with Cavallotti and Zanardelli. The conservative Visconti-Venosta had had to resign because of Zanardelli's anticlericalism. Zanardelli then resigned as a liberal protest against martial law. Transformism aimed at consensus and avoidance of divisive issues, but as soon as such a government was forced to act decisively, any coalition was almost bound to be shattered.

★

Once again, as in 1896, the king turned to a general for his next premier, and four other ministries were also placed under serving officers. Parliamentary opinion was not consulted in advance, for by a strict reading of the constitution the government was responsible not to parliament but to the king. General Pelloux nevertheless seemed an uncontroversial choice. Earlier in the year, when sent with full powers to restore order in Apulia, Pelloux had refused to proclaim martial law, for he appreciated that disorder did not arise from political rebelliousness but was a manifestation of extreme economic need. He was a conservative with liberal leanings, and he included in his coalition Fortis and Nasi from the Left Center. For seven months he governed as a liberal and refused to enforce Di Rudinì's repressive edicts.

Before long, however, Pelloux's training as a soldier and his parliamentary inexperience made him an instrument for those who advocated further strengthening the executive. As an army officer he was also subject to a direct order from the king in a way which other prime ministers were not. In February 1899 he introduced legislation to control public meetings and the press and to send political offenders to the penal settlements. When the more liberal members of the cabinet objected, he replaced them by Salandra and Di San Giuliano. Some of his opponents argued that Article 28 of the constitution explicitly guaranteed freedom of expression in the press, and indeed that the very creation of Italy had depended on this freedom as a means of educating people in patriotism. The Left urged that extraordinary powers should not be allowed save when requested by the judges, but the committee appointed to examine the bill in parliament modified its provisions to allow the executive even greater discretionary power. Still unsatisfied, Pelloux in June announced his intention of ruling by royal decrees without parliamentary debate. Never before had anything quite so extreme been suggested.

The promulgation of this decree-law forced the liberals into extra-constitutional action. Deprived by the censorship of normal modes of criticism, lacking party organization, without redress in the courts whose harsh sentences were undermining popular confidence in the judiciary, they fell back on obstruction in the Chamber and so forged a powerful but dangerous weapon. Zanardelli and Giolitti stood aloof at first from this obstructive policy, but the socialists Bissolati, Prampolini, and especially Ferri began to talk continuously through entire sittings, and when Sonnino in response proposed to introduce the same guillotine procedure which had been used to quell the Irish at Westminster, the opposition used the same filibustering in discussion of this procedural point. In a memorable session of June 1899, the Speaker, claiming to save the dignity of the House, suddenly declared that the debate was closed and the motion could be put. This arbitrary action provoked Bissolati and De Felice to overturn the voting urns. Pelloux thereupon arrested them and closed parliament for three months; and Costa when he protested against this closure was arrested himself. The socialist town council at Milan was also dissolved and replaced by a nominated royal commission.

The conflict then shifted from parliament to the higher courts. The *Corte dei Conti*, which had the right to register all government edicts, had already made certain reservations about the decree-law, and in February 1900 the high court of appeal declared it an unwarranted act of the executive. This was a notable decision, and Pelloux had to accept it if he did not want to carry out a *coup d'état*.

For another month he fell back on trying to alter the parliamentary regulations and restrict freedom of debate. At the end of March 1900 he once more attempted to cut short the interminable discussion and win parliamentary sanction for his decree-law. But rather than be party to such a violation of usage, the extreme Left walked out of the Chamber. Paradoxically, it had so far been the "anticonstitutional" groups of the *estrema* which had defended the constitution in these two years since martial law was declared at Milan. But in April 1900, Zanardelli declared that he and the Left Center would also withdraw from parliament rather than countenance such despotic governmental action.

This strike by the parliamentary opposition resembles that secession of the "Aventine" liberals which twenty-five years later was to present Mussolini with a path toward absolute power. Had Pelloux been so minded, he might have arbitrarily altered the standing orders and then used his large majority to pass any measures he fancied, but in fact he had sufficient belief in liberal and parliamentary methods to put his case to the electorate. No doubt he hoped that a general election would confirm his policy and give him a mandate for more forceful behavior.

The alliance against Pelloux was an important development. Until now, radicals and republicans had been reluctant to band together in parliament, but repression gave them a common experience and persuaded even socialists of Turati's faction not to be wholly intransigent. Indeed the socialist congress of 1895 agreed to support the more progressive liberals even to the point of voting for them on the second ballot in elections, and in 1898–99 the sixty-seven deputies of the *estrema* welcomed the aid of enlightened liberal newspapers. The important liberal-conservative daily, the *Corriere della Sera* of Milan, moved into opposition against Pelloux as it had also opposed Crispi in Africa—this was another big difference between 1899 and what took place in 1922. Even some of the conservatives objected to Pelloux's attempt to start a colony in China, just as others objected that this attempt was such a failure. A useful weathercock was the young poet D'Annunzio who, elected deputy for the extreme Right, with theatrical exhibitionism ostentatiously crossed the floor of the House. "On one side of parliament," he exclaimed, "there are many people who are half dead, and on the other a few who are alive, so as a man of intellect I shall move toward life."

This strengthening of the opposition saved Italy from reverting to a pre-1860 type of government, as a similar alliance might have saved her from Mussolini in 1922. In the elections of June 1900 the representation of the *estrema* increased from sixty-seven to ninety-five seats. At Turin a socialist lost by only six votes against the ministerial candidate, but the ballot box was then found to contain ten more voting cards than the number of registered voters. D'Annunzio, now a candidate for socialism, failed to be returned as such (a lesson he took to heart), but at Milan a socialist defeated the same conservative Speaker of the House who had tried to invoke the parliamentary guillotine against the filibusters. Pelloux still had a majority but feared to push matters to extremes, and when the new Chamber gave him a majority of only twenty-eight, he chose to resign in June 1900 so as to give the king a chance to find a stronger coalition.

Pelloux had stirred up an enormous amount of ill-feeling without being prepared to introduce that emendation of the constitution which some of his friends advocated. Sonnino and others were discussing the merits of a Bismarckian type of chancellorship, or possibly returning to the pre-Cavour tradition of strongly monarchical government. But here the conservatives were being dangerously radical. Indeed such suggestions had the perhaps unintended effect of undermining confidence in parliamentary government of any kind.

★

Unfortunately, this episode had involved the monarch in political controversy, and cries of "down with the king" were heard from deputies in the Chamber. Pelloux's resignation revealed the fact that King Umberto had kept no contact with Giolitti or other possible premiers from the opposition. Being unfettered constitutionally in his choice of a successor, the king again departed from precedent and chose another member of the Upper House, a characterless septuagenarian from Piedmont, Senator Saracco. A few days later Umberto was assassinated by a former emigrant, Bresci, who had been chosen by anarchists in the United States to avenge the deaths of those shot by the army in Milan.

In a sense King Umberto had been the victim of the ultras who sought a more authoritarian mode of government. He himself had taken no public initiative in this movement, though he was certainly intervening more actively in politics and Queen Margherita was notoriously a bigoted conservative who could not abide even the moderate liberalism of Zanardelli. In choosing two senators as premier, Pelloux and Saracco, the king had shown no regard for the recognized leaders in parliament. Admittedly the royal right of veto on parliamentary resolutions had never been used, but the issuing of regulations by royal decree had again become general practice in the nineties. Moreover the king, who was theoretically a "sacred" person above political conflict, had allowed himself to be involved (not merely through his ministers) on one side of a struggle which divided the nation.

Umberto was recognized to have a special prerogative in foreign and military policy, and the Triple Alliance was thought to be largely his handiwork. This made him unpopular not only in circles which wanted to cut the military budget, but also among irredentists who opposed Austria. Zanardelli's project to form a government in 1892 had failed because the king refused to have the irredentist General Baratieri as foreign minister, and the fact that this refusal was in response to a request from Austria made it doubly unacceptable. After Adowa, Umberto had further insisted that Di Rudinì should not yield to the demands of the victorious Menelik because "neither I nor the army will stand for it." Di Rudinì's minister of war had also been overruled by the king when he asked for a reduction in the army.

Such actions hardly amounted to a plot against the constitution for existing constitutional law gave the king considerable latitude. Umberto lacked the strength of mind and perhaps also the intention to go as far as some monarchists wished. Moreover, what the monarchy had lost in prestige and popularity was in part to be recovered during the more peaceful and prosperous years which lay immediately ahead.

26   Defects in the Constitution

The assassination of Umberto ended a decade of violence and even some republicans joined in a testimony of homage to the dead sovereign. A more tranquil and prosperous age was coming. The rapid building of factories in the North was evidence of this. So was the growing habit of seaside vacations for the well-to-do at Viareggio, Venice, and Posillipo. A great tide of emigration was partially relieving country districts of the surplus manpower which had depressed standards of living and caused unemployment. The age of electricity had begun, the first automobiles were on the roads (Queen Margherita became a great enthusiast), and the first reinforced-concrete buildings were being constructed. *Giolittismo* was something new in politics, as *d'annunzianesimo* in literature. The age of Verdi was giving way to the age of Puccini—Verdi died in 1901, and it was a sign of changing times that the young Mussolini made a speech to commemorate the event.

★

In politics the most notable feature at the turn of the century was a sad derangement in parliamentary behavior. Now that forty years of history could be reviewed in perspective, it was clear that parliament had never been robust. Italy had not been able to assimilate or supersede the experience of France, England, and America by developing stable conventions of her own. Parliament had not succeeded in controlling corruption. Nor had the *Corte dei Conti*. In 1896, more bank directors at Turin and Naples were arrested for fraud, and it was found that Palermo had not published its municipal accounts for five years—a million lire could not be accounted for by the city treasurer who was another of Crispi's shady acquaintances.

Ever since 1860 the centralization of government had proceeded apace without a parallel development in representative institutions to ensure enough public criticism. Cavour had realized the dangers to liberalism inherent in the inevitable advance of mass democracy. He had foretold how the idea of equality, once assimilated into social habits and codes of law, might end in the centralization of power. Rattazzi, Nicotera, and Crispi were examples of this leaning of radical democracy toward authoritarianism—even the great democrat Garibaldi had chosen to be a dictator during his only period of political rule.

There were similar tendencies latent on the Right. Di Rudinì and Sonnino inherited from Spaventa and Ricasoli the notion that liberty should be imposed from above, which led to the idea that the government had a right to increase its powers and ignore or censure criticism. The menace of socialism in the eighties and afterward served to increase the intolerance and authoritarianism of those who felt threatened by class war, and to reinforce the pervasive sense of disquietude about parliamentary institutions.

The king and his ministers possessed a preponderance of power under the 1848 *statuto*. Not even Cavour had been able to set up adequate checks and balances. The judiciary was not clearly distinct from the executive, and through the minister of justice the government had wide powers of nomination and promotion of magistrates. There were few political forums outside parliament, no wide circle of newspaper readers, no well-developed party organizations. The Senate rarely showed independence and came to heel at the mere threat of nominating an *infornata* or "ovenful" of new senators. In the Lower House a skillful premier could usually build a temporary majority by the patronage emanating from the ministries of the interior and public works.

Crispi when out of office in 1886 described this exercise of influence:

In parliament a kind of bilateral contract is often made: the minister gives the local population into the hands of a deputy on condition that the latter promises the ministry his vote: the prefect and the chief of police are carefully

chosen in order to support this policy of collusion. ... There is pandemonium in parliament when an important vote is expected, as government
agents run through rooms and down corridors collecting votes and promising
subsidies, decorations, canals, and bridges.

Much power was exercised covertly through the practice of promising tariffs,
government contracts, and titles. Railways, roads, barracks, drains, and aqueducts would be built wherever deputies required them to assert their own
influence, and local interests thus placated would vote for government
candidates. The authorities bargained with the *camorra*, the mafia, the local
landowners, or the banks which owned the mortgages on so much property,
and thus they managed by persuasion or coercion to control many southern
electoral districts. A friend of the government who owned large estates might
easily be elected without so much as visiting his constituents.

On the relatively few occasions when a serious contest seemed probable, the
government would instruct the prefect which candidate to favor. A corollary
was that prefects would commonly be replaced by each successive administration: in the years 1886–96 Salerno had ten different prefects (this was Nicotera's
constituency) and Girgenti twelve. Opposition voters in the South were
sometimes arrested on trumped-up charges the day before the elections;
criminals could be released from prison to use their influence on behalf of the
official candidate (Crispi in private once threatened to release all the prisoners in
Sicily); and names of opponents were erased from electoral lists on the spurious
plea of illiteracy. Government servants—under which category came schoolmasters, university teachers, magistrates, and railroadmen—might be threatened with loss of employment or removal to some inhospitable post on the
islands. On average there were only some 4,500 voters in each constituency
around the year 1900, and in country districts it was not hard for the prefect to
find a majority.

If Depretis, Crispi, and Giolitti all created what was called a parliamentary
dictatorship, this was largely due to such electoral manipulation. Very seldom
indeed did any election lead to a change of government, for it was the
government which made the election, not elections the government. The very
regularity of this practice suggests that it evolved naturally out of the
constitution, and no doubt many Italians were glad to sacrifice electoral
freedom for the order, discipline, and "sense of the state" which they felt
themselves to lack. The instinctive insubordination of so many Italians thus
produced an equal and opposite trend toward authoritarianism as a corrective.
History had shown them that necessary reforms, in education or local
government for instance, might have to wait until an emergency when they
could be effected under plenary powers: whereas, under ordinary conditions of
parliamentary life, such reforms ran the risk of perishing stillborn for want of
consensus or the habit of give-and-take.

This nostalgia for authority was always present but submerged. Some of those who dared not inform against brigands or *mafiosi* must have secretly hoped that one day they could support law and order without being thought dishonorable or having to fear the penalties of private vengeance. In like manner, many of those taxpayers who defrauded the government of millions may have hoped that a more just and efficient fiscal system would one day make it possible to reduce taxation even at the price of making subterfuge impossible. In an even greater degree the poor knew that true liberty might come only from a strong central authority which curbed the overmighty landlords. As things were, trial by jury in the South, far from safeguarding liberty, was a normal means of perverting justice on behalf of some local magnate or camarilla whose interest the jurors dared not gainsay. By another paradox, the curtailment of "constitutional rights" might appear to some people the best guarantee of freedom. The deputies themselves connived at this process and would accord a government full powers so that reforms might be made; or alternatively the government would rule by decree and then ask to be acquitted retrospectively.

The reputation of parliament naturally suffered when the process of government could be thought of as a succession of administrative edicts which deputies could criticize but rarely overturn. Parliamentary prestige also suffered when the bank scandals revealed how much the deputies, who received no payment (and life at Rome was expensive), had been connected with the Banca Romana and so were possibly the mouthpieces of corrupt financial interests. Over a hundred deputies had been implicated in the misdeeds of this bank, and Crispi and Giolitti, together with other ex-ministers or future ministers, had been censured publicly for peculation.

It was particularly disturbing that deputies were not very widely representative. In 1895, to check the influence of vested interests, all government contractors and representatives of companies subsidized by the state were made ineligible for the Chamber, and no more than ten professors and ten magistrates were allowed in the House, any excess being removed by lot. One result was that half the whole number of deputies were lawyers. So far removed were these so-called representatives from the productive life of the nation that in 1900 only eight called themselves agriculturists and a dozen engaged in industry.

The practice of filibustering naturally lowered the dignity of parliamentary proceedings. Unseemly behavior by deputies during debate was much too common. The Speaker might on occasion be showered with paper missiles or worse and forced to suspend the session. One minister of marine was assaulted by an admiral whom he had retired on half pay. More than once there was a fight on the floor of the House, and the temperature of politics could be charted by the charges for broken desks and chairs. The newspapers naturally fastened on these scenes and on tales of parliamentary corruption as being more newsworthy than normal parliamentary business, and this too helped to lower deputies in popular estimation.

Toward the end of the nineteenth century the standard of speeches declined, in part because a widening electorate favored a more rhetorical and demagogic delivery. Speeches were too often declaimed toward the press gallery, and parliamentary journalists thus became a power in the land. A deputy rash enough to go on speaking after 7 P.M. might find that his pronouncements would receive no notice in the press and his dearest objective would be frustrated.

★

The chief limitation on the power of a man such as Crispi was the lack of cohesion among groups in his majority and the consequent succession of ministerial crises. Groups were customarily composed of clients acknowledging the same patron or of deputies representing some regional interest, rather than of men (there were no women in parliament) who accepted the same political principles. As Petruccelli remarked, "a gust of wind, and these leaves which call themselves deputies will be blown about and mixed up anew." A chance insult was enough to permit one group leader to work up an artificial excitement and force the prime minister to reshuffle his cabinet. This helps to explain how, in the seventy-four years between the granting of the constitution and Mussolini's accession, seventy different cabinets held office.

One interesting constitutional custom was that a prime minister would not normally wait for defeat in either House before resigning. In 1892 Crispi estimated that during the last thirty-two years there had been twenty-eight ministerial crises of which only six had been strictly parliamentary, and of these six not one had been resolved by giving power to the man most representative of the parliamentary majority. Ministries usually resigned without waiting for a parliamentary vote against them. Crispi claimed to be quite justified in this and had the audacity to say that the interests of the state might only be damaged by a vote in the Chamber.

The king was thereby left more free to choose a successor "unhampered" by a parliamentary decision. The outgoing minister knew that, if he resigned without a vote, he might later be allowed by the king to return in some new combination, or at any rate have a say in placing his friends in the vacant ministerial posts. His justification in thus sidetracking parliament would be that the Chamber, possessing no solid basis of party, seldom knew its own collective mind and seldom objected to the royal choice. Crispi accepted that "the king is not responsible before parliament but before the country;" also that "when the king turns against a ministry, he will conspire in parliament with the deputies whom he thinks most influential and organize a hostile movement." A previous king had certainly conspired against Cavour, Minghetti, and Ricasoli, and almost certainly on other occasions where documentation is not yet available. Crispi had good reason to know this procedure at first hand.

Because of the absence of well-knit parties, politicians were normally powerless in opposition. Crispi and Giolitti when out of office took care to avoid taking an active part in political life and made little attempt to build up an organized party. It suited their interests to remain uncommitted so that they would have more scope when their turn to build a coalition came again. Crispi seldom effectively disciplined his followers, perhaps because he knew the absurdity of trying to impose political discipline; or perhaps he preferred to be free to profit from the continually shifting balance inside parliament.

Every government was a coalition, for no group was powerful enough on its own. This usually meant that when any division of principle emerged, it was driven underground in order to prevent the majority breaking up. For example, the condition of the poor scarcely seemed a subject for profitable debate in a cabinet that included Di Rudinì alongside Nicotera or Zanardelli. Relations with the papacy were likewise too delicate for the usual composite ministry. Individual ministers were usually sharply divided on the vital question of colonies and on military expenditure, yet resignation on such issues was infrequent. More disastrous was to be the way in which half a dozen successive cabinets after 1919 avoided the issue of fascism while there was time to avert a *coup d'état*, and Italian parliamentarism thus dug its own grave.

The tacit agreement to submerge conflicts of principle hinders the historian in labeling political groups and pinpointing the significance of parliamentary debate. Many politicians refused to question military expenditure or the Triple Alliance, for they knew that they could hardly reach office against active royal disfavor and they also needed to avoid the hostility of the local prefect at the next election. The Catholics, if they had not held back from parliamentary life, might have acted as a healthy challenge, and this would have forced the anticlericals, from Turati to Zanardelli and Crispi himself, into a common alliance over a point of real substance. But without such a challenge, as Villari remarked in 1902, no feature of Italian political life was in fact more remarkable that the small amount of real change effected by the succession of one government to another. The political life of the country was therefore often unreflected in parliamentary proceedings. Although some parliamentary criticism was extremely vocal and sometimes physical, the critics came from a nonconformist fringe outside the game of transformism—they were lonely eccentrics such as Bertani on the Left, Villari and Mosca on the Right, or Garibaldi and the socialists who disapproved of the elitist Italian parliament almost as a point of principle.

The lack of great political issues was associated with a lack of the kind of party that could have manufactured a real or artificial conflict of ideas. The United States and Britain had in common a two- or three-party system, and this ensured—however artificially—that each problem was threshed out in the open and presented before the public as susceptible of alternative solutions. Among Italy's more important political theorists, Cattaneo and Mazzini had similarly believed in the formation of parties with a good organization, possessing members, membership subscriptions, and newspapers; and the more pragmatic De

Sanctis and Minghetti (also Crispi and Giolitti when not in office) spoke in general approval of a two-party system. But Cavour and most Italian liberals, despite their admiration of England, tended to believe that parties were factions which put sectional before national interests. Cavour set the fashion of believing that the art of politics was to find a coalition based on a highest common factor of agreement, obscuring where possible—or else absorbing—what was controversial. That this caught on was partly due to the danger from extremists, ultraconservative or republican, communist or fascist, who wanted to alter the whole basis of politics, and against whom the groups of the Center had to combine. Cavour at least knew how to use this method of group combination for the purposes of efficient government, and was brilliantly successful at preserving his majority while not shirking the controversies of the day. His successors copied his methods indifferently and with less political courage.

Political theorists justified this concept of "government by the indeterminate middle." They easily proved how even Mazzini and Cattaneo, for all their teaching, in practice lacked the first requisite of good party men, the readiness to yield on doctrine and tactics in order to maintain party cohesion. Italian politicians, it was argued, were too individualistic, too used to a clientelistic tradition, and so failed to form parties of any durability. Even when, as in 1898–1900, issues of great moment could no longer be buried, there were no organized parties which emerged to voice them, but only broad alliances containing a wide range of view. And between these broad alliances there was a lack of mutual respect and tolerance. A healthy parliament could hardly exist where one side attempted to alter the rules and suppress criticism, while the defeated side walked out of the Chamber after upsetting the voting boxes.

It was the socialist party which made the first serious attempt to cut loose from transformism. The socialists theoretically believed in discipline, dogma, and organized opposition, and therefore brought new life into political controversy. Before long, however, their own lack of internal cohesion revealed them as yet another example of the atomic individualism of Italian politics. It remained for the fascists to show how a party could discipline its members to achieve certain selected ends, and unfortunately fascism like socialism was pledged to rewrite the constitution of 1848. Parties and parliament evidently did not coexist easily in Italy. One may note that the same means of transformism and coalition were also used initially by fascism in order to conquer its disorganized opponents.

★

To remedy the defective working of parliamentary government a number of changes in the constitution were sometimes suggested, for instance strengthening the authority of the prime minister or the prerogatives of the monarch. Experiments were made with proportional representation, with single-member constituencies and *scrutine de liste*. The English system of three readings to a bill was considered as a replacement for the French system of committees and interpellations, and regulations for parliamentary procedure were changed successively in 1863, 1876, 1888, and 1919. But such experiments still left political behavior much as before and inhibited the development of an indigenous political tradition.

Experience convinced many people that they had to blame not only procedural and institutional deficiencies, but also what a famous editor of the *Corriere della Sera* called the "political immaturity of the country." Cavour had told parliament in July 1850: "Yes, gentlemen, I tell you frankly that, until our liberal institutions are animated by real political life in the smallest villages as well as in the largest cities, we shall never have a genuinely liberal system but be driven to and fro from anarchy to despotism like the French." Centuries of rule by tyrannical governments had greatly enfeebled native traditions of local self-government. Under the new system adopted after 1861, provincial and communal government was based on prefects nominated by the minister of the interior. The alternative, whereby elected councils were given more authority, would have meant that local cliques and camarillas merely reinforced their personal power with results that would have been partisan and inequitable.

The result suggested, once again, that only strong central government would check the countertendency toward anarchism or at least excessive individualism. Since there was corruption in the progressive city government of Milan as well as in the backward communes of the South, evidently democratic methods did not grow naturally in this milieu. A year or so after the Left had upset the voting urns in parliament, Mussolini's socialist father was arrested at Predappio when one of the customary election battles in the village had ended with broken ballot boxes. Given little incentive to take their share in politics, electors often abstained: the Rome elections in 1871 were an extreme case, when only a few hundred people took the trouble to vote.

Local self-government was not a program with much popular appeal. The chief aims of the general public were less for self-government than for security and prosperity. One result was that active politics became more professionalized. Instead of portfolios going to traveled men of culture such as D'Azeglio and Cavour or to philosophers like Gioberti and Balbo, office was regularly conferred on accomplished bureaucrats such as Depretis and Giolitti, or on lawyers who coveted the deputy's title of *onorevole* to help widen their legal practice. When Giolitti once quoted Dante in parliament, there was an audible gasp of astonishment at such unexpected breadth of culture—until someone pointed out that he must have lifted his quotation from some other speech he had found in the parliamentary records.

★

Complaints against the working of parliament had been heard ever since 1860. Cattaneo registered his protest by repeatedly refusing to take his seat. Mazzini was elected more than once, and his election arbitrarily vetoed by parliament itself, but he regarded the very restricted suffrage as a corrupt and bogus method of falsifying the general will of the people. Garibaldi ostentatiously resigned three times from the Chamber and notoriously believed in the quicker methods of dictatorship. Cavour alone of these great names was a great parliamentarian but he died without establishing sufficiently solid traditions of liberal government, and after him most notable political thinkers lacked his optimism about parliamentary institutions. The 1848 *statuto* was in practice stretched to cover monarchical paternalism, enlightened liberalism, parliamentary dictatorship, mass democracy, even fascism, but most of the suggestions heard in the eighties and nineties were for reform in an authoritarian direction such as Cavour would hardly have countenanced.

In 1882 Pasquale Turiello published a reasoned criticism of Italian politics. His argument was that government would continue to be paralyzed until the Crown could act more independently of an elected majority and of a chance decision by the electorate. Turiello used to apply Darwinian terminology to politics and spoke crudely of the "struggle for life" between nations and between elements inside a nation. He not only believed, but was apparently proud, that Italy was "the most violent and bloody nation in Europe," and he hoped that, with a strong hand to quell their natural factiousness, Italians could be piloted into another European war which would stiffen their moral fiber. Turiello was an early representative of a new right-wing school of nationalism, and his views are helpful for a true understanding of Crispi's Italy.

From a different standpoint there was the criticism of parliament made by Ruggero Bonghi, a disciple of Cavour who had translated Plato's dialogues and was much admired as a journalist and pamphleteer. Bonghi maintained that copying English governmental methods was anachronistic and unwise, since Italy still lacked a widespread political education, a sense of social responsibility, and a strong middle class. Like Croce among other Italian intellectuals, Bonghi took his views to the point where liberalism became not only distinct from but opposed to democracy. He recognized that parliamentary government in Italy had worked well only when Cavour had made himself almost a dictator. He agreed with Turiello that the gradual reduction of the king's discretionary powers had left the cabinet without one essential limitation to its authority, and pointed out that, while in England parliament had become an effective countercheck on the executive, in Italy this had not happened. His solution was for a stronger monarchy with a consultative privy council chosen for their ability to put national before group loyalty, and whose age, status, and reputation would enable them to strengthen royal authority and prestige.

Bonghi had once defended the practice of *trasformismo* in the hope, shared by Minghetti, that new parties would emerge once the unreal distinctions of Left and Right had disappeared. Regretfully he had to acknowledge that these hopes had been excessive since parties were still to seek, while petty egotism and ambition for office took the place of principle. The alignment of parliamentary groups bore little relation to political forces in the country, but was rather the product of corridor intrigue; and ministers conspired to parcel out offices by private and sometimes squalid backstairs compromises instead of putting issues honestly to the electorate for its criticism and sanction.

Largely in agreement with this diagnosis was another liberal, Gaetano Mosca, who lived to raise his voice against Mussolini but who was firmly opposed to the extension of democracy. Mosca not only criticized the practical workings of parliament but posed theoretical objections against it as a method of govern-ment. He concluded that, if the problem was to find the best governors, this was obviously not being solved by the existing representative system. The will of the people never expressed itself freely and honestly in electoral contests, for elections were always won either by the ministry or the local bosses. Mosca propounded the doctrine, which subsequently became a political cliché, that in every society there was a political class or elite in control. Formulas such as "the rights of man," "liberty and equality," or "votes for the people" were merely used by that class as a device to conceal its own supremacy. With the spread of democratic methods there would still be an elite, but it was one of demagogues and wirepullers instead of detached and liberal statesmen.

Vilfredo Pareto, the economist and sociologist, developed still further this concept of a ruling class. He suggested that the decadence of parliamentarism in Italy after 1876 had sacrificed the mass of the people to the interests of a small class of rulers, and this ruling caste, by incorporating any potential leader into the system, had been able to keep a monopoly of politics. Pareto's doctrine of the transformation of ruling elites was to become of considerable importance in the study of politics. If its chief exponents were Italians, this may have been due to the fact that the ruling class in Italy was narrow and more or less clearly defined. As this class was also receptive to new blood and new ideas, young revolutionaries such as Carducci and Nicotera, Crispi and Mussolini, were eventually drawn into it.

These critics agreed that parliament was not working as it should. Fortunato regretfully concluded that Italians were authoritarian by nature. In practice, the Chamber of Deputies had had virtually no say in the accession of Di Rudinì, Giolitti, Crispi, Pelloux, and Saracco. The conservative leader Sonnino asserted anonymously in an article published in 1897 that this fact should be regularized by a formal return to the original purpose and spirit of the constitution of 1848, so that cabinets might be made responsible not to a majority in parliament but to the king. He agreed with Bonghi that the dominance of the Lower House was an idea of foreign provenance without warrant in the *statuto* and without correspondence to Italian traditions and experience. As he saw it, "parlia-mentarism will kill liberty if we cannot oppose to the concept of collectivist tyranny the ideal of the liberal state."

Sonnino disagreed with Cavour and wanted a different system of checks and balances; and since parliamentary dictatorship had grown through the atrophy of the royal prerogatives, it might best be checked by their restoration. Some politicians took their opposition to democracy so far that they impugned the very principles of liberalism itself, but others sincerely admired parliamentary government in theory and were merely perplexed at its failure in an Italian context. Their plan to return from a parliamentary regime to what they termed a constitutional regime was, however, an abortive attempt to put the clock back. Umberto and Vittorio Emanuele III were not of the caliber to restore personal rule.

Parallel with this antiparliamentarism on the Right, there was a similar trend on the extreme Left. The anarchists were a small body but their importance was considerable. Exiled or imprisoned, sometimes without trial, they declared war on society and refused to collaborate in parliament. They were especially strong in the Romagna, as were also the residual republicans who shared their attitude of non-co-operation. The more extreme socialists and syndicalists also had theoretical objections to parliamentary government, and on the Left generally there was a tendency to think of parliament as a class institution from which no good would come. The great criminologist Cesare Lombroso saw as early as 1897 that universal suffrage might even undermine freedom rather than increase it. In his study on political crimes he concluded that "parliamentary government, which has with justice been stigmatized as the greatest superstition of modern times, offers ever greater obstacles to good government, since elected representatives, by their immunity from prosecution, obtain a freedom from responsibility which allows them to break the law with impunity."

Zanardelli on the Left Center was not so pessimistic as those on the extreme Left, nor did he join conservatives in wanting more power for the crown, for he mistrusted the monarchy and attributed the constitutional malaise rather to excessive royal power than to too little. He also recognized that representative institutions alone offered an adequate opportunity for new forces in society to penetrate the ruling elite. It was the sanity of men such as Zanardelli which tided over this difficult period in Italian history, and after him Giolitti, another moderate, worked out a new system of liberal parliamentary dictatorship which went further in accepting the aims and methods of democracy.

The many criticisms of parliament nevertheless created a dangerous impression that the constitution of 1848 could and should be altered. The belief gained currency that liberal democracy could not be so fine and might one day have to give way to something more virile and authoritarian. The more prosperous conditions after 1900 postponed any crisis of confidence, but only for a few years, after which the fascists were able to look back on Turiello, even on Pareto and Sonnino, as precursors.

SECTION SEVEN: GIOLITTI AND LIBERAL REFORM, 1900–1911

27 Liberal Government Resumed, 1900–1904

Vittorio Emanuele III had been born in 1869 in the presence of ministers, generals, and the mayor of Naples; he became king in July 1900, hymned by Pascoli and D'Annunzio; he survived the rise and fall of Mussolini, and died in 1947 as an exile in Egypt. He was not a great king. Physically delicate and deformed, he possessed an obvious sense of inferiority. His father and grandfather had both married their first cousins, and a fear that the dynasty might have become dangerously inbred occupied people's minds when in 1896 the young prince was married to the daughter of a Montenegrin chieftain. Up to the age of twenty he lived under the severe military rule of his tutor, Colonel Osio, and only twice a week was allowed to take meals with his parents. His was a soldier's education and it effectively suppressed any liveliness he might have possessed.

The new king's tastes were soberer than his father's. The royal stables were quickly dispersed, as were his father's mistresses. Queen Elena herself, so it was said, liked to prepare the family meals. Only on state occasions did they appear in the Quirinal palace, for the king preferred a private residence where his children could break windows and he himself could drive a nail into the wall without bothering about its cost to the national exchequer. His one great passion was for numismatics and he personally supervised a voluminous catalogue of Italian coins. As the English scholar Bolton King noted, already on his accession "he had the tastes of an old man or a bookworm."

This was no way to popularity, and Vittorio's prosaic, cynical and unsociable nature cut him off from the common man. He was served with loyalty, but was not greatly liked. When in 1904 his heir was born, the town council of Milan refused to fly the national flag from the cathedral. Nor was he even a good Catholic, despite the prayers of his pious mother and the instruction of his Irish governess, Elizabeth Lee. Indeed, he was the most anticlerical and unreligious of a generally anticlerical dynasty. He was appreciated neither by the "black" papal aristocracy, nor by the Left, nor by the *mondain* society which went on crowding the salon of the queen mother.

If personally he was not a great success, his common sense and modesty gave the throne a solid support, at least until his love of a quiet life allowed him to surrender Italy to the fascists. His father, in the years 1893–1900, had seemed to be trying to halt the liberal development of the constitution, and in successive ministerial crises had never consulted the liberal leader Giolitti or even answered his letters. The new king, too, was never friendly with Giolitti or indeed with any of his ministers, and Osio's papers show that Vittorio in his youth had been more or less contemptuous of parliament. But he did try not to seem committed to any political group and to avoid being tainted like his father with partial responsibility for an unpopular government policy. He even abandoned some of the constitutionally recognized methods of influencing his ministers, and was never to refuse when Giolitti requested a dissolution of parliament.

*

The conservatives had been slightly weakened by the elections of 1900. The elderly Saracco was hardly the man to keep a majority intact, and the king broke with his father's example in February 1901 by turning to the Left Center liberals under Zanardelli. There was no obvious parliamentary mandate for this, but since the old ministerial majority had been broken, it was for the king to find a new combination which could settle the country after the violence of recent years. Umberto's experiment in authoritarianism had not quelled disorder but increased it. Though the conservative Saracco had to some extent restored confidence and tranquillity, he had still relied too much on censorship, while police action, and his hostile attitude toward labor organizations provoked several paralyzing strikes. That the conservatives were by now on the defensive was shown by an article Sonnino wrote for the *Nuova Antologia* of September 1900, in which he moved away from his proposal to modify parliamentary government and instead advocated the union of "all national parties" to defend the constitution against the "so-called popular party."

Giuseppe Zanardelli, who had served under Depretis, Cairoli, Crispi, and Di Rudinì, took the premiership without any departmental portfolio, thus allowing considerable scope to his minister of the interior, Giolitti. He did not hesitate to include conservatives in his cabinet, for instance Prinetti the foreign minister, but was himself a staunch liberal, an anticlerical, and something of an irredentist. His weakness was that he had not learned, as Giolitti was to learn, that a prime minister without a firm party basis could afford the luxury of strong opinions only if they were such as would bring his ministry solid support in the country at large.

Zanardelli effectively succeeded in restoring the full practice of parliamentary government and the proper discussion of state expenditure. He reduced some of the more oppressive food taxes, and refused to follow Saracco in using the army to break agricultural strikes. When landowners complained in parliament that they would then have to do the ploughing themselves, they were astonished to be told that this was not a bad thing for it would teach them to pay better wages. An important objective was to convince the peasants that the government and the troops were not always an enemy of the poor.

Although Zanardelli succeeded in making the socialists break their rule and vote for a bourgeois government, he misunderstood socialism and underestimated its importance. He flouted the extreme Left by increasing military appropriations, and kept as minister of war General Di San Martino who had served in that post under the conservatives Pelloux and Saracco. The socialists shook his government by exposing how naval contracts were placed at absurd prices to keep up the profits of the Terni steelworks; and when their paper

Avanti described how these profits soared every time Admiral Bettolo was minister of marine, not only socialists were impressed.

Zanardelli was a theoretical liberal, not a trimmer of Giolitti's quality, and so could never forge many various interests into a sufficiently malleable coalition. Giolitti realized that a more subtle policy was required, and after two years in government chose to resign as soon as the scandal over armament production weakened the government majority. Zanardelli's proposal to introduce law permitting divorce also broke one of the tacit compacts on which coalition government depended. Giolitti resigned so as to free himself for being called in as Zanardelli's successor. Although he did not vote at once against the government, he took care not to involve himself in its growing unpopularity.

★

In November 1903, Giovanni Giolitti became prime minister for the second time. He had begun his career as a civil servant under the expert tuition of Sella at the ministry of finance. After a later entry into parliament, Crispi made him treasury minister in 1889, and in 1892–93 he was briefly prime minister. He was then just under the age of fifty, whereas Crispi reached the premiership at sixty-eight, Zanardelli at seventy-four, and Saracco at seventy-eight. He was to be prime minister five times, and on four occasions held the pivotal ministry of the interior, so that the period 1901–14 can justly be called the age of Giolitti.

In administrative realism and knowledge of character, as in financial experience, Giolitti was equal if not superior to Depretis. No doubt his administrative training and phlegmatic Piedmontese background helped him eschew the rhetoric and bombast of Crispi, and his speeches have a clarity and economy reminiscent of Cavour, another northerner. This low temperature was thought by many to be un-Italian and to suggest that he did not believe in "Italy's mission in the world." Hence they gave him their respect rather than their affection. None could deny, however, that he was a crafty and masterful parliamentarian, particularly adept at manipulating any controversial issue to make it seem a simple matter of administration on which most people could agree.

Giolitti learned much from the liberal precepts and practice of Zanardelli. Together they had opposed Crispi and Pelloux and criticized the "exceptional laws." They had maintained against Sonnino "that the parliamentary regime is the method of government best able to reconcile stability with liberty and progress"—so Giolitti told his constituents in March 1897. He believed that the conservatives had endangered existing institutions quite as much as the socialists had done, and were therefore as dangerous and insidious.

Giolitti declared that social questions, being now more important than political questions, would henceforth differentiate one political group from another. In a speech of September 1900 he made his position clear:

Sonnino is right in saying that the country is unhealthy politically and morally, but the principal cause of its sickness is that the classes in power spend enormous sums on themselves and their own interests while obtaining the money almost entirely from the poorer sections of society. We have a large number of taxes paid predominantly by the poor, on salt, on gambling, the *dazio* on grain and so forth, but we have not a single tax which is exclusively on wealth as such. When in the financial emergency of 1893 I had to call on the rich to make a small sacrifice, they began a rebellion against the government even more effective than the contemporary revolt of the poor Sicilian peasantry, and Sonnino who took over from me had to find more money by increasing still further the price of salt and the excise on cereals. I deplore as much as anyone the struggle between classes, but at least let us be fair and ask who started it.

Once back in the government, Giolitti insisted that justice and expediency demanded "a policy which is frankly democratic," and not only the tax system but local government and even the legal code itself should be changed. In February 1901 he told parliament that "the administration of justice can certainly not be said to win general confidence, and everyone knows the state of our public security, and how communal administration in many places is in the hands of a real camorra." A political assassination in Sicily had lately shown how illicit interference with police and judges was perverting the course of justice. It was useless to preach the virtues of parliamentary government to people who were hungry:

If you wish to defend our present institutions, you will have to persuade these new classes that they have more to gain from those institutions than from utopian dreams of violent change.... It depends on us whether they will turn out to be a conservative force, a new element in the greatness and prosperity of the country, or a revolutionary force for its ruin.

Giolitti thought it impossible to prevent the lower classes from eventually winning some share of economic and political influence, and anyhow it would be a political, moral, and economic error to drive what was in fact a majority of Italians into irreconcilable rebelliousness.

Finding that since Jacini's inquest of the 1870s no official statistics had been collected about agricultural wages, Giolitti made inquiries through the prefects. In Lombardy he discovered agricultural laborers earning one lira a day or less, which meant that, in the intervening thirty years, wage levels had declined from a standard which had already been insufficient. Agrarian unemployment was much more serious than he had imagined, and in no other European country were taxes on food so high or the gap between rich and poor so wide.

★

While Giolitti was thus coming part of the way to meet socialist demands, a distinct current of socialism moved in his direction and proclaimed that gradual and evolutionary methods were the surest path toward social justice. From 1896 the party paper *Avanti* appeared with the moderate Bissolati as its editor, and during the struggle over martial law it was persuaded to make a tactical alliance with radicals and democratic liberals to defend personal liberty and the constitution. Under this compulsion the socialist party produced a "minimum" program which, while retaining long-term ideas of social revolution, allowed socialists to collaborate with liberals inside parliament. This program included the right to combine and strike, universal suffrage, the payment of deputies, compulsory insurance, a progressive income tax, reduction of interest on the national debt, administrative decentralization, and government neutrality in disputes between labor and capital. Most of these aims Giolitti would have found unexceptionable.

At the socialist party congress of 1900 in Rome, two programs, a minimum and a maximum, were proposed, to approve either of which might have split the party, and so Turati secured the approval of both, the one being held as a means to the other. This compromise papered over an internal division which remained fundamental. It was much the same cleavage as in other countries, where the revisionism of Bernstein and the reformism of Millerand condemned the policy of violent revolution and approved of collaboration with middle-class governments. Giolitti welcomed this cleavage and adopted much of the minimum program in order to win over its supporters and strengthen his own majority. He was not far from Turati, who in the *Critica Sociale* was urging that social reform should be achieved through slow and gradual changes in society without upsetting existing institutions.

But many leaders of Italian socialism were more interested in a utopia of their own devising than in the wage concessions that Giolitti offered. Indeed, for those who adhered to the maximum program, social reforms might even seem harmful since they would make workers more contented and less revolutionary. The maximalists rejected compromise, believing that history was on their side and the process of dialectic would bring them success without having to contaminate themselves by fraternization with the liberals.

At the Rome Congress of the socialist PSI in 1900, a more extreme group of syndicalists gathered around the Neapolitan professor, Arturo Labriola. These syndicalists believed dogmatically in violence and the general strike: their aim was to win control of the socialist party and secure the management of *Avanti* and of the party funds on behalf of their revolutionary policy. They failed and became one more example of that tendency toward schism that always beset Italian socialism. The anarchists had seceded in 1892; syndicalists, reformists, and communists were to follow suit in 1908, 1912, and 1921, and numerous other groups thereafter.

These divisions eventually left the maximalists in command of a diminutive remnant, but for the moment, in 1900 and again in the 1902 congress at Imola, Bissolati, Bonomi, and the reformists carried the day. The revolutionary leaders,

Ferri and Labriola, had to contain themselves awhile. This could only strengthen Giolitti's Center coalition.

★

Giolitti's treatment of socialism was most perceptive. He recognized that, with its concentration on class and social problems, socialism was rapidly outpacing radicalism as a political force. It had thrived on the repressive measures of Crispi, Di Rudinì, and Pelloux. Giolitti read it as a sign of the times when Milan, the wealthiest Italian city, elected a socialist mayor. The premier was a friend of Turati and had studied *Das Kapital* with application and profit. Instead of, like Crispi, attributing the Sicilian revolt of 1893 to political propaganda, he recognized it as an understandable explosion of discontent better met by reform than by repression.

Giolitti assumed that persecution would merely heal the cleavages inside socialism and make it a force to be feared. He also advanced the novel doctrine that labor unions were welcome as a safety valve against unrest, for organized forces might be less dangerous than those which were disorganized. He observed in February 1901 that

> the badly nourished industrial worker is always weak in body and mind, whereas countries which have high wages are at the head of industrial progress. A period of social justice inaugurated by the government would recall the common people back to their affection for our institutions. I do not exceptionally want privileges for either workers or capitalists: the government ought to stand above these disputes between capital and labor except where the law is actually broken.

Impartiality suited Giolitti's temperament. In the damping down of controversial issues he saw most hope of maintaining his majority, and wisely aimed to avoid a situation where groups might be maneuvered against him before he had time to prepare the next elections. He also believed that wages, like profits, were best fixed by the free working of economic laws, for example by permitting strikes, instead of by Crispi's alternative method of putting the prefects and the *carabinieri* at the disposal of employers. In this way he hoped to edge Marx off the political stage just as Bernstein and Croce were simultaneously attacking Marxism as a philosophy.

Giolitti was soon put to the test by an outcrop of strikes. On the municipal tramways, in the sulphur mines, the docks, the iron and steel factories of Liguria and Leghorn, everywhere there were strikes as the proletariat began to envisage a fairer balance between classes. In 1901 there were 629 reported strikes in agriculture and 1,042 in industry, and in the space of three years there were at least eleven armed conflicts with the authorities. Nevertheless, Giolitti persisted in thinking that employers would be more ready to compromise where both sides had to conduct the dispute on more or less equal terms. He refused to let soldiers take over the work of agricultural strikers, for the knowledge that such help was at hand had simply increased the landowners' intransigence. The peasants therefore bettered their wages, and the state won more of their confidence.

Yet toleration was combined with firmness. On the grounds that the government should always put down disorder, the anarchist Malatesta, Bakunin's favorite pupil, was arrested. Giolitti claimed that freedom to work was as important as freedom to strike, and if strikers prevented other people from working this "would set up artificial conditions which in turn would make a new conflict inevitable." A strike by railroad workers, he maintained, was in a different category since it might cause unemployment if not actual starvation, so he threatened to call up any railroadmen on strike who were liable for military service. He argued that all public officials must be subject to extra discipline, especially as they had secure contracts and pensions to differentiate them from most other workers.

When Turati accused Giolitti of opportunism in this attitude, the latter took it as a compliment. As a true empiric he claimed to be both conservative and radical, wanting above all to secure existing institutions by wise reforms. His enemies put it differently, saying that he tackled no fundamental problem but wanted just enough reform to keep people quiet—and himself in office. Whatever the reason, opportunism brought him to appreciate the transformist technique, and in 1903, renouncing his earlier belief in party government, he was ready to choose his cabinet from many different sections of the Chamber.

Once he had offered the socialists much of their minimum program he went further by asking the reformists to be logical and join his government. The age of barricades was indeed over when the very men Crispi had outlawed in 1894 were invited to take office. Some of the Fabians who believed in the inevitability of gradualism were inclined to accept this invitation, but Turati knew that acceptance would split the party, and Bissolati had to inform the premier that his offer was premature. The explanation was offered that acceptance would be misunderstood by the politically immature rank and file, so discrediting the reformists: that is to say, refusal of office was for some socialists a matter not of principle but only of expediency. Acceptance of Giolitti's offer might well have stabilized and reinforced the liberal state. Turati in private deplored that the socialists could not join Giolitti, the most effective and reformist statesman that Italy possessed, but in public had to side with the maximalists.

When both socialists and radicals refused his alliance, Giolitti turned toward the Right, appointing Luzzatti to the Treasury and Tittoni to the Foreign Office. The rest of the cabinet were liberals of the Center. Apart from Luzzatti, all were in office for the first time since it was Giolitti's intention to bring new blood into the governing class and prepare himself a new basis of political power. He and Zanardelli persuaded the king to create fifty new senators. Meanwhile, his policy of social reform was not pushed so far as to antagonize the majority in the Lower House, which was still that elected under Pelloux in 1900. By a vote of 284 to 117 they gave him their confidence.

In the meantime the reformists were losing control of the socialist party. In 1903 Ferri captured the editorship of *Avanti* from Bissolati and in the 1904 congress at Bologna became virtually the leader of the party. Many socialists distrusted Ferri, knowing him to be a late convert who was as unversed in Marxism as he was inexperienced in working-class affairs and a notorious opportunist who never adhered to one policy for very long. He was, however, a clever and dangerous man, and his growing extremism was alarming.

Still more alarming was the development of syndicalism inside the party. The Italian edition of Sorel's book on syndicalism obtained wide circulation after 1903, and the *Reflections on Violence* by the same author was published in translation soon afterwards. Popularized in Italy by Croce, Sorel was to instruct many in the cult of violence and antidemocracy. Against the milder socialists who were beginning to yield to the allure of power and compromise, he taught that workers' syndicates, instead of relying on parliamentary action and the betterment of conditions, should be a weapon of violent class war against the bourgeois state. After triumphing at the regional conference at Brescia in 1904, Arturo Labriola strongly advocated this idea.

In September 1904 the revolutionary socialists at Milan tried out for the first time Sorel's idea of a political general strike as a protest against bloody collisions between police and workers in Sardinia and Sicily. For four days life over large areas of the country came to a standstill: newspapers did not appear, public services shut down, even the gondolas suspended activity and Venice was virtually isolated. Such success surprised no one more than the strikers who enjoyed the holiday and the spectacle but had little idea what to do next.

Giolitti alone was certain what to do—which was, nothing. He avoided bloodshed, confronted the strikers with the futility of such purely negative action, and also encouraged the reformists to recapture their former leadership in the party. The *Corriere della Sera* blamed him for what appeared to be cowardice, but wiser men appreciated that his restraint effectively defused this new syndical-ist weapon. Giolitti was sensible enough to allow wages as well as prices to find their own level, and even let the magistrates form a union to increase their salaries. Instead of using force, as Crispi or Di Rudinì might have done, he dissolved parliament in October and held general elections the following month. His object was partially gained, for the *estrema* was reduced from 107 to 94, a total made up of thirty-nine radicals, thirty-one socialists, and twenty-four repub-licans. Another significant point was that a few militant Catholic deputies were elected to strengthen the conservatives. This belated intervention by Catholics was eventually, much later, to upset the whole shape of Italian politics.

★

In this, the second of Giolitti's five general elections, electoral chicanery was said to be greater than ever before, though some allowance must be made for the exaggerations of defeated candidates and in any case these sharp practices were by now a well-established custom. In the elections of 1895 Crispi had easily been able to strike many opposition voters from the electoral lists and had drawn heavily on the Banca Romana for his electoral expenses. Pareto described how a special language had already come into existence:

> It is called the *blocco* when the whole contents of the voting urns are changed, or the *pastetta* when one changes only a part of them. There is still no word for when absent people and even the dead are made to vote though one will soon appear when this usage becomes general. . . . Such practices have always been endemic in southern Italy, but for some time now they have begun to infect the whole country.

These methods were brought to a fine art by Giolitti's election managers: blotting paper was issued to voters which had to be returned showing the name of the favored candidate upon it; banknotes were torn in two and given half before and half after voting; secret service funds were appropriated to the election campaign; electoral lists included fictitious names, sometimes gathered from tombstones in the town cemetery. Mussolini's father once described in a local paper how fifty cows were registered by name for the elections in Predappio. Giolitti recalled how a mayor had once apologized for two negative votes being cast against the government candidate: "We have found out who cast those two votes," reported the mayor, "and the men have had such a time of it that they have emigrated to France." "I replied," so Giolitti recounts, "that this was going too far."

His own policy was to allow the more advanced parts of Italy to vote in relative freedom, and to confine his intimidation and corruption mainly to backward areas, where such methods worked better, and where, if he did not use them, someone else would. "There are places in Italy where the law does not operate at all," he informed parliament, and he more than once referred to a large Sicilian municipality which avoided taxes by persuading the police to register it as "missing and untraceable"—his implication being that this kind of fact had to be either endured or exploited. A later prime minister, Bonomi, estimated that three-quarters of the electoral districts in Italy were feudal enclaves or private perquisites where there was never a serious contest, and concluded that the moral significance of an election would emerge just from the hundred or so seats where there was a genuine fight. Giolitti could afford to allow a more or less free vote in these hundred cases, but elsewhere found it easier and more profitable to use the local machines than to destroy them.

28   Clerical and Radical Co-operation, 1904–1906

Papal hostility had been such that it was rare for any leading minister of the Crown to be a devout Catholic. Crispi called himself a deist, and the Freemasons claimed such names as Depretis, De Sanctis, Spaventa, Di Rudinì, Crispi, Cavallotti, Carducci, and even the king himself. The policy of such men reflected an instinctive prejudice against a Church which was a state within the state. The Vatican claimed jurisdiction in "mixed matters," arbitral authority over all moral issues, and in some cases the supremacy of its own law over that of the nation. For sixty years it refused to recognize the existence of an Italian state or the loss of Rome.

The secular authorities for their part tried to argue that, the Pope apart, every inhabitant of the Vatican might be held subject to the Italian courts. Though the crucifix still hung in some lecture rooms, an anticlerical minister in 1881 appointed the heretical ex-canon of Mantua, Ardigò, to a professorial chair at Padua, and religious seminaries were threatened with closure if they refused to permit government inspection. In the universities, theological faculties had already been suppressed before the accession to power of the Left. A decree of 1888 put the onus on parents to ask for religious education for their children instead of having to request exemption from it. Then Zanardelli's penal code of 1889 increased the penalties on clergy who preached from the pulpit against existing institutions or acts of the government.

After much opposition, the compulsory payment of tithe was abolished, and most of the remaining church charities were taken over by the state after 1890. This last was a great blow to the clergy, who had obtained much influence from the distribution of alms and doles. Crispi asserted that there were 9,464 pious fraternities with a total revenue of nine million lire a year, of which only one-tenth was devoted to public assistance, the rest being spent on masses, candles, and fireworks on gala occasions. Most wounding of all was that Crispi made an annual public holiday of September 20, the day on which the army in 1870 turned its cannon against the walls of Rome.

★

Such measures were anticlerical rather than anti-Catholic; they were, indeed, supported by many sincere Catholics who recognized that Cavour's ideal of "a free Church in a free state" had been effectively replaced by Luzzatti's more realistic formula, "a free Church in a sovereign state." By 1900 the controversy between these two institutions was looking more and more unreal. Even though liberalism was officially condemned by the pope, even though Catholic protests were heard against King Umberto's burial in the Pantheon at Rome, the lay state was untroubled by such censure. In May 1904 Giolitti laid down that "Church and state are two parallel lines which ought never to meet."

Even popes had to recognize that they were less disturbed by outside pressure since losing temporal power, and the eighty-six encyclicals of Leo XIII have been called the most important contribution to Catholic doctrine since the Middle Ages. The verbal *non possumus* having saved honor, good sense was always at hand to make a compromise in practice. The Pope had been forced to allow bishops to ask for the royal exequatur, just as he had to endure the statue of Garibaldi looking down provocatively from the Janiculum onto the few remaining acres of papal territory. On the other hand, monasteries had been re-endowed since the dissolution, and the census figures of 1881 and 1901 show that, in defiance of formal law, monks and friars increased in number from 7,191 to 7,792, and nuns from 28,172 to 40,251. Sella in the 1870s had been able to say that "the black International is far more dangerous to our liberties than the red," but by 1900 this fear could seem excessive. Both sides were developing a mutual tolerance, and the danger of red revolution gave them something in common.

There continued to be extremely conservative popes, especially those of humble origin such as Pius X and Pius XI; but the more aristocratic Leo XIII and Benedict XV intimated that the alliance of the Church with political absolutism was not irrevocable. Both of them were trained in diplomacy and, like good statesmen, ready to meet an opponent halfway or nearly halfway. It was Leo who opened the Vatican archives in 1881 and who advised French Catholics to rally in support of the Third Republic. His encyclical of 1888, *De libertate humana*, seemed almost to argue away the antiliberal syllabus of Pius IX a quarter of a century before.

Catholic socialism appeared late in Italy, for the condemnations of both Pius IX and Leo were too recent and uncompromising. Theologians had feared that the Christian virtues of patience and charity might be prejudiced if people over-stressed rights of the poor and duties of the rich. But Leo recognized that the poor were the great majority and it was inexpedient to leave the materialists a monopoly of the claim to speak on their behalf. Perhaps the encyclical *Rerum novarum* of 1891 contained no very definite doctrine, but a new spirit was abroad when a pope could give his blessing to the Knights of Labor and affirm the desirability of trade unions. Professor Toniolo and Monsignor Bonomelli, two leading churchmen, were meanwhile providing a requisite theoretical justification by distinguishing the natural and absolute right to property from the limited uses to which it might be put, and insisting that ownership carried duties as well as rights.

In the turmoil of 1898, Christian-democrat groups were formed which—to the concern of the Vatican—did not scorn alliance with the *estrema*. Other Catholics were busy organizing agricultural unions, co-operative dairies, and village banks. Padre Curci, founder of the Jesuit paper *Civiltà Cattolica*, was preaching that the Church should come to terms with democracy, though his writings were banned by the ecclesiastical censorship and he was dismissed from his order. The monks of Monte Cassino, under their famous Abbot Tosti, had already in 1870 shown that they put national unity before the temporal power of the pope. The heirs of these men were Toniolo and Meda who in the late 1890's developed the propaganda organization of Christian democracy. When this was suspended by Pius X in 1904, Romolo Murri, although a priest, founded the "National Democratic League" and entered parliament, but was defrocked and excommunicated.

Parallel with this political movement were kindred heresies which Curci and Murri did not share and which collectively earned from their orthodox ecclesiastical opponents the generic label of "modernism." The modernists suggested that dogma was not formulated once and for all, but could be expected to grow organically and change to suit the times. This suggestion was condemned outright by a new papal syllabus in 1907. The chief enemy of modernism was Pius X who reigned from 1903 to 1914 and was the first pope of modern times to be canonized—it is interesting that he was elected pope only after Austria had vetoed the election of the pro-French cardinal Rampolla. Pius felt obliged to protest against the growing materialism and positivism of the age and against the false logic which might lead through modernism to Protestant heresy. Even Fogazzaro, the most popular novelist of the day and a Catholic, had some of his writing placed on the index of prohibited books.

Fifty years earlier the state might have risen to the rescue of a minority within the Church, but Croce and the liberal anticlericals were by now indifferent and admitted that the Church should regulate itself as it wished. Furthermore, while the Vatican was careful to condemn what it thought incorrigibly erroneous, it was gradually becoming reconciled to trends in modern society that it had once censured as heretical. Once the heat of controversy had passed, the Church throughout its history has managed to come to terms with all manner of diverse philosophical and political beliefs, wisely acting to moderate the more extreme views, and warning against irresponsible flirtation with the latest fashionable craze. Its gradual and partial reconciliation with the ideals of liberal democracy was to help Giolitti bring Catholics more actively into political life.

Many churchmen now accepted that their policy of non-co-operation since 1870 had been ineffective. The Vatican had made a brave effort to challenge the secular state and prevent it from taking permanent shape, but success became less likely with every year that passed. Church abstention from politics mainly damaged the conservatives, and co-operation might be by now, if not a positive good, at least a lesser evil. There was need for Catholics to appear in parliament and present the Church's views on marriage and education, especially when the year 1904 saw the shocking fact of a world congress of freethinkers in the Holy City itself. The new king was accused of atheism. It was said that the only church he built was the Jewish synagogue at Rome, and in February 1902 the speech from the throne had announced Zanardelli's project for permitting divorce. This called for urgent political action in reply. Moreover, the black nobility could not be expected to refuse Court invitations forever, and from contemporary fiction one can see that many Catholics were now ready to take their share in national life. Far from being enemies of the new state, Catholics were beginning to think of themselves as its defenders, alike against socialism on the Left and the anticlericalism of Sonnino and Di Rudinì on the Right.

Giolitti, though personally favorable to divorce, was too realistic to antagonize Catholicism directly, and when his plans for socialist support fell through he gladly welcomed this other nonconformist faction. His election campaign of November 1904 was first opened on a liberal platform, but when the results of the first ballot proved disappointing, he made positive overtures to the Catholics. *Avanti* calculated afterward that the clerical vote caused the defeat of socialist candidates in twenty-six districts.

★

Giolitti's object was to find the highest common factor of agreement and so produce a workable majority. Hence the apparent contradiction of his offer to the socialists in 1903 and to the Catholics in 1904. His change of front left him in an equivocal position, especially as the *estrema* constituted a powerful enemy. The socialists were close to capturing that nerve center of the country, Milan, and the grand master of Italian Freemasonry, the English-born Nathan, became a highly successful mayor of Rome in 1907–13. The republicans barely existed as a party—Scarfoglio, the most prominent contemporary journalist, asked what purpose would be served by working for a republic when no one so much as noticed that a monarchy existed. But the radicals still exerted considerable influence, especially through the Milanese newspaper, *Il Secolo.* Accordingly, Giolitti made another transformist gesture. He supported the election of the radical Marcora as Speaker of the House hoping that his group might be weaned from the rest of the *estrema.* Enemies of the government read this as new evidence of Giolitti's lack of principle, but in any case the variegated basis of his parliamentary support still left him insecure.

He was further shaken when one of his ministers, Rosano, committed suicide after being accused of corruption. The cabinet was lashed from the Left by the bad-tempered oratory of Ferri, while the Right complained of the government's refusal to confront a "go slow" campaign of the railroad workers. Giolitti was therefore glad to take the opportunity of resignation afforded by a bout of influenza, his designation of the insignificant Fortis to be his successor suggesting that this was merely a temporary tactical retreat in favor of one of his lieutenants. Probably he felt himself unable to put through his nationalization of the railroads, or at least he hoped to divert to his stopgap successor any unpopularity that this measure might bring.

The railroad boom of the late nineteenth century had left behind it much inefficient and uneconomic construction, and the network was notoriously unable to cope with the growth in foreign trade. Many bankruptcies had been registered in the course of railroad building, and the profits were significantly less than in France and England. A government commission nevertheless recommended that no change be made in the system of private ownership. But Giolitti disagreed; the restlessness of the railroad employees was seriously interfering with commerce, and moreover exporters were asking for subsidized transport rates which private companies could not afford. The strikes of 1904–5 brought this problem to a head and forced the state to intervene.

An act nationalizing the principal lines was eventually put through by Fortis, though without a full study of its implications. The first director of state railways, Riccardo Bianchi, did much to improve services, but his accounts soon showed a deficit. Critics claimed that the loss was inherent in state ownership; others replied that the private companies, whether in fear or hope of state intervention, had latterly been exploiting the lines to their limit without making provision for repairs and replacement. The new administration certainly gave better service, and differential freight charges were introduced to subsidize long-distance freight traffic. But such an increase in state involvement provided scope for corrupt patronage and to many conservatives it seemed an unwise concession to the pressure of organized labor. Giolitti was prudent in leaving to Fortis the responsibility for so contested a measure.

★

The cabinet formed by Fortis was of the Left Center and met the same opposition from both extremes. One of its chief problems was to reconcile the economic interests of North and South. Northerners welcomed a commercial treaty with Spain to assist the outflow of northern manufactures, but southerners suffered from a compensatory grant of preferential treatment to Spanish wine. When this forced the government to resign, in February 1906, the inheritance fell to Baron Sonnino of the Right Center.

Sidney Sonnino was a solitary man, rigid, austere, and taciturn. He was the child of a Welsh mother and a rich Tuscan Jew, and had the reputation of combining strict honesty with a somewhat narrow conservatism. It stood to his credit that he had written a commentary on the sixth canto of Dante's *Paradiso* and had given up a foreign-office career to do research on Tuscan and Sicilian agriculture, but he came into active politics as a minister under Crispi and had then advocated a reduction in the powers of parliament. Sonnino by 1906 headed a group of about thirty deputies, and in order to form a government had to approach the *estrema* in what was hailed as the most audacious political experiment since Cavour's *connubio*. He formed his first ministry with Luzzatti, Salandra, and Boselli from the Right, all of them future premiers, and the radicals Pantano and Sacchi from the extreme Left. Although Salandra and Pantano had been at opposite political poles, Italian political tradition contained no prescription about collective cabinet responsibility, and former governments had seldom needed to possess a collective policy.

Even more surprising than this association of ministers was the support by Ferri who at the socialist congress of Bologna in 1904 had agreed with the revolutionary syndicalists in repudiating parliamentary collaboration. Among other socialist groups, Bissolati's reformists and Turati's "integralists" were on the fringe of Giolitti's group system, but Ferri chose to go one better and join the conservative Sonnino. This opportunist stroke was suggested in part by the failure of the general strike which discredited the syndicalists. Then at the socialist congress of Rome in 1906, Bissolati and Turati united under the banner of what was called integralism to put Ferri and the syndicalists in an unimportant minority.

Obviously, the socialist PSI was too impractical and doctrinaire a party. Marxism was proving more successful with lawyers and students than with the working classes of the Po Valley and had a negligible influence among the peasants in southern Italy and the islands. Most leaders of the party tended to value doctrine above tactics or tangible success, a fact which was to have serious consequences in the future.

Sonnino's policy was one of conservative reform. He condemned the use of secret service funds for bribing the press and promised to relieve the burden of taxation in the South. He also promised to give more state aid to village schools and to limit the power of prefects in confiscating newspapers or in dissolving the elected councils in communes and provinces. Pantano, as minister of agriculture, even sketched a project for breaking up and colonizing the large estates, a scheme which cannot have had much appeal for some of his colleagues. But after three months the government resigned when a conflict at Turin between workers and police led to another general strike. Sonnino was almost bound to fall if ever a fundamental controversy arose to divide his followers.

The same parliament which had just given a majority of 150 to Sonnino now applauded Giolitti as his successor. The new government was to last three years, longer than any for a generation. Almost all its ministers except Tittoni were from the Left Center, but this time Giolitti determined to ask no favors from an extreme Left which had compromised itself with Sonnino. His aim was to outdo his predecessor in reforms, to attract the working-class vote, and if possible to restore the cohesion of the Center liberals. Not only did he revive political use of the secret service funds, but he vetoed a bill which Sonnino had introduced limiting the right of the central government to overrule local authorities. Indeed in September 1906 Giolitti dissolved the civic administration of Naples for the fourteenth time since 1861 and appointed to govern the city a royal commissioner who could perhaps make Naples more *giolittiano* in time for the next elections.

One accomplishment in June 1906, profiting from budget surpluses, was conversion of the interest on government bonds from 5 to 3.75 per cent. The success of this conversion reflected a growing confidence in the stability of the state, for very few people chose the alternative of cashing their bonds at par. It enormously lessened the annual load of interest payments on the eight billions of national debt and allowed the government to borrow money more cheaply, so reducing the food taxes. This sign of greater financial independence was also reflected in the larger gold reserves and in the greater amounts deposited in savings banks. Cheaper money for the government also meant cheaper money for industry and agriculture.

But Giolitti still believed that the dominant problem was how to improve life for the working classes. Legislation was accordingly passed to regulate conditions of employment and contracts of service. Tenders for public works were accepted from workers' co-operatives, to the great disgust of richer contractors, and parliamentary commissions were set up to examine irregularities in the administration of the army and navy.

29 The "Southern Problem" and Emigration

For some time after 1860 most northerners were completely ignorant of the South, for few ever went there if they could help it. Minghetti imagined that it might well be the most fertile part of Europe, and even Cavour, who refused an invitation to go and see for himself, believed that Naples would become the richest province in Italy. Probably this illusion provided one of the reasons why some initially skeptical northerners accepted the national movement, and their subsequent disillusion was a source of weakness for national feeling. After closer acquaintance the inhabitants of the South were soon being referred to by one cabinet minister as "an army of barbarians encamped among us." D'Azeglio seriously suggested that the South should once again be separated from Italy, since other provinces were incapable of supporting such a burden and "even the best cook will never make a good dish out of stinking meat."

To correct such dangerous pessimism, politicians again took refuge in talking of a rich area impoverished by the inefficient rule of the Bourbons. It was assumed that the enlightened government of United Italy would automatically improve matters, and hence there was no need for scientific study and legislation on the "southern problem." People forgot that the island of Sardinia was in worse shape even than Sicily despite 150 years of rule from Turin. They disbelieved what the less doctrinaire economists told them of the real condition of this imagined garden of the Hesperides, and Fortunato was even reproached with having "invented" malaria as a polemical fiction. Piedmontese statesmen such as Cavour and Depretis never considered traveling to the South to investigate for themselves, and Giolitti went only once during the emergency which followed a terrible earthquake in the Strait of Messina. These three statesmen came from the far northwest, and to them Rome was as far south as was pleasant to go.

The southern question was not studied seriously until the two Tuscans, Franchetti and Sonnino, tackled it in the 1870s, and not until much later did politicians in general become aware that the South was still not righting itself under northern rule. Luzzatti warned parliament in 1901 that, if nothing were done, the North would sink to the economic level of the South, so that the future of the nation depended on solving this awkward problem. The fabled wealth of the South had evidently been a myth; it was the North that had investment capital, established industries, better education and communications, contact with the rest of Europe, a more enlightened ruling class, a better climate, more raw materials, and a complex network of irrigation works built up through many centuries. Corbino computed that the average Piedmontese in the 1890s was almost twice as rich as the average Sicilian.

Under the Italian system of government there was often a conspiracy of silence about issues which threatened to displace the balance of groups in parliament. The condition of the poor had long been such an issue, and hence there had not been much to choose between the social policy of Cavour and Rattazzi, Minghetti and Depretis. Only after 1900 did the growing importance of the proletariat force both Left and Right to compete for popular sympathy. The conservative reforms of Sonnino were thus met by the liberal reforms of Giolitti, and each faction competed to discover the facts upon which policy should be based.

The South would eventually gain from national unity by enjoying more efficient administration and a freer regime, but there had inevitably been severe economic dislocations in such a violent change, and in 1899 the economist Einaudi calculated that the damage still probably outweighed any benefits. Before 1860 the South was a country of low taxes and negligible national debt, with the collective capital asset of large domanial lands in public ownership, and having a paternal government which tried to keep food cheap. After 1861 its autonomy was gone, taxes leaped upward, and by 1865 the loss of industrial protection forced the closure of many factories at Naples, Messina, and elsewhere. The British consul at Naples reported that trade declined by 16 per cent as a result of the increase in municipal octrois between 1861 and 1866.

In 1864 Garibaldi informed the king that Neapolitans hated his semimilitary government more than they had hated the Bourbons, and ten years later a newspaper campaign was opened with the slogan "we are Neapolitans before we are Italians." Resentment was reciprocal. Northerners sometimes reproached the South for having made so few sacrifices in the struggle for unity, and, in Franchetti's cruel phrase, it was thought of not as a region to be wisely governed, but rather as a group of deputies to be conciliated and bribed.

Then in the 1880s the agricultural depression caused another set-back in the South just when the industrialized North was beginning its rapid advance under protection of government tariffs. The price of wheat fell first to 22 lire a quintal in 1888, then to 13.5 in 1894, and Sonnino as minister of the treasury chose this moment to increase the *dazio* on grain and to raise the price of salt from 35 to 40 centesimi a kilo. This hit both landowners and peasants in the predominantly rural South, for the amount collected by these taxes in Sicily was no less than that paid by the infinitely wealthier region of Lombardy. Meanwhile, the decline in agricultural prices made it increasingly difficult for southerners to pay the interest on debts incurred by their enormous increase in vineyard acreage, and hence each year many thousands of smallholders forfeited their land. The South had to pay with its depreciated products for manufactured goods which protection now made dearer. Instead of subsidizing poorer regions in order to lessen these disparities, there was a deliberate policy of accumulating capital and resources in the North where it was thought that they could be better employed.

*

It has often been said that two stages of civilization coexisted in Italy, for in the South there were more murders, more illiterates, superstition, corruption, and poverty. Alexandre Dumas *père* described what he found at Naples in 1862:

> While the *signore* feeds his dogs on white bread, the people live on roots and grass, eked out with an insufficient quantity of coarse bread. The *signore* puts his horses in stables shut in from the winds and the rain and properly paved. His peasants live in damp, unhealthy hovels open to all the winds, without windows, without a roof. The whole family will sleep on the same bed of straw, in the same room with their donkey, their pig, and their chickens.

For this accommodation they paid the equivalent of seventy days' wages. Fifty years later these people could still be found earning only half a dollar a working day, and working days meant only half the year or less. Malaria often determined the way they lived, their methods of land tenure, the type of crops, and the relative density of population. Where families had to live huddled together in hill villages raised above the malarial plains, crops were needed which could be looked after by people living at a distance, which could be left without close attention in the most dangerous months, and which did not require the help of female labor in the fields.

Fortunato fought a great battle against chemical manufacturers and drug stores to obtain state provision of quinine. He described how in his native Basilicata you could travel twenty miles without sighting a village, and could live for months without seeing an open or joyful face. The number of expropriations for tax default in this province alone was twice that for the whole of northern Italy. In the Abruzzi, Franchetti related how the *contadini* were virtually slaves: they worked on their lord's farm for a stipulated number of days, they kissed his hand, suffered the gratuitous exactions which indeterminate clauses in contracts of service allowed him, and showed a groveling deference to anyone who dressed respectably. Early in the new century he wrote:

> Peasant risings, which usually lead to bloodshed, are characteristic and normal events of public life in the South. . . . Without any middle class, even without workers who are above the poverty level or possess a rudimentary education, the practice of representative government in fact works directly against the objects it might hope to achieve.

The Neapolitan, Villari, said the same, that the peasants still thought their lord almighty and all-knowing, yet when anything happened to challenge this belief, a long suppressed hatred would flare up with all its accompaniment of vindictiveness and savagery. Only a small rise in the price of bread might lead to desperate episodes of violence. Travelers from the North, said Villari, thought southerners were idle, when in fact they merely lacked employment. He described how two-thirds of the population of Naples, still in 1881 the largest Italian city, had no certainty of daily work and daily bread. Not until after the terrible cholera outbreak of 1884 did Naples obtain a reasonably pure water supply along the Serino aqueduct.

In Sicily it was not so much a class but almost the whole region that was poor. A parliamentary commission in 1876 cheerfully reported that the Sicilian peasants were not so badly off as the Lombard rice growers or the shepherds of the Roman Campagna, but Franchetti and Sonnino criticized this parliamentary inquiry for seeking evidence only from the Sicilian gentry and only in the main provincial centers. These two northerners concluded that the idea of liberty was quite meaningless in such conditions as they found all over the island; also that violence would remain an important local industry unless and until the whole social and economic situation could be changed. No wonder that Verga left his fashionable writing and went back to his native Sicily to find a proper setting for *Cavalleria rusticana*, those sketches which he published in 1880 to describe the violent passions of a downtrodden peasantry. His novel *Mastro Don Gesualdo*, published in 1888 and later translated into English by D. H. Lawrence, likewise told of the misery and anger of Sicilian peasants in revolt against their environment.

Four-fifths of the island population were still illiterate in 1900, and nine-tenths of conscripts were medically unfit. Drains, pure water, even cemeteries were often lacking well into the twentieth century. Once the granary of ancient Rome, Sicily no longer fed itself, and a primitive system of agriculture was progressively exhausting the soil. It was a country like Ireland, of great estates, absentee landlords, secret societies, rebellion, emigration, and sometimes starvation. Sicily was not so much oppressed as neglected by Italy. Considerable support was sometimes found for separation from the continent, and Franchetti echoed D'Azeglio in saying that the island should be given back its independence if the government in Rome continued to be so ignorant and unhelpful.

The southern problem was basically a problem of poverty. Except for a few fertile areas such as the Campania around Naples and the Conca d'Oro around Palermo, the soil was burned up by the sun, frequently a barren wilderness of clay and rock. Also the generating of electricity was more difficult in the South where fuel was expensive and rivers dried up for half the year. Statistics for wheat production in the decade 1909–20 show that, compared with nineteen quintals per hectare in the northern district of Ferrara, Reggio Calabria could produce only 4.9 and Syracuse 5.5. The twelve provinces with the lowest production were all from the South, whereas no more than two provinces from the South came into the top half of the national list. The same figures show a striking annual variability of output as equally characteristic of the South.

Landslides and earthquakes were also a specialty of the lower Apennines and the islands. Some indication of this constant menace may be gathered from the fact that Croce lost his parents and Salvemini his wife and children in such awful natural calamities. In the space of a few years an eruption of Vesuvius in 1906 and another of Etna in 1910 engulfed whole villages. Hundreds were killed by earthquakes in Calabria in 1905, and in 1908 a terrible convulsion and tidal wave in the straits of Scylla and Charybdis destroyed three hundred townships, burying fifty thousand people at Messina and twelve thousand in Reggio.

Finance to repair such disasters was short in the South, and when it was available there was little spirit of enterprise. Farmers tended to conceal any savings at home, or more often their whole "surplus" income went in discharging usurious interest rates which might be well over 100 per cent. Usury was profitable enough to take capital away from industry or agricultural improvement, and landowners had to lend money to their tenants against bad harvests instead of using it to increase production. The vast sums spent in purchasing ecclesiastical and domanial lands between 1865 and 1890 also absorbed much of the free funds available and discouraged the transition to a more intensive form of agriculture.

Any remaining money tended to go into state securities. Centuries of misfortune had made security the primary requisite, and speculative ventures or even investment in public amenities were distrusted. Loans were refused by many southern municipalities when offered by the government on easy terms for use in road building, although such offers were readily snatched up by enterprising northerners who sought long-term rewards for present abstinence. A false economy led town councils, thinking more of the municipal rates than of public health, to turn down projects for drainage and water supply, while municipal theaters were given priority.

★

It was perhaps natural that southerners should try to shift the blame away from their own deficiencies and on to government. Giolitti was attacked for favoring the North. No doubt he had reason to be more afraid of social revolution among the northern industrial proletariat than among southern peasants, but to reward the rich North and penalize the poor South seemed unfair. It was even suggested that brigandage was deliberately publicized in the national press to keep tourists away from the South. After the Messina earthquake, when the government prohibited the return of fugitives for fear of indiscriminate looting, there were legitimate complaints that this had prevented the rescue of many people, and even that northern insurance firms bought up individual claims to government compensation so as to gain ownership of the best street sites.

More justifiably it was argued that, while Sicily alone among Italian provinces enjoyed a demonstrable export surplus (sulphur, marsala wine, and fruit were all export trades), the rest of Italy swallowed up its profits. The Sicilian waste land was the last to be reclaimed, and it was in Lombardy and Emilia that the state built canals and roads and carried out its biggest schemes of land reclamation. Government contributions to elementary education were assessed on the basis of existing schools rather than on the need for new ones, and this naturally favored the North. Such public works as were carried out in the South were frequently entrusted to northern contractors, and northerners had the advantage of sufficient capital and enterprise to administer the tobacco monopoly and the construction and running of the railroads.

The economist Pantaleoni computed in 1910 that northern Italy, with 48 per cent of the national wealth, paid 40 per cent of the nation's taxes; the Center was more equitable; while the South, with 27 per cent of the national wealth, paid 32 per cent. Fortunato in 1904 even said that the immense wealth being built up in Lombardy largely escaped taxation. Rural property was less heavily taxed than urban, but primitive peasant huts clustered in large southern hill villages were considered urban dwellings, while the equivalent farm buildings in the North were more obviously rural and so exempt. Again, while the old Kingdom of the Two Sicilies had possessed little national debt, after 1860 the vast increase in debt payments by the state impinged on the hitherto sheltered southern taxpayer. Rich men in the North, instead of investing in backward areas, bought national securities which bore attractive rates of interest, and the heavier taxes after 1860 therefore seemed to divert money from the South to pay the interest of northern bond holders.

★

Cavour told an English friend that "the reason why Naples has fallen so low is that laws are held not to apply to a *gran signore* or a friend of the king, or to their friends and confessors. Naples can rise again only by a severe but just application of the law." Unfortunately, Cavour's successors failed to tackle this problem. The land-tax qualification in local elections confirmed the landlords in possession of effective power, through which they could influence national elections and even the administration of justice itself. The Marquis di Rudinì virtually inherited the mayoralty of Palermo in his middle twenties, as did the Marquis di San Giuliano that of Catania.

Some mayors treated their office as a perquisite which, by its control of electoral lists, could be used to perpetuate family graft and the exploitation of communal property. We hear of another Sicilian marquis who diverted a river for the benefit of his own watermills and in return said a mass for the people on feast days in his private chapel. A survey of Calabria in 1910 found in one commune eighty-three usurpations of the common land, two of them by brothers of the mayor, seventeen by his first cousins, and a dozen by communal councilors and their friends. After the Messina earthquake, some of the relief money disappeared (the ruins were still there in 1940), and accusations were made that far too much was diverted to rebuilding the houses of the rich. Poor-law boards sometimes operated so that little of the revenue from local charities reached the real poor, and commissioners of the *monts de piété* lent themselves money from these funds, sometimes under assumed names. The prosecution of the Sicilian minister Nasi for embezzlement added to the belief that the island was thoroughly corrupt, and Ferri once said in open parliament that there existed only a few "oases" of honesty in the whole South.

Franchetti recounts how one prefect was removed for trying to stop such corruption; and another mentioned the arrival of orders that he was to wink at it. Another reported that "a mayor can arrest whom he wants." Franchetti here discerned the emergence of a new and different feudalism: instead of *corvées* and *banalités* there were communal taxes which could be rigged by the local bosses, and though the peasants were not tied to the soil in law they were still so in fact. Prefects who came from the North regarded their tenure of office as a penance, while prudent silence would earn them promotion to a more congenial area.

Among the principal instruments of oppression were the mafia of Sicily and the *camorra* of Naples. The mafia was a collection of gangs which protected pockets of graft from the law and organized smuggling and kidnapping. They exacted hush money and protection money. Their sanctions ranged from murder to the burning of ricks and killing of cattle, or to preferring trumped-up charges against opponents by suborning false witnesses. Anyone who administered justice with his own hands without recourse to the law was thought praiseworthy. In 1875 the vice-prefect of Palermo confessed to Sonnino that he was a *mafioso*, and many urban officials and lawyers took a profitable share in the racket. Landlords used it to keep their peasants in subjection, or an ambitious politician would purchase its support at election time by promising to represent the interests of the *mala vita* at Rome. Its objects were not always bad, and it gave invaluable support to the revolutionaries in 1848 and to Garibaldi's volunteers in 1860. Sometimes the government made halfhearted efforts to investigate it, but generally preferred tacit collusion with a way of life that was too pervasive and too secret to be extirpated.

The name *camorrista* was bestowed at Naples on anyone who used cleverness or strength to exploit the weak. Here, too, a perverted sense of honor enabled a criminal conspiracy to live by intimidation and blackmail. The *camorra* became a sort of unofficial police force and was sometimes engaged as such by the government. More frequently it supplied the place of the magistrate, for its justice was commonly cheaper and sometimes more just than that of the regular courts. Like the mafia, it sold its electoral support and blacklisted candidates who did not subscribe to its funds. It had considerable influence inside the Naples town council and could even send its own deputies to parliament.

The camorra was never highly organized but seems to have developed something of a hierarchy, with peculiar laws, initiation ceremonies, and conventional language. In the city of Naples it was said to take a tenth of the winnings in gambling houses and to impose a specified tariff on porters, cabdrivers, and prostitutes. A *camorrista* lurked at every city gate, at railroad stations and markets where he imposed levies at every stage on the cartage, unloading, distribution, and sale of food. Peasants bringing their wares to town would gladly pay their tithe for protection, and so would any merchant who wished for the safe unloading of a cargo. The *camorra* had its own methods of influencing customs and excise officials, and its agents even when in prison were paid a regular monthly tribute to which all other prisoners would contribute. It was the pawnshop of the poor. It might also put a tax on a priest when he said mass. If a more than ordinarily scrupulous prefect tried to crush it the organization might temporarily disappear, but the way of life remained and the prefect himself usually disappeared more permanently. No wonder if, from Minghetti to Garibaldi and Lombroso, leading Italians voiced their shame over the criminal statistics in a country where such things were normal and apparently incorrigible.

★

Not until the end of the century did the government begin to take active responsibility for reform in the South. Acts were passed in 1897 for the betterment of agricultural conditions in Sardinia, in 1904 for the Basilicata, and in 1906 for Calabria. The state now recognized that certain regions had special needs which demanded special treatment, and northern industrialists also realized that a more prosperous South would provide them with an expanding market. But action continued to be slow and expenditure far too small. In 1905, after forty years of talk, a contract was signed for an aqueduct to pierce the Apennines and carry water for two million people from the River Sele into remote Apulia; the work dragged on and was not finished until 1927. If by then the southern question was less acute, this was due not so much to government schemes of development as to the spontaneous action of southerners themselves in emigration.

★

This great exodus of Italians is among the most striking features of their recent history. Many districts had long been acquainted with a migrant life. In the Alps and Apennines there was little work to be done in the winter: people moved freely across state frontiers, and shepherds would take their flocks for seasonal grazing far away to the plains below. In the search for casual work there had always been an annual migration from Umbria and the Marches to the Agro Romano and the Tuscan Maremma, and the harvesting and polishing of rice in Lombardy has always attracted seasonal labor. In 1900 it was estimated that a million workers spent up to two months in the year working away from their families in other provinces of the country.

For permanent migration abroad there are no exact figures until later. The *Annuario Statistico* of 1861 gave 220,000 Italians as resident abroad—77,000 were in France, 47,000 in the United States, and 18,000 in Brazil and Argentina. By 1876 a hundred thousand people were leaving Italy each year, by 1901 half a million; and in the single year of 1913, 872,000 people left the country, one person in every forty. By 1914 there were five to six million Italians living abroad as compared with thirty-five million inside Italy.

The early emigrants were casual wanderers or political refugees. Mazzini, Foscolo, and Rossetti had gone to England, Pareto's father to France. Da Ponte, the librettist of Mozart, and Garibaldi himself went to America. In the middle of the nineteenth century the chief trend was from northern Italy to other European countries, the emigrants being mostly urban workers who intended to return. In the next phase casual laborers, the agricultural *braccianti* who had no property to bind them to the soil, left Liguria, the Veneto, and the coastal areas of the South. The adult males would go first, and later might summon their wives or write home to their families to choose a wife and send her out to them. Usually they would return to Italy once they had made a modest fortune. Only at the end of the century did whole families in inland districts go abroad together and for good.

The poor peasant in Italy, if he did not rebel, had no choice but resignation to his lot or else emigration. His motive in leaving was not always simply land hunger; on the contrary, it sometimes looked like flight from the ungrateful soil. Deforestation, soil erosion, and enclosures had upset his rural economy, destroying fuel supplies and grazing rights and encouraging the spread of malaria. New local and national taxation skimmed off that small margin of cash which might have made backward areas more fruitful. An Alpine valley in Italy might be poor while the next valley in Switzerland was prosperous, and this provided a reason for moving to a place where conditions were easier.

The national population rose to 42 million by the census of 1936, having doubled since 1861. Though the birth rate began to decline during this period, the fall was much slower than elsewhere, and in 1906 there was still an annual surplus of eleven per thousand in births over deaths. Agricultural families were large and, especially in the more barren and mountainous regions, fathers would send children abroad to avoid division of the family inheritance. The depression in agriculture after 1887 made unemployment acute, for fewer hands were needed if grain land were converted into pasture to serve some local cheese industry, or if a *latifondista* wanted to reduce his wage bill.

For this "surplus population" there were jobs in the mines of Lorraine and Luxembourg, in building railroads, bridges, and harbors from Scotland to Siberia, in planting coffee in Brazil or vines in North Africa, in peddling ice cream or shining shoes in New York. Navigation companies made enough profit on the traffic in emigrants to give publicity to labor shortages abroad, while those who returned brought back higher standards of living, which made their friends at home discontented and ambitious to better their own fate.

In 1876 north Italy was providing 85 per cent of the annual emigration. The Piedmontese went to France, the Venetians often spoke German and had a tradition of movement to Austria. Only after the agricultural slump was emigration predominantly from the South. By that time the industrial development of Lombardy and Umbria offered alternative employment for agricultural workers, while the depression helped to break down that attachment to the land which had hitherto deterred southerners from moving abroad.

The proportion of migrants who went overseas rose from 18 per cent in 1876 to 50 per cent by the end of the century. At first the exodus was directed to South America—mainly Brazil and the Argentine—whence, after the harvest months, a man would perhaps return in time for the spring sowing in Italy. Later the swelling stream poured instead into the United States. Garibaldi, Mazzini, and Cavour all looked to the United States as the country destined to lead the world in a new age of liberty and human progress. Cavour once threatened to emigrate there himself, and Garibaldi lived there long enough to call himself an American citizen. In 1898, of all immigrants coming into the United States, there were for the first time more from Italy than from any other country and twice as many Italians as British. In remote villages of the Abruzzi, American politics were followed even by people who had never been there and who could neither read nor write. By 1927 the Italian government computed that over nine million Italians were living abroad, including three and a half million in the United States, and one and a half million each in Brazil and the Argentine. Over half a million were in New York city alone, a hundred thousand in Philadelphia and as many in Buenos Aires.

The economies of Tunisia, Argentina, and the south of France had already been substantially altered by the work of Italians, and on Italy itself the effect of such a mass exodus was incalculable. It was a safety valve and incidentally took away many anarchists and other undesirables—Mussolini himself, when out of work in 1909–10, thought of emigrating to the United States. No doubt in early years it helped to postpone the development of an organized labor movement in Italy itself. It resulted in raising domestic wages, but also in inducing landowners to save labor by abandoning cereals for cattle. A particular benefit was that about 500 million lire—a sum larger than that produced by tourism—returned in annual remittances to the families of emigrants in the years just before 1914, and this not only helped to correct the balance of foreign trade, but by bringing capital into the countryside dealt a blow to the local usurer and made the land more profitable. The *Americani* who returned, easily recognizable from the gold and silver prominently displayed in their teeth, brought back new habits, new needs, new skills, a higher level of education, a greater sense of independence, and a consciousness of their rights against the *padrone* and the government. They were convincing proof that literacy paid. The prospective emigrant feared that he might be refused entry to America if he were illiterate. He needed to be able to write letters to his family, and his family needed to be able to read them. This was as great an educative force upon such a family-conscious nation as half a century of edicts from Rome in favor of compulsory schooling.

Apart from wanting to keep men at home until no longer liable for military service, the government cared little about emigration. Only in 1901 was an office set up to control speculators and transportation agencies involved in this traffic. When Zanardelli traveled to see conditions in the South (the first northern prime minister who thought this half of Italy worth a visit), he was shocked when the mayor of Moliterno greeted him "on behalf of the eight thousand people in this commune, three thousand of whom are in America and the other five thousand preparing to follow them." But the government's policy was normally one of *laissez-faire*, and only under fascism was every emigrant considered a potential source of manpower lost to the country.

Mussolini substituted for the word emigrant a more patriotic title of "Italian abroad," and developed the new doctrine that these *émigrés* did not reflect the poverty of his country but rather the superabundant energy of a young people with a mission to civilize the world. But by then, immigration laws in other countries were refusing illiterates and discriminating against poorer and more backward nations, so creating a new problem for Italy.

30   Economic and Cultural Revival

Although Italy was an agricultural country, few parliamentary deputies were much concerned about rural society. Professor Villari wrote: "If I try to interest a deputy in the working conditions of the poor, he is only bored, but if I talk to him about the latest shuffling of parties, his face lights up and he regards me as a sensible man of the world." Nor was the government much interested in statistics, and the census that should have been taken in 1891 was put off for ten years to save expense. It was left to individual students to fill this gap.

Villari reminded people that Italy was still one of the very poorest countries in Europe. Workmen's unions designed to increase wages had at first been considered illegal, whereas employers could legally combine to stop over-production or to bring pressure on the government. Despite persecution, friendly societies and co-operatives appeared in agriculture toward the end of the century: we have an early example in the landless *braccianti* of Ravenna who in 1883 formed a co-operative to obtain contracts for land drainage. By 1889 chambers of labor were being formed, and in 1892 there was in existence a Federation of Agrarian Co-operatives. There were co-operative dairies and wine factories, as well as co-operative rural banks; and for perishable truck-garden produce a joint sales organization was most necessary. Agricultural experts were sometimes employed by them and sent to give demonstrations on market days, to teach pruning and wine production and the use of vegetables in the rotation of crops.

Self-help and mutual help were important, but the government alone had resources large enough to tackle the problem of land reclamation, especially as marsh and mountain formed such a high proportion of Italy's land surface. Rome itself had been partially surrounded by uninhabitable land ever since Belisarius and Witige cut the aqueducts in the early Middle Ages, and the three hundred thousand acres of the Pontine marshes stretched from the Alban hills to the coast, almost as a shallow gulf of the Tyrrhenian sea. The marshland of the Maremma ran northward along the coast between Civitavecchia and Leghorn, and near Ferrara there was another large almost uninhabited swamp. In the still water of such marshes bred the mosquitoes which propagated the parasites of malaria.

Another problem calling for state action was the rapidly dwindling forests, especially in the Apennines, which had been cut down to provide timber for the railroad, shipping, and building industries, or deliberately burned to provide a soil which for a few years would be highly fertile before being washed away. In Sardinia the bark of oak trees had been indiscriminately stripped off for the cork trade or the tanneries, and much of what remained of the forests was cut down in the 1870s and 1880s to feed a flourishing trade in charcoal. By 1890, between four and five million acres of woodland were thought to have been destroyed in living memory. Great numbers of peasant families had thereby lost an important source of livelihood and severe problems of soil erosion had been laid up for the future. In the single province of Cosenza, forest inspectors reported 156 landslides during 1903 covering some five thousand acres. The River Basento in the Basilicata, a raging flood in winter, almost dry in summer, was estimated to carry 430,000 cubic meters of mud into the sea each year, washing the soil away from under the feet of the inhabitants and blocking the river mouth. Deforestation in this way destroyed capital as well as income, and was a prime cause of the barren rocks, sterile pastures, floods, avalanches, marshes, and malaria of Italy. Farmers out for quick profits had no notion that woodland might in some areas be the most profitable type of cultivation.

In the course of time, when the damage became obvious, a third of the country was to come under one scheme or another of land reclamation. Something had been done by private hands: successive popes had built canals near the old Appian way to drain part of the Pontine marshes. Prince Torlonia in 1876 brought to a conclusion the draining of Lake Fucino, later to be the scene of Silone's novel *Fontamara*—this one project involved the construction of 800 bridges and 250 kilometers of roads, and a living for thousands of families was provided on the land reclaimed. The government made a forlorn effort after 1865 to build a network of dikes for flood control, and a suggestion was made in 1873 of expropriating non-co-operative landowners. A law of 1877 encouraged reforestation, and the Baccarini act of 1882 recognized that the cost of draining large areas would have to be borne by the state.

Successive edicts of 1883, 1903, and 1910 then tried to force the landowners in the Agro Romano to drain land and settle people on it, under pain of forfeiture. Near Ferrara, two hundred thousand acres were said to have been reclaimed for productive agriculture in the thirty years before 1907. The great plain of the Tavoliere, stretching from the sub-Apennines to the gulf of Manfredonia and down into Apulia, had its medieval pasturage customs curtailed by statute to make it an area of more intensive cultivation. Bounties were given to families that settled in these newly reclaimed areas and new villages were given tax exemptions. Altogether in the forty years before 1900 it was claimed that one and a half million acres were reclaimed; even the fertile lava on the slopes of Mt. Etna was broken up for profitable cultivation.

But the figures are suspect and sometimes referred rather to projects than to completed work. The bureaucracy was slow; reclaimed land fell back only too easily into wilderness; and landowners usually were more than satisfied with the income from unreclaimed pasture lands where so little labor was required, while their lethargy and poverty made it difficult to enforce any law about expropriation. On the contrary, landlords could all too often arrange that their own estates were the chief beneficiaries from public expenditure, especially as laws put the onus of action on local authorities. The provincial authorities were in general poor and lazy, preferring to spend their money on theaters and festive occasions. Giolitti declared that state action had not secured the planting of a single tree in provinces which were hostile or indifferent.

It was long before the magnitude of the task was fully grasped. Apart from the difficulty of making laws effective, a project might be useless if it did not fit into a composite regional plan. Road building might thus be a prerequisite of expenditure on river beds and embankments, and schemes of drainage would be insufficient if they failed to introduce effective methods of land tenure and cultivation that would attract settlers for the land. Since poor Alpine areas could not be expected to pay for work in the mountains which chiefly benefited the plains, only the central government could provide the necessary finance and co-ordination of effort, or maintain the results once achieved.

★

The return of prosperity after 1897 was due only in small part to government action. The end of the tariff war with France, the growth of the co-operative movement and emigration, the increased use of electricity, all had their share. Fairer negotiation in labor disputes was now possible, and the outburst of strikes after 1901 was a symptom of improved conditions. From one lira a day, wages sometimes rose to three and even five lire in the countryside. Another indication is the comparison of mortality figures for 1901–5 with those for 1909–13, when the number of deaths in the two worst provinces diminished from twenty-seven to twenty-two per thousand inhabitants.

In the years 1899–1910 industrial production almost doubled and the annual Treasury budgets show a favorable balance of income over expenditure for the only continuous stretch in modern Italian history. The habit of travel, of taking vacations at the seaside or in the mountains, was a further indication of growing prosperity. Genoa held its place as the third port of the Mediterranean for traffic, and it was hoped that completion of the long Simplon tunnel in 1906 might further enrich Italy by creating an alternative route from Central Europe. Foreign trade, which had diminished in the decade 1880–90, grew again between 1890 and 1900 from two to three billion lire in value, and then to six billion lire by 1910. Even after corrections have been made for advancing prices after 1906, imports were judged to have risen by 61 per cent in value between 1901 and 1913, and exports by 47 per cent.

One significant qualification is that the discrepancy between imports and exports was larger than elsewhere in Europe, and from a yearly average of about 175 million lire in the period 1896–1900, the gap had increased to 1,300 million by 1912. Another qualification is that in 1913 two-thirds of Italy's maritime trade was still carried in foreign ships and the Italian merchant marine was, despite heavy protection, largely foreign-built. Income per head in Italy in 1911–13 was less than half that in France, less than a third that in Britain, and little more than a quarter of that in the United States.

Nineteenth-century Italy had produced many distinguished scientists and mathematicians, but names such as Betti and Cremona were eclipsed in popular renown by the work of those who, from Volta to Marconi, made important discoveries in the field of electricity. In 1883 the Italian Edison company set up a generating plant on the River Adda, using some of the dynamos of the defunct Holborn Viaduct station in London, and Milan became one of the first European towns to use electricity for streetcars, street lighting, and industrial power. By 1886 Meucci's invention of the telephone was being used in the Vatican. Streetcars were running from Florence to Fiesole in 1890, and two years later from Tivoli to Rome—the famous falls of Tivoli being used to supply Rome with her light and power. Marconi's great work on wireless telegraphy took place between 1896, when he took out his first patent at the age of twenty-two, and 1909 when he became a Nobel prizewinner.

After this early start, it was perhaps surprising that a country lacking in coal and with great hydraulic resources did not develop hydroelectric energy much faster. Generating stations were rather considered by the state as a new source of taxation revenue, and it was fortunate that the enormous profits attracted private capital despite all the bureaucratic difficulties encountered. As an indication of the official attitude, foreign bids for big schemes of railroad electrification were turned down in 1897 because the minister was unwilling to allow foreign companies too great a control over Italian resources. Not until just before World War I was Nitti's scheme adopted for large generating plants on the River Sila in Calabria and the River Tirso in Sardinia, and only the pressure of war forced Italy to develop other latent potentialities. Even so, Mussolini after 1919 was naïve enough to blame Nitti for allowing so much American capital to build up this vital industry. The topsy-turvy economics of the new age assumed that it was better to do without than to accept foreign help.

★

Electricity was at last to provide an abundant form of power, and this supplemented the meager deposits of lignite and the importation of foreign coal which by 1914 amounted to one million tons a month. These various sources of power gave a great impetus to Italy's industrial revolution. Hitherto, land and government bonds had been the favored form of investment, while silk and sulphur had alone been of great international importance. Now a wide range of other manufactures began to offer the same combination of profit and security.

The replacement of wood fuel by coal had originally been a severe threat to the subalpine ironworks of the Val d'Aosta and the Val d'Ossola, far away from supplies of coal. After 1878, however, government protection began to be lavishly granted and in proportion to the political weight of industries as well as to their economic need. In many direct and indirect ways the state was to bear the cost and risk of expansion in the heavy industries, and government protection was followed by the forming of cartels. A metal trust had been formed at Florence in 1896 to stop internal competition and raise prices, and in 1905 two rival companies, which had competed for mining concessions in the island of Elba, joined to form the Ilva group, linked with the Terni steelworks and the Orlando shipyards at Leghorn. A second composite group was that of Ansaldo, using the mines of Cogne in the Val d'Aosta, shipyards at Sestri Ponente, and mechanical and electrical shops at Sampierdarena. Combination, though no doubt unavoidable, was bound to result in keeping superfluous and inefficient workshops in existence, and did not suffice to prevent chaotic overproduction after 1907. In 1911 a convention had to be made between the Ilva and other smelting concerns to reduce stocks and prevent further capital being sunk in the industry.

Armament production was always closely involved with politics. The Terni factories in Umbria had a monopoly in the supply of some armaments, and a parliamentary inquiry in 1906 showed that they were misusing the heavy state subsidies in order to pay dividends of 20 per cent, as well as possessing unhealthily close contacts with Krupp and Vickers. Yet the Italian steel cartel was able to use the evidence of German infiltration to extort still further subsidies. Some of the resultant profits, guaranteed by the government, were undoubtedly spent in bribes to obtain even more favorable tariffs and bounties. The cartel was backed in particular by the Banca d'Italia and in time came to be run more by financiers than industrialists, the industrial companies sometimes appearing as pawns in an enormous game of speculation.

These new industries were never really healthy and vigorous. They did not prove remarkably efficient during World War I and often collapsed with disastrous results in the post-war slump after 1919. Without heavy protection they could not have survived so long, since the high charges for coal and other imported raw materials told against them. Heavy duties placed on imported steel and pig iron had meanwhile harmed the mechanical industries by increasing costs all round. And again with shipping, bounties based on tonnage did not encourage efficiency and economy in the shipyards. Protection brought together politicians and speculators, and with the growth of *affairisme* it is not surprising if taxpayers' money was sometimes misspent.

After 1900 the concentration of industry in the North became more pronounced. Even when laws required that one-eighth of the material used for the railroads should come from Naples, the absence of skilled labor made this quota impossible to meet. Milan continued to increase its commercial and industrial predominance and was becoming a highly efficient city which the other Italy of Puccini and Verdi was tempted to dislike for its wealth and materialism. Between Milan, Turin, and Genoa lay most of the nation's industry and wealth, and this disproportion became greater with the passage of time.

Italians had been experimenting with internal combustion engines since the 1830s. The first Italian automobile was made at Turin in 1895, and in 1899 a group of industrialists under Giovanni Agnelli created the Fabbrica Italiana Automobili Torino, or *Fiat* for short. By 1903 there was an output of thirteen hundred cars a year from four factories, and, shortly after the grant of protection in 1905, as many as seventy different concerns were engaged in the automobile industry. But this new group of factories came into activity just when a contraction of sales set in. Overhasty expansion created financial and technical difficulties, and in 1907–8 Fiat had to write off most of its capital. After the industry had rationalized itself, production of cars increased to 18,000 a year in 1914. World War I turned Fiat into the largest group of factories in Italy, responsible for over 70 per cent of the automobiles produced. In addition, Alfa Romeo at Milan specialized in racing cars; Isotta Fraschini, also at Milan, was to be one of the first firms interested in aircraft motors; Bianchi and Prinetti made bicycles; also the factories of Lancia at Turin and Maserati at Bologna became world famous; so did the names of Pirelli and Montecatini.

★

Fifty years after unification, northern and central Italy were becoming prosperous under the benevolent rule of Giolitti. Not even the experience of the 1890s had undermined his confidence in parliamentary government, and his tolerant attitude produced a less inequitable balance of social forces. Both clericals and reformist socialists were gradually drawn into the orbit of the constitution. This was a remarkably buoyant period in Italian history, and affluence brought with it optimism and greater political maturity. Giolitti did not greatly exaggerate when in 1911 he claimed that no other people had in so short a period of time gone through such a profound transformation politically, morally, and economically.

If the nation felt itself internally less divided, this came partly from a developing social conscience and the realization that conservatism might best be served by a policy of enlightened reform. Giolitti insisted that one of society's main tasks was to improve the condition of the poor. He had already more than once proposed the introduction of death duties and a progressive tax on incomes. In 1902 parliament passed a factory act to regulate the work of women and children—though only three inspectors were appointed and one of these was soon dismissed. Giolitti's proposal for a compulsory Sunday holiday was defeated in 1904, but two years later night work was forbidden for women and children in the cotton industry. Agricultural workers were less vociferous and less easily organized, but also benefited. The right to strike was confirmed. Giolitti laid down a special code for unhealthy activities such as rice cultivation, and tried to insist on workers receiving proper sleeping quarters, medical attention, good food, and drinking water. He also reduced food taxes, after being shocked to discover that salt paid fifty-five times its price in tax, while alcohol and tobacco paid only four times. Acts were passed to enforce public holidays, to provide free quinine against malaria, and to prescribe rules for accident prevention. The socialists commented that no fundamental reforms were being tackled and only enough was conceded to avoid serious disturbances; nevertheless it was noteworthy that some of these socialists were becoming far less unco-operative as prosperity spread.

★

In matters of culture, Italy had tended to lag behind France. Marinetti, Pareto, and D'Annunzio chose to write some of their works in French, as did Papini,

Soffici, and Ungaretti; and the most celebrated Italian painter, Modigliani, was French in almost all but name and origin. There had been little of great note in art or architecture during the Humbertine period, and the flamboyant style of the early twentieth century was epitomized by the tasteless Palace of Justice. This building was planned to cost eight million lire but in practice cost thirty-nine, and four deputies had to resign after a parliamentary committee reported in several volumes on this discrepancy. Far worse aesthetically was the hideous Vittorio Emanuele monument which desecrated the skyline of Rome. Covered with warlike emblems, built arrogantly and aggressively on the Capitoline hill, a typical and far too expensive product of top-heavy state enterprise, Sacconi's edifice was a monument to much of what was worst in the age.

In opera Italy had been supreme. Donizetti was dead by 1860 and Rossini's work was over, but Giuseppe Verdi was then beginning to set the fashion of a new dramatic and lyrical style which protected Italian music from too slavish an admiration of Wagner and Debussy. Verdi's enormous output was crowned in 1871 by *Aida* written for the new opera house in Cairo, by the *Requiem* in 1874 to commemorate Manzoni, by *Otello* which was first performed at La Scala in 1887, and finally, when the composer was over eighty years of age, by *Falstaff* in 1893. During the next ten years his successor in popular esteem, Puccini, wrote *La Bohème*, *Tosca*, and *Madama Butterfly*. Mascagni's *Cavalleria rusticana* appeared in 1890, and Leoncavallo's *Pagliacci* in 1892.

De Sanctis had proclaimed as long ago as 1861 that the national *risorgimento* needed to be intellectual and artistic as well as political. Mazzini, too, hoped for an intellectual movement "more stirring, more *initiating* than all French and German *systems* had been or ever will be." But in practice, far from being stimulated by the political revolution, artistic and intellectual life continued at a low ebb after 1860. French novels had a better sale than Italian with intelligent readers such as Cavour, but also with later generations.

In a famous essay, Bonghi showed why Italian literature was not and could not be popular, for the language of 1860 was too refined for simple prose. There was too wide a variety of local idiom and, in treating the life of ordinary people, realism demanded too much dialect for intelligibility. Characters in Fogazzaro's novels sometimes spoke Venetian, those in Fucini, Tuscan. In Naples, Rome, and Lombardy there continued to exist an entirely dialect literature, and D'Annunzio had to leave his native Abruzzi to learn a purer diction in Tuscany. But although many years of city life and popular journalism were needed to fix the language more firmly, by the beginning of the new century a literate public was in existence. This was for books as well as journals and reviews. Carducci died in 1907, De Amicis in 1908, Fogazzaro in 1911, and their books reached a large audience. Carducci's achievement was signalized when in the year before his death he received the Nobel prize for literature.

In philosophy there was an even more significant effort to break the narrow provincialism and characterless cosmopolitanism which distinguished much of

Italian culture. Unification had found the country with no indigenous tradition which could survive the invasion of Parisian art, English political liberalism, and German philosophy and historiography. There was nothing to justify Gioberti's boast that "because Italy is the center of Catholicism, it follows that she is the natural leader of our modern civilization and Rome the true metropolis of the world." Perhaps the very strength of clericalism deprived Italy of the stimulus which in France was to create a flourishing school of lay Catholic philosophers. Instead, the return from exile after 1860 of Bertrando Spaventa and De Sanctis had brought an invigorating injection of Hegelianism, non-Catholic and often anti-Catholic. After Garibaldi in 1860 made De Sanctis minister of education at Naples, thirty of the old timeserving professors were removed from the university and three notable Hegelians figured among their successors. Naples became the center of philosophical studies in Italy, as it had been in the time of Bruno, Campanella, and Vico.

The rival school of scientific positivism was to meet special difficulties in a country where education was fundamentally classical and literary and where the Church stood firmly against the new heresies of Darwin, Comte, and Spencer. An article by the Neapolitan Villari in 1886 marks the appearance of philosophical positivism in Italy, but although it was to be taught in some universities by Ardigò and his disciples, its chief importance was in practical application, for example through the psychological and sociological criminology of Ferri and Lombroso.

Against the somewhat arid achievements of the positivists, speculative thought was revived in philosophical idealism, especially by the Neapolitan, Benedetto Croce. Books on aesthetics and logic by Croce began to appear soon after 1900, and continued through the next half century, sometimes more than one volume a year. Eschewing all remote metaphysics, his attack on current fashions of thought from D'Annunzio to Marxism brought new life into Italian thinking. Croce never held an academic post yet his influence was enormous. His fine style and universal grasp made him read (or read about) by all intelligent people. His Sicilian friend, Giovanni Gentile, was more of a pure philosopher and had an equal following in schools and universities. Until fascism divided these two men, their common respect for spiritual values seeped down through the educational curriculum to color the outlook of ordinary individuals.

★

A morbid phenomenon that not even Croce's criticism could exorcise was the fascinating prose and poetry of Gabriele d'Annunzio. This man spent his time in sensuous and extravagant living, almost always in debt, searching always for what was spectacular. He took everything to excess, seeking always for new experiences and indulgences, for greater speed, greater passion, a more shocking private life, a more violent assault on convention than anyone else. His cult of beauty was in itself an excess. Reveling in the decadence of the aesthetic movement, he preached that everything should be forgiven the artist who was a superman above ordinary morals, just as he should also be above the payment of debts. Poets were for him the acknowledged legislators of mankind. D'Annunzio affected colored cravats, a monocle, and perfumes so pungent that some people could not stay in the same room. It was a fair warning when on the doorway of his luxurious villa he put "beware of the dog" on the left-hand pillar and "beware of the master" on the right.

As a writer, D'Annunzio claimed to be the successor of Carducci. Against the orthodox, romantic tradition of Manzoni and against the spare realism of Verga, he set a new fashion of sonorous rhetoric that was captivating even when it was not meaningful. His characters were not sympathetic or amiable; all of them lacked nobility and nearly all were more or less unbalanced. D'Annunzio gradually moved from aestheticism toward politics and to become what Nitti called "a literary Barnum." He entered parliament in 1897 in order to experience a new sensation; to experience another he crossed over from extreme Right to extreme Left at a moment well-chosen for dramatic effect. Moving quickly through socialism, he had become by 1909 an ardent nationalist, summoning his countrymen to revenge their colonial defeats and conquer their unredeemed provinces from Austria.

In a famous speech, one of the characters in his play *La nave* called on Italians to "man the prow and sail toward the world," a dubious exclamation which had an enormous *réclame* and somehow helped to make nationalism the fashion. In a poem of 1911 he reached the point of saying that "Africa is only the whetstone on which we Italians shall sharpen our sword for a supreme conquest in the unknown future." Beneath his crepuscular, delphic terminology lay half-concealed visions of unmentionable splendor and excitement, and though exposed again and again by Croce and the critics, his rhetoric and his nationalism fitted so exactly the mood of his time that he molded as well as reflected Italian taste. It was to be expected that D'Annunzio would be well to the foreground in the two dramatic moments when Italy entered World War I and then raised Mussolini to power.

31 The Last Years of Liberal Reform, 1909–1911

The elections of 1909 increased the representation of radicals, republicans, and socialists, and this extreme Left rose to 108 in the Lower House. The militant Catholics also numbered about twenty. Whether or not this advance of the two extremes convinced Giolitti that it was time for another of his temporary retirements, or whether he was planning to strengthen himself with the Left, he now brought up again his provocative plan to raise income-tax and death duties. A parliamentary tumult ensued during which a duke was moved to throw an inkpot at the prime minister, and in December, when the *estrema* still refused him their support, Giolitti ended his third and longest ministry. Without waiting to sound parliament in a vote of confidence that might have prejudiced his later return to power, he advised the king to revert to Sonnino and the right-wing liberals.

Sonnino's second administration, like his first, lacked the support of a carefully prepared majority. While Giolitti always kept some personal friends among his political enemies, Sonnino had few friends anywhere, and possessed none of Giolitti's suppleness in debate. His Jewish antecedents and Protestant faith were against him in some quarters—good Catholics were advised not to read his newspaper, *Il Giornale d'Italia*. This time Sonnino avoided association with the radicals. He also appointed thirty new conservative senators, among them Benedetto Croce himself. Croce had already been put up for this honor by the previous government, but Giolitti claimed not to have heard of him. After three months, when Admiral Bettolo ran into severe opposition over his proposal to increase the subsidies of shipping firms, the cabinet did not wait to be defeated in parliament but gave way to another under Luigi Luzzatti.

These successive cabinets are not easily differentiated. No parliamentary leader had any very distinct party support outside parliament, and inside they all claimed the title of liberal—not only Giolitti and Zanardelli, but Sonnino and Luzzatti, Crispi and Di Rudinì. As Giolitti told Salandra, they were all liberals of a sort but the word now covered so many different shades of opinion that it ought to be dropped. Most of these liberals were eventually to draw closer together when socialism became more an object of fear but, for the moment, Right Center and Left Center competed against each other with competitive projects of reform, and the radicals could without dishonesty take office under Sonnino, Luzzatti, and Giolitti in turn.

Luzzatti was, like his predecessor, a Jew. He was a famous and erudite economist and already had been five times minister of the treasury. Personally he inclined to the Right, but his cabinet included two radicals, Sacchi and Credaro, as well as several Giolittians. Laudable measures were announced to put down usury, to control food adulteration, to abolish the truck system of wages in the mines, and for compulsory insurance and cheap housing.

Early in 1911, however, when Luzzatti proposed a moderate electoral reform, Giolitti sensed a drift of opinion which gave him a new opening. Dramatically, and despite his former scruples, Giolitti outbid the government and demanded universal suffrage, for since the democratic trend of society seemed irreversible, he wanted to gain for himself the prestige of such a concession and win power in time to prepare for the next elections. The radicals thereupon helped to defeat the ministry, indicating how cleverly Giolitti had chosen the issue on which to resume office. The same Chamber that had welcomed Luzzatti by 393 votes against 17 hailed his successor by 340 votes to 87. How unreal was the change appeared from Giolitti's retention of seven out of ten of Luzzatti's ministers, even including those radicals against whom he had fought in the elections of 1904 and 1909.

★

Once again the socialist party refused Giolitti's offer of collaboration. The indecisiveness of Italian socialism, its internal divisions and continued invocation of violence and revolution, all these were to make a tiresomely complicated story but were to be of the greatest importance in the next few years. Its party congress at Rome in 1906 had recorded a victory for "integralism" when the syndicalists were heavily outnumbered, yet revolutionary socialism continued to spread, especially in Milan and in the agricultural areas round Parma, Reggio, and Ferrara. The two extreme wings of the official socialist party disagreed strongly over ends as well as means, yet even the right wing feared to split socialism still further by explicit collaboration with a bourgeois government.

The syndicalist program was to boycott parliament, to back the trade unions as a kind of anti-state, and to exert control back over production by resort to a general strike. The agricultural strikes of 1908 in Parma and Ferrara put this program to the test, but they only drove the landowners into defensive leagues and counterrevolution. It was a foretaste of the future when, in 1908, the landowners of Emilia collected a defense fund and formed a motorized volunteer force equipped with arms. This force assisted the troops in street-fighting at Parma and marched through a barrage of missiles to occupy the working-class quarter of the city. Similar scenes were to occur more frequently in the not so distant future. Some of the syndicalists, Arturo Labriola among them, saw that their best hope of revolution might lie in encouraging an aggressive nationalism. Olivetti demonstrated how easily some extremists of the Left could accept an objective of imperialism in which war and conquest became ends in themselves, and he even advocated voting for reactionary representatives so as to bring the parliamentary system into contempt.

The ordinary working man was far less extreme than these firebrand leaders, and the reformists were therefore voted into control of the trade unions when a General Confederation of Labor was formed in 1908. Reformists also proved successful when they joined radicals and left-wing liberals to win many town administrations. The positive and immediate success of this collaborative method secured a decisive victory for reformism in the socialist congress of 1908 at Florence. It was there declared that the general strike and any strike of state employees were dangerous weapons not to be lightly used. As a result the revolutionary syndicalists were expelled and the remaining extremists around Ferri were placed in a clear minority.

From 1908 to 1910, the moderates Bissolati and Treves used the pages of *Avanti* to try to educate the workers in a policy of gradual reform, and to wean them from unqualified faith in the international solidarity of the working classes. These two "reformists" held that the practice of democracy and a wider suffrage should be used as means toward persuading the electorate to accept socialism. Eventually, but more slowly than Bissolati, Turati was to agree that socialists might even consider taking office.

In the party congress of 1910 at Milan, a revolutionary remnant inside the party was led by Lazzari and the young Mussolini. The voting at the congress showed that these revolutionaries were still in a minority of about one to four, which led Giolitti to conclude that sweet reasonableness must have worked and "Marx had been relegated to the attic." The revolutionaries answered him by producing a journal called *The Attic*, and his confidence was soon made to look premature.

Giolitti's fourth ministry had some support from the moderate socialists. Although Bissolati reiterated their refusal to enter the cabinet, it was important that at last a socialist had entered the Quirinal—albeit in a soft hat and lounge suit which scandalized the Court—to advise the king over a ministerial crisis. In a private letter to Giolitti, Bissolati confessed that only a temperamental predilection for being "against the government" had motivated his refusal to become a minister, not a serious difference of principle. Nevertheless, he resigned from *Avanti* in favor of Treves, realizing that the majority of socialists still preferred a more uncompromising attitude.

The moderates had gone too far and too fast for their party. At the congress of Modena in 1911, Bissolati and Bonomi found themselves against a coalition of intransigents and "integralists," with whom were temporarily associated the other school of reformism under Turati, Treves, and Modigliani. Bissolati claimed that he was right to be pleased that the head of the state had recognized the political power of socialism. But most party leaders had been nurtured in the dogmas of class war and revolution, and it was the extremists who in 1912 were once again to capture the party organization and funds.

★

Meanwhile an act of 1911–12 greatly extended the franchise concessions of 1882. Having effectively pre-empted Luzzatti's platform, Giolitti surprised everyone by the concession of manhood suffrage and raised the electorate from three to eight million. It was arguable that the partial project which Luzzatti had proposed would mainly have enfranchised the town artisans and so aided socialism, whereas manhood suffrage included the southern peasantry whose vote would offset the radically minded workers in the North. A wider suffrage would give a firmer basis to the social structure. Giolitti admitted that a social revolution had taken place since the last electoral reform and this made necessary a much wider participation in political life.

The new law gave the vote to all males over thirty or who had served in the forces. This meant illiterates too, so pictorial symbols were included on voting cards to differentiate the various parties. Votes were not granted to women, though this had been desired by the socialists and Sonnino's conservatives. Sonnino also made a bid for proportional representation, but Giolitti disagreed on the grounds that it would benefit smaller parties and so make a working majority even harder to build. The payment of deputies was agreed to in 1911, and Giolitti also promised to check the use of fraud and violence in elections— disingenuously, as his own conduct in 1913 was to show.

One or two dissentient voices were heard. The political philosopher Mosca foretold that a wider suffrage would add to the problems which it was intended to solve, and he considered it merely a dodge by which the Giolittians hoped to keep power. His opposition to it was that of a liberal who discerned in this reform the beginning of the end of liberalism. Manhood suffrage, he said, would decrease that proportion of the electorate which had "political capacity" and increase the representation of local or class interests. The *Corriere della Sera* likewise shied at this latest step on the dreaded path to democracy and regretfully watched rival liberal groups competing for support from the uneducated masses. When a minor peasant revolt broke out late in the summer of 1911 against the "spreaders of cholera dust," many people realized belatedly how ignorant and superstitious was the new electorate.

The conservative leaders Salandra, Sonnino, and Luzzatti all approved of the law and even hoped that its provisions might be extended to make voting compulsory. This was because they hoped that the new electors in the South would overthrow the local cliques which had been used to guarantee Giolitti's majority. Manhood suffrage would, they believed, shatter the socialists' claim to speak for the people and would "contradict the argument that parliament was merely a shareholders' meeting to promote bourgeois interests." Among the Catholics similarly there were many who thought that they could rely on the peasant vote, at least until free elementary education began to produce its corrosive effects. Hence Catholics and conservatives virtually agreed with radicals and socialists, each of them hoping to exploit popular sovereignty for their own ends.

Giolitti had apparently triumphed. And yet instead of such a broad suffrage helping him, it was shortly to generate new mass parties which spelled ruin to the existing balance of politics. A larger proportion of people had been given the vote than was usual in other European states, but these newly enfranchised masses did not always possess a vested interest in the preservation of social order, and hence might have more reason to overthrow existing society than to defend it.

Democratic in appearance, the main effect of Giolitti's reform was to change the composition of the ruling elite by favoring those adept at manipulating elections and utilizing the democratic myth. It put a premium on demagogy and rhetoric by promising power cheaply to those who offered most bread and circuses—which in the end meant fascism. Giolitti himself looked upon democracy as something which should grow naturally out of liberalism, though he did not possess the skill or imagination to control the difficult process of transition. Croce and Mosca, on the other hand, were satisfied that liberalism and democracy were irreconcilable and indeed antithetical. As the liberals in general were too self-assured in their monopoly of power to yield willingly, democracy was going to develop less by evolution and gradual concessions than as something revolutionary grafted on the state from outside. Since most liberals were too proud and insensitive to court popularity, and since the socialists were too doctrinaire to collaborate in government, it was the fascists who eventually gained. Universal suffrage was thus to assist in weakening the liberal party: the old liberal ruling classes were soon so afraid of the new popular parties, whether socialist or Catholic, that to combat them they signed their own death warrant by supporting Mussolini.

As well as his franchise act, Giolitti obtained approval in April 1912 for the government to take over a monopoly of life insurance. State monopolies had already yielded a good revenue from salt and tobacco, and Giolitti was disturbed to see that the profits of private life insurance were enormous even though its risks were more or less accurately calculable. He also argued that too much capital was thereby concentrated in a few hands, and those for the most part foreign hands, so that too much money was leaving the country. Opposition to his proposal was encountered from the leading economists of the day, Pantaleoni, Einaudi, and De Viti de Marco; also from the conservatives, Sonnino and Salandra; and from the insurance companies and other financial interests who feared more nationalization to come. The chief spokesman for the bill was the southern radical, Professor Nitti. After a stormy session, parliament agreed to it, but such were the vested interests involved that its repeal was one of Mussolini's first measures after 1922.

★

Another reform which Giolitti took over from Luzzatti was an education act to supplement the Casati law of 1859 and the Coppino act of 1877. Individual teachers had often been men of great distinction, but the educational system itself was widely criticized. One complaint was that it concentrated too much on literature and the classics, another that religious instruction was neglected (or some people said over-stressed). Education was generally held to be far too centralized, since the king appointed the rector of each university and the heads of faculties, while the minister for education determined even details of the school curriculum.

The chief criticism was that the establishment of "compulsory" elementary education in 1877 had in many areas remained a dead letter. There had been little if any sanction of force behind it, and far too few school inspectors had been appointed to supervise its application. Parents preferred their children to earn money rather than attend school. They associated education with taxes, and hence protests against taxation sometimes took the form of assaults on school buildings. Local authorities were always tempted to economize at the expense of popular education; government loans for school building were sometimes refused or diverted elsewhere; and teachers, whose salaries should have increased by one-tenth every six years, were often dismissed and reappointed at their former salary. The poverty of schoolmasters certainly helped the spread of socialism, and the Church had this in mind when it opposed or retarded the development of secular state education. But in any case, so easy was it to disobey regulations that millions of children managed to escape schooling, and almost half the population was still illiterate according to the census of 1911.

One problem in the universities was that education was too cheap. Italy had not only more illiterates but also more university students than many European countries, and an intellectual proletariat was being produced that was more dangerous and multiplying faster than the real proletariat. A university education was a useful qualification even for minor government posts, and such was the social prestige of government service or the professions that parents successfully combated any attempt to increase fees or raise standards of entry.

Professors complained that they were still paid the same as fifty years previously despite the fall by a half in the value of money, and the need to find other part-time work gave them little direct contact with pupils except at examination times. We hear of students breaking up a course of lectures (since by law this might exempt them from examination), and there might be riots against professors who insisted on attendance at lectures or who dared to fail their examinees. Examples are on record of corruption or intimidation by the family of a student whose career was at stake. In Sicily there were cases of lecturers and even schoolmasters having to be given a police escort after the examination results were announced, and of prizes not being awarded because teachers did not dare differentiate between students. Moreover, the subjects favored for degrees suggested that professionalism all too often overcame the desire for either general education or disinterested speculation and research. Technological education was backward, and it was something quite new when in 1902 the famous Bocconi university, specializing in economics, was founded at Milan. Since by far the greater number of students read law or medicine, these two professions suffered from chronic overcrowding. Fortunato noted it as a morbid sign that even in 1900 there was one lawyer for every 1,300 people in Italy, and in Sardinia there was one lawsuit pending for every three inhabitants—lawsuits that almost always took years to resolve.

The radical minister of education, Credaro, had been inherited by Giolitti from the previous cabinet together with his draft of reform. Both men realized that the electorate would need better schooling if the new suffrage act were to work and a primary need was to raise the salaries and social esteem of the teaching profession. Many teachers were being worked too hard, though

Giolitti was worried that university professorships were sometimes created even where there were no pupils. He also criticized the casualness with which diplomas could be awarded even in the most recondite subjects.

Credaro's chief contribution was to make a larger grant-in-aid by the state and to give the control of elementary education to the provinces instead of to the small communes which often contrived to avoid their responsibilities. Unfortunately, a comprehensive plan had small chance of being discussed and applied when thirty-five ministers of education followed each other in the thirty-eight years after Crispi's first accession to power. Equally unfortunate was that the new regulations of 1911 had barely time to be effected before World War I upset everything, and it remained for Professor Gentile in 1923 to attempt a more fundamental reform of education.

SECTION EIGHT: THE ONSET OF WAR

32   The German Alliance, 1896–1911

The Triple Alliance with Germany and Austria was renewed in 1891 and 1902, but critics were beginning to argue that it thwarted Italy's ambitions in the Adriatic and the Balkans. Italians therefore sought to make a supplementary agreement with Great Britain, the strongest Mediterranean power. Britain had sometimes, very improbably, been thought to covet Sicily for her empire, but most Italians feared British hostility far less than British indifference, and there was no common frontier to cause trouble as there was with France. By 1900 an understanding had therefore been reached with Britain about Mediterranean affairs; also the King of Italy was called upon in 1902 and 1905 to arbitrate between Britain, Brazil, and Portugal over colonial disputes; and it was even hoped that the Triple might become a Quadruple Alliance.

In the early 1890s Franco-Italian relations were severely strained. Crispi's trade war had serious psychological as well as economic results, and latent ill-feeling burst out after riots against immigrant Italian workmen at Aigues Mortes in 1893. This antagonism lost Italy the scope for maneuver between France and Germany that offered the best chances of an independent foreign policy. The defeat at Adowa, moreover, proved that Crispi, deluded by his own dramatic gestures and flagwaving, had overestimated the country's strength and so had misjudged its true interests in picking a quarrel with France.

The Marquis Visconti-Venosta then became foreign minister. He had already held the same position in 1863–64, 1866–67, and 1869–76; and in two further periods of office between 1896 and 1901 this experienced and professional diplomat adopted the more subtle and opportunist expedients of his mentor Cavour. Visconti-Venosta had been alarmed at Crispi's submission to Bismarck and rightly feared an Austrian advance into the Balkans, so the pendulum now swung in favor of an understanding with France. In 1896 Italy at last recognized the French protectorate over Tunis, and two years later Luzzatti was sent to Paris to terminate the ten-year-old tariff war. From the other side, Barrère, who was French ambassador at Rome for the next twenty-five years, worked cleverly to weaken Italy's attachment to the *Triplice*. Early in 1900 the Italian fleet made a ceremonial visit to Toulon. Then, in December, an exchange of notes recognized the paramount French interest in Morocco and the Italian interest in Libya.

In addition, Vittorio Emanuele III was much less Germanophile than his father, while Queen Elena came from Montenegro and had been brought up in Russia, two countries that were at odds with Austria. In one of many *faux pas*, the German emperor visited Italy with a retinue of giant Pomeranian grenadiers, which delighted the cartoonists but infuriated the diminutive king. Instead of impressing Italians, this was taken as bad manners and equally bad psychology. On another visit some cruelly disparaging words by the emperor were unfortunately overheard and reported by a German-speaking Italian. As a gesture of independence, Vittorio Emanuele pointedly made state visits to Paris, London, and St. Petersburg.

More seriously, Zanardelli's foreign minister was the Milanese industrialist, Prinetti, who even went so far as to revive feelings of irredentism against Austria. In November 1902, Prinetti assured Barrère that Italian obligations under the Triple Alliance were limited: "If France is directly or indirectly attacked, Italy will maintain a strict neutrality, and it will be the same if France, as a result of direct provocation, is compelled to declare war in defence of her honor and security." This secondary entente with France, though in blatant contradiction to obligations under the German alliance, was a partial return to the traditional foreign policy of makeweight between rival power groups. Von Bülow accused Italy of flagrant adultery, but later admitted that a husband might occasionally dance with someone else's partner, especially as Austria and Germany themselves made subsidiary agreements with Russia and Turkey outside the alliance. The Triple Alliance for reasons of expediency continued in force until 1915, but some subtlety was needed to explain the import and morality of its protracted existence. An Italian foreign minister had told Barzilai as far back as 1892 that the alliance with Germany was a piece of bluff and there was no intention of ever acting on it.

Though Giolitti as prime minister in 1903 welcomed the *rapprochement* with France, it was not thought necessary to take this to the point of throwing over the *Triplice*, and the Triple Alliance was formally renewed in 1907 and 1912. The foreign minister Tittoni ingenuously repudiated any intention of being deceitful "for that would be unworthy of a great nation"; but in practice he and his successor continued to flirt with both sides. Giolitti's personal disregard for foreign affairs was proverbial, and he was criticized for spending too little money on supplying the armed services or on bribing the foreign press. If he renewed the Triple Alliance this was largely out of inertia, because it was an inexpensive piece of reinsurance, and it was not his nature to copy the far more complicated foreign policy of Bismarck or Cavour.

★

The outward continuance of the German connection reflected cultural and financial links forged in twenty years of alliance. Parallel with the political and economic breach with France, observers had noted a retreat from French rationalism and a marked preference for German scientific method in philosophy, religion, technology, and law. French influence continued to prevail in some fields: in painting through the impressionists, in literature through D'Annunzio and Soffici. In their different fields, Sorel, Maurras, Barrès, and Loisy had a sizable following in Italy. But Croce and Gentile, had a preference for orienting Italian intellectual life around Hegel and German philosophy. The study of German literature became more common and students went to

Germany to complete their education, while textbooks were modeled on, or translated from, the German. Writers of Prezzolini's generation, nurtured in French culture, began to wonder whether post-Bismarckian Germany might be politically more admirable than the France of Dreyfus and the Panama scandal. Even the Italian socialists abandoned Bakunin for Marx and named their paper *Avanti* after the German *Vorwärts*.

When Crispi's tariff war led to the withdrawal of French investment capital, Germany became the chief alternative source. Early in the 1890s the Deutsche Bank sent Siemens to make a financial agreement with Giolitti in Rome, and the renewal of the *Triplice* was accompanied by the grant of commercial facilities to Italy. Many Italian firms were soon owned by Germans, others were dependent on German patents or on the German chemical and electrical industries. Eighty per cent of the cotton machinery used in Italian factories was said to be made in Germany. German finance was heavily engaged in the construction of railroads to develop Trieste. The Banca Commerciale Italiana, for which most of the capital was Austrian and German, controlled several important shipping lines, half the electric companies and much of the steel industry; and this provided a concealed influence over the press and in politics. Simultaneously, the habit of vacations and Alpinism was bringing German settlers and travelers along the Brenner railroad and down the Adige Valley.

These changes were not unwelcome except for their political implications. It was the fear of exclusive dependence upon Germany which, at the conference of Algeciras early in 1906, caused Visconti-Venosta to lean toward France. In newspapers there was a revival of irredentist ambitions toward the cisalpine provinces of the Austrian empire, and currency was given to the name Alto Adige to describe what Austrians preferred to call the Südtirol. Special journals and learned societies were founded wherein individual Italian savants, with a deliberately political intention, proved the affinities of the local dialects with Italian, and postulated that the water system of the Trentino, like the geological formation of the Carso, made these regions essentially part of Italy. Minority rights were demanded at Trent and Bozen, but unsuccessfully. Cesare Battisti and his irredentist companions took it upon themselves to spy on the movement of war material in this Austrian province and send details to Rome. Italian-speaking professors at Innsbruck tried to lecture in Italian, so provoking student riots which triggered off violent outbursts in both Italy and Germany. Two foreign ministers, Tittoni and Di San Giuliano, felt obliged to state in public that irredentism was dead, but an instinct of self-preservation kept Italian language and culture alive in these border provinces. The Speaker of the Chamber, the radical Marcora, embarrassed the orthodox by publicly referring to "our Trent," and Giolitti later confessed that he used government money to assist the victory of the Italian element in municipal elections at Trieste just as Vienna favored the Slovenes. The alliance with Austria was clearly wearing thin.

In 1908, Austria announced the formal annexation of Bosnia and Herzegovina, thus drawing attention to the rapidly altering balance of power in the Balkans. This stirred up the peoples of that unstable area to seek revenge, and Italians in particular were resentful. It was no accident that the following year the Czar visited the King of Italy at Racconigi. Hitherto, the Left had resisted any friendly gesture being made toward autocratic Russia, so much so that Giolitti had to threaten prefects with dismissal if the Czar's visit provoked any hostile demonstration, but the event proved that even some of the *estrema* were now prepared to back Russia against the Austrians. At Racconigi an agreement was made with the Russians to keep Austria from further disturbing the *status quo* in the Balkans and to look benevolently on each other's designs in the Dardanelles and Tripoli. Thus yet another blow was struck at the spirit of the *Triplice*, and we now know that the Austrian general staff began to think about open hostilities against so uncertain an ally.

★

Italy meanwhile was being swept by the same jingoism which pervaded not only the Kaiser's Germany but Theodore Roosevelt's America and the England of Joseph Chamberlain and Kipling. To some extent this Italian nationalism was an understandable reaction against people such as Lombroso and Ferrero who tended to praise the superiority of Anglo-Saxons to Latins; but in part was trivial and almost morbid. We find protests against French menus and fashions in dress, against foreign words creeping into the language, against works of art going to America, against foreign offers of help after the terrible earthquake disasters in the South, and even against foreign generosity when the campanile of St. Mark's in Venice collapsed.

From something natural and not unhealthy, jingoism eventually became a disease for those many people who were susceptible to nationalistic vanity and rhetorical overemphasis. Mazzini and Garibaldi were Italian patriots who deplored nationalism or any encroachment on the rights of other peoples. Yet the irredentism which looked toward Trent, Trieste, even sometimes to Nice, Corsica, and Malta, was for some people a projection of *risorgimento* patriotism. Crispi spoke of Italy's need for domination in the Mediterranean. In 1894 Farini, the president of the Senate, talked of the army as alone in keeping Italy united, and ominously remarked that Italy must become a strong militarist state or cease to exist.

The wish for a strong army and navy was not merely the sovereign's personal whim but was shared by ordinary liberals and Catholics at many levels of society. In 1907, when Baron Casana became the first civilian minister of war in Italian history, the hope was that a civilian might persuade parliament to increase military expenditure. When he still insisted on saying that Italy must proportion her forces to her means, this unexceptionable statement provoked considerable disapproval, and he had to resign in favor of General Spingardi who then continued in this office through four successive cabinets. In 1908 it was decided to build four more ironclad battleships.

The military men thought this armament policy too modest, the radicals called it too grandiose, and others found it simply ineffective. In July 1906 a parliamentary commission reported on scandalous incompetence in provision for the navy. Not only did ships take six years to build, but the report exposed administrative disorder, the use of defective steel, and corruption in the placing of contracts. As high protective duties had freed domestic industry from its worst fears of foreign rivalry, there was no great incentive for cheapness or modernization, and this often left the armed forces dependent on inferior and expensive weapons. The Terni company received particular blame, heavily financed as it was by the state for the profit of influential shareholders. This report led to an angry debate and a violent tumult during which the Speaker's chair was overturned and the Chamber had to be forcibly cleared.

★

In the Florentine magazine *Il Regno* between 1904 and 1906, Corradini and a new group of extreme nationalists, alongside more moderate men such as Prezzolini and Papini, began to advocate another great age of Italian expansion. A new paper at Venice was significantly entitled *Mare Nostrum*, another in Milan *La Grande Italia*. At the Milan exhibition of 1906 a special section was devoted to the work of Italians abroad, and in 1908 and 1911 national congresses were held in the United States by Italian emigrants. Religious orders and missions from Italy were prominent in Syria as in North America, and in 1907 the Pope was persuaded to substitute Italy for France as the protecting power for Catholics in Turkey. Most important symptom of all, in 1910 the first congress was held in the Palazzo Vecchio at Florence of a new Nationalist Party, claiming the inheritance of Crispi's imperialist tradition and going far beyond the patriotism of the *risorgimento*. In the following year, on the anniversary of Adowa, Corradini and Federzoni launched its journal, *L'Idea Nazionale*.

This party was not without an admirable idealism, but its less worthy elements were soon in charge, inebriated with the vulgar imperialism of violence and conquest. Its publicity was subsidized by the big Ansaldo combine whose huge steelworks and machine shops relied on armaments for their continued prosperity. If the Nationalist Party was irredentist, this was only incidental, and until after the outbreak of war in 1914 it was not sure whether to stand with or against Austria so long as blood could be shed and victories won. Its adherents believed with D'Annunzio that paradise lay in the shadow of the sword; with Papini that war was a quick and heroic means to power and wealth; and with Corradini that the sacredness of human life was outmoded sentimental idealism. Corradini, one of the more moderate, said that with a hundred men ready to die he could give Italy new life. For him nationalism was welcome as an antithesis of democracy, and without an authoritarian state there could be no future for Italy. The ideals of liberty and equality should be replaced by discipline and obedience; instead of life being sacred, he insisted that life should be lived aggressively, dangerously, and with hardship.

Mingled with these novel ideas, nationalism learned from Sorel and the syndicalists about the political use of violence. From Darwin and Spencer were derived such terms as the fight for existence between nations, natural selection, and the survival of the fittest. Hegelians supplied the concept of an ethical state which was far greater than the sum of individuals who composed it. Alfredo Oriani represented yet another current of authoritarian thought, discontented with liberalism and believing in the right of an elite to seize power. Oriani campaigned to take the statue of Julius Caesar from the Capitoline museum and raise it in some public square as a reminder of the Roman conquest of Europe. Oriani was later hailed as a prophet of fascism, to whose tomb Mussolini was one day to lead a "pilgrimage." His remarkable and readable books are full of talk about "Roman eagles," "imperial destinies," and the "*virtù* of our race," but they are bitter in their recollection of the recent past as well as vainglorious and aggressive in their hopes for the future.

Another ingredient came from the "futurists" who thought of war as "the only purifier of the world." Marinetti's Futurist Manifesto of 1909 repudiated the criterion of justice and extolled conquest and power:

We sing the love of danger. Courage, rashness, and rebellion are the elements of our poetry. Hitherto literature has tended to exalt thoughtful immobility, ecstasy, and sleep, whereas we are for aggressive movement, febrile insomnia, mortal leaps, and blows with the fist. We proclaim that the world is the richer for a new beauty of speed, and our praise is for the man at the wheel. There is no beauty now save in struggle, no masterpiece can be anything but aggressive, and hence we glorify war, militarism, and patriotism.

In fulfillment of this theme, Carrà in 1910 produced a manifesto of futurist painting and Boccioni in 1912 one for futurist sculpture. Thirsting after novel sensations, Silvio Mix produced a futurist ballet called *Cocktail*; Russolo in 1912 began to write "noise music" for an orchestra of thirty different noises; and Folgore wrote odes to coal and electricity. Contemptuous of intellectualism, or even intelligibility, hermetic poets tried "to free words from the tyranny of syntax and meaning," and made their poems a phonetic and illogical concatenation of symbols. Papini in his futurist period described the essence of futurism as all that was fantastic, rebellious, destructive, and agitated. It was the breaking of all rules, for Italian culture had too long been copying other nations. Papini talked of wanting to burn all libraries and museums, to end the vacuous adulation of Dante and Giotto, and to throw away the traditions of university academicism represented by Carducci and Pascoli. The best concerto was the noise of a busy city, so he said, and the most profound philosophy was that of a peasant ploughing or of a carpenter whose mind was a complete blank. Marinetti went one better and started a campaign against spaghetti as too middle-class and respectable a food for a new race of *conquistadores*.

These were the petulant and rebellious manifestations of would-be artists who felt a need to create something new and yet discovered that short of this extravagant rhetoric they had nothing very noteworthy to say. It is interesting that, despite their *avant-garde* attitude toward art, in politics the futurists earned the title of reactionary. They believed in force, at home and abroad, and together with the nationalists they reacted strongly against Italian passivity in North Africa and the Balkans. They discovered that many of the younger generation had an unsatisfied longing for national grandeur. Educated on the stirring exploits of Garibaldi and of that man whom they regarded as an honorary Italian, Napoleon Bonaparte, many surplus graduates were humiliated to find themselves keeping accounts or writing for cheap magazines.

The nationalists at last gave Italy a self-confessed and active party of the extreme Right. Some industrialists provided money for its organization and its newspapers, approving both its foreign policy of expansion and its domestic policy of authoritariansim and the disciplining of labor. The socialists naturally opposed it; so did Croce on intellectual grounds, and Nitti and Salvemini from their various radical standpoints. But some liberals were converted. Maffeo Pantaleoni the economist, impelled by his compound dislike of socialism, parliamentary degeneration, and labor unrest, moved over toward a party which took pride in being antiliberal, antidemocratic, even antiparliament.

Giolitti saw what was happening, and as his policy was always to bring inside his majority as many as possible of the live forces of the nation, he pondered how to satisfy these new currents of opinion on the extreme Right, just as he had already made gestures toward the clericals and the moderate socialists. At the first nationalist party congress in 1910 Federzoni, the future fascist minister, called for the invasion of Libya which was part of the Turkish empire, and a year later Giolitti launched Italy on another colonial war of conquest.

33   The Libyan War, 1911–1912

Although the disaster of Adowa had temporarily halted active colonial expansion, Eritrea had been retained (though Luzzatti had a project for exchanging it for Cyprus), and a protectorate was established over much of Somaliland. During the South African war, though many Italians supported the Boers, some newspapers suggested aiding Britain in return for the gift of Malta and perhaps

Egypt. More practically, trade concessions were won from the sultan of Zanzibar, and Crispi had earlier tried unsuccessfully to rival France in Morocco, building warships for the sultan and securing a contract to set up an arms factory and a mint. Morocco had eventually to be written off along with Tunisia and Egypt as barred from Italian exploitation. But in Libya the Italian consul was encouraged by Crispi to intrigue with dissident Arab groups as a preliminary to occupation. Naval bases had been constructed in southern Italy at Taranto, Brindisi, and Augusta. This southward shift away from the old ports of Genoa, Spezia, and Venice was a move toward Africa.

Considerations of prestige sent Italy yet further afield. Pelloux never published the documents about his military expedition to China in 1899–1900, and Giolitti's biographer, Natale, says that Giolitti privately persuaded the opposition in the national interest not to press for information on a fiasco which was expensive and unsuccessful.

The China expedition was widely recognized as absurd, and Nitti was not alone in thinking it wasteful to go chasing after sandy deserts in Africa. Radical humanitarians remembered the embarrassing remark of Garibaldi that if Italy tried to conquer other peoples, he himself would regretfully take their side against his own fellow countrymen. Southern Italy in any case desperately needed the money that was being squandered on prestige ventures abroad, and it was ironic to see railroads being built in Africa when some Italian districts had been awaiting them for fifty years. Trade figures by no means justified these colonies, and despite the constructive work being done in Eritrea by Ferdinando Martini, they remained an economic liability—all the more so if one remembers the enormous cost of colonial wars in 1896 and 1911–12. The arguments about colonies absorbing surplus population were beside the point, for only 1 per cent of Italian emigrants would go to Italian colonies in Africa as against 40 per cent to America, and it was hardly likely that peasants would voluntarily go to Libya where soil and climate were even worse than in Sicily and the Basilicata. A commission under a British geologist, reporting in 1909 on the possibility of Jewish settlement in Libya, advised against the colonization of such arid desert, and was unable to find the great mineral deposits that it was said to contain.

Yet these bogus arguments went on being used in Italy because economic facts were buried under considerations of emotion and prestige. Turiello, for example, had strongly advocated expansion of the white races, and in the struggle for life each nation had to seek out colonies to make itself powerful and respected. Oriani about 1900 was writing that conquests in Africa and the Balkans were a duty, part of Italy's historic mission which she could not abdicate. The worth of peoples, he said, was to be measured by the extent and celebrity of their expansion—and he once offered to accompany a polar expedition as its official poet and historian.

In the pages of *Il Regno* this frenetic mood was exploited by people who glorified war for its own sake and called Italians a naturally warlike race. Dogali and Adowa, said Martini, had so depressed national morale that Italians were losing heart and confidence in themselves. Hence successful war was essential to restore self-confidence, and the fiftieth anniversary of unification must be celebrated by the conquest of Libya to prove that Italians were worthy of nationhood. Such was the spirit with which Giolitti had to reckon in 1911. When Ricciotti Garibaldi assembled some hundreds of red-shirted volunteers in that year to re-conquer an Italian empire on the Albanian coast (one of them was a youngster of fourteen, Italo Balbo, the future fascist leader) it became expedient for the government to consider if nationalist sentiment could be more safely and profitably canalized into an official invasion of North Africa.

★

By 1911, Libya had become in popular imagination a veritable Eldorado, and a book about it with the title of *Our Promised Land* appeared that same year. History and geography were invoked to establish a proprietary right over this former dependency of ancient Rome. Sicilians as diverse as Crispi, the socialist De Felice, and the conservative foreign minister Di San Giuliano, all agreed on the strange doctrine that similarities of cultivation and climate made North Africa a natural outlet for surplus Italian population.

The first plan had been one for economic penetration in this province of the Turkish empire. Hitherto most imports into Libya had come from England, while Libyan ivory and esparto grass went to England and her ostrich feathers to France. But after 1905 the Banco di Roma secured mining concessions, and launched an exaggerated propaganda campaign about the plentiful raw materials to be found there. The bank soon controlled grain mills and part of the sponge industry. But Turkish nationalists naturally feared any one European state becoming deeply involved in their empire and guessed that Italian contractors were politically subsidized. Preferential concessions were therefore given to Krupp instead of Ansaldo, Siemens instead of Marconi, and the Deutsche Bank instead of the Banco di Roma, and when an Italian firm submitted the lowest bid for the harbor works at Tripoli, the Turks preferred to drop the whole project.

Italians became even more alarmed when Britain and France took greater interest in North African shipping lines and in "archaeological research." When French troops entered Morocco in 1911, and when Germany after the Agadir crisis was thought to be picking her way toward other vacant stretches of North Africa, Italians were driven to consider military conquest if they did not want to give up what they took to be a generally recognized right of pre-emption over Libya. They did not like the prospect of another humiliation such as their loss of Tunis in 1881, nor that of Germany turning Benghazi into another Agadir. The Banco di Roma, furthermore, deliberately played on this fear and circulated a rumor about selling to Austrian and German banks its considerable interests in Libya.

Giolitti became worried. He had opposed earlier efforts at colonization, but was genuinely annoyed when the Turks, instead of yielding gracefully to economic penetration, chose instead to offer alternative concessions in Mesopotamia. Giolitti never allowed himself to fall far behind public opinion and sensed that national prestige now required a more assertive foreign policy.

In the summer of 1911 he therefore decided to act. If other countries forestalled him in Libya he might be outvoted, whereas forceful action might win over the nationalists and the new mass electorate which he was in the process of enfranchising. Hastily he prepared an offensive while the foreign ambassadors were still away on summer vacations and while the weather still permitted. Because of the need for secrecy and haste he had no time to make entirely sure that the army was ready for war, let alone for a desert campaign. He could not stop to verify his assumption that the local Arabs would be hostile to Turkey, nor could he prepare public opinion at home or governments abroad. These omissions were to prove costly.

★

Left-wing opinion mostly disliked the prospect of war, and ordinary citizens sometimes mutinied or tore up railroad tracks to stop the movement of troops. Anticlericals in general resented that the Catholic Banco di Roma, the bank of the Holy See, should benefit from state expenditure and be saved from the consequences of its ill-judged investment policy. Salvemini, in his paper *Unità*, showed that he knew far more about the unpromising conditions of Tripoli than did those who considered it potentially a great economic asset, and Ferrero saw in Italian imperialism the mark of typically German power politics. According to the radical intellectuals, Italy should renounce her idea of being that kind of great power, for she could never afford it, and Libya promised to be not an Eldorado but the grave of any Italian settlers.

The socialist party congress at Modena therefore declared against war as did the official socialist paper *Avanti* and the reformist *Critica Sociale*. Turati wrote that the war was one of aggression which would arouse brutal mob instincts and assist a return to power of the reactionaries. As for the revolutionary socialists, they were even more violently pacific: Mussolini and Nenni tried to raise the workers in a general strike against war, and both were sent to prison for a treasonous anti-imperialism which the Duce later tried to excise from the record. Leone and De Ambris among the syndicalists were also against the war, citing the bankruptcy of Italian colonialism in Eritrea and Somaliland.

But on such a major issue the socialist movement was always hopelessly divided, especially now that nationalism was beginning to cut across class interests, and on this occasion their reformist and revolutionary wings were each split internally. Among the moderates some were becoming very close to Giolitti, and the veteran Costa before he died in 1910 was even elected deputy speaker of the Chamber. Although Turati and Treves feared to give up the myths of their creed too suddenly, Bissolati and Bonomi were coming to agree that "vital interests" and expansion were proper considerations for a young state. Another current of socialist thought welcomed colonial wars as a logical development of capitalism which might hasten the ultimate victory of the proletariat. Ferri approved of the war and De Felice embarrassed the high command by asking to be the first to disembark in North Africa. Among the syndicalists, Arturo Labriola and Angelo Olivetti were behind the government. Olivetti explained that war was a school of virility and courage, and the conquest of Libya would be a wonderful example of syndicalist methods, for it would mean breaking treaties and defying international law. These various attitudes explain why, while Mussolini and Nenni were reading Sorel together in prison to study the technique of violent action, their antimilitarist campaign lacked widespread support, and Mussolini's *volte-face* in World War I was a tacit admission that Olivetti's analysis in 1911 might have been the more correct.

Support for the Libyan war came from the columns of Giolitti's *Stampa*, and from the *Corriere della Sera* which represented the more conservative liberals. The *Corriere* admitted frankly that little material gain could be expected from colonies, but was equally sure that, with France now in Morocco, it would be demoralizing if Italy did not find compensation elsewhere. Support also came from Catholics who looked forward to a crusade of Cross against Crescent. Chiesa and Barzilai stood apart from the other republicans in favoring the war, and Alessio divided the radicals by supporting it. Nonpolitical humanitarians such as the poet Pascoli were convinced that Italy needed colonies to settle her surplus population, and even the wise and moderate liberal, Giustino Fortunato, while realizing that Italy might be ruined by this "fruitless and wasteful" effort, rejoiced at what he took to be the first real proof that Italy was at last a united state. D'Annunzio, with his usual bravura and full of the joy of conquest, burst into streams of historically allusive patriotic poetry which did much to obfuscate or etherealize the rational arguments on either side, and his chief theme in *La nave* was imperialism and the white man's burden. He was echoed by other hysterical poetasters such as the futurist Marinetti. Mystical nationalists followed Corradini in promising that Libya would fall without firing a shot and that a few honest Italian laborers would then suffice to make the desert blossom like a rose. The nationalists were in their element and began to beat up their enemies in public—sometimes without Giolitti's police interfering.

★

War was declared at the end of September 1911. Giolitti first tried to justify his decision by saying that the Turks had provocatively resisted Italian economic penetration. He was also bold enough to talk of the civilizing mission of Italy and to protest that the Turks had not reciprocated the invariably frank and honest conduct of Italy toward them. When he sent a twenty-four-hour ultimatum, the Turks declared themselves ready to make concessions and asked what guarantees Italy might think necessary. But Giolitti was not to be balked of his war; any delay might give time for his allies, Germany and Austria, to intervene and mediate.

Early in October, after Tripoli was bombarded, a compromise settlement was proposed by Germany which would let Italy occupy Libya while Turkey remained nominally sovereign, but Giolitti foiled this by burning his boats, and a simple royal decree formally annexed a country that was over five times Italy's size. In thirty years of occupation in Egypt, Britain had never been so rash as to cut off all room for maneuver in this way. But Giolitti wanted to engage Italian honor so that there should be no chance of any compromise solution; a conspicuous military victory was indispensable for his own and Italy's prestige. The unexpected result was that a war, though intended to last a few weeks at a negligible cost, dragged out for very much longer and seriously depleted Italian strength.

The general unpreparedness and overconfidence was quickly apparent. Although Tripoli had been an objective of policy for decades, neither the nature of its tribal society nor even its geographical features had been adequately studied. The diplomats had been in such a hurry with their ultimatum that they gave little warning to the armed services, and it was over a week after hostilities began before an army corps was ready to embark. General Caneva had little idea how to fight a mobile war against guerrillas. His chief of staff, General Pollio, mistakenly assumed that Turkey, unable to send reinforcements, would surrender after a token protest. He also made the expensive miscalculation that the local Arabs would oppose their Turkish coreligionists or would at least remain neutral.

Caneva's first proclamation to his troops spoke proudly of the conquests of ancient Rome. Nevertheless the resistance he met was a painful reminder of Adowa and he therefore hugged the coastal strip that was under range of his naval guns. Before long he found that not twenty thousand but a hundred thousand men were needed against only ten thousand Turks and about twenty-five thousand Arabs. Nor was it easy to adjust his technique of warfare to guerrillas who knew the countryside and could quickly vanish into the desert. Heavy artillery was not much use. Bombing airplanes and dirigibles were employed for the first time in history, but the enemy had few fixed targets to destroy, and most of the bombs buried themselves harmlessly in the sand.

Contrary to all expectation, the Arabs proved far more difficult to conquer than the Turkish troops. For when irresponsible Christian bishops talked of a crusade, the Arabs proclaimed a jihad and "treacherously" defended themselves by attacking the Italian lines from the rear. This provoked Caneva into terrible reprisals, since ununiformed Arabs were by his definition spies and not soldiers, as Italians were by definition their protectors against Turkish oppression. Some grisly tales emerged which dismayed the rest of Europe. Marinetti and Boccioni traveled all the way to Surrey to challenge an Irish newspaperman to a duel for having evaded the censorship with some highly colored stories. Marinetti claimed that the war was a typical manifestation of futurism and wrote a book that positively reveled in the slaughter. Corradini spoke of the Arabs as savage beasts who should be whipped and hanged.

Although Giolitti had assumed that other countries would accept a *fait accompli*, the fact was accomplished too slowly to be well received. The government expended money lavishly on French newspapers, yet France had much capital invested in Turkey and resented this clumsy disturbance of the Mediterranean equilibrium. An attempt at blockade was disliked and so was the spreading of war toward the Dodecanese Islands and Asia Minor. In particular there was a celebrated incident in January 1912 when two French steamers were hauled into Cagliari under suspicion of carrying contraband. Great Britain also had reasons for regretting the decline of Turkey, fearing that all Europe might be sucked into the vortex, so permitting Russia to move southward to the Dardanelles. Worst of all, the other powers of the Triple Alliance resented this precipitate and unilateral action. Austria instructed her nominal ally that the war must not come near the Balkans, and Germany, smarting from Italian failure to support her in Morocco, was friendly to Turkey and openly claimed to be the protector of Islam.

There was no decisive victory in Africa, but Rhodes was taken in May 1912, and secret negotiations then dragged on throughout the summer. Giolitti put forward extreme claims so that subsequent Italian concessions would enable the Turks to yield without too much loss of face. Italy was eventually recognized as *de facto* ruler of Libya and the Dodecanese. In return she paid a large sum to the Turkish national debt (some Italians objected that this looked too much like an indemnity), and a dangerous concession was allowed by which Constantinople kept its religious authority in North Africa and hence some influence in judicial and political affairs.

★

Italian morale was greatly uplifted by this colonial success and its importance was signalized by the establishment of a ministry of colonies in 1912. Although the war brought no access of material power, it could be called proof of national vigor. Croce and Mosca insisted that even a purely moral victory was well worth the expense and loss of life on both sides. Evidently the dangers concealed behind sentimental considerations of honor and prestige were not apparent even to some highly intelligent observers.

The glamor of empire, however, could not permanently conceal that there were also disadvantages. The new provinces produced much the same crops as southern Italy, so that domestic prices were depressed and imports not greatly increased. Over half a million Italians emigrated from Italy in the first six months of 1913, but they still preferred French Morocco to Italian Libya and far more went to America than ever before. Colonies without colonizers proved an expensive concession to sentiment. Tripoli needed capital, but Italy had not enough even for herself and few notable public works could be set on foot, though an equivalent sum spent on reforesting the Apennines might have provided living space for thousands who otherwise had to starve or emigrate. Fifty thousand resident Italians were expelled from Turkey in retaliation, with great loss of business and of contacts built up over centuries. A Moslem boycott of Italian goods, reinforced by unwise Italian protectionism, made Rhodes under Italian rule lose importance as a trade emporium. For the textile centers of Biella and Schio the first result of colonial expansion was a decline in overseas orders. Commercial disadvantages were accompanied by financial ones. Not only was the Banco di Roma badly hit and forced to reduce its capital by half, but the war caused an inflationary price revolution. As Luzzatti admitted, no one had ever imagined that hostilities would last so long and cost so much. Giolitti announced this cost as 512 million lire, but he had deliberately falsified the balance sheet and the true cost was twice as much. He also boasted about non-existent military victories to make people think that the army had fought well, but in private confessed that the army commanders had been "totally incompetent." After ten years of budgetary equilibrium, a huge deficit of 1,305 million appeared, and was now to grow steadily worse with each year.

Italy, wanting colonies to exploit, was herself exploited by them. The Treaty of Lausanne was signed with the Turks, but war continued for two decades against the native Libyan population. By the beginning of 1916 the "rebel" Senussi had reduced effective Italian occupation to a few coastal garrisons, and, by the Treaty of Acroma in 1917, Italy was obliged to admit their independence. Italian prestige never recovered from this setback in the eyes of the North African population. The Turks had garrisoned the vilayet with a few thousand soldiers, but Italy found it difficult with many times this number.

Moreover, the administration of Tripoli was ineffective: the frequent change of policy and governors, the remote control from Rome by inexperienced bureaucrats who negotiated directly with local chiefs and bypassed their agents on the spot, all marked an inauspicious beginning in colonial government. Not until 1922 could enthusiasm be generated for an extension of Italian dominion into the Libyan interior, and even as late as 1928 there were apparently only 2,800 Italians resident in the 680,000 square miles of this most expensively earned colony. The argument that Libya could take up any surplus population from Italy had been used with cynical irresponsibility by the nationalists who in fact wanted colonies merely for purposes of prestige.

More important was the dangerous fanning of nationalism and the cult of violence. Italian newspapers give ample evidence of this. In Europe, by weakening Turkey, this adventure led to a succession of Balkan wars and so was among the causes of World War I. In Italy itself the liberals were rapidly losing their comfortable monopoly of politics to new groups which demanded a more assertive foreign policy. These new parties were more intractable than the other social forces that Giolitti had managed to control or corrupt and were shortly to undermine the whole Giolittian system. The prime minister had learned his lesson that war gained too little and cost more than Italy could afford, but dared not tell the nation the facts that had given him this conviction. Partly as a result of this reticence, in 1915 other politicians entered a much bigger war when his own private experience foretold disaster.

The spokesmen of tolerance and moderation had been given little chance to make themselves heard in 1911–12, especially as hostilities had been deliberately commenced at the beginning of a seven-and-a-half-month parliamentary recess. Parliament was neither called to sanction the declaration of war, nor to debate the royal decree that proclaimed annexation. When the deputies met at last in February 1912, Turati was shouted down, and the foreign minister announced that parliament ought not to be allowed to debate matters of high policy. In the flush of victory a retrospective vote was secured for the taxes already raised by decree, and there was hardly a voice so bold as to object. These were ominous signs.

34   Giolitti's System Collapses, 1912–1914

The victory of Mussolini and his faction at the socialist congress at Reggio in July 1912 reflected working-class impatience with the middle-class leadership of Bissolati and Turati. Doctrinaire concepts and Fabian tactics had less and less appeal as socialism became more of a mass party. The war of 1911 gave a fillip to those socialists who believed in violence. It also weakened those who accepted the methods of parliamentary government. Bissolati shocked the other socialists at the Reggio congress by his reformist heresies, and especially by his hope that "our country, which today is the equal of England and I think even surpasses her in matters of liberty and political institutions, tomorrow may become the forge of a great democratic movement." Because of this heretical bourgeois belief he was expelled with others who had voted in favor of war against Turkey. Also expelled from the party was Bonomi who was one day to become prime minister, and Podrecca who among other offences was overfond of attending the opera in evening dress.

Against Bissolati's democratic reformism, Cicotti proclaimed at Reggio that the socialist party was an eminently antidemocratic party and democracy was a purely bourgeois expedient. Extremists of this type were henceforward to control the party until its dissolution a dozen years later. The young Benito Mussolini, who scored a great oratorical success in this congress, said that the class war was not concerned with economic reforms so much as with revolution and the pursuit of power. At the age of twenty-nine he became, with Lazzari, the most prominent party leader, and as editor of *Avanti* in the next two years tripled the sales of this official socialist paper. Under his guidance socialism renounced any idea of co-operation with the liberals.

From the parent brood of the original workers' party there had successively split off anarchists, syndicalists, and now the right-wing reformists under Bissolati and Bonomi. Bissolati's group was doctrinally not unlike the British Labour Party, but it lacked any broad popular base. The left-wing reformists, Turati and Treves, remained as a right wing of the official party, though heavily outnumbered. A natural split along the grain might have divided reformism from revolutionism and left Turati and Bissolati both on the same side, but Turati remained loyal to the majority. At the same time he refused the seats on the party executive which were now offered to his group, arguing that the revolutionaries should be solely responsible for the failure that he hoped would attend their policy. In retrospect this seems a muddled and perhaps irresponsible attitude.

★

Giolitti, when the socialists again proved refractory, made further overtures to the parliamentary Right. Perhaps he was alarmed at the results of his policy of social *laissez-faire*. Perhaps he also calculated that the enfranchisement of the illiterate peasantry might mean a more conservative or even a Catholic vote in rural areas. Salandra described how, paradoxically, the Italian peasants would vote socialist mainly out of a desire for land, in other words so that they might cease to be socialists. More reliable as indicating a conservative trend in public opinion were the increasing sales of the *Corriere della Sera* whose circulation shortly touched 750,000, far larger than that of any other daily. Its weekly supplement, the *Domenica del Corriere*, had a readership of almost two million. In the municipal administration of Rome, Nathan's radical-democratic bloc was defeated by a combination of Catholics, liberals, and nationalists. In the country at large the nationalists had the active assistance of heavy industry and at least the sympathy of the foreign minister Di San Giuliano, as well as some support from the royal Court. The Catholics, now more prominent in public life, were also a conservative influence during the pontificate of Pius X.

With elections imminent, Giolitti needed to trim his sails to the prevailing wind. Instead of trying to absorb the new mass parties, he therefore adopted Sonnino's policy of forming a national bloc against them and his group momentarily joined with Sonnino's. In the summer of 1913 he dissolved parliament. The subsequent elections were manipulated even more than those he had already organized in 1892, 1904, and 1909, and this time the new instruments of the motion-picture projector and phonograph were employed. About half the electorate voted, and Giolitti's constitutional liberals were returned with about 318 seats instead of 370. Alongside them the first three nationalists were elected and the militant Catholic deputies increased from 20 to 29. Four different socialist groups together obtained almost one vote in four, and although their number of deputies increased only from 41 to 78, 52 of these were pledged to the subversion of parliament as an "institution devised by the *bourgeoisie* for their own interests." With proportional representation, these 52 would have been far more numerous. The cause of liberal constitutionalism was indisputably on the wane.

Giolitti still possessed a comfortable majority. He had renounced his anticlericalism sufficiently to make an electoral compact with Count Gentiloni, president of the Catholic Union, whereby those liberals who were against socialism would receive Catholic votes if they also signed a declaration to oppose divorce and favor the religious orders. Gentiloni claimed the adhesion of 228 ministerialist candidates to his pact, and estimated that without this support Giolitti might have had to resign.

★

In this one parliament the liberals were more or less to hold their own. But Giolitti's endless compromises were wearing thin. Salandra and the *Corriere* criticized his Catholic alliance, and when Giolitti made civil marriage precede the religious ceremony he simultaneously antagonized Catholics. The defection of the radicals then deprived him of office at a critical moment so that the outbreak of a world war in 1914 found him on the opposition benches. He had upset a delicate balance of forces and weakened his amorphous majority. This was a premonitory sign that the tradition of parliamentary government was breaking down, the transformist compromise becoming ever less feasible.

As the socialist Raimondo explained in parliament, under a democratic banner Italy had imperceptibly been led into what he termed a dictatorial regime. People had used this term about Cavour, Depretis, and Crispi in turn, and were now using it about Giolitti. Four times he had "made" the elections, as often as Cavour himself, and by now he had nominated most of the senators, prefects, police officers, and other administrative officers of the state. But the worm was beginning to turn, and in 1913 some of the deputies demanded his impeachment for illicit interference in elections. Salvemini vehemently, perhaps excessively, attacked what he called "*il ministro della mala vita*" and the practice of electoral gerrymandering:

> The police enrolled the scum of the constituencies and the underworld of the neighboring districts. In the last weeks before the polls, opponents were threatened, bludgeoned, besieged in their homes. Their leaders were debarred from addressing meetings or even thrown into prison until election day was over. Voters ... favoring governmental candidates were given not only their own polling cards, but also those of opponents, emigrants, and deceased voters, and were allowed to vote three, five, ten, twenty times. The Government candidates were always the winners. Any deputy who dared Giolitti had to confront a bad time at his next election. In Italy people used to say that Giolitti sold prefects in order to buy deputies. ... When in 1913 he

was confronted, in a constituency to be "managed", not with a mere two or three thousand voters but with ten thousand or more, he was forced to increase the dose of violence to ensure success. He won another of his overwhelming electoral victories. But the scandals of that campaign provoked bitter indignation everywhere. On the eve of the war of 1914–18, Giolitti was the most powerful man in parliament but the most unpopular man in the country.

In February 1914 the radicals decided to withdraw their support. Radicalism was now an indiscriminate mixture ranging from liberals to quasi-socialists, free traders to protectionists, irredentists to pacifists, and had no roots in any solid sectional interest; but its seventy-eight deputies represented a third force inside Giolitti's political system. In 1913 a group of Masonic radicals attacked the Gentiloni pact, contending that the Vatican as an international and religious body should be excluded from temporal and national affairs. The radical ministers, Sacchi and Credaro, were forced by their party congress of 1914 to resign, and Giolitti, although he still had his majority, took this as a cue for what he intended to be another temporary exit. The Libyan war in any case had created serious financial difficulties, and there were visible shoals ahead in the shape of a railroad strike and agrarian disorders. Another period of retrenchment out of office might be beneficial to his reputation and career. He had successfully used the extension of suffrage and the African war to divide the opposition groups, but socialists, Catholics, and nationalists were all increasing their representation, and these three groups were before long to upset the whole applecart of upper-class liberalism.

★

Giolitti's active career was almost over. He has been accused of being dictatorial but also of the opposite charge that he fatally let things slide, and this second charge contained some truth. No doubt Giolitti's Italy had something of the police state about it: the memoirs of Armando Borghi give examples of imprisonment without warrant and of violent repression by the police. But this was not remarkable in contemporary Europe. Giolitti made no attempt to subvert institutions but only exploited what already existed, and if he left politics in a not altogether healthy state, it was existing traditions and institutions rather than himself which were primarily responsible.

No one will deny that much was wrong with politics during this period of *giolittismo*. Several commissions of inquiry had been appointed, on electoral corruption, on misappropriation in the armed services and on the building of government offices. The Saredo commission had shown up shocking abuses in the administration of Naples. In 1908 the Sicilian professor Nasi, a former minister of education, was convicted by the Senate of embezzling the funds of his department. It did not restore confidence when the culprit was given a short term of imprisonment which he was allowed to serve in his own home, nor was it reassuring that an uprising in Sicily protested against his prosecution. Some of Nasi's adherents at Trapani even raised the French flag and proclaimed a republic, and afterward went on electing him to parliament. Few people minded very much that ministers had considerable perquisites attached to their office, and the assumption was that Nasi had been unlucky to be caught. Far from trying to reform such scandals, Giolitti made use of them for his own political purposes.

These abuses were the product of an unhealthy political system and a persistent anarchism among ordinary citizens. Political anarchism was responsible for the assassination of King Umberto and numerous other crimes of blood. Brigandage was still endemic in many provinces, and when a law was passed to restrict the length of knives, manufacturers evaded it by making hilts that would enter a wound along with the blade. Politicians set a bad example of illegality by corruptly feathering their own nests and sometimes illegally fought duels at the same time as they punished crimes of violence among their inferiors. Another aspect of this contempt of the law was the boycott of politics by the clericals. The thin attendance of deputies in parliament was occasioned by their inability to cohere as organized parties with a collective policy. The theoretical anarchism of Bakunin and Malatesta was reinforced by a widespread empirical anarchism that took a multitude of forms. It had been seen in Garibaldi's succession of private armies, in the Sicilian *fasci* of 1893, in the agrarian leagues for self-help which grew up after 1906, in the frequent student riots against university discipline. The Sicilian mafia was an extreme manifestation of such individualism, and Mosca knew from experience that the mafia itself was an anarchic confederation of gangs, each *cosca* working on its own. This general lawlessness was made worse by the fact that the magistracy was badly paid and was therefore undistinguished by intelligence or status. Both Giolitti and Mussolini were, in their different ways, natural products of such an environment. History was to show that this exaggerated individualism, though among the great glories of Italy, could also be her greatest peril. The police state was sometimes seen as a remedy, but could as easily make a bad situation far worse.

★

The most common accusation against Giolitti has not been that he was authoritarian or corrupt, but that he was prosaic and pedestrian in substance while his tactics were opportunistic and shifty. He was always feeling for his majority, selecting different tendencies and trying to synthesize them. Like Depretis, he tended to equate politics with administration, and to this extent he brilliantly made the most of a political system which favored coalitions and misprized clear commitments. Sonnino made the criticism that Giolitti's policy was to patch up each leak in turn, to placate the most noisy of his opponents, taking care of day-to-day problems as they arose.

The enemies of Giolitti continued to say that his cynicism robbed Italian politics of any idealism. Interpreting everyone's wishes in terms of self-interest, he played on people's defects rather than on their virtues. As the king later recalled, Giolitti kept a dossier on each deputy's private weaknesses so that he knew how to manage each individual. No wonder he sometimes seemed contemptuous of parliament when deputies and electors could be manipulated so easily, and indeed, like the most distinguished of his predecessors, when he was not in power he spent years without attending the House. In November 1916 he told people that there was no point in attending parliament, for it was no longer asked even to vote taxes and had become little more than a legal fiction. If this was true, it was in part his fault.

There was, however, a good deal to be said in favor of a realist who was in his way a sincere if disillusioned liberal, an enemy of magniloquence and over-emphasis. Prezzolini adjudged that this unemotional, industrious, and practical administrator was the right leader for a people who were so prone to enthusiasm and rhetorical exaggeration. As Giolitti was never eager to super-impose any theory on his practice, his variegated liberalism often deceived contemporaries, but later generations construed him as one of the foremost statesmen of United Italy. He stands along with Cavour and De Gasperi, alike in technique and temperament, scornful of doctrinaire ideologues, resourceful in parliamentary maneuver, all three fighting a vanguard or rearguard defense of a workaday down-to-earth liberalism. For nearly thirteen years Giolitti governed Italy. Even when out of office he was the most important politician in the country. Fortis, Sonnino, Luzzatti, Salandra, and Bonomi became premier on his recommendation. Although Giolitti did not receive a good press at the time, Croce was later able to conclude that Italy had reached a pinnacle of success in 1914 under his skillful and benevolent rule.

Croce was here going to the other extreme of exaggeration. The liberals like himself who served under Giolitti mistook their own well-being and that of their friends for constitutional balance and social stability. Many Italians had become more prosperous in the years before 1914. Mosca noted as one sign of change that more peasants now wore shoes and carried handkerchiefs. Some of the liberals realized nevertheless that the country was on the brink of political disaster and social revolution. Mosca pointed out the dangers of universal suffrage, Pantaleoni those of nationalized insurance, Croce those of *d'annunzianesimo*, and here they spoke as experts; but in other respects they were too close to the system to judge it correctly. From the relative detachment of Switzerland, Pareto noted the gradual defection of voters toward socialism and Catholicism and explained it by the corruption and lack of leadership of the Italian ruling class and their divorce from the rest of the nation. He thought that Italy could have chosen either military power or economic wealth, and success either way might have reconciled ordinary citizens to this system of government; but, trying for both, the country had fallen between the two. On the politicians who encouraged this or allowed it to happen, he concluded that a grave responsibility must lie.

35   Italy Remains Neutral, 1914

Austria and Italy were still allies in name but hardly in fact. Austria remembered her loss of Venice in 1866 and the danger to which this exposed her only port at Trieste. Especially after 1906, under the hereditary prince Franz Ferdinand and General Conrad von Hötzendorff, the anti-Italian party became powerful in Vienna. The Austrian foreign minister, Aerenthal, momentarily moderated Conrad's aggressive schemes. But Italian counter-irredentism toward Trent and Trieste was then fanned by the Austrian annexation of Bosnia in 1908, and by the chilly unfriendliness of Austria and Germany during the Libyan war of 1911–12.

The Triple Alliance had to be either denounced or renewed one year before its expiry in the summer of 1913. The Italian foreign ministry in 1910–14 (under three successive premiers) was presided over by Di San Giuliano who passed for a confirmed triplicist. But irredentists were dismayed at the prospect of renewing the treaty, especially as, with general war becoming more likely, Italy's hands might thereby be tied too tightly for diplomatic finesse. Denouncing the alliance after thirty years would have been too positive a foreign policy for Giolitti and might have looked like an act of hostility against Austria. Rather than devise any alternative, in December 1912 he confirmed the existing treaty for the fourth time.

Nevertheless, this treaty relationship with Germany and Austria was by now of very limited potentiality for Italy had reached an understanding with the rival Triple Entente of France, Russia, and Britain. There was also friction when, in August 1913, Trieste was ordered by Prince Hohenlohe to dismiss Italian-speaking civic employees. Formerly, the Italians in Trieste had looked to Vienna for protection against the advancing Slovenes, but a novel Austrian solicitude for the Slavs now threatened Italian livelihood as well as Italian culture and language.

Giolitti's resignation early in 1914, though at the time it seemed just another of what his enemies called calculated political vacations, in fact marked an important change in Italian politics. Giolitti was not the man who would have let animus against Austria build up into open hostility. He had gone unenthusiastically into Libya and was disinclined toward heroics and wild hopes of glory. He was aware as early as July 1913 of Austria's aggressive intentions toward Serbia, though he concealed this knowledge for more than a year so as not to alarm the public. Despite the imminence of war he resisted the financial appropriations for which the army pressed, convinced as he was that Italy's best policy was to remain neutral in any European conflagration.

Successive ministers of war had tried to reorganize the armed services within the limits imposed by the Treasury. That General Spingardi could remain minister of war successively under Giolitti, Sonnino, and Luzzatti allowed some continuity of policy under royal supervision. However, lacking adequate parliamentary criticism and enough financial support, the best he could do was not good enough, and the unpreparedness of the armed forces was to be the greatest argument for Italian neutrality when the European war broke out.

On Giolitti's resignation, and on Giolitti's advice, the king in March 1914 appointed as premier Professor Salandra who had been in Sonnino's cabinets of 1906 and 1909. Antonio Salandra was a conservative, aloof and distant, and much less ready than Sonnino to accept Giolitti's democratic reforms. Yet he made the usual pastiche administration. His appointment of one of Giolitti's enemies, Ferdinando Martini, as minister of colonies brought him some initial support from the radicals. The Court insisted on his retention of Di San Giuliano as foreign minister, and this ensured the simultaneous support of the nationalists and clericals. Misreading the situation, Giolitti even helped Salandra to form his ministry; indeed, the government could scarcely have existed without such assistance for the former still had a majority in parliament. Giolitti miscalculated that Salandra was a mere stopgap who would take the responsibility of government during a difficult period, but who had neither the political courage nor the parliamentary following to take any decisive step. Instead, Salandra proved to be an ambitious gambler who was ready to break free from Giolitti's system and throw Italy into a crippling war.

★

In June 1914 the new ministry had to cope with a near revolution. In parliament the voting boxes were again overturned, and Chiesa, the deputy responsible, was severely manhandled by his colleagues. In Emilia and the Romagna there was another peasant *jacquerie*. The landless *braccianti* in this inflammable area had developed co-operatives in order to obtain from the *mezzadri* more employment and better terms. Socialist trade unions were sometimes able to control the provision of agricultural labor. To this the landowners and *mezzadri* replied by forming mobile squads of strikebreakers to exert a counterpressure. While in the South the local tyrant was a landowner, in parts of the North the local party boss was king. One such boss was Mussolini, who at the congress of Ancona in 1914 expelled the Freemasons from the socialist party for not being sufficiently revolutionary or class-conscious. Another kindred spirit was Nenni, also from the Romagna. Pietro Nenni had once been a republican for whom the works of Mazzini were a sacred text, but by now was a militant leader of the socialist *braccianti* against the republican *contadini* as well as against the conservative estate owners.

These two firebrands were both involved in the "red week" of June 1914, and so was the chief anarch, Malatesta. At Ancona a demonstration against military service provoked firing by the police and consequent reprisals. A general strike was declared, though it was only partly effective because the moderate socialists were of two minds. Shops were sacked, railroad tracks again pulled up, telegraph poles knocked down, and the royal insignia removed. Soon the red flag was flying above a number of town halls. Ancona and other towns declared themselves independent communes. When a republic was declared by extremists in the Romagna, most of the authorities went into hiding. The future Marshal Balbo, of ill-fame, was seen leaving Ferrara with an armed posse of bicyclists to make such trouble as he could, clad in a Garibaldian red shirt. Here and there an army commander took orders from a socialist dictator, and General Agliardi of the regular army had to surrender his sword to the rebels near Ravenna. None of this was the work of Mussolini, but he justified it in the columns of *Avanti* even though in later life he pretended the opposite. Over 100,000 conscripts had to be enlisted before law and order were restored.

★

In this electrically charged atmosphere, Salandra was confronted with an Austrian ultimatum to Serbia. Giolitti had already made it clear to Austria that Italy would not join her ally in any attack on Serbia. But Salandra did not know that Austria had been warned in 1913 not to count on Italian support, for Giolitti kept the relevant papers after he left office and did not give his successor this vital information. Salandra nevertheless had good reason to repeat the warning, for the Triple Alliance required the imparting of prior information to an ally and also prescribed the offer of compensation to Italy for any Austrian territorial expansion in the Balkans. Austria defaulted under both heads when in July 1914 she sent her ultimatum to Serbia, and Italy knew nothing of this ultimatum until after it was sent.

Nine months later Italy was fighting on the side of France and Britain, but in July 1914 there was a distinct possibility that she would have to join Germany and Austria. The obligations of the Triple Alliance suggested, without requiring, such a course, and the Italian general staff had always based its strategy on joining the Central Powers with whom Italy had been formally allied since 1882. At the foreign office, Di San Giuliano believed that young and energetic Germany was in the ascendant, while corrupt France and self-satisfied Britain would lose if it came to war. Sonnino similarly thought that Italy should at once declare war on Germany's side. Missiroli of the *Resto del Carlino* and Scarfoglio's *Mattino* were also for favoring the Central Powers with a policy of benevolent neutrality at least, and Croce, like the germanophile Banca Commerciale Italiana, put his weight into the same scales.

Those who wanted war were, however, in a very small minority, for to fight on the same side as Austria—the possessor of Trent and Trieste—would be to betray Italian patriotic ambitions and the inviolable *risorgimento* itself. Austria's aggressive policy in the Balkans had technically freed Italy from her obligations, while France in 1902 had privately been promised by Rome that she could rely on Italian neutrality.

There was furthermore a possibility of internal trouble if Italy decided to fight for her Central European allies. Radicals such as De Viti de Marco, the reformist socialists around Bissolati, and the republicans Chiesa and De Andreis had no sympathy for Austria, and powerful francophile and anglophile newspapers existed, including Salvemini's *Unità* and the *Secolo*. Verdi's collaborator, Boito, represented a generalized nonpartisan patriotism which already wanted war against Germany, and two of Garibaldi's grandsons were killed as volunteers with French troops fighting in the Argonne. But for most people the immediate imperative was not so much to fight against Germany as to stop Salandra from fighting against France and Britain. France had been courting Italian sympathy and established cultural institutes at Florence and Milan. Of Italy's coal, 90 per cent came from Britain. Active participation in war against the British would dislocate trade, and the treasury minister threatened to resign rather than fight such a war. On the other hand a neutral Italy would be very well placed economically.

Giolitti, now out of office, stressed the enormous advantages of neutrality, for he knew that Italy's interest was in maintaining the balance of European power, and for this she needed to keep her forces uncommitted. Experience in Libya had taught him that the army and the bureaucracy were too weak for hostilities. He reminded his inexperienced successors that there was no obligation to fight. By simple negotiation Italy could gain a good deal, and perhaps the war might break up the Austro-Hungarian empire, so setting free its subject populations to Italy's advantage. Italy therefore ought at least to wait and see who was likely to win before committing herself.

A decision for neutrality was taken by the cabinet at the end of July. Parliament was not called to ratify it but was allowed to remain dormant through another five-month recess despite Turati's urgent request that the deputies be summoned. Full powers were arbitrarily assumed so that policy could be determined by the cabinet and the Court. At such a moment Albertini's *Corriere della Sera* was more of a political force than the Chamber of Deputies, so irrelevant had representative institutions become. Unaided and uncriticized by parliament, Di San Giuliano, timid and pro-German, the one politician whom the king really appreciated, was able to promise what was in effect a benevolent neutrality to Austria. Far from trying hard to hold Austria back from hostilities, and far from making it explicit that the ultimatum to Serbia freed Italy from any treaty obligations, he refused to denounce the Triple Alliance. He even encouraged Austria to declare war so that he might claim the compensations which by treaty were payable if Austria annexed territory in the Balkans.

To make his policy seem more patriotic, Salandra later said that as early as July 27 he asked Austria to cede her Italian provinces and threatened otherwise to break the Triple Alliance. But the German and Austrian documents record this somewhat differently, and the Austrian chancellor announced that Italy had promised "to assume a friendly attitude in conformity with our alliance." Only much too late, and not before August 4, did Di San Giuliano made his request for "compensation," that is to say only after France and Britain had decided to fight and so given Italy a more arbitral position. Even then he mentioned the Trentino alone; and this was his price not for impartial neutralism as he later implied, but for nonbelligerent complicity in support of Austria.

★

In October Di San Giuliano died. His successor as foreign minister, Sonnino, was another triplicist whose program had specifically deplored Visconti-Venosta's policy of retaining the ability to negotiate with both sides. In August 1914, Sonnino was one of the few politicians to protest against neutrality and advocate joining Austria. But once the battle of the Marne had destroyed the legend of German invincibility, he quickly changed his ground and preferred to exploit a position in which each side was competing to win his support.

Profiting from this fortunate situation, an Italian "sanitary commission" landed unopposed in Albania, and in December, as no voice of protest had been heard, the city of Valona was occupied by troops. This was a pledge to be held against the victory of either side and constituted another stage in that expansionist policy which had already engulfed Libya and the Dodecanese. Italians had lately built ports and railroads in Dalmatia, and an Italian company had secured the tobacco monopoly in Montenegro. But economic penetration encountered increasing resistance from Austria and local patriots. At the same time renewed conflict between Italians and Slavs aided German infiltration in Trieste. The Austro-Serbian war in 1914 therefore offered Sonnino an excellent excuse to improve a deteriorating position and stake out a claim on this defenseless part of the Adriatic coast.

On December 9, once Valona was securely in pledge, he officially asked Austria to discuss the compensations due to Italy under Article 7 of their treaty of alliance. In other words he was still aiming to enforce the Triple Alliance rather than discard it. Salandra later claimed that his government was playing for time, having already secretly agreed to go to war in the following spring against Austria. But, if this Machiavellian explanation was really true, more war preparations would have been made in the next few months. Italy, on the contrary, still seems to have been much closer to Germany than to France, and Sonnino still hoped to gain Trent and Trieste by gift of Austria without entering the war himself.

Meanwhile, the Central Powers rose to the bait of Italian benevolent neutrality—at a price. The German generals particularly wanted to gain several months for the development of their Carpathian offensive, and the diplomats were therefore directed to play out time in talk but not to make any premature concessions to their ally. The former German chancellor von Bülow was sent to Rome with his Italian wife, there to use, as occasion demanded, blandishments or threats. Dark hints were dropped about possible concessions over the *terre irredente*, yet also about restoring the temporal power of the pope if Italy proved recalcitrant. The considerable commercial and financial influence which Germany had obtained in Italy provided another useful weapon.

As the war dragged on, Austria moved toward meeting Italian claims, but very slowly and partially. Franz Joseph had started the war as a last resort to prevent his great multinational empire from breaking up, and would not lightly yield Trent to Italy lest this should touch off a dozen other claims from the other insurgent nationalities. He could also argue that Italy already possessed in Albania all the compensation she could expect. But the fortunes of war gradually strengthened Italy's demand for nothing less than her *terre irredente*, and by March 9, 1915, von Bülow persuaded Austria to agree in principle to make some concession. Perhaps the Germans felt hopeful that they had thus assured the continuance of Italian neutrality.

36   Intervention Against Austria, 1915

As the war gathered momentum, more Italian politicians began to fear that neutrality was undignified for a nation of their status whereas intervention would mark them indisputably as a great power. Another argument was that victory by either side would upset the balance of forces upon which Italy relied, so that as neutrals they were bound to lose. Behind these dubious arguments was the hard fact that Italy thought of herself as an unsatisfied nation. Her "natural frontier" on the Alps was still in foreign hands, while the defeats of Custoza, Lissa, and Adowa had still to be avenged.

Once intervention was decided upon, Italy could have chosen either to fight against her allies for Trent and Trieste, or with them to obtain Nice, Corsica, Malta, and Tunis. Opinion gradually hardened in favor of the first course, because the Entente powers had more to offer and were better placed than Austria to do so without damage to themselves. Victory on the side of France and Britain had the advantage that it would not only liberate Italian-speaking people, but would at last achieve a proper Alpine frontier, and gain control of the Adriatic.

The interventionists were a nondescript collection acting from varied motives. There was a minority of liberal idealists. There was the king, who had been brought up as a soldier and wanted to break free from Giolitti's influence as his grandfather tried to break away from Cavour's. Most of the Freemasons and most politically active university students seem also to have been among the *interventisti*, and the irredentists were of course with them to a man. The nationalist party, as soon as their original hope for war against France began to vanish, grouped together against Germany, considering any war better than none. Likewise, the futurists were absolute for war as "a quick and heroic means toward national power and wealth:" in September 1914 they interrupted an opera of Puccini's at Rome in order to burn an Austrian flag on the stage. Marinetti declared that futurists had always considered war to be the only inspiration of art, the only moral purifier. In his view, war would rejuvenate Italy, would enrich it with men of action and force it to live no longer on memories of the past. Strange bedfellows with this *avant garde* were conservatives perpetuating the francophile tradition of Visconti-Venosta and Bonghi, but also Salvemini and the reformist socialists who wanted a war of generous idealism waged in the name of freedom and democracy against the invader of Belgium.

The revolutionary socialists under Mussolini were surprised to find themselves in the same neutralist camp as their three chief enemies, Giolitti, Turati, and the pope. By October, however, Mussolini had modified his standpoint to one of "conditional neutrality," and by November to the other extreme of uncompromising belligerency. This strident change may have been partly due to French money, but must also have come from a realization that war might prepare revolution and accustom people to violence and arms. De Ambris, Corridoni, and other remnants of revolutionary syndicalism supported this view; so did Nenni who called neutrality a sign of impotence and humiliation. In November Mussolini launched a new paper, *Il Popolo d'Italia*, to support the cause of war against Germany, for which purpose he was subsidized by the French and by Italian industrialists.

The socialist party itself, scandalized by Mussolini's irresponsible desertion of the true Marxist position, reacted by summarily bundling their late leader out of the fold, as they had recently ejected his opponent Bissolati. Those who remained in the party were divided between the moderate Turati and Treves, and the revolutionary faction of Lazzari and Bombacci, both advocating neutrality. Deprived of its two interventionist wings, yet still divided internally, it was more ineffective than ever.

★

Support for intervention was thus found in many different directions of the political compass. All told, the interventionists were far from numerous, and more than one member of the cabinet has put on record that the government's war policy was in deliberate defiance of the great majority in parliament and the country. What was more, the motives of different groups for intervention were irreconcilable. Nevertheless their momentary agreement urged Salandra to a bold stroke of duplicity. On February 16, 1915, despite concurrent negotiations with Austria, a courier was dispatched in great secrecy to London with the suggestion that Italy was open to a good offer from the Entente. At the same time the screw was given a twist at Vienna on the assumption that both sides would now compete for Italian support. The final choice was aided by the arrival of news in March of Russian victories in the Carpathians. Salandra began to think that victory for the Entente was in sight, and was so anxious not to arrive too late for a share in the profits that he instructed his envoy in London to drop some of the Italian demands and reach agreement quickly.

The memorandum originally sent to the British demanded not only Trent and Trieste, but all cisalpine Tyrol, much of Dalmatia with its islands, and a share of the Ottoman empire, together with a monetary subsidy, the exclusion of the pope from any peace conference, and equitable treatment in any distribution of colonies. On March 27, however, compromise counterproposals were accepted for fear that the war might soon be over and because Russia as protector of the Slavs insisted on halving Italy's claims in Dalmatia. Even so, the final provisions of the Treaty of London would have taken Italy's eastern frontier down as far as Cape Planka and included most of the Adriatic islands. In return, Sonnino agreed to allow the Serbo-Croats an outlet at Fiume, for this town did not feature among Italy's ambitions.

The secret Treaty of London was concluded on April 26 binding Italy to fight within one month. The Entente powers had assumed that Italian armed assistance was not worth more than a certain price, especially when they surmised from Salandra's proposals that the von Bülow mission had failed. Nevertheless, it cost them little to be generous, as Italian demands hardly ran against their vital interests. For the next week Italy managed to be in alliance with both sets of combatants simultaneously. Not until May 4 did Salandra denounce the Triple Alliance in a private note to its signatories, surprisingly calling this Italy's first spontaneous political action since the *risorgimento*. At no point, despite a formal promise, did he discuss this fateful decision with Giolitti or any member of the parliamentary majority.

Salandra and Sonnino also deceived their own cabinet, and none of the ministers and military leaders knew that secret negotiations were proceeding at London. The text of the new treaty was known only years later when it was published from Russian sources by a newspaper in Stockholm. Salandra thus committed the nation to war on his own responsibility and (as he frankly confessed) against a large known majority in parliament and the country. He was within his legal rights, but Italy was to suffer for this constitutional anomaly. He had not even consulted General Cadorna and the general staff about a change in policy that demanded a complete inversion of their military plans.

Quite apart from the question of constitutional propriety, some people felt guilty about denouncing the *Triplice* in this underhand manner just when its termination could do most harm to their former allies. Nitti in his acid reminiscences concluded that these simultaneous negotiations with each side let Italy into the war in the most dishonorable way, and he called the Treaty of London a monumental piece of folly. Nevertheless, however clumsy the manner of this diplomatic revolution, Salandra could claim that there were good arguments for trying to sway the balance between rival power-groups in

Europe. What he failed to consider was that, even if Italy emerged on the winning side, the balance of power would be upset and her own influence thereby reduced.

Giolitti, the leader of the neutralists, was living far away from Rome on his Piedmontese estate. His long absence from the political scene was another reflection on constitutional practice. His farsighted view had been that what looked superficially like an easy and attractive war of national aggrandizement might turn out to be the first step in a domestic revolution. This most experienced of Italian statesmen believed that skillful diplomacy could in any case satisfy national aspirations without war. He had been disillusioned over the fighting qualities of the army and the morale of the civilian population, and he knew all too well the niggardliness of his own military expenditure and the inadequacy of the general staff. Unfortunately his reasonable arguments were discounted because they were thought to mask an ambition to return to power. Giolitti had a majority in parliament and had been waiting for a suitable moment to displace Salandra, but he feared to press his case for neutralism too publicly, for that would have weakened Italy's hand in negotiating with Austria, and he would not then have been able to become premier without Austria reducing the price she was ready to pay for Italian nonbelligerency.

★

Salandra could expect considerable opposition when the time came to make public the engagement he had undertaken on behalf of his country. His confession that most Italians were against intervention was based on reports from the provincial prefects. Mussolini even thought it a matter for pride that the people were dragged into war by a small minority, and his own fateful conclusion was that a dynamic minority would always prevail against the static and disengaged masses.

This was a striking lesson for the future Duce to learn at so little cost to himself, and not for nothing have historians spoken of May 1915 as a dress rehearsal for his *coup d'état* of October 1922. What D'Annunzio in 1915 helped to do by inflammatory speeches at Genoa and Rome, De Ambris and Corridoni did by agitation in the nerve center of Milan. Secret-service money was used by the government on propaganda for this purpose, and the police had long since been instructed by Giolitti in the art of contriving "spontaneous popular manifestations."

As Salandra noted, these manifestations were headed by young university students, the same *déraciné* intellectuals who featured in such other revolutionary years as 1860 and 1922. Cavour in 1860 had acknowledged that "shouts in the piazza are an unreliable test of public opinion" but it was sometimes convenient to forget this truth, and the riots of May 1915 were an artificially stimulated appeal to support Salandra's policy against the known will of parliament.

Gabriele d'Annunzio was asked to return for this purpose from his hideout in the south of France whither he had fled from his creditors. According to his own testimony, the government privately informed him about the Treaty of London before he left France, long before the parliamentary leaders knew of it, and the obvious conclusions may be drawn from the fact that his financial embarrassments now ceased for awhile. Once back in Italy he delivered a declamatory harangue at a meeting to celebrate the anniversary of Garibaldi's expedition of the Thousand, and this was only one day after Salandra's repudiation of the Triple Alliance. Great scenes of enthusiasm ensued, and nothing was left to the imagination in his exuberant apostrophe to

> an Italy which shall be greater by conquest, purchasing territory not in shame but at the price of blood and glory. . . . After long years of national humiliation, God has been pleased to grant us proof of our privileged blood. . . . Blessed are they that have, for they have more to give and can burn with a hotter flame. . . . Blessed are those young men who hunger and thirst for glory, for they shall be filled.

From Genoa the poet made a triumphal progress to Rome, where he declaimed in some of the Roman theaters and on May 12–13 staged other speeches on the Capitoline hill:

> No, we are not and do not want to be just a museum, a hotel, a vacation resort, a Prussian-blue horizon where foreigners come for their honeymoons, a market where things are bought and sold. Our genius demands that we should put our stamp on the molten metal of the new world. . . . Comrades, it is no longer time for speeches, but for action, and for action after the high Roman fashion. If it is a crime to incite people to violence, I boast of now committing that crime. . . . This war, though it may seem destructive, will be the most fruitful means of creating beauty and virtue that has appeared on the earth.

While war fever mounted, Austria made one more effort to keep Italy neutral. Late in March she had offered to cede Trent as a bribe to stop the defection of her wayward ally. On April 17 she agreed to some Italian counterdemands for regions further north in the Adige Valley. On May 7, two weeks after Italy's secret commitment to fight on the other side, Sonnino notified the Italian cabinet of still further Austrian offers in the Tyrol, with Trieste becoming a free city. The Germans carefully ensured that these final concessions were generally known, hoping that Italian public opinion would then force Salandra to back down from his rash policy of war.

★

Giolitti did not arrive in Rome until May 9, though von Bülow warned him a week earlier about what the government was doing. This was a disastrous delay, but he was waiting for an invitation to give advice to the king. Salandra's cabinet at last agreed to inform the chief parliamentary leaders how things stood, and Carcano, a friend of Giolitti, therefore went to see him on his arrival with the news about ending the Triple Alliance. Giolitti visited both the king and Salandra, and urged upon them that parliament would be against fighting, that the Italian generals were not up to it, that a German victory was not impossible, and that war might last longer than they thought, bringing invasion or even revolution in its train. He suggested that, without any loss of honor, a vote in parliament could be used to upset any unratified arrangement with the Entente, and then the government could resume negotiations with Austria on the basis of offers already made.

This difference of opinion soon became generally known, and since parliament was closed, within a few hours of his arrival at Rome over three hundred deputies left cards at Giolitti's apartment to demonstrate their opposition to fighting. The parliamentary majority had been elected on a Giolittian ticket and had to think of their newly enfranchised constituents, most of whom were believed to want peace. Bissolati, himself an interventionist, computed that no more than sixty deputies sincerely wanted war, whereas on the other side the pacifist Giolittians were an absolute majority of the Chamber and Salandra confessed that the opposition was increasing each day.

Salandra's position was highly precarious. It made things worse that (again this is from his not wholly reliable memoirs) the king asked him to try to win over Giolitti so that the war would be begun without a division inside the so-called constitutional parties. But fear of impeachment by this hostile majority made Salandra unwilling to confront Giolitti publicly and he ruled out any possibility of letting parliament decide. The decision had already been taken and the king had given his approval to a policy of war. The cabinet therefore agreed to resign and so lay responsibility upon the king for reconciling the opposition. Salandra also postponed the opening of parliament from May 12 to 20 so as to gain time. He had been particularly alarmed to find that the general staff, when informed of the switch in alliances, declared that they would need much more time to prepare a completely new military strategy.

The king himself was so far committed that Salandra felt quite safe in offering resignation. Owing to Giolitti's absence, Vittorio Emanuele had been inveigled into a war policy, and now insisted that, despite the fact that they had resigned, the former ministers should continue to prepare for war. When Giolitti heard that the king thought that the honor of the monarchy was pledged, he agreed to make things easy by withdrawing his political challenge. He even recommended appointing other ministers who would support a war policy which he personally thought would be a dangerous mistake. Giolitti had something in his nature which made him reluctant to take office when things became difficult. Once he knew of the promise to declare war by May 26, he understood that its repudiation might not only impugn Italian good faith but could result in the abdication of the king who had signed it. Salandra was therefore reinstated, and another radical weakness was exposed in the constitution of 1848.

The decision between peace and war had already been taken, and the need to cover the king resulted in the government mobilizing for war before parliament had been consulted over this complete reversal of policy. Deputies known to be neutralists were manhandled in the street and Salandra cynically connived at this. Students rowdily invaded the very Houses of Parliament, and Sonnino's *Giornale d'Italia* was not alone in abusively insinuating that Giolitti's friends were in the pay of Germany. D'Annunzio's language about Giolitti became obscene and this former premier had to be given a guard through the streets. Mussolini preferred the method of fighting duels as his contribution to showing that the promised age of violence had dawned. No weapon was illegitimate, for the honor of Italy and the king's reputation were at stake so that the views of parliament and public opinion were irrelevant. This was a result of the fact that Giolitti had not bothered to organize a parliamentary opposition, but had sulked at his country house in the hope of remaining publicly uncommitted until he could stage a comeback. Being uncommitted he was also impotent just when a challenge to the government was most needed.

So loud were D'Annunzio's shouts in the piazza that the king could recall Salandra on May 16 without the wishes of parliament mattering in the least. Nitti later looked back on this as the day when the constitution was abolished and liberty destroyed. As again in 1922, the king, placed between parliament and the demagogues, chose the latter, and there was no constitutional means of restraining him. Giolitti for his part, by not being ready to form a ministry, acknowledged defeat and on May 17 scuttled away again to far-off Piedmont whence to watch the verification of his gloomy forebodings in years of solitude. In private letters he explained that he did not dare raise his fundamental opposition in parliament because that would have seemed unpatriotic. This was a melancholy and damaging admission.

Giolitti's followers drew their own conclusions from his flight, and by May 20, when parliament met for the first time during the crisis, they had changed sides. Under severe intimidation, forsaken by their leader and knowing the extent of the king's involvement, the deputies gave the government full powers "in case of war" by 407 votes to 74. This decision was greeted by salvos of applause from all benches save those occupied by the fifty official socialists, and a patriotic hymn of the *risorgimento* was begun in the public galleries before being taken up in the body of the House. Some deputies cried "long live the war," and were to have their wish granted more literally than they intended. In the Senate the decision was unanimous, for the bandwagon was moving and he who did not jump on might be left in limbo. War was declared on May 23, and on May 24 the army marched.

★

It redounds to Giolitti's credit that his first major defeat in fifteen years was at the hands of extraparliamentary forces, the piazza mob and the royal prerogative. All his reasoned arguments and all the dangerous implications of fighting in a European war were overwhelmed by the excitement of the moment and the infectious enthusiasms which swept through the land. Salvemini was one interventionist who later regretted sharing in this enthusiasm. Parliamentary deputies, when all is said, are more intelligent than mobs and (in this case) than poets or kings, even though most of them finally succumbed to a wave of patriotic hysteria. Mussolini's followers joyfully concluded from this course of events that parliament had been superseded and would altogether disappear before long. They were right, for parliament was discredited, and the war not only disappointed many patriotic hopes but was going to create the conditions out of which Mussolini emerged a dictator.

So charged with emotion was this moment of May 1915 that some people nevertheless saw it as one of regeneration, the moment when Italy chose to fight for righteousness and to win the war for democracy. Salandra, on the contrary, in his justification to parliament at the time, stressed egoistic rather than idealistic motives for intervention. According to Giolitti, Salandra's main motive in fighting was to strengthen the conservative interest in Italian domestic politics. Salandra and Sonnino were not notoriously anti-German or antimilitarist, nor were they much in love with democracy, and the liberation of subject peoples could not deeply interest a government whose chief war aim was Italian dominion over the Adriatic and the southern Slavs.

As if to prove the point, Salandra declared war not against Germany the violator of Belgium, but only against Austria upon whom Italy had territorial claims. Apart from this being a breach of his formal promise in the Treaty of London, it gave to subsequent operations the appearance of a private grudge war rather than of a war of liberation and righteousness. This explains the mistrust of Italy which her new allies began to show, for her simultaneous negotiations with all the major belligerents hardly inspired much confidence. About Salandra's unfortunate public reference in October to his motives as being those of *sacro egoismo*, Nitti concluded that this damaged Italy as much as a military defeat. The realist Salandra may have had good reason to deride the specious ideology of the Allies, but a still shrewder realist would have seen that, with some more ideal motive, Italians might have fought better and might have deserved a better press abroad and a better peace settlement.

SECTION NINE: THE WAR AND ITS
AFTERMATH, 1915–1922

37　The Conduct of War, 1915–1918

So complete was Italy's unpreparedness that her entering the war looked irresponsible in retrospect, but Salandra imagined the fighting to be nearly over, and indeed this was the main reason for him risking the future of his country. In negotiating the Treaty of London he had requested financial help from his new allies only for two months. He had omitted to ask for assistance with oil or raw materials and defended his forgetfulness by the remarkable assertion that he did not want to dishonor Italy by bargaining over peace and war—as if this was not what he had been doing for months. He bravely called Nitti an unpatriotic pessimist for thinking that war might continue past the winter of 1915. Here was irresponsibility on a colossal scale.

Salandra admitted later that the military operations were unsatisfactory. This was partly his own fault because he thought he could make Italy a great power cheaply, and indeed General Porro in 1914 refused to become minister of war specifically because of Salandra's parsimony over the army estimates. Such was the premier's secretiveness about negotiating with both sides at once that the general staff was finally told about the reversal of alliances only on the evening of May 5, and the generals were thus given less than three weeks to prepare for war against Austria after having based their plans on an Austrian alliance. The development of hostilities then showed up their obsolete military theory. Cadorna confirmed that, when he took up the supreme command in July 1914, he found the existing campaign studies to be exclusively defensive, and the ingrained habit of invasion-mindedness continued to be an important restraining factor. The Austrians were surprised at it. There was also the fact that the Libyan war had used up reserves of munitions and finance and left military morale impaired. The chief of staff reported later that the Italian army at the outbreak of hostilities had been in no position to fight.

It hardly helped matters that the king left immediately for the front and stayed there until the end of the war as nominal commander in chief. Cadorna had never held active command before. He was a good organizer, but he and his chief colleagues were unresourceful, unimaginative, and inflexible. They inspired little confidence or affection in their men. He could not abide interference by politicians and demanded the replacement of the existing minister of war by a nominee of his own. Nor would he brook much advice from the Allied military leaders, with the result that the principle of a unified Allied command was not extended to Italy.

Salandra's ministry was more conservative than the Chamber or Senate. Though he brought in the radical Carcano and the liberal Orlando in October 1914, and the ex-republican irredentist Barzilai in the summer of 1915, this was nearer one-party government than was customary. Neither Salandra nor the king even set eyes on Giolitti for some years after May 1915, for this "leader of the opposition" did not attend parliament until November 1917. Parliament was in fact of no importance during the war, and government by decree was more extensively adopted than in other belligerent countries.

★

Italy had hoped to find Austria on her last legs and was surprised when Russia's withdrawal from Galicia after May 1915 let Austria switch troops to the south. Ironically, this German advance against Russia began the day before Italy denounced the Triple Alliance and hundreds of thousands of Russians were taken prisoner in the weeks before Italy declared war. Salandra later admitted that, had this been known in time, Italy might have remained neutral.

The main Italian activity was along the River Isonzo, and here the mountains and a lack of munitions made Cadorna's task difficult. Though his army was superior by three or four to one, the war settled down into a dozen battles for position with little to show for them. On the Carso tableland beyond the Isonzo numerous caves and other natural defenses hindered the conversion of any tactical success into a strategic victory. Cadorna based his strategy on active Serb co-operation against Austria, but Sonnino never intended this when he signed the Treaty of London. The Serbs discovered that Sonnino meant to annex Dalmatia, and since they therefore feared Italy as much as they feared Austria, they kept large forces near the Albanian frontier. Sonnino's Dalmatian ambitions had clearly been misconceived: they had been opposed by Cadorna who guessed that they would be a military liability.

The first major movement on the Italian front was in May 1916, an Austrian offensive in the Trentino down the Brenta and Adige valleys. Cadorna claimed to have known about it well in advance but believed that the mountains and the single-track railroad would prevent any great concentration against him. But the Austrians penetrated within six miles of the Venetian plain; they also captured and executed the irredentists Chiesa and Battisti as Austrian-born subjects who had supposedly "deserted" to join Italy.

As a result of this reverse Salandra fell. On his own confession, after twelve months of war the Italian defenses were still gravely defective. The faith of the country was shaken and some deputies had not forgiven the way he had stampeded them into war. The prime minister was not someone who easily made himself liked, but treated parliament with quite unnecessary disdain and quarreled seriously with Cadorna. His unforgivable error was to have gambled on the war being over by the end of 1915, and Italians soon discovered that Giolitti's warnings had been amply justified.

Salandra's successor was Boselli, an undistinguished trimmer of the Right Center, than whom no one could have been less suitable as a war leader. Giolitti's advice was not sought on this occasion, which was another breach of constitutional practice. Seventy-eight years old, perhaps the oldest deputy in parliament, Boselli was a nonentity and a stopgap. Bonomi—who was in a position to know—recorded that a younger man was avoided lest he might impose a strong will on the cabinet. Boselli's lack of personality nevertheless permitted a coalition which extended from Meda of the Catholics, through Sonnino and Orlando, to the radicals Sacchi and Carcano, and even to Bonomi and Bissolati of the reformist socialists. On paper this looked like a broad expression of national feeling, however hard it must have made the quick collective decisions needed in time of war. Only the independent socialists failed to join in the general satisfaction over these appointments.

The Austrian offensive was contained by desperate fighting, and in June the coincidence of Brussilov's offensive in the East with a British offensive on the Somme brought relief. In August a forward movement under General Capello proved that, with careful preparation, positions which had defied assault for fifteen months could be won in a few hours. The capture of Gorizia was one of the signal successes of the year. But then the war settled down once again into a situation typified by D'Annunzio's isolated and irresponsible raids by land, sea, and air. The propaganda value of D'Annunzio demanded that he be given what was virtually an independent command in all three services at once. He was ecstatically happy in this freelance life with all the limelight, though he lamented that no more than three medals were given him for gallantry, since he thought he deserved at least six.

This counteroffensive on the Carso was reassuring to the Allies. Lack of mutual confidence had been deepened through political differences. The Allies wanted Greece as a belligerent to offset Bulgaria's entry into the war, but Sonnino feared Greek aspirations in southern Albania, and antagonized the Greeks by proclaiming Albania an Italian protectorate. Another difference arose over the fact that Italy was still at war only with Austria-Hungary; and France and Britain therefore had no scruples in arranging between themselves the eventual partition of the Turkish empire. To regularize this anomaly, Boselli did what Salandra had always refused and declared war on Germany in August 1916. A settlement reached in April 1917 recognized Italian claims against Turkey, but was never fully ratified and so another source of disagreement was left over until after the war.

★

Toward the end of 1917 Italy suffered a disastrous military reverse. There had been much defeatism among both civilians and soldiers enervated by a static war that was continuing much longer than anyone had intended. Italians fought well enough, but great numbers of them had entered the war reluctantly. The prefects as well as the deputies were largely Giolitti's nominees and this helped to make local co-operation unenthusiastic. There were bread riots at Turin in the summer of 1917, with forty-one deaths recorded. Shortages and restrictions caused a lowering of civilian morale which inevitably affected the soldiers, and unsavory legends were current at the front about the *pescecani* or sharks who made fortunes out of war profiteering.

Clerical pacifism was so strong that Pope Benedict XV called for a "white peace" without annexations: his unequivocal reference to "useless carnage" received wide publicity and was much deplored in Allied circles. The pope was here strangely at one with the official socialists, but the socialists' slogan "Oppose the war, but do not sabotage it" reflected their internal differences of opinion. Turati moved toward the view that the proletariat had more to lose from defeat than from fighting. A pacifist deputation was nevertheless sent to the international socialist congresses of Zimmerwald in 1915 and Kienthal in 1916, and the maximalist majority in the socialist party created disaffection in important cities such as Milan and Bologna which had socialist administrations. Later it was found necessary to imprison Lazzari and Bombacci, the secretary and vice-secretary of the party.

The defeat at Caporetto was not unconnected with this crumbling of morale. Cadorna wrote of the cowardice of the Second Army, though his solicitude for military honor demanded that defeat be attributed to "red" and "black" propaganda. General Caneva's later inquiry into the catastrophe attributed the shattered confidence of the troops quite as much to what Sforza called Cadorna's "mystical sadism," for the commander even had soldiers shot in decimations for disobedience even when some victims had been absent. He had never believed in catering to the comfort of his men. Furthermore, senior officers were rendered nervous after scores of generals had been abruptly dismissed. Basically, however, the defeat was due to poor generalship by Cadorna himself. In October 1917 regiments under Badoglio's command gave way; and when other units retired to cover the breach thus made, an exaggerated rumor suddenly spread that all was lost, and a general rout began.

Considered dispassionately, this was a straightforward military defeat. Cadorna had been too isolated to sense the danger and Boselli was too invertebrate to criticize the conduct of operations. Lloyd George and Foch agreed that poor organization and staff work were chiefly responsible. Cadorna had disagreed seriously with his corps commander, General Capello, and the wiseacres tried to point some deep moral from the fact that the former was a clerical and the latter a Freemason. Both of them later wrote books to justify themselves against each other, and both were later dismissed for their alleged mistakes. Caneva's report showed that the Second Army had been too much a law unto itself. Too little attention had been paid to the formation of reserves or to defense in depth, and units had repeatedly been incited to gain territory even if this left them in an untenable position.

The situation was further changed by the surprise arrival of German troops on the Austrian front: one young German officer who distinguished himself was Erwin Rommel. Their attack was directed against Caporetto, a small market town where the angle made by Italian defenses was too sharp. This point was chosen because a good road and railway led back to Cividale, and once there an advancing column could quickly turn the flank of the whole

Isonzo line. The movement began in the early hours of October 24 achieving tactical surprise against demoralized troops, and by midday the Italians were in full retreat. It was a serious collapse when seven hundred thousand men had to fall back for a hundred miles and on the River Tagliamento there were not enough bridges to carry them. Only by a great effort was this penetration into the plain of Lombardy halted at Monte Grappa beyond the River Piave.

The psychological impact of this retreat was enormous. Franchetti committed suicide when he heard the news. The king even mentioned the word abdication. But among politicians, when confronted with an actual invasion, even Turati and Treves spoke of resistance to the last, and for the first time in history the Italian people stood together almost as one. Giolitti, too, gave up his backstage pacifism. The feeble Professor Boselli was replaced in October 1917 by the Sicilian Professor Orlando—once again Giolitti was not consulted—and Nitti from the radical Left was included as finance minister in a reshuffled cabinet. Cadorna was succeeded by Diaz, a Neapolitan of Spanish ancestry, who took better care of the welfare of his men and set up propaganda offices to tell the soldiers about the conduct and purpose of the war. Diaz also tried hard to make Sonnino waive his unfortunate objection to co-operation with the Slavs. The winter was then spent in consolidation, and in June 1918, to everyone's relief, the army successfully held a new enemy push on the Piave.

As the war drew to a triumphant close on the other European fronts, the government overrode the advice of reluctant generals and ordered Diaz to advance. Orlando's view was that circumstances could not be better for taking such a risk. He pointed out how the Allies had the initiative, how Bulgaria had already collapsed and a revolution was taking place in Austria, and how even the Germans were putting out feelers for an armistice. Exactly a year after Caporetto, on October 24, Caviglia's army crossed the River Piave with Allied contingents in support. By the thirtieth they had reached the village of Vittorio Veneto from which the victory would derive its name. On November 3 Trent was captured and the navy landed in Trieste. Austria-Hungary was in complete dissolution and surrendered.

★

The war was over and the belligerents could begin to count as much of the cost as was countable. By the end of 1918 Italy claimed to have put five million men under arms, fifty thousand of whom had fought on the French front, and she had made an immense industrial effort. The number of combatants killed is sometimes given as nearly seven hundred thousand, though General Caneva's commission put it as less. But financially, the drain had been enormous. The yearly imports, which in 1914 had been valued at three billion lire, were running three years later at fourteen billion, and this total was covered only to one-third or less by exports. Meanwhile the current figures for state expenditure had multiplied in an alarming ratio. The Treasury calculated in 1930 that the cost of the war had been 148 billion lire, that is to say twice the sum of all government expenditure between 1861 and 1913.

In return for an enormous consumption of natural resources, Italy at last obtained a frontier on the Alps. A great deal of idealism had gone into the war and much elevated patriotism, but one need not look many years beyond 1918 to see that the downside was incalculable. A plot hatched by Salandra and the king had irresponsibly exploited the patriotism of Italians. This prime minister had exploited weaknesses in the constitution to act in secret, without consultation. The legacy of this terrible war was one reason why Italy was now to suffer twenty-five years of revolution and tyranny.

38   The Peace Settlement, 1918–1920

Italy had made a notable contribution in the last stages of Allied victory and the euphoria of success briefly left the country united as never before, but internal squabbles soon reopened and weakened her position at the peace conference. The sharp division of 1915 between interventionists and neutralists had continued under the surface of politics, and superimposed on it by 1918 was an equally fundamental division between those who hoped to annex territory in the Balkans and those who renounced it.

Sonnino remained foreign minister continuously from 1914 to 1919 and had no use for the "renouncers." In his eyes, emancipating the submerged Slav nationalities would merely replace defeated Austria by a new enemy, since the names of Croat and Slovene recalled the hated units of the Austrian army which had played a cruel part during the *risorgimento*. Against much military and political advice, Sonnino was reluctant to meet with the Slavs and support their parallel claims against Austria. For him the Adriatic was *Il Golfo*, as in the days of Venetian hegemony. It was embarrassing as it was surprising to him that the Greeks and Yugoslavs emerged from the war as technically his allies, for the Yugoslavs wanted Trieste and Dalmatia, while Greece rivaled Italy in claiming Albania, Anatolia, and the Dodecanese.

On the other hand, at least one minister, Leonida Bissolati, had always welcomed the breakup of Austria-Hungary into its national constituent elements. As a good Mazzinian, Bissolati could not deny to the Dodecanese and Albania the same self-determination which Italy claimed in Trent. When, in June 1917, Sonnino declared his protectorate over Albania, Bissolati had resigned, especially as this declaration had not first been put even to the cabinet, though he subsequently withdrew his resignation lest a ministerial crisis should weaken Italy's position with her allies. As a result, this important difference of opinion was suppressed just at the moment when its discussion was most needed. Bissolati as a minister without portfolio heard about such decisions only after the executive departments had already settled them. The cabinet had deliberately not been consulted when the Treaty of London promised Dalmatia to Italy, nor over the occupation of Albania, and in this way a highly dangerous and controversial decision had been taken irresponsibly without proper debate. Worse still, prime minister and foreign minister disagreed on many fundamental points; yet Orlando could not dismiss Sonnino without risking the dissolution of his coalition and allowing Giolitti back into power.

The defeat of Caporetto, however, had made Slav military help suddenly desirable, and in April 1918 Sonnino permitted a Congress of Oppressed Nationalities to be convoked at Rome. From it emerged a "Pact of Rome" wherein was declared that the unity and independence of Yugoslavia was a vital interest of Italy. This declaration must have been of considerable help in the downfall of Austria, and although not promulgated officially by the government, it was welcomed by Orlando the prime minister. The Italian delegation to the congress had been widely representative, and included such people as Albertini, Amendola, Barzilai, Federzoni, Mussolini, and Salvemini.

Even though Bissolati's slavophile policy continued to meet strong opposition, some of the realists recognized that Italy would need the new Yugoslavia as a friend; hence idealism and enlightened self-interest combined to recommend renouncing some Italian ambitions across the Adriatic. The *renunciatari* included men of such diverse sentiments as Giolitti and Turati, Nitti and Salvemini, and newspapers ranging from the *Corriere* to the *Secolo* and *Avanti*. Against them, as well as Sonnino, were such groups as those attached to Mussolini, Barzilai, and D'Annunzio, who wanted their pound or more of flesh from the Treaty of London. Mussolini, though a signatory of the Pact of Rome, wished to have it both ways.

★

The peace treaty with Austria was signed in September 1919 at St. Germain, and that with Hungary in June 1920 at the Trianon. Italy's main demands were based on the 1915 Treaty of London, but the situation had changed in the interim. For one thing the unexpected breakup of Austria-Hungary made Italy's domination of the Adriatic less essential for her security than in 1915, and it might have been thought unwise to press her claims against the new successor states with whom Italy should ideally have been on terms of friendship. Furthermore the United States, not being bound by the Treaty of London, stood squarely by President Wilson's fourteen points. Of these points, the ninth was repugnant to that treaty, as it stated that "a readjustment of the frontiers of Italy should be effected along clearly recognized lines of nationality." Sonnino was not formally committed by these fourteen points in his armistice with Austria, but Italy had exploited the victory value of Wilson's idealistic war aims, and the President's tumultuous reception in Rome suggested that ordinary Italians might prefer Mazzini's ideas of self-determination to the mere right of conquest and strategic advantage. Orlando was on record as having said that the Treaty of London could not be invoked against the Serbs. But, the war once over, his colleague Sonnino increased rather than reduced his claims to the Dalmatian coast, perhaps to have something which could be surrendered in a compromise.

The American experts opposed Italian claims upon the Dalmatian coast and its islands, as well as on the Dodecanese and much of Venezia Giulia. They even urged that the Upper Adige above Trent, although south of the Alps, should continue Austrian since most of its inhabitants spoke German. Against this expert advice and despite his cherished principles, Wilson decided entirely in Italy's favor over her northern frontier. He realistically acknowledged that here if anywhere a strategic boundary took precedence over nationality and language. Italy thus obtained the Brenner for her frontier, and annexed not only the Italian-speaking Trentino but also the largely German-speaking Alto Adige. In some sectors of her northeastern frontier she obtained more than her due under the Treaty of London.

This frontier was admittedly confused, geographically, linguistically, and by historical tradition. The only safe generalization was that many cities were predominantly Italian, the countryside Slav. Trieste itself was given to Italy without much debate. As the terminus of the *Südbahn* and a great mercantile emporium for Central Europe, this annexation was a rich prize. It was not such an unqualified advantage for Trieste itself, since a political frontier now severed the Triestini from their German and Slav hinterland, leaving the city a head without a body and its inhabitants often without occupation.

To the south of the Istrian peninsula, Fiume was more difficult. It had not featured among the usual Italian irredentist claims, not even in the Treaty of London where so much of the Dalmatian coast had been assigned to Italy. But in 1919 the nationalists joined with the *renunciatari* in renouncing their treaty claims on Slav-speaking Dalmatia if in exchange they could obtain Italian-speaking Fiume. The Italian peace delegation was divided on this point. Sonnino would have liked Dalmatia without Fiume; Orlando preferred Fiume to Dalmatia. In the end they demanded both, although the arguments for one might have seemed to exclude the other. This excess of appetite did Italy no service at the conference and played into the hands of those among the Serbs, Croats, and Slovenes who wished to sink their differences and form a single state united against Italian imperialism. Orlando professed that he could not abandon Fiume lest a violent outburst in Italy should endanger the whole peace settlement. This irresponsible threat covered his real motive, which was partly one of pure prestige, and partly that if Fiume lay outside Italy it might damage Trieste by becoming the main maritime outlet for Central Europe.

There was no boundary in Istria and Venezia Giulia that would satisfy both

Italy and Yugoslavia, and Wilson was right to insist on compromise. But the so-called Wilson Line was propounded so tactlessly that Orlando withdrew the Italian delegation from Paris. Wilson's recommendation offered strategic and ethnic advantages to Italy, even exceeding her demands in some places. Thereunder she would have obtained most of the Istrian peninsula with Trieste and Pola, and all the railroads connecting Gorizia and Trieste to Italy. The fact that a quarter of a million Slavs would have come under Italian sovereignty proved that Wilson could be a realist who recognized that self-determination was no absolute shibboleth.

Italy's objection to this boundary was the omission of Fiume and the independent railroad which made that city as accessible as was Trieste to the commerce of Vienna and Budapest. Wilson replied by saying that if self-determination applied to the city of Fiume it might also apply to regions of New York City where there were many Italians. Britain and France stood with him on this point, and intimated that, if Orlando persisted over Fiume, this would impair other Italian claims under the Treaty of London. Intransigence thus led to the neglect of different Italian demands that might otherwise have gone unchallenged. The result was that Fiume became a free state, to the indignation of many patriotic Italians.

Italian pretensions to the rest of the Dalmatian littoral were so sharply urged by Sonnino that in December 1918 Bissolati once more resigned from the cabinet. Whereas Sonnino argued that both Yugoslavs and Austrians were enemies of Italy, Bissolati in a speech at La Scala in Milan drew attention to the simple fact that Yugoslavia existed and nothing Italy could do would alter the fact. This speech was made almost inaudible by nationalist agitators since it betrayed the cause of "our Adriatic." In their eyes, Slav friendliness might have been welcome in the dark days of 1917, but victory in war enabled the true national interests to be reasserted. These vocal nationalists may have been negligible numerically (and their party won only ten seats in the 1921 election), but their influence was strong at the royal Court and in army and industrial circles. D'Annunzio had loudly proclaimed that the Slavs ought to be "slaves":

> Dalmatia belongs to Italy by divine right as well as human law, by the grace of God who has designed the earth in such a way that every race can recognize its destiny therein carved out.... It was ours and shall be ours again. No German from the Alps, no Croat caring nothing for history or falsifying it, not even the Turk disguised as an Albanian, no one shall ever hold up the rhythm of fate, the Roman rhythm.... What can avail the brute force of the barbarians against the law of Rome!

Only a temporary access of sweet reasonableness enabled Italy to yield this point and sign the Treaty of Rapallo with Yugoslavia in 1920, momentarily renouncing her Dalmatian ambitions.

Italy also had designs on Asia Minor. Despite rival claims by Greece, Sonnino fought for the annexation of Smyrna. Italian troops were landed at several places in Turkey on the plea of keeping order, and plans were even made for an expedition to obtain further territory in the Caucasus. But Turkish resistance soon made it clear that there was to be no partition of Asia Minor after all and Italian troops had to be withdrawn. By the Treaty of Lausanne with Turkey, in July 1923, Italy received no more than confirmation of sovereignty over the Dodecanese Islands where she had ruled *de facto* since 1912.

The colonial settlement was affected by Article 13 of the Treaty of London whereby Italy should have *compensations équitables* if her allies extended their colonies. Italian statesmen were chiefly concerned about frontier adjustments with Tunisia and Egypt; they also would have liked Kassala in the Sudan which Italy had ceded to Britain in 1897; and if only Eritrea could be linked with Somaliland, they might have some chance of dominating Abyssinia as well. Nevertheless, during the war Italy had undertaken no colonial campaign and had even been forced to withdraw from most of Libya, which made it seem improbable that she had sufficient interest or resources for much extension of colonial territory. Moreover her delegates at the peace conference were of several minds about colonial expansion.

The Allies, not with much good grace, admitted the justice of compensations, and when Balfour announced the appointment of a committee to consider them Orlando expressed himself content. Again, when the German colonies were distributed as mandates to other countries, Orlando entered no demurrer. Personally he was not much interested. He preferred to yield on colonies so as to establish his right to compensation nearer home, for his own overmastering concern was the Adriatic, and he correctly realized that the reconquest of Libya would be expensive. He therefore signed the German and Austrian treaties before raising the colonial question. Italy eventually received only Jarabub and Jubaland from Britain, and minor French concessions on the frontiers of Libya and Eritrea. With these results fascist Italy was altogether unsatisfied.

★

In sum, as a result of these treaties, the Italian mainland was extended by about nine thousand square miles, winning most of the 1915 program but by no means all. Her frontier was extended to run along the Alps from the Brenner to Monte Nevoso, which was more than self-determination would have allowed. Mussolini's newspaper—which was to veer abruptly when the wind changed—rejoiced at this consummation, delighted that all the roads by which the German barbarians had invaded Italy down the centuries were now firmly barred. Even more, whereas France was still confronted by an undivided Germany, Italy's hereditary enemy was now but a cipher. Instead of Austria-Hungary with fifty-one million subjects, there was a much truncated Austria with six million and Yugoslavia with twelve. One of the more perceptive

Italian foreign ministers, Count Sforza, expressing a view which his predecessors would have done well to ponder, concluded that Italy was the nation to win most territory from the war.

This was not the same as being satisfied, because if judged by territorial results the outcome of modern wars must seem incommensurate with the sacrifices demanded. Inestimable potential benefits were gained but were obscured by mismanagement of the bitter controversy over Fiume and the Adriatic. As Salandra recognized, absolute national security was impossible without complete domination in that area, and this was inconceivable. The brutal fact was not that her allies deserted her, not that she had "lost the peace"—these were artificial and unscrupulous nationalistic legends—but that the collapse of the Central Powers in 1918 prevented her resuming her former role as a makeweight in the European balance of power. It was the war rather than the peace which defeated her. The war revealed what in normal times skillful diplomacy could conceal, that Italy was the least of the great powers.

Many Italians thought that they were not treated with fairness at the peace settlement, but later propaganda exaggerated their disappointment in order to exploit it. Most of the other belligerents had lost incomparably more than justice would have allowed. One must add that the Italian representatives were unbending and feckless in negotiation. It was no doubt tactless of President Wilson when, in April 1919, he appealed to Italian public opinion over the head of Orlando, seeming to imply that the latter was not representative of his country. But Orlando did not improve matters by stumping huffily out of the conference, waiting two weeks at Rome in the hope of being given an apology. Fearing that Italy might be left to sign a separate treaty, he and Sonnino had to pocket their pride and return, just in time to witness the presentation of the peace proposals to Germany without the opportunity of putting the Italian case on controversial points.

Orlando and Sonnino had hoped that their importunity would force the conference to yield and so omitted to explain the economic and strategic grounds upon which their demands were based. By comparison, the Yugoslav memoranda were more subtle and calculated to please the American president. Italy lacked first-rate leaders, not for the first time since the death of Cavour, and as usual her ruling coalition included many divergent points of view—her traditional system of government made this almost inevitable. The Italian case was therefore clumsily presented. No doubt, too, the Italian public was confused about their national interests and misled by sentimental considerations. Certainly they were no more selfish than the other belligerents. But had they renounced in 1919 what they were forced to yield to Yugoslavia in 1920, concessions might have enabled them to bargain for more serious economic advantages.

As Sonnino talked so much of territorial acquisition, the Allies were given no help in understanding that the most vital needs of Italy were economic, and neither did Sonnino begin to realize this himself. In 1915 Italy's fixation on frontiers had obscured her need for adequate financial help in the war, and again in 1919, for precisely the same reason, questions of raw materials and of wider Italian economic interests in the Mediterranean were completely neglected. In this strange world of exaggerated sentimental nationalism, Sonnino thought it undignified to ask for a loan, but not undignified to ask for someone else's territory which had not even been conquered. He had not sufficiently appreciated how far Italy had been dependent on her allies for munitions and food, nor did he realize how only credits given by her allies had kept Italian currency from complete collapse. This made the rude awakening in 1919 all the more of a shock. There are many instructive lessons to be learned from the contrast between Italy's economic collapse after victory in 1918 and her quick recovery after a devastating defeat in 1943.

39 New Political Currents, 1919

The end of the war brings us to the question of why Italy, so proud of her liberties, should have been the first important European country to succumb beneath the tidal wave of fascism. Postwar problems were everywhere difficult, but Italian politicians were so bewildered that they lost both control over events and confidence in themselves. The programs of each party show little evidence of the imagination and honesty that the situation required, but successive governments connived at illegal and revolutionary actions for dark purposes of their own and played up popular discontent for tactical reasons of domestic policy. Liberals and antiliberals alike, and particularly those who had been guilty of dragging an unwilling Italy into the war, devised the myth of an Italy cheated of her due in 1919. The immense gain achieved by the destruction of Austria-Hungary was minimized so as to create a sense of deprivation.

Italy had been psychologically damaged by the defeat of Caporetto, over-excited by the triumph of Vittorio Veneto, and then depressed again when peace did not bring advantages that irresponsible leaders had promised. Inflation was meanwhile undermining middle-class security and helped to break the tacit agreement between classes which Giolitti had fostered. One hundred and fifty thousand deserters were in hiding and once more raising the problem of brigandage in the provinces. Demobilization caused yet another unbalancing anticlimax and created widespread unemployment just when emigration was becoming impossible as a remedy, while a large number of senior military officers did not adjust easily to the pedestrian and ill-rewarded tranquillity of civilian life. Allied economic help dried up almost immediately, leaving Italy billions of dollars in debt. Wheat subsidies for farmers, steel subsidies to the heavily overcapitalized war industries, bread subsidies for consumers, all helped to increase inflation and a budgetary deficit, yet were insufficient to relieve distress.

Only a government possessed of courage, vision, and popular approval could have resolved such difficulties. But once again there was a familiar parliamentary paralysis in which no government had a reliable working majority, and politicians reacted by the usual tactical maneuvering in order to widen their parliamentary support. By ill chance there was one Italian who had the correct combination of ability, fascination, and unscrupulousness to exploit this situation.

★

Benito Mussolini was born in 1883, the son of a socialist blacksmith from an impoverished family in the Romagna. He was named after Benito Juárez, the Mexican revolutionary who had executed the Emperor Maximilian in 1867, as his brother Arnaldo was named after Arnold of Brescia who had once led a revolution against the Church. During his youth he was too insignificant for many reliable facts to have survived. But like Crispi, that other anticlerical, Mussolini was brought up in a Catholic seminary, from which he had to be expelled by the Salesian fathers after he had stabbed a fellow pupil. Again like Crispi, his upbringing made him a displaced intellectual and revolutionary. In 1901 he graduated as an elementary schoolmaster, and henceforth he passed among his socialist friends for a "professor" who knew about music and wrote jejune essays on German literature. There is some evidence that he could not control the pupils in his class.

Mussolini opposed military service and emigrated to Switzerland in 1902 to avoid the draft. There he held a quick succession of fairly menial jobs. He was arrested in July 1902 for begging in the streets of Lausanne and was expelled from one canton after another for holding a forged passport. His belief in illegal action, learned from the anarchists and republicans of his native Romagna, was now formalized by reading Sorel and Nietzsche. He attended at least one lecture by Pareto in Lausanne and was attracted to Pareto's theory of a new elite supplanting the decadent humanitarians of parliamentary democracy.

Angelica Balabanoff knew Mussolini in Switzerland and has left a graphic picture of a dirty, unkempt vagrant, who slept under bridges and cheated his fellows, but who thought of himself as a privileged intellectual and would rather do no work than manual work. He seemed to be motivated by a desire for revenge against society. He was as violent in word as he was insincere in belief. Even disparaging words made him happy provided he was noticed. He was afraid of walking home alone by night. He told her that he meant one day to write something more frightful and hair-raising than Poe, and the book would be called "Perversion." He was of the crude, loudmouthed, soapbox-orator kind, with obvious signs of instability. The picture is no doubt overdrawn, but recognizable.

Mussolini returned to Italy in 1904 and modified his principles (not for the last time) so far as to undergo military service. He then took up what remained his primary interest, journalism, and worked as a local organizer for the socialist party. At Trent he was secretary of the Chamber of Labor and at that time actively fought against Battisti and the patriots. In view of his later pose as a patriot, one may note that in 1911 he was jailed for condemning Italian imperialism in Libya and for calling the national tricolor "a rag to be planted on a dunghill." He was in prison more than once for agitation. Between 1910 and 1912 he edited a pseudo-Marxist magazine called *The Class Struggle*, and produced an anticlerical book on *John Huss, the Man of Truth*. All these activities he later tried to conceal.

As a result of socialist divisions in 1912, Mussolini, then editor of *Avanti*, became with Lazzari the most forceful personality in Italian socialism. Always an extremist, he inclined to the belief of Babeuf and Blanqui in violent insurrection by a minority in order to establish authoritarian rule. His articles reveal a retreat from belief in class solidarity and a growing attachment to revolution for revolution's sake, power for the sake of power. In this he was eventually to be joined by many miscellaneous malcontents of Right and Left.

A few weeks after the outbreak of war in 1914 he veered around abruptly from ardent neutralism to ardent intervention, instinctively sensing that war would be a highroad to revolution. In return for this change, the armaments firm of Ansaldo and the sugar and electrical industries helped him to publish a paper of his own, *Il Popolo d'Italia*, with an incendiary quotation from Blanqui on its front page. Most of the war years he spent as a journalist. For awhile he was in uniform, attaining like Hitler the rank of corporal, and the self-dramatization of his heroism was to be a feature of official biographies. With a gusty humorlessness he described to Emil Ludwig how he was "so badly wounded that it was impossible for me to be moved. One of the newspapers had mentioned where I was laid up. Thereupon the Austrians shelled the hospital." And he added that he chose to have an operation without chloroform. This dramatic posturing was another characteristic he shared with Crispi. He may have been a moderately good soldier, but the more likely story is that he was wounded during grenade practice and took no part in any serious military engagement.

Fascism began as a Milanese movement when in March 1919 two hundred discontented zealots met in the Piazza San Sepolcro. Most of them were socialists of a sort, and their program was completely different from that of later fascism—it included a capital levy, an 80 per cent tax on war profits, confiscation of ecclesiastical property, and denunciation of censorship, militarism and dictatorship. Mussolini had been envious of the bolsheviks and for a while fancied himself as the Lenin of Italy. He still talked the language of expropriating exploiters and their factories as a first step in social revolution. But in the general elections of November he discovered that this had little appeal. Not a single fascist was successful and they polled fewer than 5,000 votes against 190,000 for the official socialists at Milan. Several assistant editors of *Il Popolo d'Italia* protested against Mussolini's appropriation of funds that the paper had collected from America for D'Annunzio's conquest of Fiume. Many fascists then abandoned him and his political career seemed at an end.

This catastrophic electoral failure was partly due to fascism being such a medley of different ideas and tendencies. Balbo was a republican, Bianchi a syndicalist, but De Vecchi and De Bono were monarchists and conservatives. Marinetti wanted to expel the Pope from Italy, but Grandi and De Vecchi were to finish up with honorific titles from the Vatican. Nenni was another adherent in these early days before he became the leader of Italian socialism. Toscanini was a fascist candidate in 1919, though he later rebelled when they tried to bully him into playing the fascist song *Giovinezza* in his concerts and Puccini too in his last years welcomed the new movement.

Only when this election showed the folly of competing with the official socialists did Mussolini move over to ally with conservatives at the opposite extreme. His only consistency was in extremism and the use of violent means for the pursuit of power. The agrarian disorders of Emilia and the Po Valley then gave him the chance to launch a civil war against the socialists who in 1914 had thrown him out of their party. Gangsterism came out on top when electoral failure turned him not only against socialism but against the parliamentary system itself.

*

Far more successful than fascism in 1919 were the two mass parties, the socialists and the *popolari* or Christian democrats. The leader of the *popolari* was Don Sturzo, a Sicilian priest, whose sincerity, moderation, and administrative capacity at last welded many Catholics into a political party. This revival of Christian democracy—different only in degree from what Pius X had condemned early in the century—seemed to augur well. Unlike Murri, Sturzo had not rebelled against that condemnation, but quietly submitted until the time was ripe for a Catholic movement which also tried to be democratic.

The new party launched its manifesto in January 1919. Benedict XV, one of the wisest among modern popes, avoided ecclesiastical intrusion but gave assistance by finally lifting the *non expedit* and letting Catholics vote more freely. Technically, there was no official connection with the Church, but Sturzo, though not a conservative himself, was strictly orthodox and obedient, and his party was thus the more open to influence from the conservatives who, especially after the death of Benedict in 1922, predominated in ecclesiastical circles. The next Pope, Pius XI, did not speak *ex cathedra* on politics, yet on "mixed questions" he could often touch politics by implication. Moreover, disobedience to his private and fallible communications would rank as something very close to the sin of pride. Hence Don Sturzo's position was often rendered ambiguous and ineffective.

The *popolari* were a mass party inclined if anything to the Left. Their official program, while condemning imperialism, favored proportional representation, votes for women, and dividing up big estates. An extreme wing around Miglioli was almost Marxist. Their leaders knew that only a sympathetic attitude toward agrarian strikes would win the allegiance of the agricultural laborers. By 1920 trade unions associated with the *popolari* had one million people inscribed, and though the rival socialist unions boasted over two million, it was the Christian association that included most agricultural workers. In the fight against socialism the *popolari* would have been more sincere than Mussolini, but Pius XI eventually preferred the latter, so damaging Church as well as state.

The elections of 1919 gave this Catholic party the remarkable number of one hundred deputies in parliament, yet they spoke with no single voice. Along with genuine social reformers, they comprehended conservatives and reactionaries, and therefore each party congress fought shy of any practical policy which might cause a split. Miglioli's proposal to collaborate with the socialists was rejected, and although Sturzo resisted those at the other extreme such as Padre Gemelli who wanted his movement to become strictly confessional, political tactics suggested the wisdom of including the moderate Right as well as the moderate Left. Any clearly left-wing orientation would have been embarrassing to Pius XI. So perhaps was their emblem, a shield carrying the word *Libertas*, for this hinted at what the syllabus of 1864 had condemned as a cardinal error.

In sum, although strong enough to hamper other parties, the *popolari* were not themselves sufficiently united to have the influence on politics that their number and quality deserved. The one thing common to all of them was opposition to the anticlerical liberals who had generally dominated Italian government since the time of Cavour. They might allow a tactical alliance with liberalism, but were determined to ensure that this oligarchic liberal minority should take more note of Catholic opinion. The *popolari* too often played a negative and disintegrating role in parliament and so were easily dissolved by Mussolini after a brief life. It was a tragedy that they and the Giolittians preferred to ally with fascism against each other rather than with each other against fascism.

*

In 1919 the main rival to the *popolari* was not fascism but socialism. The socialists flourished in the big industrial centers, Milan, Turin, and Genoa where the war had concentrated many workers in factories, and also in the Romagna where they inherited Mazzinian and anarchist traditions of rebellion and unrest. By 1919 large groups in industry had won an eight-hour day. The membership of the socialist party had risen from 50,000 before the war to 200,000 in 1919, readers of *Avanti* to 300,000, and trade-union membership in the Confederation of Labor from half a million to two million. In the

November elections the official socialists raised their representation in parliament from 50 to 156. By 1920 the party and the Chambers of Labor controlled two thousand municipalities as well as twenty-six provinces out of sixty-nine. It was easily the largest party in Italy, well organized and disciplined. Here was something quite new in Italian history, and many people took fright at it.

One great pity was that socialism lacked responsible leadership, and from the benches on the Left hardly a single constructive step was proposed that went beyond unrealistic generalization. The only constant factor was the association of violent language with a timid uncertainty in deed, and this was bad tactics as well as self-deception. They positively refused to collaborate against fascism with the governments of Nitti, Giolitti, and Bonomi in turn. Yet they had little idea of effecting a communist revolution. They simply sat back under the cosy illusion that time was on their side and that universal suffrage would mean the supersession of liberalism by a dictatorship of the proletariat. There was no hurry to carry out reforms, no need to compromise or win allies, no obligation even to make their policy attractive or practicable. Even a moderate such as Turati argued that those who had involved Italy in the war should be left alone to take responsibility for its results.

The language of socialism nevertheless continued full of sound and fury signifying very little, and a fierce proclamation by the party executive in December 1918 announced that they aimed at a socialist republic and a proletarian dictatorship. The original program of 1892 had allowed the party to work inside the existing institutions of government, but this was modified in 1912 and again when the "maximalists" triumphed in the sixteenth party congress at Bologna in October 1919. The so-called reformist section led by Turati and Treves was there outvoted by four to one, and the congress decided that

> the proletariat must have recourse to the use of violence for the conquest of power over the bourgeoisie.... The existing institutions of local and national government cannot in any way be transformed into organs that will help to liberate the people. Instead we must use new and proletarian organizations such as workers' soviets, and we must adhere to the Third International.

Turati warned the congress that if their propaganda for expropriation forced the dominant class to counterattack, "then goodbye to parliamentary action and goodbye to the socialist party," for it would arouse the self-protective instincts of otherwise well-intentioned people. Unfortunately, the point was not well received.

Most of those who spoke of a proletarian dictatorship did not know what they meant or did not mean what they said: such alarmist statements merely gave them a pleasant illusion of power. The submerged half of Italy was seething with excitement in 1919 over the discovery that it could stand up to the bosses and terrify them. Minor communist risings took place but were isolated and unco-ordinated, provoking counterrevolutionary reprisals. The socialists may have taken pleasure in feeling themselves to be feared, but had to pay for it when Mussolini discovered that his gangs could break up the printing presses of *Avanti* without liberal newspapers calling on the police to stop him.

Lenin and Trotsky, like Sorel, were mystified by this folly and incompetence. Despite their great number, despite sporadic general strikes and local peasant revolts, the Italian socialists were merely waiting for the bourgeois state to surrender. After the expulsion of the syndicalists and of Mussolini they had lost their revolutionary zeal. During the war they had been pacifists and defeatists, and this damaged party morale. They went on mouthing the orthodox formulas of their religion, but many remained pacifists at heart and even developed a sneaking sympathy for liberal-democratic methods. Socialist members of parliament were more moderate than the maximalists who captured the party itself, and the powerful Confederation of Labor voted in February 1920 against hastening the day of proletarian dictatorship.

One must conclude that socialism, not believing wholeheartedly in either revolution or collaboration, merely antagonized all straightforward patriots without acting to defend Italy against an inevitable counterattack from the Right.

40   Nitti and the Rape of Fiume, 1919–1920

The war ministry of Orlando lasted until June 1919 when its mismanagement of the peace negotiations was the pretext for a parliamentary defeat by 262 votes to 78. Nitti, the southern radical, became prime minister for a year at the head of three successive cabinets. Francesco Nitti was a professor of political economy who had written profusely on economic problems. Honest and well-meaning, he was sensible enough to veto Orlando's extraordinary plan to send an expedition to the Black Sea for the conquest of Soviet Georgia. But he was too academic, too much the journalist, and became facile and rhetorical in his political views. Often hasty and unsound in judgment he was also prone to acid sarcasm, and this made many enemies among the miscellaneous radicals and liberals who might otherwise have underwritten his majority.

In an attempt to bargain with the socialists, Nitti gave way more than most liberals liked. He did not see sufficiently that Italy was in a fervor of nationalism and militant class consciousness that would make coalition government particularly hard. The former system of coalitions had been the product of small groups, and was less practicable now that a wide suffrage created mass parties of Catholics, nationalists, and socialists. These new mass parties believed more in doctrine than in personalities so that transformism was less easy, yet none of them was large enough for a truly governmental party to emerge.

Parliamentary institutions were therefore in danger of no longer working and only the emergency of war had concealed this new reality. During the military interregnum, parliament had seldom met and taxes had regularly been raised by executive decree. As a result, traditions of parliamentary behavior had been lost. Giolitti had known how to bind many selfish interests together: his complex system for controlling elections had extended everywhere, and his use of patronage yoked pressure groups, municipal cliques, trade unionists, the landed families, even sometimes the parish priest, in common harness. This machine had now broken down. Parliament was full of new men whose private weaknesses were no longer registered in government dossiers. Nitti was antipathetic to Giolitti and other liberals, while his accession to power was hailed by the communist Gramsci as the counterpart of Kerensky's in Russia, denoting the incipient collapse of the Italian bourgeois state.

★

Nitti's plan to form another Left-Center ministry made it necessary to hold a long-overdue election in 1919 for which he introduced the new method of proportional representation. By instituting large constituencies and large party lists, Nitti's electoral law aimed to sever the often reprehensible attachment between deputies and local pressure cliques, and no doubt the new method produced a more exact representation of the people. It also greatly increased the power of party machines which could choose to accept a name or omit it from their list. This reform was approved by a majority of 277 against 38, though many older parliamentary leaders including Salandra, Boselli, and Luzzatti abstained because they could see it as a threat to freedom of election.

Sonnino opposed proportional representation; so did Giolitti though he did not trouble to come to Rome and vote. The new constituencies would be far too large for the immediate sympathies or comprehension of voters. Lists of candidates were now to be pre-selected by a party caucus, and deputies would be elected en bloc without their individual character or intelligence being known to the electorate. Although the liberals were weakened, the mass parties were strengthened, and the effect was to make either transformism or single-party government more difficult. Significantly enough, Mussolini's *Popolo d'Italia* welcomed this reform; and according to Giolitti, proportional representation was indirectly a factor in ultimate fascist victory.

The elections of November 1919 were run with quite unusual fairness by Nitti, but their results showed how a working majority had once been far more easily obtained by unscrupulous use of government influence. The victors turned out to be the official socialists and the *popolari*—one reason being that they had both tended to oppose the war. Together these new parties made up just over half the Chamber, and as the socialists were always in opposition, this left the Catholics as arbiters of the parliamentary scene. Fifty years after the pope's military defeat in 1870 the wheel had come full circle. The old liberals were hopelessly riven between neutralists and interventionists, renouncers and imperialists; and clearly there was strong opposition to Salandra and those who had involved Italy in war.

Out of over five hundred seats, the right-wing liberals obtained about twenty, Giolitti in the Center about ninety. The *popolari* emerged with a hundred instead of the fifty that Nitti expected. He anticipated sixty socialists, but in fact there were 156, of which only ten came from the South and none from Sicily or Sardinia. The fascists won no seats at all and a very disappointing turn-out in the areas they contested. The radicals were down; the republicans were reduced to nine deputies; the independent socialists around Bonomi were negligible. The tragic failure of these elections was that no possibility of a liberal-democratic bloc emerged against the avowedly unconstitutional programs of socialism and fascism, and with such a parliament it would be almost impossible to reach agreement on anything. Little more than half of the electors had voted, and it is likely that many of the younger generation had small regard for parliamentary institutions: in 1915 parliament had easily and unprotestingly been overruled by the king and the piazza, and so was despised by both interventionists and noninterventionists.

An ominous sign in December was that the socialists, who were the largest party, interrupted the speech from the throne by cries of "long live the socialist republic" and marched out of the chamber singing the "Red Flag." The king was humiliated and frightened. Yet these were the true representatives of the people for this was the freest election so far in Italy (as it was the last relatively free election until 1946). Universal suffrage and proportional representation were thus building a bridge into fascist tyranny. The many-headed multitude was less intelligent than its oligarchic predecessors and much less practiced in government. If the old political class had been deficient in political education, how much more so were these new voters who sometimes lacked education of any sort?

Most of the deputies were new to parliament. Few admitted that to make effective government possible some sacrifice of interest and program was indispensable, and few showed the honesty and disinterested high principles which had governed Sella and Ricasoli fifty years before. In March 1920 the Chamber unanimously decided to continue the bread subsidies simply because no one dared antagonize the voters, even though they knew this spelled financial ruin— wheat was being fed to cattle because its subsidized price was a quarter of that on the free market in Europe. Each parliamentary group, finding the reality of power out of reach, made sure that no other group would succeed. Five ministers of education succeeded each other in the three years 1919–22, each leaving behind him a scheme of reforms that he had had no time to enact.

*

The end of the war brought not only political decomposition but economic collapse. Nitti told his electors that "present state expenditure exceeds receipts by more than three times; all state concerns are in debt and billions every year are being lost by the artificial price of bread; the national debt is increasing at the rate of one billion a month; and each month our expenditure on the army is greater than each year before the war." New York and London ended exchange controls in March 1919, and the dollar, from 6.34 lire in the second half of 1918, rose to 18.47 in 1920. Prices followed the same index and only wages lagged behind. In July 1919 there were riots against the cost of living, and the slump in heavy war industries led to widespread defaulting on wage agreements.

Another threatening trend was the growing disparity in wealth between social classes, for some people had done well out of the war while others not. Government contractors had often made fortunes, and so had many farmers, because rents were by now ludicrously small and agriculture was freed by inflation from much of its mortgage payments. It was noticeable that among the first to join fascism were many wealthier peasants, as well as landowners and war profiteers who feared the advance of socialism. Many landless laborers had meanwhile returned from the relative comfort of service life to primitive conditions, depressed wages, and unemployment, and had a burning grievance against those who had stayed at home and made their fortunes. Many workers had acquired novel standards of comparison; many could write and add, so that they could check the *mezzadria* accounts with the *padrone*. The war had like all big wars brought a revolution in habits and social relationships.

Even a professor of political economy might quail before such a prospect, and in fact the impossible task of assembling a majority frightened Nitti against proposing drastic measures to stop inflation and pay for the war. An impost on capital was decreed during 1919–20 but was to be spread over twenty years. War profits, too, were taxed heavily, but this did not affect the agriculturalists who were already threatening "a strike of taxpayers." As the British embassy in Rome reported, taxation "depends on the will of the people to contribute and on the ability of the government to collect the taxes," and both were lacking. The bread subsidies threatened national bankruptcy, yet Nitti's move to abolish them by decree only antagonized the Left, while Giolitti's subsequent tinkering with income-tax and war profits pushed many of the rich into the camp of *squadrismo* and civil disobedience. Left and Right were too much preoccupied with their own private selfishness to join in promoting the commonweal.

*

In September 1919, a calamity at Fiume should have made clear whither such progressive disobedience was leading. D'Annunzio's invasion of this somewhat unimportant town was a blatant instance of international violence. Inside Italy it prepared the way for fascism, and outside it helped to destroy the mutual confidence between states for peaceful negotiation over their differences.

The principle of self-determination, conveniently ignored by Italy in South Tyrol, had been usefully invoked during the victorious advance of October 1918 when Fiume was said to have demanded union with Italy. The Italian claim did not impress the Allied statesmen at Paris, and elections later showed that the Italian nationalists had no mandate from the local population, but D'Annunzio determined to improve the Italian case by force. An Allied commission under an Italian general decided that, to avoid local clashes, Italian soldiers in Fiume should be replaced by British police, but in September 1919, when this change was to take place, D'Annunzio made his coup as a first step toward annexing the east coast of the Adriatic.

The end of the war had left this poet laureate starved of amatory and military excitement. He was now bald, one-eyed, nearer sixty than fifty, and no longer a hero in the headlines, nor had he any government funds to preserve him from bankruptcy and keep his muse and his mistresses indulged. General Caviglia, the minister of war, told how D'Annunzio asked him to lead the army in a mutiny to overthrow parliament. This having failed, the poet petitioned Nitti for three million lire of government money with which to visit the East and there find new inspiration for his art. Finally, he succumbed to the prospect of glory and pelf that the nationalists offered him at Fiume. As usual he let himself be guided by his flair for the *beau geste*. A buccaneering expedition, which Badoglio called the finest since Garibaldi's invasion of Sicily, seemed in every respect suitable. At the end of May 1919 the nationalists in Fiume were calling him the "one and only *Duce* of the Italian people."

Support for this escapade was obtained from many patriots who had no intention of honoring Orlando's signature at Versailles, and D'Annunzio spoke for such people when in November he stated that "the Yugoslavs are excited by a savage spirit of domination and we cannot avoid perpetual quarrel with them." Scores of supernumerary generals had been under arms since 1911 and knew it would be hard to retain their standard of living on a pension. One general publicly threatened to become a shoeshiner in his uniform and decorations. The blackshirted *arditi* or shock troops were especially dangerous when demobilized, and in such circles there had been talk of a military *coup d'état* long before D'Annunzio arrived on the scene. The war had accustomed such people to the use of force. A continuation of the war under the respectable cloak of patriotism would be a godsend to them, and Fiume was the obvious place for it.

Mutineers as well as demobilized soldiers were involved, and when reminded that desertion was high treason, recalled how Cavour had secretly connived at regular troops joining Garibaldi. Perhaps this precedent was in the mind of Admiral Millo, commanding in Dalmatia, when he visited D'Annunzio and presumptuously swore to uphold Italian claims. The cause of disinterested patriotism was becoming dangerously confused when Nitti refused to dismiss this senior officer.

Worse still, public opinion was encouraged by the government to solidify in favor of annexing Fiume and the possible international repercussions were completely disregarded. Powerful interests at Venice and Trieste were determined to destroy the commerce of this rival port. Even patriotic socialists of such diverse stripe as Nenni and Bissolati called for annexation. So did the liberal Albertini of the *Corriere della Sera* however much he disliked D'Annunzio's method of conquest, and Sonnino's *Giornale d'Italia* devoted pages of lyrical excitement to both the method and its results. Giolitti's position, too, was at least equivocal for he could not help applauding in secret even while he deplored the undermining of military discipline. Members of the royal family were more open and paid visits to D'Annunzio in Fiume. The seamen's union was behind him and so was the Ansaldo munitions cartel.

A particular responsibility must rest on Nitti the prime minister. Subsequently he explained that, while appalled by these events, he did not turn D'Annunzio out because that would have risked revolution and weakened Italy's bargaining position with her Allies. Nitti hoped that these Allies would increase the government's prestige by conceding Fiume. While forced by European protests to deny the nationalists in public, in private he abetted them so as to convince Europe that there was no alternative to Italian annexation. The Yugoslav army could easily have chased D'Annunzio out, but Nitti prevented this by a direct military threat. When, after a hand-to-hand fight in parliament, the deputies affirmed that Fiume should be Italian, Nitti was not the man to court unpopularity by trying to calm them. Instead he boasted of giving government money to help keep this artificial revolt alive, and when the next prime minister showed how the rebellion would collapse at the first sign of force, Nitti's reaction was to blame him for throwing away such a useful diplomatic counter. Apparently it meant nothing to him or to the king that military indiscipline was unpunished and even rewarded.

★

D'Annunzio's "Regency of Carnaro" lasted for over a year. Although it was a petty and ridiculous affair, its example was an inspiration and a dress rehearsal for fascism, however much Mussolini's jealousy made the early fascists doubtful about it at the time. The *comandante* let few days go by without a speech, usually from a balcony, and with stage effects which later became familiar as the crowd answered his cry, "Whose is Fiume?" "Ours"; "To whom the future?" "To us." The black shirts of the *arditi* were to be seen in Fiume as people shouted the future fascist war cry, "*A noi . . . eja, eja, alalà.*" Here, too, was seen the first sketch of the "corporative state." All this was later copied without acknowledgment by Mussolini. Here at Fiume was the same amalgam Mussolini was to use, an alliance of nationalists, army veterans, dissident socialists, idealists, and adventurers who turned up at the first smell of blood, men who fought duels with hand grenades in D'Annunzio's presence. The Regency proved an irresistible attraction to undesirables, as fascism did later. Schoolboys absconded to join it as they had run away to join Garibaldi, for this was a generation which had learned D'Annunzio's poems at school. To obtain food his army relied in part on piracy, and D'Annunzio's marriage legislation incidentally drew a profitable revenue from those who could not procure a "divorce" in Italy. His effrontery and panache were superb. In a typical gesture he dropped a manifesto on Paris from the air to publicize the "foreign policy" of his state. He proclaimed that he would make Fiume the center of a world revolution. To show his contempt for Italian politicians he once flew over Rome and dropped on the parliament buildings a chamber pot full of carrots.

The end came in the last few days of 1920. The new premier, Giolitti, for six months continued to provide government money and food for Fiume. Also the minister of war, Bonomi, thought it a matter for boasting that he helped finance D'Annunzio on the budget of his ministry, But when an armed clash led to the death of a dozen soldiers. Giolitti was emboldened to order the army into action. D'Annunzio, after theatrically declaring war on Italy, withdrew hurriedly into honored retirement, a wealthy man again, and held up to the next generation of schoolchildren as a national hero. Mindful of his oath for "Fiume or death," he continued to bewail that death had not taken from him the shame of being an Italian, but then concluded that Italy was not worthy of such a loss. As Nitti remarked, this flamboyant adventurer treated Fiume as he treated his mistresses and left it exploited and exhausted. The cause had meant little to him, his own self-indulgence everything.

Meanwhile the good conscience of Italy had temporarily triumphed. D'Annunzio lamented that if only half the Italians had been of the same stamp as the inhabitants of Fiume. Italy could conquer the world. To this the *Corriere della Sera* responded: "Italy has no wish to conquer the world but does need to gain mastery of herself. . . . D'Annunzio should be warned not to provoke civil war and unmake the very nation whose territory he is trying to complete." Albertini, the editor of the *Corriere* and in private life D'Annunzio's good friend, echoed the admonition of Mazzini and Cavour that the capture of Fiume would be barren if it alienated the Slavs, and added that the use of violence would merely provoke violent revenge. But unfortunately this sensible and moderate editor still had to learn the same lesson himself when it came to domestic politics and the violence of the fascist *squadre*.

41 Giolitti and the Suicide of Liberalism, 1920–1921

Nitti's government had been submerged under an accumulation of discontents. The army deplored his amnesty for deserters; capitalists disliked his talk of nationalizing trade in sugar, coffee, coal, and oil; while the nationalists resented his unwillingness to set up a protectorate in Georgia or Armenia. Conservative liberals were alarmed by his proposal to curtail hours of work and his laws for compulsory unemployment insurance, workmen's compensation, and old-age pensions. The fascists and socialists feared his specially created security force of twenty-five thousand "Royal Guards," for this threatened all who had an interest in disorder. Nitti's personal nucleus of radicals was small, and Giolitti disliked him as he disliked all professors on principle. When even the *popolari* turned hostile, Nitti first tried to rule without them from March to June 1920, and then discreetly retired.

His immediate successor was the elderly revenant Giolitti who had first become prime minister thirty years before. Giolitti's diagnosis of the situation was interesting, if inadequate. He complained that parliamentary prestige had fallen because the deputies had surrendered their power to the executive and to government by royal decree. Parliament should recover its legislative action. The king should be deprived of his constitutional right to prorogue the legislature. Article 5 of the constitution should be repealed under which the king in 1915 had secretly reversed the system of alliances and decided upon war without resort to parliament: this last proposal was something that the king never forgave. Giolitti also spoke in favor of more local administrative autonomy, of the workers' right to share in the management of industry, of imposing a capital levy. At this price he hoped to obtain left-wing support for abolishing the bread subsidies and so balancing the budget. But his attempt to please both Right and Left antagonized both sides. Radicals, socialists, and *popolari* backed his government, but there was no longer enough in common to bind a composite Giolittian coalition of the Center. This calm, impassive, industrious *faux bonhomme* was no longer in charge of events.

One thing Giolitti inherited was a rash of violent agrarian strikes. During the war the conservative Salandra had optimistically promised plots of land to the soldiers on their return to civilian life, but no serious action was prepared or perhaps even intended, and in 1919–20 many of the peasants illegally scrambled among themselves for what they could get. In a time of inflation, ownership of land spelled security, and hunger drove people to excesses in their search for it. The state appeared helpless before strikes and civil disobedience. Nitti had to give retrospective sanction to many occupations of the land. Not only were landowners highly indignant at this, but social reformers objected that wealthier peasants obtained more than the destitute and the surrender to violence discriminated against the law-abiding. Above all, it was dangerous to show people that armed illegality would pay.

In industry a similar problem arose over occupation of some factories in September 1920. A breakdown of wage negotiations in the metallurgical industry led to a lockout by factory owners, and this aroused workers to seize some of the large factories in the North. For eight weeks the red flag flew over these buildings in what was wrongly regarded as the first step in a political revolution. Far from planning this operation, the socialists were surprised and baffled, however ready they were to profit from it. They had little idea how to apply their revolutionary theories in practice, and this sudden challenge to their bluff was spontaneous and unexpected. Neither the party nor the Confederation of Labor could agree about what to do.

There is evidence that some industrialists welcomed this incident in order to compel Giolitti to use compulsion against the workers, but the prime minister refused to be drawn in. He believed that forceful repression would only unite the socialist factions and convert industrial into political revolt. He knew that only skilled workers were participating in this occupation and without clerical and managerial staff they would find factories impossible to run. Giolitti therefore chose his moment to suggest a peaceful compromise and the occupation petered out in an anticlimax. Although much magnified by parties interested in exaggerating the danger of socialism, in reality the occupation demonstrated that Italian socialism was inept and relatively harmless. Governmental nonintervention, however, though it exposed the ineffectiveness of these strikes, gave another example of unpunished lawlessness. Insubordination spread to the railroad workers who held up trains used for transporting troops and police. Hence property owners everywhere became afraid for their livelihood, and when the protection of the law seemed to fail they engaged private armies of hooligans. The technique which Giolitti used so successfully with socialist strikers in 1904 did not work when he tried the same passive inaction with these fascist bravos in 1920–21.

Giolitti's public excuse was that he possessed insufficient police to reoccupy the factories. Yet we know that a few thousand resolute men with cudgels and castor oil were shortly to succeed in taming agrarian and industrial disorder, while in many areas the local police were siding openly with the fascists. Giolitti's real reason was not lack of policemen: he deliberately abstained from intervention in the belief that such hectic symptoms would disappear with the revival of tourism and foreign trade and investment. This passive attitude had worked well before 1914 by allowing new social forces to work themselves out or find their own level. But whereas a neutral attitude had formerly aided the working classes, it would now chiefly benefit their employers who had the means and the resolution to act on their own in a contrary sense.

★

Giolitti's affectation of neutrality at the end of 1920 gave free rein to the general economic turbulence of the times, and this played into other hands than his own. Strikes occurred even among government officials and schoolteachers, while labor unrest at Turin resulted in fatal casualties, and an incident in a football game at Viareggio caused splutters of insurrection all over Tuscany. Mussolini himself was to be the chief gainer. Although he later used both this lawlessness and the government inactivity as excuses to justify his own coup, at the time he supported both one and the other, just as at first he had openly encouraged occupation of the factories.

After his defeat in the 1919 election, Mussolini saw no future in trying to out-socialist the socialists. Without a distinct policy, without friends and backing, he was in serious danger of ending up as a confused and egocentric demagogue with a talent for histrionics. But the Fiume episode had now given him a chance to feel the prevailing nationalist mood of Italy. It was time for him to emulate D'Annunzio and "move toward life." Before Italy recovered its prosperity he needed to encourage anarchy and civil strife so that he could pose as the nation's deliverer.

The strikes of 1920–21 were later built into a justification of Mussolini's rise to power, so it is important to stress that labor unrest was found in every other country without such fatal effects. Despite what was said, the strikes had no master plan behind them and were usually unrelated. The railroad workers, who had not taken part in the so-called general strike of 1919, now decided to act but only after the post-office employees returned to work. Individualism and spontaneity was the keynote, and this makes it fairly clear that bolshevism was not the threat in Italy that it was in Germany and Hungary, fascist propaganda notwithstanding. In any case, such dangers as it did present were much less serious by 1921. Giolitti's refusal to intervene had been a principal factor in a return to more normal conditions in 1921, though the fascists could not afford to let him take the credit and soon began to blame him for the remedy as well as for the disease.

It was the bogey of socialism that made newspapers such as the *Corriere della Sera* go to the far more dangerous extreme of conniving at fascist injustice. What they saw was a pattern made up of proletarian lawlessness, of Giolitti's plan to increase income-tax and death duties, of an attack on wartime profits, an eight-hour day in industry, socialist administrations in several thousand towns, and Nitti's proposals for state ownership of fuel and power. Landowners in some areas were at the mercy of the Red Leagues and sometimes of their own employees who were in charge of local government. Labor might be doled out to them at the fiat of union leaders, and squatters were often settling on their land. Moreover, not only the socialists but also the *popolari* were serious about intending to split up the big estates.

Property owners were not alone in forming pressure groups to draw private advantage out of the common pool. Without being less selfish than other people, they were usually more individualistic and less easily organized, and by owning real estate they had survived inflation far better than most. In 1920 they were alarmed and took the offensive. A General Confederation of Industry was formed, and armed bands of retainers were enrolled from the unemployed and demobilized. These bands became the nucleus of the fascist *squadre*, and from this period dates Mussolini's *connubio* with the agrarians of the Po Valley. Under the pretense of saving the country from bolshevism, the fascists were able to attack governmental authority and foster anarchic conditions that would make people long for authoritarian government.

Contemporary plays and novels reflect this proletarian challenge against the hitherto unquestioned supremacy of the old ruling classes in public life. Giolitti found that he could be outbid in electoral appeal by both socialists and *popolari*, and was alarmed when neither would join his coalition. The liberal heirs of Cavour were unable to absorb the new forces in Italian politics, and many of them acted on the false assumption that the fascists would prove more easily digestible than Catholics or socialists. Croce and Mosca had been elaborating theories about the antithesis between liberalism and democracy, and some of Giolitti's liberals were so confused that they allied against democracy with men who were far more serious enemies of the liberal state.

The postwar generation was slow to perceive how profoundly antiliberal fascism was, and people preferred to believe that revolution could come only from the Left. Croce, who was a member of Giolitti's cabinet, explained that fascism was safe because it had no program, as though this were not a fact that should have put him on his guard. Social disorder and parliamentary breakdown sent even moderates looking for a strong leader to deliver them, and Mussolini's well-timed renunciation of republican socialism labeled him in their eyes as a comfortable transformist of the old school. Many liberals, as they analyzed the situation, felt that the primary need was for a stronger state and for this purpose Mussolini would serve, while they themselves would stand apart and retain their reputations uncontaminated against the day when they could replace him. Any alternative remedy might require probing under the surface to discover the more fundamental maladies of the body politic and expose their own social and constitutional position to criticism.

This was a failure of perception and leadership. The experience and intelligence of Croce and Giolitti would have been invaluable if only a profounder analysis had equipped them to do effective battle for liberal principles. Giolitti, now nearly eighty years old, was all for a quiet life—under no circumstances was the prime minister to be disturbed at night. When D'Annunzio collapsed so readily, this fostered the fatal delusion that fascism could be safely invoked to crush socialism, and then brushed away with equal ease to leave the liberals in control. Hence, astoundingly, Giolitti included the fascists on his own list for the elections of May 1921, telling Sforza that this would make them respectable and would enable him to assimilate fascists as he had assimilated other radicals in the past. It was this electoral alliance that guaranteed Mussolini representation in the new House whereas in the elections of 1913 and 1919 he had completely failed. Liberalism to Giolitti was a matter less of principle than of means that could be modified when necessary. Despite all his progressiveness and his contribution to the advance of his country, he had, like Hindenburg later, based his calculations on a formidable error in psychology and so helped to conjure up a monster which he could not subdue.

★

Giolitti achieved one notable success when he withdrew Italian troops from Albania. Sforza, his foreign minister, combining liberal views with astuteness, understood how sentimental considerations had made Sonnino try to annex part of the Dalmatian shore. Ever since 1914 a virtual Italian protectorate had existed in Albania which had cost much money and yielded nothing. In 1920 a hundred Italian soldiers were dying there each day from malaria and the railroadmen again refused to transport reinforcements. In June 1920 mutiny broke out in an Italian regiment about to embark for Albania. This was another sign of the prevailing spirit of insubordination and government paralysis, but at least it persuaded Giolitti to retreat from such an unprofitable venture.

This withdrawal outraged D'Annunzio and the nationalists. They were even more infuriated when in November Giolitti signed with Yugoslavia the Treaty of Rapallo, renouncing Dalmatia and recognizing an independent state of Fiume. The nationalists noisily persisted in regarding Yugoslavia as an artificial creation invented to cheat Italy of her due, and General Caviglia threatened to resign his command if the eastern shore of the Adriatic were not annexed. Giolitti paid no attention to such nationalist bluster, and thought that if anything his new treaty included too many Slovenes inside Italy who might cause trouble in the future. When Salandra criticized him for abandoning Fiume, Sforza answered with a reminder that Salandra had failed to mention Fiume in his war aims of 1915. Sforza was able to boast that at Rapallo he kept the Dalmatian town of Zara for Italy. The agreement also confirmed Italy in possession of Istria, Gorizia, Trieste, and several important islands. Best of all was that this advantageous compromise was settled by negotiation. It is interesting that Mussolini was not yet a supporter of the nationalist party, and his approval of the Treaty of Rapallo was another fact that he later tried to make others forget.

★

A still better omen for Giolitti was the defection of the communists from the socialist party. Ever since the Russian Revolution in 1917, the communists of Turin had tried to capture the party from the maximalists entrenched at Milan. The word had come from Russia that the socialist utopia required a violent revolution to overthrow capitalism. But Turati replied with the heretical statement that conditions in Italy were not the same as in Russia and he still hoped to achieve socialism without passing through the horrors of civil war. He was supported by the trade unionists who decisively turned down a communist motion for a general strike.

Disturbed by such a turn of events, the Third International chose this critical moment to split the largest party in the Italian Chamber, and the socialists were ordered by Moscow to expel the last remnants of reformism along with all who believed in a bourgeois parliament. They were also required to sever relations with the co-operative moment and the Confederation of Labor. This astonishing directive was still more astonishingly endorsed by the party executive, but in January 1921 the party congress decisively repudiated their executive. The defeated left wing then trooped from the hall chanting the *"Internationale"* and seceded to form a new communist party, thereby depriving the main socialist body of its most courageous, single-minded, and unscrupulous leaders. Because of this ill-considered gesture, a hundred thousand socialists gave up their party membership altogether, so remaining one more obstacle in the way of a counterrevolution from the Right.

This communist secession left the nonco-operative and illiberal elements around Lazzari and Nenni still in charge of what remained of the socialist party. The Leghorn congress recorded 58,000 votes to the communists, against 98,000 for the majority decision, while only 14,500 voted for the democratic reformists represented by Turati, Treves, Modigliani, and Matteotti. Yet the maximalist majority possessed little obvious *raison d'être* on their own. Mere logic would have demanded a choice between reformism, with its faith in compromise and co-operation, or else Gramsci's uncompromising call for class-conscious revolt. But the majority preferred to avoid this choice.

Events were moving toward the destruction of Giolitti's political equipoise. The failure of the 1920 harvest was a disaster and two-thirds of wheat requirements had to be bought abroad at a price far above what Italian consumers would pay. Agricultural subsidies aggravated the existing deficit, yet any move to increase taxation was bound to alienate Left or Right and undermine Giolitti's coalition. He had at first been backed by every large group save the official socialists, but he foundered when financial difficulties at last forced him to challenge the tacit connivance in tax immunities for the wealthy.

On Giolitti's estimate, securities of some seventy billion lire in value were escaping income-tax and death duties through being held as unregistered bonds made out to the unnamed bearer. In September 1920 the Chamber agreed to his law making these shares compulsorily registered and taxed. This law was one of elementary fairness, but it threatened the rich and those ecclesiastical bodies which used bearer bonds to evade the law. The Vatican pressed the *popolari* to break from Giolitti and protect the assets of religious corporations. As a result, the Catholics moved into opposition, and their subsequent refusal to join any coalition with Giolitti was to be of the greatest help to fascism in 1921–22. An immediate collapse on the Stock Exchange forced Bonomi in August 1921 to suspend application of the law on bearer bonds, and Mussolini abrogated it altogether. This form of investment was thus allowed to keep its tax immunity, though the national income was wildly out of balance and although the poor had to give up bread subsidies in February 1921. Giolitti thus offended Left as well as Right and the one serious attempt to balance national income with expenditure collapsed.

Uncertain about his majority, Giolitti held elections in May 1921. He had won four elections already and did not guess that a fifth was beyond him. By a gross tactical error he appealed to the electorate by organizing a national bloc including nationalists and fascists and using the fasces as one of his electoral symbols. This was a protest against Nitti's law introducing proportional representation. Wanting fascist help against socialists and Catholics, he even briefly considered offering Mussolini a cabinet post. In his memoirs he lamely justified this alliance with Mussolini as of real benefit to the country, arguing that fascism was now a live political force which ought to be represented in parliament. Mussolini, as a result, won thirty-five seats, for he had the powerful aid of Giolitti's prefects and an official toleration of terrorist action. This gave Mussolini an accolade of respectability. Fascists with clubs were responsible for dozens of deaths on polling day and rendered socialist propaganda impossible over large areas. Giolitti must bear full responsibility for this ugly fact, and there can be little doubt that the police had orders to wink at anything which weakened socialism. Nevertheless these elections were freer than any others for the next twenty-five years, and yet fascism obtained only 35 deputies out of 535.

Dino Grandi described how the fascists looked upon this electoral struggle as only one more episode in their civil war against socialism; and that war was not won yet. Twice in succession, and despite this fascist violence, the rump of the socialist party emerged as the largest group in parliament, and the Right learned the dreadful lesson that socialism could not be eliminated unless they could alter the system of parliament and elections. Grandi, one of the leading fascists, began to criticize Mussolini for not overthrowing parliament and the liberal state. Mussolini himself recognized increasingly that this course of action might at last be possible.

The numerical strength of parties in the new House was variously estimated. There were about 123 socialist deputies, apart from 29 independent reformists and 15 communists who ran on separate slates. The *popolari* actually increased their representation to 107, and there were 68 radicals under their new name of liberal democrats. Since the national bloc won little more than a hundred seats, Giolitti was nowhere near obtaining a majority. What he called the "constitutional parties" captured about half a million votes that had formerly gone to the "subversive parties," but inside his bloc he lost far more to the extreme Right who were shortly to prove far more subversive.

Mussolini, elected at Milan, was determined to exploit and canalize the counterrevolutionary enthusiasm that he had observed behind D'Annunzio. He himself boycotted the opening of parliament, though some disobedient monarchic fascists turned up to sing "*Giovinezza*" on this inauspicious occasion. When Mussolini first addressed the Chamber he explained to an unheeding or uncomprehending audience that his speech would be reactionary because he was against parliament and against democracy. Though elected inside the government bloc, he at once ranged himself with the opposition and Giolitti's coalition was thereby stillborn. Mussolini, despite continuing to call himself a republican, chose to sit on the extreme Right where normally no deputy liked to be seen for fear of being thought an impossible extremist. In fact he seldom appeared in parliament for he preferred the more powerful and less competitive rostrum of his editor's office in Milan.

One by one the various groups were turning against Giolitti. Salandra and the nationalists criticized his "renouncing" policy over Albania and his support of the League of Nations. Another important class was antagonized by his proposals for surtaxes, a capital levy, expropriation of war profits, and a campaign against tax evasion. The *popolari* and the Left could never forgive his electoral compact with the reactionaries. Nitti and Salandra he disliked on personal grounds, not least because of his objection to university professors. So Giolitti had to conclude that the traditional practice of coalition government was unworkable in a parliament produced by proportional representation. In a final effort he asked for full powers to cut down the number of state employees and so put some sense into the national budget. But parliament refused to sign away its prerogatives, at which Giolitti resigned. The full powers which they refused him, this same parliament uncritically gave Mussolini in the following year.

42   Bonomi and Facta, 1921–1922

It is surprising that so many liberals took fascism at its own valuation, not as a positive element of disorder but as the incarnation of legality. When a fascist deputy drew his revolver in parliament, one of Giolitti's ministers was bold enough to protest, but Giolitti pulled that same minister back into his seat and told him not to take sides in the developing civil war. Mussolini came from the Romagna where a tradition of armed banditry went back to time immemorial. Here and in Tuscany the practice of *squadrismo* developed to defend the agrarian leagues against socialist co-operatives, and spread rapidly when its leaders found that they went unpunished and socialist opposition was crumbling. Italo Balbo was typical of ex-*arditi* from the army who smuggled bombs and machine guns back into private life, and he strutted about Ferrara making passers-by take off their hats when the black flag of fascism went by. Every Sunday, fascist shock troops followed Dumini and his fellow murderers in punitive expeditions through the Tuscan villages with a death's head embroidered on their black shirts.

Sometimes these sorties were pointedly political, sometimes just anarchical, sometimes an urban revolt of the *petit bourgeois* against peasant uppishness and price-fixing in the countryside. Alternatively it exemplified the traditional struggle for control of town administration. At Bologna fascism had a minor triumph in November 1920 and caused many casualties, since the socialists had to be punished for winning in the local elections. In January 1921 the social-democrat Matteotti expostulated in the Chamber: "The government and local authorities are assisting unmoved at the overthrow of law and order. Private justice is in operation substituting public justice. . . . So the workers are saying that the democratic state is a joke and has renounced its duty of guaranteeing the same law for everyone." But when Giolitti did nothing to stop illegality, neither did parliament try to make him stop it, for the socialists were trying to sabotage parliament and so were a fair target. In the two years before October 1922 it was computed that three hundred fascists and three thousand of their opponents were killed in riots. There are no completely reliable figures, but political assaults by the end of 1921 were happening at the rate of a dozen a day.

That the fascists went unpunished must be read as evidence of government complicity, for a few hundred gangsters could have been controlled with the greatest ease. In December 1921 there were 240,000 men in the services, plus 65,000 *carabinieri* and 40,000 *guardie regie*, all at the government's disposal in addition to the ordinary police, but they were not used, not even when the fascists gave ample notice of their nefarious intentions. The police and magistracy seemed to be in collusion against law and order, and one clue may be found in a threat by the fascist-party secretary that he might "put his cards on the table and embarrass certain politicians." Often the squads were organized by army officers and obtained arms and trucks from the military authorities. Possibly this assistance was more by negligence than design, yet it was not easy to explain an official circular of advice to local military commanders in September 1920 that fascism should be supported. Bonomi, the war minister, claimed that there had been some mistake, but Bonomi was to fight the next election on the same slate as the fascists and it would not be surprising if some elements in his department used government influence to help their political friends.

Socialist counterviolence was no doubt equally horrible and inexcusable, only it was not so systematic, nor was it deliberate policy. Whoever started the reign of terror, the fascists were better organized, better armed, and had far more money; their raids were more numerous and infinitely more successful. A legend later created around the fascist martyrs done to death in the "massacre of Sarzana" and the "butchery of Modena" was designed to deceive later historians and justify the fascist "counterattack." Whereas the official socialist party, irresolute and defeatist, was advocating nonresistance or passive resistance in order to give the government no further excuse for a mere pretense of neutrality.

There remained to the socialists only their strong parliamentary representation, and this they refused to use. Freedom might have been defended if the Left and Center had stood together as in 1898–99, and the communists were able to taunt their socialist ex-colleagues with the folly of nonresistance. The only alternative would have been to join Giolitti's coalition, but that would have defied a doctrine sanctified by decades of party congresses. At the congress of Milan in October 1921, Modigliani, brother of the painter, again put the case for collaboration in a new social-democratic alliance, but again Lazzari's maximalist counter-proposal carried the day.

Since the liberals refused to govern effectively, and as the socialist party was a slave to dogma, fascism had to cope only with local trade unions and co-operatives. Without leadership and organization, these were helpless, and the Left was expelled forcibly and piecemeal from hundreds of municipal councils and chambers of labor. So successfully did this break the spirit of the opposition, that as the blackshirt lorries were seen approaching, the Red Guards and union officials used to fly into the fields. No doubt many people in and near the government were secretly pleased to see the unions broken. Perhaps they intended that fascism should wear itself out and disband once its purgative mission was complete, but if so they were egregiously optimistic and simple-minded.

★

Giolitti's successor was Bonomi who held office from July 1921 to February 1922. Ivanoe Bonomi was the same who had been expelled from the socialist party for supporting the Libyan war in 1911–12. In character he was honest and good-natured and he had some reputation as a historian, but in politics he was colorless, imperceptive, and irresolute. The other socialists saw him as a renegade, and among his supporters the *popolari* and democratic liberals did not see eye to eye. Bonomi's cabinet was another broad coalition, though tending more to the Left than its predecessor. His finance minister has recorded that, when the *popolari* objected to a plan for the expensive military reoccupation of Libya, Bonomi authorized this expenditure on his own authority and did not tell the cabinet for fear of a split. This was the compulsive logic of coalition government. But Bonomi was oddly naïve and credulous as a politician. He thought he could remain impartial between fascists and socialists, and even made an attempt to reconcile them, hoping to find himself a new government majority in this unpromising quarter.

That a coalition between fascism and socialism was conceivable is witness to Mussolini's opportunism and tactical skill. The man who in May 1921 proclaimed his republican views to the *Giornale d'Italia* was shortly to take from the nationalists their cult of monarchy. At one moment he threatened to join the communists if the police acted against fascism; at another he mobilized his handful of deputies to beat up the communist deputy Misiano inside the parliament building. In his autobiography he warmed at the memory of this latter gesture of strength and recalled how it had brought some reality into the fetid atmosphere of parliament.

These oscillations reflected the split mentality of fascism. Many of its provincial organizations retained an individual character. In Trieste they were anti-Slav, in Sicily they were particularly against land occupation by the peasants, in Apulia they were linked with the *mazzieri* organized by a notorious clique of political bosses. Fascist leaders could be either republican or monarchist, quasi-socialist or conservative, Catholic or Masonic, anarchical or *étatiste*. This was a diversity of practice rather than of rational belief, for apart from the futurists and perhaps the *salon* of Margherita Sarfatti at Milan, there was a notable lack of intellectuals (as distinct from students) in the party, and its directorate was professedly and arrogantly irrational.

Mussolini was shrewd enough to embody in his own thinking many diverse elements and this was one reason why he remained head of the party. Merely tactical considerations led him to stress different ideas in turn. In June 1921 in parliament he declared his support for both Catholics and liberals. He even said that government should confine itself to little more than foreign policy and the police. Italy should abolish the collectivist state which had been a legacy of the war and return to the *laissez-faire* state. In the same month he also changed tack when his colleagues overruled his extreme republicanism. He was trying to become more respectable. He now shaved every day, abated his excessively sordid language, and for a few years sometimes wore a stiff butterfly collar and spats. From being an anti-imperialist he gradually came to advocate a nationalist foreign policy.

Simultaneously with this more seemly trend on the part of the leader, there continued inside fascism a rowdy element represented by the *ras*, local leaders who took their suggestive name from the tribal chieftains of Ethiopia. There was Grandi's variety of fascism at Bologna, Balbo's at Ferrara, and that of Farinacci the labor boss of Cremona. It was a symptom of the changing times when Farinacci, who as a socialist had seen nothing of World War I, began to talk emotionally of national grandeur. The *ras* usually distrusted centralization of power in the hands of Mussolini. They were also against too much respectability because they were men of violence, and *squadrismo* had won them a profitable enclave of local graft in their several regions.

Mussolini could be vulgar and disorderly when he wanted to, none more so, yet he could also be charming and correct; and Bonomi and Giolitti pinned their political faith on this fact. Moreover Nenni, then a journalist on the socialist *Avanti*, records that even Gramsci and Turati believed until early 1921 that fascism would soon lose its more boisterous elements. As prosperity returned and the Left became manifestly impotent, it was thought that the trimmers in fascism were likely to adapt themselves to the more moderate tenor of public opinion. Mussolini was the first of the trimmers, and resenting the independence of Grandi and Balbo with their technique of uncontrolled gang warfare, he suddenly signed a pact of pacification with the socialists in August 1921. "It is ridiculous to talk as though the Italian working class were heading for bolshevism," he argued in this transient and uncharacteristic phase. "I shall defend this pact with all my strength," he asserted, "and if fascism does not follow me in collaboration with the socialists, at least no one can force me to follow fascism."

Socialism and fascism still had something in common and a coalition of these two "anticonstitutional" parties must have seemed to him a possible path to power. But Mussolini was not strong enough to swing his followers. The *ras* rebelled against making a pact with the very people they had lately been hired to massacre, and they would not be deprived of their punitive weekend expeditions into the countryside. More important, their rebellion against the leader was apparently backed by landowners and businessmen who held the purse strings and could call some of the tunes. Mussolini momentarily had to resign from the executive of his fascist movement, and some regional meetings passed resolutions to renounce his leadership altogether.

He was, however, too skilful a tactician not to be able to eat his words, and at the fascist congress in November 1921 he capitulated and buried this stillborn pact with socialism. Subsequently he fabricated the legend that there had been some attempt at fascist schism which he had removed with a wave of his wand, but others described these events as an abortive attempt by Mussolini to break free from the agrarians and industrialists. He failed and skilfully altered course, for it was power and not program that mattered to him. "We are relativists par excellence," was what he told this congress. Unfortunately, the other groups in parliament did not yet see him as a professional adventurer and did not exploit this momentary split in his party. Although fascism was still not strong except in a few provinces and had made little impression on Rome and southern Italy, the poison was spreading day by day, abetted by one liberal government after another.

★

Early in 1922 the socialists decided to vote against Bonomi, presumably in the hope of upsetting the whole parliamentary system for there was hardly any other party combination which they can have preferred. The king was at a loss and asked Bonomi to force a vote that might indicate a possible successor, but parliament failed dismally to give any such indication. All party leaders were summoned to the palace for their advice, but with parliament divided into a dozen diverse groups, each leader feared to compromise his political future by any positive statement that might weaken his negotiating position. So this twenty-sixth legislature in the history of Italy signed the death warrant of liberal government, and after four weeks without a government admitted to power another of those nonentities traditionally reserved for such moments of impasse.

Luigi Facta was designated as another stand-in for Giolitti. He had little experience of heavy responsibility, being a timid, ignorant provincial lawyer whose appointment at first was taken almost as a joke. Facta's stopgap ministry completely failed to persuade the groups in parliament to agree on any policy, and fascist violence meanwhile continued with astonishing impunity. In five months, remonstrated Turati, daily outrages against life and property had taken place without a single one of them being punished. In July the *popolari* therefore joined the socialists in a vote of no confidence.

For several weeks the country again lay helpless without any government while sporadic gang warfare continued all over northern Italy. Orlando, De Nicola, Bonomi, Meda, and Giolitti each declined the poisoned chalice, though any one of them might have called on the patriotism and right-mindedness of deputies and summoned them to unite in self-defense while there was yet time. The Catholic Meda declared that he would join a ministry but not lead one. Nitti, the doctrinaire, was flirting with both D'Annunzio and Mussolini, and said he would not take office again until there was a parliament likely to approve his paper reforms. Salandra preferred to sketch out a plan to link his conservative-liberal remnant with the fascists and nationalists on the extreme Right. Turati the socialist at long last crossed the threshold of the Quirinal to give advice with the other party leaders. Had he shown such flexibility earlier it might have saved Italy.

Mussolini, too, was consulted by the king and apparently recommended another Giolitti administration. He knew that the more chaotic the situation the more call for an autocrat, so was content to bide his time. An article he published in February had ostentatiously advocated a military dictatorship, and he now told parliament that he would initiate a full-scale revolt if any attempt were made to suppress fascism. But not even this was taken seriously by other parties. Giolitti was at Vichy, determined not even to give advice in such a situation. He hoped one day to become premier again, but wanted his hands free to make a coalition with Mussolini and meanwhile waited to be summoned back into power—only to be foiled when the gratuitous folly of the socialists permitted Facta's return to office on August 1.

★

At this moment of all moments a general strike was declared. Apparently this was intended to help the government against the growing unruliness, but it was pathetic to see a negative and pacifist strike used as an answer to active fascist terrorism. In this case the public was merely exasperated and the last vestige of socialist credibility was nonsensically thrown away. No one even knew whose decision the strike had been, and the editor of *Avanti* was on the point of denouncing it as a plot by the reformists. In fact it originated from an irresponsible secret committee of action set up by a group of unions, so secret indeed that its existence was not generally known.

Mussolini had hitherto been uncertain in his movements, witness his negotiations with both Left and Right. But with an intuitive understanding of a revolutionary situation he realized that the socialists had played into his hands, and he announced that the fascists would break the strike if the government did not immediately intervene to stop it. This would enable his gangs to pose as defenders of law and order. On August 2 at Ancona his squads moved in from the countryside and razed all buildings occupied by the socialists. The same thing happened at Leghorn and Genoa. This was a planned movement, and the choice of these arterial cities was well made.

The biggest prize of all was Milan, the brain center of Italian socialism. Here on August 3 and 4 there was street fighting during which the fascists destroyed the printing presses of *Avanti* and burned its buildings. To the satisfaction of the *Corriere* and many Milan industrialists, Farinacci then ejected the socialist civic administration, and from the balcony of the town hall D'Annunzio spoke to exhort the multitude. The commercial classes of Milan detested any transportation strike and were duly appreciative when the fascists took over trains and operated a reduced service for the public. Their gratitude undoubtedly took a tangible monetary form. They were alarmed at rumors that Italy was on the edge of economic collapse, whereas in fact the year 1922 was witnessing a decline in the number of strikes, an improved balance of trade, and an important revival of tourism. It was these economic improvements which no doubt made Mussolini in a hurry to act lest they should destroy the justification for his revolution.

Once again, government passivity in face of this criminal rowdyism is what requires explanation. Irresolution, cowardice, criminal conspiracy have all been advanced as explanations and all of them plausibly. The very ease of Mussolini's success against this strike, coupled with the fact of public approval of his action, is a condemnation of Giolitti and the others who feared the unpopularity of trying to enforce the law. The strike put the fascists on the same side as the police and public opinion. It also showed that Italy was leaderless. Facta promised Turati that no action would be taken against the strikers if they returned to work at once; but Mussolini vetoed this pardon and Facta had to wriggle out of his promise—possibly it had been designed only to split Turati still further from his fellow socialists.

SECTION TEN: MUSSOLINI'S REVOLUTION, 1922–1925

Map 1. Italy

43   Italy on the Eve, Summer 1922

Facta presented his new cabinet to parliament early in August. An American visitor noticed revolvers brandished in the Chamber, for the sirocco was blowing from Africa and the tremendous heat made politics particularly tense. Facta was now confirmed in office by 247 votes to 122 though two weeks earlier these same deputies had rejected him by 288 to 103.

Even among his cabinet there were some who later regretted their folly in accepting his leadership a second time. It was not an administration to inspire confidence and ministers had been selected to satisfy the eight groups whose support was necessary to avoid defeat. Taddei had the reputation of a strong man, and he, together with the liberals Amendola and Alessio, was the main hope of the constitutionalists. On the other hand, Riccio at the department of public works seems to have vetoed any action against fascism and kept Grandi informed about cabinet discussions. There were thus several irreconcilable factions inside the same cabinet, yet no one dared expose this fatal flaw by resignation. The absence of collective cabinet responsibility was once again to prove expensive. Alessio said that he would not resign unless Riccio did. This was bad doctrine and bad tactics.

Much depended on Taddei at the vital ministry of the interior. This man recounted how one of his first actions was to advise the prefects on August 4 to use arms against disorder if necessary, but the prefect of Milan, Lusignoli, sent a defeatist rejoinder in acknowledgment. Senator Lusignoli had been a follower of Giolitti, but, as the government representative at Milan, was now veering toward the city's fascist captors by whose sufferance he maintained his prefecture. He was in fact playing a triple game between Facta, Giolitti, and Mussolini, ready to back whoever emerged victorious.

Lusignoli on August 6 sent a telegram to Facta after long talks with the fascist leaders. He described how Milan had become the center of a widespread revolutionary movement and how the fascists intended to invite the king to constitute a directorate with dictatorial powers. Here was another example of the state authorities treating with the fascists as with an independent sovereign power. Taddei himself met another fascist leader to plead for a reduction in bloodshed and apparently regarded such a petition as nothing very extraordinary. He noted that Bianchi, the secretary of the fascist party, was a real fanatic and therefore not so amenable to negotiation as was Mussolini. To this nadir had liberal Italy descended on the eve of its eclipse.

*

It is important to note the king's attitude, for this was one of those moments when his actions were decisive. If he and his government had acted in concert against fascism, all might yet have been retrieved, for he retained the loyalty of the army and the Senate, as the cabinet did that of the police. But Vittorio Emanuele had not kept in touch with the opposition groups which one day he might have to invite into office—for many years he never met Sonnino or Giolitti when they were out of office. So much had his political conscience been attenuated in two decades of transformist practice that he could not understand why Turati and Mussolini should not solve the crisis by joining the same cabinet. The minister of the royal house, Pasqualini, seems to have been an opponent of fascism, but Margherita the queen mother was an overt fascist enthusiast, and both of them were alarmed when republican socialists became the largest party in parliament. The king was also afraid that, if he opposed the fascists, they might depose him and give the crown to the far more spectacular and personally attractive branch of the family led by his cousin the Duke of Aosta.

The king's misjudgment eventually precipitated the revolution, and for the impropriety of his final act he must bear full responsibility because he was acting against ministerial advice. There nevertheless is some truth in his defense that, when he invited Mussolini into power, this appealed to a growing number of people in every class of society. Everyone must have known of the barbarities which from the second half of 1920 had devastated Emilia, Tuscany, and the Po Valley, yet many moderate citizens had psychological and economic reasons for welcoming a movement of revolt and reaction against anarchic socialism. Students and ex-soldiers discovered in *squadrismo* the same outlet that their grandfathers had found with Garibaldi. Fascism for them meant a uniform and a job in the party hierarchy or the squads. Many white-collar unemployed joined the nationalists, the futurists, the violence-loving syndicalists, and other malcontents with a grudge to settle. Many peasants and small farmers had an animus against the liberals who in sixty years had done so little for their welfare. Landowners wanted strikes broken and their laborers kept in order. Shopkeepers disliked competition from socialist co-operatives.

Along with blatant plebeians such as Starace and Farinacci, fascism had a large following among men of property, for example the enormously rich banker Count Volpi. Industrialists wanted a strong government to force through a new strike law, to keep wages low and raise tariffs for protection against the postwar slump, while others had private information that the government monopolies in railroads, telephones, and insurance would be released by fascism to private enterprise. Mussolini's first speech in parliament in June 1921 informed these people that "the history of capitalism is only just beginning"—this from the man whose newspaper had only recently dropped its front-page sub-title of "a socialist daily," the same man who would become the archpriest of state collectivism once he had found enough innocents to put him in power.

Support also came from poorer people whose fixed incomes were depreciating in economic inflation. There were also patriots who had been humiliated by socialist opposition to the war and liberal "renunciation" of the peace. Many

Catholics looked upon Mussolini as a defense against red atheism: when he courted Vatican support, ecclesiastical influence was employed to divide the *popolari* and win some of their leaders to alliance with fascism. Other groups were moved by irritation at an incompetent and corrupt parliament where politicians jockeyed for place and connived at illegalities. To such people fascism offered some hope of an efficient administration which would act more and talk less and make the trains run on time.

★

The co-existence of these various motives indicated the weaknesses of liberalism. Many liberals evidently put riches and comfort before liberty, and the philosopher Gentile accused his liberal friends of conniving at fascist cruelty wherever it served their purpose. Not only the conservative *Giornale d'Italia*, but the big liberal and radical dailies, the *Corriere della Sera*, the *Secolo*, La Stampa, and *Il Messaggero*, all on occasion showed distinct sympathy for the squads against the Reds. When *La Stampa* began to suggest that, since socialism was now palpably beaten, the liberals in self-defense might veer back again toward the social democrats, the *Corriere* refused to follow.

Albertini, the editor of the *Corriere*, boasted that he was an intransigent liberal, but in fact his paper did not seriously oppose fascism in these early, decisive years. After (or even because of) more dreadful acts of fascist prepotency, he even advised in August 1922 that the handful of fascist deputies be asked to form a government, for he thought this the best way to avoid a *coup d'état*. Like the London *Times* on which it was modeled, Albertini's paper was a powerful influence with the governing classes. It had taken a not unworthy share in liberalizing the conscience of its three-quarters of a million readers, and Albertini, like Croce and many of his other contributors, later regretted that he had supported Mussolini at a time when his anathema would have carried enormous weight. But psychologically this type of liberal was unprepared for the possibility of revolution from the Right.

The fascist gangs must have cost a good deal, and so must their paper, *Il Popolo d'Italia*. Some contributions came from Ansaldo and the shipowners of Genoa; others from Milan, the town of bustle and reinforced concrete, where many big concerns were pledged to the fight against strikes, bolshevism, and nationalization. The saying went that both fascism and socialism obtained their money and brains from Milan, their thugs from Tuscany, and their orators and agitators from the Romagna. Fascism had already been supported by the agrarians, who were now doubly alarmed since a new law of June 1922 threatened to break up large estates. Now finance and industry began to see that their own vital interests were involved. Although national prosperity was returning, Terni and Fiat only just managed to weather the postwar economic crisis. The big industrial cartels of Ilva and Ansaldo were forced into liquidation in 1921, and this caused a succession of bank failures. The General Confederation of Industry kept in close contact with Mussolini, since a party that promised to underwrite Italian prestige had obvious attractions for the war industries with their excess capacity. Mussolini himself, who had gone to prison as a pacifist in 1911, now trimmed his sails to the nationalist breeze. In the middle of August he is said to have borrowed heavily from the Roman banks which were closely involved in financing heavy industry. By backing fascism to win, bankers purchased a useful financial interest in its success. The industrialist Pirelli later recollected how a committee of the *Confindustria* met Mussolini at the office of the *Popolo d'Italia* two days before the fascist "march on Rome."

The socialists were now a parody of their former selves detesting liberalism very much more than they feared Mussolini. The official party no longer had any resources to protect itself against fascism. Yet Serrati reasoned that to join a bourgeois government would be the end of the party: socialism might be overpowered by violence and still recover, but there would be no recovery if they surrendered their revolutionary principles. Their one serious weapon was the general strike, yet this had now failed dismally. Unable to face their enemies they turned petulantly on their friends, and in October by a bare majority expelled Turati, who thereupon formed a separate Labor Party with Treves, Modigliani, and Matteotti. Turati had at long last accepted the wisdom of collaboration with the Catholics and Giolitti, so that his expulsion was therefore correct in dogma even if pointless in practice. The residuum of the official socialists were tempted to follow Bombacci who later supported fascism but who, by October 1922, had deserted to join the communists. Many socialist as well as communist leaders were away in Moscow where they could have no influence over a rapidly developing crisis.

This fatal month found the extreme Left completely ineffective and unimportant, divided into squabbling factions around Bonomi, Turati, Bombacci, Labriola, Bordiga, and Gramsci; and Ferri was already trying to persuade some socialists to support fascism.

★

Meanwhile, the fascists acquired a plan of campaign. Ferrara, Cremona, Parma, Ravenna, Leghorn, all had their town councils forcibly taken over for they were strategic points in the coming insurrection. When a fascist was killed at Fiume, his fellows even seized a destroyer and captured the city from the antinationalist party which had won the civic elections of April 1921. Bologna was besieged and its prefect forced to flee the city under cover of night. Yet, almost unbelievably, the government took no action and ministers did not resign. The fascists were given a free rehearsal in mobilizing their legions after being presented with proof of the paltry temper of Facta's cabinet.

On a much larger scale, an invasion was planned of the Alto Adige where Senators Credaro and Salata, the acting high commissioners, had been sensibly trying to win the affection and loyalty of the recently annexed German-speaking population. Farinacci and De Stefani simply took over the government of this region in protest against such a feeble and un-Italian policy. The occasion and the particular area were admirably chosen to secure nationalist approval for fascist depredation. The moral position of both government and governed was further weakened as they first connived at lawlessness in little, then suddenly found themselves to be accomplices in large.

Mussolini later recalled how every day brought him the growing conviction that he alone was in charge of events. Success was due in part to luck, in part to the fact that neither Giolitti, Bonomi, nor Facta had the sense and fortitude to say that this daily slaughter was illegal; but in part it was also due to Mussolini's own personality. His success in popular journalism led him to think that he could solve problems which baffled everyone else, and this superficial self-confidence was reinforced by an opportunism that was ready to accept any kind of alliance. His hand was sometimes forced—for example by the ex-syndicalist Bianchi, who as party secretary was the real drive behind the "march on Rome" when Mussolini was too timid and uncertain to force the pace. It was, however, Mussolini's deliberate inactivity which cleverly or from fear left open to the very last moment the choice between collaboration and insurrection, a strategy that kept everyone guessing and allowed him to pose as a potential ally of all and sundry.

One by one he neutralized other politicians by threat or bribe, and left them hoping to join a coalition with him. Mussolini was in touch with Facta and Giolitti through the prefect of Milan; with Salandra and the Right through Federzoni and the nationalists; with the radical Nitti through General Capello; and also in contact with D'Annunzio, with the Court and the queen mother; with the Duke of Aosta through General De Bono; with both the Church and the two branches of Italian Freemasonry. This was a grand new transformist attempt to darken the waters of politics. He was even ready to make another move toward the socialists until this was vetoed by Federzoni, and he played up to the conservatives by at last accepting the monarchy in a speech of September 20. In typical fascist verbiage he justified this latter *volte-face*, saying that the reason why he had hitherto been republican was that the monarchy had not been sufficiently monarchical.

Many fascists must have genuinely believed that they and they alone could save the country. But most of their leaders were adventurers of the worst sort, either ignorant bullies or mercenaries in search of booty. D'Annunzio, the archadventurer, had no hand in the final blow, but only because he had been incapacitated in August by a mysterious fall from a window after an assignation with a lady. He had nevertheless declaimed to a congress of his Fiume legionaries that the parliamentary system was a mephitic sewer which had to be destroyed; and this was the man whom Nitti, in a presumably aberrant moment, hoped would join a coalition with himself and Mussolini. Jealousy, if nothing else, made such a coalition most unlikely. Although only a febrile imagination like D'Annunzio's could have conceived the choreographic *mise en scène* of a march on Rome (as Mussolini later admitted), the poet could hardly have led such a march himself; he had no tactical sense and was worried that he might not know what to do on arrival. The fascists wanted power but otherwise neither knew nor cared about what they would do, a fact that was now their strength, as later it was to be their ruin and the ruin of Italy.

By early October, Mussolini and his handful of deputies were virtually masters of the situation even though the other parties were slow to recognize as much. The government writ scarcely ran, though pockets of state authority still survived around the police and the prefects. Taddei emptily threatened that he would resign unless the cabinet approved stronger measures; but when they still could not agree he withdrew his resignation, arguing with unconscious irony that for him to leave now might have provoked a crisis.

If Taddei's behavior was futile, his colleagues' refusal to act as he advised was criminal negligence. That a strong policy to punish illegalism might possibly have failed is no excuse for not having tried it; and moreover, from what we know today, it is extremely unlikely that repression could have failed. Fascism was still a small minority, and the state authorities had not even been allowed to go into action against them. What the government lacked was not the strength but the will. Facta's secretary noted that several ministers were expecting the cabinet to fall and were determined to see that they themselves fell on their feet. In the expectation of a new government, everyone intended to play their cards so as to have a good chance of inclusion, and offending Mussolini was something they would try to avoid.

44   The March on Rome, October 26–30, 1922

The machinery of government was fast running down when Facta, who had hitherto implored other ministers not to precipitate a crisis by resigning, on October 26 himself proposed a collective resignation. Alessio and Taddei were horrified, for at this very moment a fascist congress at Naples was proclaiming revolution. Resignation before now might possibly have worked against fascism, but at this particular moment could not have been better timed to suit Mussolini by its implication of surrender. All Italy knew what was being said at Naples. One fascist delegate at the congress delightedly observed that government had ceased to exist except a few prefects who would follow the prevailing current. Another declared that the fascists, though a minority, had the right to govern because they had saved the country from bolshevism. And yet, according to Soleri who was minister of war, Facta on October 26 decided to shuffle his cabinet and bring in the fascists, and to this a majority of ministers presumably agreed.

Late on the twenty-sixth, the prefect of Pisa reported the beginning of fascist mobilization and added that telephone lines were cut and men leaving in small groups for Rome. Their strategic headquarters was at Perugia, where Bianchi, De Vecchi, Balbo, and General De Bono were a quadrumvirate directing operations. Mussolini was a notable absentee. Had he been sure of success he might have fought where the glory was greatest, but until all was over stayed close to the Swiss border. Balbo used to say in private that the other leaders forced Mussolini to act and only by the threat that otherwise they would proceed without him. For the moment, however, Mussolini kept his options open and relied on bluff, because bluff was needed to conceal that the fascist militia was often without arms or food and had orders not to fire on the troops even if they themselves were fired on. Mussolini's chief fear was that the army might shoot, and this was one reason why he was eager to enroll retired generals in uniform.

Facta nevertheless insisted upon resignation and was delayed only by the extraordinary fact that at this turbulent moment the king was still away on vacation near Pisa. While awaiting his return, Facta and Taddei consulted the military authorities, and General Pugliese guaranteed that, if given precise written orders, absolute trust could be placed on the troops to suppress fascism. Facta, it must be assumed, was still hoping for a coalition with Mussolini, and simply assured Pugliese verbally that such orders would be issued when needed. This was a confession of weakness, and the army leaders must have taken it as a caution against overzealousness.

At about 8 P.M. on October 27, Facta met the king on his arrival at the Rome station. Then again an hour later after Lusignoli at Milan had telephoned to say that no mere cabinet reshuffle would be acceptable to Mussolini, Facta took to the king's private residence the resignation of his ministry. During the evening, prefects reported trains and telegraph offices illegally requisitioned, so it was agreed that, until a new cabinet was in office, ministers should remain responsible for law and order to the best of their ability. Facta told Senator Bergamini that the king consented to this and had authorized a declaration of martial law if necessary. So, astonishingly, the prime minister went to bed. There was no general alarm so far, and the telephone service at the ministry of the interior was not operated through the night.

★

We still do not know with certainty the motives of the chief actors in this tragedy. It is generally assumed that Facta had been secretly working for the return of Giolitti, but he was also in touch with the fascists. Giolitti himself, the man who had the best hope of saving the country, was celebrating his eightieth birthday hundreds of miles away and never came near the scene of action. He later regretted that he had not returned to Rome, and give it as his belief that

Facta had been won over to the fascists by the hope of some place in a new coalition. A telegram was sent on the twenty-seventh telling Giolitti that the king wanted to see him. But this venerable statesman would not leave home without an express command to form his own ministry. Mussolini had been in touch with Giolitti to keep the old man quiet, but now told the fascists at Naples that he did not mean to come into power "by the servants' door." He well knew that Giolitti had ordered the army to fire on D'Annunzio at Fiume and might act against fascism if ever the Giolittians were back in government.

Of other party leaders, Salandra was the most likely candidate for the premiership. He led a conservative group in parliament some thirty strong who sat next to thirty-five fascists and ten nationalists on the extreme Right. His bitter rivalry with Giolitti was now fatal for Italy. Hoping to form his own ministry with Mussolini's collaboration, he worked to overthrow Facta. He was supported in this by Senator Albertini of the *Corriere*, by Senator Bergamini of the *Giornale d'Italia*, and also it seems by Senator Frassati who owned *La Stampa* of Turin. He was also backed by his friend Federzoni of the nationalist party. Mussolini had visited Salandra's house on October 23 when passing through Rome to Naples, and the fascists Grandi and De Vecchi came to see this former prime minister more than once on the twenty-seventh.

The loyalty of the army leaders to the king, as well as the nonintervention of the army in politics, had been features of Italian history. But the generals were far from being irremovably wedded to a parliamentary regime, and a succession of ten war ministers in five years was hardly calculated to appease them. Demobilization had created a dangerous class of needy men accustomed to battle and military discipline. Generals De Bono, Fara, Ceccherini, and Gandolfo helped to organize and lead the "march on Rome," and numerous other generals, for instance the more important Giardino, were marginal sympathizers. Salvemini adds that Diaz, the wartime commander, addressed the fascists of Florence on October 27. At a critical moment in the night of October 27–28, the king is said to have consulted General Diaz and General Pecori Giraldi as to the loyalty of the troops in the event of civil war, and Diaz is supposed to have answered that the army would do its duty, but had better not be put to the test.

There is, however, no evidence to suggest that the army would have disobeyed the king, and twenty years later Vittorio Emanuele said that this particular story about Diaz was fictitious. At Fiume the military had fired on other Italians when ordered to do so and D'Annunzio's rebellion had thereby been dissolved in an instant. In October 1922, General Badoglio, who had succeeded Diaz as chief of staff, said that at the first shot the whole edifice of fascism would crumble. Badoglio asked to be given full powers and a determined government would have granted his request at once. His opinion was confirmed by General Pugliese, the military commandant of Rome, who told Facta at the time and subsequently repeated that he could have put down any attempt at revolt. Road blocks and *chevaux de frise* were ready on the roads, and even some of the blue-shirted nationalists had asked to help defend the capital against the blackshirts. The deficiency was in political sense and in morale, not in the force available for repression.

About midnight on October 27–28, Taddei telephoned Pugliese ordering him to assume military powers over Rome, for the ministry had decided this unanimously after the king agreed. But Pugliese, fearing to be disowned like other Italian generals in the past, insisted on written instructions, and no such instructions were sent. Bianchi then telephoned from Perugia, pretending to be the prefect, and informed the government that bloodshed could be avoided only by surrender. This at last caused Facta to suspect that Mussolini had deceived him, and he was heard to remark that revolt must be resisted. A cabinet meeting was urgently summoned for 6 A.M.—one minister was untraceable in a hotel on some *affaire de cœur*—at which everyone, even Riccio, agreed that violent revolution must be repressed. Written orders were finally sent for the army to stop the fascists by every means at their disposal. The form of decree used for martial law at Milan in 1898 was hurriedly consulted—it is interesting that this had been neglected until so late—and soon was in the newspapers and on the walls of Rome. At once, says Pugliese, the fascist bands began to dissolve. The order even went out for the arrest of the fascist *quadrumvirs*, but the telegraph office at Perugia had been captured and the order was received by De Bono himself.

★

Then came the shock: for when, soon after 9 A.M., Facta went to obtain the promised royal ratification, the king refused to sign. Vittorio Emanuele knew that the rebels were moving on Rome. His ministers were unanimous and his military advisers told him that order could be restored if he signed. His refusal was not only a grave infraction of constitutional procedure, it clinched the success of the revolt. Some people have argued that Facta may have dissuaded the monarch from signing and certainly he cannot have pressed very hard for the fulfillment of this constitutional duty, but the prime minister would hardly have published the decree overnight had the king not approved it the previous evening. There is even some evidence that the latter had at one point threatened to abdicate if martial law were not proclaimed.

There is little doubt that the king changed his mind during the night. His glamorous cousin the Duke of Aosta, perhaps secretly aspiring to the throne, had conspicuously stationed himself near Perugia and was said to have recently reviewed fascist militiamen. The king therefore had to go warily. Very early that morning, on his own responsibility, he had been talking to the wrong people. He had not consulted Badoglio who wanted to arrest the ringleaders, but he had spoken with at least one fascist, and with Federzoni who left his presence to put a call through to Mussolini at Milan. Judging from Federzoni's tone of conversation immediately afterward, the nationalist leader probably mentioned to Mussolini over the telephone that the king was afraid of civil war and hoped to prevent it by allowing a peaceful fascist arrival in Rome.

This was apparently the first time in twenty-two years that the king had acted against his ministers' advice. The fact that some reputable parliamentarians defended his action is perhaps a commentary on the dubieties of the Italian constitution. But most people have agreed that the ministers were still in office and the king should have accepted their advice until a new cabinet had been sworn in. It was not a valid excuse to say that proclaiming an emergency by decree would have been unconstitutional, for this had been done often in the past. A better, not publishable, excuse was that in 1898 the villains had been the Left, whereas in 1922 they were the Right, and by definition the Right represented law and order, property and the establishment, Church and state.

The King of Italy had learned a dangerous lesson in 1915, namely that he was entitled in emergencies to short-circuit parliament and appeal directly to the man in the street. He saw that fascism claimed the allegiance of many leading liberal newspapers and deputies of Center and Right. Local elections in October were undeniably turning in favor of fascism—aided by the powerful electoral argument of castor oil and the cudgel or *manganello*. Croce, the liberal high priest, advocated Mussolini's assumption of power as better than the existing anarchy and believed that fascism might be gently directed into good constitutional usage. There was nothing new in the king calling into power a minority group without the prior authorization of a parliamentary vote. On the other hand, a more sensible sovereign might have seen that the use of bludgeons and hand grenades indicated that fascism was still a minority opinion, and he must have realized that refusal to act against self-confessed murderers would bring his judgment into question.

The king on October 28–29 still did not perceive that the stable door was open, and asked Salandra to form a ministry. Salandra, too, hoped for a coalition with fascism and supported the king in refusing to sign the martial law decree. But he was being duped like everyone else. Mussolini used Federzoni and the pivotal prefect of Milan to notify Rome that, if he were not called upon to form a fascist government, things would become ugly. Once the king's revocation of the martial-law decree indicated that the government was powerless, noncooperation became general since no prefect who hoped for promotion would oppose fascism until he could see which way the cat would jump.

This was the worst consequence of the king's refusal. Local authorities were convinced thereby that the government would do nothing to stop fascism, and adjusted their loyalties accordingly. In the second place Mussolini now knew that the king, having once yielded to a threat, would be obliged to do so again for he had been made an accomplice in illegality and his only alternative would be abdication. Mussolini was always uncertain in later years whether to implicate the throne by publicly insisting on its collusion at this moment or to ascribe the success entirely to his own courage and intuition: with typical inconsistency he usually tried to have it both ways.

★

The most effective means of undermining public confidence during this fatal weekend was through the newspapers. The *Corriere* was therefore ordered by the fascists to drop all mention of a coalition under Salandra; and on proving obstinate it received a direct threat. For one vital day the paper ceased publication and the next morning it surrendered. Albertini feared for his wonderful new typesetting machinery, and in face of Mussolini's veto thought it more dignified to write nothing at all than to voice his objections to this ungentlemanly behavior. Events were showing how right Mussolini had been to concentrate his intimidation and bribery on Milan, the "moral capital" of the kingdom. One of his discoveries was that intimidation was more than half the battle, and he studiously cultivated an outward mien of inflexible determination in order to conceal the indecisiveness which some of his best friends knew lay underneath. Albertini was frightened enough to ask the prefect and the army for protection, but the answer came that this was impossible and he would have to let his newspaper's offices be occupied by the blackshirts.

A different technique was used with *La Nazione* of Florence. There was an urgent need to control Florence which held the largest garrison on the highroad to Rome. So the journalist Malaparte led a deputation to "encourage" the editor of this newspaper to print the premature story that the king had invited Mussolini to form a cabinet, and two hours after this interview, fascist trucks were distributing the news in a special edition all over Tuscany. The tale was believed, perhaps because many people wanted to believe it, and by thus implicating the king, the army was neutralized. The military commander at Florence, Prince Gonzaga, thought that he could quiet his conscience by a personal visit to fascist headquarters in order to hear the rumor confirmed.

Meanwhile Salandra, when charged to form a government, pleaded with Mussolini to come to Rome for consultations. De Vecchi and Grandi came instead and spent the evening of October 28 discussing a possible coalition of the Right. By midday on the twenty-ninth they were able to advise Mussolini not to hold out any longer. Mussolini, however, thought otherwise and once again his instinct was right. In the security of Milan he did not appreciate that the few fascist squads encamped around Rome were sitting in the rain, hungry and on the point of going back home to work on Monday morning. Mussolini required complete assurance of victory before he moved. He also wanted to show that he was responsible to no one for office and could therefore be absolute in his exercise of power. A well-staged coup would better satisfy the hooligan element than simply joining someone else's coalition, and it would be good theater as well as a good self-indulgence.

Whether from timidity or calculation, Mussolini would not budge from the safety of Milan unless invited to form a cabinet himself, and without him a coalition of the Right proved to be impossible. So Salandra, disgruntled at finding himself a pawn in someone else's game, renounced his attempt. At the king's request, De Vecchi telephoned from the palace and invited Mussolini to Rome, but Mussolini still insisted on a positive invitation to form a ministry, and even the offer of a special train did not move him. A discreet hint was dropped by the fascists to the *Giornale d'Italia*, and that evening all Italy knew through a special edition of the virtual ultimatum they had sent to the king. This was clever journalism and helped build up the illusion that Mussolini was a necessary man.

The required telegram was finally sent, and during the night of October 29–30 Mussolini crossed the Rubicon in a sleeping car, arriving the next morning at Rome station. Meanwhile, a group of about twenty-five thousand fascists—the king claimed that there were a hundred thousand—was mobilized into "columns" within forty miles of Rome, many of them unarmed and quite out of touch with headquarters at Perugia. The troops at Rome could easily have put them to flight. But the Duce arrived at Rome before his men, and, surrounded by a few blackshirts dirty with mud and rain, singing and brandishing their sticks, made his way to the palace. The "march on Rome" was a comfortable train ride in response to an express invitation from the monarch.

Subsequently Mussolini managed to twist appearances to indicate a violent conquest of power. When the squads refused his order to disband, he persuaded the king to allow his desperadoes to come in ten special trains from their encampments, ostensibly to make a demonstration before the palace in homage before being packed off home; but photographers were in place on October 31 to give this some semblance of a dictator's private army overpowering the constituted authorities of the state. There were priests among the crowd, and the Duke of Aosta later told Mussolini's wife that he too was with them. Many senior officers were observed among the fascists, including the war hero General Capello who wore a half-army, half-fascist uniform. Peopled noted that there was something South American about the whole business, and the *caudillo* Garibaldi with his red shirt and poncho would surely have seen the humor of it.

45   Dictatorship Emerges, 1922–1924

At the age of thirty-nine, Mussolini was the youngest prime minister in Italian history. In November 1922 he still had only his three dozen fascist deputies in the House, less than 7 per cent of the whole, and he wisely chose to proceed slowly and gently in the best traditions of transformism. While keeping in his own hands the foreign office and ministry of the interior, he included ten nonfascists and only four fascists in his cabinet. Three of these ten called themselves liberals, two were *popolari* (Gronchi, who in 1955 became president of a democratic Italian republic, was an undersecretary), and two social democrats. The king said that Mussolini's first suggested list included the name of Einaudi, another future republican president, and that the royal permission was also asked for including a socialist. The armed forces were rewarded by choosing the popular Admiral Thaon di Revel and General Diaz for the service ministries. Diaz had hoped, unsuccessfully, to obtain from Nitti some public recognition to signalize his war services, and was now delighted to find himself more appreciated.

When parliament met in November, Salandra noted that the benches on the extreme Right were unexpectedly becoming almost crowded, as deputies of the Center experienced a timely conversion. Mussolini's first speech in parliament, along with equally timely invocations of God's help, threatened in Cromwellian tones to "make an armed camp of this House" if he met resistance. He boasted that his government had been formed without reference to parliament and was therefore not accountable to it. His numbed audience, far from challenging such a statement, took it without protest. Giolitti, bizzarely, approved of this speech and said that parliament at last had got the government it deserved: as the deputies had not known how to find a workable administration, the country had found one for itself. Even De Gasperi and the *popolari*, even dedicated democrats such as Salvemini, preferred Mussolini to Giolitti whom they had become accustomed to regard as the arch-corrupter of political life.

No doubt many of these deputies were only too relieved to find that someone at last knew his own mind and was prepared to act. One moderate socialist, Matteotti, was among those who protested, and Modigliani was bold enough to cry "long live parliament." But the communists led a shout of "down with parliament" in reply, and their prayer was to be answered sooner than they perhaps wished. The Marxists had been misled by their dogma into misreading the situation: their diagnosis that fascism was the last counterattack of the conservative classes was less than a half-truth.

In the Senate the liberals were quite disoriented when Mussolini asked rhetorically: "Who could have stopped me from making myself a dictator? Who could have resisted a movement that represented not just 300,000 party ticket holders but 300,000 rifles?" The liberal senator Albertini gave a favorable vote and tried hard to convince himself that there had been a normal constitutional accession to power, "since the spirit of the country is evidently in favor of fascism and its leader." He wistfully cautioned Mussolini not to abuse his victory and to disband his armed squads. "Mussolini has given to the government freshness, youth and vigor, and has won favor at home and abroad.... He has saved Italy from the socialist danger which had been poisoning our life for twenty years." Coming from a true liberal of the old school, these words are a sad commentary on how the great party of Cavour had sunk to supping short-spooned with this populist demagogue.

The Senate voted confidence in Mussolini by a larger majority than any liberal ministry had received in a long time, and the fact has an undeniable significance. In the Lower House, Giolitti, Salandra, Bonomi, De Nicola, as well as the *popolari*, joined other liberals in the government majority, and by no means all the 160 socialist deputies seem to have voted negatively. Pareto had written to reassure Mussolini that, parliament being divided into so many groups, fascism would find an easy majority, and he was right. Both Houses accorded Mussolini what they had refused Giolitti, the exercise of extraordinary powers for twelve months, despite (or because of) his threat to use force if they refused. The parliamentary committee that approved this concession included Bonomi, Salandra, and a number of other liberal ex-ministers.

The elected representatives of the people were by now inured to government by decree and had become fully convinced of their own incapacity to rule. By condoning the monarch's refusal to promulgate a state of emergency the deputies took on themselves a responsibility for future events. Albertini rightly ascribed the fascist victory to a love of *quieto vivere* by the liberal parliamentarians. What adds up to the most serious criticism of liberal Italy is that he and they opposed fascism only later when serious opposition had become impossible. Even Nitti in April 1923, one of the few who refused to support Mussolini, cravenly refused to criticize him and argued that the fascist experiment should be allowed to continue undisturbed.

For the next two years some people were able to hope that parliament and the king were still free to believe in Mussolini as a new Giolitti who stood for national union against the subversive parties. Friends and critics alike had their reasons for trying to make out that there had been no revolution. Fortunato, that aged relic of liberalism, coined the epigram that fascism was not a revolution but a revelation—a revelation of servile, boastful, bigoted Italy that derived from the Counter Reformation and the Spanish occupation and in whose history liberalism had been a mere parenthesis. From a very different point of view Mussolini convinced others that he was not the destroyer but the defender of the constitution, whereas Facta had violated constitutional convention by urging the king to an illegal act.

Cautiously and cleverly, Mussolini lulled people into a sense of false security, giving himself time for the opposition groups to be singled out for piecemeal and surreptitious destruction. His immediate aims were to stress continuity and tradition and to develop the myth that he spoke for the "general will" and knew the true interests of Italians better than they did themselves. He was quite within tradition in governing by decree. Nor was there anything illegal or novel in depriving Rome of its elected municipal council on the pretended grounds of bad administration. Gradually, during 1923 and thereafter, prefectures, police offices, and the state administration were restaffed with fascists. A batch of new senators was created in March 1923, including De Bono, Pareto, Pantaleoni, Corradini, Martini, Casati, and Agnelli the director of Fiat. The structure of a new state was being built up unobtrusively and as far as possible without recourse to revolutionary methods.

★

Mussolini tried for a time to remain committed to only a few positive policies. He had few constructive ideas but needed to hold together the diverse elements in his party and give himself time to test popular reactions. At least until the 1924 elections he had to tread carefully. There was the big problem of how to balance Left against Right, the extreme fascists against his liberal sympathizers, monarchists with socialists, clericals with anticlericals, idealists with rogues and *affaristi*. Volpe, the enthusiastic historian of the movement, trod delicately over this muddle. Fascism, said Mussolini, was not a party but an anti-party. It was a synthesis of every negation and every affirmation, and he admitted that the precise objectives for which it was fighting were none too clear—which struck Volpe as neither surprising nor deplorable.

Mussolini in time found that people expected a policy from him, indeed that policy was a prerequisite of useful action, but he preferred to let any general political ideas emerge empirically from *ad hoc* responses to the problems of administration. Circumstances made it expedient for him to create a party militia which made *squadrismo* into a legal institution of and transferred to the government payroll the hoodlums he did not dare dismiss. This done, he then claimed that the militia made redundant the Royal Guards which Nitti had instituted as an extra force of police. These Royal Guards he condemned as a "blind instrument of national hatred," and the angry tone reveals his vindictiveness against one of the few public bodies which had been available to maintain public order in the civil war of 1920–22.

The dissolution of these *guardie regie* provoked armed resistance and fatal casualties in some places, as did the dissolution of the nationalist blueshirts, but no one was ready to exploit the fact, and the socialists disliked these bodies for precisely the same reason the fascists did. Mussolini's enemies were allowing themselves to be picked off one by one. There was minor friction even inside the fascist party during 1923, and armed conflict occurred between various factions for the possession of buildings and funds. But the hierarchic element soon overcame the democratic inside fascism, just as the state became ever more closely identified with the party.

Fascist policy was constructed from a wholesale borrowing of ideas, the intention being to make the regime look progressive and yet sound. Measures and ideas did not need to be consistent so long as they were popular, showy, easy to administer, preferably noncommittal, and pre-digested enough to need no extra thought or definition. Mussolini picked Gentile's brains for the education act of 1923 which became "the most fascist of all reforms," until soon afterwards it was replaced by other educational reforms which were each said to be more fascist than their predecessors. In foreign policy the same man who had offended many patriots by his socialistic anti-imperialism now appropriated from the nationalists their flagwaving and drumbeating. A pact of fusion was made with the nationalist party in March 1923 and so a potential rival was annexed together with support from high finance, heavy industry, and the nationalist intellectuals around Federzoni and Corradini. This also brought him ten more deputies, to make forty-five in all.

Mussolini was politic enough to take from the Catholics such readymade ideas as fitted his own brand of anticommunism. The Catholics formed the vast bulk of the Italian electorate, and without benevolent neutrality from them and the Vatican he could not hope for easy success. So he jilted Marinetti, renounced his own extravagant idea to expel the pope from Italy, and overrode Farinacci by declaring that both factions of Italian freemasonry were incompatible with fascism. Red atheism was decreed the common enemy. Influential prelates readily took the hint that a few well-directed political sermons would help promote the new Catholic university at Milan and the introduction of compulsory religious instruction in schools. Salvemini found evidence that in January 1923 Mussolini secretly met Cardinal Gasparri, the papal secretary of state, and discussed an alliance with the Church and possible help for the Catholic Banca di Roma. Certainly Pope Pius XI turned against Don Sturzo's Catholic party and so helped to confound one of Mussolini's few potential rivals.

With an eclectic, empirical policy it was hoped to keep all classes happy. While on the one hand some of the syndicalists were attracted by a mock version of guild socialism, on the other hand Mussolini pandered to the monied interests. A few days after October 28, the General Confederation of Industry put out a manifesto welcoming the new government. One of Mussolini's first acts was to decree the abrogation of Giolitti's law on registering bonds in the owner's name, a decision that sent the stock market soaring, and his suspension of the law on land reform was welcomed with acclamation by the agrarians. A few months later another decree reduced death duties by half and the commission of inquiry on wartime profits was dissolved, in both cases reversing what had been fascist policy in 1920.

Mussolini's former socialistic speeches were now withdrawn from the official canon, and De Stefani, an economics professor close to the old-fashioned liberal school, was brought into the cabinet with a policy of denationalization to free industry and trade and to repeal quasi-socialist land legislation. It was De Stefani's policy to withdraw government subsidies from co-operatives, to abolish the government life-insurance monopoly, and to hand the telephone system over to private enterprise. Einaudi and his liberal friends heartily approved and so did the *Confindustria*. The railroads remained under state control, partly as a sop to the ex-railroad worker Farinacci and the other "national socialist" elements in fascism, but also because the railways were unprofitable. Nevertheless a policy of decontrol and financial stringency continued until De Stefani's dismissal in 1925, and this helped to win the initial support of industry and finance.

Policies quickly succeeded each other, more for reasons of public relations than of intellectual coherence. Up to 1919 Mussolini had been a socialist. In April 1920 he had so far changed that his newspaper claimed to believe only in the "religion of anarchy." "I am for the individual and against the state," he said at this stage in his career: "Down with the state in all its forms and permutations." Subsequently he posed as a free-trade liberal. Then after 1925 he reversed this trend and proceeded through an exaggerated phase of monopoly capitalism to end up after 1938 reverting back to his original views as a class-conscious, revolutionary socialist. Similar oscillations characterized fascist policy in almost every field.

*

Mussolini's chief object in 1922–24 was to entrench his party in power but without acting so fast that his enemies were frightened into premature resistance. His most revolutionary step was taken not by decree but by parliamentary vote, the passing of the Acerbo electoral law at the end of 1923. This law declared that the party or coalition obtaining the largest number of votes, provided this was at least 25 per cent of the votes cast, should automatically have an absolute majority with two-thirds of the seats in the Chamber. When this utterly decisive matter came up for discussion there were no more than forty-five fascist deputies in parliament, but the law received the support of Salandra, De Nicola, Orlando, Giolitti, and their respective groups, for these liberals had come to the conclusion that transformism was unworkable and must be replaced by party government, even if that party should be the fascists.

Most of the *popolari* disapproved of this electoral reform as also did Bonomi's reformist socialists and Amendola's democratic liberals, yet as they retained general confidence in the government these groups decided to abstain from the vote. Thirty-nine *popolari* deputies opposed this decision to abstain and some of them had to leave the party. Other senators connected with the Vatican resigned their party membership so that they could support Acerbo's bill, and this was interpreted to mean that the Church had decided against the continuance of a popular Catholic party that was threatening to break free from its earlier collaboration with fascism. The disintegration of such a large group suited Mussolini admirably.

His vote of confidence on this occasion was carried by 303 to 140, and the Senate majority was 165 to 41. While the representatives were voting, black-shirted troopers in the galleries of the Palazzo Montecitorio ostentatiously toyed with pistols and pared their nails with daggers, while the *onorevoli* pretended that this childishness meant nothing. A minority was thus presented with dictatorial powers and the assurance of at least 356 seats out of 535, because the fascists, if they used Giolitti's techniques of electoral gerrymandering, could hardly fail to obtain the necessary 25 per cent poll. There was no hope of a parliament elected under these conditions giving an adverse vote, let alone any chance of a change of ministry. The parliamentary system had simply been voted out of existence by a large but intimidated liberal majority. Speaking on the first anniversary of the "march," Mussolini said that his government would last five years, but corrected himself and said "or rather twelve times five."

The subsequent elections showed that, political practice being what it was, the Acerbo law had hardly been necessary. The elections were fought on a national not a constituency basis, and the fascists contrived to form a transformist electoral coalition containing the names of Salandra, De Nicola, Orlando and other liberals, together with the first batch of trimmers and *arrivistes* from socialism and the *popolari*. Against this single government bloc, the communists suggested organizing a broad alliance to try to win the necessary 25 per cent of the vote, but the other parties would not hear of it, and six individual opposition slates were formed, none with any possibility of success. There was also a seventh independent slate led by Giolitti which flanked fascism and was not technically in opposition. Mussolini told his men not to take these "election sports" too seriously, for good fascists should despise such a survival of an old outworn order. Nevertheless, in the elections of April 1924 the party militia was on duty inside the polling booths and the familiar tale of casualties and killings was repeated. The principal opposition newspapers were systematically intimidated all through the campaign, and armed raids inflicted heavy financial losses on them.

Perhaps it was remarkable that as many as 2,500,000 votes were cast for nonfascist parties. But Mussolini's coalition obtained four and a half million or 65 per cent of the vote. The *popolari* obtained 640,000 votes; the reformist labor party which had broken off in 1922, 420,000; the maximalists who controlled the socialist rump, 360,000; the communists, 268,000; and the independent liberals, 233,000. The twenty-seventh legislature in Italian history had 403 ministerial deputies, apart from qualified supporters in the 15 independent liberals, 10 social democrats, and 4 deputies of the so-called peasant party. The opposition included 39 *popolari*, 24 reformist socialists, 22 maximalists, 19 communists, 2 deputies of the Sardinian party of action, and 1 dissident fascist. Even opponents of Mussolini such as Salvatorelli admit that, despite manifest illegalities, fascism could probably claim to represent "a relative majority" in the country, and this gave retrospective sanction to Mussolini's conquest of power. Fascism already had behind it the authority of the king and the two Houses of Parliament; from now onward it also could claim, rightly or wrongly, to represent the will of the electorate.

46   The Defeat of Parliament and Press, 1924-1925

Now that he was backed by the largest majority since the time of Cavour, Mussolini had less need for caution. Opposition deputies were assaulted and sometimes horribly tortured. A personal telegram from Mussolini ordered the prefect of Turin to "make life difficult for Gobetti"—a leading journalist who was uncompromising in his courageous opposition. Worst of all was the assassination of Giacomo Matteotti. This man was a moderate socialist deputy who was brave enough to point out how Mussolini had once fought for many things which fascism now opposed on principle. Matteotti published in foreign newspapers the shocking details about how fascism relied for its success on violent intimidation and unprecedented financial corruption. He even dared to accuse Mussolini in parliament of being determined to use force if the elections turned hostile, at which remark a triumphant cry of "Yes!" went up from the fascist deputies and Mussolini nodded his head. Why, asked Matteotti, did fascism make it a matter of pride that Italians alone in the world should be incapable of running their own affairs and must be ruled by force? The reply came that he "must be taken out of circulation," and a gang led by Mussolini's associate Dumini murdered him for his outspokenness. Only a few months had gone by since the Italian representative at the League of Nations had poured public scorn on Greece as a primitive nation where assassination was still an instrument of politics.

So great was the outcry at this crime that Mussolini had to stand in sackcloth. He tried hard to put all the blame on others, but his own involvement was confirmed in detail by Dumini. Some leading fascists were sufficiently scandalized to turn king's evidence. Other politicians, including Sforza and Albertini, even contemplated a *coup de main* when they saw the incriminating memorandum compiled by undersecretary Finzi. But unfortunately Amendola, who had succeeded Giolitti as head of the independent liberals, decided that the monarch could be relied on to take any action that might be necessary, and only a few days after Matteotti's murder the Senate, in which fascists were a small minority, passed a vote of confidence in Mussolini by 235 to 21.

Some leading fascists were sure that the king at this point could easily have ousted fascism, but his own fortunes were now bound up with the revolution, and the only alternative to fascism would involve the socialists whom he disliked far more. Giolitti, too, stated in so many words that only a government under Mussolini could restore social peace; and in the eyes of the ruling classes in Italy, social peace was an overriding consideration. Both Giolitti and Salandra, so the king told Bergamini in 1945, advised him at this moment to support Mussolini. Other politicians presented Vittorio Emanuele with Finzi's implication of Mussolini in Matteotti's murder, but the king said he could not act without a decision in parliament. A few months later the sovereign returned unread to Bonomi other inculpating evidence presented by dissident fascists. Too late, and contrary to his behavior in 1915 and 1922, he now affected to play the constitutional monarch who could do nothing without his ministers' advice. When a deputation of veterans came to protest at fascist crimes, he changed the subject at once.

Faced with a majority of blackshirts, in June 1924 most of the opposition deputies decided to abandon the Chamber altogether. This was called the Aventine secession, after the plebs in ancient Rome who once withdrew from the city to the Aventine hill. It was led by Amendola, one of the finer minds and more attractive characters in Italy's modern parliamentary history. Amendola had already been assaulted in Rome during 1923 and would receive fatal wounds from a second manhandling in July 1925. A final speech from him in parliament listed the sins of fascism—using state funds to pay the armed party militia, intimidating the parliamentary opposition, and truculently boasting of his reliance on violence. Mussolini interrupted twenty-seven times during this forty-minute speech using typically uncouth and quite unparliamentary language.

Amendola hoped that the Aventine secession would give the king an excuse to intervene. But in practice it was yet another example of the ineffectiveness of constitutional opposition: it could only have worked had there been a general abstention, whereas Giolitti told Amendola that salaried deputies had no right to absent themselves from parliament—perhaps forgetting the precedent he himself had set in 1894 and 1916. At this particular moment when fascism was confused and hesitant, its remaining opponents were passing the buck in turn, and so were severally defeated.

Even though the parliamentary opposition ran away from the scene of battle, fascist uniforms and badges now began to disappear, party membership cards were returned, Mussolini's *anticamera* was deserted, and criticism became outspoken. Worse than a crime, the murder of Matteotti was proving to have been a blunder. De Bono and Balbo had to resign. Yet some of the liberals continued to insist that they had no wish to unseat the man whom they had elected to guarantee effective rule and social order. When the Senate over-whelmingly supported Mussolini there were some respected names among the opposing minority—Albertini, Bergamini, Ruffini, and Sforza. Even so, only three senators dared to speak against fascism on this occasion, and Albertini's speech contained many words of cautious praise. Facta was soon afterwards made a senator in return for his help, and Salandra's opinion was still that fascism was the best available representative of the liberal tradition.

★

It was this attitude of many so-called liberals that betrayed the hollowness of parliamentary Italy. The liberal party congress had lately given its blessing to fascist rule. Casati and another liberal were somehow persuaded to join the cabinet in July 1924, unmoved either by Matteotti's murder or by a decree of that month which introduced restrictions on press comment. The fear of socialism among these men was greater than their love of liberty, and they still regarded Mussolini as a useful antisocialist instead of someone with a positive ambition for power on his own illiberal terms.

Don Sturzo commented most unfavorably on the inaction of Giolitti, Orlando, Salandra, and the other former prime ministers who all voted for fascism. According to Sturzo there were many timeservers in Mussolini's party who would have been glad to desert the government coalition if only these parliamentary leaders had set an example. The electoral coalition with fascism shows that the liberals feared not Mussolini but rather the mass parties threatening to oust them in popular favor, and by this they meant the *popolari* as well as the socialists. Christian democrats, said Croce, were doubly to be feared in that they were both democratic and papal, and this monstrous blend of irreconcilables meant that they must be foolish or insincere. Giolitti had harsh words for Sturzo and Salandra, but was never heard to make any disparaging remark about Mussolini. Croce had publicly sanctioned the violence used in the 1924 elections for it was the only way to obtain a fascist majority. In January this philosopher had made an explicit and public statement:

The heart of fascism is love of Italy, the safety of the state, and the true conviction that the state without authority is no state at all.... Fascism is overcoming the traditional indifference of Italians to politics ... and I value so highly the cure which Italy is undergoing from it that I rather hope the patient will not get up too soon from his bed and risk some grave relapse.

Croce's name would have carried great weight if used to condemn what a few months later he was to revile as an "onagrocracy" or government by wild asses. But in the confusion of the postwar world the liberals had lost their bearings. Giolitti and his friends had tried to use the fascists to give the Left a few salutary rebuffs in punishment for its non-co-operation and its attempt to reduce class privilege. The *Giornale d'Italia* was beginning to be more critical, but its rival the *Corriere* was still reluctant to print hostile comment against fascism lest this should imperil the newspaper's existence, and because of such timidity neither the general public nor foreign observers could properly judge what was happening. Giolitti attended parliament with unwonted regularity to show his solidarity with the government; he listened deferentially to Mussolini's speeches and was seen to applaud them. The king noted this and pretended that all must be well. Among a few brave dissenters, Gobetti asserted the need to make liberalism more radical and democratic, as Gramsci already saw the need for socialists to discard some of their inflexible myths, but these were heretics and a small minority; and their protest came too late.

The fate of fascism was still uncertain in October 1924 when the war veterans association refused to take part in anniversary celebrations for the "march on Rome." But as soon as it became obvious that the opposition did not mean business, the job hunters and timeservers re-emerged with their fascist insignia. Men of every party sincerely or insincerely began anew to bow to the rising sun: Romolo Murri who had once been a leader of Christian democracy, the philosopher Gentile, the former liberal prime minister Boselli, senators of renown such as Marconi, Scialoia, Tittoni, and Pantaleoni, all confirmed their allegiance to the regime. This was a testing time during which many consciences were racked and many friendships broken.

In November Giolitti was bold enough to object that freedom of the press had been abolished by a simple decree, for this violated an express provision of the constitution. When Orlando made a similar criticism, Mussolini launched a challenge in the Senate to see if his critics were prepared to back words with deeds. If the king were to ask for his resignation he would salute and obey, but his allegiance was to King Vittorio Emanuele, not to "his majesty the *Corriere della Sera.*" In the absence of the Aventine seceders there was unfortunately barely a handful of liberals and communists left in parliament to take up this challenge. During a noisy session, in which Mussolini himself was several times called to order, Albertini tried to pretend that all the leading politicians were by now secretly in opposition; but Federzoni, minister of the interior, pertinently shouted, "except the majority in parliament." By 208 to 54 the Senate again supported the government. Mosca and Croce could not suddenly restore confidence in the parliamentary democracy whose theoretical justifications they had spent so long helping to undermine.

★

At the end of December 1924, another memorandum implicating Mussolini in assault and murder was publicized by Amendola in his paper, *Il Mondo.* The author, Cesare Rossi, had been perhaps the closest of all leading fascists to Mussolini. There was an awed hush for a few days, and Salandra and Riccio at last joined the opposition. Amendola assured his friends that they need only keep quiet and do nothing since Mussolini was now bound to resign. But on January 3, 1925, the Duce dealt characteristically with this pitiful parliamentary remnant, at last discarding his earlier excuses and claiming personal responsibility for Matteotti's murder:

> I declare before all Italy that I assume full responsibility for what has happened.... If fascism has turned out to be only castor oil and rubber truncheons instead of a superb passion inspiring the best youth of Italy, I am responsible.... Italy wants peace and quiet and to get on with its work. I shall give it all these, if possible in love, but if necessary by force. In the forty-eight hours after my speech the whole situation will be changed.

He proceeded to taunt his hearers by reminding them that Article 47 of the constitution allowed the Chamber to impeach ministers before the High Court. But no one dared to take up his defiance; on the contrary, the speech was accepted with acclamation and only thirty-three votes in the Chamber were cast against him. The two remaining liberal ministers, Casati and Sarrocchi, at last resigned, the second not very willingly it seems. Sforza told a friend that a new ministry would have to be formed with Giolitti, Orlando, and Salandra because it was unthinkable that a self-confessed murderer should continue to govern the country. But the king had other ideas.

Forty-eight hours after this speech of January 1925, Mussolini's government had ceased to be merely a ministry and had become a regime. He had isolated his opponents and defeated them individually so that he could now drop all pretense and reveal his true colors. Salandra withdrew from politics in bitter disillusionment, even though fascism still retained the more or less enthusiastic allegiance of most of his conservative-liberal friends who represented the landowners and northern industrialists. The liberal party of Giolitti and Croce, without whose explicit or tacit consent Mussolini might not have won power, was outlawed along with all other independent parties. The 123 deputies of the Aventine, when they lamely tried to return to parliament, found the door shut: they were in 1926 declared to have made "an anticonstitutional and revolutionary secession," so forfeiting their seats. This decision was carried unanimously. In the words of one historian the opposition now left the Aventine for the catacombs, among them the liberal Amendola and the *popolari* leaders De Gasperi and Gronchi. Some antifascists fled abroad. Most were left unmolested so long as they abjured politics.

★

After January 1925, it was no longer easy to deceive oneself about fascism. Mussolini had publicly acknowledged his responsibility for torture and murder. Clearly he was far more interested in power than good government, and any criticism in parliament or the newspapers was now declared intolerable. In a last flicker of protest on January 4, Amendola's *Il Mondo* wrote: "This man Mussolini constitutes a pathological case not foreseen in the constitution. ... Everything is subordinated to his mad ambition. ... Apart from his personal coarseness, he is altogether alien to what the English call 'fair play.'" This illumination came too late, and independent journalism was thenceforward silenced.

Nenni, former friend of Mussolini and editor of the socialist *Avanti*, had already been arrested for "defamation of the fascist government." His paper proclaimed to the last that antifascist victory was certain "if only we remain quite intransigent. ... This is not the first time that our party has been dissolved, but persecution has never held up the march of socialism." Such a philosophy may have consoled, but did not heal, and *Avanti* paid the penalty for its intransigence. The radical *Secolo* also fell into fascist hands. Repeatedly the *Corriere della Sera* had whole issues confiscated in an attempt to ruin its profitability. The liberals who remained on the municipal council of Milan had already been frightened into disavowing their paper, and in November 1925 the owners of the *Corriere*, the Crespi family who were cotton manufacturers in Milan, were persuaded by Farinacci to dismiss the Albertini brothers from its editorship. Liberal writers such as Einaudi, Parri, and Croce were banned from its columns, and a less recalcitrant editor, Ojetti, was appointed on the Duce's special designation. So fell one of the most admirable newspapers in Europe. Likewise Frassati had to hand over *La Stampa* to fascist control.

A new generation of journalists was appearing to replace Salvemini, Gobetti, Salvatorelli, and other notable figures who had striven to keep liberal thought and criticism alive. Hitherto the opposition journals had been selling ten times as well as the official press. Henceforward journalism was standardized, and Farinacci, Grandi, Bottai, and Balbo found it profitable to launch newspapers in their respective fiefdoms which obtained a guaranteed sale as the mouthpiece of government policy.

Mussolini himself, always a journalist at heart, spent much more time and thought on publicity and public relations than on devising policy. Not only did journalists form an absolute majority on the Grand Council of fascism, but daily instructions came to the press from the dictator's personal office in order to mold opinion and ensure that a uniform and ideologically correct impression was created. It would be ordained for example that no mention should be made of his birthday, of his being a grandfather, of him dancing; for the authoritative impression was to be one of youth and serious-mindedness. He was said to excel at every sport, skiing, fencing, even tennis and boxing. By some unfortunate miscalculation figures were sometimes given to show that the hours he spent at the controls of his plane were greater than those permitted to a full-time professional pilot. Photographs of himself smiling were not to be printed. "Say that the *Duce* was called out on to the balcony ten times." "Put out a special edition with his speech under an eight-column headline." "You may comment on his speech, and we shall shortly circulate the requisite comment for inclusion."

This behavior was in the long run contraproductive, and though there is no means of testing sales resistance one may guess that the individualism and humor of Italians made them less susceptible to this kind of treatment than Mussolini can have wished. Even his own paper, *Il Popolo d'Italia*, never reached at its peak a circulation of 500,000, a figure which the liberal *Corriere della Sera* had far surpassed in the old days.

SECTION ELEVEN: THE THEORY AND PRACTICE OF FASCISM

47 The Machinery and Personnel of Fascism

Having overcome the independent organs of public opinion by 1925, Mussolini could spend the next few years transforming the nature of the state, making it more authoritarian and personal. All over Italy the nominated *podestà* was to supplant the elected mayor in each town and village. A committee of "eighteen Solons" was appointed in January 1925 to reform the constitution. In December a law gave the prime minister a new legal existence, no longer the first among equals but singly responsible to the king alone. Whereas under the 1848 constitution the king nominated and dismissed ministers, in practice he now did this only on Mussolini's proposal, and every motion for parliamentary debate had first to be approved by the Duce. Mosca was a lone voice in opposition to this. A law of January 1926 gave Mussolini power to issue decrees having the full force of law—there were to be more than one hundred thousand decree laws issued under fascism, which would have made administration and justice impossibly complicated had they been obeyed. Mussolini's person was declared inviolable, and after the attempts on his life by Major Zaniboni in 1925 and the Irish Miss Gibson in 1926, capital punishment was prescribed for anyone who so much as contemplated his death.

By a law of December 1928 Mussolini was to enter the plentitude of power when the king lost some of his right to select the prime minister. When the Grand Council of fascism was empowered to list the names from among whom Mussolini's successor should be chosen, the king did not dissent. This promotion of the *Gran Consiglio* into an organ of state was a constitutional innovation of which Mussolini was particularly proud. Its secretary was always secretary of the fascist party. Mussolini alone could convene it and determine who should attend; he was its president by right, could decide its agenda, and use it as a check on the cabinet. He even gave it a nominal right to intervene in the succession to the throne, since the heir Umberto was reputedly lukewarm in supporting the regime. Behind these theoretical attributes, however, there is no evidence that the Grand Council had much importance until in July 1943, almost inadvertently, it turned on its creator and toppled him.

A new electoral law of May 1928 also changed the representative system once again. Parliamentary candidates in future were to be selected from a list drawn up by unions of workers and employers. From the names on this list the *Gran Consiglio* would choose the candidates who were then put to the electorate for approval or rejection en bloc. Only in the impossible event of their rejection were second elections to be held in which, hypothetically, other competing lists could be presented.

Mussolini when introducing this bill told the Senate that universal suffrage

337

was merely a conventional fiction; also that the constitution was dead and buried, not because it had been abolished, but because Italy was now profoundly different from what it had been in 1848. The senators who sat quietly through this kind of talk were still very largely the liberals appointed by Giolitti and Orlando, but a counterresolution by Ruffini received only forty-six signatures. Albertini bravely argued that the victors in World War I had been the free peoples,

> while those ruled by more or less despotic forms of government were either defeated or else fell out of the struggle before its end. . . . I am a survivor of a liberalism that even though defeated cannot accept dishonor, and mindful of the oath taken in this very hall of the Senate, I feel it my duty in this hour to reaffirm my unshakable faith in those principles which the bill before us denies.

Hundreds of new senators soon swamped these antediluvian survivors, and because it sometimes became *de rigueur* for the whole body to wear fascist uniforms and shout ritual slogans, the liberals usually preferred to stay away.

In 1929 when elections were held, 136,000 votes were officially declared to have been cast against the national list of candidates, but this number may well have been a pure fabrication. The next elections in March 1934 showed only fifteen thousand votes for the opposition though 95 per cent of the electorate was said to have voted. These were improbable figures in view of the number of policemen required to suppress any manifestation of dissent. Plebiscites of this sort were a bogus test of public opinion and merely indicate how easily such elections could be manipulated to give a required result.

But this is not to say that Mussolini was unrepresentative of his country. Opposition there may have been, but it could not be very vocal, and where most people wanted security and prosperity above democracy, Mussolini used his undeniable skill in propaganda to persuade them that he had these gifts at his disposal. The plebiscitary dictatorship was in its own way a manifestation of democracy. Other politicians in history had already discovered that liberty and equality could be antithetical rather than complementary, and that by careful handling the mob could be used to make a dictator more autocratic. The argument for Leviathan often became more attractive as international relations became more perilous and as the problems of government grew more complex. Internal liberties might seem too expensive if they could be portrayed as meaning delay, division, perhaps inefficiency. And so Mussolini was able to establish what he called an "authoritarian, centralized democracy" in which he could talk contemptuously of the "putrefying corpse of liberty" to the applause of a uniform nation.

★

The central organ of the revolution was the fascist party itself, and alongside each existing institution of state there grew up a parallel institution dependent

338

on the party: the fascist militia alongside the army, the Roman salute alongside the military salute, the special party tribunal cutting across the ordinary law courts, and the party *federale* at the side of each provincial prefect. There was also the Palazzo Venezia which after 1929, when Mussolini made it his private office, overtook the Quirinal palace as a fount of patronage and power, and there was the party song *"Giovinezza"* which, to the king's disappointment, began to oust the *"Marcia Reale."* At the apex, the Duce of fascism was simultaneously Head of Government, and these two offices were soon considered identical. Gradually, the party was identified with the state. Fascist law became the only effective law. The nationalization of the fascist militia transferred an onerous burden from the shoulders of party backers onto the taxpayer. Emblazoned on the state coat of arms was the party emblem of the lictor's fasces. The party secretary eventually assumed ministerial rank and attended cabinet meetings; he came to be a *de jure* member of the defense council and the board of education; he also took precedence in ceremonial processions and Court functions.

Another tendency was for the party to become increasingly centralized; and throughout 1923 there was a purge of its provincial directorates as local fascist units were subordinated to the center at Rome. Several times before 1925 the local *ras* had rebelled and overruled their leader, but never again until 1943. After 1926, instead of the *Gran Consiglio* being elected at the annual party congress, nomination was introduced from the top—"supermen elect themselves," declared Mussolini. The *Gran Consiglio* was empowered to choose the party secretary, who appointed the provincial secretaries who together made up the fascist national council. These provincial secretaries then appointed the lesser officials of the local *fasci*.

Membership of the party fluctuated considerably in number, for there was an oscillation between considering it as a mass or treating it as an elite. The *tessera fascista* was usually a document requisite for many types of employment. But sometimes large expulsions were decreed when the party was thought to be unwieldy or factious. Its hard core was the "fascists of the first hour," the *sansepolcristi* who had inaugurated the movement in 1919 and often continued to set the tone. These obtained special privileges and financial perquisites, as did all "pre-march" fascists (whether genuine or self-styled), and this helped to perpetuate the hooligan element at the summit of Italy's new ruling class.

★

Few of the party leaders were more than mediocre. Most were unintelligent, grasping, incompetent, and jockeyed for place by telling tales against their rivals, or else boosted each other's morale by organizing "spontaneous" crowd demonstrations for one another. With the possible exception of D'Annunzio and Marconi there was no living Italian for whom Mussolini felt any admiration. When he later claimed that the party leaders had let him down, the answer must be that he had the subordinates he deserved and whom he had himself advanced. Indeed he deliberately promoted their rivalries and conflicting policies. Frequently he replaced ministers and party leaders in a sweeping "change of the guard," and publicly boasted that he liked to announce these wholesale changes without first informing the people he intended to appoint or dismiss. This was a revealing manifestation of what became known as *ducismo*.

Most party secretaries were quickly superseded so as to prevent anyone winning too much influence or building up a private following of their own. In 1923 Bianchi was displaced as general secretary by Sansanelli, he in 1924 by Giunta. In 1925–26 the post was held by Farinacci, one of the more crude and brutish of the hierarchy, anticlerical and (when it suited him) anti-semitic. His successor, Augusto Turati, was eventually charged with immorality, suspected of lunacy, and confined at Rhodes. Then followed Giuriati, Starace, Muti, and Serena; of these only Starace reigned long enough to have much influence—"a cretin," said Mussolini, "but an obedient cretin." Then, with Vidussoni in 1941, was appointed a party secretary still in his early twenties of whom no one knew anything at all except that he had failed his examinations and had a medal for valor. After him came Scorza, another murderous leader of the early fascist gangs.

Mussolini's sons were but shadows of their father. Bruno was involved in running an airline to South America, and Vittorio tried to assume direction of the film industry. Edda, their sister, had a more forceful character. Mussolini's younger brother Arnaldo was a man of some conscience and religion, and one of the few to keep Mussolini's affection and confidence. His main job was to edit *Il Popolo d'Italia*.

Of the other leaders the Duce was always a little suspicious, sometimes with reason. Emilio De Bono was fifty-six years old in 1922, an undistinguished army general who helped organize the militia and whom Mussolini was to execute in 1944. Italo Balbo in 1922 was only twenty-six, thirteen years younger than Mussolini. The most genuine and gallant of the fascists, he was always a *frondeur* with his own private ambitions and was suspected of courting Prince Umberto in the hope of one day succeeding to supreme power. Mussolini was a little afraid of Balbo as well as envious of his youth. Eventually, this potential rival was shot down by Italian antiaircraft guns in 1940, probably by accident. A more senior and laughable figure was Cesare De Vecchi, created count of Val Cismon, poetaster and pseudo academic, who was the general butt of his colleagues and helped to remove Mussolini in 1943. Dino Grandi was another young "first hour" fascist and a callous squad leader in his youth. He too had some ambition to succeed or replace Mussolini. His chief official task was to fill the ministry of foreign affairs with party hacks; and later he took over the London embassy. Grandi was a competent diplomat but fawning and obsequious toward Mussolini until he too deserted the sinking ship in July 1943.

The younger generation was represented by Galeazzo Ciano, whose father did very well financially out of running the ministry of communications. The younger Ciano rose rapidly to become foreign minister in 1936 at the age of thirty-four. He compared moderately well with his associates, having something of wit and even intelligence to make up for lack of education, but he was corrupt and self-indulgent, superficial to a degree, idle, frivolous, and quite without weight of character. He had the reputation of giving away public secrets to friends in high Roman society who found in him almost alone of the fascist leaders a man of conversation and polish, and he defended their interests against the quasi-socialist elements which occasionally threatened to dominate the party. The old-guard fascists of the first hour resented him as an upstart and were upset when in 1930 he was chosen by the Duce as a son-in-law. For years Ciano remained the dictator's favorite, until in 1944 his father-in-law had him shot in the back on a trumped-up charge of treachery.

On the left of the party was Rossoni, leader of the fascist labor unions, who had once been a revolutionary agitator in the United States. Bianchi and "Professor" Bottai also inclined toward this left wing, together with other ex-socialists such as Farinacci. The importance of such men is hard to gauge, but union leaders gained in power from the centralized organization of trades and professions. Anyone in search of a job would, if sensible, abandon the socialist or Catholic unions and join the fascist syndicates. Under government pressure, in October 1925 Rossoni agreed to the Vidoni pact which obtained industrial peace by outlawing strikes and penalizing labor unrest. Clearly, the left wing of the fascist party was not strong until Mussolini reverted to his earlier socialism toward the end of his life.

★

One fascist novelty that obtained wide publicity was the Corporative System to regulate the national economy. Mussolini was eager to demonstrate that his movement was not simply conservative but had new and seminal ideas. The party intellectuals were therefore enlisted to expound and apply his oracular assertion that "our Corporative System is destined to become the main theme of the twentieth century."

This was an idea that he borrowed from the nationalists and Catholics. Its author, the nationalist Rocco, became justice minister in January 1925; the following year a new ministry of corporations was created, and in 1930 a National Council of Corporations was called into theoretical existence as a deliberative assembly. To it, again in theory, were attached all the workers in the state through their respective trade organizations. When the system took more positive shape in 1936 there were said to be twenty-two separate categories for various trades and industries—for instance, the fifth for the sugar and beet industries, the ninth for metallurgy, the twenty-second for the professional classes and artists. All workers had their appropriate category and each category had political as well as economic functions. The officials in charge of each corporation were appointed from above, partly because well-paid jobs were needed for prominent fascists. The rank and file had but to pay their subscriptions and do what they were told, for instead of being citizens with rights and independence, they were now cogs with a function. Having abolished political liberalism by 1925, Mussolini thus buried economic liberalism soon afterward.

This idea of corporativism was so attractive that he once called it the single essential component in fascism. In 1933 he promised the National Council of Corporations that they might one day replace the Chamber of Deputies: "The Chamber has never been to my taste; it has now become anachronistic even in name; as an institution it is foreign to our fascist cast of thought and presupposes a plurality of parties which no longer exists." Two years later he shamelessly assured this National Council that it was "the most imposing assembly in the whole history of Italy." Finally, in 1939 the Chamber of Fasces and Corporations was created, to replace the old parliamentary system which disappeared in name as well as in fact.

Imposing though the name of this new body may have sounded, the corporations were more an aspiration than an actuality and Salvemini rightly called them an elaborate piece of humbug. The machinery of corporativism was tremendously expensive and this invited much jobbery and corruption, while a vast new organization was thereby created to duplicate (and hence hinder) operations carried out by the civil service.

Mussolini in March 1936 told the Council of Corporations that he "did not wish to bureaucratize the entire economy of the nation," but in practice the extension of governmental activities created a top-heavy organization, slow, unresponsive, and out of close touch with ordinary people. Party members and officials constituted a huge new vested interest, since the party, the militia, and the corporations provided tens of thousands of jobs for secretaries and organizers. This helped to satisfy that deep-rooted desire for a respectable job in government service, poorly paid, but easy work and a sure pension. The census returns of 1931 and 1936 reveal how the greatest increase in occupation was made in administrative and professional categories. The bureaucratic capital, Rome, now regained the lead in size (lost about 1875) over the industrial capital, Milan. A writer in the London *Economist* described the position in 1935: "The new corporative state only amounts to the establishment of a new and costly bureaucracy, from which those industrialists who can spend the necessary amount can obtain almost anything they want, and put into practice the worst kind of monopolistic practices at the expense of the little fellow who is squeezed out in the process."

With all this increase in government expenditure and patronage, corruption became the besetting sin of the regime, though the Duce did nothing to profit personally from the graft which riddled every department of state. On the island of Ponza in 1943 he was surprised to find that there was no running water because grants for an aqueduct had been channeled into the pockets of good party members and their friends. In every locality the party hierarchs or *gerarchi* were petty tyrants with an unlimited call on public money and the assurance of being acquitted of any crime. As most of them were selected because of their flaws in character, this immunity was especially damaging.

Authenticated and unauthenticated stories of malversation were legion. Mussolini's supporters included people interested in the marble trade from Carrara, and the extravagant public buildings erected in the best *stile fascista* all over Italy and its colonies are not unconnected with this fact. Fictitious "industrial zones" were declared to exist so that state subsidies would be forthcoming, and mock factories were built for this same purpose though sometimes they never went into production. There was a lively trade in titles. In another field, Farinacci the railroad clerk easily picked up a doctorate in law, and the incontrovertible nature of his forensic arguments secured him the rewards of an exceptionally lucrative legal practice. The Ciano family was also said to have used inside knowledge to buy up ships prior to the Ethiopian war. And thus the ungodly flourished.

In most cases this corruption was no doubt petty and unimportant. Even an unfriendly American press agency could buy up a monopoly of pictures from a party official on any newsworthy event, and a foreign reporter with ready cash could jump an important story even when a simultaneous release had been promised. But high civilian and military officials diverted funds away from aircraft development and there were always enough people who would keep silent for a consideration. Mussolini was told by his chief of police and others that corruption was the main cause of his regime's inefficiency, but he preferred to turn a blind eye rather than admit to public opinion that his own choice of subordinates had been at fault. Dishonesty, he once said might be a positive qualification for appointments.

★

That this rickety machine kept running so long was due largely to the personality of its leader. Mussolini lacked all nobility of character, but he knew the Italians and knew how to make them serve his ambition. He was always able to inspire confidence and make people think him sincere, whatever his beliefs or lack of them. Skill consciously employed was allied with a fascination he exerted almost unconsciously.

In 1932 Mussolini dropped some revealing remarks to Emil Ludwig:

Today people have not so much time to think as they used to have. The capacity of the modern man for faith is unlimited. When the masses are like wax in my hands, when I stir their faith or when I mingle with them and am almost crushed, I feel myself to be a part of them. All the same there persists in me a certain feeling of aversion, like that which the modeller feels for the clay he is moulding. Does not the sculptor sometimes smash his block of marble into fragments because he cannot shape it to represent the vision he has conceived? Now and then this crude matter rebels against the creator.

His interlocutor asked whether a dictator could be loved. "Yes," answered Mussolini; "provided that the masses fear him at the same time. The crowd loves strong men. The crowd is like a woman."

Mussolini was a play-actor who knew how to produce himself in public. With his bulbous and unsmiling face he created a legend of the strong man who was victorious and always right, the wise man who knew the inmost thoughts of people, the industrious servant of the public photographed toiling in the harvest field stripped to the waist. Foreign diplomats were either impressed or disturbed when they had to move past a double column of his pugnacious-looking black-uniformed musketeers with daggers held out at arm's length, and any reception in Mussolini's gigantic marble study was carefully staged to humble the visitor. His most important quality was that of being a stupendous poseur. His mixture of showmanship and vulgarity appealed to the common people who liked to hear of his adulterous relationships and illegitimate children because he then became more human and virile. They were not allowed to know about his ill-health or failing eyesight, and foreign journalists were expelled if they mentioned his digestive troubles.

Balbo and Grandi both referred to Mussolini's inferiority complex. Others noted his extraordinary timidity and reluctance to decide between alternative lines of conduct. What was stressed at the time was the carefully contrived swagger and braggadocio, on top of which was superimposed the different legend of a temperate man who did not smoke and who seldom drank wine. A light would burn in his study far into the night to persuade people that he was at work, when in reality he was asleep, or dallying with Signora Petacci. Stories circulated of his skill on the violin and his abiding affection for Dante—it was even claimed that he knew whole cantos of the *Divine Comedy* by heart. His fencing and horsemanship were legendary for he had to excel in everything, and a public fall from his horse or on the skiing slopes would be stringently concealed from the newspapers. Since there was no possibility of contradiction, he even convinced himself of his ability as a great strategist and war leader. In his "autobiography" he was childishly vain about driving cars so fast that experienced drivers were astonished, while mention by the foreign press of his involvement in road accidents could lead to a formal diplomatic protest.

Some of this deceived nobody except himself, and even the witless party leaders had their private laugh when requested to record some flatulent *mot* for posterity. But propaganda makes people gullible and fascism bred a low average of sense and discrimination. After one visit Mussolini paid to Genoa, a journalist was not ashamed to write: "To die without lament, with a vision of light in one's eyes and an infinite sweetness in the heart, that is what we should be glad to do after the experience of today, while our hands still keep some of the warmth of his masculine hand which we kissed, our hearts in tumult and full of a sense of liberation." When people such as Croce turned against fascism, it was not for its tyranny and bellicosity so much as for the embarrassing triviality and tastelessness that permeated the whole of public life.

There was perhaps some slight excuse for foreigners to misjudge Mussolini from a distance when Italian press and parliament found so much to applaud. Croce later tried to exculpate himself for supporting Mussolini in 1922–24 by describing fascism as a disease which came to Italy from abroad and largely because of foreign help. He even took this piece of patriotic consolation to the point of arguing that fascism was wholly alien to Italian traditions and temperament. No doubt there was some comfort in pointing out that Bernard Shaw whimsically defended the Ethiopian invasion, or that Winston Churchill in 1927, after an hour with Mussolini, tactfully spoke of his charm and gentleness and praised him for backing anticommunism. From the United States many useful loans were advanced to fascist Italy, and Mussolini's "auto-biography" was ghost-written by a former American ambassador.

Foreign approval was mostly found among those who hoped to use Mussolini as a front-line defense against communism; but their approval was artificially magnified by fascist propaganda to impress opinion in Italy, and sometimes was actually invented at Rome. The regime took pains to influence opinion abroad, whether by planting stories in the foreign press or deporting hostile newspaper correspondents, and the shopwindow aspect of fascism was deliberately dressed with an eye to foreign inspection. When Axel Munthe asked him to make Capri into a bird sanctuary, Mussolini saw the value in this idea to impress sentimental foreigners—though his forgetfulness or discourtesy was such that he is said to have given Munthe skylark pie for lunch when the latter arrived to thank him for his benevolence.

★

Mussolini's flair for publicity is undoubted but it masked a profound lack of skill in policy and administration. His journalistic bent is revealed in the anonymous articles he continued to write for the press, and it was on the profits of journalism, authorship, and newspaper ownership that he lived, for it was claimed that he never took his ministerial salary. Press clippings from abroad, if favorable, were diligently reproduced and became lamentably influential on policy, while Mussolini's own mental processes never ceased to be governed by journalistic slogans and eight-column headlines. This was to prove disastrous. He was a facile assimilator of superficialities and possessed an ephemeral secondhand culture—"forgive my learned references" was a phrase which once amused his entourage. He preferred to declaim and speechify rather than to penetrate behind words to reality. Fascism affected to despise speeches and talk, but was itself essentially rhetoric and blather. Mussolini was a moderately good talker and some good listeners found his conversation delightful, but he was a bad administrator, and his policy was too often empty, contradictory, or misapplied.

The motto "Mussolini is always right" was nevertheless stenciled on wayside houses all over Italy, winning credence by repetition—it was even embossed by *devots* on their notepaper. And yet his opinions were inconsistent as well as shallow. On and off he preached and then abandoned socialism, anti-clericalism, republicanism, anti-imperialism, pacifism, and in April 1919 he had denounced every kind of dictatorship. At one moment he claimed to be the categoric antithesis of democracy, at another its most perfect manifestation. His one constant belief was that action was for the sake of action while consistency mattered not a whit: ideas and opinions were of minor importance, no more than tactical means to win the alliance of the Church or the conservatives or the trade unionists. Patriotism meant far less to him than one might suppose and, to judge from his abuse of them, he despised Italians as much as he did humanity in general. He glorified Italy only in so far as this redounded to his own glory, and readily handed her over to German occupation and civil war when she fell short of that purpose.

Mussolini was easily influenced, and his lieutenants quickly discovered his habit of agreeing with the last person he had spoken to. But perhaps no one held any continuous influence over him, not even the Petacci family who cornered him in his declining years. He had little sense of loyalty to former friends. Indeed he despised friendship. He boasted that he had never possessed a friend in his life, and almost no one was ever asked home to the Villa Torlonia. Despite having an impressive interview technique, he could be awkward in dealing with individuals, whereas he loved crowds and felt enlarged when addressing them. He was as self-consciously unsure of himself in private as he was self-consciously aggressive in public.

Always he was careful to take all the credit for any success, because this not only fed his vanity but prevented his lieutenants from gathering any popular support and becoming anything but abjectly subservient to his person. For the same reason he discouraged them from taking any political initiative. In return they were allowed to strut in fine uniforms and amass private fortunes, the chief losers being the Italian people who consequently were exploited and mis-governed by a new mediocre ruling class. Yet though he tried to monopolize any credit for success, he always found someone else to blame for failure, and perhaps reached that last pitch of delusion where he thought he could do no wrong. This divorce of power from responsibility was ruinous, and it allowed him to declare war without full appreciation of Italy's unpreparedness: such was the concentration of power in himself that he had only himself to blame. In 1926 he held the offices of Duce of facism, premier, and head of government, foreign minister, minister of the interior, minister for the Corporations, minister for all three service departments, and commander of the militia. At other times he was also minister for colonies and for public works. Mindful of the Code Napoléon, he also put his own amateurish stamp on new law codes said to be his personal handiwork and which were distributed in translation for the benefit of foreign imitators.

This was quite absurd, for no one could attend to so many jobs, and power thus became confusedly dispersed through a jungle of undersecretaries, *gerarchi*, and *ras*, who were frequently changed and were seldom given either the time to carry out any reform or the authority to consider policy over a broad enough field. The dictator's personal permission was needed before the police could change into their summer uniforms, but high policy sometimes went by default, and as minister of war he confessed to Bottai in 1939 that he had no idea that the artillery dated from World War I. Again and again he buried his head in the sand, either from ignorance and carelessness, or from a genuine fear of having to take the responsibility for policy decisions. Yet he told a British newspaperman that he controlled the whole life of the nation "from eighty-two keys on the switchboard of my desk."

48   Economic and Social Policy

Fascism began with no particular economic policy: its doctrines of planned economy were one day to be called typically fascist, but in fact they came as an afterthought. The first minister of finance, De Stefani, started rather by reducing government intervention and expenditure. He partly rationalized the tax system, and in the years 1924–26 the budget once again was balanced. Italy was meanwhile sharing in the general prosperity of contemporary Europe and liberal economists could approve of government policy.

In July 1925 De Stefani was replaced by the financier and industrialist Count Volpi and many vested interests at once began to profit from protection and central planning. First, import duties were heavily increased on grain, sugar, silk, and other commodities. Then the currency was heavily overvalued to put the lira on a par with the franc. Note circulation was heavily reduced and credit so restricted that the value of the dollar fell from 32 to 18 lire in the single year 1926–27. This raised export prices and damaged trade, though it benefited the bureaucrats and some of the middle classes whose salaries had depreciated during the postwar inflation. Meanwhile trade unions were forbidden to strike, and thirty vapid aphorisms were officially coined in 1927 with the grandiose title of a Charter of Labor. Mussolini in 1926 began his national "battle for grain," followed by another "battle to increase the population." The new trend can be seen in decrees issued for reducing the size of newspapers to save wood pulp, for diluting gasoline with alcohol made from wine or grain, and for once again

allowing a nine-hour working day. Gradually a planned economy was introduced, at least on paper. Self-sufficiency had become a principal aim by the
early 1930s, and the Leader declared that *"laissez-faire* is out of date." No one
could obtain employment without a worker's pass on which were included
details of political as well as personal industrial experience.

The postwar economic recovery began before fascism came into power and
reflected no very exceptional credit on the government. But the slump in Italy
started earlier than the collapse of the bull market on Wall Street and must be
ascribed in part to Mussolini's policy of revaluation and autarky. Tourism and
the trade in luxury commodities fell off. The rich complained that the lira was
valued too highly and a multiplying bureaucracy ate up too much of the
community's taxable wealth. Accordingly the salaries of government employees
were cut by 12 per cent. Those affected by this cut and by parallel wage
reductions found cold comfort when Mussolini told the Senate in December
1930 that "fortunately the Italian people were not accustomed to eat much and
therefore feel privation less acutely than others." When recovery commenced
after 1933, he contrived to attribute it to fascism, but he then started preparing
for war and began a progressive dislocation of the whole economy.

Fascism found it hard to alter Italy's dependence on foreign imports—in
1925 this dependence included 99 per cent of her cotton and mineral oil, 95 per
cent of her coal, and over half of her metals. Industry did make considerable
progress but mainly in fields related to military supply. Electricity was
subsidized and increased fivefold between 1917 and 1942. Sixty thousand
automobiles were produced in 1926, a figure not reached again until 1937. In
an attempt to modernize shipping, bounties were given for the scrapping of old
vessels, though uneconomic investments were made in big prestige liners such
as the "Rex" and the "Conte di Savoia" which might win records for a brief
period but could not compete profitably in transatlantic traffic. Moreover,
shipping construction seems to have declined in the 1930s, owing to the high
cost of steel plate which resulted from exorbitant protection and the lack of
competition. Schemes were devised to build oil refining installations at Bari and
Leghorn, and perhaps Mussolini believed his own statement that he would
make Italy self-sufficient in oil and gasoline by 1938. But achievements fell
ludicrously short of this aim, and had he understood the precariousness of
Italian heavy industry, he might have been less bellicose in foreign politics.

★

Mussolini was no mere instrument of business and agrarian interests, yet his
ignorance about economics and human nature left him a target for sharks who
wanted protective duties or who extracted money from the state for unrealistic
schemes of industrialization. Fascism had a close reciprocal understanding with
the big industrial trusts from which both sides gained, and several presidents of
the *Confindustria* became ministers. When Count Volpi, the leading industrialist
of Venice, took over the ministry of finance there was further talk of scandalous

relations between banking and politics. The industries of the Ansaldo group, which had collapsed in 1921, lent support to a government that would stimulate armament production and "nationalize" their losses. A new steel cartel arose in the early thirties which helped to keep inefficient firms alive, its express intention being to maintain high prices and control production, and consumers thus subsidized inefficiency in order to prevent a large uneconomic investment from losing its value. With such help, the Edison electricity company, Montecatini chemicals, Snia Viscosa artificial silk, and Pirelli rubber lost none of their dominant position. The Agnelli family, which controlled Fiat, became responsible for four-fifths of Italian automobile manufacture, as well as for numerous other operations that ranged from mining and smelting to making vermouth, cement, and newspapers. These were private concerns. Italian economy under fascism was not typified by direct state ownership, but in 1933 the Istituto per la Ricostruzione Industriale (IRI) was founded by the government to subsidize ailing industries and save those banks that had been too liberal in giving long-term credit. IRI by 1939 controlled many of Italy's leading firms in the heavy and mechanical industries and had interests stretching over a very extensive field of banking and manufacture.

Nevertheless, as employers found it increasingly necessary to go to Rome for credit, permits, and protection, they were bound to be irked by the delays and restrictions involved in dependence on such a government. Milanese business-men had welcomed fascism's nationalization of labor unions, but in the thirties they felt the brunt of capital levies, compulsory loans, and the high taxes which imperialism demanded. The war industries continued to thrive, though Italy's weakness in 1940 suggests that billions of lire may have been misappropriated. By a paradox, the obverse of dictatorship was inefficiency, and such a fact cannot have helped to ingratiate this type of government with the generality of businessmen.

An overvalued currency led to devaluation of industrial wages, and as early as 1926 the hard-earned eight-hour day was surrendered. The official index of wages told such a tale that its publication was suspended in 1927. Figures given by the International Labor Office in 1930 suggested that real wages in Italy were lower than anywhere in western Europe, and Professor Chabod, after trying to reconcile conflicting statistics from various ministries, later concluded that between 1926 and 1934 farm laborers lost 50 per cent of their real wages. Unemployment figures showed a million out of work in 1932–35.

By a typical about-turn Mussolini abandoned his boast to increase prosperity, and in May 1936 bragged instead that he was enforcing a more austere way of life: "We must rid our minds of the idea that the days of prosperity may return. We are probably moving toward a period when humanity will exist on a lower standard of living." By this time he had engaged on a policy of war and was taking money away from welfare in order to invest it in imperialism. People have estimated that three or four hundred thousand Italians at this time were still living in hovels made of earth and sticks, and others in caves or crowded up to ten in a room. To the abjectly poor a showy apparatus of social services was offered which was much more than the liberals had ever considered, but in great part was another piece of window dressing, and expenditure on social services probably absorbed less of the national income than in other European countries. Foreign visitors might not notice the increase in child labor but would be impressed by punctual mainline trains and police action against beggars.

★

These twenty years saw a new exodus from the land. The census of 1921 gave three-fifths of the working population as employed in agriculture, but that of 1931 gave only half. Mussolini strongly disliked this drift to the cities because industrial labor was factious and socialistic, and a law was passed in 1930 to stop workers moving except by permission of the prefects. Landowners were grateful for this because it kept their peasants tied to the soil and wages low. But industry suffered and rural overpopulation became worse, so much so that proprietors were sometimes instructed to employ a fixed proportion of workers per unit area of land. Not surprisingly this degree of coercion was only spasmodically obeyed.

Mussolini maintained that Italy was a land of smallholdings. But some seven thousand small properties a year continued to lapse to the exchequer for failure to pay land tax and nothing was done to divide up the large estates. A bill had already passed through the Lower House in 1921–22 to give part of these large estates to the peasants, and indeed this was a policy which Mussolini's personal newspaper had specifically supported, but after 1922 he was too much in thrall to the agrarians and the bill was quietly dropped. Fifteen noble families such as the Borghese, Caracciolo, Chigi, Colonna, and Torlonia continued to hold between them over a million acres of land, which was a sizable proportion of the total agricultural area. It was estimated that in 1930 there were some 3,500 *latifondi* each over 1,200 acres in size, comprising perhaps a fifth of the land under cultivation, while estates of 250 acres or more covered half the cultivable area of Italy. No doubt many large farms could not be split into small holdings without loss in productivity. Nevertheless, satisfaction of land hunger would have been the only way to prevent that flight from the countryside that Mussolini so deplored.

Some idea of the principal imports and exports of Italy at this time may be gained from the following tables for 1933:

Imports (in million lire)

Raw cotton	737
Coal and coke	685
Wheat	504
Machinery	365
Wool	361

Exports (in million lire)

Fruit and garden produce	1,091
Raw and artificial silk	820
Cotton fabrics and yarn	676
Cheese	241

These figures indicate how far Italy was still an agricultural nation and yet how dependent she was upon imports of grain.

The most striking alteration in her economy under fascism was in production of wheat. Ever since 1870 this had been little more than forty million quintals a year, but by 1930 Mussolini had raised this to sixty million, and by 1939 to eighty million. His *battaglia del grano* was highly successful. Medals for the most successful farmers were distributed each April 21—this date being chosen to rival the socialist May Day—and wheat imports were cut by 75 per cent in the ten years after 1925. The price was, however, dangerously high. Cereals were a product that was not particularly economical for Italy, and the result was to lower the gross output of agriculture and with it the national income. Mussolini's obsession about self-sufficiency drove him to produce the maximum quantity of wheat at any price instead of as much as could be produced economically. Marginal land was changed from cattle pasture and fruit trees, quite distorting the economy, and Italian wheat cost 50 per cent more than American.

While large-scale cereal growers grew fat on government subsidies, consumers were less able to make their voices heard. As wheat cost more, many Italians simply had to eat less, and the switch in land usage damaged olives, vines, and livestock. Political motives thus played havoc with Italian agriculture, and autarky mostly added to Italian economic problems instead of solving them as Mussolini had assumed. The relative index of variations in consumption per head given in the *Enciclopedia italiana* shows the effect of a rising cost of living:

	1922–29	1930–38
Wine	123	101
Wheat	100	91
Tobacco	99	81

With a decline in consumption of basic foodstuffs, small wonder that the infant mortality figures remained more than twice those in Scandinavia.

★

Another fascist "battle" was that for land reclamation under the generalship of undersecretary Serpieri. Mussolini soon discovered the advantages of *bonifiche* as proof of his own skill and enterprise, and in 1928 large government funds were appropriated to schemes of water regulation and mountain conservation. Positive achievements were the Emilia canal and the partial colonization of the

Volturno Valley and the Pontine marshes. The Agro Pontino was near Rome, and hence its reclamation was a particularly useful advertisement with foreign visitors. Several hundred thousand acres were reclaimed and hundreds of peasant families settled in a more successful scheme than any previous ruler of Italy had attempted. Here again, however, the work was marred by its political motivation, and it was said that proprietors who had the ear of some *gerarca* diverted subsidies to improve land that was already in good shape. When Mussolini turned away to pursue grandiose schemes of imperialism after 1934, payments on land reclamation dried up. Many of his improvements were lost in World War II, for as soon as dikes were unrepaired, marshland returned. Farm buildings scattered irrationally over the Sicilian *latifondi* also had to be abandoned when insufficient investment was forthcoming to change the prevailing type of extensive agriculture.

Progress was maintained in the development of communications. The mainline tourist trains ran more punctually than before and by 1939 some five thousand kilometers of track had been electrified. Fast traffic roads, or *autostrade*, were built to connect some of the principal towns in northern Italy. The aircraft industry never developed as successfully as Italian skill in automobile manufacture might have predicted. Italian planes won the Schneider trophy in 1920, 1921, and 1926, and Major de Bernardi set new world speed records in 1927 and 1928 with a Macchi seaplane powered by a Fiat motor; but subsequently the blight of fascism was a great hindrance to progress. Prizes and subsidies were liberally offered and by 1939 Italy's civil airlines covered a considerable mileage, but World War II found her deficient in types of warplane and industrial capacity. Mussolini boasted that he could blot out the sunlight with his air force, but he had no idea of the inefficiency and corruption attending his sort of totalitarianism.

The eighth national census in 1936 showed that Italian cities had absorbed two million more people during the previous fifteen years. Between 1871 and 1943 Rome grew to seven times its former size and Milan almost as fast. The coastal towns Taranto, Bari, Genoa, and Spezia also expanded considerably. The drying-up of overseas emigration contributed powerfully to this movement, and urbanization continued despite Mussolini's attempts to stop it by legislation.

The damming of the stream of emigration was one of the biggest changes in postwar Italy. In 1920 the current still ran strongly and about 350,000 Italians entered the United States alone. Then came the American immigration law of 1921 which laid down an annual quota for every nation, namely 3 per cent of its share in the U.S. foreign-born population as of 1910. The Italian quota was reduced to about forty thousand a year, and another law of 1924 cut this figure to about four thousand. After other countries followed suit, there were often more former emigrants returning to Italy each year than new ones leaving, especially as Mussolini was shortsighted enough to encourage this trend. Hence the standard of living diminished in many areas and the remittances sent home by emigrants were reduced. By 1939, as links with the homeland became severed, the sum of these remittances dropped from five billion lire to about five hundred million a year, a not inconsiderable loss in the balance of payments.

★

This drastic fall in emigration was made less catastrophic by a fall in the birth rate. Mussolini for some reason thought that national honor demanded a high rate of fertility and launched a "battle for births" with the optimistic target of increasing the population by one-third to sixty million before 1960. When the incredulous asked how such a number could live in Italy, the reply came in typical fascist language that they would live because they could not die, adding that such questions revealed a weary or anemic mentality. A large population meant more cannon fodder and would perhaps impress foreigners with Italy's need for colonies; it would also keep wages conveniently low. Faced with one of Italy's most chronic and intractable problems, it is interesting that Mussolini aimed to make it worse and not better.

He therefore subsidized matrimony. Fathers with conspicuously large families received higher wages, and the most prolific mothers in each region were made honorary members of the fascist party. Loans were advanced to newlyweds, to be repaid only if there were no children or not enough, and insurance policies were distributed by the officiating priest along with a copy of Pius XI's encyclical *Casti connubii*. Being unmarried was a serious impediment in most careers and in February 1939 was declared an absolute bar to promotion in government service. A progressive bachelors tax was introduced in 1926, exemption being allowed only to clergy and disabled veterans. Other interference in family life was taken to the point where parents were forbidden to give their children names which might sound like an offence to fascism. Women were encouraged to stay at home so as to have more time for children and to reduce unemployment. There was a fear that women as schoolteachers might be too religious and too pacific for the planned indoctrination of Italian youth. The potential labor force of the country was in this way heavily reduced just at the moment when war preparations forced a complete reversal of this particular policy.

Results were once again incommensurate with intentions. Excluding the exceptional war years of 1915–18, 1932 was the first year since 1876 in which there had been fewer than one million live births—a fact which perplexed and infuriated the Duce.

49 Fascist Doctrine

Fascism at first boasted of being a movement and not a doctrine. Action, said Mussolini, was of primary importance even when it was a blunder, and the theory or purpose behind action was less relevant. The battle was what mattered. "Believe, obey, and fight" was his motto for Italians, inscribed in Article 4 of the fascist party constitution, though the belief to which he was referring was in himself personally rather than in a creed.

The success of fascism in 1919–22 was due less to any interior logic or merit of its own than to the vacuum left by the failure of other Italian parties. Hence doctrine was not a main requisite, and indeed victory was even helped by a merely negative philosophy for fewer people were thereby antagonized. Mussolini's life had been a succession of negations, against the state, the socialists, and the Libyan war; against law and order and then against disorder; against parliament and liberalism, the Treaty of Versailles and the League of Nations, bolshevism and democracy. When asked to replace these negations with something positive he was often evasive and contradictory, for he had no fixed beliefs of his own and any positive statement was likely to offend some possible ally. Astoundingly enough, Mussolini came into power before people had more than a vague idea of what principles he stood for. The fact that Croce could think fascism empty of doctrine and therefore innocuous helps to explain how potential opposition was neutralized.

The most original contribution of Mussolini's kind of fascism was in technique, for instance, the use of castor oil to intimidate opponents. Nevertheless he skillfully maneuvered into a position where he was actually claiming that for the first time in modern history the Italians were giving the world a doctrine, a philosophy, a new style of living. This he did by making a patchwork of bits and pieces collected from friend and foe. He had learned the theory and practice of revolution from the socialists; his foreign policy, after a few false starts, was taken from the nationalists; the liberals around Gentile contributed a pseudophilosophical terminology; and from authoritarian parties in France he discovered how Catholicism could be used to underpin a strong state built on order and obedience.

This amalgam was never given quite enough time to set, and Mussolini went on mouthing imprecise slogans of doubletalk long after he had decided that fascism was after all a doctrine as well as a movement. Sometimes he instructed fascists to live with a high seriousness and passionate conviction; sometimes they were prescribed the "could not care less" attitude summed up in their uncivilized motto *me ne frego*. Relying on people's forgetfulness, he said that he was a friend of England and yet her irreconcilable enemy. He was the only disinterested champion of the League, yet also its destroyer—both these facts being treated as matter for boasting. He meant to bring both peace and a sword:

> We represent a new principle in the world, the clear, final and categoric antithesis of democracy, plutocracy, Freemasonry, and "the immortal principles of 1789."

> The ideals of democracy are exploded, beginning with that of "progress." Ours is an aristocratic century; the state of all will end by becoming the state of a few.

> Fascism is the purest kind of democracy, so long as people are counted qualitatively and not quantitatively.

The clearest statements can be found in an article on fascism in the *Enciclopedia italiana*, an article written about 1931 and signed by Mussolini but obviously composed by Gentile and perhaps others. Here at last it was boldly asserted that fascism had a doctrine: that of the Ethical State which manufactured its own system of morality and owed no allegiance to anything outside itself; also that of the Nation in Arms which had to fight in order to justify its own existence:

> The fascist conception of the state is all-embracing, and no human or spiritual values can exist outside of the state.

> Perpetual peace would be impossible and useless. War alone brings all human energies to their highest state of tension and stamps with the seal of nobility the nations which dare to face it.

Mussolini's article became the last word in philosophic speculation, just as his speeches had already become a bible from which texts could be extracted to suit all occasions. Every few hundred yards along the roadside the traveler would see emblazoned in large letters on the whitewashed walls of a house the terse and pregnant quotations that every schoolchild knew by heart: "He who has steel has bread"; "Better to live one day as a lion than a hundred years as a sheep"; "Nothing against the state, nothing outside the state"; "Nothing is ever won in history without bloodshed." In order to immortalize these gnomic prescriptions a fascist faculty of political science was established at Perugia in 1927, followed by the creation of a "School of Fascist Mysticism" at Milan to debate what they signified. The true fascist, said a decree on the militia, must have his mind "pervaded by a profound mysticism." Groups of professors were instructed by visiting party bureaucrats about not trying to put their own reasoning capacity on a level with the Duce's, for between them and the leader was "a simply astronomical gap."

One of Mussolini's chief mentors in establishing the intellectual content of fascism was the Sicilian philosopher, Giovanni Gentile, who had split away from Croce and his fellow liberals. In 1925 Gentile drew up a fascist manifesto to send to foreign intellectuals, signed by Pirandello, Ungaretti, Soffici, Pizzetti, and Panzini among others. This was in reply to Croce's antifascist manifesto signed by Einaudi, Ferrero, Fortunato, Mosca, Salvemini, Salvatorelli, Jemolo, Ruffini, and Calamandrei who formed an even more distinguished list. Gentile became minister of education, member of the *Gran Consiglio*, president of the Istituto Fascista di Cultura, and general editor of the *Enciclopedia*. He was a person of great intelligence, but his vanity was tickled when fascism temporarily adopted the philosophical jargon of Actual Idealism. Croce also believed in the strong state, yet drew back as soon as he realized its practical implications. Gentile on the contrary turned somersaults to prove that all true liberals must become fascists, and he had insufficient self-respect to rebel when Mussolini contemptuously declared that "one *squadista* was worth two philosophers."

Gentile's task was to justify fascism theoretically, to rationalize its boasted anti-intellectual bias, to demonstrate how its proclaimed lack of a philosophy might be itself a philosophy, and how its frequent changes of policy could be comprehended into a program of higher opportunism:

> Often the Duce, with his profound intuition of fascist psychology, has told us the truth, that we all participate in a sort of mystic sentiment. In such a mystic state of mind we do not form clear and distinct ideas, nor can we put into precise words the things we believe in, but it is in those mystic moments when our soul is enveloped in the penumbra of a new world being born that creative faith germinates in our hearts. ... The fascist spirit is will, not intellect. ... Intellectual fascists must not be *intellectuals*.

Again, with another paradox, Gentile adapted Croce's Hegelianism to attract right-wing Italian liberals into the fascist party:

> The Duce once discussed whether action should be by force or consent, and concluded that the authority of the state and the liberty of the subject are counterparts and inseparable. ... Fascism does not oppose authority to liberty, but sets a system of real and concrete freedom against an abstract and false parody. ... Even in the nineteenth century people were beginning to think that a strong state was necessary in the interests of liberty itself. ... One can even say that the new Corporative State, by stressing the identification of liberty with authority, and through a system of representation which corresponds better with reality, is more liberal than the old.

There was apparently sufficient speciousness in all this to appeal to many who were steeped in the fashionable idealist philosophy. It was easy to make fun of the skeptical prewar liberalism

... which dared do nothing because it believed in nothing and saw no point in sacrifice; which used to measure the national fortunes by the standard of individual well-being, but never liked to compromise itself or to get heated about anything, preferring to put on one side any question that might imperil *quieto vivere*; which threw the cold water of prose upon the enthusiasm of poetry, and recommended moderation at all costs.

Nevertheless, Gentile leaned over backward to the other extreme, justifying the cruelties of *squadrismo* and writing pages of nonsense about the austerity of the *stile fascista*. He was bold enough to say that in the corporative system the Italian genius was once again leading the world, for the first time since the age of the Renaissance.

Gentile's ideas were later repudiated by the regime. Fascists did not like clever people, and Gentile's use of an umbrella showed him to be out of touch with the true fascist style. When he made an unguarded remark about fascism being a minority movement he was publicly disavowed, and the breach became wider after Mussolini signed a treaty with the Vatican in 1929. Gentile's own educational reform of 1923, which Mussolini once called the essential fascist reform, had been inspired by the belief that the dogmas of the Church were no more than a useful halfway house to the truth and suitable for teaching only in primary schools. When fascism sensed the need of full alliance with the Church, Gentile fell from grace. He remained on and off an officeholder, and was eventually assassinated by antifascists in 1944.

★

Mussolini's inspirational method of extempore speechmaking sometimes led him to pose as a philistine and say that he cared nothing for the past, but in his contrary pose as an intellectual he set great store by rooting his movement in Italian historical traditions. Research was vigorously organized for this purpose under De Vecchi who lectured university professors about how fascism should be differentiated from everything in Italian history that was unwarlike, parliamentary, or bourgeois. Their job, said De Vecchi, was to explain that history knew no more profound revolution than fascism. At the same time the regime had to be linked with Mazzini, Foscolo, Dante, and other great names of the past, because in history and politics their movement was somehow simultaneously ultra-conservative and ultra-revolutionary.

Imperial Rome was a favorite hunting ground for moral lessons and heroic exemplars. Mussolini thus announced that Caesar was the greatest man who had ever lived, and he innocently and comically called Shakespeare's *Julius Caesar* the finest school for statesmen. He took the fascist symbol from the *fasces* carried by the lictors of ancient Rome, and such words as consul, cohort, and centurion were now self-consciously resuscitated. Archaeology therefore came into its own. "Fascism," said the minister of education De Vecchi, "has solved the most formidable problems of archaeology and art through the mind and will power of the Duce." An ambitious excavation of the Forums at Rome was started in 1924, and in ten years completely altered this region of the city, bringing to light what was Roman at the expense of what was Christian and medieval. A monumental Via dell'Impero was built as an ugly scar through these excavations, and there was even vandalistic talk of opening up another imperial route between the Pantheon and the monument to Marcus Aurelius in Piazza Colonna. Meanwhile, large outdoor maps in marble relief showed the extent of the Roman Empire, with the implication that what Rome had done once she could do again. In the new penumbral jargon, life had to be lived *romanamente*. Mussolini in October 1928 instituted a ceremony for patriotic citizens to present their national savings certificates as a burnt offering on an ancient altar of Minerva brought out of its museum for the purpose.

Other periods were likewise investigated to find forerunners. The Middle Ages were played down as a period of weakness, though Dante was excepted as being a premature nationalist. The Duce said he read Plato and Dante every day and knew all the works of Shakespeare and Molière. He used to recall listening to his father read Machiavelli's *Prince* aloud, and he himself chose the theme of this book when he lent his name to a slight disquisition for an honorary doctoral degree at Bologna. The Renaissance itself was not, however, uncritically accepted in the new canon, as it was said to have diverted Italians into a ruinous individualism. Renaissance rulers were faulted for spending money on beauty instead of on making a strong and victorious state.

The nineteenth-century *risorgimento* exemplified more of the authentic fascist ebullience and encouraged Mussolini to believe that he was the fulfillment of a logical process of history. Garibaldi had been a Duce with a colored shirt and was marked as a precursor by his acts of piracy, his balcony speeches, and his militarized youth corps. Benevolent and liberal-minded though he was, Garibaldi chose the title of dictator when he ruled over half the peninsula, believing that "the only way to get Italians to agree with each other was by using armed force; nothing less."

The official professors were also instructed to praise Mazzini, who spent much of his life crusading against socialism and against a parliamentary system that he saw as corrupting and undemocratic. Mazzini was praiseworthy for stressing that the individual had duties before he could claim rights. Mazzini and Garibaldi, though both would certainly have opposed fascism, had a vision of national grandeur that the fascists could appreciate.

Fascist historiography could also, with some difficulty, find antecedents among conservative liberals. Some right-wing liberals had always wanted an extension of governmental controls, and it was the Right not the Left which first advocated nationalization of the railroads. Bonghi, although a good liberal, had concluded that Italian parliamentary government worked well only when a man of genius such as Cavour had coerced it into operation. Sonnino and Mosca were equally dubious about the practice of representative government.

The young Orlando, likewise disillusioned with parliament, had written in 1884: "Our only hope is in the appearance of a *deus ex machina*, that is to say a man of such demonstrably superior qualities and such determined intention that he would seize the rudder of the state and pervade every aspect of people's lives with a sense of positive government action." The arrogant Crispi had been vain enough to imagine himself just such a superman and had reason to think that Italians would welcome a disciplined authoritarian state. Unlike northern Europe where many people inherited a disbelief and an individualism from the Reformation, Italians had been brought up in an ecclesiastical tradition that demanded perfect obedience.

These past memories help in part to explain why parliamentary government broke down in 1922. Fascist historians were able to find precursors everywhere and to suggest that arbitrary rule came naturally to the national temperament. From Rienzi to Masaniello and D'Annunzio there had been many notable demagogues before Mussolini. Enlightened despots, Jacobins, Bonapartism, national unification by conquest and plebiscite, irredentism and imperialism, all were wrought into a pattern by obedient official historians. The intent was to confer an aspect of inevitability on the events of 1922 and to make Italians feel that by nature and history they were destined for this high fate. All roads led to Rome, to what Mussolini liked to call the Third Rome, in which he aimed to outdo all the Caesars and popes of the past two millennia.

50   The Standardization of Culture

Artists and intellectuals can be as irrational as anyone in their political judgments. Pirandello signed the manifesto of fascist intellectuals and put on the gaudy fascist uniform of Mussolini's new Academy. Shortly before his death, Puccini gave his blessing to fascism and was made a senator. The *doyen* of Italian economists, Pantaleoni, was also made a senator and so was the sociologist Pareto. Marconi, too, had his pride caressed when he was created a marquis and his advice was asked on politics. Mussolini later remembered this as "the time of the carrot and the stick," and experience taught him that these two weapons were effective with most people. A decree of 1933 prescribed, on paper at least, that party membership was necessary for any administrative post, and Croce agreed with the pope that an oath of allegiance to fascism was a formality which could be accepted even by nonfascists if needed for promotion.

Croce himself, though his writings might be removed from schools and libraries, possessed an integrity and an economic independence that allowed him to remain adamantly distinct from fascism after 1925. D'Annunzio, on the other hand, easily capitulated to the grant of a pension, and a palatial villa was bestowed on him as a national monument in which he could indulge his unamiable eccentricities. Mindful of the absolute power he had enjoyed as Regent of Fiume he was presented with the forecastle of a naval ironclad which he erected in his garden by Lake Garda; sentries stood by it on duty, and the poet used to welcome visitors by a salute of guns corresponding to their merit or title, as though he were still a sovereign power. D'Annunzio was created Prince of Monte Nevoso, one of the few examples of princely rank conferred in modern Italian history. Mussolini invented several new titles for himself, and made De Pinedo a marquis for flying around the world in 120 days.

The intellectuals were drilled into corporations like everyone else, because fascism hoped to prevent any untidy leftovers or people who claimed some vestigial independence of thought. After 1933, compulsory uniforms were introduced even for professors and civil servants as a symbol of their new uniformity of mind, and medals were distributed annually for "fascist" achievements in art, culture, and sport. A National Council of Research was created, over which Marconi and Marshal Badoglio presided with considerable powers of patronage, while Gentile's Fascist Institute of National Culture subsidized periodicals and set up libraries for the study of what fascism meant.

Between 1926 and 1929 the Fascist Academy was conceived, to co-ordinate all work in the arts and sciences, to "preserve for our intellectual life its national character according to the genius of our race, and to favor its expansion abroad." There were to be sixty academicians, all chosen by Mussolini, paid a generous salary, addressed as "Your Excellency," receiving free first-class travel, and given a mock-antique uniform complete with plumed hat and gilt sword. Pirandello and Marinetti were obvious choices as inaugural members. Tittoni, Marconi, D'Annunzio, and Federzoni, successively its presidents, had perquisites on an even more luxurious scale.

Their duties were negligible. They awarded titles and decorations, banned words of foreign derivation, and decided that everyone ought to address his neighbor only in the stilted language of the second person plural. A few academicians became as much at home in fascist parades as in the arts and sciences, and the photographs of them goose-stepping at the Roman salute have a macabre fascination. Papini and the composer Mascagni look oddly placed in this *galère*. But the honor and remuneration without doubt caused a crisis of conscience among an important class of people. Some signatories of Croce's antifascist manifesto in 1925 had become apologists for the regime ten years later, because Mussolini used the carrot to good effect.

A rap with the stick was also used when professors in 1931 were required to swear an oath of loyalty to fascism. This oath was generally considered a mere formality and nearly all the professors did as they were bid. Orlando and De Viti de Marco preferred to resign. Eleven others made their names celebrated by refusing to swear, and forfeited their salaries. These included De Sanctis the ancient historian, Lionello Venturi the art historian, Ruffini the canon lawyer, and Buonaiuti the modernist theologian who had come under ecclesiastical ban. Students were incited to mob those teachers who refused to burn their pinch of incense, but sometimes had the sense to respect such signal courage and integrity. If there had been hundreds of refusals instead of eleven it would have carried weight with public opinion and abroad.

When the racial laws were introduced in 1938, some ninety scholars were dismissed for being "racially impure." Of the two leading Italian mathematicians, Volterra had already refused the oath, and now Levi-Civita was dismissed. Others who had Jewish friends and relatives were pushed into voluntary or involuntary retirement and exile. The physicist Fermi refused to return home after receiving his Nobel prize in Oslo, and as two of his leading colleagues in Rome followed him, the loss to Italy in the field of nuclear physics was incalculable. Together with the bureaucratization of universities and the blatant selection of professors for political reasons, this persecution helps to explain the backwardness of Italian science in assisting the war effort after 1939.

In literature and history some of the party bosses put their names to—and perhaps even wrote—books purporting to be serious contributions to scholarship. In Croce's magazine, *La Critica*, a true scholar such as Omodeo was able to expose some extraordinary examples of plagiarism in such work, but he had to pay for his courage and not many others were ready to risk their careers. The vagaries of the censorship were notorious. Fisher's *History of Europe* was confiscated from bookstores in 1939 by order of a new dignitary called the Minister of Popular Culture. An index of prohibited books was also drawn up for libraries, in which, along with Robert Graves and Axel Munthe, Machiavelli and Boccaccio were in 1939 declared "unsuitable to the fascist spirit." By that time the lunatic elements of fascism were in full control. But fortunately a pervasive inefficiency, plus a certain amount of good-natured tolerance, allowed for more freedom of expression than was possible in nazi Germany.

★

It is unlikely that posterity will greatly value most of the artistic and cultural achievements from this quarter of a century. Pascoli and Fogazzaro had died before World War I; Modigliani the painter died in 1920, Pareto in 1923, Puccini and the Duse in 1924. The leaders of the next generation were of smaller stature, and the central controls of fascism were inevitably a brake and a hindrance on creative work. Political motives helped to weaken links with France and so to cut off Italy from the most vital source of challenge and renewal. German influence was more encouraged, especially as Mussolini himself had acquired a fair superficial acquaintanceship with German culture and took German lessons to the end of his life. Beethoven and Wagner he much preferred to Puccini, or so he said; but Vittorio Mussolini often saw his father asleep during Wagner's operas.

Mussolini intended fascism to be strikingly creative and sought hard to discover for it a cultural identity. Successive experts restlessly pursued one novelty after another, though the results usually lacked individuality and character. The ubiquitous but hazy "fascist style" was dragged into art as well as into manners and even religion. Dragged is the only word, for Mussolini had no love of art and once praised Marinetti's suggestion to dispose of the national galleries in exchange for foreign currency. What he would have liked, he told Ciano, was museums with fewer pictures or statues and more enemy flags captured in battle. He boasted of never having set foot in a museum or art gallery until Hitler took him on a minute examination of the Pitti and Uffizi, and the boredom of that occasion remained a painful memory.

Marinetti the futurist had been the earliest literary influence in fascism, but futurism was *passé* before the fascists had caught on to its usefulness. The religious conversion of Papini about 1918 was symptomatic of an already existing return from futuristic excesses back to order, discipline, and traditional language; and Papini became a keen fascist. Bacchelli, Baldini, and Ungaretti were turning to more classical models of prose and poetry after the crude paroxysms of yesterday's *avant garde*, but they were too intellectual for Mussolini. In an attempt to exemplify the fascist style in literature, the Duce himself became a much applauded playwright, and so did the barely literate Farinacci, with unimpressive results.

Pirandello's best work was already written by the end of 1921, in which year he composed *Enrico IV* and *Six Characters in Search of an Author*. In 1934 he won a Nobel prize for literature. But he was not outstandingly popular in Italy and after the first performance of *Sei personaggi* had been hissed into the street. In his lugubrious characters it is possible to glimpse something of the spiritual emptiness of postwar Italy; they believed that life was a bad joke, vain and useless, and private illusions alone afforded any protection—an apt enough commentary on fascism, even though not Mussolini's idea of the *stile fascista*. Among the younger generation, Moravia's brilliant novel of 1928, *Gli indifferenti*, held another mirror up to fascist Italy, describing a cynical, existentialist world, peopled with characters devoid of belief and purpose; but its irony was wasted on the *bien pensants*.

In sculpture and painting there was an artificial culture that awarded prizes to those who depicted fascist successes and martyrology. Fascism inherited no ready-made school or tradition and not much success was registered in creating a new style to reflect the inner nature of Mussolini's revolution. Futurist artists such as Carrà, metaphysical painters such as De Chirico and Morandi, the sculptors Marini and the younger Manzù, with neocubists, neorealists, tonalists, hermetic poets, and the rest, managed to exist alongside the safe academic art which flourished on official patronage.

In architecture the fascist period showed much more character. It has been said that architects flourish under a dictatorship as much as lawyers in a democracy. Buildings can become good publicity, and countless post offices and town halls proved to be effective vehicles for the grandiose and magniloquent impressions that fascism hoped to convey. Compared with the baroque Rome of Bernini, the much larger "Humbertine" Rome palpably lacked a consistent character and is remembered mostly for its gigantic official follies. The new fascist style was unashamedly modernist. It transplanted, or rather translated and traduced, Gropius and Le Corbusier, using harsh geometrical lines and large white plain surfaces to replace the pilasters, loggias, and elaborate façades which had for so long been used to soften the glaring sunlight of Italy. At its most successful there was Michelucci's railroad station at Florence, and a younger school of engineers led by Nervi and Ponti was to show an artistry in reinforced-concrete hangars and office buildings that won world-wide admiration after 1945. At its worst, Mussolini's taste showed a reversion to the classical and "Roman," almost always spectacular and violent, and often vulgar. At international exhibitions the Italian pavilion had if possible to be higher and showier than others, and the unfinished tower of Babel on the outskirts of Rome is an impressive but melancholy reminder of pretentiousness and vainglory.

The history of these twenty years was not synonymous with that of fascism. There were Toscanini and the other exiles abroad, and even in Italy there was always some nonconformity to interrupt the monologue that issued from Palazzo Venezia. It is tempting to say that the best creative work came from the non-co-operators. There were fine works of historical scholarship by Omodeo, De Sanctis, De Ruggiero, Chabod, and many more. The better novelists of Bacchelli's generation showed no purely official qualities in their novels, and much of Treccani's huge and impressive *Enciclopedia italiana* is free of political slant. Einaudi and Gramsci were major figures outside the system. Above all there was Croce, who as writer, thinker, critic of art and literature had an immeasurable influence on all intelligent people. In a hundred ways Croce exposed the bad taste and shoddy thinking which threatened to characterize a whole generation of Italians, and luckily he had too big a world reputation to be suppressed.

Fascism was too casual, and perhaps too self-consciously on the defensive, to be as insidious and deep-rooted an evil as nazism. Nevertheless, despite the few creative artists who had the courage, integrity, and means of livelihood to hold aloof from official direction, the damage done was incalculable. Many writers, artists, and thinkers depended on official money, and this made it the more disastrous that a policy of artistic autarky ran parallel with political and economic autarky. The music and drama of "sanctionist" states was thus forbidden during the Abyssinian war, while jazz was always deprecated as something alien to the race, and the use of foreign words was not permitted.

Such a doctrine of cultural self-sufficiency betrayed a lack of confidence and an unwillingness to compete that was both symptom and cause of artistic decay.

*

The education of the young was vitally important for a government which boasted of upsetting conventional standards of morality, justice, and civilized behavior. Official policy laid down that Italians must be brought up to be more warlike and tough, less artistic, less "nice" or likeable, and to be always "desperately serious." Above all they had to become less individualistic and more amenable to discipline.

The education act of 1923 sponsored by Gentile was passed before Mussolini developed ideas of his own. It allowed considerable freedom to private schools and universities. It stressed the value of humanist education and promoted the teaching of philosophy at every level. It also laid down that examinations were to test not facts learned by rote, but understanding and expression. Gentile's philosophical method became vacuous and rhetorical in the hands of lesser men, and perhaps Italy's chief need was not more philosophy but that very scientific and technological education which Croce and Gentile thought to be of minor importance. Nevertheless, Gentile's reform contained few of the usual fascist banalities, and it helped to preserve some independence of mind in education during the dark days to come.

It was typical of fascism that one reform should cancel out another. Instead of the stability which Mussolini had promised, he soon had to invert his thesis and proclaim that fascism was not a revolution once and for all, but a perpetual revolution. His ministers changed quite as rapidly as their predecessors. Eight ministers of education, eight ministers of public works, nine ministers for the colonies followed each other in the fourteen years after 1922. The syllabus for schools was repeatedly changed; textbooks were rewritten when Fedele wanted more religion, or when Ercole wanted more economics, and yet more radically when De Vecchi ordained that every detail of education must be infused with the highest fascist principles. Bottai then discountenanced mixed-sex schools since male supremacy was a fascist principle. But the basic problems of education remained unsolved, and the seventh national census in 1931 still gave 48 per cent of illiterates in the backward region of Calabria, while the eighth census in 1936 pointedly omitted to give any figures at all.

"Fascist culture" and "corporative law" were introduced into the schools, though teachers must have been puzzled what these topics meant. Professorships of political economy were renamed professorships of corporative political economy. The subject of history was disciplined and twisted in order to illustrate Italian "primacy" in many diverse fields. Over a hundred history textbooks were forbidden by a special commission in 1926, and ten years later a few standardized texts were in compulsory use. The polarization of history around the year 1922—*anno primo*—was indicated by a new calendar superseding the outmoded reckoning of dates from the birth of Jesus Christ. Balbo's description of his flight across the Atlantic in 1933 became Italian literature and a set text for secondary schools. The Italian language was enriched with new words coined by Mussolini, and whole books were written to analyze the subtlety and vigor of the leader's literary style. The words chosen for spelling lessons were connected with fighting. Children were taught how Italy had saved Britain and America in World War I and how Mussolini had made Italy "the first nation in the world."

Selected phrases from the compulsory reader issued for eight-year-olds in 1936 give some indication of the kind of education which fascism now intended to impart.

The eyes of the Duce are on every one of you. No one can say what is the meaning of that look on his face. It is an eagle opening its wings and rising into space. It is a flame that searches out your heart to light there a vermilion fire. Who can resist that burning eye, darting out its arrows? But do not be afraid; for you those arrows will change into rays of joy.

A child, who, even while not refusing to obey, asks "Why?," is like a bayonet made of milk. ... "You must obey because you must," said Mussolini, when explaining the reasons for obedience.

How can we ever forget that fascist boy who, when near to death, asked that he might put on his uniform and that his savings should go to the party?

To the victor who has conquered the Abyssinians we owe eternal gratitude and obedience for winning the greatest colonial war that history has recorded. ... The Empire has been created by our rooted conviction that "Mussolini is always right."

An essential part of fascist education was the conscription of youth into quasi-military units. At the age of four a child became a "son of the she-wolf" and wore his first black shirt; at eight he joined the *Balilla*, at fourteen the *Avanguardisti*—Balilla was the nickname of a Genoese boy who was said to have started a civic rebellion against the Austrians in 1746. These children were trained to military discipline, and toy machine guns were manufactured for their entertainment. They were instructed in *cultura fascista*, which they were then expected to retail among their families. Official chaplains were attached to the *Balilla*, and this partially appeased the Church after a monopoly on youth clubs had been obtained by organizations which were pagan in fact and militaristic in theory. Millions of young Italians passed through this poisonous process of indoctrination.

★

Other methods of propaganda were limited, since most Italians had not acquired the habit of listening to the radio or reading newspapers. Even the provincial Catholic press filled most of its pages with fascist hand-outs in order to be able to print the bishop's letter and events of the ecclesiastical calendar. Mussolini made his first broadcast speech over Marconi's new system in 1924, but a technical hitch made his words difficult to hear and he was cut off. Radio was a strict government monopoly and a law of 1927 set up a special organization which later became *Radio Italiana*. A policy was eventually laid down for radio programs to be governed by "a rigorously autarkic cultural spirit" and parliament greeted this order with loud applause. Mussolini rarely gave talks specially for the radio because he discovered that fireside chats did not suit his style of oratory.

The Italian film industry was not organized until relatively late. Historical films were always a favorite with their pageantry and reminders of national greatness. Lucrezia Borgia, the battle of Lepanto, the last days of Pompeii, Nero, Julius Caesar, even Dante, all were made into films at least once. On the introduction of talkies after 1926, another speciality was opera and dramatizations of the lives of composers such as Verdi and Bellini. After 1929, films with a fascist bent became more common, but people found them dull when compared to American importations. Mussolini had films shown for him most evenings at home. He preferred comedies and especially those featuring Laurel and Hardy. He tried at first to forbid films with foreign dialogue, and then allowed foreign products a quota of only one to ten. This caused American companies in 1939 to withdraw from Italy, and the consequent decline in competition gave Italian producers a guaranteed market however poor their efforts. For this reason, and because of the demands of propaganda, good films such as the *Siege of Alcazar* were exceptional. Yet subsequent development of the new realist school with De Sica and Visconti revealed a fund of latent talent, and with the removal of central direction and ideological prejudice, Italy after 1945 was ready to take a front place in the world of cinema.

*

A totalitarian regime had to stake out moral dominion over every sphere of individual life including recreation and sport. Here national prestige could be asserted ostentatiously and the nation's physique could be improved against a day of bloodier battle. The vogue of sport, like the word itself, had been introduced from Britain late in the nineteenth century. Sella in 1863 helped to organize the first Alpine society two years before the first ascent of the Matterhorn. In 1870 the first cycling club was founded in Milan, and after 1909 the *giro d'Italia* became one of the big events of the year. The second favorite sport was football, for which a club was started as early as 1890 in Genoa. From 1908 when the first Italian championship was held, football spread rapidly until there were ten thousand recognized clubs. Fox-hunting also was brought in from England, and there was a golf society in Rome by 1903.

Mussolini did his best to organize these importations and even tried to instill the fascist style into sport through a new and short-lived game called *volata*. The organization of leisure was a paramount aim of the new ideology, so *"il weekend"* was abolished and in 1935 became by law *"il sabato fascista."* Sport eventually was made into another fascist monopoly: for example, the Olympic Games committee had to be affiliated with the party, and the president of the Italian chess association was another party appointment. The physical education of the young benefited from official encouragement, and the *Dopolavoro* institution provided excellent cheap vacations and recreation for workers. Many international victories were also won in bicycle and motor racing, and in 1933 the carpenter Primo Carnera beat Sharkey at New York to become world heavyweight boxing champion, the newspapers being instructed never to show pictures of him knocked down in the ring. Boxing, said Mussolini, "was an essentially fascist method of self-expression." In February 1939 the Italian lawn tennis association decreed that all players in international matches should wear fascist uniform and respond with the fascist salute when their opponents offered to shake hands—like many other orders it was disobeyed.

The football industry was purged as early as 1926 and reorganized on lines "more consonant with the new life of the nation." This sport was said to be not an importation; it was rather a development of the old Tuscan *calcio* which had long ago been forbidden because of the casualties it caused. Its control now passed from local clubs to a central body with a honeycomb of divisional, zonal, and federal directors. By 1937 there were 52,000 players licensed to play and 2,700 authorized referees under the chief referee at Rome with his gold whistle. As a "typically Italian creation" there was to be a new official, the *commissario di campo*, sent by the federal director to "invigilate" the behavior of players and the public. He drew up a private report on each game and sent it to the zonal Directorate of Football where it was then compared with that of the referee. Sport, as in other countries, was thus encouraged to pass from dilettanti to professionals, from the countryside to the large metropolitan towns, for only big stadiums could pay for the grand spectacles that were part of the choreography of fascism.

51   Persecution and Its Effects

The tale of misery caused by fascism will never be fully known. Humanitarian feelings prevented anything remotely resembling the wholesale murder practiced in Germany or Russia, and there was a sentimental side to Mussolini's character which had unexpected if unimportant manifestations. Yet fascism exalted brutality into an officially imposed creed and the police did not usually interfere when the squads were on a weekend spree. Harmless citizens, if they escaped being beaten by the *manganello*, might have their heads shaved and painted with the national colors, or they might have to perform some revolting act to humiliate them as a means of intimidation. More commonly they would be forced to drink half a pint of castor oil in the fascist "baptism" designed to purge people from the sin of opposition by imposing the maximum public indignity on its victims.

This purgative action was so capricious and unsystematic that in one province a man might be in danger of his life and yet be a minor public figure in another. In general the liberals and *popolari* were left in peace so long as they abstained from open political action, but occasional severities were designed to generate fear and make a public example of any lukewarmness. People who joined the Aventine secession in 1924 or who signed Croce's "antifascist manifesto" in 1925 suffered in their profession unless they later groveled in penitence, and any former Freemason or socialist might find himself at the mercy of some private enemy who could pay off a grudge without cost to himself.

In November 1926 a special police body was created to prosecute antifascism. A special tribunal was also set up as an organ of the fascist party rather than of the state, from which there was no appeal and which could hear cases *in camera*. While the *carabinieri* were a semi-military police force that kept some loyalty to the king, the more highly paid OVRA, or secret police, was essentially an arm of the party. Luckily Bocchini, the head of police, was a not disagreeable cynic who saw through Mussolini and kept a residual sense of legality and decency that was sometimes used to modify the letter of the law. Luckily, too, the characteristic carelessness of fascism created what the head of the OVRA says were as many as twenty separate and rival police forces, often unknown to and sometimes working against each other. Senise, who was Bocchini's sucessor in 1940–43, recorded that he was answerable to no one for the very large sums at his disposal. Bocchini and Senise were seldom mentioned in the press. Their political prisoners were confined on the penal islands, while lesser suspects, as, for instance, the painter-novelist Carlo Levi, might be sent under surveillance to live in some remote and primitive village.

★

Between 1924 and 1926, many people had to decide whether to take the path of exile. Among the first political expatriates were Nitti, Sforza, Don Sturzo, Amendola, Gobetti, Salvemini, and De Ambris. Then followed Turati, Treves, Nenni, Saragat, and Modigliani. Of the communist leaders, Gramsci returned from Russia to live the rest of his life a captive, in Italy while Togliatti replaced him as representative of their party in Moscow. One or two exiles came back later, as Labriola returned from New York to support the Abyssinian war. In a different category was the gifted young writer Lauro de Bosis, who first went to scrape a living in Paris, and then met a heroic and mysterious end in 1931 after dropping antifascist leaflets over Rome from the plane he had barely learned to fly.

The story of these exiles is tragic, not least in exemplifying the doctrinaire extremism, political fecklessness, and mutual intolerance between parties that had already helped fascism into power. The bitterness and idleness of exile were enough to break the spirit of all whose quality was not of the finest, and there was a continuous succession of quarrels and splits between the various parties and inside each party. Nevertheless, those who survived were to bring back a priceless experience of freedom after 1943.

Of those who died, the most famous antifascist martyr was Carlo Rosselli. He had been driven into active politics by his horror at the murder of Matteotti. In association with Salvemini and younger liberals such as Bauer and Ernesto Rossi, he edited a clandestine paper called *Non mollare* (*Don't Weaken*), which had to be printed in one house after another to avoid discovery. In 1926, Rosselli and Parri (who survived to become prime minister in 1945) smuggled the elderly Turati by motorboat to Corsica and then chose to return to imprisonment. In 1929 a famous escape was organized from the Lipari Islands by Rosselli, and thereafter he lived a precarious existence in Paris editing that most famous of antifascist papers, *Justice and Liberty*.

Mussolini could not let this pass unpunished. Close watch was kept on these exiles in Paris, and a grandson of Garibaldi was employed as an *agent provocateur*. When Mussolini intervened in the Spanish civil war, Rosselli went to Spain with Nenni and the communist Longo to fight for the republic against General Franco, as did five thousand other Italian antifascists. But political differences diminished their military effectiveness. Rosselli returned to France disillusioned with this particular fight for freedom. Soon afterwards he and his brother Nello were assassinated near Paris by Mussolini's hirelings.

★

Fascist persecution was also directed against the two hundred thousand southern Germans in the Alto Adige whom the Treaty of Versailles had given to Italy, and even more against the half million Slavs who had been annexed in the five provinces of Gorizia, Pola, Trieste, Fiume, and Zara. Fascism proclaimed that there could be no minorities in Italy, only Italians. As early as 1923, German place names were changed, use of the German language was restricted, and Italians were imported to dilute the German character of the Trentino–Alto Adige and its "ethnographical relics." When monasteries were forcibly handed over to Italian abbots, the Prince Bishop of Trent, Endrici, did more than connive at this, and in 1926 he ordered that religious instruction was to be given only in Italian. The local priesthood appealed to the Pope, and two hundred priests refused to obey this order when the Vatican would not or could not reply. Fortunately Gentile's education act in the early and more anticlerical days of fascism allowed children of dissenters to opt out of religious instruction, and devout Catholic German parents preferred to invoke this provision rather than submit. When Austria asked for more lenient treatment of these unfortunates, the Italian minister was indignantly recalled from Vienna; but Hitler eventually intervened and persuaded Mussolini to offer people the choice of emigration to Germany if they wished; and some seventy thousand applied to leave.

Bishop Fogar of Trieste, unlike Endrici, showed himself a courageous champion of minority rights, but the Vatican found that obedience to Mussolini was a lesser evil and in 1936 replaced this bishop. Slav inscriptions in the churches and on tombstones were forcibly removed, and it was even prohibited to call children by the names of Slav saints. Whereas Hitler could speak for the German minority, the Slavs had no powerful champion. Italy had once been indignant over the treatment given to the Italian-speaking minority in the Austro-Hungarian Empire and had even justified her own *risorgimento* by the immorality of this persecution. But her own treatment of minorities was no less cruel. By 1938 the French-speaking parts of the Val d'Aosta were also being forcibly Italianized, and in 1942 the fascist party secretary spoke of wanting to exterminate a million Slovenes. Italy was to suffer for this after 1943 when the Slavs and the French were in a position to fight back.

★

The reaction of Italian public opinion to fascism cannot be easily gauged. But without the active or passive collaboration of most Italians, Mussolini could hardly have been so successful. Economically and politically his regime ended in a complete disaster, but at the time it gave them reassurance and a sense of importance. There was no need to be enthusiastic, for so many inconsistencies and half-truths existed in the official claptrap that people could choose any one interpretation of fascism, and some of its aspects appeared harmless enough.

Many people were convinced by the appearance of success. Some clung to the illusion that autocratic government would moderate itself once the emergency was over. One way or another, so long as fascism offered an ordered regimen, an end of class war, and the fruits of victory without war itself, many ordinary citizens were content. Individual liberty was sacrificed as the price of purchasing collective power and renown, and there was a flattering sense of being feared abroad. There were fine parades and speeches. Great hopes were constantly fostered and sometimes partly realized. Some people later looked back with nostalgia on these twenty years as a golden age, for much of what is unpleasant may be forgotten in retrospect.

Up to 1936, so far as one can see, support for Mussolini grew rather than diminished. In the early days a few more people as bold as Matteotti might have sufficed to overturn the hollow colossus which bestrode Italy, and when in May 1925 a false rumor spread at Reggio Calabria that fascism had fallen, there was general celebration in which even party members joined. But forcible suppression of press and parties after 1925 proved unanswerable. Consciences were gradually dulled as people were driven from one small connivance to another.

THE THEORY AND PRACTICE OF FASCISM

From the king downward they found that, once the first surrender had been made, there was no point of retreat, no unviolated principle worth a battle, until the means of opposition no longer existed. Antifascist activity diminished through the 1920s as it became more obviously useless, and fascist violence dwindled proportionately. A circular from the Duce to prefects in January 1927 said that *squadrismo* had by now become "anachronistic" and "the period of reprisals, devastation, and violence is over." By this time, according to Nitti, sentiment, necessity, and calculation combined to make almost all Italians content and loyal. It was enough that Mussolini could fool most of the people most of the time. They were convinced Mussolinians if nothing else, and antifascism had been reduced to negligible proportions.

The liberals of the old school were the most easily deceived, and some escaped from any personal responsibility by looking on events as inevitable, as something that merely needed analysis and justification. "It may be," said Albertini in the Senate, "that the Italian people were not sufficiently penetrated with the sanctity of liberal principles and needed a reactionary experiment in order to appreciate them." Opposition would therefore be politically sterile and a useless severance from the active life of the country.

Indeed, it could be maintained that the task of intellectuals should not be to oppose, but rather to try to influence fascism for good, to develop the healthy conservatism in this new movement and show its relation to the rest of Italian history and culture. Their own surrender could in this way be justified, and fascism would appear as necessary and logical. Given the reluctance of these older liberals to stoop to conspiracy, this was a not unworthy attempt to salvage something from the wreck of the past and make fascism safe and respectable. Placing the cause of Italy above that of its rulers, they hoped to serve fascism with their fingers crossed.

★

Giolitti and his liberals had in 1922 admitted the need for authoritarian government, and such opposition as they now allowed themselves was intellectual rather than political. By 1928, the year Giolitti died, their party had been proscribed. Croce, Ruffini, Casati, Bergamini, and Albertini had been compelled to reconsider the fundamentals of their political philosophy. The few people who gathered for Ruffini's funeral in 1934 had mostly given indispensable support to fascism in its earlier and more difficult years, but they now seemed survivors of a forgotten world. Croce found that his philosophical ideas were losing ground to the neoscholasticism of the Catholics and the heresies of the renegade Gentile. While at first he had welcomed the authoritarianism of the regime, Croce could not abide its bad taste and materialism, its brute ignorance and muddleheadedness. People who had received his kind of liberal education could not be expected to approve a creed of irrational mysticism, nor the fact that Mussolini encouraged culture mainly for reasons of prestige in the outside world.

The younger liberals, Gobetti, Parri, and Bauer, were prepared to go one stage further, to revise their creed to meet these new conditions, fighting and if necessary suffering for it. Gobetti was a remarkable journalist who endured assault and arrest from the fascists and died in Paris in 1926 at the age of twenty-five. A pupil of the great liberal economist, Einaudi, he worked on Gramsci's communist paper *Ordine Nuovo*, and in 1922 edited the weekly magazine *Rivoluzione Liberale*, which became for several years the liveliest opposition journal in Italy. Gobetti remained in close touch with the communists but found them too rigid and exclusive. He spent the few active years of his life trying to make liberalism more combative, more democratic, more aware of social problems. His was an inspiration which fired many leaders in the future war of liberation.

After 1926 there was hardly an antifascist movement, only a few divided antifascist groups. Outside Italy these ranged from the communism of Togliatti, through the liberal socialism of Rosselli and Salvemini, to the radicalism of Nitti, the Christian democracy of Don Sturzo, and the republicanism of Sforza. A broad Anti-Fascist Concentration was formed temporarily at Paris, but the republicans broke away from it, and the reuniting of Nenni's maximalists with those reformists adhering to Saragat did not last.

Inside Italy a skeleton communist organization continued in secret existence, but other parties completely disappeared. There were individual antifascists, for instance the ex-premiers Bonomi and Orlando who as titled "cousins of the king" had a right of access to the throne which they were able to use with effect in 1943. There were liberal aristocrats such as Duke Gallarati Scotti and Prince Doria, aghast at the vulgarity and irresponsibility of the fascist leaders; also scholars such as Luigi Einaudi, whose intellectual honesty was beyond doubt and whose international position kept them in touch with world opinion. Croce's magazine, *La Critica*, and books from the publishing houses of Laterza and Giulio Einaudi gave currency to a shadowy and allusive antifascism that surreptitiously helped to preserve some independence of mind and teaching. It was impossible to suppress altogether the occasional pasquinade, and some illegal manifestos were even printed in the offices of *Il Popolo d'Italia*.

*

Educated public opinion had no possibility of manifest opposition until Mussolini overreached himself and success failed him. But like all governments in Italy he could not escape private criticism. What many people particularly resented was the increasing interference in private life, for this was far more obvious than the cruelties of the *squadre* and the penal settlements. Mussolini forbade people to shake hands, despite the fact that this used to be one of his own favorite poses in front of the camera. He introduced instead the ostentatious armlength Roman salute which made them feel ridiculous—he described it as more hygienic than a handshake. Addressing a group of doctors in 1932, he said he meant to change popular habits of eating, dressing, and even of sleeping. Italians were told to gesticulate less. They should date their correspondence as from *anno primo* (October 1922), and had always to use *Voi* instead of *Lei* in private address. As well as their vocabulary, their clothes and the style of bathing suits were subject to political control. Such intrusion into private behavior was disliked and despised. It was also very widely disobeyed.

The superficiality of the system was further exposed in the fondness among party members for uniforms, civilian state employees being obliged to wear uniforms by a law of 1938. It was also seen in the importation from Germany of the goose step under its inadequately disguised name of the *passo romano*. The height of absurdity was reached when public gymnastic exercises were prescribed for elderly party leaders who were made to scramble up walls and jump through flaming hoops in the Mussolini Forum. With a whimsical humorlessness, films of this activity were publicly shown in cinemas as propaganda for physical fitness. It was indeed hard to take these party leaders seriously. And their malpractices were notorious. Wealthy citizens, who had approved of fascism so long as it confined itself to strikebreaking, became maddened by its extravagance and bureaucracy; and the government, which they had originally welcomed for its boasted efficiency, no longer had the same appeal when it proved to be thoroughly corrupt and inefficient.

Such intellectual and moral opposition may have been widespread, but could never have had any political effect until the king, or a general insurrection, or foreign armies could undermine the edifice of fascism. Absolutism was tempered only by inefficiency and minor private disobedience. Nevertheless the bureaucracy which multiplied in the corporations and government departments did put a restraint on action by its very unwieldiness, and this gave scope to a traditional inclination toward non-compliance. The unruliness and insubordination which had been major forces behind the *risorgimento*, and also behind the original success of fascism, were Mussolini's undoing. Funds were often misappropriated by self-seeking officials—to the king's private satisfaction. In June 1942 a revealing entry in Ciano's diary explained that ministers were for the first time considering the possibility of penal sanctions for tax evasion, but the proposal had to be withdrawn because, whereas it might work in more advanced countries, in Italy everyone would continue swearing to their false statements. This would just make fascism look ridiculous, and the extra revenue would be wasted on building prisons for the disobedient. As Mussolini later lamented, fascism failed because it was not totalitarian enough. "I am the most disobeyed man in history," was the pathetic confession in private of this absolute dictator.

Even more than wealthy taxpayers, many farmers and laborers must have sometimes resented fascism as just another invasion from the towns, bringing more taxes and more wars in which the peasants would do most of the fighting. Indifferentism and passive conformism or nonconformism were instinctive remedies for such people. Sicilians transferred to Mussolini's government their ancient insular resentment against the mainland. The prefect Mori was sent to crush the Sicilian mafia by ruthless measures, only to find in it something more durable than fascism, the habit ingrained in all classes of falling back on self-protection and self-help. Such was Mussolini's irritation against Sicily that in 1941 he took the strange and impossible decision to transfer all its local officials to the mainland. The more backward a province, the more flourishing was this conspiracy of non-co-operation—against rationing and monopolies, against requisitions and the compulsory dispatch of crops to government storage centers. The shrewd Sardinian peasant regarded official requisitioning and fixed prices as primarily a means to enrich the local party hierarch, and fascism pitted itself in vain against unco-operative rustics who hid their wheat and sometimes assaulted government officers sent to collect it.

This example of rebelliousness may stand as symbolic of the shrugging shoulders, the caustic *bon mot* and *barzellette*, the amused skepticism at fascist claims, and an unchronicled passive resistance at all levels of society. Unfortunately these were all compatible with great enthusiasm for other more dangerous aspects of fascism. Unfortunately, too, the general indifference, the habit of dissimulation and passive disobedience were going to prove one of the most evil and ineradicable legacies of the regime once liberal government was restored after 1945.

52 Surviving Institutions

Mussolini's ideal was to have everything organized under state control. As he told the judges in 1939, "in Italy we have no longer a division of powers, only a division of functions." But some more or less independent institutions survived, including the monarchy and the Church; and the armed forces were never completely identified with the party.

The army played only a small part in Mussolini's revolution: it remained broadly loyal to the throne, sometimes aloof from fascism or even mildly critical, though open mutiny was inconceivable. Diaz, Caviglia, and Badoglio were each placated by the offer of a marshal's baton, but General Capello was dispatched to the penal settlements, and even the Chief of General Staff Badoglio—to judge by his own special pleading—retained some independence. When Balbo in 1926 was suspected of heading a republican pressure group inside fascism, the monarchist Badoglio was apparently strong enough to force its dissolution.

The fascist militia had been created with the deliberate intention of offsetting the regular army, and an important rivalry developed from this fact. The regulars disliked going short of weapons that were given to the militia. Sometimes militiamen duplicated the army's duties in the field, and blackshirt divisions were active in Ethiopia and Spain. Their officers were given rank equal to army officers, and this caused jealousy among those who had attended the crack military school at Turin.

The increased use of civilian uniforms and the growth of civilian militarization in any case undermined the caste consciousness enjoyed by the services. When General Gazzera, the minister of war, resisted this process of depreciation, Mussolini in 1933 permanently took over the war department himself— he had also held it until 1929. His undersecretary, General Baistrocchi, was a fascist who obeyed orders. Many entrenched susceptibilities were offended when old regimental distinctions were abolished, when the goose step and the fascist salute were introduced, and when undignified songs and war cries were demanded of the troops. The recipe for advancement in the military profession was to have many children, to join the party, and to applaud the Duce's hyperbolical speeches about breasts of steel and forests of bayonets.

This effort to *fascistizzare* the army introduced favoritism and corruption as well as allowing promotion to the wrong type of officer. Any diminution of the army's *esprit de corps* undermined morale, and the results appeared after 1940 in a lack of self-reliance and initiative among the generals. The air force was yet more demoralized, having been born under fascism and its first loyalty having always been to the regime. Here was further proof that fascism discouraged honesty and individual enterprise. But the navy remained an efficient fighting force, and many admirals retained enough independence to disobey Mussolini in 1943.

★

If the king had been a more vital personality, the loyalty of the armed services might have saved Italy before her final defeat. Vittorio Emanuele III was an unsympathetic man with little of the character and spirit of his forebears and none of their popular vices. Queen Elena kept her Slav accent and preferred to speak French. She was a woman of simple tastes who preferred living in the mountains far from Rome—"my cousin the shepherdess," so the Duchess of Aosta called her. Such unsophistication made them the happiest royal family in modern Italian history, but did little to win popularity or ensure good government.

The king was pedantic and pettily scrupulous over the details of uniforms, but relatively uninterested in policy or politicians. To his ministers he appeared cynical and cold, without enthusiasm, without any capacity for friendship. Despite his obstinacy he was easily frightened, as he was also sensitive about his diminutive height—people noted that when seated at audiences his feet used to dangle in the air. Whereas his grandfather had ordered the army to fire on the

375

national hero Garibaldi, Vittorio Emanuele was awed by Mussolini and shrank from any difficult decisions which might compromise the dynasty. He would always swim with the tide, whether of liberalism in 1900, nationalism in 1915, reaction in 1922, or panic in 1943. He was not a man from whom any courageous determination could be expected, and until far too late he never contemplated rebelling against the man whom he sometimes must have regretted lifting into power.

There was no love lost between Mussolini and the king. The minister was seldom if ever invited to a meal, and the king almost never visited the Duce. Etiquette was usually observed, and a Mussolini in civilian clothes would call officially at the palace on Monday and Thursday mornings. But we hear of many petulant threats to abolish the monarchy. It was resented that when Hitler visited Italy he reviewed parades beside the king, while Mussolini had to stand behind. It was also resented that the king placed much of his large private fortune in safe custody with Hambro's bank in London (where in 1940 it was invested in British War Loan). Prince Umberto, too, even though conforming outwardly, was not seen in a black shirt. The press was instructed not to use his title of "Hereditary Prince" and hints were given that the Grand Council was going to alter the succession.

Right-wing antifascists clung to the monarchy as an anchor when it was in fact the frailest of reeds. If the king ever protested, it was not in defense of the constitution that he had sworn to uphold, but against trivial invasions of his royal prerogative or some disrespectful treatment of his majesty. His independence was limited to raising objections when decorations were presented to Ribbentrop and Goering, or when Starace entered the presence in his black shirt-sleeves, or when parliament without any notice gave Mussolini the new title of First Marshal of the Empire—on this occasion the king threatened to abdicate. The Duce made jokes about a diarchy, but in fact he himself had effective power and both of them knew it. The fasces were sometimes superimposed on the royal cross of Savoy, and Mussolini's portrait displaced that of the queen in schools and barracks, at the same height and in the same-sized frame as the king's. The Duce pardoned criminals on his own initiative, and laws were said to have been "approved" before receiving the royal signature.

As Mussolini became increasingly unhinged toward 1939, he reverted to his earlier republican sympathies and even prepared a dossier on the private lives of the royal family in which Umberto was accused of unspeakable vices. But this ammunition was never used because the approach of war made the co-operation of army and monarchy indispensable to fascism. The king, moreover, was troublesome rather than dangerous. He had severed all contact with the opposition after the murder of Matteotti, and it was almost impossible for a man of his aloofness and indecision to renew it. In his isolation he could hardly ally with the Church when he himself was so little inclined toward religion. Only in

Piedmont and Naples did he have broad popular support, while the Roman aristocracy seem to have thought him a bore and a boor.

The monarchy, unlike that of Great Britain, had been less successful in retaining both power and the appearance of powerlessness. It was saddled with responsibility for events without effectively controlling them, and was therefore discredited in the eyes of fascists and antifascists alike. Abdication would have focused world attention on Mussolini's iniquities and would have divided Italy (perhaps even fascism). But though his great-grandfather had abdicated to save the country, Vittorio Emanuele III had no great regard for the duties of his office or the liberties of his country. Cut off from good advice he failed to save his dynasty. One of his daughters perished tragically in a German concentration camp; he himself died an expatriate in Egypt; and his son too was condemned to exile as soon as a free popular vote could again be held.

★

Parliament was far less independent than the king. Mussolini as late as June 1939 republished the *statuto* of 1848 as the fundamental constitution of the realm. Without being abolished, it simply atrophied as his party absorbed the state. Both Senate and Chamber learned to break into fascist songs and war cries. Every member stood up when the Duce entered or left. Voting was generally by acclamation, even at the passage of the racial laws or, ironically enough, when the Chamber of Deputies abolished itself in January 1939. An extract from the proceedings of the new Chamber of Fasces and Corporations on April 27, 1940, reveals the quality of Italian politics at a time when the rest of the civilized world was overwhelmed with dismay and apprehension:

> The Chamber and public galleries broke out into an intense and enthusiastic ovation. The cry of "Duce, Duce" resounded through the hall again and again. The Duce responded with the Roman salute. The Assembly then sang "*Giovinezza.*" Again vibrant acclamation. The president ordered that the Duce should be saluted, and the Chamber answered with a powerful "*A noi.*" When the Duce left his seat, the National Councilors crowded around him with enthusiastic and continual acclamation.

After January 1939, members sat not by election but by virtue of holding some office in the corporations or the party. They had no importance except as window dressing for a regime that was personal and strictly unconstitutional. Laws were passed about the status and competence of official institutions, but they were empty words. The Duce of fascism was declared not only *ipso facto* head of the government, but the press was told to spell out DUCE in capital letters. By that time constitutional niceties had ceased to matter.

★

The Church was another institution which remained autonomous. Few leaders of fascism were practicing Catholics. Mussolini himself boasted of being an unbeliever who ruled over an irreligious nation, and his personal servant, Navarra, never knew him to have attended mass. One of his early works had been a eulogy of the heretic Huss, and he named his son after another heretic, Giordano Bruno. A scurrilous novel by him appeared in an American translation in 1928 entitled *The Cardinal's Mistress*. Yet he was prudent enough to realize how indispensable was ecclesiastical support. His first program in 1919 had called for the confiscation of Church property, but the prospect of power made him change direction, and by 1922 his party had come to a tacit arrangement with the Church.

Before the election of 1924 he played for clerical support. The crucifix came back into schoolrooms, chaplains were appointed to the party militia, Freemasonry was abolished. Wide exemption from military service was given to clergy and seminarists, and a timely increase was made in the state subsidy for clerical stipends. This was something quite new in Italian history. The Laodiceans were confounded and the prestige of the parish priest augmented when religious ceremonies were at last officially attended by political leaders and religious blessing was given at party functions. The anticlerical Gentile was replaced as minister of education by a Catholic, Professor Fedele, who inaugurated a more sympathetic educational policy in the years 1925–28 and at the pope's request deprived the excommunicate modernist Buonaiuti of his teaching post in a state university. Mussolini began to have his children baptized, and in 1928 yielded sufficiently to go through a religious form of marriage with Donna Rachele.

This friendly policy toward the Church helps to explain the powerful support which Mussolini received when he needed Catholic help in establishing his power. Church encouragement was withdrawn from the Christian democrats in 1922, and Sturzo had to resign his secretaryship of the party lest as a priest he should compromise the Vatican. When many of the *popolari* collaborated with the socialists in the Aventine secession, the *Osservatore Romano* condemned this impious association. Mussolini seemed more trustworthy; he could at least be relied on to oppose the Reds, and it could not yet be guessed that fascism would inadvertently encourage the spread of atheistic communism in Italy. After all its secular experience of tyrants, the Church refused to say that fascism with its ruthless bludgeoning, its glorification of the state and of war, was incompatible with Christianity. The Vatican had in 1864 protested uncompromisingly against liberalism, and eventually determined that no communist could remain in the Church, but most rank-and-file fascists were Catholic in name at least, and some high prelate was always at hand to bestow a public blessing on all the main events in the fascist calendar.

For the past fifty years the pope had refused to leave his "prison" or even to recognize the existence of Italy. So when reconciliation was at last announced in 1929, this was rightly hailed as a great victory for Mussolini and brought him a great accession of support—though the British foreign secretary, a Methodist and a socialist, refused to send his congratulations. In one papal pronounce-ment, Pius XI paid tribute to "the man sent to us by Providence" and who fortunately lacked the "preconceptions of liberalism." These casual phrases marked the culminating point of Mussolini's career and help to explain how one month after this reconciliation a plebiscite showed overwhelming support for the regime.

This reconciliation in 1929 comprised a treaty and a concordat by which the Church at last recognized the existence of Italy and the Italian occupation of Rome, retaining for itself only the sovereign territory of the Vatican. The Vatican City, with a population of a few hundred, was allowed its own army and police force, its own courts, railroad station, radio, and newspaper. The Church obtained confirmation of its establishment as the state religion with a call upon government protection. The compact was sealed with a huge sum of money which made the Church the largest holder of Italian state bonds with a much-criticized financial interest in the success of Mussolini's regime.

Other concessions were also obtained. There was to be no further distribu-tion of Protestant bibles, and evangelical meetings in private houses were forbidden. The state promised to take its marriage laws from the Church. Ecclesiastical schools received preferential treatment and religious teaching in state schools was extended. Ecclesiastical corporations were exempted from taxes, and legal personality was again allowed to religious orders. A national holiday on every February 11 would commemorate this conciliation, replacing the provocative September 20 which in every previous year had celebrated the conquest of Rome in 1870.

Croce alone spoke in the Senate against this concordat. While he welcomed the reconciliation, he strongly disliked the manner and the details of this "surrender" by the lay state. "Against those who think Paris is worth a mass, there are still some who must protest on grounds of conscience." These were the last words of serious criticism in parliament that Mussolini heard.

The Church soon realized the barrenness of its victory. On his first ceremonial visit to the Vatican after the reconciliation, Mussolini refused to kneel or kiss the Pope's hand and forbade the photographers to picture him as the humble servant of the Church or the mild man of religion. He explained to parliament that he had conceded nothing of note. In the field of education, he added, he would show himself intractable. Mussolini the realist had given up his claim to out-of-date jurisdictional rights and was quite ready to modify the fascist encouragement of women's sports so as to meet objections from the Vatican; he would even bring his wife from Milan and pose, implausibly, as a model family man; but in an "established Church" the state retained its voice in ecclesiastical nominations. This was no longer Cavour's "free Church in a free state," for ecclesiastics knew that the government could block their promotion or even secure their dismissal. Mussolini could not afford much latitude to any institution outside his machine. Almost immediately he launched a violent attack on the lay organization Catholic Action, and the pope was forced to yield over the activity of Catholic organizations in the training of youth.

This conflict over Catholic Action produced a renewal of that rivalry between Church and state which had been one of the great forces working for liberty. In particular it prompted the outspoken encyclical *Non abbiamo bisogno* in 1931 which asserted the independence of the Church against totalitarianism, though the fascist party was said to be not specifically in question. The authoritarian state was welcomed by the Church, with reservations: as Pius stated, "We cannot allow freedom of discussion, for that might imperil the faith of less enlightened hearers and damage the established religion." But authoritarianism on a Mussolinian scale was worse than expected. The racial laws and the fascist attempt to monopolize youth education, though approved of by some prominent churchmen, were bound to be anathema to most Catholics.

This encyclical was the most categorical public challenge that Mussolini had received inside Italy since Croce's manifesto in 1925, but for politic reasons criticism had to be partial and indirect. As a rule, Mussolini knew that he could rely on Church support. In the plebiscitary elections of 1929, the president of Catholic Action instructed all members of his organization to support fascism, and the Jesuit organ, *Civiltà Cattolica*, which had been so relentless in its criticism of liberal governments, looked with far greater benevolence on this military dictator. The secretary of the fascist party was in 1930 received by Pius XI in solemn audience, a favor never previously conceded to other parties in government. Pius XII in March 1939 mentioned explicit appreciation of the beneficent effects and the success of fascism." In sum, while Mussolini's more strident heresies were unacceptable, no previous administration had received anything like so much ecclesiastical approbation. Thousands of sermons exhorted the faithful to be loyal to their great leader and a cardinal inaugurated the school of "fascist mysticism" in Milan, while in the world at large Mussolini became for a time, until the appearance of General Franco in Spain, the ideal pattern of a Catholic statesman.

SECTION TWELVE: DECLINE AND FALL OF A ROMAN EMPIRE

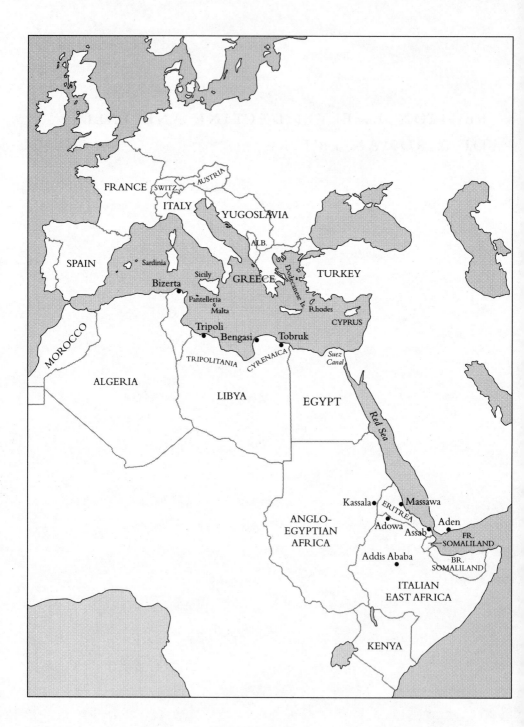

Map 2. Italy in the Mediterranean and the Italian Empire

53 Foreign Policy, 1922–1936

Mussolini gave a foretaste of the fascist style in foreign policy when he bombarded Corfu in 1923. An Italian, General Tellini, had been assassinated on the borders of Albania and Greece while with an Allied mission. Without waiting to discover the facts, Mussolini sent a truculent ultimatum to Greece and ordered his warships to shell the island. He wanted to eclipse D'Annunzio and earn the reputation of someone who would make Italy feared throughout the Balkans.

Despite a warning from Britain and acceptance by Greece of a settlement arranged in Paris, the episode was to rank as a success in Italian eyes. It set an ominous example of unpunished violence at the same time as it defied the League of Nations, and Mussolini pretended to his compatriots that the rest of Europe was admiring and jealous. It was not in his nature to see that there might be disadvantages for Italy if he earned the reputation of a bully and a trickster.

Until he could assert himself more emphatically, Mussolini nevertheless tried to reassure the world that fascism was not an article for export and that ideology would not influence foreign policy. His sympathies and antipathies were well known, so he said, but he did not base policy on them. In his less restrained moments, however, he announced his intention to bring about the downfall of the British Empire, to turn the Mediterranean into an Italian lake and drive out its "parasites." The antithesis was palpable, but foreigners were not to know that the export of fascism was something close to his heart. He secretly subsidized Oswald Mosley, the rexists, the cagoulards, the Italian party in Malta, and other fascist organizations all over the world.

Little by little he moved toward a policy of treaty revision. In 1923 he backed French occupation of the Ruhr. He signed a pact with Yugoslavia in January 1924, by which Italy took Fiume and recognized Susak as Yugoslavian—all without reference to the League, of which Italy was a member. He did what he could to penetrate into Balkan politics and prevent any close alliance of states there. He also signed commercial treaties with Germany and Soviet Russia, on whose support any revision of the Versailles settlement would ultimately depend.

Mussolini held the office of foreign minister until June 1936 (except for the years 1929–32), but his first departmental secretary, Contarini, was a career diplomat for whom national interests came before fascism. Contarini tried to continue Sforza's foreign policy, to restrain the intrusion of ideology and whimsy, and to prevent the giving of gratuitous offence to other nations. In this spirit of accommodation the Treaty of Locarno was signed in 1925. Contarini resigned in 1926, for by then the party machine was beginning to permeate the foreign service with men who lacked intelligence, honesty, or even much knowledge of the outside world. In their blindness to genuine national interests and ignorance of how lines of retreat could be kept open from every diplomatic position, these party placemen would do grave harm to the prestige of Italy and begin an unhappy chapter in foreign politics.

Miscalculations and confusion in foreign policy were to be Mussolini's undoing. He was dangerously muddled between on the one hand trying to convince foreign admirers that Italy was a stabilizing force in Europe, and on the other proclaiming that the settlement of 1919 must be smashed to allow Italian expansion. The urge for expansion won in the end and by 1927 his statements should have left Europe with little room for doubt. In that year he explained that between 1935 and 1940 Italy would arrive at a crucial point in history and see her rights at long last prevail. By that time, he added, Italy would possess five million soldiers under arms and enough warplanes to blot out the light of the sun. Italy was made out to be an unsatisfied power with a grievance that would justify the most barefaced acts of imperialism.

Once firmly in the saddle, Mussolini could not resist the temptation to cut a figure, and it was merely a blind when in 1928 he adhered to the Kellogg pact to renounce war. By 1930 fascism was being declared of universal application and very much for export. "Though words are beautiful things, rifles, machine guns, planes, and cannon are still more beautiful." Two years later Mussolini told an audience at Milan that the twentieth century would be the century of fascism during which Italy would return to be the directing force in human civilization. In ten years' time, he insisted, all Europe would be fascist. In 1934 he announced that Italians had to be a militarized nation and all citizens between the ages of six and fifty-five should be trained as soldiers.

Fascist foreign policy had above all to be different. Sometimes it veered unstably from ideological arguments to momentary whims, but usually it was compounded with a modicum of shrewd realism and a virtuosity in propaganda and showmanship. Though he had come to power on the pretext of opposing bolshevism, Mussolini was realistic enough to be among the first to recognize the revolutionary government in Russia. "Both we and the Russians are opposed to liberals, democrats, and parliaments." Not until Russia supported the League of Nations and seemed to abandon revisionism did Mussolini turn to prefer German help. Evidently the central core of fascism was not antibolshevism, but a deliberate intention to cut a figure and undermine the peace of Europe; antibolshevism had been a pretext for tricking the *ingénus* at home and abroad into becoming his accomplices.

Italy and Germany had similar ambitions but were kept apart by failure to agree about Austria. Austria was a cushion on Italy's sensitive frontier, and the fascists therefore furnished arms and money to help Dollfuss maintain Austrian independence against Germany. When in July 1934 Dollfuss was murdered, an infuriated Mussolini mobilized troops at the Brenner to check any threatened

German advance, and momentarily crossed back from revisionism into the camp of the League. This was a fateful moment for Europe. Britain and France joined Italy at the Stresa conference in May 1935, and Mussolini hoped that, in return for his support against a rearming Germany, the democracies might guarantee Austria and support his conquest of Abyssinia. The crucial issue was Abyssinia, and here a chapter of accidents intervened which aligned fascist Italy in a fatal marriage with the nazis.

★

General De Bono has put on record that Mussolini had been preparing to invade Abyssinia for some years, though the invasion was subsequently sold to the world as an answer to "unprovoked aggression" by the Abyssinians in 1934. The fascists needed to score some very public success no matter what so long as it was large and provocative. Italian history since 1922 seemed to belie their promise of grandeur to come. Apart from the Lateran Treaty there had been no spectacular achievements. Furthermore, the economic depression made it desirable to divert people's gaze from home discontents and unite the nation around its common patriotism. "We have a right to empire," said Mussolini, "as a fertile nation which has the will to propagate its race over the face of the earth." Colonial expenditure was already up five-fold since 1921, but this had mostly been dissipated on the profitless desert of Libya. Hence arose the idea of a more glamorous colonial war against the last unoccupied region of Africa, the same country whose defeat of Italy in 1896 still rankled. So often had Mussolini extolled war and conquest that he had if possible to find an easily beaten opponent in order to practice what he preached.

While the new undersecretary Suvich providently stressed the overriding need to defend Austria against the Germans, the amateur politician Mussolini calculated that there was no hurry and he had plenty of time to acquire an African empire, hoping he could then regroup his forces on the northern frontier before Germany was ready to risk hostilities. Already he had looked with benevolence on the nationalist movement in Egypt against Britain, but in the Italian colonies of Tripoli and Cyrenaica he was naturally against local patriotic movements, and these provinces were gradually reconquered from the Berbers and Senussi. The "revolt" of such newly conquered peoples took many years to suppress before the Senussi chief was captured and publicly hanged before the eyes of his followers. Mussolini promised that a million Italian settlers would be sent to establish in North Africa a stronghold of *italianità*, but after many years and much expense he could never persuade or coerce more than thirty thousand to carry out this unprofitable experiment.

Meanwhile Italy, trying to reassert her patronage over Abyssinia, introduced this independent country into the League of Nations and in 1928 signed a pact of friendship with the Negus. But the latter was anxious to remain strictly independent and soon was said to be hindering the development of roads and trade connections with Italian Somalia and Eritrea. This opposition turned

Italian patronage into hostility. Mussolini repeated that there was no question of wanting territorial conquest and he was no collector of deserts. Both these statements were untrue but many people believed him.

A preliminary step toward the conquest of Abyssinia was to obtain in January 1935 a general statement of French approval. The British refused to support this, though if Italy persisted they were ready to compensate Abyssinia with a corridor to the sea through British Somalia. But Italy objected to Abyssinia keeping an independent outlet to the sea that would free her from Italian economic pressure. Mussolini was quoted as saying that he would not take Ethiopia except by war, not even if offered as a gift. The Hoare-Laval plan, which proposed to give Italy a large part of Abyssinia while still preserving it as a separate state, was for the same reason unacceptable. In any case the unexpected outcry against this plan by British public opinion effectively split the "Stresa alliance" and drove Mussolini to seek the friendship of Hitler. Germany was thus able to reoccupy the Rhineland and then engulf Austria without more than a token protest from Italy. From this moment the Italian dictator was doomed to play a subordinate and even servile role in Europe as Hitler's ally.

★

Mussolini began military operations in October 1935. He knew from an intercepted message that the threat of British naval action against him was bluff, and Grandi at the London embassy claimed to have private information from members of the British conservative party who opposed their own government and favored the Duce. It looked all too simple, for the fascist cause stood to gain a maximum of effect with a calculated minimum of risk.

Condemnation by the League inevitably followed the outbreak of hostilities but the imposition of economic sanctions suited Mussolini very well: this half-hearted gesture was exploited to show Italians that it was their nation not the regime which was in danger, and that the austerity campaign for self-sufficiency had been no mere caprice but a vital national interest. Sanctions in any case did not cripple his war effort. Ridiculously enough, coal and oil were exempted, although without fuel he would on his own confession have been brought to a halt. Soviet Russia provided a considerable part of Italy's requirements for this imperialistic war, and Germany also refused to join other nations in their embargo, while the United States' oil companies were not bound by a League decision. The Germans were delighted at this diversion of Italian energies so far away from Austria, especially as in the process it destroyed the self-confidence and mutual trust among members of the League.

The Italian people showed considerable enthusiasm over this call on their patriotism, and the war strengthened Mussolini's internal position. Wedding rings were sacrificed to provide foreign exchange and Prince Doria's Scottish wife was assaulted when she refused this tribute. Some former political exiles now rallied to the regime, while Orlando, Albertini, and Croce welcomed a continuation of the former policy of African expansion. Imperialistic poetry poured from Soffici and prose from D'Annunzio. Even the Papacy, which had angrily condemned World War I as a "useless carnage", said nothing to give offence to fascist imperialism, and most bishops bestowed their public blessing on the self-styled Protector of Islam in his war against the Christian Abyssinians.

Military operations began under General De Bono, who as a first-hour fascist had the honor of capturing for the party any laurels there were to be gained. Mussolini flooded him with telegrams of instruction, all top priority even when they dealt with the tiny details over which the Duce was anxious to show his masterly sense of control. But after a few weeks of desultory fighting, De Bono had to be replaced by a commander from the regular army, Badoglio. Thenceforward, the war progressed smoothly, about half a million Italian soldiers being needed, and in six months Addis Ababa fell. This was a workmanlike job of strategy, and the engineers and roadbuilders in particular proved remarkably efficient, although unpublicized but sizable military operations had to continue against "rebels" and "brigands" for many months longer.

Admittedly the enemy could put up no more than a token resistance, and victory was achieved almost too easily, giving Mussolini a dangerous feeling of overconfidence. He even lamented that only 1,537 Italians had been killed, and the war had been won at too small a cost without hardening the national character. Italian prestige in the outside world suffered because of the supererogatory use of poison gas, and young Vittorio Mussolini published a much admired account of the fun of bombing native horsemen, describing how they looked like a budding rose as his bombs exploded. While justifying the war by denouncing the barbarity of the Abyssinians, fascism thus attracted this label of barbarism to itself.

Further bad publicity was created by the pettiness and corruption of the party bosses who appeared in droves in order to earn their campaign medals and fill their pockets. In February 1937, stories circulated of a pitiless massacre of thousands of Abyssinians, for the Duce expressly ordered Graziani to shoot all captured "rebels," to use gas to destroy whole villages, and to enforce the law of "ten eyes for an eye." There were demoralizing stories of fortunes being made by companies engaged in building roads, and exaggerated reports were sent home about the resources of Abyssinia in order to obtain investment funds from Rome. Political jobbery ensured that there was little competition for public contracts, and the new colonial governor reported that half of his fascist civil servants were incompetent and half of the rest corrupt. Effective supervision was lacking to remedy this deficiency, and when a new ministry of Italian Africa was created, the Duce simply added it to his own profusion of overlapping responsibilities.

Much fine work continued to be done by individual Italians in Africa, but it was obscured and ultimately ruined by mistakes of the regime. If Italy gained no economic benefit from what she invested in colonies, this was not only because the empire was mostly unprofitable land, but also because desultory misman-agement was the invariable companion of fascist exploitation, and great sums were squandered each year on "fascist" objectives concerned with prestige and propaganda. Despite Mussolini's arguments for expansion, in 1939 Italy's trade with her colonies was only 2 per cent of her total trade. She was spending on them ten times their economic value to her, and the Italian population of New York City was still ten times that of the entire Italian colonial empire.

★

Some Italians who welcomed Mussolini's domestic policy began to fear the inebriation of superficial success after 1936, and with reason. Financial exhaus-tion, moral disrepute, and diplomatic isolation were all threatening. Yet his victory in Africa seemed a glorious success at the time. It mortally wounded the League. It defied a vote by fifty-two nations and rocked the prestige of Great Britain. It cost few casualties and provided many medals. Since 1860, many an attempt to cut a more heroic figure in the world had crumbled, but at last there seemed to be something substantial to show and Mussolini was succeeding precisely where parliamentary government had failed.

This parody of an empire gave many Italians a false impression of their country's potential strength and their leader's abilities. After reconciliation with the pope in 1929, the creation of an African empire in 1936 was the second deceptive peak in this rake's progress. Instead of seeing that the campaign had depleted military reserves, the illusion spread that victory over half-armed tribesmen could be repeated against France and Britain. Instead of recognizing that the war had been won on credit, bad habits of lavish expenditure had been acquired and retrenchment was psychologically ever more difficult.

The tragedy of Italy in the next ten years was the fruit of these misconcep-tions. Mussolini shared both the illusion and the subsequent disillusion, though no one was better placed for knowing the truth. Flattery went to his head. He was extolled by the king for winning the greatest colonial war in all history and so increasing the prestige of the "fascist fatherland." Many years later the Duce recalled in Ciano's hearing how everything had gone well until 1937 and how he wished that his stomach ulcer had killed him at that moment of success.

In truth, however, Italy was well on the road to destruction by 1937. The Ethiopian war had created an exaggerated religion of *ducismo* which proved fatal. Ambition led to the extortion of compulsory loans, a capital levy, and irremediable budgetary deficits. It also isolated Italy and compelled her to accept an alliance with Hitler that proved her ruin. By teaching her to under-estimate Britain it broke the Anglo-Italian entente which for eighty years had remained an essential premise of foreign policy. The results of a search for prestige could already be seen in the fate of Trieste and Fiume under fascist rule, cut off from their natural trade routes, the one city declining despite heavy protection, while the other had grass growing on its railroad track and its port installations in decay. Money spent in Africa was badly needed at home.

Fifteen years of fascism had left most Italians too confused for honest self-criticism and the internal contradictions in the system were bewildering. Mussolini persuaded them that the Ethiopian war was defensive, fought against a savage and brutal aggressor, despite simultaneously arguing that war should be welcomed and provoked as a good in itself. The Ethiopians were to be condemned for their cruelty and failure to conform with the Geneva conventions of 1924–25 on the conduct of warfare, whereas he was to be praised for his realistic recognition that humanitarianism was mere cowardice and international law a fictitious device invented by decadent powers. At one moment he was the champion of tradition, at another the herald of a new age.

> Stiff in opinions, always in the wrong;
> Was everything by starts, and nothing long:
> But, in the course of one revolving moon,
> Was chemist, fiddler, statesman and buffoon.

At once revolutionary and conservative, Catholic and antireligious, socialistic and bourgeois, the champion of law and the negation of all law, Mussolini's cynicism and opportunism were characteristic of Italian fascism. Understandably the general public ceased to possess much capacity for firm belief and trusted only that the Duce, with all his apparent contradictions, was merely using these stratagems to delude the enemies of Italy. The delusion was rather his, and theirs.

54   Lack of Restraint, 1936–1938

Two such dissatisfied countries as Germany and Italy were natural allies, and the two regimes in many ways resembled each other. Hitler seems to have admired Mussolini as much as he admired anyone, and both dictators surrounded themselves with so many sycophants that one needed the other to alleviate his own isolation. There was a relief in having someone else with whom they could communicate on something like level terms.

Hitler had been using the Roman salute by the middle twenties and the word *Führer* copied that of *Duce*. The unknown Hitler is said to have been refused when he requested a signed photograph from his successful prototype, and yet Salvemini collected evidence to show that nazism was being subsidized from Italy long before its victory in 1933.

Mussolini was so convinced of his intellectual superiority that he believed he would be the senior partner in any alliance with Hitler. He was delighted to find someone outside Italy who took him seriously and aped his dogmas and institutions. Nazism flattered his vanity by confirming the negation of liberalism and democracy and by accepting much the same combination of state socialism and state capitalism. Nazism employed the same belief in aggression and conquest and echoed his mystical belief that "only blood can turn the bloodstained wheels of history." Hitler took from Italy the military organization of youth, as indeed he took some of the posturing and the hysterical crowd scenes. Mussolini was already by 1930 allowing nazi military units to train on Italian soil where this violation of the 1919 treaty could not be observed.

As time went on, Hitler proved immeasurably more successful and fertile in ideas, while Mussolini degenerated physically and intellectually. On paper the two ideologies may have looked alike, but in practice fascism lacked the ruthlessness, the organizing capacity and willingness to take theory to its logical extreme. It became the turn of the Italian fascists to admire the efficiency, the "know-how," national discipline, and the supposedly shattering thoroughness of the nazis. Mercifully, the very individualism which prepared the way for Mussolini constituted an invaluable differentiation from the totalitarian methods of Hitler. Mussolini could casually order the coldblooded murder of Matteotti, Rosselli, and antifascists captured in the Spanish Civil War, but his ferocity was far more in word than deed. Croce's conclusion was true in part:

> There was a deep and important distinction between nazism and fascism, because the first was a terrible crisis which had been brooding through centuries of German history, and the second was a superfetation quite alien to the history of Italy. . . . The first had a tragic and diabolical aspect, but the second kept an incorrigibly clownlike appearance even in the crimes it committed, and anybody could see this difference by contrasting the appearance of the two chiefs.

In comparison, Mussolini was a lightweight, a novice in the political arts. There was an undeniable pettiness about the man who ordered Italian journalists at Geneva to hiss Haile Selassie when he came to defend Ethiopia before the League. Mussolini's abrupt changes of policy were sometimes accepted at his own valuation as brilliant strokes of Machiavellian deceit, part of a superplan which the fullness of time would reveal; but Ciano's diary suggests that they were casual, illogical, and sometimes almost pathological. At one moment he vetoed the *Anschluss* and began to fortify the Brenner; at the next he announced to the world that he was standing beside Germany in shining armor. At one moment he was ranting against Hitler and hoping that the Russians would defeat Germany; then he suddenly changed when a recollection of Chamberlain reminded him how contemptible were what he called the pluto-democracies. He was by turns antiracialist and racialist.

Sometimes when the issue of peace or war appeared to lie in his hands and the world stood breathless to know his will, Mussolini had no policy at all and sought his information from the press like everyone else. National and international politics were often directed to subserve a personal vanity and on a level of irresponsibility which passes belief. Again and again, when trying to explain the collapse of his regime, the vanity and irresponsibility of this one man obtrudes. Hitler was great enough to endure powerful subordinates and deserve their fear and loyalty, but there were very few top-level fascists with a strong will and personality of their own. Indeed, surprisingly few of Mussolini's chosen apostles had any admirable qualities even of a purely technical order.

★

Evidently, the western democracies had nothing to offer Italy comparable with what she thought she might obtain from Germany. Italian territorial claims against the German peoples had been largely satisfied in 1919; hence any ambitions which remained were directed against France, Britain, and French client states in the Balkans. Mussolini failed to appreciate that revising the 1919 treaty might upset the balance of Europe to Italian disadvantage. He preferred to reason that, since Germany refused to impose sanctions in 1935–36, she must have Italian interests at heart.

In the summer of 1936, despite or even because of German rearmament and reoccupation of the Rhineland, there was a *rapprochement* between Italy and Germany. Mussolini christened it when he remarked that the Berlin–Rome vertical was not a diaphragm but an *axis* around which other states would be obliged to group themselves. Once the Austrian question was "solved," once Germany could forget Italian "treachery" in 1915, and as soon as fascist doctrine could be modified to include Italians within the Aryan race, all was ready for what in 1939 became the Pact of Steel. Mussolini went on protesting that he never imitated anyone or anything, and when people grumbled that the goose step was Prussian, he humorlessly replied that the goose was a Roman animal which had once saved the Capitol from the Gauls. But he also promised that he would never stop his campaign to "prussianize" Italy. His feelings toward Germany were a mixture of admiration, envy, fear, and dislike; but envy predominated.

The traditional foreign policy of noncommittal was therefore discarded. Instead he spoke of preparing for an inevitable war against the western powers. A cleverer man would have retained sufficient independence to play the *tertius gaudens* and so extort more consideration from his new ally. Instead, Italy became a camp follower in the march of German expansion, and whether victorious or defeated she stood to lose. Even when fate restored her to the position of mediator between two power groups in September 1939, Mussolini obtusely threw away this undeserved good fortune, and since he had crushed all opposition there was no one to show him his error. Bottai murmured against the Axis, as Balbo against the Roman salute, but these murmurs were drowned in the artificially amplified chorus of praise which encouraged Mussolini to believe that his own instinct must be infallible.

★

One can follow this lack of restraint developing after June 1936. In another "change of the guard," and without the least preliminary discussion with anyone, Mussolini handed the foreign ministry to the thirty-four-year-old Ciano. In previous years the Duce's many other preoccupations had allowed foreign affairs to be in part directed by his undersecretary Suvich but, as in other departments, the restraining influence of permanent officials was increasingly ineffective. Suvich was dismissed and Ciano now went further in the "fascistization" of diplomacy that Grandi had already begun. The existence of an Italian empire was proclaimed in 1936 and Italy was pronounced to be a satisfied power. In yet another contradiction, satisfaction was then declared to be a bourgeois and unfascist sentiment, and Ciano needed to attach his name to some new conquest.

This was the moment when Franco, relying on Italian support, initiated his revolt against the Spanish republic. The Spanish republicans had challenged Mussolini by supporting free speech and parliamentary government at a time when fascism was supposed to be winning everywhere. His military intervention, disguised as a campaign against communism, would punish them as well as acquiring military bases in the Balearic Islands for Italy. Another military victory for the party militia would also be good for fascist prestige. Italians had been told to expect success after success, and any failure to repeat the prescription might expose the shallow foundations upon which fascism was built.

In return for the money and effort expended in Spain, Mussolini received nothing. When his forces suffered a minor defeat in the region of Guadalajara, foreign papers began to suspect that fascism was more bark than bite and this irritated him excessively, because not being taken seriously was his greatest fear. He therefore made Roatta's expeditionary force less "voluntary" and replaced the black-shirted militiamen with regular soldiers just as he had been forced to do in Ethiopia. Seventy thousand Italians were engaged in Spain during 1937 as the initial promise of arms led to an inextricable involvement. While victory would bring little reward, defeat would mean a loss of face which he dared not contemplate.

Completely misinformed by incompetent fascist diplomats, Mussolini continued to believe that this Spanish war might end at any moment, whereas it dragged on for three years until the fall of Madrid in March 1939. Apparently, he did not even use the fighting to learn any much-needed lessons on weapons or tactics. The Germans, on the other hand, seized a greater political and economic hold on Spain in return for a much smaller effort. Germany was not averse to seeing Italian troops tied down, for this gave Hitler a freer hand in Austria and made the breach between Italy and France so wide that Germany could be assured of an Italian alliance without the need of any concessions.

Mussolini's remoteness from this kind of political reality emerges from a strange speech to the Senate in March 1938 in which he claimed that the Abyssinian and Spanish wars had increased and not weakened Italian military strength, and he even claimed to have learned that modern armies should not be heavily motorized. Few delusions could have been more disastrous—or more typical of this political dilettante.

★

Britain had meanwhile been gambling in the hope that appeasement would prevent a European war, guessing from experience that Italians would try to keep a foot in each armed camp. But Mussolini, by his so-called Gentleman's Agreement with the British in January 1937 merely aimed at concealing the fact that fascist Italy was geared to upsetting the Mediterranean *status quo*. Fortifications were built in Pantelleria, Tobruk, and the Dodecanese. Italian newspaper correspondents were withdrawn from London, and no Italian representative attended the coronation of George VI because the deposed Negus of Ethiopia was also invited. In March 1937 Mussolini made a provocative speech at Tripoli in which he again claimed to be the defender of Islam.

In September, wearing a specially designed uniform, Mussolini set out for Germany where he was given a tremendous reception. The display organized for his benefit, especially at the Essen factories and the army maneuvers in Mecklenburg, convinced him, as intended, that Germany would win the inevitable war. The 800,000 Germans listening to his speech on the Maifeld were impressive beyond anything he had ever imagined, and Hitler's personal admiration was intoxicating. From now onwards Mussolini clung to the myth of probable German invincibility, and this reception in 1937 was a fateful and fatal event in his life.

In November he therefore joined the anti-Comintern pact with Japan, and an Italian ship carrying armored cars to the Chinese was even ordered to wreck itself off the Chinese coast so as not to offend his new ally. In December, after an unserious two-minute meeting of the Grand Council, he announced Italy's withdrawal from the League of Nations. Quite apart from the sin of being dominated by the Western powers, the League was obnoxious by being democratic in procedure and by its antiquated aim of securing peace, friendliness, and the maintenance of international law.

In this same mood Austria was sacrificed as the price of German friendship, and in March 1938 Hitler was allowed to swallow the rump state which had once looked to Italy for protection. This caused the immediate collapse of the friendly Danubian bloc that Italy had tried to construct. It also lost Italy her chief advantage under the 1919 settlement since a strong European state was now back again on her Alpine frontier. Here was the most unanswerable condemnation of Mussolini's foreign policy, and this was an important moment in the progressive enslavement of Italy to the Germans. What must also have annoyed many Italians was the promise to give Germany the famous Discobolus of Myron. They could not know that many other masterpieces would follow later, but the Duce said he wanted fewer statues in Italy and more military trophies captured from defeated enemies.

★

As dictatorship became more firmly established, there was less need for showing consideration to the monarchy, or to the Church, or big business; and the dictator was increasingly ruled by whimsical intuition. Criticism, destructive or constructive, became rarer, and even his old cronies found him unapproachable and impervious to discussion. The chief weakness threatening any personal dictatorship is the lack of critical discussion. Some people trace the beginning of Mussolini's decay to his appointment of Starace as party secretary in 1931 (the same man Mussolini had called an "obedient cretin"), and of the cynical Buffarini as undersecretary at the ministry of the interior in 1933. But only in 1937–38 was decline obvious, aided by the fatal illusion of cheap success in Ethiopia and Spain.

As his tactical alliance with the men of wealth became less necessary, Mussolini reverted to type, to his plebeian associates and his former socialism. In the autumn of 1938 he escalated a campaign against the Italian bourgeoisie for preferring private gain to national victory. He thus gratuitously provoked the enmity of a most powerful class which had hitherto been a source of strength. Many first-hour fascists had always been nostalgic for the quasi-socialist program of 1919. Achille Starace, who was principally responsible for this anti-bourgeois campaign, was typical of all that well-to-do northerners detested in the proletarian South. In payment for their contempt he attacked their "bourgeois mentality" and tried to make it a scapegoat for fascism's failure to permeate the whole of national life. This mentality he defined as pacifist, pro-League, pro-England, and antisport; it was a preference for conserving gains already made, not risking in order to gain more; it was the habit of mind which always counted the cost and considered Balbo's propaganda flights in formation across the Atlantic as only a waste of aviation fuel.

Mussolini became surprisingly fierce on this point. Looking back to his socialist youth, he wondered what he would have done if he had truly under-stood the Italian middle classes instead of having a second-hand knowledge of them from books, and he concluded that he would have outdone Lenin himself in the cruelty of a totalitarian class war. He now turned with inverted snobbery against the top hat, butterfly collar, and spats that he had once affected. Party hierarchs were told to avoid night clubs, to stop drinking coffee (he himself loved coffee but his indigestion forbade it), not to use formal evening dress, nor to starch the collars of their black shirts; for these things were bourgeois. He also tried to abolish sleepers, dining cars, and first-class compartments on the rail-roads, and talked once more of closing the stock exchange. A later party secretary, Vidussoni, even tried to prohibit golf, to the vexation of the social climbers, Ciano and Grandi, who had his decision overruled.

One intention in all this was to toughen up the Italian people and be revenged on their soft middle-class mentality. Mussolini told Ciano that in reforesting the Apennines his idea had been to make the climate more severe, for this would kill the weaklings and make others more robust. Toughening the race was also one reason given in all seriousness for his entry into World War II, and again he expressed the astonishing wish that more Italians might be killed so as to bring home to them the glory and the sacrifice of war. Too few of them had been killed in Ethiopia and Spain. Too many automobiles made them soft and unwarlike. Italians, he used to say, must become less *simpatico*, more hard and ruthless; he would even like to see them hated and above all feared.

The Italian middle classes, however, hardly appreciated this intention. Nor did they like the higher death duties imposed in 1939, nor the attempt to compel the registration of bearer bonds in order to close up a major tax loophole. Nor would they have approved if they had known that Mussolini talked obscurely in his socialist vein about changing the system of private property. The growing unbalance in the national accounts was already alarming taxpayers without these new threats to middle-class prosperity.

Vastly increased government expenditure at home and imperialism abroad were creating huge debts which not even prestidigitation with the budget and "deferred payments" could altogether conceal. In only fifteen years since 1861 had revenue apparently balanced expenditure, but not until after 1934–35 was the unbalance catastrophic. The following table of published state expenditure reflects the loss of control in fascist foreign policy (the excess of expenditure over revenue is given in parentheses):

	(in million lire)	
1934–35	20,926	(2,199)
1935–36	33,057	(12,687)
1936–37	40,932	(16,230)
1937–38	38,642	(11,174)
1939–40	60,389	(28,039)

Thereafter, the deficit doubled each year. Evidently, totalitarian absolutism had not resulted in more accurate payment of taxes, and the increasing complexity of so many laws may even have made evasion easier. The minister of finance, Guarneri, who had been president of the Banca di Roma, repeatedly told the Duce that imperialism was ruining the country, but the latter became too accustomed to these jeremiads to listen, and the job hunters politicly tried to conceal facts which he evidently preferred not to know. A new ministry of the press and propaganda, created in 1935, reflected the fact that fascism depended not on efficient action, but on pretense and on attempting to persuade people of the illusion that the government was more efficient than its liberal predecessors.

Gradually the deficit lost Mussolini the confidence of the financiers who had once found him a good investment. Volpi continued in public to thank the Duce on behalf of Italian industry for his policy of imperialism and national self-sufficiency, but not all the big industrial barons were so naïve, and Pirelli, Cini, and Agnelli must have been becoming increasingly restive. As for ordinary citizens, another heavy devaluation of the lira in 1936 led to an increase of 20 per cent in the cost of living by May 1937.

★

Another symptom of Mussolini's aberrant behavior was his imitation of the German racial laws. According to the 1931 figures, there were only fifty thousand Jews in Italy, though others were later welcomed as refugees from Hitler's persecution. Mussolini had earlier boasted that there was no racial problem in Italy. The article on anti-Semitism in the *Enciclopedia* had even been written by a Jew. Some fascist *gerarchi* were Jews. Mussolini in the early 1930s talked disparagingly of Hitler's anti-Semitism, for it was a sore point that the German racial doctrines also excluded Italians from the *Herrenvolk*. Then came conquest in Africa which led to unfortunate miscegenation and a new sense of race consciousness. No doubt Mussolini's journey to Germany in 1937 accentuated this trend. On Hitler's return visit in May 1938 the two countries agreed to harmonize their internal as well as external policy. In July every newspaper had to print a declaration by well-known university professors who suddenly discovered that Italians were Nordic Aryans; and it warned people against the "peril" from Jews who were only one-tenth of 1 per cent of the population. Mussolini in private expressed the hope that the resultant persecution would make Italians more hated abroad.

Many world-famous scholars had to leave their posts. Admirals and generals were dismissed and Mussolini had to change his dentist. The law said that Jews could not become journalists, teachers, or notaries; recent immigrants were to be expelled; Jews could not attend state schools; they could not go to university or possess listed telephone numbers, and some of their property was forfeit. The "Italian race" had to be kept pure from corruption by "inferior elements," and hence contaminating marriages with people of other "races" were no longer valid without special permission—it was prudently forgotten that one of Marconi's parents was English and one of Cavour's Swiss. Marriage or concubinage with "natives" in Africa was punishable by five years in prison.

As with all fascist legislation, these laws were ineffectively enforced, especially as many people, fascists such as Balbo included, were shocked by such unscientific, shameless imitation of the barbarian nazis. The fact that a dictator could suddenly change his mind and decree that this much-conquered Italian peninsula was inhabited by a pure race must have given the more intelligent fascists something to ponder. But perhaps by this time there were not many intelligent fascists left.

55   The Drift Toward War, 1938–1940

British politicians still credulously hoped that Mussolini was too sensible to join Hitler, and the Anglo-Italian pact of March 1938 marked another stage in a futile policy of appeasement. A few days before signing this pact Mussolini confidently told the Germans that he would fight England, singlehanded if necessary. Once Italy had become united, he explained, she was obliged to expand further and become an empire, forced by an internal logic to dominate other neighboring countries: fascist imperialism was the culmination of the *risorgimento* and not its antithesis. Neighborly concessions by Britain merely encouraged him to calculate that the British by now must have been corrupted by wealth and comfort and their empire was moribund. This view was confirmed by the Munich conference in September where Mussolini posed as the savior of peace and the virtual arbiter of Europe.

This success was an illusion, but it was also intoxicating. Ciano's reference in parliament to Italy's "natural aspirations" was a prearranged cue for the well-drilled deputies to rise to their feet and shout "Nice, Corsica, Tunis," as the French ambassador watched from the gallery. Since Germany had won control of Austria, fascist Italy felt obliged to do something comparably ruthless, and France was the chosen victim. When more evidence was received of the falling French birth rate, and when Chamberlain even asked Mussolini's opinion on the text of a speech which he intended to make at Westminster, the Duce was further convinced that the western democracies were decadent and defeatist. Appeasement thus had a contraproductive effect, for it gave Italy the inaccurate conviction that she had nothing to lose by pulling down the pillars of European society. Annoyance was added to Mussolini's disdain when another diplomatic intercept informed him that certain uncharitable remarks had been made at his expense by the new French ambassador. Instead of being useful, these secret pieces of information always made Mussolini too angry to act sensibly, and when the Belgian ambassador sent home reports on pacifist feeling in Italy, the embassy received an anonymous letter of protest drafted personally in the Palazzo Venezia. Early in 1939, a vicious press campaign was opened against France, though the only people to suffer were the hundreds of thousands of Italian seasonal emigrants who earned their living across the French frontier.

The ambassador to Berlin, Attolico, was one of those Italian diplomats who put the interests of his country above those of the regime, and did what little he could to keep Italy from complete subjection to the Germans. He repeatedly sent warnings that Hitler was deceitful and would drag Italy into the wrong kind of war, but Mussolini's capriciousness and self-delusions made these warnings vain. On a sudden impulse in May 1939, enraged by an American press report about disaffection in Milan, Mussolini telephoned Ciano to conclude an immediate formal alliance with Germany. Ciano was astonished, for no detailed plans had been prepared for such a contingency, and it seemed merely a decision on instinct by someone who placed points of dignity and prestige before national interest.

So unready was Ciano that the text proposed by Germany for an offensive alliance was accepted with minor verbal amendments, and unexpectedly Mussolini found himself pledged to support Germany in an aggressive war. Ribbentrop reassured Ciano that Hitler looked forward to three years of peace, but no steps were taken by the Italians to include any precautionary clause, and by the time that the Duce realized his mistake the German generals had orders to prepare war against Poland. This was irresponsibility on a colossal scale. Thus easily could a self-styled realist be fooled. At least Mussolini's action should be contrasted with that of General Franco who managed to retain some independence and so saved his country from the horrors of another war.

Ciano admitted that the Pact of Steel was unpopular in Italy, though the fact was partly concealed by numerous missions pouring into Germany to exchange decorations and compliments. He also privately revealed his own doubts about its desirability. The foreign minister's diary shows how trivial and irresponsible were the architects of policy. Essential decisions were not made at all, or were based on gossip, or on personal animosities. Ciano said he would not read any memorandum if it were over a page long, and his "diplomacy" was often carried out on his almost daily visits to the golf course or at cocktail parties. Neither he nor the king seemed to be aware of impending tragedy, and up to June 1939 he was still talking in private of London's aggressive intentions against Italy. The Italian ambassador in Moscow spent three years without being once consulted or instructed on policy; yet every day Mussolini spent valuable time reviewing press photographs of himself and he boasted of reading three hundred newspapers. The Duce had discovered that he could do at a pinch without substantial successes so long as he could slant the news by propaganda, and he increasingly sought refuge in a make-believe land where he was insulated from the truth by mass meetings and eight-column headlines.

★

The invasion of Albania on Good Friday in April 1939 bore the hallmark of fascist Machiavellism and carelessness. Fearful that Germany might become a satisfied power before Italy achieved any success, and piqued at not being informed about Germany's invasion of Czechoslovakia in March, Mussolini determined to fend for himself. It could have been objected that Albania was hardly worth conquering, for it was already a vassal state and useful as such for asserting Italian influence in the Balkans. Subsidies and connivance at the financial irregularities of the puppet king Zog had so far proved much cheaper and perhaps more effective than actual occupation of the country, and already the small Albanian army was partly commanded by Italian officers. But the logic of fascism demanded another military victory.

The attack had to be improvized and the actual decision was made at the eleventh hour. There was in fact a total absence of calculated planning and hitches over disembarkation revealed an astonishing carelessness by the army. The Italian press, too, was unsure whether Italian strength had overcome fearful odds, or whether the Albanians were welcoming with open arms their delivery from the tyrant Zog. It was a familiar piece of fascist confusion.

The conquest of Albania apparently met some opposition from the king. It was widely resented in Europe and destroyed what was left of the confidence that Italy had tried to inspire in the Balkans. When the simple feudal patriarchs came to greet Starace, they were given a good dressing down because they offered to shake hands instead of using the Roman salute. This was obtuse and heavy-handed, and its effects were probably the reverse of what Starace had in mind.

★

The mismanagement of this invasion convinced Mussolini that he would need three years to prepare for general war. Apart from his armament requirements, he needed time to pacify Albania and Ethiopia and to repatriate the million Italians resident in France. He was already running out of foreign exchange and knew that a major war would dry up the proceeds of tourism. He was also planning to obtain foreign currency from a big exhibition for the twentieth anniversary of fascism in 1942. A quite excessive reliance was placed on this exhibition. But the chief argument for delay was military and industrial unpreparedness. Between 1860 and 1939, a third of state expenditure had apparently been used for military purposes, and yet this was now seen to have been insufficient or else had been most corruptly applied. In his saner moments, Mussolini appreciated how completely unprepared Italy was for a general war, but his capacity for self-deceit was unlimited, and it was an essential part of fascist dogma that politicians must act without counting the cost.

The measure of Mussolini's competence was that he continued to proclaim the inevitability of war and yet had no idea how to prepare for one. The Italian nation had not become military-minded, despite drilling children with the goose step and miniature machine guns, and despite the weekly half-holiday which workers were meant to spend on the parade ground. Mussolini later confessed to Admiral Maugeri that Italy was better equipped for war in 1915 than in 1939, so that the seventeen years of fascism had been to no purpose. The long and painful struggle for autarky, far from increasing Italian strength as had been promised, had done the reverse. Fascism, indeed, was being defeated by its own dogma.

As Mussolini had personally directed all three service ministries in 1925–29 and again after 1933, his later claims to have been misinformed about rearmament merely reflect his own incompetence. When things went wrong he put the blame on his chief of staff. But Badoglio protested at being unconsulted and completely left in the dark about vital questions of peace and war—to which protest, the answer came that military men could not appreciate the complex issues involved. Hitler used to bring his own chiefs of staff to meetings with Mussolini, but Mussolini usually came alone in case Italians should think he needed advice on strategy. In 1938, journalists were told that military matters took up most of the Duce's time, as they were also told that his working day was twelve to fourteen hours long. The reality was, however, different. Pretending to run half a dozen departments at once, he inadvertently made incompatible decisions in different ministries at the same time, for he had to rely on subordinates who were not seldom incompetent and untrustworthy. His undersecretary of the navy, Admiral Cavagnari, told him the true state of affairs but was not believed. His undersecretary of the army General Pariani, and of the air force General Valle, both failed to disillusion him when he claimed that "by a single order and in a few hours I can mobilize a force of eight million men." This delusion was a symptom of *folie de grandeur* and was a fatal product of a centralized regime where criticism or independence of mind were discouraged.

World War II would reveal the weaknesses of fascism, its carelessness and corruption, its insincerity and lack of criticism. With the army, for instance, training was not built around the hypothesis of a possible enemy, and the target date for military preparations was far in the future. Marshal Graziani grumbled about the plethora of generals and party placemen who held high military command with no qualifications for active service. Graziani was made army chief of staff, but with little power or responsibility, and even held a simultaneous operational command in Africa. Italian artillery in 1940 was still mostly of 1918 vintage and included guns captured from Austria in that year. The rifle issued was that of 1891. There was a serious shortage of antiaircraft ammunition, and people grumbled that this was due to the firm of Breda having acquired a lucrative monopoly of its manufacture. Colonel Canevari in October 1939 sent a memorandum to Mussolini which described the motorization of the army as derisory and tried to convince him that, despite what propaganda was claiming, his armored divisions did not exist. When serious parades were required, Senise describes how his police had to lend trucks to the army and have them painted khaki for the occasion. Never in fifty years, said General Favagrossa who was in charge of the rearmament program, had Italy been so weak.

The air force, according to Graziani, was antiquated and ill-equipped, though interservice rivalry may lie behind this criticism. A project for making torpedo bombers had been turned down in 1938, and Italy had no aircraft carriers because Mussolini rejected technical advice and said they were unnecessary. There were no plans to build a heavy tank, no naval air arm, and no tactical co-operation between navy and air force; hence no plans were ready to attack Malta. Captain Bragadin of the naval staff has confirmed the incredible fact that no study was made of Malta's defenses which shows that the navy had not been warned to prepare for war against England. This unpreparedness was also industrial, psychological, and administrative. When Italian experts drew up for Hitler a list of essential requirements, Mussolini doubled some of their estimates before forwarding the figures to Germany, so revealing to his ally an inability to estimate the consumption of raw materials on a rational basis. He could hardly grumble when the Germans in future cut Italian requests by half.

No doubt the Duce too often let himself be gulled by subordinates who deluded him into thinking that money was spent honestly and efficiently. The Albanian mobilization surprised him by revealing that many divisions were only about a regiment strong, and he had to admit that the effective front-line troops numbered ten divisions instead of his boasted seventy. Ciano in April 1939 questioned Valle's boast about possessing 3,006 effective aircraft because his own information put the number at only 982. A census was taken and planes were flown from one station to another so as to be counted twice. But Mussolini, who would easily lose his temper at a feeble display of drill in front of German generals, paid little attention to these military deficiencies, and Ciano's devastating comment was that he was afraid to face the truth. No doubt he also feared that the truth would expose the hollowness of his regime. Hence the calculation of peace or war was based on evidence that was entirely defective.

★

The Pact of Steel, signed in May 1939, obliged the Italians to fight alongside Germany if war broke out, and this gave Hitler an unconditional warrant that he could present at any time. Attolico's reports from Berlin about German double-dealing had been unheeded in Rome. Since Mussolini had not the courage to confess to Hitler that his own warlike posturing had been bluff, the Italian ambassador was instructed to confuse the issue and gain time. Mussolini's psychology thus became an ingredient in one of the most gigantic catastrophes in world history. He was acutely sensitive lest the world's newspapers might suggest that he was afraid to fight or that he was betraying his ally, and his own hope was that there would be another conference like that at Munich to avert war, since the democracies were too decadent to take up arms and he would win more cheap prestige as an intermediary. At the end of August he therefore began partial mobilization to make it look as though England had yielded to his threats, whereas it merely removed British confidence in his mediation and so eliminated one of the last chances of averting war.

Mussolini eventually realized that he had lost control over the situation. His associates found him old and touchy and ill, fearful that the Italians would laugh at him, grumbling that Hitler treated him with scant respect and merely sent him another message as Germany conquered each country in turn. One message arrived on August 21 saying that Hitler was signing an agreement with Russia, despite the anti-Comintern pact, despite the crusade in Spain to save civilization from bolshevism. This caused some difficult moments before the Italian press could be swung into line. A second casual note announced the German invasion of Poland just when Mussolini had cast himself as the brilliant mediator who was dramatically saving the world from war.

Hitler, bent on hostilities, cared not a rap for Italian opinion. Ciano may have been a convinced neutralist, but he lacked the moral courage to assert his views and in fact held his post of foreign minister only because of his constant submission to Mussolini. Ciano confessed that he was disgusted with Germany. Hitler had lied to the Italians and was now dragging them into an adventure which they had not wanted and which might ruin fascism. It was hard for them to know whether to hope for German victory or defeat. The Duce's reactions were first to say that Ciano was right; then to declare that honor obliged him to march with Germany, and he added that he wanted his share of the booty in Croatia and Dalmatia. On the other hand, the king, the general staff, Balbo, De Bono, Bocchini, Federzoni, and Bottai all recognized the need to stay neutral. So low was morale in September 1939 that a resolute move by the king might have crumbled the whole edifice of fascism. But perhaps people were so inert after years of dictatorship, so numbed and uncritical, that war came as an inevitable fifth act to conclude the tragedy.

Mussolini was never at his best on the rare occasions when subordinates dared to give conflicting advice, and in September 1939, while De Bono insisted that army morale was terrible, Alfieri and Starace reported on the contrary that the Italians were rejoicing at the prospect of war. For the moment Mussolini supported the peace party, because Britain and France had unexpectedly sided with Poland, and he grudgingly recognized that discretion should come before valor until he could see who was winning. Starace was therefore replaced as party secretary by Muti, the immediate pretext being that Signora Mussolini had seen Starace's dogs being taken for a walk by a uniformed official. Pariani, Valle, and Alfieri (in charge of propaganda) were also supplanted, and the neutralists remained temporarily in command.

It was too much to hope that the dictator would not change his mind at least once more, for after all his talk of war and national virility this discrepancy between word and action was a confession of weakness. On September 24, smarting at the memory of Salandra's double policy in 1914–15, he explained that Italy would have to intervene or lose her good name. Not appreciating the unfascist word "neutral," he invented the more manly term "nonbelligerent." On October 3, however, the pendulum had swung again. He told Ciano that he was jealous of the glory which Hitler was winning and it was to be hoped that Germany should meet with some salutary setback. A few months later he took bad faith to the point of warning Holland and Belgium after the Germans confidentially gave him advance notice of their invasion.

Mussolini had learned from his brother dictator that bold intuitive decisions were a hallmark of the *Führerprinzip* and he convinced himself that his own sudden changes of opinion were a true sign of Napoleonic genius. Bocchini, the chief of police, gave this inconstancy a different interpretation, suspecting that Mussolini was becoming deranged and should take another syphilis cure. Clearly the Duce was not himself. Bottai once saw him quite convulsed with pain and so did his son Vittorio. Clara Petacci had by now left her husband, who had been prudently exiled to Japan, leaving her as mistress of a secret apartment inside the Palazzo Venezia. Some people noted this as another sign of her paramour's increasingly eccentric behavior.

Mussolini's more sensible acolytes were convinced that neutrality was the only sensible attitude, with both belligerents competing for Italian interest and support. Trade statistics were rocketing. Nevertheless, this artificial prosperity, like the tactical relaxation of the British blockade in his favor, merely increased Mussolini's illusion of strength and he was eager to punish those Italians who were so unfascist as to prefer peace and affluence to war and conquest. His regime still depended on a journalistic mastery of propaganda to make people believe in his infallible intuition. He had lately spoken to his biographer De Begnac of how he needed to keep up a spectacle and impress the public. He could endure neutrality only until he suspected that people might be sneering at him as a coward, or until he thought that they needed a new conjuring trick to keep up the illusion of his own omnicompetence. This was why, after waiting through the winter to pick the winner, he was tempted, and eventually would choose the wrong side.

★

Some historians argue that this was the point where, after years of skillful and beneficent government, Mussolini accidentally miscalculated and took the wrong road. Against such a view one must consider whether war was not the logical conclusion of totalitarianism and of the propaganda which taught Italians that they and the Germans constituted a mighty master race destined to inherit the earth. Mussolini had publicly said he was ready "to make *tabula rasa*" of all civilized life, and by leading Italy into battle he was now fulfilling a long series of such promises. Here he was a victim of his own rhetoric. He even quoted Bernard Shaw to prove that dictatorship was the central theme of the age and also that never in history had conservatism triumphed over revolution, so that the democracies were bound to crumble at a touch. Juggling with words took the place of informed argument. It was part of the same logic when, instead of eight million men, only one and a half million soldiers could be mobilized in June 1940 at tremendous cost to the economy and only by accepting very low standards of equipment. The chickens were coming home to roost at last.

Misinformed as to his own strength, Mussolini had also been misled about foreign opinion, about the readiness for war of the Spanish republicans in 1936, and of the British in 1940, not to mention the Greeks. Most of his ambassadors feared to give their true opinion about foreign countries. It has even been said that fascist diplomacy was tested more in the relations of these ambassadors with the regime in Rome than in their relations with foreign governments. Once again one must conclude that war was declared because fascism could not free itself from its own intricate network of deceit.

Not only the foreign service but the intelligence service was also untrustworthy. The *Servizio Informazione Militare* seems to have had a passable information service inside Germany, but Ciano asserted three months after the outbreak of war there was still not a single reliable agent in Great Britain. According to the head of military intelligence, each of the services had distinct counterespionage organizations which sometimes planted false documents on each other and even arrested each other's agents. The complexity of such deceitfulness soon becomes bewildering. The army chief of staff in February 1938 had stated that munitions production would be completely ready for war by the spring of 1939, yet the director-general of munitions found himself in June 1940 with only one month's supply. Mussolini no doubt was often deceived by officials trying to cover up their corruption or inefficiency, or by the provincial secretaries of the party who told him how Italians were agog for war. But he was responsible for choosing such officials and they were a characteristic product of the *stile fascista*. To dismiss corrupt officials would have exposed his personal fallibility and misjudgement, so challenging the one essential precept that "Mussolini is always in the right."

56   Military and Political Defeat, 1940–1943

Averse from accepting any advice and information, Mussolini gambled with his country's fate as he changed his mind from one extreme view to another and then back again. In January 1940 he wrote sensibly to Hitler that they might gain most from peace, though much less sensibly he added that war might profitably be fought against Russia. Hitler did not reply for two months, and by that time Mussolini's intuitive sense had divined that the time for intervention was near if he did not want to be "left behind by history." The thought of leading a victory parade through an enemy capital was irresistible, and he now envisaged annexing an enormous area in central Africa and the Middle East. It was humiliating to stand with arms folded while others were writing history. To make a people great, he said, they must be forced into combat by a kick in the backside. He feared he was becoming the laughingstock of Europe, but informed Ciano that he would make the British sorry for their continued resistance and Italy's intervention would be the signal for their defeat. A month later he repeated that he would fight only when there was, as he put it, a mathematical certainty of winning. Yet his preparations were niggardly: air-raid shelters were given barely a thought, no plans were prepared for the evacuation of civilians, no industrial mobilization was decreed (there was no ministry of production until 1943). Mussolini even continued to export essential armaments in 1940. He sent some of his scanty supply of airplanes to help Finland, and munitions were even exported to England.

The king apparently realized for a brief moment that many Italians would rely on him to prevent this final miscalculation, and the chief of police thought that he could have arrested Mussolini at this point. Vittorio Emanuele was timidly supported by Badoglio and the general staff, who pointed out in May that there were very few tanks or armored cars and little more than a thousand combat planes available. But military men are trained to obey orders and Badoglio hardly pushed his objections very far. The tremendous sweep of the Germans through France seemed to offer glory to the Italian army with a minimum of effort, and unfortunately this gave a fatal example of how the intuitive genius of Hitler had successfully overridden technical objections by the military experts.

At the end of May, Mussolini appointed himself supreme military commander despite the constitutional claims of the king and the military claims of Badoglio to this position. Ciano had seldom seen him so happy for at last he had his dearest wish, to be a military leader in time of war. No advice was sought from the *Gran Consiglio*, which in fact did not meet until 1943. Nor did Mussolini consult other ministers, for he wanted the credit of victory for himself as much as he later wanted to saddle the generals with responsibility for failure. The army was given only two weeks' notice of war because the surrender of Belgium and the Dunkirk retreat meant that there was no time to lose before peace was declared. "It is suicide," so Badoglio told Mussolini, and received the extraordinary reply that the army need prepare only for a defensive war and the fighting would be over by September: he needed only a few thousand dead so as to be able to attend the peace conference. It had not entered his calculations that Britain might continue to fight after the fall of France. He himself was joining in the war to obtain the profits of victory, not to risk a serious military engagement.

★

On June 10, war was announced from the balcony of the Palazzo Venezia. The exiled socialist, Pietro Nenni, wrote in his diary:

> This is a war without any reason, for no real Italian interest is at stake; it is without excuse, because a German victory would mean for Italy and the rest of Europe just the brutal and intolerable hegemony of Hitler; and it would be without honor because Mussolini is attacking a France which already languishes on the point of defeat.

Italian intervention did the Germans no good, but only closed a useful aperture in the blockade system and committed Germany to the schemes of an incompetent megalomaniac. Hitler later admitted that Italy's intervention was less than helpful for Germany, and it was a disaster for the Italians. On a mistaken hypothesis about the war's duration, they suddenly threw themselves into a conflict from which they had little to gain and almost everything to lose.

A full-dress war was a fair test of whether behind all the rhetoric of fascism there lay anything substantial. After months of threatening talk there were still no adequate plans for the invasion of France, and Prince Umberto's troops were by Mussolini's express order still in defensive positions when he suddenly instructed them to attack. The generals explained that this would need twenty days to prepare, but the Duce would allow only three, for France had already asked for an armistice and he had at all costs to appear on the stage before the curtain rang down. Without adequate clothing, with "cardboard" boots that became legendary, many soldiers froze to death in this Alpine campaign. Mussolini was determined to use his single motorized division even in unsuitable mountain fighting. The general staff thought this to be farcical since the army was in fact praying that the French would not attack. Armellini called Mussolini's decision the desperate bluff of a poker player, and the Duce was described as ordering war as he would ask for a cup of coffee, with no idea of first providing the right plans and munitions. Jealous of the army leaders he even gave detailed orders to their subordinates without telling them, and then blamed them for the disorganization which ensued.

Luckily the Germans had already beaten the French before the Italian advance began, and only a slight penetration into Savoy had been made when, as Ciano said, fortunately for Italy an armistice was signed. But Mussolini was much upset. A tenth of Italy's submarines was lost in the first weeks, a quarter of her mercantile marine, and 217 soldiers had been killed. But Italy received neither Nice, Savoy, Corsica, nor the French Tunisian ports which would have been so useful later in the war, because Hitler needed the friendship of a defeated France more than that of his Italian ally.

Mussolini was still certain that the war would not drag on into the winter, and without consulting his Chiefs of Staff he began demobilizing. Three hundred thousand men returned to civilian life, and resources were diverted from arms production to the thousand-acre site designed to carry the immense marble weight of the "Third Rome" being built for the twentieth anniversary of fascism in 1942. When Mussolini repeatedly asked for the honor of assisting in the invasion of England, the German reply was a grudging acceptance. Fiat bombers were attacking Britain by the end of October, but a counteroffer by the Germans to help Italy bomb Suez showed Hitler's more realistic sense of priorities. A resentful Mussolini refused this offer and even betrayed pleasure over German defeat in the Battle of Britain.

In particular, lack of plans made it impossible to profit from Britain's critical position by invading Egypt; and this had an important effect on the course of the war. Three hundred thousand men in Africa were equipped with only 300 combat planes. Precious time and supplies were also wasted on occupying British Somaliland in August with the intention of annexing the largest possible expanse of territory before Britain sued for peace. When the army made every excuse for not moving toward Suez, Mussolini drove a reluctant Graziani into an offensive with ill-equipped troops in order to win the glory which (so he said) Italy had been seeking for three centuries. But fascist pride led him to reject another offer of help from German armored divisions, and the only result of this miscalculated offensive in North Africa was to leave Graziani's army in an untenable salient.

One subsequent success was that interception of American messages betrayed detailed figures to the Italians about British armor in North Africa and about the Malta convoys. But this came too late to prevent Graziani's ten divisions being beaten in January 1941 by two divisions perilously supplied from distant England, and the Italians were then chased out of Egypt in a five-hundred-mile retreat with the loss of a hundred thousand prisoners. Eritrea fell in February, Somalia in March, Addis Ababa in April when the Duke of Aosta surrendered with an even larger force. Courage and patriotism could not compensate for gigantic political errors, nor for military unpreparedness, nor for the fact that fascism had filled so many posts with party placemen, nor that it had crushed individual initiative and taught people to rely blindly on an organization which was bureaucratic, corrupt, and inefficient. A court of inquiry censured Graziani's conduct, and Badoglio reported that this rival general had proved thoroughly incompetent. The man who had lost one reputation through his cruelties in Ethiopia now lost another through sheer military incapacity. But the incompetence was quite as much that of Badoglio himself, who for fifteen years had been in charge of staff planning as well as industrial research and had little to show for it. Graziani went into disgruntled retirement, and Badoglio was shortly to follow him.

★

Those chiefly responsible were not the generals but fascism and the politicians. This is exemplified in Ciano's scheme to invade Greece. Once again a principal motive was irritation against Germany, this time against her sudden occupation of Romania. Mussolini complained that Hitler always confronted him with a *fait accompli*, and this time he meant to pay the Germans in their own coin by making them learn from the newspapers that Italy had taken Greece. Mussolini added that he would resign from being an Italian if anyone found difficulties about fighting the Greeks. It never occurred to him that German secretiveness might be justified by the deliberate leakages of information at Rome. He likewise never dreamed that Greece had any chance of successful resistance but assumed that a few days would bring victory.

The chiefs of staff pointed out the obvious objections but were overruled and given only a fortnight and allowed three weeks to switch their plans to this difficult campaign. Mussolini changed his mind repeatedly about its timing. The date he eventually chose was October 28, the anniversary of the "march on Rome," though it was madness to begin mountain warfare so late in the rainy season. Armellini adds that staff headquarters learned about the final ulti-matum only by listening to the London radio. As an ultimate absurdity, on October 5 another order had been issued for demobilization, and large numbers of troops were sent home at the very same time as others were being hastily remobilized.

This Greek adventure led to Italy's greatest military disaster of the whole war because after a few days the Italian army was in full retreat. Hitler was furious that Mussolini had provided the British with bases in Greece from which they would be able to bomb the oil wells of Romania. In November half the Italian battle fleet was put out of action while anchored at Taranto, since the lack of reconnaissance planes allowed a British aircraft carrier to come within a few miles unobserved. Almost as bad, Franco had lately intimated the possibility of Spain entering the war and it was the Italian failure in Greece which restrained him. Mussolini and Ciano were personally to blame for this military defeat though they pretended that the general staff had incompetently botched the invasion. Ciano lamely assured Mussolini that he had bribed the Greek forces to give way, but probably much of the money had been diverted into fascist pockets *en route*. Even the replacement of Marshal Badoglio by General Cavallero could not save the Duce's reputation, especially as Cavallero had been a director of the Ansaldo munitions trust and therefore was deeply suspect in army circles.

Hitler had the pleasure of pointing out the folly of acting without German advice and assistance. German troops had to be brought in to rescue Mussolini, or otherwise the Italians would have been driven out of both Africa and the Balkans. The arrival of German planes in Sicily after January 1941 altered the pattern of war in the Mediterranean, and Germany henceforward called the tune in both strategy and politics. From these early defeats in the winter of 1940–41 the Duce never recovered, and his regime suffered accordingly in popular esteem. Fascist propaganda could not conceal that the British navy was even able to bombard Genoa unmolested.

*

The closer that relations with Germany became, the more Italians admired German successes, and the deeper their fear of German domination. It was natural for the ruling power in Austria to seem a potential enemy. Italians were staggered by nazi cruelties, and even Mussolini was surprised that his allies could surpass him in brutality while feeling no compunction. Moreover he had staked everything on Hitler's assurance of a quick German victory and never forgave the *Führer* for letting him down. Owing to their very totalitarianism, it was never possible for these two Axis powers to develop a joint military command such as the democracies constituted naturally among themselves, and this was a vital factor in the final result. Hundreds of thousands of Italian workers were drafted into labor service in Germany to replace Germans sent to the front, and were often treated like prisoners of war or another subject race. Italy became almost a colony of the Reich, and this built up a huge fund of anger and resentment.

Mussolini sorrowfully described himself as only "the rear light" of the Axis and was not pleased when the king told him his nickname of "the Gauleiter for

Italy.". Had the alliance not been the last prop to his personal dictatorship, he might have tried to extricate himself. In June 1941 his entourage heard him say that he just about had enough of that man Hitler and of being summoned to conferences like a waiter by a bell. On such occasions Mussolini had to listen to boring monologues that he could hardly understand or question. He therefore decided to continue fortifying the ridge of the Alps: one day those fortifications might be useful against Germany. He now began to find the *Führer* less heroic, more lachrymose and hysterical. He was justifiably piqued when Hitler's personal messages were timed with obvious deliberation to arrive so that he would have to be wakened at night to receive them. So vain was Mussolini that in his meetings with Hitler he refused an interpreter lest this should bring into question his own imperfect knowledge of foreign languages; hence the Germans had it all their own way and the Italian staff sometimes barely discovered what was being planned. In July 1941 Mussolini told one of his ministers that he foresaw an inevitable crisis in relations with Germany. He even occasionally wondered if it would not be better for the western allies to win the war. He was glad that they were bombing Germany by day and night, because Italy would at some point be fighting Germany and so must not build up any legend of her invincibility. He also said he would keep fifteen divisions on the northern frontier ready for the day of reckoning against his nominal ally.

This was crazy talk. In fact his personal security depended on the presence of the Germans in Italy. The Gestapo was in Rome; Rommel virtually took over the Libyan campaign early in 1941 though nominally under Italian command; and Kesselring set up his headquarters at Frascati in December. German help offered the last hope of winning the war, yet Mussolini knew that the Germans represented a force stronger than himself and it was his nature to resent the fact. They had not only duped him into signing a blank check in the Pact of Steel, but had then duped him into a war several years before he was ready and into staking the whole future of his people on German talk of a lightning victory. Finally, they were now taking over the Italian war effort because fascism was so incapable. The pill was a bitter one, especially when administered so publicly.

★

Italians, whether fascist or antifascist, fought loyally in their country's defense. Yet many felt from the outset that their cause was wrong, and as visions of a quick victory receded the war grew increasingly unpopular. Mussolini was forced to admit that he had little faith in the "Italian race," since at the first bombardment that destroyed a famous picture "they would be overcome by a crisis of artistic sentimentalism and throw in the towel." He even said that the Italians of 1915 were better than those of 1940, though this was a poor commentary on the achievements of fascism. Italians he now described as being a race of sheep. Eighteen years had not sufficed to change them; it would need eighteen centuries or more. His attempt to mobilize the civilian population and pervade them with a fascist style of life had evidently failed.

By July 1941 the undersecretary for the interior, the rascally Buffarini Guidi, described how antifascism was rooted everywhere, threatening and implacable even though unostentatious. Newspapers were ordered not to mention queues and shortages. People were becoming torpid and cynical as the theory of fascism was obviously belied by the facts, and the soldiery were openly sarcastic against a government which had led them into such a war irresponsibly and ill-prepared. What Italy stood to gain from fighting was not clear. Everyone listened to the London radio, even the generals and fascist leaders who wanted to know the facts that propaganda might be concealing from them.

By the spring of 1942 there was news of strikes once again, of clandestine newspapers, and of *carabinieri* firing into the air over crowds of hungry citizens. A sudden fascist decision to reduce prices by 20 per cent merely led to the disappearance of foodstuffs from the stores, and a black market grew up in every commodity as a necessary counterpart to official disorganization. The price of land soared as people defied regulations and scrambled to invest in something solid, and a general inflation of prices progressively undermined the loyalty of fixed-income groups.

Further signs of disaffection appeared in a renewed struggle with Catholic Action in 1941, and from May 1942 onward in successive purges inside the fascist party. Ciano, Bottai, Grandi, Farinacci, and Starace, had already in 1941 been suddenly ordered to leave their comfortable sinecures and undertake active service in the front line: some of them appreciated the chance to earn more decorations, but others were not so keen, especially when the number of medals was limited because of evident abuse. An unknown young man was appointed to run the fascist party, whose sole qualification was hero worship of the Duce, and under whom organization and discipline became quite out of hand. Only the army and the Germans held the country together. Discontent must have been widespread, particularly after military failure and the growing subordination to Germany; yet there was a residual faith in Mussolini's charisma and not the least glimmer of revolution could be perceived.

★

The fortunes of war had meanwhile gone to and fro. Rommel's offensive in North Africa was launched in March 1941 and caught Wavell unguardedly trying to stretch his limited forces in support of Greece. Bypassing Tobruk, the Afrika Korps reached the Egyptian frontier after barely a fortnight. In April an Axis offensive against Yugoslavia was started, provoking a fierce nationalistic uprising against Italy which was to obliterate all the gains won by prefascist diplomats at Rapallo. Two weeks sufficed for the Germans to conquer Greece where the Italian army had failed in six months.

In June 1941 began a German invasion of Russia. Mussolini had been given only the vaguest intimations of this move and was caught in the middle of negotiations with Russia for a commercial treaty. Once again, however, he accepted Hitler's confident assurances of easy victory and eventually he sent

200,000 Italians to the Russian front—contrary to Hitler's wishes and without consulting his own ministers and generals. He even pretended that these divisions were superior in equipment to those of Germany. But in fact this poorly equipped Italian army in Russia had an impossible task. If used in Libya, so many men might possibly have tipped the scales of war against Britain.

In December 1941, Japan wantonly brought America into the war and so sealed the fate of the Axis. Mussolini was delighted and at once declared war on the United States, apparently under the illusion that this would make victory more simple. The more grandiose the war, the more he felt himself to be the destined man of history. He declaimed against Roosevelt as someone who for years had been planning a war with aggression, and his continuing under-estimation of the Americans was the product of a mind that had become accustomed to work by intuition and not intelligence.

For a brief moment, victory seemed within sight. After a second offensive by the British through the western desert in November 1941, by May 1942 the British front in Cyrenaica had again crumbled. Tobruk fell with thirty thousand prisoners. In June the Germans reached El Alamein. Mussolini again thought that his hour had come and flew to Africa, intending a triumphal entry into the Egyptian capital; but his premature arrival aroused the mocking ridicule of the Germans, and after waiting three weeks he had to return home.

In reality the battle of supply was already lost. Before the war, 80 per cent of Italian imports had come through Gibraltar or Suez, and both routes had now been closed for two years. Hitler's altered directives and Mussolini's lack of forethought had left Malta impregnable though only twenty minutes' flying distance from Sicily, and a few battered British reinforcements continued to reach the island. Yet Italian convoys in the short passage to North Africa sometimes lost every ship through the Allies' complex system of intelligence, and overall up to half of the supplies for the Afrika Korps were being sunk. Rommel was checked for lack of fuel at El Alamein whither all his supplies had to be brought for hundreds of miles under enemy fire. Montgomery's victory in November 1942, coming together with the American landing in French North Africa and the battle of Stalingrad, must have convinced most Italians that the war could not be won.

Mussolini had lately suffered what was possibly the recurrence of his stomach ulcer (though post-mortem medical reports suggested a psychosomatic illness). Bottai noted this combination of intellectual and physical decline and reported that the Duce no longer possessed his former fascination but was increasingly dependent on flattery. People were surprised to find him indecisive and superstitious, afraid of the evil eye, afraid of being ridiculed. Even his flair for publicity was gone, and his war bulletins were less happy in their effect. He compared himself more frequently to Napoleon and even to Jesus, as delusions of grandeur grew to compensate for his weakness. He grumbled to Ciano that Italians were letting him down and "even Michelangelo needed marble before he could make his statues." He was glad to see so many German casualties in Russia and positively vexed that so few Italians were killed. He rejoiced at a heavy snowfall or a reduction in food rations because that would kill off the weaklings and strengthen the fiber of what he termed this mediocre Italian race. He expressed a ghoulish delight that Naples was being heavily bombed: the race might thus become harder and more Nordic. This, it must be remembered, was the man who was not only prime minister but head of six out of seventeen ministries in the cabinet and was also military commander in chief. Megalomania could go no further. Another measure of his declining ability was the scandalous power that his mistress's family came to exercise. They evidently secured an influence in some appointments ranging from ambassadors to professors and were thought to have built up a fortune that was dispatched to safekeeping in Spain by way of the diplomatic bag.

By January 1943, half Mussolini's armies in Russia were lost; the navy, whose fine ships had been immobilized for lack of fuel, was now working on only 24,000 tons of oil a month; and in May, Marshal Messe surrendered with the remaining Italian forces in North Africa. In early July the Allies landed in Sicily. There were only 500 effective aircraft left. Nevertheless Mussolini retained the loyalty of many. Perhaps he had given false encouragement with sinister references to a secret weapon which he forbore to particularize, and by his delusions about an imminent revolt by his friends in India against the British and of blacks in the United States. He had assured Hitler that Sicily was impregnable, and in June made a fantastic speech to tell Italians that "the enemy has no further card to play." He was wrong and few people can have believed him, yet disaffection never became active revolt and there was still little practical indication that he was imposing himself on a country burning to be free.

★

Under these crushing blows, cracks were nevertheless appearing inside the fascist ruling class. Elderly party leaders did not like being put through assault courses, nor being sent to fight in the Balkans. The least dishonest among them must have been amazed at the revelations of industrial and military weakness. Bottai mentions that the Duce, when he informed the cabinet of the loss of North Africa, could defend himself only with the argument that the Germans had retreated first and that events would soon turn in Italian favor. Bottai, De Bono, De Vecchi, Grandi, even Ciano were increasingly afraid that their leader was leading them to disaster. In February 1943 Mussolini dismissed the *frondeurs* and any remaining ministers who preserved some independence of mind. They were replaced by insignificant, unknown men, one of whom was suffering from a serious mental disorder. The new party secretary was Carlo Scorza, a first-hour fascist implicated in the mortal attack on Amendola in 1925.

Some of the dissident fascists began to edge toward the king and to wonder whether the Allies might accept them as a new government if they managed to defenestrate Mussolini. As early as November 1942, Vittorio Emanuele privately urged Ciano to discover some link with the enemy, but even after the North African defeat the king was not prepared to take any positive initiative that might compromise or endanger his own position. He was waiting for a move by some subordinate who could be repudiated in the event of failure.

Working along parallel lines with these dissident fascists were the old-school liberals, some of whom still kept in remote touch with the Court, and all of whom remembered with nostalgia the prefascist era of political liberty. Hitler thought in May 1943 that certain Italians would be glad to become a British colony if this were the only way to free themselves. Most people must at least have resented being treated as a German colony. Early in June 1943 Bonomi called on the king; so did Soleri; Orlando and Casati were also consulted. But Vittorio Emanuele was quite out of touch with liberal opinion and was embarrassed and hesitant when dealing with prefascist politicians whom he had once betrayed.

A long-standing tradition of the dynasty was to turn in an emergency to the army leaders. General Ambrosio, who in February 1943 succeeded Cavallero as chief of staff, saw the king every week and is known to have pressed Mussolini to make peace. Marshal Badoglio, too, had a national reputation and a known loyalty to the throne. But these officers had been schooled to await orders and to insist on being covered by the responsibility of higher authority. Admiral Thaon di Revel and General Zupelli also saw the king, but no one was ready to risk serious action without a positive written command or at least a fairly distinct understanding that they would be supported.

The final impulse came rather from malcontent party leaders, especially those dismissed earlier in 1943. At the center of this plot was the Duke d'Acquarone, the minister of the royal household, who had recovered a political importance for this office similar to that won by Gualterio in the 1860s and Rattazzi in the 1890s. Through him the king learned that some of the chief lieutenants of fascism were considering ways of saving themselves by the removal of Mussolini, and hints were dropped in return that the king might act if a public appeal were made to him.

So strongly entrenched was Mussolini in power that not until the invasion of Sicily was anyone ready to rebel. The bombing of Rome in July was another fact that startled many civilians into rebelliousness, for hundreds of thousands had swarmed to the Holy City as a place immune from attack. Mussolini arranged a meeting with Hitler on July 19, their thirteenth encounter. But he did not dare carry out his private undertaking that he would use this occasion to break loose from Germany. Hitler made acid references to the conduct of Italian troops in Sicily and was unwilling to send extra help against the Allied invasion because doubtful if it would be properly used. If Mussolini, despite all his boasting, was not able to defend Italy and not even able to retain the confidence of her German allies, no hope remained, and Acquarone therefore intimated to Badoglio and Ambrosio that the king was at last ready to intervene.

★

In the night of July 24–25 came the meeting of the *Gran Consiglio* in which Grandi guardedly suggested that Mussolini should invite the king to resume his old prerogatives as commander of the armed forces. A number of different accounts have been given of this dramatic occasion for no stenographer was allowed to attend. Grandi brought a live grenade in case of emergencies and gave another to De Vecchi, but unnecessarily. Mussolini was ill and tired, and again had little better argument than an obscure reference to a secret weapon which he had in store to resolve the situation. After ten hours of discussion, Grandi's motion was carried by nineteen votes to seven, not to remove Mussolini but only to limit his authority. De Bono, De Vecchi, Federzoni, Ciano, Alfieri, Bottai, and De Stefani were among the majority nineteen, five of whom were executed a year later for this "betrayal" of their leader.

Mussolini tried to defend himself by claiming that opinions of the *Gran Consiglio* were no more than advisory, but the king quickly seized his chance and decided to go one step further than most council members can have wished. Before midday on the 25th he had signed the appointment of Badoglio as premier. The *carabinieri* were ordered to arrest Mussolini outside the king's private residence, and this was done without fuss or difficulty. A royal proclamation announced that the king "intends to resume effective command of all forces according to Article 5 of the constitution, and also to resume the supreme initiative of decision which our institutions allow him."

The Great Dictator had collapsed and the emptiness of his whole system was suddenly exposed. He had been ousted with astonishing ease, not by popular revolution, nor by the antifascists, but by a royal edict coming on top of action by the fascist leaders themselves. Mussolini told a friend a few months later that the Italian people hated him in defeat as much as they had loved him in victory. Despite the oath taken by millions of party members that they would die in his defense, there were unprecedented scenes of public rejoicing and only a single fascist committed suicide at the news of his removal. Historians have concluded in retrospect that no regime in all history had fallen under such unaminous condemnation.

This may well be true, but it leaves unresolved why in that case this fall had been so long delayed. By waiting so long, people had allowed fascism to lose Italy's colonial empire, devastate her homeland, and temporarily throw away her good name. Mussolini had perverted politics, destroyed very many lives, undermined national self-confidence, and perverted the education of two generations. For twenty years he had educated people in subservience and corrupt practices, and now he was to divide the nation in a painful and shocking civil war. It needed far more than the joyful shouting and illumination of that fatal Sunday in July 1943 before this incalculable damage could be repaired.

SECTION THIRTEEN: THE TRANSFORMATION OF ITALY, 1943–1969

57   Liberation, 1943–1947

For his new prime minister, the king did not choose an antifascist, nor Marshal Caviglia whom Grandi urged on him, but Badoglio who had consistently held immensely lucrative offices under Mussolini. Fascism was thus replaced not by the old liberals but by a monarchical autocracy founded on the army, the police, and the ex-fascist civil service. Ordinary citizens had to rest content with the promise of free elections once hostilities were over.

Meanwhile the fighting continued for another six weeks, since the king was afraid to break from the Germans and indeed he gave Hitler his word of honor that he had no intention of deserting the Axis alliance. The fascist party was declared illegal, but the political censorship continued, most fascist appointees remained unpurged, and Badoglio did not at first disband the fascist militia. Such an ambiguous policy had one grave failing, for it forced both Germans and the western Allies to treat Badoglio as a potential enemy. Evidently he hoped to wriggle free from both sides without further fighting and without risk to either throne or army. But this was a grave miscalculation and made a bad situation much worse.

On September 3, when the Allies were poised to attack the Italian mainland, Badoglio agreed to an armistice. Two landings were made, in Calabria and south of Naples, but the king and Badoglio, after first promising to help the invasion, reneged on this promise and at the last moment even requested the allied leadership to cancel a planned attack against Rome. On September 9 they fled precipitately to the South, and the Italian army, left without orders, without even a commander, resisted the Germans for a few hours but then was forced to surrender. Although the bulk of the navy escaped from German hands and sailed for Malta, the generals allowed their forces to be disarmed with little positive resistance, for a totalitarian education under fascism had effectively destroyed any sense of personal initiative and individual responsibility or obedience. German forces quickly occupied Rome and the whole peninsula down as far as Naples, meeting little reaction. Only in Naples did a popular insurrection help the Allied forces check this advance—and in retaliation for that brave effort the Germans destroyed much of the priceless Neapolitan archives, permanently obliterating many chapters of Italian history.

★

Mussolini spent his sixtieth birthday a prisoner of the king. He passed the time practicing his German, skimming through twenty-four volumes of Nietzsche sent by the Führer, and trying to discover how the blame for defeat could be pinned on either Hitler or the Italian people. On September 12 a brilliant operation by German glider troops set him free, while Badoglio's Italian police in his mountain prison, despite orders to guard him, stood to attention and saluted his captors. Nothing much remained now of Mussolini's political flair, none of the skill in propaganda, nothing of the swagger and braggadocio. Physically, he looked a beaten man, hollow-cheeked, often in pain. There remained only the colossal conceit which claimed his recapture to be one of the most dramatic moments in the whole course of human history.

★

When the king reformed his government at Brindisi, one unfulfilled hope was that Italian politicians had learned in bitter years of persecution to underplay the factious dissensions which had helped Mussolini into power. Eventually, in June 1944, Badoglio's "nonpolitical" administration gave way to a broad coalition under Bonomi in which six reconstituted parties, from liberal to communist, were all represented. A number of familiar names from pre-fascist Italy now reappeared. Among the conservative liberals, Einaudi, Orlando, De Nicola, and Croce had survived to contribute a sense of continuity to a younger generation with no experience of self-government. Among other survivors were Sforza, Nitti, and Don Sturzo. At the head of the Christian democrats was not the elderly Sturzo but Alcide de Gasperi, who had spent much of the fascist period as a papal librarian in the Vatican City.

Unlike the Christian democrats, Italian communism had retained some clandestine organization under fascism; and, equally important, the cohesion and combativeness of the communists enabled them to form excellent partisan units in the final stages of the war, from which they therefore emerged with a special prestige. Palmiro Togliatti was an able politician, and his deputy, Luigi Longo, was an active leader in the armed Resistance against Germany. Togliatti had once supported some of the worst excesses of Stalinism, but now showed unexpected tactical mobility by joining Bonomi's government, as well as by promising to respect religion and not to collectivize land or industry. This was communism with a difference, a far more positive political force than in 1921–22, and the party remained inside the government coalition for three years. Very close to this extreme Left were the socialists whose leader, Pietro Nenni, proved more intransigent and less agile a tactician than Togliatti; he usually ranged his supporters alongside the communists in a united popular front, though refused to stay with them in government when Bonomi formed a new administration in December 1944.

Another much smaller group with a radical program was a new Party of Action, which tried for a brief while to act as a "third force" between this popular front and the conservatives. These "actionists" were prominent among partisan forces fighting against the German occupation of northern Italy. Their leaders were greatly respected for their courage and integrity—among them Ferruccio Parri, Ugo La Malfa, and Ernesto Rossi. Most of them had been disciples or companions of Salvemini, Gobetti, and Rosselli. Their hostility to the monarchy and to the Church was far more doctrinaire and uncompromising than that of Togliatti. As perhaps was inevitable with a party of intellectuals, they liked to make fine distinctions which eventually undermined their political solidarity. But until elections could be held, the degree of popular support behind their or any other party was anyone's guess.

★

Meanwhile, the war dragged on. The Allies advanced very gradually and made a further landing at Anzio in January 1944. In May the "Gustav Line" collapsed and Cassino fell. Rome was entered in June, Florence in August, after the Germans refused Mussolini's request to sacrifice civilians in a street by street resistance. There was then a halt to the Allied advance, which had tragic results in prolonging what was now a civil war. In part this resulted from the allied policy to draw German forces into the peninsula and so weaken their chances of resisting an invasion of France.

Mussolini was thus given time to establish a new puppet administration—as its various departments were mostly scattered around Lake Garda it became known as the Republic of Salò. The trimmers and the opportunists had already abandoned fascism in 1943, and there were left only the rogues and the dreamers, among them Farinacci, Buffarini Guidi, and General Graziani the embittered rival of Badoglio. The German army allowed little scope to this fascist rump, for Hitler had no further interest in Italy except as a battleground on which to fight the Allies and the Italian partisans.

Though Mussolini went on grumbling against the Germans, he nourished a desperate faith in ultimate German victory by the use of secret weapons. He even spoke of a "death ray" which might possibly turn the scales. Another naïve hope was that the western Allies would break with Russia. He sometimes said he was ready to abandon Germany by making a separate peace with either West or East, though he thought it would be preferable to become a Russian satellite than an American colony. He was comfortably sure anyway, win or lose, that fascism had by now destroyed the British Empire: his defiant assertion was that above all he had been against Britain, and he fancifully recalled how British and French ill will had foiled his self-sacrificing efforts in the 1930s to support peace in Europe.

The prospect of defeat accentuated Mussolini's bitterness against his fellow Italians for shattering his imperial dreams. He lamented their factiousness which he had failed to correct, though he was glad to think that this same factiousness would equally undermine any attempt to restore liberal government. He conceived the idea that he had not created fascism but merely exploited fascist tendencies existing subconsciously in all Italians. It comforted him to believe that, even if he should be beaten, they would one day return to his methods.

Two traits noted by Mussolini's new German doctor in 1944 were an extreme credulousness and an absolute inability to say no to anyone when face to face: these characteristics help to explain why his encounters with Hitler had been one-sided and why his preparations for war had been so hopeless. His last months of life revealed a stupendous incapacity for self-criticism. He was seldom seen in public but played solitaire by the lake and tried unsuccessfully to secure obedience from the many discrepant factions in this Republic of Salò. Buffarini Guidi was even tapping the Duce's telephone. Dozens of new uniforms casually appeared. So did private police forces that freely used torture and assassination. The chief internal enemy he identified as no longer communism but capitalism, and he therefore proclaimed sweeping measures of nationalization to "liquidate" the bourgeois classes whose inertia and defeatism had been too strong for him. He let it be known that he was applying himself to the study of Plato's *Republic*, and made searching inquiries of a French visitor about the astrological predictions of Nostradamus.

This fascist republic is of little importance and the Duce's office was later found to contain mostly photographs and newspaper clippings about himself. Some Italians were still willing to launch their country into further civil strife on his behalf. Some of the last-ditch adherents, the philosopher Gentile among them, were assassinated in a growing fever of reprisal and counterreprisal. Other fascists came to a different sort of violent end, for Mussolini had De Bono and his own son-in-law, Ciano, shot in the back as traitors, because of their lukewarm vote in that final meeting of the *Gran Consiglio*. Grandi escaped to Lisbon where he gave Latin lessons; De Vecchi took refuge in a monastery; and other *gerarchi* quietly followed Mussolini's son to South America. In April 1945 the partisans caught Mussolini near Lake Como, disguised in a German greatcoat, clutching packages of mysterious documents which he theatrically asserted could be used to win Italy the peace. Only the faithful Clara Petacci remained with him. Both were summarily shot, and their bodies strung upside down with those of a dozen other fascist leaders in the Piazzale Loreto at Milan.

With this gruesome scene the curtain fell on the period of fascism. Italy, which had endured and assimilated so many barbarians, had been forced to support yet another cruel tyrant and a twenty-year sack as bad as any in her history. The fascist regime had in some respects penetrated deeply into Italian life but mostly had been empty pomp and vacuous speech. Benedetto Croce satisfied himself, despite his theories of historical continuity, that fascism had been essentially extraneous to Italy and its history. This was a dangerously simple view; and yet totalitarianism in Germany had been infinitely more thorough and hateful. In his last years Mussolini fondly manufactured a legend with which disciples might be able to justify his life and prepare a second more nationalistic *risorgimento*. He could not be expected to admit that aggressive fascist nationalism had held Italy back from greatness, nor that his countrymen were poised to break free of this incubus and thereby achieve unprecedented development and prosperity.

*

In April 1945 the Anglo-Americans overran northern Italy, and a popular patriotic movement helped to bring about the German capitulation in May. Although there had been little sign of a resistance organization in Rome or the

South, antifascist cadres of fighters had subsequently been formed all over the North: working sometimes on their own, sometimes with the Allies, these partisan groups tied down a number of German divisions. Parri, one of their commanders, claimed that in August 1944 there were 80,000 fighters on this clandestine front, and perhaps nearly 200,000 by April 1945. Certainly their achievements were a big factor in restoring Italian morale and self-confidence. Some of the best elements in the country were prominent in the Resistance, and it provided a fine training in social consciousness as well as a new manifestation of idealistic patriotism. No one who lived through such an experience could forget it; never before had ordinary citizens participated so actively in national life. From many sources—neo-realist films, the poetry of Quasimodo, or in the writing of Pavese, Vittorini, and Pratolini—the impression emerges that this liberating war against Mussolini and Hitler penetrated far more deeply into the conscience of contemporaries than the nineteenth-century *risorgimento* had done.

Although individuals of many political beliefs fought together in the Resistance movement, most partisans were well to the Left, so capturing considerable influence in local government and hence in what would soon become the electoral machine. This posed a strong political challenge to the ideals and leaders of old-style liberalism; and one result was that, during the five-months premiership of Parri who followed Bonomi in June 1945, Italy came closer to a radical process of social and political change than at any time since 1861. That the country stopped short of drastic social changes was due to the conservative instinct of so many of her people, the entrenched strength of vested interests, and the presence of an allied army occupation.

★

The aftermath of war proved to be extremely difficult, not least because the partisans put a keener edge on the class struggle and gave many people a new political awareness; but gradually the country returned to something more familiar. Of particular interest is that it was the communist Togliatti who, as minister of justice, granted an amnesty for all the many crimes and brutalities of the previous regime. The problem of political purging was less divisive than in France, since in Italy nearly everyone had been involved in fascism and therefore the apportionment of guilt seemed less relevant. Cobelligerency alongside the Allies helped to mitigate the terms of peace that Italy was obliged to accept in 1947. Because of Mussolini's earlier misdeeds, the peace settlement awarded Istria and Fiume to Yugoslavia and the Dodecanese islands to Greece, but at least Trieste was saved for Italy, and so were the German-speaking areas of the South Tyrol. In the northeast, De Gaulle tried to occupy the Val d'Aosta for France, but the other Allies stood firm, and French annexations were ultimately confined to several small Alpine villages. The colonial empire in Africa, which had cost so much in men, money, and emotional commitment, had to be surrendered despite De Gasperi's anguished protest. Croce tried to argue that, since in his view fascism had been extraneous to Italy and imposed on her by outside forces, it was unfair to penalize Italians for fascist mistakes. As a good patriot, Croce did not accept that other countries, having suffered at Mussolini's hands, would not accept this argument but might want compensation for immense losses that they had suffered.

On top of the mortification of defeat and the agony of civil war there had been tremendous damage to the physical endowment of Italy, to buildings, shipping, and internal communications. Nearly half of governmental expenditure remained uncovered by revenue, and politicians were all anxious to avoid severe measures of austerity. By 1947 the wholesale price index had risen to fifty-five times its prewar level. There were millions of unemployed whose conditions of life were desperate.

On the credit side, well-organized partisan action enabled the port installations of Genoa and the factories of Milan and Turin to suffer relatively little damage in the final German evacuation. Even more important, the Allied occupation, though distressing, was effective in lessening the internal divisions which had made the previous postwar period after 1918 so unhappy. Defeat in 1943, paradoxically but mercifully, proved less disturbing than victory in 1918. This time there was less social unrest and far less political anarchy. Another bonus was that the United States and Britain forwent their claim to reparations, and American generosity was to make reconstruction much easier than after World War I. Not only was much-needed food supplied, but a billion dollars in American aid helped the country onto its feet, and a defeated Italy ended the war with considerable credits owed her by victorious Britain. One incidental gain was the gift of new insecticides which brought the centuries-old scourge of malaria under control—in terms of human happiness this must rank among the more important events in modern Italian history.

★

Had Vittorio Emanuele III abdicated in 1943 as did Carlo Alberto at another moment of defeat in 1849, the monarchy might have survived. Instead, he self-righteously denied the indictment of his own unconstitutional collusion under Mussolini, arguing that a parliamentary sovereign was not responsible for his ministers' actions. His son, Umberto, publicly blamed the events of 1922 on the Italian people, and imprudently stated that public enthusiasm for fascism had forced the king to accept Mussolini's appointment. This unrepentant attitude made many former monarchists reverse the charge and blame Vittorio Emanuele as a scapegoat for fascism and military defeat.

Too late, when public opinion demanded a referendum on the monarchy, did the king grudgingly anticipate matters by abdication, hoping that the greater popularity of his son would tip the vote and save the dynasty. In May 1946 Umberto therefore became the legal sovereign for thirty-four days. The following month a referendum decided against him—by twelve millions to ten millions. Enrico de Nicola became provisional head of a new republican state, at last realizing Mazzini's prophetic dream. Umberto, under protest, followed his father into exile, to continue from abroad a moderate but ineffective campaign for a monarchical restoration; and subsequently his son, another Vittorio Emanuele, remained a half-hearted pretender in Switzerland.

★

Elections were held in June 1946 for a Constituent Assembly to choose a new constitution. In these elections, to which women were at last admitted, the Christian democrats obtained 35 per cent, the socialists 20 per cent, the communists 19 per cent. This was a notable victory for De Gasperi and the Catholics, marking a decisive reversal of *risorgimento* anticlericalism, and the women's vote was no doubt an important factor. Of the remaining fractions, the old liberals won only 6 per cent, a neo-fascist group 5 per cent, and the Party of Action just over 1 per cent. These results not only confirmed the defeat of the liberals who inherited from Giolitti and Cavour, but proved that a "third force" had little backing: the intellectuals of the Left Center were already breaking up into half a dozen doctrinaire factions more interested in splitting hairs with each other than finding an agreed middle way between communism and clericalism.

The only threat to the Christian democrats was that communism and socialism might join to push Italy into the Russian camp; but this fear proved illusory. Indeed, the communists went out of their way to work with the conservatives, helping for instance to undermine Parri's Center-Left government in December 1945, supporting De Gasperi when even the socialists were reluctant to do so, and stressing that they meant to follow a parliamentary not a revolutionary road to power. Nevertheless De Gasperi decided that it was not safe to accept this change of heart as genuine; and as soon as he had obtained Togliatti's support for the unpopular treaty of peace, he yielded to pressure from America and the Vatican, and against advice from some other Christian democrats he expelled the communists from his coalition in May 1947.

This was an important moment in the process by which Christian democracy acquired a more conservative label and Italian politics were polarized into two irreconcilable, almost uncommunicating, extremes. The forces of the Left were never strong enough or united enough to form an alternative government. Among the socialists, some were trying to be more proletarian and revolutionary than the communists themselves; others were reformist, evolutionary, and more inclined to join De Gasperi in government than Togliatti in powerless opposition. Leading the former "maximalist" group was Nenni who decided to run a common electoral slate with the communists, but Saragat led a "minimalist" faction of social democrats nearer the Center. Money came to Nenni from Russia, to Saragat from America.

In 1947 the Constituent Assembly, presided over by a communist, approved a new constitution by a remarkable majority of 453 to 62. The Left managed to insert in this fundamental law that there existed a right of citizens to a job, to a living wage, to free education and health treatment; also the right of workers to share in profits and management was guaranteed. To balance these somewhat theoretical generalizations, the Christian democrats obtained what was most important to them, namely a renewal of Mussolini's concordat of 1929 recognizing Catholicism as the official state religion, together with special privileges for the clergy and the repudiation of divorce. The communists earned sharp criticism from socialists, *actionists*, and Benedetto Croce who disliked this illiberal concordat. Togliatti had agreed to it as an earnest of his determination to work with the Church in a world where democratic majorities must be accepted; but although De Gasperi gladly accepted the communist vote on this crucial point, he could not afford to yield anything substantial in return.

The constitution stated that the head of state should be a president elected for seven years, chosen in joint session of both houses. Einaudi served a term in this post, followed by two Christian democrats, Gronchi and Segni, and then by the social democrat, Saragat. After bitter experience under fascism, it was decided to keep the presidential office more honorific than powerful, though some of its incumbents succeeded in exerting a residual power of intervention. Among other constitutional innovations, senators were to be elected instead of nominated. Legislation by decree would lapse if not sanctioned by parliament within sixty days, and the promotion and relegation of judges were subtracted from control by either government or parliament. Italy was also to be divided into nineteen regions, each with a greater or lesser degree of administrative autonomy, though this innovation remained largely ineffective for twenty years.

In January 1948 the constitution came into force and elections for parliament were held in April, almost a hundred parties presenting candidates. The recent communist coup in Czechoslovakia created a general panic that helped the Christian democrats to obtain an absolute majority, with 48 per cent of the popular vote and 53 per cent of the seats in the Chamber, while socialism and communism together were supported by only 31 per cent of the electorate. This was an outstandingly large majority in the history of Italian party politics and represents the high watermark of Christian-democrat fortunes. It showed that the monarchists and the liberals could each count on barely 3 per cent of the vote. It also signified a further defeat for the "third force" represented by Parri, Sforza, and the radical *actionists*, and hence called a halt to their attempt to make Italy more secular, radical, and egalitarian. It was presumably a vote against authoritarianism and in favor of moderate, even conservative, reform. Unclouded by the confusing tactics of Giolitti, or by the bludgeonings of Mussolini, Italian politics seemed to offer some chance shaking down into a roughly bi-polar system and a sharply uncompromising conflict between red and black. An absolute majority was, for the moment, accorded to the Center Right, moderately conservative, reasonably tolerant of everything which did not touch religion or property, but above all Catholic and sometimes clerical.

58   Postwar Recovery

In May 1948, De Gasperi was confirmed in office by the first postwar legislature and at once proved to be the most effective parliamentary leader since Giolitti or indeed since Cavour. He was also one of the most high-principled. Like Cavour, De Gasperi was seen by some Italians almost as an outsider, coming from the region of Trentino in the extreme North and having lived almost forty years as an Austrian subject. He had studied at the Austrian university of Innsbruck and his parliamentary education was in Vienna not Rome. Unlike Cavour he was a devout, practicing Catholic, yet his fine political instinct enabled him to resist the urgings of those who wanted a one-party Catholic government. Realizing how important it was to heal the breach between Church and secular society that had caused so much damage since 1861, he always included other minor parties in his eight successive governments and this made him distrusted in Vatican circles. The Papacy had once tried to prevent the creation of a liberal and united Italy; thereafter for many years it had forbidden Catholics to enter national politics, and in the 1920s chose to throw its weight behind the fascists rather than Don Sturzo's Christian democrats. In 1946 a Catholic party at long last won political power, but De Gasperi was wise enough not to push victory as far toward the antiliberal Right as Pope Pius XII wanted.

The Christian-democrat party included different groups that were divided over such matters as tax reform, land redistribution, economic planning, and freedom of conscience. Many voters welcomed this party as a defender of Catholic prerogatives; others voted for it only as the best defense against a communist revolution; and hence its left wing of advanced social reformers remained more of an eccentric embarrassment than an effective force. The tensions inside such a broad political grouping were not easy for outsiders to decipher though usually its center of gravity was slightly to the Right. Another problem for voters was that a similarly wide range of opinion could be found inside the Liberal and Republican parties, each of which subsequently split. The small monarchist remnant would also eventually divide over trivial points of principle, and the minuscule Party of Action dissolved into many even tinier fractions as early as 1947, while the various socialist groups sometimes seemed to be in an almost incomprehensible state of flux. Even the apparently monolithic communists would reveal internal divisions of their own as Togliatti's authoritarian policy of what he called "democratic centralism" was in later years modified to accept the advantages of a pluralistic society.

De Gasperi remained prime minister between 1945 and 1953. Being on most issues to the left of center inside his own party, he distrusted attempts by the *Confindustria* and the Vatican to turn Italian politics into a simple conflict of

Right against Left. Alongside Catholics his coalitions included liberals, republicans, social democrats, and at first even communists. This helped to preserve political stability and a rough consensus during a period of rapid social and economic change, but such a co-partnership put a premium on avoiding controversial decisions that were much needed but might have undermined cabinet solidarity. Powerful vested interests, for instance landowners and the higher echelons of the bureaucracy and senior university professors (most of them fascist appointees), were for this reason able to resist or delay change in their own spheres of activity. Little could therefore be done about modernizing the civil service, without which most reforms were likely to be ineffective; nor could enough be done to improve the educational system so as to eliminate illiteracy and promote greater technological expertise. The privileged position of the Church was likewise beyond any constructive political debate, and this inhibited reforms relating to education, divorce, censorship, and individual liberties. Such problems were left over for a future debate.

★

The Christian democrats were not for the most part so conservative as to welcome inclusion in their coalitions of the monarchists and the small neofascist party. These fringe groups on the anticonstitutional Right could sometimes attract 10 per cent of the popular vote but failed to produce a leader of ability. At the opposite extreme of the political spectrum, the communists were far more of a problem, for as well as having strong leadership they won between a quarter and a third of the total popular vote and, until 1953, were supported by most of the socialists. Active communist party membership, as a direct result of fascism, was very much larger than in other western countries, and in addition there were people in every social class who, without being ideologically committed, supported the extreme Left as an outlet for disaffection and alienation in many different layers of society. The communists were often backed as a defense of secularism against clericalism and this helped to keep alive a serious debate in the press. Successive elections would show that communism had no chance of becoming the majority party or of ever forming an alternative government, and though this fact was widely welcomed, such a marginalization of so many voters was not entirely healthy for either the Christian-democrat party or for Italian politics in general. The communists and revolutionary socialists never managed to persuade a large enough part of the electorate that they had genuinely accepted the democratic process; so they fell back on their residual function to criticize the government and keep issues of principle from being swamped by transformist pragmatism. Here they had a salutary if not very effective role to play.

Outside national politics the extreme Left had a clearer field of action, especially when the posthumous publication of Antonio Gramsci's prison writings in 1947–50, by offering a more flexible and sophisticated version of Marxism, helped to edge the conservative Croce out of his cultural dominance over intellectual life. Many distinguished writers and artists were strong supporters of the secular Left. Among writers this included Moravia, Pasolini, Pavese, Carlo Levi, Vittorini, Quasimodo, Calvino, and in later years Umberto Eco. It also included the musician Luciano Berio, the artists Renato Guttuso, Pietro Consagra, Giacomo Manzù, and famous film producers such as Roberto Rossellini, De Sica, Visconti, Bertolucci, and Francesco Rosi. Communism also made considerable inroads into local government, especially in central Italy and the big cities of Bologna, Turin, Milan, and Genoa, where the administrative ability of its elected representatives was often impressive. One important force it lacked was the support of a powerful trade union movement, for in 1949 the Confederation of Labor split along party lines and was replaced by separate groups, Catholic, communist, and social democrat. This was as grave a disadvantage for industrial and agricultural workers as it was welcome to their employers.

★

A notable contribution to Italy's economic revival was the appointment of Luigi Einaudi in 1945 as governor of the Bank of Italy, then as budget minister, and in 1949 to the highest political office as president of the Republic. This champion of economic freedom and financial orthodoxy risked popular opprobrium by placing monetary stability before immediate economic expansion. Perhaps, as some economists have argued, he took this policy to excess. But by severely tightening credit, and at the cost of maintaining unemployment and restraining industrial development, he managed by 1948 to stem inflation (which had risen to an annual 50 per cent) and peg the currency. Approval in 1947 of De Gasperi's expulsion of communist ministers from the coalition government brought a continuance of massive financial grants from America which helped to support the value of the lira and minimize social unrest. Einaudi was obliged to retain Mussolini's huge public ownership of banks, shipyards and steelworks, because the market lacked sufficient resources to privatize or repurchase them from the state-controlled IRI. But memories of the not very impressive experience of state planning under fascism made it easy for him— despite strenuous opposition from hitherto protected industries as well as from the extreme Left—to restore more of a free market economy.

Now that Mussolini's grandiloquent rhetoric had been exposed as a sham, it could be recognized that fascism had squandered resources in war and wastefully twisted the economy toward prestige, or rather toward a tragically deceptive illusion of prestige. Hence there was general support for replacing the excessive nationalism of economic self-sufficiency by an expansive confidence in freer international exchanges. Even many former supporters of fascism belatedly admitted that Mussolini's bellicose foreign policy had not helped Italy toward ranking with the other Great Powers, and indeed that his aggressive foreign policy had greatly lessened Italian prestige and restrained her material prosperity. De Gasperi's foreign minister, Carlo Sforza who belonged to the small Republican party, had proved himself a good European before 1922 and became even more of an internationalist during twenty years of exile. Einaudi, too, was well ahead of his time in advocating the creation of a federal Europe. Together these three men ranged Italy firmly on the side of the new Atlantic community. In March 1949, after one of the longest and most dramatic debates in parliament with the communists in strong opposition, Italy joined NATO. Nationalism, said Sforza, was out of date, and most Italians agreed with him.

Italian society remained basically agricultural. Mussolini had by law tried to stop farm laborers from moving to the towns. When De Gasperi visited the South he was surprised to find families still living in caves and subterranean cellars or crowded into a single room with their children and farm animals. Grisly shanty towns had during the war appeared on the outskirts of most cities and this alarmed anyone concerned with problems of social welfare. Consciences were stirred by denunciations from the Church and the political Left as well as from the more liberal newspapers and publishing houses, especially by periodicals such as *Il Ponte*, *Il Mondo*, and *L'Espresso*. Calamandrei, Ernesto Rossi, and Jemolo were names in this field that could stand comparison with any in public life since 1861. A contributory educative force was exercised indirectly by nonconforming, eccentric individuals such as Adriano Olivetti, an enlightened industrialist; by Danilo Dolci who set up an institute to encourage self-help in the poor villages of western Sicily; by Carlo Levi, who in his book *Christ Stopped at Eboli* showed many northerners for the first time something of the realities of southern Italy; and by Giorgio La Pira, the maverick mayor of Florence, a militant Catholic who defied religious superiors and current shibboleths to create a positive colloquy with communism.

De Gasperi was among those who understood the urgent need for a fairer deal between classes and regions so as to remove some of the tensions that had hampered economic development since 1861. No truly radical changes were possible without risking a split in his party, but some concessions to social reform were permitted by its conservative wing in an attempt to defeat communism and attract mass support. He was able to introduce rent controls, modest family allowances, and a partial inflation-indexing of wages. Many agricultural and industrial workers were given security of tenure for an emergency period until unemployment could be reduced. Furthermore, in perhaps the boldest attempt at agrarian reform in any noncommunist country, more than two million acres of uncultivated land were compulsorily acquired from *latifondisti* in the 1950s and distributed to create a larger class of smallholders. This reform was far from popular with landowners, and the further objection was raised that it was not only an inefficient use of limited financial resources but was quite beyond the ability of the civil service to administer. Nevertheless its partial success helped to mitigate some hardships caused by the war and Einaudi's policy of deflation, while in some places the *latifondo* system of cultivation gave way to more intensive methods and more profitable crops.

★

One of the most hopeful contributions to the postwar economy was the discovery of natural gas in Lombardy. This raised some expectation of satisfying the need for a domestic source of power. Coal imports, on which Italy had been obliged to lean heavily, were expensive and a great burden on the balance of payments, whereas gas was easily transported and much cheaper. Mussolini had made some attempt to find oil or gas but nationalist arrogance deterred him from using foreign expertise: success had therefore to await the return of liberal government with its less regulated economy, and this is a pertinent commentary on the self-justifying rodomontade of the fascist regime. Mussolini's failure to discover the huge oil fields of Libya was an instructive lesson.

Success was due above all to one man, Enrico Mattei, who in 1945 was given the task of closing down Mussolini's unprofitable oil exploration agency. Repeatedly disobeying orders, Mattei persisted in drilling, finding fair supplies of methane in 1946 and large quantities in the next three years. In 1953 this discovery was usefully supplemented when an American company found oil in southeastern Sicily. By that time Mattei was producing two billion cubic meters of natural gas a year, and before his death in a mysterious air accident he had raised this figure to nearly seven billion, which in an Italian context was a real revolution. A brilliant if unconventional and autocratic organizer, he was also an excellent publicist and an agile puller of political wires. By deliberately exaggerating and sometimes fabricating the existence of indigenous fuel supplies he stampeded parliament into taking decisions on incomplete evidence. Despite strong political pressure from rival entrepreneurs and international oil companies he was therefore allowed a monopoly on further exploration in the most promising areas. Using this monopoly to charge a high price for his product, he was able to finance what became an enormous economic conglomerate that included chemicals, cement, textiles, tourism, transport, telephones, nuclear energy, and one of the better newspapers in Italy. He also purchased considerable influence in all the main political parties, not excluding the revolutionary Left and also the small group of neo-fascists. Though nominally a state corporation his highly idiosyncratic economic empire was barely accountable to parliament or government. Though idealistic and honorable in private life, he broke the law with apparent impunity and set an unfortunate example of political corruption that was later copied by lesser men with disastrous results.

Despite his cavalier attitude to competition and the market economy, Mattei proved that a reduction in fascist controls would make possible an astonishing outburst of entrepreneurial activity. Another helpful factor for the economy was the many new industrial processes imported from other countries and which had not hitherto been exploited because of fascist arrogance and its target of self-sufficiency. Yet another advantage was that, with so many unemployed and a large surplus of agricultural workers, a vast labor reservoir was available for industry and hence there was little immediate risk of wage increases that would make production uncompetitive. A long tradition of skilled craftsmanship was speedily converted to the needs of large-scale industry and novel production techniques. The traditional companies, Fiat, Pirelli, Montecatini, and Olivetti, made up lost ground and before long had few rivals in Europe. New firms also appeared to satisfy a strong home demand for such articles as motor scooters, household appliances, artificial fibers, and office machinery. From this basis the country soon and for the first time developed into a major exporter of manufactured goods.

Industrial production was more or less up to prewar levels by 1950 and there then followed a dozen years of sustained economic progress. This was on a scale that Italy had never known before. Alongside an annual growth rate of about 5.9 per cent, one of the highest anywhere in the world and which even in bad years hardly fell below 5 per cent, there was an additional advantage that prices for awhile remained comparatively stable. No longer burdened by the excessive protectionism and wasteful expenditures of fascism, Italy was ready to make full use of her economic potential and profited from possessing more underdeveloped capacity as well as greater reserves of labor than other countries. Unlike Spain, which at first preferred to remain in protectionist isolation, De Gasperi and Einaudi also shared Mazzini's prophetic idea of a truly federated Europe. In 1951 they joined the European Coal and Steel Community and in 1957 their successors signed the Treaty of Rome which inaugurated a European common market. Beyond Europe too, scores of Italian civil engineering firms began to win substantial contracts all over the world.

★

Regional inequalities were inevitable in a country with the historical antecedents and geographical diversity of Italy, but their reduction was seen as an imperative need, especially since provincial sentiment and local loyalties too often took precedence over the sense of national identity. On the islands of Sardinia and Sicily, not only detached physically but with a history as much Spanish as Italian, movements appeared after 1943 that aimed at regional autonomy and sometimes at complete political separation from the Italian mainland. Special situations also existed in the partly French-speaking Val d'Aosta, in the largely German-speaking Alto Adige, and in the partially Slav hinterland of Trieste.

So long as the Christian democrats had been an opposition party, as in the immediate years after 1919, they had strongly supported regional autonomy and condemned centralization, but this was reversed once they held power after 1948. It was rather their communist opponents who promoted the regional devolution that was prescribed by the 1947 constitution, whereas De Gasperi feared that, especially in the "red" areas of Tuscany, Umbria, and Emilia, regional autonomy would give the extreme Left power and the patronage that accompanied power. Although he could not avoid creating elected regional assemblies in the peripheral provinces of Sardinia, Sicily, Trentino/Alto Adige, and the Val d'Aosta (in none of which the Left seemed likely to achieve electoral victory), in practice he managed to restrict their autonomy within fairly narrow bounds, and elsewhere he refused to create the other regional governments whose existence was required by the new republican constitution.

In the few areas where regional self-government was tried the experiment proved to be only moderately successful. This was notably so in Sicily where there was a tragic refusal to confront the mafia. To a lesser degree it was true in the Trentino/Alto Adige where a demand by the German-speaking element for even more self-determination was sometimes backed by acts of terrorism. Undeniably there proved to be some value in bringing the processes of government nearer to the ordinary citizen in each region, as there was also a good deal of point in training local politicians and a local civil service to deal with problems that did not have much impact on the nation at large; but the regional administrations were overmanned and not particularly effective. Since they raised little of their own revenue and relied on state funding, it was not hard for the government to restrict their competence. Moreover the Constitutional Court, when belatedly it was set up in 1955 to resolve clashes in jurisdiction, did not like the untidiness of different legal systems and usually took decisions in favor of centralized state authority.

It was easy to see that this might be making the worst of two worlds. Italy retained the many disadvantages of over-centralization because the bureaucracy in Rome remained as complicated, as constricting, as dilatory, and in some respects as corrupt as it had always been, while clientelism and boss rule received new vigor at a local level where regional bureaucracies provided luscious plums of patronage. Jobbery and pork-barrel handouts by the regional assemblies were regularly employed to reinforce the local notables and create suspect enclaves of illicit influence and financial immunity. Regional elected deputies could vote themselves large salaries; they passed special tax laws to favor interested parties and used their position to obtain financial credits for many operations that brought local politics into disrepute.

★

The main regional disequilibrium was still between North and South. The South had some twenty million out of the fifty-three million inhabitants of Italy. It was short on natural resources and free capital. Geographically it was far from the main industrial and agricultural markets, and this distance was all the greater in that rail and road communications remained inadequate. Historically, whereas the North had over the centuries developed networks of local associations and civic loyalty, the South had fewer traditions of social or collective action but rather ingrained habits of exploitation and mutual distrust.

Overpopulation, a high birth rate, poor educational facilities, archaic agricultural techniques, and a primitive land tenure system all contributed to keep this
large area backward and so delayed national economic unification. The bigger
industries, often privately controlled by individual families, remained in the
much richer North—Fiat at Turin, Italsider and Ansaldo at Genoa, Olivetti in
Ivrea, and at Milan the giant companies of Pirelli, Edison, Montecatini, and
Snia Viscosa.

The fairly consistent policy of successive governments, whether intended or
not, had hitherto kept this dual economic system in being. During the first years
of united Italy the government had largely been in the hands of northerners
who identified the national welfare with their own: they had understandably
preferred to accumulate capital for their own industrial take-off, and the
agricultural South was therefore kept overtaxed and underinvested so as to
provide extra funds for northern industry. Northerners subsequently used
political power to reinforce this regional advantage even where such behaviour
might seem to result in retarding overall growth of the national income and the
rate of capital accumulation. Duties on imported steel suited some northern
industries as well as discriminating against the South through the increased price
of manufactures. Agricultural protection at the same time kept alive in the
South the sometimes inefficient practices of the *latifondi*. Just as high steel prices
acted as a drag on any expansion of engineering, so the artificially high price of
cereals delayed the diversification of southern agriculture into more profitable
channels. More seriously, the political unification of Italy had not resulted in its
economic unification but had even tended to widen the gap between the
capitalist North and the semi-feudal, traditional and often self-sufficient South.
Mussolini's armaments policy in the 1930s had increased this gap still further.
He had even made matters worse by dogmatically censoring any public
reference to the existence of a "southern problem."

Post-war governments made a determined effort to reverse the process and
integrate the backward South into the mainstream of Italian society. The
potential dangers were dramatically revealed when in 1946 a referendum
showed 76 per cent at Naples and 85 per cent at Lecce in favor of retaining the
monarchy, while the North voted heavily for a republic. Another index of the
difference was that the armed Resistance movement in 1944–45 had been
almost entirely confined to the North; and hence the South missed out on a
vital force for renovation that might otherwise have displaced some of the
retrograde local elites. What was almost worse, the Anglo-American military
administration in 1943, having more urgent problems to deal with, permitted
mafiosi to reacquire their former authority over many areas of Sicilian society.

In De Gasperi's party there were many who were alarmed at the possible
"southernization" or "clientelization" of Italian political life and were the more
anxious to extirpate this dual system of economics and morality. Yet politicians
were deterred from acting against the mafia because the electoral support of that

criminal confraternity was found to be useful, especially by the Christian democrats. But in 1950 a Southern Development Fund was created, the *Cassa per il Mezzogiorno*, as a special investment agency with substantial sums for building roads, dams, aqueducts, and irrigation works. In 1954, a year when unemployment was particularly bad, the "Vanoni plan" outlined a scheme by which direct public investment and incentives to private industry aimed at creating in the South some four million more jobs over ten years and doubling the rate of income growth.

Much play was made with these well-intentioned proposals but the Vanoni plan was not even presented to parliament. It was little more than a statement of intent because northern businessmen had other priorities and in particular had good reason to dislike Ezio Vanoni's simultaneous campaign against tax evasion. Industrialists and landowners preferred the kind of state help that attracted private investment to the South by offering cheap credit, freight reductions, and tax incentives; but even these measures encountered the objection that, while profitable for northern contracting firms, they diverted money from where the nation could advantageously use it, as well as being partly motivated by a desire to win votes in political elections. The same criticisms were raised when a special Ministry of State Shareholdings was created in 1956, and when the large sector of publicly owned firms was instructed that 60 per cent of all new investment must be located in the South.

This figure of 60 per cent was impossible to enforce because no minister had enough time and authority to cut through the tangle of conflicting bureaucracies, or even to obtain the basic statistical data on which to take action. In practice a confusion also arose between development projects and measures designed for social relief. Vast sums were spent in the South: roads and clean water supplies were brought to villages for the first time, many schools were built and large sections of the rural population at last came within sight of a decent standard of living; but many of the experts objected that reforms were tackled piecemeal with far too little co-ordinated planning between the Southern Development Fund and other official agencies. Moreover the rivalry between politicians (and political groups) affected the allocation of money, with the result that development organizations were often staffed by second-rate politicians or clients of some local boss who was ready to trade his electoral support. Villages were built in which no one came to live, and dams constructed from which the water trickled profitlessly into the sea instead of providing irrigation. A fairly high percentage of the money, some said a good third, was probably wasted, and much of it ended up in the hands of *mafiosi* and *camorristi*. Much the same had happened under fascism—and earlier.

Private industry in the North did not enter with much enthusiasm into such projects for southern development. Some larger firms contributed their share— Olivetti set up an office machinery factory near Naples and Montecatini spent a great deal on petrochemicals and fertilizers in Sicily—but Fiat, arguing that the South lacked the market and raw materials and power supplies for an automobile industry, had economic reasons for at first preferring investment nearer its home base in Turin. Mostly it was state-controlled firms which under political pressure moved south; it was also capital-intensive rather than labor-intensive industries, because the South lacked skilled labor whereas officially sponsored credit made capital cheap and this left standards of life only moderately improved. Many northern industries preferred to rely on a continuance of southern unemployment from which they could draw labor as needed into their northern factories, and hence saw strong arguments for keeping the South dilapidated and relatively poor.

For these reasons there began another period of substantial emigration from the South, an emigration that gradually imposed remedies of a much more drastic kind. Over a million people left for Australia and the Americas; another million, less permanently, for northern Europe; perhaps three million moved to northern Italy in the late 1950s and early 1960s. Mussolini's law preventing labor from leaving agriculture, which had been unconstitutionally retained after 1945 to protect northern trade unions, was repealed. Vast new social problems were thus transferred to the North, such as the urgent need to provide houses, schools, and hospitals for the new arrivals; and this created ill-feeling on both sides. The emigrants did not at first mix easily in northern society and many did not even speak Italian. Eventually this painful and disruptive process succeeded better than a century of legislation by creating something closer to a common culture and system of values throughout the whole nation. But in the South, though unemployment was reduced and wages improved for those who remained, by taking away men of working age and leaving behind the old, the young, and the women, emigration partly solved one problem only to create another.

Southern Italy made far more progress after 1950 than ever before, though how far this was because of, or irrespective of, government action was in dispute. Everyone agreed, however, that progress was disappointing in view of its formidable cost, and not even all this vast investment of thought and money was able to prevent northerners increasing their comparative advantages in income and industrial development.

59 Constitutional Problems in the 1950s

Finding answers to these problems was all the more difficult because, though the Christian-democrat party remained permanently in office, its overwhelming electoral success in 1948 was never repeated and politics therefore became less manageable. The passage of time also revealed unsatisfactory aspects of the new republican constitution. In particular the memory of fascist dictatorship had made the constituent assembly of 1947 anxious to curb executive authority, forgetting how a weak premiership in 1922 had helped Mussolini into power. Also the rivalry between parties led to restricting the prime minister's powers and those of the presidential head of state. It was even decided to revive an extreme form of proportional representation for parliamentary elections in order to prevent any single party from ever again becoming too powerful. Einaudi and De Gasperi would ideally have preferred the very different practice of a first-past-the-post voting system so as to reduce the number of parties and produce a clear majority in parliament. Croce, Orlando, and Sturzo would also have liked single-member constituencies as in Britain. But after prolonged discussion their views were rejected.

This created further recurrent problems. Proportional representation was favored because it would reflect the full variety of public opinion and give adequate expression to minority views; but an obvious disadvantage was the impossibility of welding a patchwork of minority political groups into a stable and homogeneous majority. With ten or more parties represented in the legislature and with most of them divided still further into competing factions, a cabinet might include members of three or four parties and half a dozen minor groups or *correnti*, a fact which discouraged any proposal of legislation that might be divisive. Because such coalitions lacked discipline and easily disintegrated, the average duration of governments would be less than a year. This gave insufficient time for any cabinet to formulate policy on important issues, so creating the paradox that cabinet instability was compounded by legislative immobilism. Another disadvantage was that coalition governments, in defiance of a clause in the constitution that made expenditure dependent on adequate funding for any proposed law, found it much easier to agree over spending than over taxation, and eventually this led to the accumulation of a huge national debt. A further problem was that every prime minister was so busy resolving power struggles among his coalition colleagues that policy and necessary reforms took second place.

In other countries where there was a first-past-the-post electoral law, small parties were excluded from the legislature and the two largest parties tended to alternate in power. Such a practice had disadvantages but did permit strong government. It also provided for a fairly regular renewal of persons and policies by presenting the electorate with a choice between different programs, and it usually enabled electors to chose a government instead of delegating this decision to negotiated bargaining between a multiplicity of party secretariats. But in Italy, where one legacy of fascism was a polarization of society and the creation of a strong communist party, any alternation in power would play into

435

the hand of extremists who, after winning an election, might alter the rules of democratic politics. For this reason Italy was unique in that for almost fifty years the Christian democrats, usually with little more than a third of the popular vote, presided over fragile and unstable "transformist" coalitions that lacked a clear mandate for positive reforms. De Gasperi privately feared that this absence of a potential alternative government would hinder the development of a healthy parliamentary system, because he knew that his own party, since it lacked any fear of losing office, might become unresponsive to popular wishes and succumb to the inevitable corruption of being permanently in power. In practice, however, the fear of communism gave him little option but to juggle with a series of coalition administrations in order to deprive his only serious opponents of any useful function; and equally unfortunate was that the Left, excluded permanently from power, lacked the incentive to formulate the practical policies that might have been expected from a party aspiring to government.

By another decision of the constituent assembly, instead of creating single-member constituencies, votes were solicited not for individual candidates but for collective rosters of names drawn up in each electoral college by the various parties. This enabled five or six party secretaries to acquire exceptional authority and become far more powerful than other politicians, often almost as powerful as the prime minister who had to accept their nominations to his cabinet and their decisions about policy. This *partitocrazia* or "tyranny of parties" was already a subject of apprehension as early as 1947 but became far more alarming over the course of time. Governments rarely fell over a precisely motivated vote of no confidence in the way that Article 94 of the constitution prescribed, but usually when one or more party secretaries or faction leaders chose to abandon the coalition. This gave extraordinary power to an unrepresentative professional oligarchy of half a dozen individuals whose position was unrecognized in the written constitution but who on their own initiative could determine the composition of each administration. During twenty-five years after 1945, only two out of twenty-seven governments fell as a result of a motivated parliamentary vote, and some thoughtful observers thought that liberal democracy was bound to suffer when parliament and the electorate were so discounted.

★

Implementation of other articles in the constitution was deliberately delayed for similar reasons of political expediency: Articles 114–19, for instance, which demanded decentralization to the individual regions, and articles 134–7 that demanded the institution of a Constitutional Court to clarify conflicts of jurisdiction and oversee the actions of government. Other articles seemed anomalous or contradictory. One apparent contradiction was between Article 7, which recognized Catholicism as a privileged state religion, and Article 8 which guaranteed equality of all religions before the law. On such issues as divorce and birth control the law imposed Catholic penalties on everyone. Catholic Action, an official body of laymen subordinate to the hierarchy, took a strongly conservative line on politics and its three million members wielded great influence in elections. Bishops sometimes demanded that Christians should vote for the Christian democrats.

Pope Pius XII who reigned between 1939 and 1958 had even stronger conservative views than his predecessor, and wherever politics touched on religion or morals he claimed a right to pronounce on policy and expect obedience. Voters were even threatened with withdrawal of the sacraments during the crucial election of 1948. In July 1949, Pius issued a collective excommunication against the millions of Italians who continued to vote for the communist party, and subsequently he opined that socialism, having the same materialistic philosophy as communism, was irreconcilable with Christianity.

De Gasperi agreed with Pius at least to the point of distrusting Togliatti's claims about bringing "atheistic communism" within the ambit of democratic politics. Moreover, where articles of the constitution seemed to conflict with each other, he would give the Church the benefit of any doubt and if necessary would even allow the bishops some immunity from legal sanctions. In private this Christian-democrat prime minister nevertheless criticized Catholic Action and spoke strongly against clerical intervention in politics. When informed of papal wishes that he desert the social democrats and move toward the neo-fascists, he sensibly demurred, for with the existing balance of parliamentary parties this would have invited defeat in the perilously balanced election of 1953 and would have given gratuitous respectability to the communist opposition.

Instead, one of his last political initiatives was to persuade the three other parties in his coalition that effective government would require a radical modification in the practice of proportional representation if they wanted a workable parliamentary majority. His interesting but provocative proposal was that any alliance of parties winning a clear 50 per cent of the votes should receive an extra 15 per cent in the allocation of parliamentary seats. Perhaps he was tactically at fault in suggesting so large a bonus, and there was unprecedented opposition to his proposal in fifty successive sessions of parliament. Criticism came mainly but not only from the Left, and there were angry episodes of physical violence such as had not been seen in the legislature since the early years of fascism. Eventually his proposal was adopted, but when elections were held in June there were many defections from Christian democracy and De Gasperi's coalition failed by a few thousand votes to secure the necessary 50 per cent. His new electoral law was therefore abrogated. Instead of winning a bonus of extra seats he lost much of the support he already possessed and this brought his parliamentary career to a close. He had tried and failed in a attempt to educate what the conservative *Corriere della Sera* was already denouncing in March 1953 as "a retrograde and incompetent political class that was failing in its duty to the nation." Unfortunately none of his

Christian-democrat successors enjoyed the same political supremacy or his reputation for rectitude and sound judgment. None of them for almost forty years dared repeat his attempt to give parliamentary government a more solid basis with a workable majority, and some of his critics came to regret their failure to support him on this crucial issue.

★

The 1953 elections dealt the four-party alliance a damaging jolt and in the new parliament their reduced margin gave the Christian democrats much less freedom for maneuver. Out of 590 seats in the Lower House this one party now had 261 instead of 304. Furthermore they were an ill-disciplined, ramshackle group of sometimes squabbling factions so that support from other parties would be more necessary than ever. Four Christian-democrat prime ministers formed administrations in the next two years to see if they could find a working formula, but there were personal differences between them, and other center parties were unenthusiastic about anything so transient and indecisive.

This second postwar legislature lasted until 1958. A succession of prime ministers learned under difficult circumstances that their most requisite skill was that of mediating between political groups and if possible avoiding controversial action. After Giuseppe Pella and Amintore Fanfani who experimented with temporary *monocolore* cabinets of only Christian democrats, Mario Scelba and Antonio Segni managed to reassemble coalitions that once again included liberals and social democrats. But these cabinets hardly differed from each other on major points of principle. The reality was one in which different notables inside a single party, each with his own individual group of dependent followers, tried to find a nuance of policy or tactics that would mark them out from their rivals and permit the creation of a new majority. One group leader, Bernardo Mattarella who in western Sicily could guarantee a bloc of parliamentary votes, remained a minister in fifteen cabinets, so helping to prevent action against the Sicilian mafia. Giulio Andreotti, during thirty-five years, held office in thirty different governments and was criticized for doing the same.

Each individual Christian-democrat group had its own central office, its own sources of finance and separate news agency, but kept its own identity not so much through ideological objectives as by jobbery and the competition for lucrative patronage inside the administrative machine. The largest group solidified into what became known as the *Dorotei*, among whose younger leaders were Emilio Colombo and Mariano Rumor; barely distinguishable were the *Morotei*, so-called from their leader Aldo Moro. To the right of these were Scelba's *Centrismo popolare* and Andreotti's *Primavera*, while to the left of center were other *correnti* such as *Iniziativa democratica*, and the *Nuove cronache* that supported Fanfani. All these politicians held the office of prime minister at some point in the years leading up to 1976, Moro and Rumor on five occasions each, Fanfani on four. Other smaller groups, the *Forze nuove*, the *Basisti*, and *Rinnovamento democratico*, had a greater or lesser degree of durability and effectiveness. Each group had some claim to be represented in any cabinet and to impose its own nominees for ministerial office. Any prospective prime minister had to secure a broad balance between them and men nominated by other coalition parties. There also had to be a balance between representatives from each of the various regions and this further restricted a prime minister's freedom of choice. Only when negotiations reached a stalemate would the party fall back on a noncompetitive *monocolore* "administrator" to lead a weak temporary administration until the various factions could regroup themselves.

Personal rivalries among these party leaders were fueled by the competition to obtain influence and patronage that would provide salaried positions for their followers. The same rivalries explain the lack of cabinet solidarity that was always a hindrance to decisive government action. Such were their differences that in 1955, when a new head of state had to be elected, the official Christian-democrat candidate failed to get the required number of votes. One problem was that Fanfani was ambitious to secure this office for himself and the *Fanfaniani* broke ranks in a secret ballot. Other rivals in the party, with outside support from both communists and neo-fascists, then outmaneuvered both candidates. The surprise choice to succeed President Einaudi was Giovanni Gronchi, a much more controversial figure who had entered politics as a junior minister in Mussolini's first cabinet before changing to join the antifascists.

As the years went by, the perils inherent in this lack of party solidarity became more apparent. When in 1957 a government led by Segni lost the support of the republicans and social democrats, chiefly over agrarian reform, parliament had to accept another *monocolore* administration under Adone Zoli; but Zoli found himself dependent on the neo-fascist vote, a fact that to some of his colleagues was most unwelcome. Equally intolerable to others was Fanfani's tentative proposal to win power through an alliance with Nenni's socialist party: indeed this suggestion was vetoed by the Vatican. An election in 1958 gave the Christian democrats 273 deputies, still well short of a majority, but since this strengthened Fanfani's following in the party he became prime minister for six months with support from the social democrats round Saragat. Fanfani was followed by Segni again, who was displaced in 1960 by yet another Christian democrat, Fernando Tambroni.

The choice of Tambroni, though intended as an emollient stopgap, gave the whole system another jolt, for he too had a bare majority and depended on the twenty-four neo-fascist deputies. One suggestion had already been mooted that, since such a quick succession of governments was unsatisfactory, the constitution should be modified in favor of a presidential regime on the model set by General de Gaulle in France. Some countenance was given to this idea by President Gronchi who was hoping to win greater political initiative for the presidential office and who publicly criticized the "dictatorship of the parties" as a threat to representative democracy. It was Gronchi who chose Tambroni as prime minister and thereby incurred criticism for offering the extreme Right a chance to recover political power against the manifest wishes of the electorate. When severe rioting broke out, with a number of fatal casualties, Tambroni was forced by his own party to resign. The conservatives had tried and failed to push the balance of power toward the Right. It was difficult to escape the conclusion that a quite different grouping of parties was urgently needed if parliamentary democracy were to thrive.

★

In 1958 the election to the Papacy of the elderly John XXIII did not at first seem particularly significant; but in 1962 when the second Vatican Council met, there were surprising indications that Catholicism might be moving toward greater changes than in the last four hundred years. Pius IX, in his allocution *Jamdudum cernimus* of 1861, had formally condemned "progress, liberalism and modern civilization;" Pius X, in *Lamentabili sane* of 1907, gave a list of further "modernistic" errors that the Inquisition decided were as deadly as those of Luther; and then Pius XI after 1922 had encouraged authoritarianism in both Church and state. But now Pope John, in welcoming what he called renovation or *aggiornamento*, went toward what many churchmen called the opposite extreme. Expressing a preference for the methods of liberal democracy and episcopal collegiality he encouraged a more tolerant pluralism, and this would greatly lessen the conflict between clericalism and anticlericalism that had been so divisive an influence in Italian society. Papal excommunication of the extreme Left was renewed in 1959 but John then realized the need to rebuild some of the bridges that had been burned, and the hierarchy was even urged toward hesitant acceptance of socialism as a possible partner in government. The rights of individual conscience, which in 1864 had been condemned as almost heretical in the papal Syllabus of Errors, were now praised as a Christian virtue. In the encyclical *Mater et magistra* of 1961 with its plea for social justice, as in that of *Pacem in terris* of 1963 with its advocacy of international conciliation and dialogue with other faiths and ideologies, Pope John showed that the Church could move toward a fruitful co-operation with secular society.

Another factor in changing some of the old stereotypes was the rapid progress of an economic boom that brought a faster process of industrialization and urbanization than Italy had ever known. One result of this was to promote discussion about state intervention and national economic planning. The right wing of the small liberal party received strong backing from the *Confindustria* in a delaying battle against governmental *programmazione*, pointing out that prosperity was increasing despite the lack of national planning. On the other hand some radical liberals argued that economic growth and the methods of *laissez-faire* were eliminating neither unemployment nor the disparity between North and South: the implication being that only governments could provide those elements of economic infrastructure that the private sector was unwilling to supply, and only legislation could restrict the exploitation of consumers by private monopolies and near monopolies such as existed in the provision of electricity. Even if government action was generally less effective and profitable than private entrepreneurs, at least it might be more socially beneficent by enacting antitrust legislation and intervening where free enterprise was deficient or socially harmful. Thirty years of experience with the state-controlled IRI had shown that this public holding corporation could if necessary use normal market methods to raise money and run a number of competitive industries in which the public interest was overriding.

By 1960 the Christian democrats had moved further away from the doctrine of *laissez-faire* formerly championed by Einaudi. The so-called "Green plan" allocated a great deal of public expenditure to the modernization of agriculture and improvement in rural living conditions. Some economists and many industrialists wondered if enough investment opportunities could be found for such a huge expenditure on agriculture, but tentative approval came from the *Coltivatori diretti*, a powerful and somewhat disreputable organization of small proprietors that was a right-wing pressure group supporting Christian democracy. Some of the conservative factions inside this party could thus welcome greater government intervention in the economy when it suited them, as they also recognized that subsidies and cheap credit provided by the taxpayer, especially when funneled through themselves, would provide useful jobs and patronage at the same time as turning voters away from communism.

★

Even De Gasperi, despite his own personal honesty, had not halted his party's growing reputation for treating public life as a benefice rather than a service. Such a reputation was acquired and made more durable by the fact that his party had little to fear from any political challenge. Corrupt politics were in part a legacy of fascism whose ruling class had often been unconscionably lawless, and old habits from the 1930s were hard to eradicate. Numerous governmental and para-governmental agencies created by Mussolini continued to exist in post-fascist Italy, some of them with absurdly anachronistic purposes such as organizing fascist youth, colonizing Ethiopia, or even for administering property confiscated from the Jews. These organizations still had funds to disburse, particularly on the supposed expenses of administration. Moreover new agencies were now created, partly in the expectation that pork-barrel politics would help to win electoral votes and provide salaries for party officials and placemen. Total lack of supervision meant that no one had any idea about how many of such organizations were in existence, but a figure of up to thirty thousand was sometimes quoted, many of which were probably a sheer waste of money, unregulated and covert. Alongside the private sector of the economy, which showed an extraordinary capacity for enterprise and wealth creation, the growing public sector in the 1950s was often crippled by being misused deliberately as an instrument of party politics. This reinforced another disturbing legacy of the fascist past, namely for public opinion to regard any government as probably corrupt and hence to be disobeyed or exploited without impropriety. Surveys of public opinion reflected a popular belief that people became politicians chiefly for motives of personal gain.

Newspapers during the 1950s and early 1960s reported many examples of public funds being misappropriated, sometimes on a huge scale and always involving ministers or political parties. A major scandal over an agency for collecting local taxes (INGIC) was among the most notorious. Other much publicized scandals concerned the construction of Rome airport at Fiumicino, the distribution of penicillin, and the regulating bodies for savings banks (ITALCASSE) and social security (INPS). Others involved special agencies set up to import bananas and tobacco which, as monopolies, could fix prices at will and purchase the silence or active collusion of ministers and senior bureaucrats. Quite as much as under fascism, politicians rather than professional managers were chosen to operate such giant holding companies as IRI, the national oil company ENI, the radio corporation (RAI), and the national airline (Alitalia).

This process meant a loss in managerial efficiency was a rich source of jobbery for the party machines in proportion to their representation in each coalition government. Most operations inside the public sector were gradually colonized by second-rank politicians, including the directorship of the more important banks which were all state-owned. The new bank managers often lacked any technical qualifications. At a lower level the same practice prevailed with municipal authorities controlling the money allocated to hospitals, transport, and water supplies. Even at the lowest level, political patronage regulated the employment of garbage collectors, *concierges*, and parking-lot attendants. Immense patronage was also provided by political appointees who controlled the allocation of building licenses and allocation of personal pensions, all at great cost to the taxpayer. The pejorative word *sottogoverno* was coined as early as 1950 to describe this diffusion of sovereignty through a jungle of uncontrollable political clienteles which had little incentive to limit expenditure and often had no fear of malpractice being investigated.

In February 1960 the Speaker of the Senate, Cesare Merzagora, whose office made him the senior politician in Italy after the head of state for fourteen years, threatened to resign because of what he called "the atmosphere of corruption that weighs heavily on our political life." But although his words were greeted with loud applause and strange cries of "long live parliament," in practice the senators had plenty of reason to let sleeping dogs lie. During the third legislature from 1958 to 1963, although the judiciary asked for permission to investigate 295 parliamentarians and ministers on charges of corruption, in only fifty cases did the two chambers waive parliamentary immunity and permit the magistrates to proceed. Another supervisory body, the Court of Accounts which on paper had a constitutional duty to oversee the expenditure of para-governmental agencies, had been emasculated when Mussolini placed it under the direct authority of the executive, and its powers were further limited by law of 1958.

Nor were the ordinary courts of law an effective barrier to corruption. Not only had many of the judges learned their trade in the heyday of fascist malpractice but the judicial system was notoriously slow and hesitant. Civil cases often took six years before being decided and it was not unusual for two million cases to be pending. Nor were the courts entirely free of interference by the ministry of justice. Other criticisms were directed against the Constitutional Court itself which for many years continued to apply anachronistic articles of the fascist legal code in flagrant breach of the new republican constitution. Instead of enforcing equality between the sexes as the constitution prescribed, this supreme court at first confirmed Mussolini's differentiation by punishing adultery more harshly in women. Not for many years after 1960 was the fascist law abrogated that criminalized criticism of the social order or any offense given to the state authorities.

60   A Move to the Left: the early 1960s

Merzagora's forthright denunciation reflected a growing sense of unease throughout the country. A succession of blatant public scandals suggested that the political system was functioning badly and might be a hindrance to the development of a more healthy society. Failure to change might, in Merzagora's view, push middle-of-the-road voters to support the communist opposition. Yet the alternative options were few. The failure of Tambroni in 1960 taught that any alliance between Christian democrats and the Right would fail to produce a viable transformist coalition. Nor could a safe parliamentary majority be created by alliance with minor parties of the non-socialist Center Left. After the disintegration of the Party of Action, Parri and Calamandrei fought the 1953 elections as a separate group but had no success. In the 1958 elections, a new Radical party championed secularism, civil liberties and minority rights, but despite intellectual distinction and back-stage influence it obtained not a single seat in the Lower House. Mazzini's old Republican party, now under the distinguished leadership of Ugo La Malfa, won six seats in 1958 and its leader was eventually recruited by Fanfani as minister in charge of the budget. Together with the twenty-two social democrats who followed Saragat, this gave the ruling coalition a bare majority, though it was a perilous equipoise because some individual deputies in the main Christian-democrat party regularly defected in any secret parliamentary vote.

One possible alternative was to push the alliance leftward to include Nenni and his eighty-four socialists, because this would lift the government majority to over 380 against an opposition of 140 communists and about 60 deputies on the Right. Though a quarter of these socialist deputies were still unwilling to join any "bourgeois" government, Nenni had persuaded them in 1952–53 to drop their common slate with the communists, and this change was strongly reinforced after Khrushchev's revelations about the horrors of Stalinism. Also a gradual improvement in living standards helped to convert more socialists away from revolutionary ideas toward a belief in gradualism and free enterprise. Meanwhile in local government Nenni's followers sometimes joined conservative municipal administrations wherever this was the only means of creating a working majority. Such an alliance took place at Milan and Genoa in 1961, while in the Sicilian region some Christian democrats defied Vatican protests and accepted socialist, even sometimes communist, support. As Cavour and Giolitti had shown earlier, governments by allying with moderate elements on the Left could sometimes absorb or submerge a potentially dangerous opposition, and much now depended on whether any Christian-democrat leader was skillful enough to carry out such an operation at national level without wrecking his party or his own political future.

A first attempt was made by Fanfani who followed Tambroni and became prime minister in July 1960. As secretary of his party between 1954 and 1959, Fanfani had brought younger politicians to greater prominence and given them the backing of a reinforced party organization. Some in this new generation set their minds to a leftward realignment of political alliances that would capture the middle ground and isolate the communists in opposition. At first they met renewed criticism from the Church hierarchy, but Pope John, after initial doubts, prevailed against the conservative curia cardinals. Fanfani's fourth administration in February 1962 was at last able to offer a partially left-oriented policy that the socialists might accept. For example he was ready to discuss more intervention by government in the economy, in particular nationalization of electricity provision and raising the school leaving age to fourteen, and also a withholding tax on dividends to make tax evasion less easy. He was even prepared to study the possibility of creating the other fifteen regional assemblies already promised in 1947, despite the fact that some of them were bound to fall under domination by the communist Left. Higher pensions and minor measures of social welfare were also part of the package.

The socialists agreed to support this program though they would not accept appointment as ministers before seeing what it meant in practice. But Fanfani had gone too fast for his colleagues and discovered that by diluting the centrist policies of his party he had aroused too much antagonism. The *Dorotei* preferred Aldo Moro whose support for a Center-Left administration was more cautious and inspired by a Giolittian skill in patient negotiation rather than by imposing a pre-arranged solution. Other right-of-center Christian democrats eventually backed Moro as part of a deal whereby the conservative Segni was chosen as the official party candidate to succeed Gronchi as head of state. Fanfani was displaced after the communists picked up a million extra votes in the elections of April 1963. The obvious successor would have been Moro, but when Fanfani's supporters made difficulties, another caretaker government had to be formed under Giovanni Leone. Only at the end of 1963 did the Nenni socialists at last agree to enter a coalition cabinet, for the first time since 1947, and Moro formed an administration with Nenni as deputy prime minister. The "opening to the Left" was a reality.

★

The issue chosen to seal this new alliance was nationalization of the electricity cartel. Edison, for the biggest electrical company, had acquired considerable political power which it used to support the Right. Another argument for nationalization was that any near-monopoly in an essential service ought to be under public control. Another reason was the need to provide electricity as cheaply in southern Italy as in the North where it was mostly produced. On the other hand major industries in the *Confindustria* were strongly critical of nationalization, arguing that it would mean inefficiency and the granting of important jobs to inexperienced party hacks. Moreover shareholders would have to be bought out with money better spent on schools and hospitals. Another bad result of the decision to nationalize was that, to protect themselves against state controls and the new withholding tax on dividends, rich Italians smuggled hundreds of billions of lire out of the country in a major flight of capital that helped to cause a collapse of the stock market. The Church, too, claimed immunity from this tax on its large shareholdings and the government agreed to ignore parliamentary objections by not enforcing such a payment.

An economic recession that began after 1962 had deeper origins than this flight of capital. Equally important was the continuance of weak, compromise governments without a fully agreed economic policy. More particularly, shortages of skilled labor were now beginning to cause wage increases that made costs rise faster than production. This recession was in part a natural downturn after an excessive expansion of credit, but was serious enough to cause a deficit in the balance of payments and there was talk of possible devaluation. One political result was that the new Center-Left alliance was obliged to curtail its reform policy and use anti-inflationary measures to reduce consumer demand. By the end of 1964 this deflation had largely succeeded in its objective, but the socialists had not liked it and a rift in the coalition could be discerned, while any further program of reforms would risk another refusal by industry and the rich to co-operate.

Some of Nenni's colleagues were soon convinced that he had made a poor bargain by joining the government, and they wondered whether, like Depretis and Crispi before him, he had been disarmed by the insidious logic of transformism and was becoming *embourgeoisé*. By separating Nenni from Togliatti the Christian democrats had certainly been hoping to make socialism innocuous, and some socialists therefore broke away to form a separate Party of

Proletarian Unity. Others who stopped short of such desertion did so with reluctance: while accepting that socialism should free itself from the taint of Stalinism, they wanted much more than a slow advance along the primrose path to a welfare state. At the socialist congress of 1965 these dissidents were not strong enough to force a withdrawal from the coalition and Nenni was even empowered to accept back into the party those social-democrat *Saragatiani* who had left the main body of socialism in 1947; but many of their companions looked on this tentative reconciliation as a doubtful measure that could hardly be justified unless it gave socialism more weight in deciding the coalition's legislative program.

For his part, Moro was aware that lack of cohesion among the Christian democrats made it unwise to move any further to the Left. Indeed some in his party looked on Nenni's partial discomfiture with complacency. Their own internal feuds were again exposed when in December 1964 a new president of the republic was elected to succeed the ailing Segni. The official party candidate, sprung on the party by the *Dorotei*, was Giovanni Leone; but other factions rallied to push the alternative candidature of Fanfani; and once again individual jealousies were such that after twenty-one ballots enough Christian democrats deserted both candidates to decide the election in favor of the social-democrat Saragat. That this choice was supported by the communists was an additional embarrassment to the main government party.

The same wrangling and rivalries affected questions of policy. Moro's first cabinet collapsed in June 1964 over the issue of school reform, because party discipline failed and the socialists, nettled by tax exemption for the Vatican, refused to vote for state support to private Catholic schools. His second cabinet fell in January 1966 when some Catholic deputies again took advantage of a secret vote and turned against him. Moro in each case managed to assemble another Center-Left cabinet, but there were some notable defections over the issue of Church prerogatives and over a fear that the *Dorotei* were trying to push the coalition back in a more conservative direction.

★

The fourth postwar legislature (1963–68), despite a large government majority on paper, drifted to a finish with few achievements to its credit and so proved that the correct formula for a working alliance between the center parties had not yet been found. Each year brought promises of major reforms but the results were meager. Inability to liberalize and modernize the state universities was another of the failures that weakened Moro's third administration. The fact that sixty parliamentarians were simultaneously enjoying a virtual sinecure as university teachers (Segni, Moro, and Fanfani among them) helps to explain why reform in this critical field was difficult. University faculties were regularly governed by a self-perpetuating oligarchy that resented any attack on its privileged position. Newspapers had stories of blatant nepotism in professorial appointments and of party loyalty being a primary criterion of selection; also of notorious absenteeism by teachers, as well as a superabundance of graduates in medicine and law, and of doctoral theses being purchased from professional researchers who publicly advertised their services. At the other end of the educational scale almost half of the population never completed elementary school, and a national census revealed the existence in 1961 of eight million illiterates.

Another uncorrected abuse was the quite chaotic process of urban development. Ten successive projects to regulate urban sprawl were blocked by interested parties because a big rise in land values led to highly profitable speculation at the expense of the environment and of the general public. A quarter of the houses built in Rome and Milan were in breach of the existing inadequate regulations, and so were half those in Naples. Critics spoke of the "sack of Rome" and the "sack of Palermo." In Venice, substantial sums of money were allocated by the government and the international community for conservation and repair of ancient monuments, but the industrialists of nearby Mestre and Marghera had different ideas and much of the money simply disappeared while the pollution of air and water by industrial waste continued its work of destruction. Likewise Moro's projected law on regional self-government met consistent right-wing obstructionism because it threatened other vested interests. Nor was any remedy proposed for the great backlog of cases that jammed the law courts. Moreover simplification of the immensely complex tax structure, which had repeatedly been promised as urgent and imminent, was too controversial an issue for the Center Left to settle. Parliament succeeded in agreeing to renegotiate with the Vatican those sections of the 1929 concordat that conflicted with the 1947 constitution, but this was merely another declaration of intent. After fifteen years of repeated requests by opposition deputies the first of successive parliamentary commissions was at long last appointed to investigate the mafia, but a vast accumulation of evidence by this commission was subsequently buried in the archives unread by almost anyone, and evidently some politicians had private reasons for evading legislation on this delicate but crucial subject.

Moro had been secretary of the Christian-democrat party between 1959 and 1964, then prime minister continuously from 1963 to 1968, but differences inside his party left him unable to use his alliance with socialism to confront any of these urgent problems. Although a fine tactician and mediator, he lacked the statesmanship of De Gasperi and in private was pessimistic about reforming what he called a deeply corrupt system. His instinct was rather to temporize, to seek compromise and avoid divisive decisions that might threaten the unity of his party. He was fortunate in that his socialist allies could not match his political skills and lacked governmental experience. They had joined him in the hope of being able to challenge the system but instead were absorbed into it and adopted its ways of behavior. Cynicism increasingly replaced idealism. Instead of attacking the practice of clientelism, all too often the socialists' priority was to share in the spoils of office by obtaining well-paid directorships in public corporations and welfare agencies, and numberless other jobs in the *sottogoverno*.

One alarming revelation that weakened this Center-Left alliance was a newspaper report in 1967 about a threatened military coup three years earlier. Nothing had come of this mysterious threat, but enough information was eventually revealed to indicate that in the summer of 1964 a potentially dangerous conspiracy had been organized. Its leading figure was General De Lorenzo who after controlling the secret services had been promoted to command the *carabinieri*, and then used his position to prepare a military unit armed with tanks for some hypothetical and unspecified emergency. The *carabinieri* were the militarized police force that in 1943 had played an indispensable part in organizing the royalist coup against fascism. This same force was now used by De Lorenzo with something very different in mind.

What became known in 1967 was that, during years of secret surveillance, senior military officials had been collecting dossiers on the private life of 150,000 citizens prominent in public life. De Lorenzo not only had some sympathy with neo-fascism but had contingency plans to arrest some of these citizens and confine them on the island of Sardinia; also to take control of prefectures, radio stations, and government offices. Apparently he was relying on the fact that President Segni, whom he met frequently, spoke in private of wanting to terminate the Center-Left experiment, and it is a safe assumption that these elaborate preparations must also have been known (if not actually authorized) by one or more ministers in government. What particularly aroused apprehension was that a subsequent parliamentary report on this possible coup was published only after many deletions had been made by Moro. Other mysterious episodes would later confirm that the military secret services were often a law unto themselves and were almost entirely concerned with internal rather than foreign politics. Further revelations later demonstrated that an undercover military organization had existed ever since 1948–49 to prepare for resistance against a possible communist insurrection. This organization, code-named "Gladio," had received arms and finance from NATO and the United States. For forty years its existence remained unknown to the Italian public, even apparently unknown to some prime ministers, and certainly never authorized by parliament; but it continued in being even after communism ceased to present any revolutionary threat, for reasons that can only be surmised.

The election results of May 1968 reflected public alarm over De Lorenzo's behavior and also disappointment at the poor achievement of the Center Left. The vote made any prospect of an effective majority even more doubtful. In the new parliament the Right was weaker and there was a significant move inside this Right away from the neo-fascist Italian Social Movement (MSI), but the socialist party as a penalty for failure in government lost a quarter of its popular support and so imperiled continuance of the coalition. Intransigents in the new Party of Proletarian Unity obtained almost a million and a half votes, and the communist vote went up to eight and a half million, so that non-co-operators on the extreme Left again held a third of the parliamentary seats.

The Center-Left alliance could still be said to represent 55 per cent of the vote after May 1968 and there was no obvious alternative to it, but the socialist leaders recognized that to continue as allies of Christian democracy might further erode their own electoral support. Although Nenni himself would have liked to remain in the government, some of the other socialists were jockeying for position inside four party factions that differed only marginally in policy but found difficulty working together. To prevent a split they agreed on retaining party unity by collective resignation from the government, which left another *monocolore* administration under Leone to continue on sufferance. A more obvious candidate than Leone might have been Mariano Rumor who since 1964 had held a commanding position as secretary of the Christian-democrat party; but Rumor would not stake his reputation on a losing cause. Short of his party accepting a more radical program, it would not be easy for him or anyone to reassemble the one coalition that might command an effective majority, and the party notables would not commit themselves so far. Once more there was an impasse in national and local politics, which permitted a variety of problems to build up as government action had again to be postponed.

★

Many solid achievements had been registered in the economy by the late 1960s. Standards of life for most people had greatly improved. Though islands of extreme poverty remained, average incomes had risen more in twenty years than over the previous century. One index was that the number of television sets doubled in four years to seven million and the number of telephones in Milan was said to be proportionally as great as in London. As well as the lira being one of the world's stronger currencies there was a substantial trade surplus. Italy had by now become a heavy exporter of capital—much of it illegally as a means of tax evasion. Workers in agriculture had in the past twenty years declined by half to little more than four million, and those remaining on the land were more prosperous than ever before. A traditional peasant world of handicrafts and bare subsistence was rapidly giving way to a consumer society with a new demand for manufactures and a higher standard of living.

At long last Italy was experiencing a genuine industrial revolution. Though consumption of energy per head was only half that in most north European countries, the steel industry, which before the war produced two and a half million tons a year from scrap, was now producing six times as much. Zanussi, Ignis, Indesit were new names in an efficient refrigerator and washing-machine industry that outdistanced competition in the rest of Europe, and Olivetti was the leading European manufacturer of typewriters and office machinery. Another index of change was that foreign tourism, the largest source of foreign exchange, probably earned more in Italy than anywhere else in the world and the number of visitors increased each year. In 1938 38,000 private automobiles had been produced, but the figure was 100,000 in 1953, 500,000 in 1960, a million in 1963, and reached over a million and a half by 1967. Russia in 1966 chose Fiat to build one of her first mass-production car factories; automobile plants were also being planned for Poland and Romania. Montecatini and Edison, which became one of the biggest European chemical industries when they merged in 1966 to form Montedison, had contracts to construct other large factories in Russia.

Despite Mattei's exaggerated claims, domestic supplies of oil provided less than ten per cent of Italy's needs. New sources of methane had been found in Sicily, Basilicata, and the Abruzzi, but increasing amounts of gas and oil had to be imported, mostly from North Africa and the Middle East. Italy was well placed for such imports and by 1969 had the largest oil refining industry in Europe with a capacity of up to 130 million tons a year. Over four thousand miles of pipe lines had by then been laid for transporting gas supplies inside Italy. The National Hydrocarbons Institute (ENI) continued to invest heavily in the search for new sources of supply abroad, with only moderate results.

★

The promised economic expansion in southern Italy was a casualty of the 1962–65 recession. A new plan—presented in 1965 but interminably postponed—laid down once more the aim of eliminating the differentiation in living standards between North and South; but even after investment revived, the increase in incomes continued to be lower south of Rome than in the northwest, and industrial investment in the South was disappointing. Not only were existing incentives insufficient to attract enough private capital from northern investors, but government machinery was neither flexible nor powerful enough to act as a compensatory instrument of planning or control. Much of the allocated funds was either misspent on buying political favors or continued to lie idle in credit with the Treasury because of bureaucratic incompetence and because agreement could not be reached on how to use it. Months and sometimes even many years passed before adequate help could arrive to repair the damage done by a succession of earthquakes.

As a result the aim of creating a self-propelling process of industrial growth in the South seemed as remote as ever, and the gap between the two Italies, far from being eliminated, continued to widen. Some people wondered if fine promises had been meant seriously or only as electoral propaganda, and it was increasingly hard to credit officially inspired slogans (still heard in the 1990s) about the South being potentially "the California of Italy." Successive coalitions were obliged to pay verbal obeisance to the southern lobby and promise redress, but the very nature of coalition government forced the authorities to gratify the even stronger northern industrial lobby whose solution to the southern problem was far more ruthless. To this extent the continued backwardness of the South was a casualty not just of economic recession but of the governmental system.

Even if the North was progressing faster, life in southern Italy was far easier than before. The old kind of *latifondo* was well on the way to disappearance wherever more intensive cultivation was profitable. Unemployment and underemployment were being reduced by emigration, and the yield of agriculture was three times what it had been fifty years earlier despite a smaller work force. Welfare benefits and compulsory insurance as well as television sets were progressively reaching out into the southern countryside. A fine motor-way from the North came nearer each year to joining Calabria with Milan and at last a double-track railway was built down to the Straits of Messina. In Apulia the 1960s saw the southern towns of Bari and Taranto becoming more industrialized, and in a well-timed visit to Naples before the 1968 election Moro inaugurated work on a large automobile plant for the government-owned Alfa Romeo company. Not everyone believed that these investments in the South were economically justifiable. It is also true that Sardinian banditry was never so obtrusive and intractable as in the years after 1967, and the Sicilian mafia had little trouble finding protection in high places which enabled it to move into far more lucrative and damaging operations than gang warfare. Nevertheless there was more and more local indignation against these twin scourges of the South and at last public opinion was beginning to change from passive acceptance to more active resistance against them.

Gradually the different Italian regions, despite their economic diversity, were becoming socially more homogeneous and more aware of their common national identity. The process was made easier by invigorating cultural movements that spread from Milan and Rome to every province of the peninsula. The statistics were still poor for school attendance and newspaper readership, and another retarding factor was that for almost a quarter of the population the customary spoken language was still not Italian but a dozen mutually unintelligible dialects. But the pace of change was increasing, especially through the standardizing medium of television. Italian citizens moreover, especially as the European Common Market allowed many to work abroad, were becoming more conscious of events and ideas in other countries and hence better able to understand their own society. Also the outside world became much more aware of contemporary Italian architecture, painting, and sculpture. There was an ever greater market for Italian fashions and industrial design. In film-making the work of Michelangelo Antonioni, Visconti, Pier Paolo Pasolini, De Sica, and Federico Fellini became a familiar part of western culture. In literature, not only would Moravia, Tomasi di Lampedusa, and Umberto Eco become best-sellers all over the world, but readers in other countries began through translation to know the names of Italo Svevo, Carlo Gadda, Eugenio Montale, Italo Calvino, Primo Levi, Leonardo Sciascia, and Norberto Bobbio.

SECTION FOURTEEN: ITALIAN DEMOCRACY IN CRISIS

61   Terrorism, Corruption, and Consociation, 1968–1981

A minor political and cultural revolution took place in the wake of a militant movement of protest that swept through universities and schools in 1967–68. Initially students were protesting against poor teaching and authoritarianism inside the educational establishment, but soon they moved toward challenging authority everywhere, in family life as well as in state and Church. During the autumn of 1969 there were other violent disputes over poor working conditions in industry and against the delays by government over promised reforms in housing, health, and public services. Both movements, by industrial workers and students, were disruptive and traumatic while they lasted, but had positive results in challenging some of the residues of fascism and in revealing popular wishes for a more equitable and open-minded society. But sometimes the use of violence provoked retaliation or imitation by parallel movements of protest that were more mysterious and far more than merely disruptive. In December 1969, when a bomb outside a Milanese bank killed sixteen people, automatically the authorities strove to blame the extreme Left, discovering only later that the likely culprits were individuals on the extreme Right who had suspect connections with the secret services. Worse still, it emerged later that evidence was fabricated by the police in order to block investigation and protect whoever was responsible, as a result of which a series of condemnations and then acquittals on appeal continued over the next twenty years.

For some time after 1969 the country was torn apart by hundreds of minor and a few major terrorist attacks. Revolutionaries on both Left and Right were apparently trying to destabilize the country. At each extreme fringe of the political spectrum a small nucleus of idealists was involved, but for other revolutionary groups such violence was almost an end in itself. Hundreds of individual victims were kidnapped for money or else "knee-capped" as a means of social revenge and intimidation. Victims were occasionally assassinated even after large ransoms had been paid. Nor were some of the perpetrators ever identified.

Among activist political factions on the extreme Left the Red Brigades made their appearance in 1970. They and other kindred groups were hoping to attract mass support and win a share of power through revolution, but events showed this to be a pathetic misjudgment and they never obtained much popular backing. While proclaiming a belief in different versions of Marxist-Leninism, some were in practice much closer to anarchism. They were condemned by the official communist party which in turn they traduced for its unexpected rejection of revolution and its preference for winning power through parliamentary democracy. At the opposite political extreme were dozens of small groups on the Right that had learned from Mussolini to believe in the morality and utility of political violence. In December 1970 a futile comic-opera attempt at a political coup was launched by a former fascist hero, Prince Borghese. In 1974 eight people were killed in the center of Brescia by terrorists trying to disrupt an anti-fascist meeting. A few months later there were twelve fatal casualties when an express train was derailed by a bomb near Bologna. Some individuals, including members of the secret services, were prosecuted after these grisly events, but the courts moved so slowly and indecisively that succesive convictions and acquittals left a great deal unexplained.

Although the revival of any fascist party was forbidden by the constitution, the Italian Social Movement (MSI) was properly called neo-fascist and its party secretary Giorgio Almirante had been a leading organizer of Mussolini's anti-Semitic campaign. The MSI usually polled less than 6 per cent of the electorate and was ostracized or at least marginalized by the other parties, but the existence of support for such an extreme group was unusual anywhere in Europe. Exploiting ambiguities in the law, Almirante continued to proclaim in the 1970s that the fundamental principles of fascist doctrine remained valid and Mussolini's regime represented "the highest degree of human morality." On occasion he continued to defend terrorist action on the unconvincing pretense that he was thereby halting the spread of communism. As well as regretting the replacement of authoritarianism by liberal democracy, he at first demanded the return to Italy of her African colonies and denounced the "iniquitous" loss to the Yugoslavs of Mussolini's conquests in the Balkans. Nevertheless support from this small anachronistic party was sometimes needed to give the Christian democrats a majority in parliament.

★

The Partito Comunista Italiana (PCI) was a far more substantial dissident party, and as well as being supported by a quarter or more of the popular vote it continued to enjoy secret and substantial annual subsidies from soviet Russia. Its first postwar leader Togliatti, though he had been a dedicated Stalinist when living in Moscow during the 1930s, later tried to distance himself from the blind obedience and brutalities of his own past. But this change was too slow for some of his colleagues and in 1956 there were important desertions from his party when he enthusiastically welcomed soviet aggression against Hungary. It took many years before the communist leadership could accept that Marxist dogma was increasingly irrelevant to developments in society whereas capitalism was far more economically successful and less socially malevolent than they had ever imagined.

On the positive side of the ledger the communists gained much credit for their effective administration of local government in the provinces of Emilia and Romagna, as also for their realism and common sense which helped governments to enact a great deal of necessary legislation. But not even after 1968, when their party condemned the soviet invasion of Czechoslovakia, did they convince the Italian electorate that they could be safely allowed into government or that their acceptance of democracy was more than a deceitful tactical expedient. This failure kept the Christian democrats permanently in power and was a main ingredient in blocking the development of a workable political system. While France accepted a new constitution under De Gaulle, and while Spain changed radically after General Franco's death, in Italy the Christian democrats with less than 40 per cent of the parliamentary vote continued to control most of the levers of real power and lacked the stimulus for a major change in attitude that might have been provided if the parliamentary opposition had any chance of forming an alternative government.

★

Some of the reforms enacted during the fifth postwar legislature of 1968–72 were an unenthusiastic reply to the agitation by students and trade unions or else were a delayed recognition of developments in public opinion. In December 1970, at the end of another marathon debate lasting continuously for nearly a hundred hours, parliament at last legalized divorce after some Catholic deputies joined the opposition and defied a contrary ruling from the Vatican. Italy was rapidly becoming a more secular society. Church attendance was still impressive but for some time had been falling. Also, more dramatically, the birth rate was declining very substantially despite clerical injunctions against the use of contraceptives. Worst of all were startling figures quoted in the press about there being as many illegal abortions as live births. Fanfani and the Christian-democrat leadership miscalculated when they appealed to the electorate against legalization of divorce. To do this they invoked a hitherto unused article in the constitution that allowed abrogation of legislation by a popular referendum. In 1974 when a vote was held, 88 per cent of the population voted among whom over 59 per cent favored divorce. Public opinion had evidently moved way ahead of the political and ecclesiastical establishment.

Other laws at this period helped toward creating a welfare state through more job security and a reduction in working hours. There was a promise to aim at higher standards in education, housing, and health services. A law of 1970 at last set up fifteen new regional administrations in addition to the five already in existence, and this was an acknowledgment that government had become overcentralized. Each individual region would elect an assembly that possessed some rights of legislation, though in practice these bodies were still given only limited powers and proved to be costly as well as not notably efficient. Nor was their creation accompanied by a proportional reduction in the central bureaucracy at Rome. It was Italy's misfortune that administration remained more centralized, more costly and much more inefficient than in other western countries. Many laws were enacted that could never be properly enforced. Almost all public services continued to be notorious for lethargy and maladministration.

According to one minister who had the specific task of administrative reform, Italy would never become a truly liberal state without greater concessions to autonomy at the level of township, province, and region. Cavour in 1861 had said exactly the same, but even in the 1970s there was opposition from vested interests inside the administrative machine and from national politicians who depended on a centralized control over local patronage. Parliament in Rome continued to be bogged down in petty legislation on local problems, and hence many important laws had to be enacted by executive decree without discussion or vote. Decrees required validation by parliament within two months, but if this failed they could be simply reissued in the form of another temporary decree. Newspapers reported that, while deputies were eager to vote a large increase in salary to themselves, they often appeared in parliament merely to sign their attendance sheets, leaving only a handful of members to take part in debates. One deputy recalled only two serious debates on important issues in the four years 1968–72. Partly this was the old story of coalition cabinets which shied away from both controversy and collective decisions, each minister having his own partisan interests to protect. Ministers were each conditioned by dependence on a different local power base: Moro in Apulia, Fanfani in Tuscany, Rumor in the Veneto, Antonio Gava in Naples, Andreotti in Rome and Sicily, Colombo in Basilicata. When in 1971 a new head of state had to be chosen, ten Christian democrats competed against each other to obtain support from other parties for their own candidature; and for a whole year this internal rivalry crippled the normal processes of decision-making until, after twenty-three frustrating ballots, Giovanni Leone was elected president as a compromise between the various factions.

★

What chiefly held this party together was its determination to prevent the formation of an alternative left-wing government. Communist support in parliament was welcome and often necessary, but the prospect of communists in government was unthinkable. Few people outside the extreme Left were worried that the permanent ostracism of such a large sector of public opinion might be inexpedient and possibly dangerous. Only a minority in the mainstream of politics believed that democracy required parties to alternate in office so as to prevent the stagnation and degeneration that corrupts any permanent ruling elite. The philosopher Benedetto Croce, though strongly conservative in his politics, had already before 1950 foreseen that communists might be more likely than Christian democrats to move toward genuine acceptance of liberal methods; and Guido Carli, an influential governor of the Bank of Italy between 1960 and 1976, believed that communists would one day act like social democrats if only they were given practical responsibility in government and were no longer marginalized. For too long, however, Russian policy in eastern Europe made such beliefs seem overoptimistic. In the meantime anticommunism was a useful pretext for winning American financial support as well as for keeping an elderly generation of Italian politicians permanently in power.

Aldo Moro, the most prominent Christian-democrat leader, was among the few who agreed with Carli (and with De Gasperi's earlier conviction) that a truly effective democracy would require Left and Right to alternate in office. In the short term the most he hoped for was to negotiate a consociation or co-partnership, first with the socialists after 1962, then after 1972 with communism, in each case on condition that his own party retained the substance of power. Moro, as prime minister five times between 1963 and 1976, had good reason to fear that after a further series of damaging financial scandals his Christian democrats were in danger of losing support in the country. Alarmed by student riots, workers' strikes and the persistence of terrorist attacks, he accepted the need to broaden the basis of popular consent and to recognize that a greater degree of positive support from the trade unions was necessary. This became urgent when in 1973 his party had to cope with an enormous increase in international oil prices and a consequent rise in the cost of living. Compromise with the Left was all the more needed after the referendum on divorce in 1974 showed that Fanfani's intransigent Catholicism no longer had much appeal to an increasingly secular electorate.

For their part the communists, now led by Enrico Berlinguer, were already moving toward this same idea of a possible co-partnership or what he called a "historic compromise" with Moro. One reason was his belated realization that communist dogma was being progressively invalidated by the successes of a market economy. A more practical reason was the obvious fact that, even if he were joined by the socialists, there was only a slender chance in the foreseeable future of such a left-wing coalition winning an electoral majority and forming an alternative government. Yet he also recognized the danger of remaining in ineffective opposition. He remembered that in 1922 the refusal by left-wing parties to co-operate with Giolitti had handed power to Mussolini, and this same lesson was recently reinforced by a militarist counterrevolution in Greece, while the victory of General Pinochet in Chile was another warning of the dangers from right-wing reaction. Berlinguer had in any case learned that the Russian model of proletarian dictatorship was not applicable to the more prosperous and pluralistic circumstances prevailing in Italy. His best hope of creating a more equitable and less corrupt society lay in renouncing unrealistic talk of revolution and avoiding gratuitous antagonization of the middle classes. Instead, his best option would be to work inside parliament, co-operating with reformists in other parties to discover if minor changes in the system might be feasible. Some of his colleagues were already suggesting that they should drop the word "communist" and accept in practice that they were rapidly becoming another social-democrat party.

Berlinguer's talk of a "historic compromise" with the Christian democrats was assumed by his opponents to be merely tactical, but in fact it marked a change in communist policy and required considerable courage on his part. One almost inevitable result was that dissident Marxists abandoned him in 1974 to form a separate revolutionary party, but he received strong support in the local administrative elections of 1975 when moderate communists won control of most big cities. Understandably this caused alarm among conservatives, and in the national elections of the following year many people rallied to the Christian democrats who once again obtained nearly 39 per cent of the vote; but the communists increased their own share to over 34 per cent and together with other parties on the Left were not far short of winning half the seats in parliament.

★

Berlinguer's moderate and co-operative policy, strongly disliked by Moscow, was not given credence in Washington. A report to the American Congress revealed that in recent years more than a hundred million dollars reached Italy from America to support the anticommunist cause. Most of this money went to the Christian-democrat party but some was sent directly to the Italian secret services whose commanders had close links to neo-fascism. How much other American money was funneled through the covert military organization of Gladio cannot be known, but more than once the Italian government imposed a veto on disclosures to parliament about the financing of mysterious groups suspected of involvement with right-wing terrorism. Policy-makers in the United States genuinely intended to support political stability and parliamentary government in Italy although they assumed that this could best be done by obstructing Moro's tentative approaches to the hard Left. But some people criticized American intervention for encouraging subversive elements on the extreme Right and for helping to perpetuate the blocked political system that Moro and Berlinguer were hoping to change.

While this debate was continuing there appeared press reports with further damaging revelations, one of them about how the American Lockheed company bribed Italian politicians in order to sell its Hercules aircraft. This discovery was made in America, otherwise nothing might ever have come to light. Names were not mentioned, but two former Italian prime ministers came under grave suspicion and one ex-minister went to prison since he belonged to a minor party and lacked political protection. Worse still, the head of state, Leone, was forced to resign because he and his family were implicated. Public opinion was shaken by this indication that the financing of parties and party factions was secret, uncontrolled and sometimes illegal through slush funds held abroad. Don Sturzo had not been heeded when in 1958 he pointed out in parliament that large amounts of money came to the parties from industry, public corporations, foreign companies, and governments, all of whom no doubt expected and received something in return; nor was there any means of knowing how much of this money was privately diverted by some less scrupulous politicians to augment their already substantial emoluments. By the 1970s such allegations could no longer be ignored. The main parties had each developed a very extravagant bureaucratic organization that depended on suspect donations and bribes. Each party in power also continued to rely on being able to reward its supporters through the lavish patronage provided by jobs or sinecures in the large area of the economy under government control.

Moro inherited these practices and was obliged to connive at them in order to keep the various coteries of his own party in common harness. What was new was his decision to resist American advice and, without bringing communists into his government, to treat them as a coalition partner and discover if their suggestion of a historic compromise might produce a partial political consensus. They too were therefore given a few jobs in the *sottogoverno* and greater expectation of being consulted over legislation. One leading communist, Pietro Ingrao, was even appointed Speaker of the Chamber and others were chosen to chair some of the permanent parliamentary committees. In return, as well as continuing to denounce left-wing terrorism, the communist party acknowledged in public that Italy was safer as a member of the western defense system inside NATO than as part of the soviet bloc. By common agreement a new law allowed tax revenue to be used for funding the various parties in the overoptimistic hope that this would reduce reliance on outside finance. A further item in the deal was that an ambitious national health service was institutionalized. Concessions were made to the Left over pensions and the expensive escalator clause (*scala mobile*) that raised wages in line with inflation; also over the fund (*cassa integrazione*) that provided dismissed workers with 80 per cent of their former earnings.

This consociation lasted only from 1976 to 1979, during which time Giulio Andreotti led two *monocolore* Christian-democrat governments of "National Solidarity" supported by communists as well as by parties of the Center. A welcome degree of accommodation was thus obtained. Even if Italy was not ready for communism to be accepted in government, distinct benefits derived from partially correcting the virtual disfranchisement of a large sector in the electorate. But there was a price to pay for consociation, and part of the price was that legislative reforms were not always submitted to the critical scrutiny over costs that a less consensual parliament would have applied. Carli and other economists voiced their fears that the national debt would increase uncontrollably if adversarial politics were again replaced in this way by the transformist practice of buying off potential opposition through reforms that were bound to prove expensive.

★

Other very different objections to the historic compromise came from the anarchist fringes on the Right and Left where extremists had become accustomed to use violence as a means of preventing reconciliation and undermining social stability. Moro began to receive threats of death. In March 1978 the outside world was astounded when this most prominent of Italian politicians, on his way to parliament, was kidnapped by the Red Brigades in a crowded Roman street and his five police bodyguards were killed. Andreotti as prime minister, supported by the communist party, refused to negotiate with Moro's clandestine captors and the police failed to discover where in Rome he was hidden. Two months later while still in captivity he was assassinated by these self-appointed executioners.

Such a shocking murder, though intended by the Red Brigades as a step toward the general collapse of law and order, galvanized public opinion into rallying behind the government. But it also helped to persuade Andreotti against continuing Moro's attempt at consociation with the extreme Left, and the suggestion was even made that some conservatives had not been altogether sorry to see Moro removed from the political scene. A parliamentary commission of inquiry spent four years investigating the assassination but could not agree and finally produced a number of irreconcilable reports. In each of the years 1978–80, dozens of other Italians were killed by terrorists and hundreds wounded, including journalists, policemen, judges, industrialists, and professors. Yet the outraged reaction of the public once again demonstrated the tragic futility of such wanton and juvenile revolutionary action. One immediate and quite unexpected consequence was that, when Leone was forced to resign as head of state, the surprise choice to succeed him in 1978 was the elderly socialist Sandro Pertini, a man whose integrity, courage, and unpretentiousness made him the most admired and best loved of all postwar presidents. Pertini did a great deal in a period of dangerous tension to revive respect for institutions and encourage popular counteraction not only against terrorism but against the mafia and corrupt politics.

Another effective reaction was the setting up of a specialist unit to coordinate police repression of terrorist violence. Its first commander, General Dalla Chiesa, in addition to being given emergency powers, was helped by a succession of laws offering lenient penalties to any *pentiti* who might repent and co-operate with the authorities. Almost immediately this produced positive results, and when the Red Brigades captured an American general who was a senior NATO commander, information from *pentiti* led to his liberation by the authorities. Other revolutionary groups on the extreme Right were either less easy to identify or possibly enjoyed a degree of secret political protection. There was another terrible outrage in August 1980 when eighty-five people were killed by a bomb in the railway station at Bologna: right-wing terrorists were convicted, then acquitted on appeal, so leaving another case to be added to a growing list of state mysteries. Not only was the efficiency of both the judicial system and the police called into question, but yet another parliamentary commission spent the next ten years investigating these events without ever producing a generally accepted explanation.

Equally mysterious and much more murderous was the mafia in Sicily where rival "families" continued to fight each other for control of the enormous subsidies sent from Rome to boost the southern economy. These gangs had discovered in the 1960s that vast profits could be made from the trade in narcotic drugs, but they also used corruption and intimidation to establish a lucrative control over the allocation of contracts for public works, and unlike left-wing political terrorists these criminals were rich enough to buy support from a few unscrupulous politicians, judges, and policemen. Two *pentiti* of the mafia in the 1970s revealed frightening details of this collusion but their revelations were disbelieved or at least disregarded, and both were soon executed by their former associates in crime.

Such was the conspiracy of silence about the mafia that a national opinion poll taken in 1962 found a third of the Italian population still admitting to never having so much as heard of it, while another third knew nothing more than its name. Nor did the government lack effective weapons that could have been used against a small group of a few thousand malefactors, but wealthy delinquents controlled so many votes in western Sicily that the political will to act was lacking. After many years of investigation, successive parliamentary commissions continued to produce voluminous majority and minority reports from which it is clear that *mafiosi* could rely on collusion with some politicians and judges, thereby securing their own immunity from prosecution. But the substance of these reports never received much publicity. Some outspoken members of parliament were conveniently assassinated after they tried to insist on greater outspokenness over mafia crimes, and it had already been learned that any over-inquisitive journalist might simply disappear without trace.

Two Christian-democrat politicians became emblematic of corruption in some local Sicilian administrations: both served as mayors of Palermo after years spent in running the highly remunerative office that controlled the issue of building licenses in the "sack of Palermo." One was Salvo Lima who was also a director of the Bank of Sicily and in five governments during 1972–76 represented mafia interests as a junior minister in Rome. The other was Vito Ciancimino who rose from poverty to great wealth by presiding over an orgy of land speculation. Both became part of Andreotti's political machine in Sicily, and both led a charmed life protected by mafia intimidation until reports by a parliamentary commission belatedly brought some of their misdeeds to light. Palermo by the end of the 1970s was probably the chief world center for the sale of heroin. Hundreds of Sicilians were being assassinated each year in this small island, usually because of conflicts between rival gangs competing for the lucrative trade in drugs and licenses, but the victims also included communist and Christian-democrat politicians as well as some senior policemen and magistrates who refused to turn a blind eye on what was happening.

★

Elsewhere in the national economy another problem was that some industrialists in the publicly controlled sector exploited the lack of anti-trust legislation in order to build big conglomerate structures that did not always operate in the public interest. Eugenio Cefis was one of the most influential Italians throughout the 1970s. After becoming head of ENI on the death of

Mattei, Cefis had won control of the petrochemcial group Montedison, so creating a large clientelistic empire by methods that did not always bear close scrutiny and eventually led to disaster. Following Mattei's example but without any of Mattei's idealism, Cefis subsidized the main political parties to buy their support. He also purchased newspapers so as to defend himself against accusations that he used enormous sums of public money to win a dominant position in the national economy.

Another scandal involved politicians and police bribed by international oil companies who wanted to avoid payment of tax, and parliament blocked a judicial investigation into the conduct of deputies who were thought to be involved. Later it emerged that documents about this case were falsified with the complicity of the most senior customs and excise officers in order to conceal the import of large quantities of oil without paying tax. In 1979 another journalist who threatened to expose this and other sensitive political scandals was assassinated by mafia hit men who claimed or pretended to be acting on behalf of Andreotti and other prominent politicians.

Steel manufacture was another state-owned parasitic enterprise that weighed heavily on the Italian economy, and its losses were among the greatest in the hundreds of companies controlled by the IRI. A powerful lobby ensured that Italy after 1960 became one of the world's largest producers of steel, and this at a time when other countries thought it prudent to contract production. An enormous new plant was built in the 1960s at Taranto in the entirely false expectation or pretense that this would at last create an area of economic growth in the southeast of the country. Ten years later another large steel complex was planned in the southwest, once again for dubious reasons and despite a large existing surplus of capacity. An entirely new port was built for this purpose at Gioia Tauro in Calabria to the immense profit of local *mafiosi* and of some regional politicians. Not only was a rich agricultural area thereby devastated, but the allocation of building contracts led to further gang warfare in which hundreds of people were killed; yet no steel was ever produced because the project was abandoned after an astronomic expenditure of money.

Italy was unlike most countries in still having nearly half its productive economy in the public sector, and this proportion had even increased after World War II. The IRI, as a giant holding company, had been created by Mussolini as an emergency and temporary measure. The original intention was for its component companies to be subsequently returned to private control, but this never happened and by 1980 the IRI had become one of the largest corporations in the world. As well as steel, it controlled airlines, shipbuilding, radio and television networks, telecommunications, important banks, and some automobile factories. Almost inevitably its operative considerations as a state-owned business were dictated by political expediency rather than the market, and often the expediency was party-political rather than in the national interest. Always it was vulnerable to political pressure to save jobs by keeping unprofitable industries in operation, especially in regions where top politicians needed votes. Almost every year IRI reported mounting financial deficits. Privately owned industries would have collapsed without profitability, but the public sector was cushioned against failure and, being increasingly uncompetitive against its foreign rivals, on balance acted as a brake upon the country's economic development.

Private enterprise was generally far better able to weather difficult economic conditions and often was outstandingly successful. Not only large family firms such as Fiat, Olivetti, and Pirelli, to which number was later added those of Gucci, Benetton, and Armani, but a great contribution to national prosperity was made by much smaller new companies. In the financial sector some ambitious entrepreneurs nevertheless did positive harm by exploiting the lack of legislative controls. Far worse than Cefis was the Sicilian Michele Sindona who, on the back of support from the mafia as well as from the Vatican and the Freemasons, created another of the biggest financial empires in Europe. As early as 1967 the American police warned their counterparts in Italy that Sindona was involved in drug trafficking and in laundering mafia money, but he had powerful protection and Italian governments took no action. Only when an American bank in Sindona's ownership collapsed did the more stringent regulations in the United States expose suspected illegalities and the fragility of his underlying financial position. He was prosecuted in the United States, but for many years his contributions to the main Italian parties enabled him to avoid arrest in Italy and requests for a parliamentary inquiry were once again refused. In 1979 a Milanese lawyer appointed to investigate his activities was assassinated, an event that led at last to an official inquiry and eventually to Sindona's conviction and imprisonment. Two days after arriving in prison he was dead from cyanide poisoning: possibly this was suicide, but the mafia was powerful inside prisons and had already demonstrated how easily convicts could be killed to prevent them revealing awkward facts under interrogation.

Roberto Calvi, a disciple of Sindona, was another leading financier to meet a mysterious death. He used his position as head of the largest private bank in Italy, the Ambrosiano, to buy political support in Rome and recycle mafia money on the international markets. In 1981, huge debts led to the collapse of this bank and his conviction for fraud and illicit currency dealings. The magistrates also opened proceedings for criminal investigation against Archbishop Marcinkus in the Vatican whose Institute for Religious Affairs had been employed by Calvi as a means of evading the laws controlling export of currency, but the papal authorities, while agreeing under pressure to compensate creditors of the Ambrosiano, claimed immunity from secular legislation and refused to help the investigation or permit the archbishop to appear in court. Many relevant facts were therefore never brought to light. Calvi fled to London where in June 1982 his corpse was found hanging underneath Blackfriars Bridge. The verdict in the British coroner's court was suicide, though this was almost certainly wrong. Some of his clients, notably the mafia, could not forgive anyone who misused or purloined their money.

★

Meanwhile judicial investigations into the activities of Sindona and Calvi quite unexpectedly uncovered another of the major scandals in postwar Italy. Two law officers in 1981 obtained a warrant to search the house of Licio Gelli who turned out to be the grand master of a secret masonic lodge—although secret societies were forbidden by Article 18 of the Italian constitution. A list was discovered which showed that the members of this P.2 lodge included bankers, parliamentarians, cabinet ministers and ex-ministers, newspaper editors, *carabinieri*, prefects, judges, senior ambassadors and civil servants, army and naval officers. Most ominous of all, the list included the commanders of Italy's secret services. Gelli himself had a fascist past, and documents found in his office connected him to Sindona and Calvi who were fellow members of P.2. He was also linked to General De Lorenzo, Prince Borghese, and other suspects in the previous twenty years of right-wing subversion. Other documents showed a connection with arms smuggling as well as with laundering money on behalf of Calvi and the mafia.

The government at first tried to keep secret what had been found, and this led to the prime minister's resignation when the news leaked out. Parliament appointed another commission of inquiry which over the next twelve years produced numerous volumes with detailed evidence indicating that the leaders of P.2, though some individuals might have joined it innocently, had created a dangerously corrupting organization which possessed political as well as financial objectives. In order to thwart Moro's plan for partial reconciliation with communism, this masonic lodge had evidently been hoping to introduce a more authoritarian form of government. Gelli fled abroad but was arrested in Switzerland when trying to withdraw large sums of money from one of his many bank accounts. Inside Italy the investigating magistrates ran into all kinds of difficulty; otherwise they might have uncovered incriminating details about the financing of political parties that ten years later, after infinitely more damage had been done, brought the country close to political collapse.

Public opinion was electrified by the evidence of covert political operations at the very highest levels of society and by the fall from grace of three trusted financial advisers to the Holy See. There was further unease over other mysterious events. An official cover-up prevented anyone discovering who in 1980 shot down a passenger plane near the island of Ustica with the loss of eighty lives, though many reputations suffered and a number of suicides took place during a series of contradictory inquiries that continued for the next sixteen years. Nor did anyone ever succeed in tracing much of an enormous relief fund collected after an earthquake of 1980 in the hinterland of Naples. This earthquake damaged hundreds of towns and villages killing six thousand people in Italy's biggest natural disaster since World War II. After initial delay a sum equivalent to more than a billion dollars was paid by the government to repair the damage, but ten years later many people were still homeless, much of the money having fallen into the hands of local politicians and the criminal underworld. Many murders were committed in the competition to pilfer these funds and huge personal fortunes were built out of one of Europe's major financial scandals.

This episode confirmed most observers in the opinion that the south of Italy had unusual standards of social behavior, and invidious comparisons were made with an earthquake four years earlier in the northern region of Friuli where far less public money quickly revitalized a large area. In the region round Naples the *camorra*, in some respects similar to the Sicilian mafia, had existed for centuries but only now became immensely rich and powerful by taking a percentage from relief funds. Public works in the Neapolitan region were nominally in the hands of a minor Christian-democrat politician, Ciro Cirillo, and in April 1981 the Red Brigades kidnapped this man after killing his two guards. Once again, as with the kidnapping of Moro, the police had little reliable information. But politicians were so anxious to prevent embarrassing revelations that the secret services were permitted to negotiate with both the *camorra* and the Red Brigades for Cirillo's release. Nor is there any doubt, despite official denials, that an enormous ransom was paid as a result—though a kidnapped prime minister had recently been left to die at the hands of the same Red Brigades without negotiations or payment of ransom. Such behavior was hard to explain without raising extremely awkward questions, and in fact no explanation was forthcoming.

62 The Old Regime Begins to Collapse, 1981–1992

President Pertini, speaking as head of state and as a socialist, publicly denounced the corrupt practices that permitted such misappropriation of resources, and in 1981 reacted by appointing as prime minister the first non-Christian democrat since 1945. His choice was Giovanni Spadolini, an academic historian and newspaper editor whose republican party was widely respected despite support from only 3 per cent of the electorate. Spadolini had to form a coalition with other larger parties but enjoyed the advantage of being seen as more trustworthy and disinterested than his predecessors. In a welcome breach of precedent he not only tried to choose his own team of ministers without accepting nominees from the various party secretaries, but also appointed experienced specialists to head the state-owned industrial conglomerates instead of using these jobs to reward political placemen. Another of his first decisions was to investigate the Freemasons of the mysterious P.2, after which he declared this masonic lodge to be illegal and dismissed those of its members who commanded the armed forces.

A further problem for Spadolini was that the Sicilian mafia was proving to be far more murderous and difficult to defeat than political terrorism. The mafia and the Neapolitan *camorra* could now be seen as among the main reasons why the South was remaining poor and underdeveloped. Northern industrialists were unenthusiastic about investing in areas where the underworld not only demanded protection money for their factories but regularly took a large cut out of the substantial subsidies sent from Rome and Brussels to encourage development in backward regions. Quite as alarming was that the various mafia clans of Palermo and Corleone had for years been fighting each other to obtain the largest share of these grants and of the lucrative traffic in narcotic drugs. Hundreds of people continued to be assassinated each year in this civil war, especially by the *corleonesi* who were more ruthless and seemed to enjoy better political connections. Few witnesses were brave enough to break the traditional mafia code of silence and give evidence in court. Judges and policemen who tried to maintain the rule of law continued to be assassinated. Equally alarming was that individuals inside the law enforcement agencies had sometimes been terrorized or bribed into active connivance with crime.

Spadolini responded by appointing a senior military officer to be prefect of Palermo. His choice was Dalla Chiesa who had already devised a successful strategy against the terrorists in mainland Italy. Some local politicians invited suspicion by protesting against what they called this attempt by the government to "criminalize" Sicily, and once again an absurd legend tried to depict the mafia as a myth invented by northerners to discredit the South; but Dalla Chiesa quickly discovered that such local protests were bogus and politically motivated. In his view the main cause of Sicilian poverty was that politicians in Palermo and Rome were protecting this vicious scourge in return for its electoral support, so he urgently asked for increased powers in order to scrutinize its mysterious political links. Unfortunately the response from Rome was delayed because of a fierce conflict inside Spadolini's oddly sorted coalition, and Dalla Chiesa a few months later was assassinated, along with his wife, by criminals who feared to lose their immensely profitable way of life. This murder, though a major tragedy, may have been a miscalculation by the mafia because it alerted Italians and foreign journalists to horrifying facts that hitherto had been concealed or disregarded. At once three important countermeasures were taken that had been successful in the United States but which previous Italian governments had preferred to avoid. A high commissioner was appointed to co-ordinate all antimafia action, and the mere fact of association with the mafia was made a crime, while the police were at last given authority to investigate private bank accounts.

★

Elections held in June 1983 registered an extensive fall in Christian-democrat support, and after many weeks of anxious negotiation a new five-party coalition was formed under the socialist Bettino Craxi. This man had the handicap of leading a divided party backed by less than 12 per cent of the electorate, but had the advantage of relative youth, enormous ambition, and a strong personality. He soon proved to be the most forceful political leader since De Gasperi and briefly became the most popular politician in the country. His cabinet included Spadolini as well as seventeen Christian democrats and only six socialists. Some members of his own party differed from him in hoping that one day an increase in the socialist vote would allow them to break free from Christian democracy and preside over a left-wing alliance that included the new and more moderate communist party, so making possible at long last an alternation between governments of Right and Left. This hope was given plausibility when the communist leader Berlinguer, before his death in 1984, moved further away from his soviet mentors by condemning their invasion of Afghanistan and their suppression of the independence movement in Poland. Yet Craxi knew that his socialists would be subordinate in any such left-wing alliance and he also judged that a united Left would in any case fall short of winning a majority.

Public opinion was becoming more important as an active and variegated ingredient in politics, one result of which was that the two largest parties were beginning to lose some of their predominance. The communist vote fell in successive general elections of 1979, 1983, 1987, and 1992. The Christian-democrat electorate fell over the same period from 38 per cent to 27 per cent, a change that was quite without precedent. In 1979 a new Radical party had already won eighteen seats in the lower house of parliament with policies that were individualist, anticlerical, and libertarian; and in 1987 a new Green party won fifteen parliamentary seats by campaigning on environmental issues. At the same time a feminist movement was winning unusual attention from the newspapers. Radicals and feminists now invoked the hitherto rarely used constitutional right to demand a popular referendum as a means of compelling a dilatory parliament to accept reforms and as an index of views held by an increasingly politically conscious public. Such would-be reformers had to contend with the Church, which after 1978 had a much more authoritarian leader in the Polish Pope John Paul II, the first non-Italian pontiff for four centuries, but a referendum in 1981 revealed that papal opposition to abortion was shared by only 33 per cent of an ostensibly Catholic population. This was further proof that the Vatican's earlier anathematization of liberalism and democracy had been a losing battle. Craxi in 1984–85 was therefore able to win the Pope's agreement for changes in the concordat between Church and state, altering the law that gave Catholicism such a privileged position in the state and reducing the legal rights of the Church over marriage and religious instruction in schools.

Craxi soon acquired the reputation of being himself somewhat authoritarian, and the caricaturists had an easy task depicting him, unfairly but not unsuccessfully, as another potential Mussolini. He preferred to govern with only a minimum of discussion between his coalition partners or among his own socialist colleagues. Parliament and opposition he frequently treated with disdain, relying on his undoubted personal ascendancy and the general wish for a leader who would take firm decisions instead of always seeking a watered-down compromise with other parties. But his vaunted *decisionismo* turned out to be more a style of behavior than an ability to govern effectively. Though promising to reduce the cost of government he greatly and irresponsibly increased the mounting public deficit in an attempt to buy electoral support. Nor, to take one special case, did he see the need to check the proliferation of spurious invalidity pensions that were increasingly conceded in return for votes; and such pensions, especially but not only in southern constituencies, were becoming a major item in the rapidly growing national debt. Some of these presumed invalids were active members of parliament who already received a very substantial income.

One success was a decree modifying the escalator clause that automatically tied wage contracts to the cost of living: and this brave defiance of the communists and trade unions was endorsed by a national referendum in 1985. Another partially successful reform was a measure proposed by the small Republican party to reduce tax evasion among the self-employed. Craxi also carried out a decision by his predecessor to permit the installation of American missiles in Sicily and supported Spadolini's decision to send a small Italian unit as part of a peace-keeping force in the Middle East where he strongly supported the Palestinian cause. Many Italian patriots were pleased when in 1985, after an American tourist was killed by Palestinian commandos on an Italian cruise ship, Craxi stood up to pressure from Washington by insisting that this was a matter for the Italian courts to judge; and when a plane carrying these same terrorists was forced by American military aircraft to land in Sicily, he refused their extradition to America and set them free on the strange argument that they had diplomatic immunity. Two months later, encouraged by this irresolute and politically motivated response, Arab terrorists attacked Israeli passengers at Rome airport killing a dozen people among whom were more Americans.

★

Many optimists had assumed that a socialist prime minister would favor a cleaner style of politics. But in practice the logic of coalition government persuaded these newcomers in office to demand an increasing share of jobs in the *sottogoverno* and much more of the *tangenti* or bribes that were becoming a recognized method of paying for the apparatus of the various parties. Socialist politicians and their personal clienteles expected a much bigger quota of well-paid posts in the huge public sector of the economy, whether in banks, credit institutions, welfare agencies, broadcasting, or even university professorships and the judicial bench. There existed a roughly agreed tariff by which jobs were parceled out to political appointees according to the electoral strength of each party or party faction. Still more reprehensible was that some less scrupulous ministers continued to take for themselves or their party a percentage from the contracts awarded for the building of hospitals, universities, motorways, and other public works; and contractors could not afford to question this accepted practice, especially as not they but consumers would ultimately foot the bill. Although Spadolini in 1987 denounced what he called an escalating "klepto-cracy" in public life, many months elapsed before the general public grasped the extent of what was happening, but there was increasing confirmation that people were entering politics because it was a financially rewarding profession, even though most of the illicit profits went toward paying for elections and party administration. During the 1980s there were financial scandals involving socialist politicians in the northern towns of Milan, Turin, Genoa, and Venice, but fraudulent accounting and lack of publicity meant that most examples of malpractice went unpunished and unobserved.

In response to occasional accusations, Craxi responded by shamelessly insisting that no socialist would ever become involved in illegality or corrup-tion, and was indignant when French and German newspapers wrote of Italy being the most corrupt state in Europe. But rumors multiplied and prominent members of his party were living way beyond their ascertainable income. His own personal style of life was excessively prodigal and on visits to foreign countries his large retinue of relatives and admirers caused concern and offense. Not until after his fall from power could the magistrates discover incriminating proof about his own and his party's sources of finance, not to mention the scandalous misappropriation to less worthy purposes of large sums granted by parliament to relieve poverty in Africa and India. When a few alert magistrates in Milan and Trent began to investigate the involvement of the socialist party in extortionate slush funds from banks and Gelli's Freemasons, Craxi was able to secure the transfer of investigations from Milan to Rome where political influence could be used to ensure that the accusations were conveniently buried, and appeals for a public judicial inquiry were again blocked.

In Sicily there was better progress in investigating the crimes of the mafia because it was impossible to ignore a series of carefully planned murders of judges, police, and prosecuting lawyers. Moreover, while Craxi could nearly always obstruct muck-raking in his personal power base at Milan, he was less bothered about Sicily. Over the previous twenty years, several parliamentary antimafia commissions had continued to accumulate a mountain of incriminat-ing evidence, and equally important was the information patiently collected by a courageous team of investigators in Palermo. After 1984 this was supple-mented by revelations from *pentiti* or repentant *mafiosi* who had suffered in the civil war between rival criminal groups and had good reason to fear for their own lives and the safely of their families. One result was the unprecedented prosecution of nearly 500 Sicilians in a maxi-trial that lasted throughout most of 1986 and 1987. Over 300 were found guilty; 100 were acquitted, of whom 17 were then murdered by the mafia in case they had purchased their acquittal by helping the police. Unfortunately most of those convicted were subsequently released on one pretext or another, many of them by a complaisant Sicilian appeal judge who later was himself under judicial investigation for connivance with the mafia.

Further difficulties were created for the police by some senior politicians, mainly Christian democrats with an electoral constituency in western Sicily who were worried that revelations by *pentiti* might unravel links between crime and the political establishment. One cryptic message arrived from a minister telling the courts in Palermo to go easy over prosecutions, and the most active and experienced investigator, Giovanni Falcone, was actually warned by the authorities that otherwise Sicily might lose some of its financial grants from Rome. As a result, according to a senior judge in charge of the antimafia campaign, the late 1980s found the southern third of Italy under the "absolute control" of the criminal underworld. Under pressure from local politicians and rival police investigators, Falcone was transferred from Sicily to other duties in Rome.

★

A proposal heard with greater frequency was that the constitution of 1947 needed revision to make government more effective. A poll taken in 1986 among deputies and senators showed almost no one who believed that the constitution was functioning well: 62 per cent regretted the lack of any alternation of parties in power, 42 per cent blamed the slowness of parliamentary action, 40 per cent singled out the resort several times each week to legislation by executive decree which was something that the constitution permitted only in cases of real emergency. Another 26 per cent pointed out that the existence of many small groups in parliament made it impossible to find a reliable parliamentary majority, and this could only change by renouncing proportional representation. There was further agreement that the prime minister had insufficient authority and the party secretaries far too much. Also there was clearly an inadequate balance of power between executive, judiciary, and parliament.

Another inhibiting flaw in the system was that the average duration of governments was even shorter than in the years 1861–1922. Indeed for forty years it had been under twelve months, and the protracted negotiations after each governmental resignation could leave the country without effective administration for many weeks on each occasion. These debilitating facts were due to the existence of so many minority political parties and their frequent inability to agree over policy. Craxi lasted longer than any premier except De Gasperi and Moro, but met a hostile parliamentary vote almost every week and individuals in his own party exploited the practice of secret voting to join other parties in opposing him. Any minister was therefore discouraged from proposing controversial reforms. Furthermore every cabinet contained politicians who had held office repeatedly since the 1950s or even earlier, and such people had little desire to unblock the system or replace a time-worn political class which had become accustomed to monopolize the levers of power. In many other European countries it was possible for Left and Right to alternate in office with a renewal of policies and political elites, but Italy, despite repeated minor changes in its governmental coalition, lacked this component of a credible democracy.

There was no shortage of suggestions for constitutional changes that might repair such functional disorders. One possibility was to end the anomalous secrecy of parliamentary voting that allowed individual deputies to break party discipline and topple a government. Another was to reduce the complexity of the legislative process by drastically lessening the number of deputies and senators. A further suggestion was to find better legal means of financing the parties and to increase the independent authority of parliament by reducing the "unconstitutional" powers of the various party secretaries. Many politicians were beginning to advocate more decentralization to regional assemblies so as to reduce the time wasted in parliamentary discussion of trivial and local matters. Others wanted a presidential regime as in France or America with much greater powers for the executive, possibly helped by direct popular election of either head of state or prime minister. Much criticism was also leveled at the wholesale absenteeism among parliamentarians that often compelled the suspension of important debates for lack of a quorum. Another obvious target was that Senate and Chamber had an almost identical competence which meant that time was wasted in duplicated discussion. Almost as objectionable was the practice of individual ministers riding their private hobby-horses and disregarding cabinet solidarity, further weakening the prime minister and inhibiting co-ordination of policy.

These difficulties were discussed in 1983–85 by another parliamentary commission that unfortunately divided along party lines, and regrettably its meetings were often poorly attended. Most of its forty members refused to sign a final conclusion, preferring to submit six different minority reports and so leaving public opinion with insufficient guidance. Persuasive arguments were nevertheless raised in its discussions: for having fewer decree-laws, less secret voting, giving greater authority to the prime minister, and reducing the intrusive powers of party secretaries who habitually dictated policy. Only moderate enthusiasm could be found for single-member constituencies or for replacing proportional representation by a first-past-the-post practice of voting, because although this might have produced governments with a working majority, the smaller parties saw it as a threat to their very existence while larger parties feared it might end the comfortable consociation that let them plunder both the private and state-controlled economy. Such an instinct for self-preservation helps to explain why the various reports by members of this Bozzi commission received insufficient publicity and led to little action. One positive result was a law restricting use of the secret vote. More important, however, was that the electorate could now see how the leading politicians, as beneficiaries of the existing system, were unlikely to introduce any reforms which would allow that system to operate in the public interest.

★

Between 1985 and 1992 the presidential head of state was Francesco Cossiga, a respected middle-of-the-road Christian democrat who had briefly been prime minister and whose election as president was supported even by socialists and communists. Craxi presided over successive governments until 1987 and his exceptionally long period in office gave the country another welcome period of relative political stability, but little was done in this period to advance the cause of political or constitutional reform. He was followed by three short-lived administrations under the Christian democrats Fanfani (premier for the sixth time), Giovanni Goria, and Ciriaco De Mita; after which their colleague Andreotti presided over his sixth and seventh governments during the critical period 1989–92 when the whole political system came close to collapse.

Giulio Andreotti had first become a junior minister in 1947, since when, in thirty different governments, he had held most of the major cabinet posts and was rarely out of office. Though a devoted churchman as well as an unusually shrewd political operator, he had an extraordinarily cynical attitude to politics and often needed to claim parliamentary immunity in order to escape judicial investigation of his personal conduct. What especially damaged his reputation was association with sinister financiers such as Sindona, Calvi, and Gelli, quite as much as his dependence on electoral votes provided by the infamous Lima and Ciancimino who were closely involved with the Sicilian mafia. Not only American diplomats but also Margaret Thatcher gave him "top marks for political ambiguity" and a "positive aversion to principle." Yet this enigmatic politician knew better than anyone how to operate the secret levers of power and survive many crises in postwar Italy.

Andreotti and Craxi worked together after 1989 in resisting demands for radical change. Both continued to protest that accusations about ministerial malpractice were totally without foundation, and not until after 1992 did the official public prosecutors possess enough information or enough courage and public support to act. The cabinets of De Mita and Andreotti in 1988–92 included a dozen ministers who were already suspect but who only subsequently became household names for peculation and embezzlement. One premonitory sign had been an accusation against two former ministers for profiteering from the construction of prisons, but protected from prosecution they were convicted only some years later. A further revelation involved another senior Christian democrat who was chairman of the state railways, and in his case the full extent of a huge swindle became known only when in August 1989 this hitherto respected citizen was assassinated by Calabrian criminals for failing to pay them a percentage. Shortly afterwards a major state-owned bank caused another scandal by secretly and illegally sending 2 billion US dollars to Saddam Hussein for Iraq to use in buying war materials.

This exposure was almost fortuitous and, once again, came from information revealed through the less secretive conditions prevailing in the United States. Other transgressions were concealed, either by removing any investigation from over-zealous prosecutors to a different and more amenable court, or by claiming the parliamentary privilege of judicial immunity. Ever since 1974 each party had received some funding from the Treasury and by 1988 this amounted to 150 billion lire a year. But their expenditure was estimated as being nearer 5,000 billion. Some of the extra money came from America and Russia, some from secret payments by Italian businessmen or public institutions, and for this purpose governments ensured that not only the heavy-spending ministries of public works and state participations but also the giant holding companies of IRI and ENI were always controlled by reliable acolytes. The communists and minor parties of the center could sometimes follow this bad example where they shared power in local government. Yet the socialists and Christian democrats were far and away the chief beneficiaries, justifying themselves by the claim that the exaction of *tangenti* and "forced loans" would help to win elections and exclude the communists from power. By 1990, however, this justification was looking like an excuse for something much less defensible. A few politicians were becoming very wealthy, whereas the presumed danger of a communist revolution was increasingly regarded as anachronistic and unserious.

★

The communists had been co-operative ministers in De Gasperi's first three cabinets and thereafter had often given indispensable help in parliament to Christian-democratic premiers. But ever since 1947 they had been rigorously excluded from any share in government, and this exclusion, understandable so long as they remained ideologically and financially dependent on Moscow, was increasingly seen as a distorting interference with the proper functioning of democratic politics. Under the leadership of Berlinguer, then of Alessandro Natta and Achille Occhetto, the communists were moving slowly toward becoming more like a reformist social-democratic party, frankly admitting the failures of Marxist-Leninism and accepting participation in NATO and the pluralist values of a mixed capitalist economy. In the elections of 1976 they had won more than a third of the popular vote and for the next three years were again temporarily accepted as a credit-worthy ally by Christian democracy. Also in central Italy, where regional governments remained largely under their control, communist officials continued to demonstrate an enviable capacity for fair and efficient administration, so earning the enmity of not only the Right but also of the extreme Left which spurned them for becoming part of the bourgeois establishment. Yet after Moro's death the governments of Craxi and Andreotti reverted to ostracizing communism, partly because of its demand for radical social reform, but also for its denunciation of the jobbery, the corrupt practices and connivance with the mafia that kept a discredited political class in power and affluence.

At this point the end of the cold war and demolition of the Berlin wall at last made the Left much more electable. In October 1989, the communist Occhetto advocated dissolving his party and soon afterwards persuaded a congress of its members to accept his proposal. Most of them agreed to create a much less extremist Democratic Party of the Left (PDS), leaving a small hard core of revolutionaries and dedicated Marxists who broke away to form what was called the Party of Communist Refoundation. At once this altered the balance of politics. One important result was to weaken the cohesion of the Christian democrats who had kept their hegemony over Italian politics by exploiting the fear of communism. In Sicily the Catholic mayor of Palermo, Leoluca Orlando, had already broken ranks by forming a municipal government in alliance with the Left, and after being forced out of office by his own Christian-democrat leadership, Orlando seceded to launch a new and anti-mafia party called the Network. A second dissident movement inside Christian democracy was led by Mario Segni, son of the former national president, who campaigned for a new electoral system that would eventually help to unseat the older generation of politicians and destroy the party that for over forty years had dominated Italian politics.

A further symptom of this desire for radical change was the appearance of other small localist parties in Lombardy, Venice, Piedmont, and Genoa, which under the leadership of Umberto Bossi joined to form a union named the Northern League. This League quickly achieved a surprising electoral success. It represented a populist movement of protest against corruption, against dependence on a discredited central government in Rome, and against the fact that northerners had to pay heavily and disproportionately in assistance money to what they called the unprofitable and parasitic southern provinces. Bossi spoke of wanting to found an autonomous Republic of the North inside a federal Italian state and even held out the possibility of forming an altogether separate republic in northern Italy. These four politicians, Bossi, Segni, Orlando, and the former communist Occhetto, reflected different grass-roots movements of public opinion that heralded the disintegration of a static political system. Each exposed deficiencies in the old *partitocrazia* and revealed the existence of a dissatisfied electorate eager for change.

One immediate result was that reformist elements in the judiciary, hitherto muzzled by politicians, were encouraged to take action on their own initiative. In 1990 a young Venetian magistrate, while probing into extremist right-wing movements, stumbled across the existence of Gladio. This clandestine and semi-official military organization had existed since the early 1950s without the knowledge of parliament. Its exposure now created considerable trepidation, which became worse when President Cossiga, who had originally helped to set up Gladio as a defense against communism, pleaded state secrecy and refused a request to testify in court about its existence or its purpose and finances. Further alarm was caused by new evidence that arms and explosives belonging to Gladio had somehow been acquired during the past twenty years for use in terrorist activity by the extreme Right.

Cossiga added to the general anxiety when he responded to criticism by intervening more actively in politics than any previous president, sometimes sensibly, but often with unexpected acerbity that led people to suspect his motives and intentions. Since the country's institutions, as he told one friend, needed to be reformed "from top to bottom," he demanded greater presidential powers in order to make this possible. Individual politicians who disagreed with him were attacked by the president in unusually offensive language. He even spoke provocatively against his own Christian-democrat party for holding up the process of change and against Andreotti the prime minister whom he had himself appointed. The ex-communists, he believed, were now less dangerous than their predecessors in the PCI and might be allowed a more active role in helping to end the transformist consociations that for so long had been blocking political development. Yet he defended Gladio and the P.2 masonic lodge that many people assumed were two serious dangers to the state. Most surprising of all he openly criticized the senior judges and in particular the law officers in Sicily who under great difficulties were striving to subdue the mafia. Any criticism of himself he took as an outrage even when it came from the chief justice of the Constitutional Court. He even condemned some parliamentary leaders for being "cretins" and "zombies" whose criticism of his behavior was, in his view, a negation of democracy. In reply there was a move in parliament to have him impeached for being a possible threat to constitutional government.

In 1991 the general sense of unease led to another referendum, this time on a proposition by Mario Segni to reduce the "preference votes" that each elector could use to support an individual candidate by name. This apparently minor proposal was in reality a major attack against clientelism, against boss rule and machine politics, and against *mafiosi* who by intimidating electors had used preference votes to manipulate elections on behalf of friendly politicians. The proposal was strongly opposed by Cossiga as well as by Craxi, Bossi, De Mita, and politicians who had relied on election by these preference votes, but the referendum produced a remarkable 95 per cent in favor and this was rightly interpreted as demanding a thorough change in the way parliament was elected. After having once been the most popular politician in Italy, Craxi found that he no longer had the full support of even his own socialist party. His high-handed and corrupt nepotism in local government at Milan, his opposition to constitutional reform, and his authoritarian attitude to colleagues, all these were at last provoking a popular reaction.

★

Such was the demand for a new direction in politics that the legislature was prematurely dissolved by Cossiga in February 1992. The three most prominent politicians in the country were Andreotti, Craxi, and Arnaldo Forlani the secretary of the Christian-democrat party, all of whom knew that their political future rested on victory in the next elections because their two parties were vulnerable to accusations of corruption and needed to win power in order to resist further revelations by the courts. Craxi was convinced that he had a good chance of returning as prime minister, and to buy enough support he was ready to back either Forlani or Andreotti to succeed Cossiga whose term as president of the republic was nearing its end.

This projected condominium might possibly have succeeded were it not for the arrest on February 17 of Mario Chiesa, a minor official inside Craxi's socialist machine who had been caught siphoning a regular percentage from a charitable foundation which he managed in Milan. Craxi reacted too hastily by denouncing his junior colleague as a common criminal, and Chiesa in self-defense explained with a wealth of detail the corrupt practices that funded the socialist party. This at last gave the police and the courts a chance to exploit the growing mistrust of politicians and act on what they already suspected to be profiteering in the Milanese municipal administration. Prospective contractors for public works had been obliged to pay a regular tariff to the party. Many companies, ranging from Fiat and Olivetti down to humble funeral parlors and street-cleaning operators, had become accustomed to paying these bribes without protest until Chiesa made the mistake of trying to exact more than the market would tolerate.

Another event that influenced the elections in April was the collapse of Andreotti's political base in Sicily. One of his associates, Ciancimino the former mayor of Palermo, was in January condemned to ten years in gaol for corruption and collusion with the mafia. In the same month Judge Falcone was encouraged to reinforce earlier plans for co-ordinating antimafia activity, and the Supreme Court proceeded to confirm sentences on scores of *mafiosi* who had recently been freed by lower tribunals. In retaliation, Andreotti's chief agent in Sicily was assassinated on March 12. This man, Salvo Lima, had for many years secretly represented mafia interests in Rome, but after failing to protect his clients from action by the judiciary he was murdered as a reprisal and a warning to others.

Voting for the eleventh legislature indicated that the old parties had lost much of their popular support. Ten previous elections since 1948 had shown the Christian democrats successfully exploiting the presumption that their defeat would mean chaos, but at last it was becoming obvious that they themselves and Craxi's socialists might be the main obstacle to good government. Gains were registered by new protest movements, including Bossi's Northern League with fifty-five seats in the Chamber, Orlando's Network with twelve, and the ecologically minded Greens with sixteen. Sixteen different parties were represented in the new Chamber and seventeen in the Senate, though a third of these parties each received less than 2 per cent of the national vote. Such a parliament had little chance of producing a government that could act decisively, and even less chance after the judiciary warned other leading politicians that they were under investigation for criminal misbehavior. Although Cossiga had apparently been hoping to reappoint Craxi as prime minister, Chiesa's revelations made this too hazardous, and the head of state preferred to leave to his successor the selection of a more presentable alternative. In a farewell speech Cossiga hoped that whoever succeeded him would challenge a discredited political oligarchy and overcome an institutional paralysis that was leading the country toward financial ruin.

The new head of state was Oscar Luigi Scalfaro, a Christian democrat who had been an outspoken critic of political corruption. Not his party's official choice, Scalfaro was selected only after fifteen inconclusive votes by the electoral college failed to agree on any of the leading candidates. What finally shocked politicians into a decision was that two days earlier, on May 23 when Falcone was revisiting Sicily, this chief antimafia investigator was assassinated together with his wife and their police escort. Traumatized by such a provocative defiance of state authority, public opinion demanded the election of a president from outside the main party machines who was respected for his honesty and could be trusted to act with both prudence and firmness. An added advantage was that Scalfaro was not only something of an outsider but was less irritable and rancorous than his predecessor. He was elected by an unexpected and overwhelming majority.

63   Four Attempts at Reform, 1992–1995

Society had continued to change in the past twenty years and greater prosperity led to ever increasing frustration with old-style politics. Though there still existed areas of great deprivation, the country had overcome temporary recessions and outdistanced the rest of Europe through another impressive rate of economic growth. Italy had become one of the major industrialized countries in the world and workers in agriculture were now less than one-tenth of the population. The gross domestic product was as high or possibly slightly higher than in Britain, and this brought greater expectations, a better-educated work force, far greater employment of women, and a more diffused political consciousness. But an enlarged middle class had reason to fear that progress and prosperity were being held in check by ministers more interested in their own political survival than in rooting out corruption or balancing the books—a much more serious danger than either terrorism or communism.

Increasingly obvious was that Craxi and Andreotti, sometimes in collusion with each other, had purchased electoral victories by extravagant expenditure which more than doubled the national debt. This imposed a fearsome burden on future generations and was already damaging Italy's credit abroad. Each year on average saw governmental expenditure exceeding revenue by 10 per cent, as compared with nearer 3 per cent in Germany and Britain, and this resulted in the consolidated public debt rising from 38 per cent of annual GDP in 1974 to the unsustainable figure of over 100 per cent. The deficit each year was met by issuing Treasury bonds which became enormously popular among savers because they carried high rates of interest and escaped tax. Most of the rentiers who bought these bonds came from northern Italy, and one incidental result was to transfer more wealth from the impoverished South to already richer northerners. But a more important result was that, since the proceeds were needed by governments for servicing debt, insufficient was left for improvements in Italy's threadbare public services, or else preference was given to subsidizing public-sector, loss-making industries and to providing salaries in the *sottogoverno* for clients of the major parties. Another electoral bribe was the payment of pensions to a fifth of the total population, twice as large a proportion as twenty years earlier, and this generous entitlement to pensions encouraged very early retirement from work. In some areas more than 10 per cent of the population was in receipt of disability pensions, often distributed to party adherents who were far from being disabled. Any responsible minister must have been aware that, however politically expedient, this was another quite unsustainable expenditure.

Such extravagance and favoritism were much criticized by Italy's partners in the European community. Andreotti had agreed in 1978 to join the European monetary system, a bold move that some people optimistically hoped might bring more coherence and responsibility into the national accounts. In February 1992 he had gone further and signed the Maastricht Treaty which undertook to adapt Italy's financial and economic practices to those agreed in Brussels, halving her rate of inflation, allowing freer competition for imported goods and services, phasing out excessive public deficits and subsidies to domestic producers. The confident decision to accept these goals was taken on advice from the governor of the Bank of Italy who privately expressed his hope that it would compel politicians to accept obligations which they would never have dared to assume on their own initiative. Henceforward, to keep abreast of other countries and retain full membership of the European community, they would be bound by European law to introduce savage economies and bring the excess in annual public expenditure down to 3 per cent of GDP, at the same time halving the national debt to a more realistic 60 per cent. But whether Andreotti was brave enough to impose the requisite austerity measures was widely doubted, especially since his hopes for re-election depended on continued deficit-spending to attract votes. Italy already had a poor record over introducing European legislation into domestic law and for policing the fraudulent application of financial grants sent from Brussels to selected areas of deprivation. Inability to enforce the decisions agreed at Maastricht was soon to become a further factor in a mounting political crisis.

★

After the general election of April 1992 and its failure to produce anything remotely resembling a parliamentary majority, ten frustrating weeks elapsed before President Scalfaro found a prime minister. Giuliano Amato's new cabinet included six ministers from his own socialist party and twelve Christian democrats. But prominent politicians in both these parties soon learned that they were under judicial investigation for corrupt practices and accepting *tangenti*. So began what before long became a gigantic exposure of misconduct in public life, and it was inauspicious that not parliament, not ministers, not even the Church, but rather journalists and the courts of law instigated the cleansing operation known as *tangentopoli*. Two investigating magistrates in Milan, Francesco Saverio Borelli and Antonio Di Pietro, led a team of lawyers who became popular heroes, whereas the accused politicians showed little if any remorse but mainly incredulity and resentment at the public airing of dirty linen. These law officers, though supported by Scalfaro, were denounced by Craxi for interfering in politics as month by month they began to uncover a sorry story of how some of Italy's leading citizens, not only ministers but senior civil servants and businessmen, believing themselves immune from investigation, were illegally enriching themselves and their friends at public expense, so leading the country toward bankruptcy. One unusually scandalous bribe had been ninety million dollars paid to political parties by the Ferruzzi agro-industrial company in return for this failing business being rescued by state help, and presumably the auditors must have sanctioned this as a legitimate expense.

Meanwhile other investigating magistrates in Sicily, notably Paolo Borsellino and later Giancarlo Caselli, conducted a parallel and painstaking campaign to continue Falcone's work in uncovering the evil empire of the mafia. In July the whole nation was shocked when Borsellino and five of his police guards were assassinated: and it became evident that, as with the killing of Falcone, their whereabouts must have been betrayed to the mafia by traitorous informants inside the police department. Amato at once sent seven thousand soldiers to Sicily and introduced a law imposing further penalties on *mafiosi*. More importantly he also offered additionally favorable treatment to those who agreed to break their law of silence and give evidence in court. Four of these *pentiti* were instrumental in procuring the arrest of a senior official in the security services for suspected collusion with the mafia. Then in January 1993 the police arrested Totò Riina, millionaire and mafia superboss, who although accused of a hundred murders had contrived for twenty years to direct criminal operations from secret hide-outs in Palermo. Quite as significant were popular demonstrations in support of the police which showed that many more Sicilians were publicly disassociating themselves from the small group of criminals responsible for these outrages. Other successes were scored against the *camorra* in Naples and the equally murderous *'ndrangheta* in Calabria, many of their leaders being arrested and their property confiscated. A number of prominent politicians including former ministers must now have begun to fear that their own tacit complicity with the immensely rich criminal underworld might not remain secret much longer.

Amato was a close friend of the disgraced Craxi but was quick to realize that the emergency would require radical changes in policy and administration. To bring government expenses under control he proposed cuts in social spending by raising the retirement age for pensions and persuading the trade unions to agree on abolishing the remnants of automatic wage indexation. He was courageous enough to propose new taxes on the self-employed who were often still responsible for massive tax evasion. In September 1992 he accepted the inevitable and devalued the currency even though this meant withdrawing from the European monetary system. To reduce the budgetary deficit and partly jobbery he speeded up privatizing state-funded industries that had been cushioned from market competition and were grossly overmanned; and he hoped that this would eventually include not only the conglomerates IRI and ENI but the postal service, the railways, and telecommunications. Since many white elephants in the state sector had been exploited as vehicles for political patronage, these reforms encountered considerable opposition from some members of the political elite. Former Treasury ministers since 1945, Einaudi being one of the few exceptions, had damaged their liberal credentials by being predominantly protectionist, corporatist, and *dirigiste*. But Amato's challenge to the *ancien régime* received enthusiastic backing from a younger generation of Christian democrats, among them Romano Prodi who soon afterwards was given the task of continuing the privatization of IRI and a welcome fact was that Amato was supported by many former communists in the Democratic Party of the Left (PDS) who by now had committed their colleagues to more private ownership and a more pluralistic organization of society.

★

In September, parliament acted on an invitation from President Scalfaro to appoint sixty of its members to form another commission for studying possible changes in the constitution. The chief need was to give governments the stability to last longer and enough authority to act without being in thrall to parliamentary maneuvers by the party secretaries. A stronger executive would surely have a better chance of reducing public expenditure and making public services more efficient. During a year of discussion by this commission many of its members argued once again for increasing the authority of the prime minister and devolving more power to the individual regions. There was also some support for changing the electoral law in the hope of producing a clear parliamentary majority and an alternation of governments between Center Left and Center Right; but, just as with the Bozzi commission twenty years earlier, large parties feared losing their capacity for transformist maneuver if proportional representation was replaced by a majoritarian system of election. Eventually a compromise was suggested by which three-quarters of the elected representatives would be chosen in single-member constituencies where the candidate with the largest share of the vote would win, while the other quarter was elected in proportion to votes gained nationally. Though far from an ideal solution, this proposal was in principle given overwhelming approval by another popular referendum in 1993.

Such a compromise was perhaps an over-hasty reaction to a rapidly developing emergency as each week brought further revelations of sleaze in high places. In February 1993, four senior cabinet ministers had to resign because of police investigations. Craxi, too, resigned from his post as general secretary of the socialist party after being accused on forty counts of corruption and illicit party funding. In particular his socialists had profited financially from the unofficial agreement that allowed them control of the petrochemical monopoly ENI, and they were now found to possess a Swiss bank account into which seven million dollars had been mysteriously deposited ten years earlier in connection with the fraudulent bankruptcy of Calvi's Ambrosiano bank. A former president of ENI was arrested in March. Evidence was also produced against Fiat and Olivetti which confirmed the suspicion that all the major industrial concerns had been tempted to pay substantial bribes in order to win contracts. So numerous were such payments that the courts, understaffed and without adequate funds, were faced with the prospect of years of investigation and prosecution during which politics would be destabilized and parliament inevitably discredited. In an attempt at damage limitation, on March 5 the government issued a decree to decriminalize the illicit financing of parties provided that heavy fines were paid and offenders were barred from public office. But this decree was widely interpreted as politicians conspiring to defend each other from the law, and after violent scenes in both houses of parliament President Scalfaro refused to countersign it.

★

At the end of April, the president appointed a new premier, Carlo Azeglio Ciampi, who unlike all his predecessors was not a member of parliament but who as governor of the Bank of Italy had presided over one of the few major state organizations that was beyond reproach. Quite unusually, twelve other ministers were chosen from outside parliament, and it was a pungent criticism of Italian politics that their presence made this the most competent and

483

respected government in the forty years since De Gasperi's death. Another taboo was broken when three former members of the ex-communist PDS joined the cabinet without any objection arriving from Washington against this rehabilitation of the Left. But in what many people saw as a great misfortune, all three resigned almost immediately when a majority in the chamber of deputies, while accepting Craxi's acknowledgment of guilt, dishonorably voted to prevent his prosecution. Evidently most members of parliament assumed that they should still be allowed to violate the law with impunity. Although Ciampi himself was a long way from being a man of the Left, he and his ministers were in favor of fundamental reforms and opposition to him came mostly from the conservative Right. Either right-wing extremists or the mafia, or perhaps both in collusion, were responsible in May and June for an intimidating series of bomb outrages that did great damage in Rome, Milan, and Florence.

The new premier succeeded in one of his main objectives which was to put the new method of election into a formal law. With more difficulty he also succeeded in persuading the deputies to waive some of their legal immunity from prosecution. In the next two years the courts made requests to investigate a quarter of the parliamentary representatives. Meanwhile individual ministers, notably Sabino Cassese and Luigi Spaventa, studied how to make state machinery more functional, for Ciampi discovered almost at once that bureaucratic inertia and obstruction were still a major obstacle to good government. In July the Court of Accounts listed hundreds of contracts for public works that had never been completed, and no doubt some or possibly many of these had been intended only as a corrupt manipulation of official grants. Craxi himself, though a former prime minister, was at last interrogated by the courts on what eventually became 170 counts of criminal misbehavior. Three other former prime ministers, Andreotti, Forlani, and Goria, were warned that they were under police investigation. Senior judges were suspended or even arrested for using their position to protect criminals; and so were some ambassadors for diverting to unspecified purposes some of the generous grants allocated to relief operations in third-world countries. A former president of IRI was arrested. A dozen suicides included senior officials of Ferruzzi and ENI. A chief executive in the health services was found after his arrest to have accumulated a private fortune worth hundreds of millions of U.S. dollars from his control over the provision of medicines. Such examples of dishonesty were, it was hoped, exceptional, but the possibility that they were merely the tip of a concealed iceberg became the subject of earnest debate and apprehension.

Most damaging of all were accusations leveled against Andreotti, because for more than forty years this man had been at the very center of government and, although notorious for his deviousness, had usually been regarded as a well-intentioned politician prompted by righteous Christian principles. Already in April he had been formally accused of illegal methods in financing his party. Much more seriously, the parliamentary antimafia commission which included

Christian democrats suspected him of making deals with the mafia; and a number of repentant *mafiosi*, if they could be believed, agreed that this former prime minister had employed them to intimidate the electorate. He denied this categorically but there was at least a *prima facie* case to answer.

★

These revelations and allegations added weight to a substantial change in public opinion and party allegiance. The former communists in the PDS were much less tainted by scandal than other parties and their support held up fairly well, but the socialist party virtually disappeared in the course of 1993, while the dominant Christian democrats were deserted by half of their electorate and broke up into four small squabbling factions as disillusioned voters redistributed themselves to both Right and Left. In no other democratic country was there such a total collapse of a ruling elite. So tarnished was the displaced political establishment that local elections in this year indicated a sizeable growth of two parties that hitherto had been only marginally important, the centrist Northern League and the MSI on the extreme Right.

The Northern League was chiefly successful in the relatively rich areas of Lombardy and the Veneto, in particular inheriting Craxi's control over Milan. Its appeal continued to derive from denouncing other parties for the corrupt clientelism that was paralyzing government, and above all it continued to criticize the way that northern taxpayers were being forced into subsidizing the impoverished South. Its leader, Umberto Bossi, was generally disparaged as a crude demagogue but he gave voice to powerful feelings among small business enterprises against an inefficient state bureaucracy mainly staffed by southerners. Sometimes Bossi talked of leading another "March on Rome" like Mussolini in 1922, and he continued to threaten secession from the rest of Italy unless the North was given much greater financial autonomy.

The ex-fascists in the MSI on the other hand were strongest in the South. In only one election since 1948 had this party polled as much as 8 per cent of the vote: it was also handicapped by the fact that many of its members remained proud of their fascist origins and continued to subscribe to racism, nationalism, and physical violence as a legitimate method of political action. But its more responsible members accepted that, since fascism had led their country to military defeat and ruinous civil war, the success of any avowedly right-wing party would depend on more moderate tactics and on inserting their movement into the quite different democratic dialectic of parliamentary government. An extremist group of neo-fascists had won by a bare majority in their party congress of 1990. Then in 1991 a more moderate faction succeeded in re-electing as party leader the young Gianfranco Fini who realized that their only hope of winning enough votes would be by repudiating totalitarianism, racism, and the violent methods that until now had relegated their party to the margin of politics.

A degree of ambiguity nevertheless remained inside the MSI because the new leader could not deny his own earlier fascist enthusiasm and, needing to keep the authoritarian wing of his party in common harness, imprudently referred to Mussolini as the greatest world statesman of modern times. In October 1992 there had been a particularly embarrassing scene in the Piazza Venezia when his followers celebrated with black shirts and "Roman salutes" the fiftieth anniversary of Mussolini's "March on Rome." But Fini eventually succeeded in persuading most of his party that they should call themselves "post-fascist" rather than "neo-fascist" and should merge their MSI into a new party to be called the National Alliance. Its policy would include a defense of "national and Catholic values," opposing divorce and social permissiveness, with a modicum of "anti-Americanism" and only a qualified enthusiasm for the European community or the Atlantic alliance. It should stand unequivocally for a strong centralized state against the regional loyalties of the Northern League. It also distrusted the capitalist market economy that was favored by Ciampi and Amato, and strongly opposed their attempt to reduce the welfare payments that were so important for its electorate in the South. Above all it should be dedicated to preventing any electoral victory by the PDS on the Left.

Ciampi's administration had been recognized from the time of its appointment as being extra-parliamentary and hence only a stopgap until elections could be held under the new electoral law. The strength of new and old parties had to be tested in a popular vote so that Italy could return to normal representative government. After winning approval for the annual budget, Ciampi therefore resigned in January 1994. In the previous eight months he had valiantly continued Amato's attempt to rebuild confidence in honest and efficient administration despite the almost daily revelations of *tangentopoli*. He and Prodi had succeeded in privatizing two major banks, the Banca Commerciale and the Credito Italiano, though this left most banks still in the public sector. Exports were well up and so were prices on the stock exchange. The interest on Treasury bonds had been successfully reduced from 11.7 per cent to 7.5 per cent and this, helped by a surplus on the balance of payments, checked the accumulating national debt. Everything would now depend on whether the next parliament could produce an effective majority and a leader capable of restoring confidence in representative institutions.

★

Disillusionment with the old parties was so widespread that the next prime minister was another man who hitherto had shown no interest in becoming a politician or being elected to parliament. Silvio Berlusconi, one of the richest men in Europe, made his first fortune in Milanese real estate during the unregulated building speculation of the 1970s, since when he had branched out into insurance, supermarkets, advertising, newspapers, and most importantly into television. Fininvest, his family-owned holding company, was sometimes thought to carry as much political weight as Fiat, but unlike the Fiat of Agnelli it was not quoted on the bourse and, for this reason its accounts and myriad ramifications were concealed from public scrutiny. Though admired as an entrepreneur and generally liked as a person, Berlusconi's business methods attracted much criticism and mistrust. Many years earlier he had joined the secret masonic lodge P.2 whose leader had since been convicted of serious crimes. Paolo Berlusconi, his brother and business partner, was arrested in February 1994 for involvement in *tangentopoli*, and it was no secret that Fininvest had prospered because of its association with Craxi's disreputable financial operations.

One fact that forced this family into politics was that Craxi's eclipse left them dangerously lacking in political protection. Another relevant fact was their enormous debts to public-sector banks. Berlusconi therefore had an interest in bringing those banks under his personal political supervision and preventing electoral victory for his critics on the Left. Unfriendly ministers in the departments of justice and finance might penalize financial irregularities more rigorously than previous governments and they might even discontinue the frequent amnesties for tax evasion and illegal urban development upon which many private fortunes depended. Berlusconi's commercial television stations were also at issue because this lucrative near-monopoly was criticized by the Constitutional Court in Rome and by European politicians in Brussels.

Italian radio and television (RAI) had developed out of a state-controlled enterprise established by Mussolini, and after 1945 it remained a state monopoly under Christian-democrat administration until a major reform in 1975 allowed the socialists some influence in one television channel and the communist party in another. This monopoly was further attenuated in the following year when the Constitutional Court sanctioned competition at local level by numerous commercial television companies. All the more successful of these private com-panies were eventually purchased by Berlusconi who, with questionable legis-lative help from Craxi's socialist government, turned them into three national channels which together won as large an audience as the three operated by RAI. The court had been hoping that competition would introduce more diversity, but this hope was frustrated by the absence of any serious antitrust or anti-monopoly legislation. What emerged instead was a duopoly between RAI and Fininvest, with the difference that the former was obliged by law to give at least a minority voice to opposition parties whereas the commercial channels could be used by Berlusconi as organs of popular entertainment with a more or less uniform political message of his own choosing. In addition to television he bought newspapers and two of the most important publishing houses as well as creating an agency to control most of the entire TV advertising market. Nowhere else in Europe was the proprietor of such an enormous media empire able to create a highly personal political party and aim at forming a government.

As late as February 6, 1994, a few days after Ciampi resigned, Berlusconi announced the program of a new party called Forza Italia which at the end of March won a quite unexpected electoral success with over 20 per cent of the national vote. This remarkable achievement was due to Forza Italia being joined by many refugees from the recently discredited parties, especially conservatives alarmed by victories of the Left in municipal elections at the end of 1993. Success was undoubtedly helped by Berlusconi's expert use of propaganda through his ownership of all the important commercial television stations, but it was also due to his skill in making an electoral pact with Bossi's League in northern Italy and another pact in the South with Fini's National Alliance. These three parties, agreeing to limit competition against each other, emerged as strong enough to form a coalition with a majority in the lower house of parliament, and this earned Berlusconi the premiership. Nevertheless he still lacked a majority in the Senate, and another difficulty was that Bossi's federal views were fundamentally opposed to the centralizing nationalism of the ex-fascist Fini whose party won six ministerial posts. A further problem was the continued existence in parliament of a dozen smaller parties which showed that the new electoral law, by permitting a sizeable element of proportional representation, had entirely failed in its objective of producing a cohesive, disciplined and durable majority. Two-thirds of those elected, including Berlusconi himself, had never been in parliament before. Many of his ministers had no previous experience of politics and some appointments were of senior executives in his private industrial conglomerate.

★

The new prime minister was surprisingly confident that a successful business-man would succeed equally in politics, not realizing that quite different talents and temperament might be required. Instead of the austerity proposed by his two predecessors he appealed to the electorate with promises to alleviate the burden of taxation and to create a million new jobs. His program spoke of deregulation and liberalizing the economy, of more privatization in the state sector, of reducing bureaucracy, ending corruption, and making government more efficient. These stated objectives no doubt won many votes, but later events suggest that they were unserious or even fraudulent. His private instincts were those of an eager monopolist who had prospered through eliminating competition, sometimes (it was suspected) even by corrupting public officials and circumventing the law. Nor, despite promises to do so, did he create an acceptable blind trust to meet criticism of a conflict of interest between being premier and his large-scale ownership of the media. On the contrary the impression he gave was of wanting political power so as to further his private business concerns. Instead of at once tackling Italy's major problems such as unemployment, the mafia, corruption, and the national debt, time was spent on minor and equivocal matters. Decrees remitting previous penalties for tax evasion and illegal building construction could not fail to be seen as self-interested. Suspicion was also aroused by his breach of recent precedent in not permitting parties outside his coalition to hold the speakership in one house of parliament or to chair any of the fourteen committees in the Lower House that acted as a watchdog over government action. Worst of all was an endeavor to assert his authority over the hitherto independent Bank of Italy and to shackle the magistrates who had good reasons for wanting to investigate the account books of Fininvest.

This attempt to control all the levers of power was especially anomalous in someone whose party represented less than a quarter of the electorate and who claimed to champion the values of competition and private enterprise. Particularly aberrant was that the owner of all the main channels of commercial television should also take extra powers to control the state-owned RAI which was his only significant competitor in producing news programs and seeking television advertising revenue. At the beginning of July, using the eccentric argument that it was wrong for national TV channels to criticize acts of government, the governing body of RAI was replaced by his own political appointees. Later in July, again by decree rather than by parliamentary legislation, he restricted the powers of the judiciary and procured the release from prison of almost two thousand people, many of whom had been arrested for bribery and corruption. A week later, when Di Pietro and other investigating magistrates protested by offering their resignation and when even some of Berlusconi's coalition partners refused to support this decree, it was withdrawn. But inevitably his motives were suspect, all the more so when his brother was again arrested with other directors of Fininvest for bribing the financial inspectors to reduce the tax assessment on their multifarious private companies.

Many people had begun by taking the new prime minister on his own valuation as an effective operator who could solve difficulties that eluded the skill of professional politicians. Yet almost at once his coalition government was seen to be more divided and indecisive than its predecessor and possessing less of a coherent political strategy. Chiefly for this reason he lasted in office for a below-average eight months, during which time he preferred to enact controversial legislation by executive decree so as to avoid the trouble and risk of debates in parliament, and meanwhile any attempt to solve Italy's main structural problems was evaded or postponed. Promises to reduce taxes and create a million new jobs were not kept. Nor did the economy become noticeably more liberalized, especially since his partners in Fini's Alleanza Nazionale had little enthusiasm for privatization. Instead of supporting the courts in rooting out corruption, Berlusconi tried to reduce the authority of the judges on the grounds that they were exceeding their powers by improperly interfering in politics, and the leading prosecutor Di Pietro was driven out of his job in December. Industrial production and exports continued to rise but so also did the budget deficit as the government continued to live well beyond its means, which meant that any prospect of rejoining the European monetary system was disappearing into the distance.

Berlusconi remained full of outward confidence, speaking of himself as "the anointed of God" and "the only Italian politician who knows how to govern."

But public opinion as revealed in local elections turned against him when he was seen to be clearly out of his depth. Far from creating confidence in the business community, the stock market fell heavily; so did the value of the lira; and large amounts of investment capital again left the country. In October and November his sensible proposal to cut expenditure on pensions and health provoked massive street demonstrations on a scale never seen before, partly because it was imposed without prior discussion with the unions. Even many individual parliamentarians inside his coalition voted in December with the opposition after the Constitutional Court ruled that his ownership of so many television channels was illegal and a threat to pluralism of information. Most damaging of all, a public statement from the magistrates in Milan revealed that the prime minister was himself under judicial investigation for false accounting in his business operations. After trying desperately to retain office so that he could "manage" the next elections, on December 22 he resigned while publicly proclaiming his belief that the president would have no alternative but to reappoint him. In an extraordinary series of public declarations he blamed everyone else: the national president for unconstitutional action in not reappointing him, Bossi for "treachery" to their alliance, the courts for aiming at a judicial *coup d'état*, and parliament for acting illegitimately when it proposed a vote of censure against his conduct. His strange political belief, as he told *Newsweek*, was that opposition to an elected government was a denial of popular wishes and hence a negation of democracy.

★

In January 1995, his successor as prime minister was Lamberto Dini, another political newcomer and a moderate who had served in Berlusconi's cabinet after being a much respected general manager of the Bank of Italy. Once again, for want of an obvious parliamentary majority, the country found itself with a cabinet of technical experts who this time were drawn entirely from outside parliament. An early parliamentary vote indicated that Dini, while opposed by the few surviving communists, was supported by the democratic Left (PDS) and most deputies of the Center, while Berlusconi's Forza Italia and Fini's Alleanza Nazionale both abstained. This novel alignment of forces, though precarious, allowed the government to face the unpopularity of again trying to reduce the huge deficit in the national accounts. In particular Dini succeeded where others had failed in negotiating with the unions to curtail some of the escalating expenditure on pensions. But even more than his predecessor he had to govern by means of executive decrees. Though he introduced some measures to make elections fairer by correcting or counterbalancing the political bias of the television stations belonging to Fininvest, this was strongly resisted by Berlusconi's supporters and in practice was ineffective.

Other successes were nevertheless scored in the field of law and order. Mafia and *camorra* murders in southern Italy had recently been running at over five hundred a year, but after the public reaction against Judge Falcone's assassination in 1992 this secret world was progressively exposed to the light of day, especially when figures given to parliament in June 1995 showed that 968 repentant *mafiosi* were now collaborating with the police. Elsewhere, mainly in northern cities but also in Naples and Bari, the other secret world of *tangentopoli* was gradually being uncovered. The arch-corrupter Craxi, who in May 1994 had escaped to dishonorable exile in Tunisia, was in his absence given two long prison sentences. Many other front-rank politicians and financiers were arrested during 1995. Berlusconi himself, now the leading figure in the parliamentary opposition, was in October formally committed to trial for corruption. Andreotti too, Italy's longest-serving prime minister, was brought to court in September for complicity with the mafia and even of suspected involvement with the murder of a journalist who was trying to blackmail him.

The underfunded justice system did its best to cope with a huge load of work in cases that were likely to drag on for years before a final verdict could be reached. Another obstacle was that the courts were once again attacked for undermining parliamentary authority, attacks that especially came from other politicians who had reason to fear what might be revealed. Yet parliament had only itself to blame if for so long it had refused to take remedial action or even set up a public inquiry into what for many years had been generally known to be Italy's most serious problem; and this refusal was quite deliberate because the main parties had too much to conceal. Admittedly criminal prosecutions could deal only with individual cases and could never by themselves remedy what by default had become a pervasive and indurated way of life. Admittedly, also, some judges were accused of exceeding their powers of arrest. But Italy was at least fortunate in possessing courts able to bring facts to light that sooner or later would compel the legislature to act. Increasingly there was an expectation that a solution might have to be found in some kind of amnesty for all except the most serious offenses, though this was no less alarming because a succession of previous amnesties had in practice encouraged crime by indicating that offenders could rely on being reprieved.

64 An Interim Solution, 1996

Dini's cabinet of "non-political technicians," like Ciampi's two years earlier, had been intended as temporary until new elections in a calmer atmosphere gave an indication of which way public opinion was moving. But though Dini offered to resign in December 1995, a further four months elapsed while elections were held and the familiar search continued for a successor that parliament would accept. After protracted discussion the choice fell on Romano Prodi, an economist and university professor who was a noted opponent of corruption and had formerly supported the left wing of the now dissolved Christian-democrat party.

Prodi earned cross-party respect as a technocrat who had successfully arranged the privatization of businesses in the public sector. Hitherto he had not been particularly active in politics, but he knew that Italy's future depended on whether parliamentary government could be made to work better than in the past. He therefore spent the year 1995 organizing half a dozen political parties into a new coalition calling itself the Ulivo or Olive Tree. The largest of its component groups was the Party of Democratic Socialism led by the one-time communist Massimo D'Alema, who had already established a reputation as one of the foremost politicians in the country. When elections were held in April 1996 this PDS became the biggest party in parliament with over 20 per cent of the vote. Success for the Ulivo in these elections led to the formation of what became the fifty-fifth government in the fifty years since the founding of the Republic. The great novelty was that this government gave Italy the novel experience of an administration with a center of gravity well to the left of Center. Nine of Prodi's ministers belonged to the PDS and this was something entirely new. The cabinet also included the most admired and experienced representatives of the Center or Center Right, among them Dini, Ciampi, and Di Pietro, all of them champions of economic and constitutional reform.

This combination of forces suggested that Italian politics might have moved a stage closer to a bipolar alternation in office between two coalitions, the reformist Ulivo and the more conservative Freedom Alliance led by Berlusconi and Fini. But Prodi, lacking an absolute parliamentary majority like all his predecessors, was still forced to spend much time on the difficult task of searching for the highest common factor of agreement between friends and opponents because without such agreement his government would be power-less. He was committed to reducing the enormous budget deficit so that Italy could return to the European monetary system, but this obliged him to cut down on pensions and health, two measures that both Fini and the small unrepentant communist party round Fausto Bertinotti would try to prevent. The prime minister was also pledged to privatize the uncompetitive state-owned monopolies and near-monopolies, including ENI in the oil and gas industry, but also ENL in the supply of electricity and STET in tele-communications. Such drastic measures would mean job losses that the extreme Left and extreme Right would both resist. Many banks were still in public ownership; so were the railroads and the loss-making national airline Alitalia; and although the giant holding company IRI had by now sold its stake in three hundred affiliated businesses, others remained unsold and IRI had debts of fifteen billion dollars to settle.

These economic questions provided the main obstacle to finding a consensus in parliament. Prodi increased taxes, enough to hurt, but only in the teeth of much popular resentment and unfortunately not enough to create an acceptably balanced budget in the foreseeable future. On the contrary the administrative machine had no easy means of tackling the massive evasion of tax which by itself was possibly equivalent to the total annual deficit. Some observers even calculated that the hidden and illegal "black" economy, though ignored in official statistics, accounted for almost a quarter of the gross domestic product, and each year it was attracting the cheap labor of tens of thousands of clandestine immigrants from North Africa and the Balkans—a fact that created entirely new social problems. Yet overall unemployment, though comparatively small and manageable in northern Italy, had grown to over 20 per cent in the South. Differentials between North and South, which in the 1970s had seemed to be narrowing, were now widening again. The fact that incomes in Lombardy were nearly double those in Calabria was bound to create tension and blunt the sense of national solidarity.

No government had yet produced a satisfactory answer to this "southern question," but Prodi was hoping that unemployment in the South would in the long run be mitigated by reducing government controls and pursuing the deflationary financial policies agreed at Maastricht. Others disagreed, since any severe contraction in state expenditure, by aggravating unemployment in the short term, would further divide and impoverish the country. Nevertheless participation in the European union had so far been of great value and a heavy price would be payable if Italy were now to be excluded for failing to meet the agreed financial criteria. Even more obvious was that the greater financial austerity promoted by Amato and his two successors was helping to put the economy on a much sounder footing and ought to be continued. The old regime of Andreotti and Craxi had been undermined by the ending of the cold war and the fight against corruption, but its ending had also been brought about by European laws promoting competition, austerity, and restricting state debt, because politicians now had far less chance of using public funds to purchase votes and finance the clientelistic practices that had kept them in power.

★

A different problem was posed for the government by Bossi's Northern League which, disappointed by minor electoral reverses but still supported by 10 per cent of the voters, stood aside from both parliamentary coalitions and became more extreme in its demands. In May, Bossi summoned his followers to a separatist "parliament of Mantua" in which he claimed the right to secede from the rest of Italy and create a "Republic of Padania" in the North. One of his arguments was that Padania (which took its name from the large area fed by the River Po) would because of its wealth qualify much more easily than Rome or the South for rejoining the European financial system. Some of his other ideas were offensively racist, directed not only against poor immigrant laborers but against what he derided as "the Latin peoples of southern Italy"; and for instance he was already asking for southerners to be excluded from northern schools. Throughout the summer months of 1996, Bossi used his great gifts as a publicist to monopolize headlines in all the newspapers with this attempt to reverse the achievement of the *risorgimento*. But to his great surprise he failed to attract the support that he had expected from other members of his party, and his threat to national unity was for the moment removed.

A more serious adversary of the Ulivo coalition was the media magnate Berlusconi who, with a fifth of the electoral vote, headed the second largest party after D'Alema's PDS. Berlusconi's Forza Italia was still run autocratically. So far he had always refused to allow his party to hold a congress in which members could discuss policy or elect their leaders. His position as head of the parliamentary opposition gave him some hope of one day returning as prime minister, even though this hope diminished as police investigations into his business operations led to his being indicted on charges of bribery and false accounting. Political power was something that he urgently needed to regain in order to keep his virtual monopoly of commercial television, whereas Prodi was insisting that all parties should have equal access to the mass media and no single person or company should possess more than 30 per cent of the television network. Another reason for Berlusconi to want political power was his need to control magistrature and muzzle what he called the illicit attempt to prosecute elected representatives of the people. But his position was weakened when other senior officials in his business concerns were arrested, on suspicion of tax evasion or for collusion with the mafia and attempting to corrupt the judiciary. Further incriminating evidence came to light in London where the police in April found documents relating to forty mysterious off-shore companies and slush funds under Berlusconi's control, as a result of which he was himself served with another notice of prosecution. Evidently this money had evaded tax and much of it had been used to subsidise his former socialist friend Craxi.

More than four years had gone by since the scandal of *tangentopoli* surfaced, yet although in Milan the courts had worked effectively, elsewhere there was sometimes a reluctance to emulate them, and everyone knew that the system of justice still lacked adequate resources to deal with such a huge problem. At any one moment two million criminal cases and three million civil cases were still pending, yet political rivalries had resulted in many positions on the judicial bench remaining vacant. Another quite extraordinary result was that almost no one arrested for paying or receiving *tangenti* had yet received a final judicial sentence. The senior executives of Fiat, Olivetti and Fininvest were among many involved in protracted prosecutions, but evidence was mounting to suggest that many or possibly most instances of corruption were still unknown and uninvestigated. The arrest in March of the senior investigating magistrate in Rome was another monitory sign of how much remained to be discovered. At La Spezia in September the chief executive of the state railways was arrested on very serious charges, which opened up a quite new area of enquiry and was a further indication that important departments of national life might be quite out of control. From a survey of shopkeepers in the bigger towns it even appeared that a quarter were having to pay protection money, often to racketeers.

One of the difficulties was that many politicians continued their attempt at trying to frustrate action by the courts and were fiercely attacking the police investigators for intrusion into what were said to be purely political decisions. These attacks were not always unreasonable. Inevitably, however, they were seen as a defense of covert malpractice by interested parties or else as an attempt to sweep disreputable incidents under the carpet. Far better was the situation in Sicily, partly because mafia crimes were much harder to whitewash, and partly because Sicilian criminals unlike those in Milan lacked much of their former political protection. Over the previous ten years the mafia had forfeited its aura of invincibility, and another important fact was that the reduction in subsidies to the South was severely curtailing mafia profits. No longer was Sicily the major world-wide center of drug trafficking. More than 1,300 repentant *mafiosi* were talking to the police by the end of 1996, and though the evidence provided by these *pentiti* was suspect, a new and very expensive system of witness protection encouraged the collection of an immense amount of detailed information that could usually be checked and collated. There were good reasons for hoping that one of Italy's most dangerous and intractable problems was on the way to a solution.

★

On the other vexed matter of constitutional reform there was little consensus among politicians and yet almost everyone agreed that changes were required. Possibly another Constituent Assembly like that of 1946–47 would be needed to decide what alterations were desirable. But instead this task was given to yet another parliamentary commission under the presidency of D'Alema and a great deal would depend on how far it could reach agreement. Prodi announced that he would rely much more on parliament and would enforce the rule that only exceptional circumstances justified legislation by executive decree—in which proposal he was supported when the Constitutional Court decided that many decrees had hitherto been *ultra vires*. He also promised to decentralize much more power from Rome to the twenty individual regions. At the same time he meant to tackle the huge problem of how to correct the universal impression that the central and regional bureaucracies were dilatory and inefficient, especially after several of his ministers complained of finding their departments staffed with hundreds and even many thousands of super-fluous employees who had little serious work to do. There was some demand for eliminating the residue of proportional representation in elections, because that would help to exclude very small parties from parliament and make it easier for progressives and conservatives to succeed one another in government. Such an alternation had been foreseen and in principle desired by many leading politicians in the past, by Cavour and Minghetti, by Crispi and Giolitti, by De

Gasperi, La Malfa, and Spadolini. The fact that until now it had remained merely a pious hope was a useful reminder that any legal and constitutional reforms would almost certainly be insufficient if good will among ordinary citizens and politicians was lacking.

★

Any history of recent and contemporary politics is bound to reach an inconclusive finale where many loose ends remain and there is potential for development in different directions. Italy today, like every other country, has many political questions unresolved. It has unemployment at an unsustainable level; organized crime and corrupt business practices still in process of correction; a national debt and an annual deficit that leave re-entry into the post-Maastricht Europe in doubt; an unmended and dangerous fracture between North and South; a constitution in course of perhaps drastic change; and not least an insufficient pluralism in ownership of the mass media that distorts the practice of liberal democracy.

Despite these continuing problems, there is possibly more reason for optimism than in any previous period. Italy in the past fifty years has known far more freedom and prosperity than in all its long history. It has avoided any major war and is today a more just society than ever before. The twin questions of the mafia and political corruption, instead of their existence being denied outright, are now becoming understood and exposed, with immense moral and economic gain for the country. The educational system may have its defects but now includes far more students at every level than in the past. In particular the greater prominence of women has allowed them for the first time to reach senior positions in state and society: one breach in a masculine world was prized open when Tina Anselmi became minister of labor in 1976, and the speakership of the Chamber of Deputies was occupied by Nilde Iotti in 1979 and Irene Pivetti in 1994, Such social changes may one day be seen as the most interesting and promising facet of recent Italian history. Yet politics remains as an essential conditioning factor that can either inhibit or promote development, and here, too, a welcome novelty is that since 1992 there no longer exists a blocked political system. An entrenched ruling class has for the most part been removed from power, without bloodshed or revolution, and this has demonstrated that opposition parties are no longer excluded from taking their turn in office. Another positive fact is that Prodi, despite being hamstrung by the lack of a reliable parliamentary majority, has assembled a more talented team of ministers than most other governments of Europe.

History is concerned with the past and while helping us to understand the present, it provides no more than very imperfect pointers to the future. There is no certainty whether or how far a united Italy can continue to make its contribution to the future unification of Europe. There also remains some residual doubt whether different parties will be able to succeed one another in government with a clear mandate while sharing a common belief in the basic principles of liberal democracy. Nor can we be sure that a career in politics will ever attract enough of Italy's most responsible and intelligent citizens. These and other anxieties have confirmed some authoritative commentators in pessimism about the future, yet there are also grounds for believing that the dreams of Cavour and Mazzini have never been so justified and close to realization as they are today.

Appendix

Luigi Luzzatti	March 1910 to March 1911
Giovanni Giolitti	March 1911 to March 1914
Antonio Salandra	March 1914 to June 1916
Paolo Boselli	June 1916 to October 1917
Vittorio Emanuele Orlando	October 1917 to June 1919
Francesco Nitti	June 1919 to June 1920
Giovanni Giolitti	June 1920 to July 1921
Ivanoe Bonomi	July 1921 to February 1922
Luigi Facta	February 1922 to October 1922
Benito Mussolini	October 1922 to July 1943
Pietro Badoglio	July 1943 to June 1944
Ivanoe Bonomi	June 1944 to June 1945
Ferruccio Parri	June 1945 to December 1945
Alcide de Gasperi	December 1945 to August 1953
Giuseppe Pella	August 1953 to January 1954
Amintore Fanfani	January 1954 to February 1954
Mario Scelba	February 1954 to July 1955
Antonio Segni	July 1955 to May 1957
Adone Zoli	May 1957 to June 1958
Amintore Fanfani	July 1958 to February 1959
Antonio Segni	February 1959 to March 1960
Fernando Tambroni	March 1960 to July 1960
Amintore Fanfani	July 1960 to June 1963
Giovanni Leone	June 1963 to December 1963
Aldo Moro	December 1963 to June 1968
Giovanni Leone	June 1968 to December 1968
Mariano Rumor	December 1968 to July 1970
Emilio Colombo	August 1970 to January 1972
Giulio Andreotti	February 1972 to July 1973
Mariano Rumor	July 1973 to November 1974
Aldo Moro	November 1974 to July 1976
Giulio Andreotti	July 1976 to August 1979
Francesco Cossiga	August 1979 to October 1980
Arnaldo Forlani	October 1980 to June 1981
Giovanni Spadolini	June 1981 to November 1982
Amintore Fanfani	December 1982 to August 1983
Bettino Craxi	August 1983 to April 1987
Amintore Fanfani	April 1987 to July 1987
Giovanni Goria	July 1987 to April 1988
Ciriaco de Mita	April 1988 to July 1989
Giulio Andreotti	July 1989 to June 1992
Giuliano Amato	June 1992 to April 1993
Carlo Azeglio Ciampi	April 1993 to May 1994

Silvio Berlusconi   May 1994 to January 1995
Lamberto Dini   January 1955 to April 1996
Romano Prodi   May 1996–

HEADS OF STATE

Vittorio Emanuele II, 1861–78   Antonio Segni, 1962–64
Umberto I, 1878–1900   Giuseppe Saragat, 1964–71
Vittorio Emanuele III, 1900–46   Giovanni Leone, 1971–78
Umberto II, 1946   Alessandro Pertini, 1978–85
Enrico de Nicola, 1946–48   Francesco Cossiga, 1985–92
Luigi Einaudi, 1948–55   Oscar Luigi Scalfaro, 1992–
Giovanni Gronchi, 1955–62

POPES

Pius IX (Mastai-Ferretti), 1846–78
Leo XIII (Pecci), 1878–1903
St. Pius X (Sarto), 1903–14
Benedict XV (Della Chiesa), 1914–22
Pius XI (Ratti), 1922–39
Pius XII (Pacelli), 1939–58
John XXIII (Roncalli), 1958–63
Paul VI (Montini), 1963–78
John Paul I (Luciani), 1978 (August to September)
John Paul II (Wojtyla), 1978–

Bibliography of Books in English

1861–1920

Absalom, R. *Italy since 1800: a nation in the balance*, London 1995.

Adamson, W.L. *Avant-garde Florence: from modernism to fascism*, Cambridge 1993.

Adler, F.H. *Italian industrialists from liberalism to fascism: the political development of the industrial bourgeoisie 1906–1934*, Cambridge 1995.

Agócs, S. *The troubled origins of the Italian Catholic labor movement 1878–1914*, Detroit 1988.

Albertini, L. *The origins of the war of 1914*, 3 vols., Oxford 1952–57.

Albrecht-Carrié, R. *Italy at the Paris peace conference*, New York 1938.

Alloway, L. *The Venice Biennale 1895–1968*, London 1969.

Askew, W.C. *Europe and Italy's acquisition of Libya 1911–12*, Durham 1942.

Balabanoff, A. *My life as a rebel*, London 1938.

Bell, D.H. *Sesto San Giovanni: workers, culture and politics in an Italian town, 1880–1922*, Rutgers 1986.

Berghaus, G. *Futurism and politics: between anarchist rebellion and fascist reaction 1909–1944*, Providence 1996.

Blok, A. *The mafia of a Sicilian village 1860–1960*, New York 1974.

Bosworth, R.J.B. *Italy: the least of the Great powers. Italian foreign policy before the First World War*, Cambridge 1979.

Bosworth, R.J.B. *Italy and the approach of the First World War*, London 1983.

Bosworth, R.J.B. *Italy and the wider world 1860–1960*, London 1996.

Bull, A.C. and Corner, P. *From peasant to entrepreneur: the survival of the family economy in Italy*, Oxford 1993.

Burgwyn, H.J. *The legend of the multilated victory: Italy, the Great War and the Paris peace conference 1915–1919*, Westport 1993.

Cardoza, A.L. *Agrarian elites and Italian fascism, the province of Bologna 1901–1926*, Princeton 1982.

Carner, M. *Puccini: a critical biography*, London 1992.

Cinel, D. *The national integration of Italian return immigration 1870–1929*, Cambridge 1991.

Clark, M. *Modern Italy 1871–1982*, London 1984.

Clough, S.B. *The economic history of modern Italy*, New York 1964.

Clough, S.B. and Saladino, S.M. *A history of modern Italy: documents, readings, and commentary*, New York 1968.

Cohen, J.S. *Finance and industrialization in Italy 1894–1914*, New York 1977.

Coppa, F.J. *Planning, protectionism and politics in liberal Italy: economics and politics in the Giolittian age*, Washington 1971.

Coppa, F.J. *Dictionary of modern Italian history*, Westport 1985.

Coppa, F.J. (ed.) *Studies in modern Italian history: from the risorgimento to the republic*, New York 1986.

Coppa, F.J. and Roberts, W. (eds.) *Modern Italian history: an annotated bibliography*, New York 1990.

Crispi, F. *The memoirs of Francesco Crispi*, 3 vols., London 1922.

Croce, B. *A history of Italy 1871–1915*, Oxford 1929.

Davis, J.A. *Conflict and control: law and order in Italy in the 19th century*, London 1988.

De Grand, A.J. *The Italian nationalist association and the rise of fascism in Italy*, London 1978.

Di Scala, S. *Dilemmas of Italian socialism: the politics of Filippo Turati*, Amherst 1980.

Drake, R. *Byzantium for Rome: the politics of nostalgia in Umbertian Italy 1878–1900*, Chapel Hill 1980.

Duggan, C. *A concise history of Italy*, Cambridge 1994.

Edmonds, J.E. *Military operations: Italy 1915–1919*, London 1949.

Falconi, C. *The popes in the twentieth century*, London 1967.

Finley, M., Mack Smith, D., and Duggan, C. *A history of Sicily*, London 1986.

Foerster, R.F. *The Italian emigration of our times*, Cambridge 1919.

Forsyth, D.J. *The crisis of liberal Italy: monetary and financial policy 1914–1922*, Cambridge 1993.

Gay, H.N. and Alberti, M. *Italy's Great War and her national aspirations*, London 1917.

Ghiringhelli, R. and Albertoni, E.A. *Elitism and democracy: Mosca, Pareto and Michels*, Milan 1992.

Gibson, M. *Prostitution and the State in Italy 1860–1915*, New Brunswick 1986.

Giolitti, G. *Memoirs of my life*, London 1922.

Gooch, J. *Army, state and society in Italy 1870–1915*, London 1989.

Gonzalez, M.G. *Andrea Costa and the rise of socialism in the Romagna*, Washington 1980.

Hales, E.E.Y. *Pio Nono: a study in European politics and religion in the nineteenth century*, London 1954.

Halperin, S.W. *Diplomat under stress: Visconti-Venosta and the crisis of July, 1870*, Chicago 1963.

Halperin, S.W. *The separation of church and state in Italian thought from Cavour to Mussolini*, New York 1971.

Hearder, H. *Italy in the age of the risorgimento 1790–1870*, London 1983.

Hentze, M. *Pre-fascist Italy: the rise and fall of the parliamentary regime*, London 1939.

Hostetter, R. *The Italian socialist movement: origins 1860–1882*, Princeton 1958.

Hughes, H.S. *Consciousness and society*, New York 1958.

Hughes, S.C. *Crime, disorder and the risorgimento: the politics of policing in Bologna*, Cambridge 1994.

Jemolo, A.C. *Church and state in Italy 1850–1950*, Oxford 1960.

Kent, P.C. and Pollard, J.F. (eds.) *Papal diplomacy in the modern age*, Westport 1994.

Kertzer, D.I. *Family life in central Italy 1880–1910*, Rutgers 1984.

Kertzer, D.I. and Hogan, D.P. *Family, political economy, and demographic change: the transformation of life in Casalecchio 1861–1921*, Madison 1989.

King, B. and Okey, T. *Italy today*, London 1901 and 1909.

Ledeen, M.A. *The first Duce: d'Annunzio at Fiume*, Baltimore 1977.

Lovett, C. *The democratic movement in Italy 1830–1876*, Cambridge 1982.

Lowe, C.J. and Marzari, F. *Italian foreign policy 1870–1940*, London 1975.

Mack Smith, D. *Garibaldi: a great life in brief*, London 1956.

Mack Smith, D. *Modern Sicily*, London 1968.

Mack Smith, D. *Victor Emanuel, Cavour and the risorgimento*, London 1971.

Mack Smith, D. *The making of Italy 1796–1870*, London 1988.

Mack Smith, D. *Italy and its monarchy*, London 1989.

Mack Smith, D. *Mazzini*, London 1994.

Malatesta, M. (ed.) *Society and the professions in Italy 1860–1914*, Cambridge 1995.

Martin, M.W. *Futurist art and theory, 1909–1915*, Oxford 1968.

Meeks, C.L.V. *Italian architecture 1750–1914*, New Haven 1966.

Megaro, G. *Mussolini in the making*, Boston 1938.

Miller, J.E. *From élite to mass politics: Italian socialism in the Giolittian era 1900–1914*, Kent, Ohio 1990.

Morris, J. *The political economy of shopkeeping in Milan 1886–1922*, Cambridge 1993.

Neufeld, M. F. *Italy: school for awakening countries: the Italian labor movement in its political, social and economic setting from 1800 to 1960*, Ithaca 1961.

Osborne, C. *Verdi: a life in the theatre*, London 1987.

Patriarca, S. *Number and nationhood: writing statistics in nineteenth-century Italy*, Cambridge 1996.

Pernicone, N. *Italian anarchism 1864–1892*, Princeton 1993.

Procacci, G. *History of the Italian people*, London 1968.

Renzi, A.W. *In the shadow of the sword: Italy's neutrality and entrance into the Great War 1914–1915*, New York 1987.

Rhodes, A. *The poet as superman: a life of Gabriele d'Annunzio*, London 1959.

Ridley, J. *Garibaldi*, London 1974.

Rosselli, J. *The opera industry in Italy from Cimarosa to Verdi*, Cambridge 1984.

Rosselli, J. *Singers of Italian opera: the history of a profession*, Cambridge 1992.

Salandra, A. *Italy and the Great War: from neutrality to intervention*, London 1932.

Salomone, A.W. *Italy in the Giolittian era: Italian democracy in the making 1900–1914*, Philadelphia 1960.

Salomone, A.W. (ed.) *Italy: from the risorgimento to fascism. An enquiry into the origins of the totalitarian state*, New York 1970.

Salvatorelli, L. *The risorgimento: thought and action*, New York 1970.

Seton-Watson, C. *Italy from liberalism to fascism 1870–1925*, London 1987.

Snowden, F.M. *Violence and great estates in the south of Italy: Apulia 1900–1922*, Cambridge 1986.

Snowden, F.M. *Naples in the time of cholera 1884–1911*, Cambridge 1995.

Sponza, L. *Italian immigrants in nineteenth century Britain*, Leicester 1988.

Spriano, P. *The occupation of the factories: 1920*, London 1975.

Tannenbaum, E.R. and Noether, E.P. (eds.) *Modern Italy: a topical history since 1861*, New York 1974.

Thayer, J.A. *Italy and the Great War: politics and culture 1870–1915*, Madison 1964.

Tilly, L.A. *Politics and class in Milan 1881–1991*, New York 1992.

Tomasi di Lampedusa, G. *The Leopard*, London 1960.

Toniolo, G. *An economic history of liberal Italy 1850–1918*, London 1990.

Toniolo, G. *One hundred years: a short history of the Banca Commerciale Italiana*, Milan 1994.

Villari, L. *The expansion of Italy*, London 1930.

Villari, L. *The war on the Italian front*, London 1932.

Webster, R. *Industrial imperialism in Italy 1908–1915*, Berkeley 1975.

Whittam, J. *The politics of the Italian army 1861–1918*, London 1976.

Zamagni, V.N. *The economic history of Italy 1860–1990*, Oxford 1993.

1920–1960

Absalom, R. *A strange alliance: aspects of escape and survival in Italy 1943–1945*, Florence 1991.

Adams, J.C. and Barile, P. *The government of republican Italy*, Boston 1961.

Alcock, A.E. *The history of the South Tyrol question*, London 1970.

Alfieri, D. *Dictators face to face*, London 1954.

Allum, P.A. *Politics and society in post-war Naples*, Cambridge 1973.

Amyot, G. *The Italian communist party: the crisis of the popular front strategy*, London 1981.

Baer, G.W. *The coming of the Italian–Ethiopian war*, Cambridge 1967.

Baer, G.W. *Test case: Italy, Ethiopia and the League of Nations*, Stanford 1976.

Baldassarri, M. (ed.) *Industrial policy in Italy 1945–1990*, Basingstoke 1993.

Banfield, E.C. *The moral basis of a backward society*, New York 1958.

Barkan, J. *Visions of emancipation: the Italian workers' movement since 1945*, New York 1984.

Barros, J. *The Corfu incident of 1923: Mussolini and the League of Nations*, Princeton 1965.

Baskerville, B. *What next O Duce?*, London 1937.

Battaglia, R. *The story of the Italian resistance*, London 1957.

Barzini, L. *The Italians*, New York 1964.

Bellamy, R. *Modern Italian social theory: ideology and politics from Pareto to the present*, Cambridge 1987.

Bellamy, R. and Schecter, D. *Gramsci and the Italian state*, Manchester 1993.

Bessel, R. (ed.) *Fascist Italy and Nazi Germany: comparisons and contrasts*, Cambridge 1996.

Binchy, D.A. *Church and state in fascist Italy*, Oxford 1941.

Bobbio, N. *Ideological profile of twentieth-century Italy*, Princeton 1995.

Bojano, F. *In the wake of the goose-step*, London 1944.

Bonomi, I. *From socialism to fascism: a history of contemporary Italy*, London 1924.

Borgese, G.A. *Goliath: the march of fascism*, London 1938.

Bragadin, M. *The Italian navy in World War II*, Annapolis 1957.

Cammett, J. M. *Antonio Gramsci and the origins of Italian communism*, Stanford 1967.

Cannistraro, P. (ed.) *Historical dictionary of fascist Italy*, Westport 1982.

Cannistraro, P. and Sullivan, B. *Il Duce's other woman*, New York 1993.

Cappelletti, M., Merryman, J.H., and Perillo, J.M. *The Italian legal system: an introduction*, Stanford 1967.

Cardoza, A. *Agrarian élites and Italian fascism: the province of Bologna 1901–1926*, Princeton 1982.

Carocci, G. *Italian fascism*, London 1975.

Carrillo, E. *De Gasperi: the long apprenticeship*, Notre Dame 1965.

Casale, G. *Benedetto Croce between Naples and Europe*, New York 1994.

Casella, M.C. *Religious liberalism in modern Italy*, London 1965–66.

Cassels, A. *Mussolini's early diplomacy*, Princeton 1980.

Cassels, A. (ed.) *Italian foreign policy 1918–1945: a guide to research and research materials*, Wilmington 1981.

Cermelj, L. *Life-and-death struggle of a national minority*, Ljubljana 1945.

Cervi, M. *The hollow legions: Mussolini's blunder in Greece 1940–41*, London 1972.

Chabod, F. *A history of Italian fascism*, London 1963.

Chadwick, O. *Britain and the Vatican during the Second World War*, Cambridge 1986.

Cianfarra, C.M. *The War and the Vatican*, London 1945.

Ciano, G. *Ciano's diary 1937–1943*, London 1947 and 1952.

Ciano, G. *Ciano's diplomatic papers*, London 1948.

Clark, B.R. *Academic power in Italy: bureaucracy and oligarchy in a national university system*, Chicago 1977.

Clark, M. *Antonio Gramsci and the revolution that failed*, London 1977.

Coles, H. and Weinberg, A.K. *Civil affairs: soldiers become governors*, Washington 1964.

Coppa, F.J. and Repetto-Alaia, M. *The formation of the Italian republic: proceedings of the international symposium on post-war Italy*, New York 1993.

Corner, P. *Fascism in Ferrara 1915–1925*, London 1975.

Coverdale, J.F. *Italian intervention in the Spanish civil war*, Princeton 1975.

Crespi, A. *Contemporary thought of Italy*, London 1926.

Croce, B. *An autobiography*, Oxford 1927.

Croce, B. *The king and the allies: extracts from a diary July 1943–June 1944*, New York 1950.

Darrah, D. *Hail Caesar*, Boston 1936.

Davis, J.A. (ed.) *Gramsci and Italy's passive revolution*, London 1979.

Deakin, F.W. *The brutal friendship: Mussolini, Hitler and the fall of Italian fascism*, revised edn, New York 1966.

Dechert, C.R. *Ente Nazionale Idrocarburi: profile of a state corporation*, Leiden 1963.

De Felice, R. *Fascism: an informal introduction to its theory and practice*, ed. M.A. Ledeen, New Brunswick 1976.

De Felice, R. *Interpretations of fascism*, Cambridge 1977.

De Grand, A.J. *Italian fascism: its origins and development*, London 1982.

De Grand, A.J. *The Italian left in the twentieth century: a history of the socialist and communist parties*, Bloomington 1989.

De Grazia, V. *The culture of consent: mass organization of leisure in fascist Italy*, Cambridge 1981.

De Grazia, V. *How fascism ruled women: Italy 1922–1945*, Oxford 1992.

Del Boca, A. *The Ethiopian war 1935–1941*, Chicago 1969.

Delzell, C.F. *Mussolini's enemies: the Italian anti-fascist resistance*, Princeton 1961.

Delzell, C.F. (ed.) *The papacy and totalitarianism between the two world wars*, New York 1974.

Diggins, J.P. *Mussolini and fascism: the view from America*, Princeton 1972.

Di Nolfo, E.D. *The Atlantic Pact forty years later: a historical reappraisal*, New York 1991.

Dolci, D. *To feed the hungry: enquiry in Palermo*, London 1959.

Duggan, C. *Fascism and the mafia*, London 1989.

Duggan, C. and Wagstaff, C. (eds.) *Italy in the cold war: politics, culture and society 1948–1958*, Oxford 1995.

Earle, J. *The Italian co-operative movement*, London 1986.

Einaudi, M. and Goguel, F. *Christian democracy in Italy and France*, Notre Dame 1952.

Ellwood, D.W. *Italy 1943–1945*, Leicester 1985.

Etlin, R.A. *Modernism in Italian architecture 1890–1940*, Cambridge 1991.

Evans, E.H. *Coexistence: communism and its practice in Bologna 1945–1965*, Notre Dame 1967.

Falconi, C. *The silence of the pope*, London 1970.

Farneti, P. *The Italian party system 1945–1980*, London 1985.

Femia, J.V. *Gramsci's political thought: hegemony, consciousness and the revolutionary process*, Oxford 1981.

Ferrero, G. *Four years of fascism*, London 1924.

Fiori, G. *Antonio Gramsci: life of a revolutionary*, London 1970.

Foa, B. *Monetary reconstruction in Italy*, New York 1949.

Forgacs, D. (ed.) *Rethinking Italian fascism: capitalism, populism and culture*, London 1986.

Forgacs, D. *Italian culture in the industrial era 1880–1980: cultural industries, politics and the public*, Manchester 1990.

Frankel, H. *Mattei: oil and power politics*, London 1966.

Franzosi, R. *The puzzle of strikes: class and state strategies in postwar Italy*, Cambridge 1995.

Fried, R.C. *The Italian prefects*, New Haven 1963.

Garland, A.N. and Smyth, H.M. *Sicily and the surrender of Italy*, Washington 1965.

Gat, M. *Britain and Italy 1943–1949: the decline of British influence*, Brighton 1996.

Gentile, E. *The sacralization of politics in fascist Italy*, Cambridge 1996.

Graham, D. and Bedwell, S. *Tug of war: the battle for Italy 1943–1945*, London 1986.

Gramsci, A. *Selections from political writings 1910–1926*, ed. Q. Hoare, London 1978.

Gramsci, A. *Prison notebooks*, ed. J.A. Buttigieg, New York 1992.

Gramsci, A. *Letters from prison*, ed. F. Rosengarten, New York 1994.

Gramsci, A. *Pre-prison writings*, ed. R. Bellamy, Cambridge 1994.

Gregotti, V. *New directions in Italian architecture*, New York 1968.

Griffin, R. *The nature of fascism*, London 1991.

Hachey, T.E. (ed.) *Anglo-Vatican relations 1914–1939: confidential annual reports of the British ministers to the Holy See*, Boston 1972.

Harper, J.L. *America and the reconstruction of Italy 1945–1948*, Cambridge 1986.

Harris, C.R.S. *Allied military administration of Italy 1943–1945*, London 1957.

Hay, J. *Popular film culture in fascist Italy*, Bloomington 1987.

Hess, R.L. *Italian colonialism in Somalia*, London 1966.

Hildebrand, G.H. *Growth and structure in the economy of modern Italy*, Cambridge 1965.

Holbik, K. *Italy in international cooperation: the achievements of her liberal economic policies*, Padua 1959.

Holland, S. (ed.) *The state as entrepreneur: the IRI state-shareholding formula*, London 1972.

Horowitz, D.L. *The Italian labor movement*, Cambridge 1963.

Hughes, H.S. *The United States and Italy*, enlarged edn, Cambridge 1983.

Hughes, H.S. *Prisoners of hope: the silver age of the Italian Jews 1924–1974*, Cambridge 1983.

Jacobitti, E.E. *Revolutionary humanism and historicism in modern Italy*, New Haven 1981.

Joll, J. *Gramsci*, London 1977.

Katz, R. *Death in Rome*, London 1967.

Katz, R. *Black sabbath: a journey through a crime against humanity*, London 1969.

Keene, F. (ed.) *Neither liberty nor bread: the meaning and tragedy of fascism*, London 1940.

Kelikian, A. *Town and country under fascism: the transformation of Brescia 1915–1926*, Oxford 1986.

Kent, P. *The Pope and the Duce*, London 1981.

King, R. *Land-reform: the Italian experience*, London 1973.

Knox, M. *Mussolini unleashed 1939–1941: politics and strategy in fascist Italy's last war*, Cambridge 1982.

Kogan, N. *The politics of Italian foreign policy*, New York 1963.

Kogan, N. *A political history of Italy: the postwar years*, New York 1983.

Koon, T.H. *Believe, obey, fight: political socialization of youth in fascist Italy 1922–1943*, Chapel Hill 1985.

Lamb, R. *War in Italy 1943–1945: a brutal story*, London 1993.

Lange, P.M. and Samuels, R. *Studies on Italy 1943–1975: select bibliography of American and British materials in political science, economics, sociology and anthropology*, Turin 1977.

LaPalombara, J. *The Italian labor movement: problems and prospects*, Ithaca 1957.

LaPalombara, J. *Interest groups in Italian politics*, Princeton 1964.

Ledeen, M.A. *Universal fascism: the story and practice of the fascist international 1928–1936*, New York 1972.

Levi, C. *Christ stopped at Eboli*, London 1948.

Lewis, L.I. *Echoes of resistance: British involvement with the Italian partisans*, Tunbridge Wells 1985.

Lo Bello, N. *The Vatican's wealth*, London 1968.

Ludwig, E. *Talks with Mussolini*, London 1933.

Lussu, E. *Enter Mussolini*, London 1936.

Lutz, V. *Italy: a study in economic development*, Oxford 1962.

Lyttleton, A. *The seizure of power: fascism in Italy 1919–1929*, London 1973.

Lyttleton, A. (ed.) *Italian fascisms from Pareto to Gentile*, London 1973.

Macartney, M.H.H. and Cremona, P. *Italy's foreign and colonial policy 1914–1937*, Oxford 1938.

Mack Smith, D. *Mussolini's Roman empire*, London 1976.

Mack Smith, D. *Mussolini*, London 1981.

Mammarella, G. *Italy after fascism: a political history 1943–1965*, Notre Dame 1966.

Matteotti, G. *The fascisti exposed: a year of fascist domination*, London 1924.

Maugeri, F. *From the ashes of disgrace*, New York 1948.

Maxwell, G. *God protect me from my friends*, London 1956.

Maxwell, G. *The ten pains of death*, London 1959.

McGuire, C.F. *Italy's economic position*, New York 1926.

Meenan, J. *The Italian corporative system*, Cork 1944.

Michaelis, M. *Mussolini and the Jews*, Oxford 1978.

Michel, H.J. *The shadow war: resistance in Europe 1939–1945*, London 1972.

Migliorini, B. and Griffith, T.G. *The Italian language*, London 1966.

Minio-Paluello, L. *Education in fascist Italy*, Oxford 1946.

Moloney, T. *Westminster, Whitehall and the Vatican: the role of Cardinal Hinsley 1935–1954*, London 1985.

Molony, J.N. *The emergence of political catholicism in Italy: partito popolare 1919–1926*, London 1977.

Moore, M. *Fourth shore: Italy's colonisation of Libya*, London 1940.

More, J. *The land of Italy*, revised edn, London 1961.

Morgan, P. *Italian fascism 1919–1945*, Basingstoke 1995.

Morison, S.E. *Sicily-Salerno-Anzio: January 1943–June 1944*, Boston 1954.

Morley, J.F. *Vatican diplomacy and the Jews during the holocaust 1939–1943*, New York 1980.

Mountjoy, A.B. *The mezzogiorno*, London 1973.

Mussolini, B. *My autobiography*, New York 1928.

Mussolini, B. *Fascism: doctrine and institutions*, Rome 1935.

Mussolini, B. *Memoirs 1942–1943*, ed. R. Klibansky, Boston 1949.

Newby, E. *Love and war in the Apennines*, London 1971.

Novak, B.C. *Trieste 1941–1954: the ethnic, political, and ideological struggle*, Chicago 1970.

Origo, L. *War in the Val d'Orcia*, London 1947 and Boston 1984.

Packard, R. and Packard, E. *Balcony empire: fascist Italy at war*, London 1943.

Padellaro, N. *Portrait of Pius XII*, London 1956.

Pantaleone, M. *The mafia and politics*, London 1966.

Pasquino, G. *The decline of the first fascist regime and Italy's transition to democracy 1943–1948*, Washington 1980.

Passerini, L. *Fascism in popular memory: the cultural experience of the Turin working class*, Cambridge 1987.

Poggi, G.F. *Catholic Action in Italy: the sociology of a sponsored organisation*, Stanford 1967.

Pollard, J.F. *The Vatican and Italian fascism 1929–1932*, Cambridge 1985.

Posner, M.V. and Woolf, S.J. *Italian public enterprise*, London 1967.

Prezzolini, G. *Fascism*, London 1926.

Randall, A.W.G. *Vatican assignment*, London 1956.

Randall, A.W.G. *The Pope, the Jews and the nazis*, London 1963.

Roberts, D.D. *The syndicalist tradition and Italian fascism*, Chapel Hill 1979.

Roberts, D.D. *Benedetto Croce and the uses of historicism*, Berkeley 1987.

Robertson, E.M. *Mussolini as empire-builder: Europe and Africa 1932–36*, London 1977.

Rossi, A. *The rise of Italian fascism 1918–1922*, London 1938.

Rusinov, D.I. *Italy's Austrian heritage 1919–1946*, Oxford 1969.

Sachs, H. *Toscanini*, New York 1978.

Sachs, H. *Music in fascist Italy*, London 1987.

Salvadori, M. *The labour and the wounds: a personal chronicle of one man's fight for freedom*, London 1958.

Salvemini, G. *Under the axe of fascism*, London 1936.

Salvemini, G. and La Piana, G. *What to do with Italy*, London 1943.

Salvemini, G. *Prelude to World War II*, London 1953.

Salvemini, G. *The origins of fascism in Italy*, ed. R. Vivarelli, New York 1973.

Sarti, R. *Fascism and the industrial leadership in Italy 1919–1940*, Berkeley 1971.

Sarti, R. (ed.) *The ax within: Italian fascism in action*, New York 1974.

Sbacchi, A. *Ethiopia under Mussolini: fascism and the colonial experience*, London 1985.

Schachter, G. *The Italian south: economic development in Mediterranean Europe*, New York 1965.

Segré, C.G. *Fourth shore: the Italian colonisation of Libya*, Chicago 1974.

Segré, C.G. *Italo Balbo: a fascist life*, Berkeley 1987.

Seldes, G. *Sawdust Caesar: the untold history of Mussolini and fascism*, London 1936.

Sforza, C. *Contemporary Italy: its intellectual and moral origins*, London 1946.

Shepperd, G.A. *The Italian campaign 1943–45: a political and military reassessment*, London 1968.

Smith, B.F. and Agarossi, E. *The secret surrender*, New York 1979.

Snowden, F.M. *The fascist revolution in Tuscany 1919–1922*, Cambridge 1989.

Spencer, H.R. *Government and politics of Italy*, New York 1932.

Spriano, P. *Antonio Gramsci and the party: the prison years*, London 1979.

Sprigge, C.J.S. *Benedetto Croce: man and thinker*, Cambridge 1952.

Steinberg, J. *All or nothing: the Axis and the holocaust 1941–1943*, London 1990.

Sturzo, L. *Italy and fascismo*, London 1926.

Sturzo, L. *Italy and the new world order*, London 1943.

Tafuri, M. *History of Italian architecture 1944–1985*, Cambridge 1989.

Tannenbaum, E.R. *The fascist experience: Italian society and culture 1922–1945*, New York 1972.

Tarrow, S.G. *Peasant communism in southern Italy*, New Haven 1967.

Thompson, D. *State control in fascist Italy: culture and conformity 1925–1943*, Manchester 1991.

Togliatti, P. *Inside Italy*, New York 1942.

Togliatti, P. *Lectures of fascism*, London 1976.

Togliatti, P. *On Gramsci and other writings*, ed. D. Sassoon, London 1979.

Toscano, M. *The origins of the Pact of Steel*, Baltimore 1968.

Toscano, M. *Designs in diplomacy*, London 1970.

Toscano, M. *Alto Adige – South Tyrol: Italy's frontier with the German world*, Baltimore 1975.

Trevelyan, R. *Rome '44: the battle for the Eternal City*, London 1983.

Villari, L. *Italian foreign policy under Mussolini*, New York 1956.

Votaw, D. *The six-legged dog: Mattei and ENI*, Berkeley 1964.

Walter, K. *Co-operation in changing Italy*, London 1934.

Walter, K. *The class conflict in Italy*, London 1938.

Webb, L.C. *Church and state in Italy 1947–1957*, Carlton 1958.

Webster, R.A. *The cross and the fasces: Christian Democracy and fascism in Italy*, Stanford 1960.

Welk, W.G. *Fascist economic policy*, Cambridge 1938.

Whittam, J. *Fascist Italy*, Manchester 1995.

Wilhelm, M. de B. *The other Italy: Italian resistance in World War II*, New York 1988.

Willson, P.R. *The clockwork factory: women and work in fascist Italy*, Oxford 1993.

Wiskemann, E. *The Rome–Berlin axis: a history of the relations between Hitler and Mussolini*, Oxford 1949.

Wiskemann, E. *Fascism in Italy: its development and influence*, London 1969.

Wiskemann, E. *Italy since 1945*, London 1971.

Woolf, S.J. (ed.) *The rebirth of Italy 1943–50*, London 1972.

Zuccotti, S. *The Italians and the holocaust: persecution, rescue and survival*, London 1987.

1960–1996

Acquaviva, S. and Santuccio, M. *Social structure in Italy*, London 1976.

Acquaviva, S. *The decline of the sacred in industrial society*, Oxford 1979.

Aharoni, Y. and Vernon, R. (eds.) *State-owned enterprise in the western economies*, London 1981.

Allen, K.J. and Maclennan, M.C. (eds.) *Regional problems in Italy and France*, London 1970.

Allum, P.A. *Italy: republic without government*, London 1973.

Amyot, G. *The Italian communist party: the crisis of the popular front stategy*, London 1981.

Arlacchi, P. *Mafia, peasants and great estates: society in traditional Calabria*, Cambridge 1983.

Arlacchi, P. *Mafia business: the mafia ethic and the spirit of capitalism*, Oxford 1988.

Baldassarri, M. and Modigliani, F. (eds.) *The Italian economy: what next?*, Basingstoke 1995.

Baranski, Z.G. and Lumley, R. (eds.) *Culture and conflict in postwar Italy: essays on mass and popular culture*, London 1990.

Baranski, Z.G. and Vinall, S. (eds.) *Women and Italy: essays on gender, culture and history*, London 1991.

Barnes, S.H. *Representation in Italy: institutionalized tradition and electoral change*, Chicago 1977.

Barkan, J. *Visions of emancipation: the Italian workers' movement since 1945*, New York 1984.

Bedani, G. *Politics and ideology in the Italian workers' movement: the changing role of the Catholic and communist subcultures in postwar Italy*, Oxford 1995.

Behan, T. *The Camorra*, London 1996.

Blackmer, D.L.M. and Tarrow, S. (eds.) *Communism in Italy and France*, Princeton 1977.

Bobbio, N. *The future of democracy*, Cambridge 1987.

Bobbio, N. *Which socialism? Marxism, socialism and democracy*, ed. R. Bellamy, London 1987.

Bobbio, N. *Liberalism and democracy*, London 1990.

Bobbio, N. *Ideological profile of twentieth-century Italy*, Princeton 1995.

Bondanella, P. *Italian cinema: from neorealism to the present*, New York 1983.

Bono, P. and Kemp, S. (eds.) *Italian feminist thought: a reader*, Oxford 1991.

Briani, V. *Italian immigrants abroad: a bibliography*, Detroit 1979.

Bull, M.J. *Another revolution manqué: the PDS in Italy's transition 1989–1994*, Florence 1994.

Bull, M.J. *The European community and "regime parties": a case study of Italian Christian Democracy*, Florence 1994.

Caesar, M. and Hainsworth, P. (eds.) *Writers and society in contemporary Italy*, Leamington 1984.

Caldwell, L. *Italian family matters: women, politics and legal reform*, Basingstoke 1991.

Catanzaro, R. (ed.) *The red brigades and left-wing terrorism in Italy*, London 1991.

Catanzaro, R. *Men of respect: a social history of the Sicilian mafia*, New York 1992.

Certoma, G.L. *The Italian legal system*, London 1985.

Cheles, L., Ferguson, R. and Vaughan, M. (eds.) *Neo-fascism in Europe*, London 1991.

Chubb, J. *Patronage, power and poverty in southern Italy*, Cambridge 1982.

Chubb, J. *The mafia and politics: the Italian state under siege*, Cornell 1989.

Cicioni, M. and Prunster, N. *Visions and revisions: women in Italian culture*, Oxford 1993.

Collin, R. *The De Lorenzo gambit: the Italian coup manqué of 1964*, Reading 1976.

Cornwell, R. *God's banker: an account of the life and death of Roberto Calvi*, London 1983.

De Cecco, M. *Italian monetary policy in the 1980s*, Florence 1983.

De Franciscis, M.E. *Italy and the Vatican: the 1984 concordat between Church and State*, New York 1989.

De Grand, A. *The Italian left in the twentieth century: a history of the socialist and communist parties*, Bloomington 1989.

Della Porta, D. *Social movements, political violence, and the state: a comparative analysis of Italy and Germany*, Cambridge 1995.

Della Volpe, G., *Rousseau and Marx*, London 1978.

Di Palma, G. *Surviving without governing: the Italian parties in parliament*, Berkeley 1977.

Di Scala, S. *Renewing Italian socialism: Nenni to Craxi*, Oxford 1988.

Diani, M. *Green networks: a structural analysis of the Italian environmental movement*, Edinburgh 1995.

Dogan, M. (ed.) *The mandarins of Western Europe: the political role of top civil servants*, New York 1975.

Dogan, M. *How to become a cabinet minister in Italy: unwritten rules of the political game*, Florence 1983.

Drake, R. *The revolutionary mystique and terrorism in contemporary Italy*, Bloomington 1989.

Drake, R. *The Aldo Moro case*, Cambridge 1995.

Earle, J. *Italy in the 1970s*, Newton Abbot 1975.

Falcone, G., Farrelly, E. and Padovani, M. *Men of honour: the truth about the mafia*, London 1993.

Foà, V. *Italian social democracy yesterday and today*, Reading 1968.

Forgacs, D. and Lumley, R. (eds.) *Italian cultural studies: an introduction*, Oxford 1996.

Francioni, F. (ed.) *Italy and EC membership evaluated*, London 1992.

Frei, M. *Getting the boot: Italy's unfinished revolution*, New York 1995.

Fried, R.C. *Planning the eternal city: Roman politics and planning since World War II*, New Haven 1973.

Friedman, A. *Agnelli and the network of Italian power*, London 1988.

Furlong, P. *Modern Italy: representation and reform*, London 1994.

Galli, G. and Prandi, A. *Patterns of political participation in Italy*, New Haven 1970.

Gambetta, D. *The Sicilian mafia: the business of private protection*, Cambridge 1993.

Gatt-Rutter, J. *Writers and politics in modern Italy*, London 1978.

Giavazzi, F. and Spaventa, L. (eds.) *High public debt: the Italian experience*, Cambridge 1988.

Gilbert, M. *The Italian revolution: the end of politics Italian-style?* Boulder 1995.

Ginsborg, P. *A history of contemporary Italy: society and politics 1943–1988*, London 1990.

Golden, M. *Labor divided: austerity and working-class politics in contemporary Italy*, Ithaca 1988.

Groenewegen, P.D. and Halevi, J. (eds.) *Altro polo: Italian economics past and present*, Sydney 1983.

Gundle, S. and Parker, S. (eds.) *The new Italian republic: from the fall of the Berlin wall to Berlusconi*, London 1996.

Guzzini, S. *The implosion of clientelistic Italy in the 1990s: a study of "peaceful change" in comparative political economy*, Florence 1994.

Hebblethwaite, P. *Introducing John Paul II, the populist pope*, London 1982.

Hebblethwaite, P. *Paul VI: the first modern pope*, London 1993.

Hebblethwaite, P. *John XXIII: pope of the Council*, London 1984 and revised edn 1994.

Hellman, J.A. *Journeys among women: feminism in five Italian cities*, Cambridge 1987.

Hellman, S. *Italian communism in transition: the rise and fall of the historic compromise in Turin 1975–1980*, Oxford 1988.

Hellman, S. and Pasquino, G. (eds.) *Italian politics: a review* (on the two years 1991–92), 2 vols., London 1992–93.

Hess, H. *Mafia and mafiosi: the structure of power*, Farnborough 1973.

Hine, D. *Governing Italy: the politics of bargained pluralism*, Oxford 1993.

Holmes, D.R. *Cultural disenchantments: worker peasantries in northeast Italy*, Princeton 1989.

Ignazi, P. *Extreme right-wing parties in Europe*, London 1992.

Italy today: social picture and trends, Rome (CENSIS) 1992.

Italian Republic: constitutional administration, ed. Presidency of the Council of Ministers, Rome 1976.

Italian system of state participation, ed. Presidency of the Council of Ministers, Rome 1977.

Jamieson, A. *The heart attacked: terrorism and conflict in the Italian state*, London 1989.

Katz, R. *Days of wrath: the public agony of A. Moro*, London 1986.

Katz, R. and Ignazi, P. (eds.) *Italian politics: the year of the tycoon*, Boulder 1996.

Kertzer, D.I. *Comrades and Christians: religion and political struggle in communist Italy*, Cambridge 1980.

Kertzer, D.I. *Politics and symbols: the Italian communist party and the fall of communism*, New Haven and London 1996.

Kertzer, D.I. and Salter, R.P. (eds.) *The family in Italy: from antiquity to the present*, New Haven and London 1991.

King, R. *The industrial geography of Italy*, London 1988.

Kunzle, M. (ed.) *Dear comrades: readers' letters to "Lotta Continua"*, London 1980.

Labour protection in Italy, ed. Presidency of the Council of Ministers, Rome 1977.

Lange, P. and Tarrow, S. (eds.) *Italy in transition: conflict and consensus*, London 1980.

Lange, P. and Vannicelli, M. (eds.) *The communist parties of Italy, France and Spain: postwar change and continuity*, London 1981.

Lange, P. and Regini, M. (eds.) *State, market and social regulation: new perspectives on Italy*, Cambridge 1989.

LaPalombara, J. *Democracy, Italian style*, New Haven and London 1987.

Leonardi, R. and Nanetti, R.Y. (eds.) *Italian politics: a review* (on the year 1985), London 1986.

Leonardi, R. and Wertman, D.A. *Italian Christian democracy: the politics of dominance*, London 1989.

Leonardi, R. and Corbetta, P. (eds.) *Italian politics: a review* (on the year 1987), London 1989.

Leonardi, R. and Anderlini, F. (eds.) *Italian politics: a review* (on the year 1990), London 1992.

Leonardi, R. and Nanetti, R.Y. (eds.) *The Regions and European integration: the case of Emilia–Romagna*, London 1990.

Leonardi, R. and Nanetti, R.Y. (eds.) *Regional development in a modern European economy: the case of Tuscany*, London 1994.

Lepschy, A.L. and Lepschy, G. *The Italian language today*, London 1991.

Lercaro, G. and De Rosa, G. *John XXIII: simpleton or saint?*, London 1967.

Levy, C. (ed.) *Italian regionalism: history, identity and politics*, Oxford 1996.

Locke, R.M. *Remaking the Italian economy*, Ithaca 1995.

Low-Beer, J.R. *Protest and participation: the new working class in Italy*, Cambridge 1978.

Lumley, R. *States of emergency: cultures of revolt in Italy from 1968 to 1978*, London 1990.

Marengo, F.D. *Rules of the Italian political game*, Aldershot 1981.

Markovits, A.S. and Silverstein, M. (eds.) *The politics of scandal*, New York 1988.

McCarthy, M. *Evolution and implementation of the Italian health service reform of 1978*, London 1992.

McCarthy, P. and Pasquino, G. (eds.) *The end of post-war politics in Italy: the landmark 1992 elections*, Oxford 1993.

McCarthy, P. *The crisis of the Italian state: from the origins of the cold war to the fall of Berlusconi*, New York 1995.

Meade, R.C. *Red Brigades: the story of Italian terrorism*, London 1990.

Mershon, C. and Pasquino, G. (eds.) *Italian politics: ending the first republic*, Oxford 1995.

Moss, D. *The politics of left-wing violence in Italy 1969–85*, London 1989.

Moss, D. *Italian political violence 1969–1988*, Geneva 1993.

Nanetti, R.Y. *Growth and territorial policies: the Italian model of social capitalism*, New York 1988.

Nanetti, R.Y. and Catanzaro, R. (eds.) *Italian politics: a review* (on the year 1988), London 1990.

Napolitano, G. *The Italian road to socialism*, ed. E.J. Hobsbawm, London 1977.

Nichols, P. *The politics of the Vatican*, New York 1968.

Nichols, P. *Italia, Italia*, London 1973.

Onida, F. and Viesti, G. (eds.) *The Italian multinationals*, London 1988.

Partridge, H. *A one-sided bargain: the pact between the communist party and the Italian ruling classes in the 1970s*, Manchester 1994.

Piccone, P. *Italian marxism*, Berkeley 1983.

Pike Report, The, ed. P. Agee, Nottingham 1977.

Pinto, D. (ed.) *Contemporary Italian sociology: a reader*, Cambridge 1981.

Podbielski, G. *Twenty-five years of special action for the development of southern Italy*, Milan 1977.

Pollard, J. and Quartermaine, L. *Italy today: patterns of life and politics*, Exeter 1985.

Porter, W.E. *The Italian journalist*, Ann Arbor 1983.

Pridham, G. *The nature of the Italian party system*, London 1981.

Pridham, G. *Political parties and coalitional behaviour in Italy*, London 1988.

Putnam, R.D. *The beliefs of politicians: ideology, conflict and democracy in Britain and Italy*, London 1973.

Putnam, R.D., Leonardi, R. and Nanetti, R.Y. *Making democracy work: civic traditions in modern Italy*, Princeton 1993.

Ranney, A. and Sartori, G. (eds.) *Eurocommunism: the Italian case*, Washington 1978.

Raw, C. *The moneychangers: how the Vatican enabled Roberto Calvi to steal $250 million for the heads of the P.2 masonic lodge*, London 1992.

Sabetti, F. and Catanzaro, R. (eds.) *Italian politics: a review* (on the year 1989), London 1991.

Sartori, G. *Parties and party systems: a framework for analysis*, Cambridge 1976.

Sartori, G. *Comparative constitutional engineering*, London 1994.

Sassoon, D. *The strategy of the Italian communist party from the Resistance to the Historic Compromise*, London 1981.

Sassoon, D. *Contemporary Italy: politics, economy and society since 1945*, London 1986.

Schneider, J. and Schneider, P. *Culture and political economy in eastern Sicily*, New York 1976.

Sciascia, L. *The Moro affair and the mystery of Majorana*, New York 1987.

Serfaty, S. and Gray, L. (eds.) *The Italian communist party*, London 1981.

Silj, A. *The new television in Europe*, London 1992.

Spinelli, A. *Battling for the union 1979–86*, Luxembourg 1988.

Spotts, F. and Wieser, T. *Italy a difficult democracy*, Cambridge 1986.

Stille, A. *Excellent cadavers: the mafia and the death of the first Italian republic*, New York 1995.

Suleiman, E.N. (ed.) *Bureaucracies and policy making: a comparative overview* (chapter by S. Cassese), New York 1984.

Tarrow, S.G. *Between center and periphery: grass roots politicians in Italy and France*, New Haven 1977.

Tarrow, S.G. *Democracy and disorder: protest and politics in Italy 1965–1975*, Oxford 1989.

Urban, G.R. *Euro-communism: its roots and future in Italy and elsewhere*, London 1978.

Urban, J.B. *Moscow and the Italian communist party from Togliatti to Berlinguer*, London 1986.

Wagner-Pacifici, E.E. *The Moro morality play: terrorism as social drama*, Chicago 1986.

Walston, J. *The mafia and clientelism: roads to Rome in post-war Calabria*, London 1988.

Weinberg, L.B. *After Mussolini: Italian neofascism and the nature of fascism*, Washington 1979.

Weinberg, L. *The transformation of Italian communism*, New Brunswick 1995.

White, C. *Patrons and partisans: a study of politics in two southern Italian comuni*, Cambridge 1980.

Willan, P. *Puppetmasters: the political use of terrorism in Italy*, London 1991.

Willis, F.R. *Italy chooses Europe*, New York 1971.

Zamagni, V. *The economic history of Italy 1860–1990*, Oxford 1993.

Zariski, R. *Italy: the politics of uneven development*, Hinsdale 1972.

Zuckerman, A. *The politics of faction: Christian-Democrat rule in Italy*, New Haven and London 1979.

Index